Paul Apostle to the Nations

Paul Apostle to the Nations

An Introduction

Walter F. Taylor Jr.

Fortress Press
Minneapolis

PAUL: APOSTLE TO THE NATIONS
An Introduction

Copyright © 2012 Fortress Press. All rights reserved. Except for brief quotations in critical articles or reviews, no part of this book may be reproduced in any manner without prior written permission from the publisher. Visit http://www.augsburgfortress.org/copyrights/contact.asp or write to Permissions, Augsburg Fortress, Box 1209, Minneapolis, MN 55440.

All Scripture quotations are from the New Revised Standard Version Bible, copyright © 1989 by the Division of Christian Education of the National Council of Churches of Christ in the USA, and are used with permission.

Maps 2-4 and 6-7 and Figures 2.2, 4.3, 4.5, 5.2, 6.1, 6.2, 8.1, 8.2, 8.3, 9.1, 10.3, and 11.1 are reproduced courtesy of the President and Fellows of Harvard College. Other photographs are published under a Creative Commons license as credited, or are in the public domain.

Cover image: Paul Preaching at Athens, V&A Images / The Royal Collection, on loan from HM The Queen; V&A Images, London / Art Resource, NY
Cover design: Alisha Lofgren
Book design: PerfecType, Nashville, TN

Library of Congress Cataloging-in-Publication Data
Taylor, Walter F., 1946-
  Paul, Apostle to the nations : an introduction / Walter F. Taylor.
    p. cm.
  Includes bibliographical references (p.   ).
  ISBN 978-0-8006-3259-5 (print : alk. paper) -- ISBN 978-1-4514-2446-1 (ebook)
  1. Bible. N.T. Epistles of Paul--Criticism, interpretation, etc. 2. Paul, the Apostle, Saint. I. Title.
  BS2650.52.T36 2012
  225.9'2--dc23
                                2012017936

The paper used in this publication meets the minimum requirements of American National Standard for Information Sciences—Permanence of Paper for Printed Library Materials, ANSI Z329.48-1984.

Manufactured in the U.S.A.

Contents

List of Figures ix
List of Textboxes xi
Acknowledgments xiii

Part One: Who Was Paul and What Did He Do?

Introduction: Why Study Paul? 3
    Positive and Negative Evaluations of Paul 3
    Why Study Paul? 6
    How to Use This Book 8

1. How Can We Study Paul? 11
    Historical Study 11
    Political Study 13
    Social-Scientific Study 13
    Rhetorical Study 15
    Literary Study 15
    Feminist Study 17
    Theological Study 17

2. What Sources Can We Use to Study Paul? 21
    Letters of Paul 21
    The Book of Acts 27

Contents

	Noncanonical Sources	31
	Sources: A Proposal	31
3.	**Where and When Did Paul Live and Work?**	**35**
	The Problems of Outlining a "Life" of Paul	35
	Where Did Paul Live and Work?	39
	How Did Paul Travel?	46
4.	**What Kind of Person Was Paul?**	**51**
	A Judean	51
	A Greco-Roman	58
	A Christ-Believer	81
5.	**What Did Paul Do?**	**91**
	What Was the Heart of Paul's Social Network?	91
	How Did Paul Begin Congregations?	98
	How Did Paul Nurture Congregations?	102

Part Two: What Did Paul Write?

6.	**1 Thessalonians: The End Is Near—but Not Yet**	**127**
	Paraenesis	127
	Conclusion to the Letter	129
	Historical Situation	130
	4:13-18	132
	5:1-11	135
	Chapters 1–3	138
	Summary	140
7.	**Galatians: Free To Be Children of God**	**143**
	Why Is Paul So Upset? (1:1—2:21)	143
	How Does Paul Prove His Thesis? (3:1—4:31)	147
	Historical Situation	153
	The Rhetorical Genre of Galatians	155
	Paraenesis and the Letter's Conclusion (5:1—6:18)	155
	Summary	157
8.	**1 Corinthians: Life in the Body**	**161**
	How Are New Believers to Live?	161
	Founding of the Congregation	162
	Why Corinth?	162
	Composition of the Congregation	164
	Why Write Now?	166
	What Issues Does Paul Need to Address?	167
	How Does Paul Approach Them?	169
	From Where and When Did Paul Write?	170

Final Introductory Questions	170
Chapters 1–4	171
Chapters 5–7	173
8:1—11:1	176
11:2-34	178
Chapters 12–14	180
Chapter 15	183
Chapter 16	185
Summary	186
9. 2 Corinthians: Treasure in Clay Jars	**189**
Where Do We See God's Power?	189
Seams	190
Proposed Solutions	194
Time and Place	200
Genre	201
Crises and Opponents	201
Reading through 2 Corinthians, Fragment by Fragment	204
1:1—2:13	205
2:14—6:13	208
Interpolation in 6:14—7:1	212
7:2-16	212
8:1-24	213
9:1-15	214
10:1—13:13	215
13:1-13	219
Effect and Summary	220
10. Romans: God Justifies the Ungodly	**223**
Not Ashamed of the Gospel	223
Introducing Paul and His Gospel	224
Why Did Paul Write to the Romans?	229
What Genre(s) Did Paul Use?	234
Where and When Did Paul Write?	235
1:18—3:20	236
3:21—5:21	238
6:1—8:39	241
9:1—11:36	244
12:1—15:13	246
15:13—16:23 [25-27]	248
Summary	250
11. Philippians: Citizenship in Heaven	**255**
A New Home	255
The City of Philippi	255
Founding of the Congregation	256

    Reasons for Writing   256
    How Many Letters Do We Have?   257
    What Does Paul Want from the Philippians? The Question of Genre   260
    Where and When Did Paul Write?   260
    Opponents   263
    1:1-26   264
    1:27-30   266
    2:1-30   266
    3:1—4:1   271
    4:2-23   272
    Summary   275

12. Philemon: Life in the Christ Believing Family   277
    How Did People Live in the Family?   277
    The Story behind the Letter   277
    Genre   279
    Location and Date   280
    Verses 1-7   281
    Verses 8-16   283
    Verses 17-25   284
    Summary   288

13. How Did People Develop What Paul Wrote?   289
    The Eschatological Paul (2 Thessalonians)   290
    The Universal Paul (Colossians, Ephesians)   292
    The Ecclesiastical Paul (Acts, 1–2 Timothy, Titus,
        Ignatius of Antioch)   295
    The Radical Paul (Marcion)   299
    The Spiritualized Paul (Gnosticism)   301
    The Ascetic Paul (*The Acts of Paul and Thecla*)   303
    The Apostate Paul (The Pseudo-Clementines)   305
    Conclusion   306

Glossary   *311*
Abbreviations   *319*
Notes   *323*
Index   *373*

List of Figures

Map 1	Paul's World.	xiv
Map 2	Thessalonica (chapter 6 opener).	126
Map 3	Galatia (chapter 7 opener).	142
Map 4	Corinth (chapter 8 opener).	160
Map 5	Rome in the Time of Augustus (chapter 10 opener).	222
Map 6	Philippi (chapter 11 opener).	254
Map 7	Colossae (chapter 12 opener).	278
Fig. P1.1	Paul under arrest, from a Roman sarcophagus.	xvi
Fig. P1.2	*The Apostle Paul*, by Domenikos Theotokopoulous (1627).	xvi
Fig. P1.3	*The Apostle Paul*, by Anton Rublev (ca. 1410).	xvi
Fig. Int.1	Early third-century fresco of the apostle Paul, from Rome (chapter opener).	2
Fig. 1.1	Roman slaves being led by iron collars. Marble relief from Smyrna, about 200 C.E. (chapter opener).	10
Fig. 2.1	Papyrus 46 (P^{46}), from Egypt, about 200 C.E. The earliest surviving manuscript of the letters of Paul (chapter opener).	20
Fig. 2.2	The Areopagus.	29
Fig. 3.1	The perils of seafaring, from a third-century sarcophagus.	36
Fig. 3.2	The Capitoline Triad (Minerva, Jupiter, and Juno).	46
Fig. 4.1	Activity in a Roman workshop.	52
Fig. 4.2	Fresco of Moses being drawn from the Nile.	57
Fig. 4.3	The Stoa of Attalos, Athens.	66

Fig. 4.4	A lararium, from Herculaneum.	69
Fig. 4.5	Votive carving dedicated to Asclepius.	70
Fig. 4.6	The Nag Hammadi books.	75
Fig. 4.7	Bust of Livia, Augustus's wife.	78
Fig. 4.8	Mother Earth reclines in abundance with her children; relief on the Altar of Augustan Peace, dedicated by the Senate in 9 B.C.E.	80
Fig. 5.1	The Appian Way, approaching Rome (chapter opener).	90
Fig. 5.2	A spacious private home in Athens.	94
Fig. 5.3	A thermopolium from Pompeii.	101
Figs. P2.1–6	Funerary portraits of first- and second-century men and women, from Roman Egypt.	124
Fig. 6.1	Roman coin honoring the foundation of Philippi as a Roman colony.	131
Fig. 6.2	Statue of Augustus as divine.	136
Fig. 8.1	Inscription indicating a "synagogue of the Hebrews" in Corinth.	164
Fig. 8.2	An inscription near the theater of Dionysos in Corinth declaring that Erastus, a public official, funded the pavement.	165
Fig. 8.3	A spacious banquet hall from the sacred precinct of Demeter in Corinth.	168
Fig. 9.1	The *bēma*, the platform for public speaking, at the heart of the Corinthian forum.	190
Fig. 9.2	Amphoras arranged for shipping.	210
Fig. 10.1	The emperor Claudius; bronze bust from about 50 C.E.	230
Fig. 10.2	A third-century C.E. funeral inscription for Salo, daughter of Gadias, "father of the synagogue of the Hebrews."	234
Fig. 10.3	Stadium at Olympia.	245
Fig. 11.1	Coin of Augustus and Julius Caesar.	268
Fig. 13.1	The apostle Paul depicted as a miracle worker.	290
Fig. 13.2	Slaves being led to the slave market; stone relief from Miletus, second or third century C.E.	293
Fig. 13.3	Paul depicted arguing with Judean authorities.	296

List of Textboxes

A Note on Terms	4
The Greek of Ephesians	26
The Pauline Letters	28
Paul and His Activities: Differences between the Undisputed Letters and Acts	32–33
Listing Dates	37
A Basic Chronology of Paul's Life and Career	40
"The Miracle of the Bedbugs"	49
What Did Paul Look Like?	62
Gods of Greece and Rome	76
Did Paul Have a Wife?	86
Voluntary Associations and Paul's Churches: A Comparison	98
Paul's "Coworkers"	104
Types of Rhetoric	111
Diatribe in Paul	113
Pen, Ink, Paper, and Desk	118
1 Thessalonians: The End Is Near—but Not Yet	140
Excursus: Faith "in" or Faith "of"	146
Galatians: Free to Be Children of God	158
1 Corinthians: Life in the Body	186
Proposals concerning the Composition of 2 Corinthians	194
Paul's Correspondence with Corinth	200
Attacks against Paul	202

Paul's Opponents as Defined by Themselves—and by Paul	203
The Letter Fragments in 2 Corinthians, in Sequence	204
Letter E: Letter of Reconciliation (1:1—2:13, 7:5-16, perhaps 13:11-13)	205
2 Corinthians: Treasure in Clay Jars	206
Letter C: Apostolic Defense Letter (2:14—6:13; 7:2-4)	209
Interpolation (6:14—7:1)	212
Resumption of Letters C and E	213
Letter G (8:1-24)	213
Letter H (9:1-15)	214
Letter F (10:1—13:10 [11-13])	215
Letter E, Resumed (Perhaps)	219
Why Did Paul Write Romans?	235
"Works of the Law" and the New Perspective on Paul	240
Adam and Christ in Romans 5	241
Flesh and Body	243
Romans: God Justifies the Ungodly	250
Connections between Thanksgiving and Rest of the Letter	261
Shame and Glory in Phil 2:6-11	270
Philippians: Citizenship in Heaven	274
A Note on Slavery	282
Philemon: Life in the Christ-Believing Family	287
The Word *Christian*	299
"Catholicity" and "Orthodoxy"	301

Acknowledgments

The giving of thanks was important for Paul (see below on "Structure of Hellenistic Letters"), and it is important for me as the author of this study. To Gerhard Krodel and John Reumann go thanks for the excellent courses that introduced me to Paul.

To Hans Dieter Betz go thanks for the insights and encouragement he gave as my doctoral advisor. To students at Trinity Lutheran Seminary from 1981 until today go thanks for probing questions and fundamental queries. To my New Testament colleagues at Trinity—Merlin H. Hoops, Bruce E. Schein, Mark Allan Powell, and N. Clayton Croy—go thanks for spirited discussions and support. To K. C. Hanson, formerly of Fortress Press, go thanks for suggesting this project. To Neil Elliott go thanks for shepherding it through to completion. And to Dyann Adele Gottula Taylor, my wife, go thanks for upholding me in this endeavor as in all others: "without whom, not."

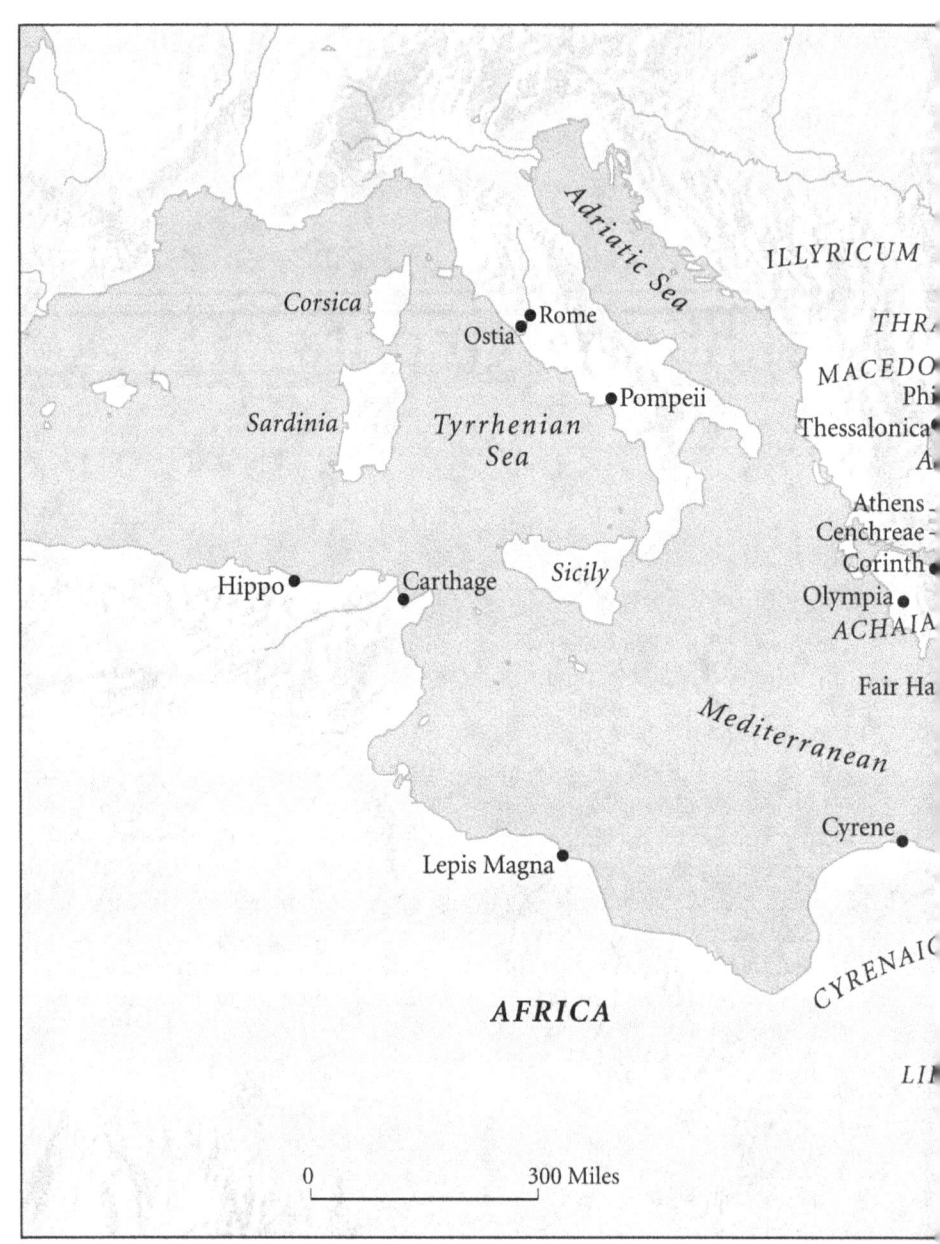

Map 1 Paul's World

Fig. P1.1 (top left) Paul under arrest, from a Roman sarcophagus (third century). Palazzo Massimo, Rome. Photo: Neil Elliott.
Fig. P1.2 (center) *The Apostle Paul*, by Domenikos Theotokopoulos (El Greco, sixteenth century). Original in the Casa y Museo del Greco, Toledo, Spain.
Fig. P1.3 (top right) *The Apostle Paul*, by Anton Rublev (ca. 1410). Original in the Tretyakov Gallery, Moscow.

Part One

Who Was Paul and What Did He Do?

Fig. Int. 1 Early third-century fresco of the apostle Paul, from the catacomb of St. Domitilla, Rome.

Introduction

Why Study Paul?

Positive and Negative Evaluations of Paul

Think of a well-known but controversial public figure from the present or the past: Barack Obama, Hillary Rodham Clinton, Lady Gaga, Eleanor Roosevelt, Ronald Reagan. Each person has passionate supporters—and equally ardent opponents. Paul, an early Christ-believing missionary, **apostle** (or "messenger," see chapter 3), theologian, and author, has elicited the same kind of sharply opposed reactions. Over the centuries, he has been appreciated as the most important apostle and vilified as virtually the Antichrist.

For Christian thinkers like Augustine (354–430) and Martin Luther (1483–1546), Paul and his thought are at the very heart of the Christian theological enterprise. Thus, Luther wrote that Paul's letter to believers in Rome "is in truth the most important document in the New Testament, the gospel in its purest expression. . . . It is the soul's daily bread, and can never be read too often, or studied too much. . . . It is a brilliant light, almost enough to illumine the whole Bible."[1] John Wesley (1703–1791), the founder of Methodism, at a crucial point in his development felt his "heart strangely warmed" when he heard Luther's words about Paul read. Throughout his career, Wesley repeatedly returned to Romans in his sermons and writings. In the twentieth century, Karl Barth (1886–1968) and Rudolf Bultmann (1884–1976) acknowledged the importance of Paul for ongoing Christian witness. For such thinkers, Paul's radical analysis of human nature and sin, coupled with his profound emphasis on God's unmerited love given to humanity in the cross of Jesus, provided clear answers to questions about the meaning of life in general and the God-human relationship in particular.

For others, however, the view of Paul has been quite different. In his own lifetime, Paul not only was opposed by Judeans who did not believe in Jesus—which might seem natural—but also was fiercely opposed by other Christ-believing missionaries (see the chapters on Galatians, Romans, 1 and 2 Corinthians, and Philippians). After his death, some ancient Judean-Christ-believing communities denounced him as the "enemy" or the "messenger of Satan," apparently because he relaxed the requirements of the Law of Moses (see chapter 13 on "The Apostate Paul"). In the nineteenth century, many scholars saw Paul as the corruptor of the simple ethical system of Jesus. For Paul de Lagarde, for instance, Paul was the one who burdened Christianity with Israel's Bible.[2] Even thinkers with no claims to being biblical scholars have had their opinions about Paul. The philosopher Friedrich Nietzsche wrote of Paul as the "dys-evangelist," that is, the negative evangelist, the proclaimer of *bad* news. The playwright George Bernard Shaw wrote in 1913 a section on "The Monstrous Imposition upon Jesus" as part of his preface to *Androcles and the Lion*. The "monstrous imposition" is Paul's theology.[3]

For opponents of slavery in the American South, Paul seemed a fickle resource: in tandem with ringing endorsements of freedom and equality (Gal

---

A Note on Terms

Israel's Bible instead of *Old Testament*

The term *Old Testament* is frequently used to designate the portion of the Christian Bible that includes the documents from Genesis to Malachi (in the Protestant Bible). Paul, of course, did not have the Christian Bible, and the documents that were available to him were not known as the "Old Testament," since there was as yet no "New Testament." Generally, he used the Greek translation of Israel's authoritative scriptures, but he also had knowledge of the Hebrew. It is therefore misleading to refer to Paul's use of the Old Testament, the Greek Old Testament (over against the Hebrew Bible), or the Hebrew Bible (over against the Greek translation). For those reasons, this study will use the terms *Israel's Scriptures, Israel's Bible, Judean Scriptures,* and *Judean Bible* to refer to this body of writings. Paul ordinarily called them simply *hai graphai,* "the writings" or "the scriptures," or *hē graphē,* "the writing" or "the scripture."

Judean instead of *Jew*

For many years, English-speaking people have translated the Greek word *Ioudaios* as *Jew*. Recently, scholars have questioned that decision, arguing that the term *Jew* ought not to be used to translate first-century documents like the New Testament. Philip Esler is an articulate representative of that approach.[4] His basic argument is that ancient Greeks named ethnic groups in relationship to the territory in which they or their ancestors originated—whether or not they still resided there, or even if they had never resided there. Romans, too, almost always identified ethnic groups in the same way, as did the people of Israel.[5]

The Greek student will recognize in the word *Ioudaios* the geographical place name *Ioudaia*, or *Judea*. *Ioudaioi* (Judeans) are people from *Ioudaia* (Judea)—because either they or their ancestors were born there. (Compare in the United States people who proudly bear their ancestral home in their preferred designations as Irish Americans, Chinese Americans, or Americans of African descent.) In the case of Judeans who lived outside Judea, many ties continued to bind them to Judea: they paid the temple tax to the temple in the Judean capital city of Jerusalem, they often celebrated feasts when Jerusalem celebrated them, and they prayed facing Jerusalem.

Esler offers several supporting arguments:

- *Judean* retains by its very name the connection with the temple and the ceremonies practiced there.
- *Jew*, in contrast, signals an identity based not on the temple and its sacrificial system, which were still very much alive during Paul's lifetime, but a later form of Judaism in which identity centered around the *Torah* (Law).
- Also, the term *Jew* carries for modern readers many later connotations, such as the persecution of Jews in medieval Europe and, above all, the twentieth-century Holocaust under the Nazis, that were not part of the experience of first-century *Ioudaioi*.

In Esler's model, *Jew* can be used as the translation of *Ioudaios* only for texts written after any realistic hope of rebuilding the temple had been abandoned—so 135 at the earliest and certainly by 200. In this book, *Judean* is the preferred translation.[6]

Nations? Gentiles?

The word *ethnē* (nations or Gentiles) also presents challenges to the translator. It can refer to all people in general, that is, the *nations* of the world. It can refer to those who are not part of a given speaker's or writer's group of people who share common culture, traditions, and kinship; those outside that group are the *nations*. And it can refer more specifically to people who do not belong to the people of Israel, in which case the term is usually translated *Gentiles*. Paul uses the first and third meanings. The word means *Gentiles* when he writes about non-Judeans in contrast to Judeans (Rom 2:14; 3:29; 1 Cor 1:23; Gal 2:12, 14-15). At other places he uses it to refer in a collective way to the *nations* of the world (Rom 4:17; 15:18; Gal 3:8b). Context is the key in determining which translation to use.

Christ-Believer instead of *Christian*

The word **Christ** itself is originally a title. It is the Greek term for the Hebrew concept of **Messiah**, which refers to a promised descendant of King David of Israel. Some Judeans believed he would restore the people of Israel to their previous glory, while others looked forward to a powerful spokesperson for God. By the time of Paul, the term *Christ* also functioned as a name for Jesus of Nazareth, with special reference to his cross and resurrection as the way through which God had restored people to a positive relationship with God.

> Paul, however, never uses the terms *Christian* or *Christianity*. The first recorded uses of *Christian* (and the only ones in the New Testament) are in Acts 11:26; 26:28; and 1 Pet 4:16. In Acts, the term comes from outsiders and is not meant as a compliment. The usage in 1 Peter is almost certainly negative, also.[7] The term *Christianity* was first used by Ignatius, the bishop of Antioch in Syria, who wrote between 110 and 117 (Ign. *Magn.* 10:1, 3; Ign. *Rom.* 3:3; Ign. *Phld.* 6:1). He may well have invented the word. In any event, the terms do not belong to the ways first-century believers in Christ identified themselves.
>
> The words *Christian* and *Christianity* also encourage the reader to envision first-century believers in Christ as understanding and organizing themselves just as Christians do today. But this can be misleading. During Paul's ministry, many churches continued to have ties to Judaism, for example, while others never had close ties with Judaism or had moved away from them. There was no united, centralized movement that sprang up on Easter Monday with a fully developed theology, mission, and organization. That is one reason Paul's work was so important to the Christian church that emerged in part because of him: he offered a clear understanding of what belief in Jesus as the Christ meant, he outlined a strategy for mission, and he took initial steps in organizing groups of believers. In this textbook, we will use terms such as *Christ-believer*, *Christ-follower*, and the *Christ movement* instead of *Christian* and *Christianity*.[8]

3:28; 5:1) went his positive use of the slave image (Rom 1:1; 6:15-23), his direction to a runaway slave to return to his master (Philemon), and his apparent lack of opposition to the whole system of Roman slavery. Although Paul's views on women and thus his larger theological system are "redeemable" for some feminist theologians when read in new ways,[9] others see Paul's thought as so hopelessly opposed to the leadership of women in the church that Paul and indeed the Bible in general must be rejected.[10]

Perhaps Paul still suffers from a strange malady identified by Robin Scroggs: "The trouble with Paul is that he has too many friends and too many enemies. The one thing that the friends and enemies tend to have in common is that they do not really know what Paul is all about. At least the Paul I hear defended and the Paul I hear attacked is not the Paul that I have come to know and appreciate."[11]

Why Study Paul?

Such diametrically opposed evaluations of the same person indicate either that some people have totally misunderstood him or that he was a complex and perhaps at times inconsistent author—or both. In either case, the sheer diversity of opinion points to a figure well worth studying. Further, Paul's thought was (and remains!) seminal. The variety of evaluations and the Christian theologians and other believers who over the centuries have been inspired and challenged by Paul point to a creative source who generated idea after idea as he sought to be faithful to what he had experienced in Jesus. And, of course, what he wrote is considered by many Christians to be God's revealed word.

Another important reason to study Paul is that he was the first theological author of early Christianity. Most if not all of Paul's literary activity that has survived was generated in the 50s of the first century. The Gospel of Mark—the other New Testament writing with a widely acknowledged claim to early dating—was written in the late 60s or early 70s. The other gospels, and indeed all other documents in the New Testament, came later. Thus, Paul, even though he did not write a life of Jesus and probably did not know the earthly Jesus, stood nearer to the beginning of the Christ movement than any other Christ-believing author whose writings have survived from antiquity.[12] Paul therefore gives us a window into the early decades of the Christ movement. In doing so, he is a key figure in the development of a new religious movement that had deep roots in an ancient religion (Judaism) and that at the same time sought to interact with and witness to a surrounding society that was substantially different from it. We also know more about Paul than about any other New Testament author, so that we are able much better to see the interplay between what Paul wrote and who he was.

Nor should we fail to note that much of the New Testament is connected to Paul. Of the twenty-seven documents that constitute the New Testament, thirteen claim to be by him. A fourteenth book, Hebrews, was included in the New Testament in large part because people thought Paul had written it—even though the document makes no such claim. The book of Acts, which outlines the growth of the early church, makes Paul the central character—and for good reason. Paul was an absolutely key figure in the spread of belief in Christ from a small Palestinian Judean sect into a religion that, by the time of Paul's death, had spread into Syria, Turkey, Greece, Italy, and many places in between. Part of the reason for the rapid spread of Christianity was the major theological move Paul made in crossing the ethnic barrier between Judean and Gentile. By arguing that Gentiles could believe in Jesus as the Christ and could become part of the community of believers without first becoming Judean converts, Paul made the salvation won by Jesus available to all people. He broke previously existing paradigms in ways just as innovative as paradigm shifters in technology, such as Bill Gates and Steve Jobs. And in an interesting development, early twenty-first-century European philosophers including Giorgio Agamben and Alain Badiou have been stimulated by Paul's vision, even when they do not share all of his faith commitments.[13]

Part of Paul's way of doing theology was to think in apocalyptic terms, that is, focusing on the coming end of the world. A glance at the daily newspaper or online news indicates how current such interests are, even if Paul had a perspective different from that of most contemporary American apocalyptic thinkers. Paul wrote at a time of great intellectual, religious, and social ferment. The Mediterranean world was dominated by the Roman Empire and its *Pax Romana* (peace of Rome). For many people, it was a relatively good time, but for others, the prosperity of the empire merely highlighted what they did *not* have, in terms of both material possessions and basic rights. So, for example, women were oppressed yet in some cases were able to explore new freedoms. Different ethnic and linguistic groups could live at times in harmony but could also be in great tension with each other. Local religions and philosophies found new competitors in teachings that crossed previous boundaries. In the midst of such realities, it was Paul's ability to think through the issues of the emerging faith in Christ and to issue relatively clear-cut formulations that helped keep the church on track in a syncretistic age. Seeing how Paul navigated such complex issues may give readers models of how to do the same in their own time.

A final reason to study Paul is that for twenty centuries, he has been one of the premier Christian theologians. His letters are still being read, still being debated, still being preached. He must have had intriguing things to say! And his insights may well tell us something about ourselves and our relationships with God, self, and others. As Calvin Roetzel remarks in relationship to the New Testament letters that Paul certainly wrote, "No other seven letters have had such an impact on human history."[14]

How to Use This Book

The goal of this book is to introduce readers to the life, struggles, letters, and thought of the first-century apostle Paul. The book is designed to encourage students to read the letters of Paul and to set them within the cultures and societies of which Paul and the letters' recipients were part—and not just read *about* the letters. By reading this book, a person should be better able to enter Paul's worlds, learn from Paul's letters, and appreciate Paul's innovative and challenging contributions to Christian life and thought. Each letter of Paul's will be explored in some detail and will function, in addition, as a case study for selected major Pauline themes. Thus, Paul's theology will arise from study of his writings, rather than being imposed on them.

Each chapter includes "Study Questions" designed to encourage reflection and discussion, as well as "Suggested Reading" for students who want to explore a topic more fully. A glossary of terms is available in the back of the book; terms defined in the glossary are printed in boldface when they first appear in a chapter.

This textbook has many endnotes. They are designed to give references but also to provide further examples as well as bibliography for those who want to do more research on a given topic. Crucial information is not placed in the notes, so the reader can read the text without constantly referring to the notes or worrying that a key explanation or insight will be missed.

Suggested Reading

Meeks, Wayne A., and John T. Fitzgerald, eds. *The Writings of St. Paul*. 2nd ed. Norton Critical Edition. New York: Norton, 2007. Presents differing views of Paul over the centuries. Also prints NIV annotated text of Paul's letters and letters written in his name.

Fig. 1.1 Roman slaves being led by iron collars. Marble relief from Smyrna, about 200 CE. Original in the Ashmolean Museum, Oxford.

Chapter 1

How Can We Study Paul?

If we had posed thirty years ago the lead question of this chapter, "How can we study Paul?" the answer would have been that we can do it by using history, with theology not far behind. In the twenty-first century, we have those options plus several others. While the larger number of interpretative options complicates the task of studying Paul, proper use of them opens the letters of Paul to new insights and points of application.

Historical Study

Modern scientific historical study is the systematic study of the past. Historians set clear boundaries when working according to the rules of historical study. They are able to deal only with that part of the past that is accessible to them. If there is no text, no monument, no coins, no archaeological artifacts, there is no history. Take the question of whether Paul ever married. From a historian's perspective, we do not know. And the reason we do not know is that the data available to us do not tell us. In 1 Cor 7:1-7, Paul talks about marriage. Although he permits marriage and says some beautiful things about it, he still indicates, "I wish that all were as I myself am" (1 Cor 7:7). Well, how was he? Virtually all scholars agree that Paul was unmarried when he wrote 1 Corinthians. But had he ever been married? Was he perhaps divorced? Or widowed? No historical source, including his own letters, tells us. People have speculated that since he was a **Pharisee** (a member of a particular Judean sect, Phil 3:5) and since Pharisees usually were married, Paul must at some point himself have been married. That could be true. But as historians, we do not know, since we have no historically verifiable data. All we can say is that when he wrote 1 Corinthians, Paul was unmarried.

Just as historical study is the systematic study of the past in general, so historical study of the Bible is the systematic study of the specific past evidenced in the Bible. Historical study tries to explain all references in the text to events and persons and in general seeks to determine the date and place of writing for the document under study, its author, the author's purpose, the identity of the recipients, the recipients' circumstances, and the religious, historical, social, and political factors that encouraged the author to write the document. Historical study pays much attention to the meaning of individual words and their relationships with each other, and therefore it pays constant attention to the context of statements within the literary context of the document. Ideally, it involves studying the text in its original language (for Paul, Greek); for experts, that linguistic ability is mandatory. Such concern with details from the past can emphasize the distance between the contemporary reader and the ancient text. As a result, according to Carl Holladay, interpretation requires the reader to "bridge this gap" by "becoming acquainted with the earlier historical period, its languages, customs, and political and social history."[1]

Consider an example. In Rom 1:1, Paul begins his letter, "Paul, a servant of Jesus Christ" (NRSV).[2] The reader of the New Revised Standard Version text will notice a footnote sign attached to the word *servant*. The note reads, "Gk *slave*," which means that in the Greek-language original, the primary meaning of the word is *slave*. The person who has studied Greek will remember that the Greek word for *slave* is *doulos*. While *servant* is a possible translation, *servant* signals to the North American ear someone who chooses to be in a position of service to others, such as a butler, maid, or public servant. That, historical study suggests, is *not* what Paul means when he calls himself a *doulos*. He wants to indicate that in relationship to Jesus Christ, he is a slave. Moreover, the whole phrase clearly signals that Jesus Christ is his master. Once that is determined, Bible students are able to ask what the text means now.

There are two chief potential limits to historical study. First, in its classical form, historical study of the Bible claims scientific objectivity for its observations and conclusions—in much the same way laboratory chemists claim scientific objectivity for their work. One of the contributions of feminist study has been to question the validity of that claim to objectivity. All scholars see things from their own perspective.[3] A second potential limit is that the scholar, having amassed a wealth of historical data about a given word or person, applies all of that knowledge to each occurrence of the concept being studied, without thinking through the particular context of this specific usage.[4] In a sense, a potential limit of historical study, then, is becoming so caught up in the interesting historical data gathered that one overwhelms the text with it.

While the student of Paul needs to be aware of these limitations, historical study provides access to the author, original recipients, and documents in ways foundational to most contemporary methods of Bible study. Leander Keck and

Victor Paul Furnish are on target when they write that historical study of the Bible "has been an astounding success, for repeatedly, the biblical text has been understood more accurately than before."[5] Historical study will be the basis for our study of Paul—albeit not the only method to be used.

Political Study

Political study is basically a subcategory of historical study and an obvious method, it would seem, for twenty-first-century readers, who are attuned to the political meaning of everything from commercials to newspaper editorials to blogs. But because of the religious nature of the New Testament and because of the North American mind-set that church and state ought to be separated (and thus religious texts ought to have nothing to do with politics), biblical interpreters have often been very slow to read the New Testament as in any way political. The theological movement called liberation theology has challenged the separation of the New Testament from its potential political implications, as have many historical and social-scientific students of the Bible.

Returning to Rom 1:1, for example, what are the potential political implications when Paul says that he is "a slave of Jesus Christ"? Paul is writing to people who are living in Rome, the capital city of the empire. Does Paul mean to flaunt that he is a slave of Jesus Christ, thank you—and not a slave of the emperor? If so, his statement carries significant political weight, especially when we recall that separation of church and state, or religion and politics, was essentially unknown in antiquity.

The potential dangers of political study are reading political meanings into texts that do not have them and reading modern political agendas into ancient texts. Attention to solid historical study mitigates those tendencies, and appropriate use of political study helps place New Testament texts within the world in which they were produced.[6]

Social-Scientific Study

Social-scientific study of the Bible investigates the Bible using models and tools developed in the social sciences. It understands the text as part of its social and cultural world. Three basic social-scientific approaches will be utilized in this study:

1. **Social history** refers to the historical work that describes and analyzes the social matrix of ancient literature, history, and archaeology. Such historical work describes the sort of endeavor that dominated New Testament studies in the nineteenth and most of the twentieth centuries. To use the example of slavery again, people using social history explore texts, artwork, and inscriptions to understand better the roles and functions of slaves in antiquity, as well as how people became slaves and what the "careers" of various kinds of slaves would normally involve.[7]

2. **Sociological study** (or sociological exegesis) refers more narrowly to the utilization of sociological theory in the study of a text. Which modern sociological theories of power and leadership, for example, might help us to grasp more fully how Paul's self-identification as a slave of Jesus Christ was heard by first-century Romans? Or how might theories of social class help us in evaluating the social level implied by the use of the term *slave*?[8]
3. **Cultural anthropology** is the social-scientific study of human culture. It is particularly interested in the values of a given culture. At the same time, it has "an overlapping concern . . . with the study of regularities in observed social organization and the ideas held by a society about such organization—how the domestic and public activities of social groups are organized and the consequences of this organization for such concerns as social inequality, gender relations, and political authority."[9] One of the core values of ancient Mediterranean cultures, say proponents of cultural-anthropological study, is honor and shame: "'Honor' is a claim to worth (on the part of an individual, family, or group) accompanied by the public acknowledgment of, and respect for, that worth."[10] Honor, therefore, has two parts, one internal and one external: "Honor is the value of a person in his or her own eyes (that is, one's claim to worth) *plus* that person's value in the eyes of his or her social group."[11] Shame is the loss of honor and thus the loss of status. Cultural-anthropology students will want to investigate the honor and shame dynamics of Paul's self-designation as a slave (even though, to our knowledge, he had never legally been a slave), and they may notice other examples of honor and shame language that could be illuminated by cultural anthropology, such as "I am not ashamed of the gospel" (Rom 1:16), and "hope does not disappoint us" (literally, "put us to shame"; Rom 5:5). Readers who do not understand Paul's cultural assumptions when he uses such language will be unable to understand him and will unconsciously recast him to fit their own culture.

The application of a theory developed in one discipline and applied to another runs the danger of overwhelming the new data (in our case the New Testament) with an interpretative framework that is alien to it. Use of the social sciences to interpret the New Testament has in particular been labeled as reductionistic; that is, these methods of study can be understood inappropriately to explain everything in the text. While such reductionistic tendencies could be present during the first years of social-scientific study, few today would claim that sociological or cultural-anthropological models explain everything. In our study of Paul, social-scientific study—especially cultural anthropology—will be important in placing our author and his documents and concerns more firmly within the realities of their first-century world and in understanding the dynamics of the texts themselves. Use of the social sciences also reminds us that Paul and his first readers were always parts of social systems both within the church and in the larger society. Although historical study and social-scientific study can be conceived as enemies, our study will emphasize the ways in which they work profitably with each other.[12]

Rhetorical Study

Rhetorical study is closely related to the methods already outlined. It seeks to understand how authors structure the presentation of their thoughts in order to instruct, entertain, or persuade a given group of listeners/readers at a specific point in time and within a given cultural setting.[13] Indeed, as Luke Timothy Johnson has written, "A major breakthrough in the study of New Testament epistolary literature . . . has been the recovery of an appreciation for ancient rhetoric not simply as a matter of style or ornamentation, but above all as a form of argumentation and persuasion."[14] As with the social sciences, so with rhetorical study the work of modern theoreticians of rhetoric can be applied to ancient texts.[15] But in addition, there were theoreticians of rhetoric in antiquity whose works and views were widely known by those trained in speaking and writing. Thus, Aristotle, Anaximenes, Cicero, and Quintilian produced major resources.[16] Already in the century prior to the birth of Jesus, "the practice of rhetoric had been thoroughly enculturated, the system of techniques fully explored, the logic rationalized, and the pedagogy refined. Rhetoric permeated both the system of education and the manner of public discourse that marked the culture of Hellenism on the eve of the Roman age."[17]

Given that reality, students of rhetoric might ask how Paul's self-title of slave functions rhetorically within Romans. Does it create an identification between Paul and any slaves in the congregation (including possibly imperial slaves who worked in the bureaucracy centered in Rome)? Does it bring forth sympathy for Paul as a person and thereby increase his authority? How does his use of *slave* in Rom 1:1 function when viewed together with his uses of slave imagery in Rom 6:15-23?

The chief temptation of rhetorical study is overanalysis—that is, seeing things that may not be present. At times, that problem is manifested when scholars impose an ideal construct on a biblical text even if the construct does not fit. But when used with some restraint, rhetorical study aids us immeasurably in discerning how Paul put together his arguments and how each element functioned. The fact that rhetoric functions within a given cultural setting helps to tie rhetorical study closely to social-scientific study.

Literary Study

Literary study of the Bible has been practiced for many decades. Much of what we have outlined so far could be viewed as literary study, namely, studying the biblical text as literature. The term *literary study* is used in most New Testament scholarship in a narrower way to refer to "a set of assumptions and approaches commonly associated with critical literary theory, especially New Criticism, but also a range of other approaches that either directly challenge the historical paradigm or provide plausible alternatives for modern biblical readers."[18] Key to understanding this approach is to realize that for literary students of the Bible, what is in the forefront of interest is the text as text—not the author, historical circumstances, or cultural context. As Carl Holladay describes this focus, "The text is understood as having its own voice, and as the words of a text are read, this textual voice speaks. What the term *literary* is intended to capture is this focal emphasis on the words of the text and the conviction that the message and meaning of a text somehow inhere within the literary texture."[19] The result is that many literary students view the text ahistorically, that is, nonhistorically. The text itself is autonomous, and its meaning is located within the text itself and not in a presumed world of the author, community, or society. The text is studied as a freestanding aesthetic or artistic object that is essentially timeless.

Thus, a literary approach to Rom 1:1 and Paul's self-label as "slave of Jesus Christ" might turn to other literature over the centuries that has dealt with slavery, whether or not it is from Greco-Roman antiquity. An antislavery sermon from the nineteenth century, a pro-slavery sermon delivered to slaves in the American South, and a speech of Martin Luther King Jr. could all be used to help understand the literary dynamics of Paul's use of slave language. Such an approach works closely with the axiom that "the meaning of literature transcends the historical intentions of the author."[20]

Of the subcategories of literary study, the one that has borne the most fruit to date in the study of Paul is **narrative criticism**. Narrative criticism or narrative study "focuses on stories in biblical literature and attempts to read these stories with insights drawn from the secular field of modern literary criticism. The goal is to determine the effects that the stories are expected to have on their audience."[21] It is particularly concerned with plot, movement, characters, setting, point of view, implied author, ideal reader, and discourse.[22] Most readers will realize quickly that such narrative study will find the New Testament works of Matthew, Mark, Luke, John, and Acts to yield narrative results most readily—because they are indeed narratives. The letters of Paul are not. Nevertheless, scholars using narrative study have been able to "tease out" the implied story of a single document[23] and have worked at re-creating Paul's larger "narrative world."[24]

Since the present volume works chiefly with a historical paradigm, literary study in its broader sense will not be much used. In its most extreme form, it seems to assume that the reader has some kind of immediate access not only to the text itself but also to the era in which it was written—and thus to its cultural understandings and language. So, for example, while the same word *slave* might be used both by Paul and by a biographer of Abraham Lincoln, the cultural contexts are very different. American slavery was racially based, usually permanent, and kept virtually all slaves in menial positions. Greco-Roman slavery was militarily and economically based (people became slaves because of war, debt, or birth), often included provisions for eventual freedom, and invested training and responsibility in slaves who ran businesses, staffed much of the empire's bureaucracy, and in some cases became quite wealthy. That is not to say that slavery in Paul's time was positive. Innumerable slaves were mistreated and died in the mines or on vast farms. But it is to say that without historical and cultural study, a reader has every chance of reading past any reasonable range of meaning Paul could have had in mind when he called himself "a slave of Jesus Christ." Scholars using narrative study tend to deal more regularly with historical questions and tend to see narrative study and historical study as supplementing each other rather than replacing each other. At appropriate points, therefore, we will use narrative study to help us understand Paul.

Feminist Study

Feminist study has developed to counteract the indisputable fact that male interpreters in male-dominant societies have controlled biblical studies essentially since the beginning. A goal of feminist study of the Bible is to look at the texts from women's perspectives, asking questions that have to do with women and are particularly important to women. Feminist students of the Bible are what Carl Holladay deems "disenfranchised Bible readers."[25] Such readers have experienced marginalization and oppression, often based on the Bible. Feminist readers therefore look at texts from the viewpoint of those who are marginalized; in addition to other approaches, they frequently use specifically feminist theories of interpretation. Not all women scholars are feminist interpreters, and male scholars can use feminist approaches.

Feminist study is also interested in what we might call "power relations," referring to how power is distributed and how different individuals or groups relate to each other in terms of their relative degrees of power. Thus, a feminist student of the Bible would investigate whether, by calling himself "slave of Jesus Christ" in Rom 1:1, Paul was asserting power in relationship to the Romans. The feminist scholar would further want to study the power(lessness) of slaves in Rome and would want to know more about the position and roles of female as well as male slaves. A feminist student might also want to explore why Paul apparently did not oppose the oppressive system of slavery.

A potential danger for feminist study is finding in the Bible what it wants to find rather than what is in fact there (a potential danger for any approach). It can also ignore the possibility that ancient texts cannot always be read as support for contemporary concerns. But feminist study has consistently raised legitimate questions that previous students of the Bible have failed to ask.[26] Therefore, feminist interpretation will inform our study at a number of points because it opens up texts and provides new insights.

Theological Study

The New Testament is composed of documents that are not historical documents only. They also are theological documents that interpret God, humanity, the world, and their interrelationship with each other. To interpret Paul from historical, political, social-scientific, rhetorical, literary, and feminist perspectives without attending to the theological is in fact to cut Paul off from the reason he wrote: to further the mission of God. When Paul, to resurrect for a final time our example of Rom 1:1, calls himself a slave of Jesus Christ, he is signaling a host of theological associations and questions. He is the "slave of Jesus Christ." Who then, the reader will ask, is this Jesus Christ to whom Paul is subject? Why is he the master? (And what does Paul mean later in the passage when he calls this Jesus Christ "Lord" [Rom 1:4]?) What, for that matter, does Paul indicate when he designates Jesus as "Christ"? And what does he imply when—as opposed to passages from Israel's Bible in which Moses, Joshua, David, and the prophets are slaves/servants of *God*—Paul writes of himself as the slave of Jesus Christ?[27] Answers to those questions help us understand what Paul is saying theologically.

Which of the seven methods of study shall we use? The answer is, all of them. While the fundamental approaches in this book are historical, political, social scientific, and rhetorical, one of the ultimate goals is theological interpretation, and all methods will be used in varying degrees so that a broad range of questions can be engaged.

Study Questions

1. Which methods of study are most attractive to you? Why?
2. Which one method seems to have the most difficulties associated with it?
3. Which methods would you like to study more?
4. What are some reasons for using a combination of methods rather than using only one?

Suggested Reading

Surveys of Different Ways of Reading the Bible

Green, Joel B., ed. *Hearing the New Testament: Strategies for Interpretation*. 2nd ed. Grand Rapids: Eerdmans, 2010.

Holladay, Carl R. "Contemporary Methods of Reading the Bible." *NIB* 1.125–49.

Historical Study

Krentz, Edgar. *The Historical-Critical Method*. GBS. Philadelphia: Fortress Press, 1975.

Political Study

Elliott, Neil. *The Arrogance of Nations: Reading Romans in the Shadow of Empire*. Paul in Critical Contexts. Minneapolis: Fortress Press, 2008.

Horsley, Richard A., ed. *Paul and Empire: Religion and Power in Roman Imperial Society*. Harrisburg, PA: Trinity Press International, 1997.

Social-Scientific Study

Elliott, John H. *What Is Social-Scientific Criticism?* GBS. Minneapolis: Fortress Press, 1993.

Malina, Bruce J. *Christian Origins and Cultural Anthropology: Practical Models for Biblical Interpretation*. Atlanta: John Knox, 1986.

———. *The New Testament World: Insights from Cultural Anthropology.* 3rd ed. Louisville: Westminster John Knox, 2001.
Neyrey, Jerome H. "Social-Scientific Criticism." In *The Blackwell Companion to the New Testament*, ed. David E. Aune, 177–91. Chichester, UK: Wiley-Blackwell, 2010.
Pilch, John J., and Bruce J. Malina, eds. *Handbook of Biblical Social Values.* Peabody, MA: Hendrickson, 1998.
Taylor, Walter F., Jr. "Cultural Anthropology as a Tool for Studying the New Testament—Part I." *TSR* 18 (1996): 13–27.
———. "Cultural Anthropology as a Tool for Studying the New Testament—Part II." *TSR* 18 (1997): 69–82.
———. "Sociological Exegesis: Introduction to a New Way to Study the Bible—Part I." *TSR* 11 (1989): 99–110.
———. "Sociological Exegesis: Introduction to a New Way to Study the Bible—Part II." *TSR* 12 (1990): 26–42.

Rhetorical Study

Kennedy, George A. *New Testament Interpretation through Rhetorical Criticism.* Chapel Hill: University of North Carolina, 1984.
Mack, Burton L. *Rhetoric and the New Testament.* GBS. Minneapolis: Fortress Press, 1990.
Majercik, Ruth, Thomas B. Dozeman, and Benjamin Fiore. "Rhetoric and Rhetorical Criticism." *ABD* 5:710–19.
Porter, S. E., and T. H. Olbricht, eds. *Rhetoric and the New Testament.* JSNTSup 90. Sheffield: Sheffield, 1993.
Watson, Duane F. "Rhetorical Criticism." In *The Blackwell Companion to the New Testament*, ed. David E. Aune, 166–76. Chichester, UK: Wiley-Blackwell, 2010.

Literary Study

Beal, T. K., K. A. Keefer, and T. Linafelt. "Literary Theory, Literary Criticism, and the Bible." *Dictionary of Biblical Interpretation*, ed. John H. Hayes, 2:79–85. Nashville: Abingdon, 1999.
Beardslee, William A. *Literary Criticism of the New Testament.* GBS. Philadelphia: Fortress Press, 1970.
Petersen, Norman R. *Literary Criticism for New Testament Critics.* GBS. Philadelphia: Fortress Press, 1978.
Powell, Mark Allan. *What Is Narrative Criticism?* GBS. Minneapolis: Fortress Press, 1990.

Feminist Study

Levine, Amy-Jill. "Feminist Criticism." In *The Blackwell Companion to the New Testament*, ed. David E. Aune, 156–65. Chichester, UK: Wiley-Blackwell, 2010.
Newsom, Carol A., and Sharon H. Ringe, eds. *The Women's Bible Commentary.* Expanded ed. Louisville: Westminster John Knox, 1998.
Polaski, Sandra Hack. *A Feminist Introduction to Paul.* St. Louis: Chalice, 2005.
Schüssler Fiorenza, Elisabeth. *Bread Not Stone: The Challenge of Feminist Biblical Interpretation.* Boston: Beacon, 1984.
———. "Feminist Hermeneutics." *ABD* 2:783–91.
———. *In Memory of Her: A Feminist Theological Reconstruction of Christian Origins.* New York: Crossroad, 1983.

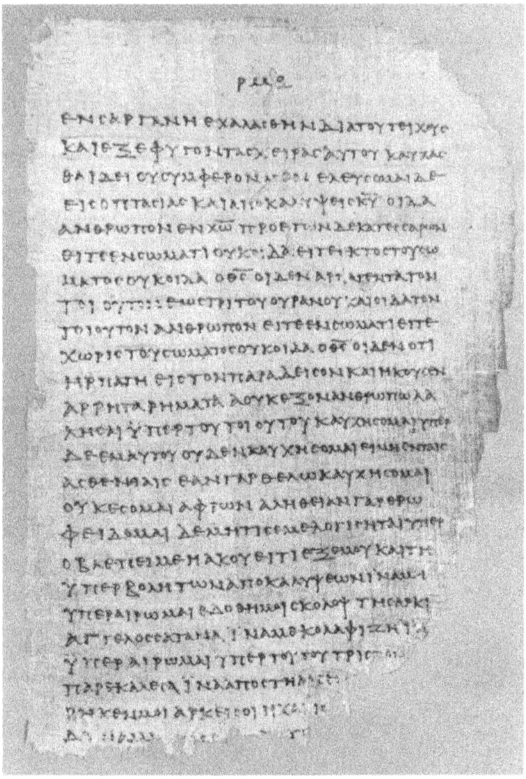

Fig. 2.1 A page from Papyrus 46 (P⁴⁶), from Egypt, about 200 C.E. The earliest surviving manuscript of the letters of Paul.

Chapter 2

What Sources Can We Use to Study Paul?

We have explored reasons why the study of Paul is both intriguing and informative, and we have investigated different ways of studying ancient texts from Paul. Now we need to be more precise about the sources available for studying him. The major sources that have been used are his letters, the New Testament book of Acts, and various noncanonical sources.

Letters of Paul

A first and obvious place to begin is with the letters of Paul. They provide us a unique opportunity. From the hand of Jesus, for example, we have not one written word. Whether any of the gospels was written by the men whose names are attached to them is much disputed, with most scholars answering negatively. But in the case of Paul, we have a large collection of letters in which Paul's name appears as the sender or co-sender (listed here in the order in which they appear in the **canon** (that is, the list of authoritative writings): Romans, 1 Corinthians, 2 Corinthians, Galatians, Ephesians, Philippians, Colossians, 1 Thessalonians, 2 Thessalonians, 1 Timothy, 2 Timothy, Titus, and Philemon.[1]

AUTHENTIC AND PSEUDONYMOUS LETTERS

Unfortunately, things are seldom as simple as they seem. During the past three centuries, debate has ebbed and flowed and sometimes even raged regarding whether or not all thirteen of the letters associated with Paul's name in fact originated with him. Traditionally, the church had simply assumed that any letter containing Paul's name as a sender was actually written by him. The rise of historical scholarship ended that easy certainty and raised the possibility that at least some of the letters that are attached to Paul's name were not written by him.

How could that be? A common phenomenon in antiquity was writing in the name of another person—invariably someone more important or better known than the actual author. Such a practice is called **pseudonymity**, from the Greek words *pseudēs* (false) and *onoma* (name). As soon as twenty-first-century people hear about writing in the name of another person, they think of copyright laws, lawsuits, and forgeries.[2] Certainly, forgeries in the negative, deceptive sense were found in antiquity. Often, the authors of such documents were trying to make money by claiming that their just-written works came from a philosophical or literary master. But many pseudonymous writings were valued in a positive way and were understood to be a way to keep current the influence of an important figure. The writing of pseudonymous letters was common both in Judaism (the Epistle of Jeremiah, Epistle of Aristeas) and in Christianity (1 and 2 Peter, Jude, James, 2 Clement, Barnabas, 3 Corinthians, Epistle to the Laodiceans, correspondence between Paul and Seneca). The Pythagorean philosophical school passed on the teachings of their master in a large number of works that were written as though they were from the historical Pythagoras—even though it was widely known that he did not write anything. Part of the perspective of the Pythagorean authors was their deep sense of indebtedness to Pythagoras: without his teaching, they would have had nothing to say, so they honored him by writing in his name. There are also writings connected with the name of Plato, especially letters. They, too, came from followers who lived centuries after his death. Indeed, a normal exercise in ancient schools was for the student to write a speech or letter as the speech or letter would have been composed by a famous person or mythical figure.[3]

Why would an early believer write in Paul's name? For two basic reasons: (1) to gain immediate credibility for one's thoughts and document; and (2) to update Paul for a new time and situation, so that Paul's themes and basic theological commitments could address new people and new life circumstances. The author of the document thereby claimed Paul's *authority* for his or her work.

DETERMINING AUTHORSHIP

How do scholars determine that a given document is probably pseudonymous? Admittedly, the discernment process involves some circularity. There has been a high degree of scholarly consensus for many decades that certain letters of Paul are indisputably by him. These seven letters are often called the "**undisputed letters of Paul**" or the "**pillar epistles**." They are Romans, 1 Corinthians, 2 Corinthians, Galatians, Philippians, 1 Thessalonians, and Philemon. Their vocabulary, style, and theology are similar, and the problems and concerns they address are easily placed in the Christ movement of the 40s and 50s. These seven constitute the control group against which the other six letters containing Paul's name as author are tested. The two other letters that garner the strongest support for authorship by Paul are Colossians and 2 Thessalonians. Ephesians still has some learned proponents of its being authored by Paul, but this letter has in recent years increasingly been viewed as pseudonymous. 1 Timothy, 2 Timothy, and Titus, often lumped together as the "**Pastoral Epistles**," are widely seen as pseudonymous (see the table that follows).

What distinctions between the "control group" and the remaining six Pauline letters lead many scholars to evaluate these six as pseudonymous? While the specifics vary from letter to letter, the following categories are the most important when discussing authorship. (Examples will come from Ephesians and the Pastoral Epistles.)

Vocabulary

Several concerns involve the vocabulary used:

- Words that replace terms often found in the undisputed letters suggest a different author. So, for example, in Eph 1:3, 20; 2:6; 3:10; and 6:12, the author talks about "heavenly places" (*ta epourania*). The term occurs nowhere else in the New Testament. In the undisputed letters, the comparable term is *hoi ouranoi* (the heavens). In the undisputed letters, Paul uses the word *eucharisteō* (I give thanks), but in 1 Tim 1:12 and 2 Tim 1:3, a different phrase is used: *charin echō* (thanks/grace I have). Similarly, in the undisputed letters, Paul uses *kyrios* (lord) for the owner of slaves (Rom 14:4 and Gal 4:1, for example), whereas the Pastorals have *despotēs* (master; 1 Tim 6:1-2; Titus 2:9).
- Words used differently when compared with their use in the undisputed letters also suggest the author may be different. In the Pastoral Epistles, the primary example is the word *faith* (*pistis*). Although it can mean obedient trust (as it does in the undisputed letters), normatively it is used in the Pastorals to designate "the Christian faith" as a distinct religion, with emphasis on its teachings (1 Tim 1:2; 3:9, 13; 4:1, 6; 5:8; 6:10, 12, 21; 2 Tim 2:18; 4:7; Titus 1:4, 13; 3:15) or faith as a Christian virtue (1 Tim 1:5, 14, 19; 4:12; 6:11; 2 Tim 2:22; 3:10; Titus 2:2, 10). The word *dikaiosynē* (righteousness; justification) does not refer to justification as it does, for example, in Rom 3:21-28, but means being upright or moral (1 Tim 6:11; 2 Tim 2:22; 3:16; 4:8). In Ephesians, words such as *mystērion* (mystery), *ekklēsia* (church), and *sōzō* (save) all have meanings different from their use in the undisputed letters.
- Words not found in the undisputed letters raise further questions about authorship. Certainly all New Testament documents contain words not found elsewhere in the New Testament. The Pastoral Epistles, however, use such words at a rate two and a half times the rate of such words in

the undisputed letters. Words and phrases found in the Pastorals but nowhere else in Paul are frequent and theologically significant. "The saying is sure" (1 Tim 1:15; 3:1; 4:9; 2 Tim 2:11; Titus 3:8), "a good conscience" (1 Tim 1:5, 19) and "clear conscience" (1 Tim 3:9; 2 Tim 1:3), *godliness* or *religion* (*eusebeia*; 1 Tim 2:2; 3:16; 4:7-8; 6:3, 5, 6, 11; 2 Tim 3:5; Titus 1:1), and *modesty* (*sōphrosynē*; 1 Tim 2:9, 15) are all absent from the undisputed letters. We have a similar experience when we turn to Ephesians: *beloved* (*ēgapēmenos*) as a reference to Christ (1:6), *commonwealth* (*politeia*; 2:12), and *debauchery* (*asōtia*; 5:18) are just three of the terms occurring in Ephesians but not in the undisputed letters.

- Words missing from the letters in question are a final vocabulary issue raising doubts about authorship. While, admittedly, arguments from silence need to be looked at carefully, the fact remains that, in the Pastoral Epistles, for example, important words and phrases from the undisputed letters are missing: *righteousness of God, cross, freedom, body of Christ, proclaim the gospel, boast, wisdom, soul/life,* and *revelation*. Even short, seemingly insignificant terms are missing from the Pastorals: *therefore, yet, so that, ever, whether, each, now, no longer, again,* and *just as*. Often, in such short words, the style of an author comes through in its most characteristic form. Thus, in the undisputed letters, Paul uses the word *with* (*syn*) twenty-eight times, frequently with great theological weight, but that word never occurs in the Pastorals.

Many other examples of differences in vocabulary could be listed. The sheer quantity of the occurrences raises for many scholars serious doubts about Paul as the author of the six letters in question.

Writing Style

Scholars often identify differences in the writing style between the six disputed letters and the seven undisputed letters. The differences deal with structure and length of sentences. Thus, the author of Ephesians loves to pile up synonyms and loosely connected phrases that are dependent on a far-distant verb. He also appreciates long and complex sentences. Thus, in Greek, Eph 1:3-14 is all one sentence, as is 1:15-23. (Editors of modern Greek editions of the New Testament as well as translators have added periods to make these sentences easier to read.) In terms of sentence structure, the author of Ephesians may be history's first known German author! Sanday and Headlam characterized the writing styles of Ephesians and of Romans (one of the undisputed letters) in this way:

> We may take Eph. and Rom. as marking the extreme poles of difference within the epistles claimed for St. Paul. . . . The language [of Romans] is rapid, terse, incisive; the argument is conducted by a quick cut and thrust of dialectic. . . . [In Ephesians] the rapid argumentative cut and thrust is gone.

In its place we have a slowly moving onwards-advancing mass, like a glacier working its way inch by inch down the valley.[4]

The Pastoral Epistles, for their part, have ten to twenty times as many constructions that come from more sophisticated Greek than do the undisputed letters of Paul.[5]

Theology

The disputed letters often make statements that theologically are at odds with what Paul writes in the undisputed letters:

- In Eph 2:4-6, we read, "But God, who is rich in mercy, . . . made us alive together with Christ—by grace you have been saved—and raised us up with him and seated us with him in the heavenly places in Christ Jesus." Believers are already saved, and they have been raised to heaven. That is significantly different from Rom 5:9-10, where salvation is clearly in the future; see also Rom 6:5 and 8. And in Rom 6:4, Paul writes that Christ has been raised from the dead, but he stops short of saying that believers have already been raised. As opposed to what Paul says in Romans, the writer of Ephesians says believers are to consider themselves in some sense already resurrected and already saved.
- In Eph 1:22-23, Christ is the head over all things for the church, which is his body. Also, in 4:15-16 and 5:21-33, the "headship" of Christ is used in a hierarchical way: that is, Christ is the head over the body. That is quite different from the body imagery of Rom 12:3-8 and 1 Cor 12:12-31, in which Christ is not viewed as the head of the body.
- In the Pastoral Epistles, the Spirit is much less significant than in the undisputed letters. Only twice is the indwelling Spirit mentioned (2 Tim 1:14; Titus 3:5).
- The Pastoral Epistles unabashedly call Jesus God (Titus 2:13), a move that Paul, despite the very exalted view that he has of Jesus Christ, never makes in the undisputed letters.

Although a given scholar may latch onto one example or another as the key example, part of the strength of the argument for those who see the six disputed letters as written in Paul's name by someone else is the sheer cumulative effect of the many occurrences of significant differences in vocabulary, style, and theology.[6]

Do these distinctions (which can be replicated for Colossians and 2 Thessalonians and multiplied for Ephesians and the Pastoral Epistles beyond the examples given) prove absolutely that Paul is not their author? No. But for many scholars, they point to the strong probability that Paul himself was not the author of these six letters. The disputed letters are important sources for theology and for the periods after Paul, but we will not use them to reconstruct the life and thought of Paul himself. For that purpose, we will rely on Romans, 1 Corinthians, 2 Corinthians, Galatians, Philippians, 1 Thessalonians, and Philemon.

The Greek of Ephesians

The following is the author's translation of Eph 1:3-14, which is one long sentence in Greek.

(3) Blessed be the God and Father of our Lord Jesus Christ, who has blessed us with every spiritual blessing in the heavenly places in Christ, (4) just as he chose us in him before the foundation of the world to in order that we might be holy and blameless before him in love, (5) having predestined us for adoption through Jesus Christ into him, according to the good pleasure of his will, (6) for the praise of the glory of his grace with which he engraced us in the beloved, (7) in whom we have redemption through his blood, the forgiveness of transgressions, according to the richness of his grace (8) which he lavished on us, in all wisdom and understanding, (9) having made known to us the mystery of his will, according to his good pleasure which he proposed in him (10) as a plan for the fullness of the times, to sum up all things in Christ, the things in the heavens and the things on the earth in him; (11) in whom also you were appointed, having been predestined according to (the) plan of the one who works all things according to the purpose of his will (12) in order that we might be for the praise of his glory, having been the first to hope in Christ, (13) in whom also you, having heard the word of truth, the gospel of our salvation, in which also having believed you were sealed with the Holy Spirit of promise, (14) which is a down payment of our inheritance, for redemption as (God's) possession, for the praise of his glory.

Here is Eph 1:15-23—again, one long sentence in Greek.

(15) On account of this, I also, having heard of your faith in the Lord Jesus and the love for all the saints, (16) do not cease giving thanks for you, remembering (you) in my prayers, (17) in order that the God of our Lord Jesus Christ, the Father of glory, might give to you a spirit of wisdom and revelation in full knowledge of him, (18) having had the eyes of your heart enlightened in order that you might know what is the hope of his call, what is the richness of the glory of his inheritance among the saints, (19) and what is the surpassing greatness of his power for us who believe according to the working of the power of his might, (20) which he worked in Christ Jesus, having raised him from dead ones and having seated (him) at his right hand in the heavenly places (21) high above every ruler and authority and power and lordship and every name that is named, not only in this age but also in the coming (age); (22) and he put all things under his feet and made him head over all things for the church, (23) which is his body, the fullness of the one who fills all things in all.

The Book of Acts

The second source that traditionally has been used in the study of Paul is the New Testament book of Acts. Acts is the second half of a two-part work that includes the Gospel of Luke (the two volumes were separated when they were placed in the New Testament canon). Luke is about the life of Jesus, and Acts deals with the early church. Paul appears in Acts already at 7:58 (where he is called Saul), and in the second half of the book, he is the central human actor. It is natural, therefore, that people have read Acts as a source for studying Paul.

PAUL IN ACTS VERSUS PAUL IN HIS LETTERS

Opinion on the value of Acts as a source for Paul is divided, however. Some scholars evaluate Acts as a good historical record that was written by Luke the physician, the traveling companion of Paul (see Col 4:14; see also 2 Tim 4:11 and Philem 24). Certainly, there are many points of agreement between Paul's letters and Acts.[7] But others identify why it is improbable that Acts was written by someone who was a close associate of Paul's.

Paul's Apostleship

Paul's fundamental claim that he was an apostle lies in, with, and under every epistle and indeed his whole life's work. In contrast, Paul is called an apostle only once in Acts (14:14; implicitly in 14:4). Furthermore, when the author of Acts defines *apostle*, he limits the office of apostle to the original twelve disciples or, in the case of Judas Iscariot's replacement, Matthias, the office is extended to one who accompanied Jesus from the baptism of John until the ascension (Acts 1:21-26). Such a definition would immediately exclude Paul. The book of Acts also pictures Paul as heavily dependent on the Judean Christ-believing authorities in Jerusalem, but in Gal 1:11-12 and 2:6, Paul says quite otherwise.

Chronology

In Acts 9:26-29 and 11:27-30, Paul goes twice to Jerusalem before a major meeting called the Apostolic Council (15:1-29). Eventually, he makes two other trips to Jerusalem (18:22 and 21:15—23:30). In Gal 1:18-19, however, Paul himself says he went to Jerusalem only once before the Council (Gal 2:1-10) and saw only Peter and James. In Acts, he is introduced to the apostles and goes in and out among them. Yet in Galatians, he says he was there just two weeks and was unknown to the churches in Judea. Overall, as Bart Ehrman asserts, "in virtually every instance in which the book of Acts can be compared with Paul's letters in terms of biographical detail, differences emerge."[8]

Missionary Methods

We have already discussed the difference in perspective regarding the level of Paul's dependency on Jerusalem. In addition, Acts and Paul's undisputed letters view differently his way of carrying out his call to be a missionary apostle:

The Pauline Letters

Undisputed Letters (the Pillar Epistles): almost all scholars agree that Paul is the author	Deuteropauline Letters:	
	(a) scholars are fairly evenly divided on whether or not Paul is the author	(b) a significant majority of scholars view these as pseudonymous
Romans		
1 Corinthians		
2 Corinthians		
Galatians		
		Ephesians
Philippians		
	Colossians	
1 Thessalonians		
	2 Thessalonians	
		1 Timothy
		2 Timothy
		Titus
Philemon		

- *Speaking.* In Acts, Paul is an eloquent speaker in front of any group, from Judeans in the synagogue (13:15-43), to philosophers in the city of Athens (17:16-34), to the Roman governor (24:10-21). (Admittedly, one person fell asleep and tumbled out the window, 20:7-9, but see the next point concerning miracles.) In his own letters, Paul downplays his oral abilities (2 Cor 11:6) and acknowledges that others think he is not a strong speaker (2 Cor 10:10). At the same time, he does not want people to believe because of his oratorical abilities anyway, but rather to believe because of the message of the cross of Christ (1 Cor 1:17). But are the speeches of Acts actually from Paul? Many speeches in Acts have the same structure, whether they are given by Peter or Paul. They originate with Luke, not with Peter or Paul, in much the same way that authors of ancient histories regularly put speeches into the mouths of the main characters.[9] In the speeches in Acts, we hear the voice of Luke, not the voice of Paul.
- *Miraculous actions.* Similarly, in Acts, Paul performs healings and exorcisms as part of his ministry (19:11-20; 20:7-12, where the young man who fell out of the window and was taken for dead is brought back to life; 28:1-10). In the letters, however, Paul deemphasizes his ability to

perform such signs and wonders and points rather to preaching the cross (1 Cor 2:1-5; Rom 15:19; 2 Cor 12:12).
- *Letters.* The Paul of Acts is not a letter writer. Although scholars debate whether or not Luke knew Paul's letters at all, what is indisputable is that there are no references in Acts to any of Paul's letters. As the scholar John Knox once wrote, "Paul's letters represent him as a forceful and effective writer but as having few gifts as a speaker; Acts, on the other hand, presents him as an able orator but makes nothing of his letters—indeed does not give the slightest hint that he wrote any at all."[10]
- *Church organization.* In Acts, Paul organizes congregations by appointing elders (14:23). The term does not occur in the undisputed letters, appearing again in the New Testament only once 1 Timothy is reached.

Theology

In Acts, Paul avoids saying that Christ died for humanity, but in the letters, that is *the* crucial event in the life of Jesus. Similarly, for Luke, the death of Jesus is a miscarriage of justice (Luke 23:47; Acts 13:28), whereas for Paul, it is *the* salvation event (1 Cor 1:18-25; 2:1-2; Rom 5:1-6).[11] In terms of Judean dietary laws, Paul agreed, as part of the agreement worked out at the Apostolic Council (according to Acts 15:29), to have Gentile believers follow a minimum of Judean dietary restrictions, including not eating meat sacrificed to idols. In Gal 2:5, however, Paul indicates that he refused any such restrictions, and when in his letters he discusses meat sacrificed to idols, he views the eating itself as undefiling, even if

Fig. 2.2 The Areopagus, scene of Paul's speech to the philosophers (Acts 17).

for other reasons he urges believers to exercise care in eating such meat (1 Cor 8:1-13; 10:25-30; Rom 14:13—15:6). In general, the Paul of Acts is devoted to maintaining the Judean Law and is depicted as fulfilling all its requirements (see his protest in Acts 28:17). Although Paul's view of the Law of Moses is very complex and at times inconsistent, he had no reservations about violating the Law when he needed to do so. Thus, he could live like a Judean when he needed to, and he could live like a Gentile when he needed to do that (1 Cor 9:20-21). He also discusses a sharp confrontation with Peter (Cephas) when Peter failed to violate Judean dietary laws to enable him to eat with Gentile believers (Gal 2:11-14). As we might already anticipate from the discussion of the speeches, Acts generally includes little of Paul's theology.

Many more such examples could be described. Whether a close associate of Paul's or not, the author of Acts has an understanding of Paul's history and theology that differs sharply from Paul's letters. The differences are so great that many scholars do not think the author of Acts was closely connected with Paul at all, and for them, serious questions are raised regarding the historical reliability of what Acts says about Paul.

THE "WE" SECTIONS OF ACTS

There is still the matter of the "we" sections in Acts (16:10-17; 20:5-16; 21:1-18; 27:1—28:16). In those four sections, the author shifts suddenly from using the third person plural (what "they" did, referring to Paul and his companions) to the first person plural (what "we" did). When readers first encounter the "we" language, they may naturally conclude that the author of Acts shifts to that language because he was directly involved. The reasons just detailed on the relationship between Paul and the author of Acts argue against such a conclusion. More likely, the author of Acts is using as a source a travel diary (perhaps available to him only in sections, rather than as a complete document).[12] His use of such a source could also explain the way he shifts so abruptly between using "we" and not using "we."

That the author uses sources is something he tells us at the beginning of Luke (1:3), his first volume. Might that mean that Acts does indeed contain at least some historically authentic information? Opinions vary among scholars, as one might anticipate, but scholars today are not as quick to discard everything about Paul that is not countered by the letters as they once were. The basic standard for what material in Acts deserves suspicion is outlined by Mark Allan Powell: "The overriding consideration for evaluating the historicity of unparalleled material . . . is the question of whether the material appears to serve Luke's own agenda: if it does, its historicity is immediately suspect."[13] His example is the geographical and citizenship designation of Paul in Acts. In 21:39 and 22:3, Paul is identified as being from Tarsus; in 16:37-39 and 22:25-29, he is labeled as a citizen of Rome. Scholars can identify no Lukan theological tendency in the first identification, but they see important reasons for Roman citizenship, since that serves the author's larger agenda of fostering positive relationships between Christ-believers and the

Roman Empire. Thus, many conclude that yes, Paul was from Tarsus, but no, he may well not have been a citizen of Rome.

Noncanonical Sources

Starting with the disputed New Testament Pauline letters (Ephesians, Colossians, 2 Thessalonians, 1 Timothy, 2 Timothy, and Titus), a good number of authors understood themselves to be "Pauline" in the sense of wanting to continue Paul's basic theological and ecclesiastical program. Authors as different as Ignatius of Antioch and Marcion utilized Paul in their own writings, as did authors from certain strands of Gnosticism. Other documents, such as the *Acts of Paul and Thecla* and the *Pseudo-Clementines*, relate stories about Paul and state definite opinions about him (*Thecla*: positive on Paul; *Pseudo-Clementines*: very negative).[14] Many of the stories told in these documents differ from anything we read in the New Testament. While it is quite possible that some of the stories (or traditions) are quite old, it is unlikely that any of them gives us historically dependable data on Paul. We will therefore not take them into account when we are seeking to reconstruct Paul's life and thought.

Sources: A Proposal

Where are we, then, with regard to sources for studying Paul? People generally take one of three basic approaches:

1. **Acts as chief source.** Traditionally, people who understand Acts as historically reliable have started with that document. In turn, they integrate Paul's letters into the chronological framework of Acts.[15]
2. **Letters as sole source.** In reaction to the traditional approach, people who question the historical dependability of Acts have often totally omitted the book when writing about Paul. They have sought to work exclusively with Paul's letters.
3. **Letters as chief source.** Others have tried to work mainly with the letters of Paul when studying his life and theology but have also endeavored to fit in material from Acts when, according to their best judgment, the material in question is historically relevant and apparently accurate.

The third approach is the method we will follow in this book. When Paul's letters contain no evidence, we may gingerly cite Acts, having made historical judgments about the veracity of what it says. When Paul's letters and Acts conflict, we will choose Paul. His letters predate the book of Acts by three to four decades and are, after all, primary data from the hand of Paul himself. That is not to deny that Paul has his own theological perspective, just as Luke has his, but the significant difference is that Luke projected his theological views onto Paul. In the case of the letters, we have Paul's own words about himself and about his thinking.

Paul and His Activities

Differences between His Undisputed Letters and Acts

Paul's Letters	Acts
Paul makes three trips to Jerusalem (Gal 1:18-20; 2:1-10; Rom 15:25-29).	Paul makes five trips to Jerusalem (9:26-29; 11:27-30 and 12:25;[1] 15:1-29; 18:22;[1] 21:15—23:30).
After his conversion/call, *Paul does not immediately consult with apostles in Jerusalem*; he goes to Jerusalem *three years later*; he sees *Peter and James only* (Gal 1:15-19).	After his conversion/call, Paul leaves Damascus some days later; he *goes straight to Jerusalem* and *meets with the apostles* (9:26-29).
Apostolic Council (Gal 2:1-10): • Council occurs *after 14 years* of missionary labor. • Paul goes with Barnabas and *takes Titus* with them; Paul goes in response to a *revelation*. • Council is a *private meeting*. • Those at the Council agree on spheres of missionary work; and that • There will be *no dietary regulations* (cf. Gal 2:4-5).	Apostolic Council (15:1-29): • Council occurs *much earlier* in Paul's career. • Barnabas and Paul are *sent by* Christian community in Antioch. • Council is a *public meeting*. • Those at the Council agree on spheres of missionary work; and • *Issue a decree about dietary regulations for Gentile believers*.
A monetary collection *among Gentile believers* is to be given to Jerusalem believers as a sign of unity and to relieve their suffering: • The collection is an important part of the *latter portion* of Paul's ministry (Gal 2:10; 1 Cor 16:1-4; 2 Cor 8–9; Rom 15:25-28).	A monetary collection is taken *in Antioch, at the beginning* of Paul's ministry, and delivered by Paul and Barnabas (11:27-30): • It is *not* discussed as *part of his final journey to Jerusalem* (21:15—3:30).[2]

---

[1] The unparalleled visits.
[2] For a more detailed comparison of the chronologies of Paul's letters and Acts, see Karl P. Donfried, "Chronology: New Testament," in *ABD* 1:1017–19.

Paul and His Activities *(continued)*

Similarities between His Undisputed Letters and Acts

Paul's Letters	Acts
Conversion/call near Damascus (Gal 1:17, implied)	9:1-22; 22:6-11; 26:9-23
Flight from Damascus (2 Cor 11:32-33)	9:23-25
Travel to Jerusalem (Gal 1:18-20)[3]	9:26-29
Travel into the regions of Syria and Cilicia (Gal 1:21)	9:30 (Caesarea and Tarsus)
After 14 years, travel to Jerusalem; Apostolic Council (Gal 2:1-10)	15:1-29[5]
Conflict in Antioch between Peter and Paul (Gal 2:11-14)	15:30 (Paul in Antioch)[6]
Ministry in Galatia (Galatians, especially 4:13; 1 Cor 16:1)	16:6
Ministry in Philippi (Philippians; 1 Thess 2:2; 2 Cor 11:9, referring to Macedonia, the region where Philippi is located)	16:11-40
Ministry in Thessalonica (1 Thessalonians, especially 2:2; Phil 4:15-16)	17:1-9
Ministry in Athens (1 Thess 3:1)	17:15-34
Ministry in Corinth (1 Corinthians, especially 1:26-28, 2:1-5)	18:1-18
Ministry in Ephesus (1 Cor 16:5-9)	19:1—20:1; 20:31
Ministry in Macedonia (northern Greece; 2 Cor 2:13; 7:5; 9:2-4)	20:1-2
Ministry in Achaia (southern Greece; Rom 15:26; 16:1;[4] 2 Cor 13:1)	20:2-3
Plans to visit Jerusalem . . .	21:15—23:30 (visit in Jerusalem and arrest)
and Rome (Rom 15:22-29)	27:1—28:15 (journey to Rome as prisoner); 28:16-31 (under house arrest in Rome)

---

[3] But only "after three years."
[4] Cenchreae is in Achaia.
[5] No reference to 14 years.
[6] But no conflict with Peter.

Study Questions

1. What in this chapter surprised you? Why?
2. What arguments made the most sense to you? Which arguments did not? Why?
3. What is your evaluation of the proposal regarding sources for Paul?

Suggested Reading

Pseudonymity

Aland, Kurt. "The Problem of Anonymity and Pseudonymity in Christian Literature of the First Two Centuries." *JTS* new series 12 (1961): 39–49.

Charlesworth, James H. "Pseudonymity and Pseudepigraphy." *ABD* 5:540–41.

Authorship of Disputed Pauline Letters

ABD. Articles on individual books.

Hayes, John H., ed. *Dictionary of Biblical Interpretation*. Nashville: Abingdon, 1999. Articles on individual books (for 1–2 Timothy and Titus, see "Pastoral Letters").

Krodel, Gerhard, ed. *The Deutero-Pauline Letters: Ephesians, Colossians, 2 Thessalonians, 1–2 Timothy, Titus*. Proclamation Comentaries. Rev. ed. Minneapolis: Fortress Press, 1993.

Acts as a Source for Paul

Barrett, C. K. *Luke the Historian in Recent Study*. London: Epworth, 1961.

Haenchen, Ernst. "The Book of Acts as Source Material for the History of Early Christianity." In *Studies in Luke-Acts*, ed. Leander Keck and J. Louis Martyn, 258–78. Reprint ed., Philadelphia: Fortress Press, 1980.

Marshall, I. H. *Luke: Historian and Theologian*. Grand Rapids: Zondervan, 1970.

Powell, Mark Allan. *What Are They Saying about Acts?* Mahwah, NJ: Paulist, 1991.

Vielhauer, Philipp. "On the 'Paulinism' of Acts." In *Studies in Luke-Acts*, ed. Leander Keck and J. Louis Martyn, 33–50. Reprint ed., Philadelphia: Fortress Press, 1980.

Chapter 3

Where and When Did Paul Live and Work?

Although scholars have often viewed Paul as a timeless figure issuing theological pronouncements independent of his own era, today scholars work hard to set Paul within his own world. Indeed, not to do so runs the risk of misunderstanding him by reading him as though he wrote in the fourth century, the seventeenth century, or the twenty-first century, instead of the first century. In this chapter, we will focus on details of Paul's life: when he lived, where he lived, and how he traveled.

The Problems of Outlining a "Life" of Paul

As long as we approach Paul from a historical perspective, we will find it difficult to write a biography or a chronology in great detail. The reason for this inability is simple: we have precious little historical data with which to work. As we have seen, we do have the seven undisputed letters, and we do have the book of Acts. Unfortunately, none of the letters is dated. Nor are they numbered by Paul or placed by him in chronological order. When we turn to Acts, we find ourselves confronting the same three choices we encountered for identifying reliable sources in chapter 2: (1) take Acts, including the three missionary journeys of Paul discussed there, as a historically authentic framework for Paul's life into which the seven letters are inserted;[1] (2) reject Acts as a source for Paul and work only with the seven letters;[2] or (3) take the letters as the primary but not exclusive source for Paul's

Fig. 3.1 The perils of seafaring are illustrated in this relief from a third-century sarcophagus, discovered in Ostia; copy at the Museum für antike Schiffahrt, Mainz, of the original at the Ny-Carlsberg Glyptothek in Copenhagen.

career, utilizing Acts when it does not conflict with Paul's letters and when Luke's theological goals seem not to have overridden whatever historical data he had.[3]

In Acts and in Paul's letters, there are two potentially important references to people who can be placed chronologically from sources outside the New Testament. These people give us verifiable dates around which to build our outline of Paul's life.

The first reference is to the Roman proconsul of Achaia (southern Greece),[4] a man named Gallio. In Acts 18:12-17, Paul is hauled before him by non-Christ-believing Judean opponents. The location of this scene is Corinth. In the twentieth century, an inscription was discovered in Delphi, Greece. It mentions Gallio and can be used to date his time of office in Greece. The inscription reads as follows (words in square brackets are conjectured readings where words are missing):

> Tiberius [Claudius] Caesar Augustus Germanicus [Pontifex Maximus, in his tribunician] power [year 12, acclaimed Emperor for] the 26th time, father of the country, [consul for the 5th time, censor, sends greeting to the city of Delphi.] I have long been zealous for the city of Delphi [and favorable to it from the] beginning, and I have always observed the cult of the [Pythian] Apollo, [but with regard to] the present stories, and those quarrels of the citizens of which [a report has been made by Lucius] Junios Gallio my friend, and [pro]consul [of Achaea]. . . .[5]

To determine the date of the inscription, we can apply what we know of the Roman Empire's history and narrow the possible date range:

> **Listing Dates**
>
> For many centuries, Christians have used this system to indicate to which era of human history a date belongs: B.C. ("before Christ") and A.D. (*anno Domini*, meaning "year of the Lord"). Non-Christians quite appropriately have raised concerns about that way of identifying dates. As a sign of respect for people of all religious traditions, many scholars have moved to the abbreviations B.C.E ("before the Common Era") and C.E. ("Common Era"). C.E. dates are the same as dates identified by A.D., and B.C.E. dates are the same as those identified by B.C. We will use B.C.E. and C.E. in this book.

- The various names listed for the emperor identify him as Emperor Claudius, who became emperor on January 25 in the year 41. There was no pattern to the acclamations, but from other inscriptions, we know that acclamations 22, 23, and 24 were made in the eleventh year he was emperor (51). We also know that acclamation 27 was made some time in the second half of his twelfth year (52, before August).[6] Applying that information suggests that acclamation 26 was likely late in Claudius's eleventh year or during the first half of his twelfth year (scholars think the latter is more likely). That gives us a date range of January 25 to August 1, 52.[7]
- The Roman senate appointed proconsuls of senatorial provinces like Achaia to one-year terms that usually began in early summer. We know that under Emperor Tiberius (14–37), the terms began on July 1.
- Assuming the same terms for the date of the inscription gives us a range of July 1, 51, to July 1, 52.[8]

These dates work with Paul's eighteen-month ministry in Corinth and place him there in 50–52 or 51–53 CE.

The second reference is from Paul's hand and mentions the Nabataean king Aretas IV. In 2 Cor 11:32, Paul writes, "In Damascus, the governor [Greek: *ethnarchēs*; English: *ethnarch*] under King Aretas guarded the city of Damascus in order to seize me." He also places himself in Arabia (in the first century, a name for Nabataea) and Damascus after his call experience (Gal 1:17). Nabataea was an area east and south of the Dead Sea (see the map on pp. xiv–xv). It is in present-day Jordan, and its capital was Petra. Aretas IV ruled from 9 BCE to 40 CE (Josephus, *Antiquities* 16.9.4 [294–99]; 18.5.1-3 [109–25]), so the latest date for the search and subsequent escape (2 Cor 11:33) is the year 40, although it could well have been earlier. The flight from Damascus probably happened just before Paul's first visit to Jerusalem.

In addition to the Aretas reference, what about Paul himself? While we learn much from Paul's letters regarding the problems of his congregations and his responses to them, we do not find much information that helps us construct an outline of his career. Most of what we do have from Paul is contained in Galatians 1–2. In 1:15-17, Paul refers to his conversion/call and to its immediate aftermath: "But when God, who had set me apart before I was born and called me through his grace, was pleased to reveal his Son to me, so that I might proclaim him among the Gentiles, I did not confer with any human being, nor did I go up to Jerusalem to those who were already apostles before me, but I went away at once into Arabia, and afterwards I returned to Damascus." So God reveals Jesus to Paul, and then Paul does not go to Jerusalem; instead, "at once" he goes to Arabia (which means Nabataea, as we have seen), probably to do missionary work, which arouses the ire of Aretas IV, and then he returns to Damascus.

The next indication of movement we have from Paul's own hand is in 1:18-19: "Then after three years I did go up to Jerusalem to visit Cephas and stayed with him fifteen days; but I did not see any other apostle except James the Lord's brother." From there he went into Syria and Cilicia (1:21). Paul gives one more piece of chronological data in 2:1: "Then after fourteen years I went up again to Jerusalem with Barnabas, taking Titus along with me." Most scholars equate the Jerusalem meeting of Galatians 2 with the Apostolic Council discussed in Acts 15:1-29.[9] But there is lack of clarity in Paul's time reference. Does he mean fourteen years after his first visit to Jerusalem (1:18) or fourteen years since his conversion/call (1:15)?[10]

The result of this limited information is that any attempt to outline a chronology of Paul's life is hypothetical and inevitably to some extent speculative. Still, there is widespread agreement on these basic parameters: the apostolic conference took place in the 40s, and Paul's surviving letters were written mainly in the 50s. It is also clear that a fuller chronology cannot be constructed from the letters alone but must use Acts, even if we need to use Acts carefully.

Two final chronological notes concern Paul's birth and death. On his birth, we have no information about the date. In Philemon 1, written between 55 and 62, he refers to himself as an old man. The term for old man (*presbytēs*) was used for someone fifty-five or older (so Philo, *Creation* 105), which would result in a birth date around 5 BCE to 1 CE. That range of dates places his birth near the birth of Jesus.

Concerning Paul's death, the process leading up to it extended over several years. In approximately 57 CE, Paul traveled to Jerusalem with the "love offering" he had been collecting from Gentile believers. The offering was to be given to the Judean Christ-believers in Jerusalem, and it had a twofold purpose. It was, first of all, meant to relieve real suffering and financial hardship. It was also meant to be a sign of unity between Gentiles and Judeans who believed in Jesus as the Christ (on the collection, see Rom 15:25-28; 1 Cor 16:1-4; 2 Cor 8–9; Gal 2:10). When Paul came to Jerusalem, he was seized in the temple by a mob and subsequently taken into custody by the Romans (Acts 21:27-36). When the Roman officials learned about a plot to kill Paul, they transferred him to the port city of Caesarea (23:11-35), where he was kept for two years (24:27). Eventually, he appealed to the emperor (25:10-12) and was taken by ship to Rome (27:1—28:16). The trip began in late summer or early fall of 59. The journey lasted too long, extending into the season of greatest sailing danger and resulting in a shipwreck at Malta (27:39—28:1). Three months later (28:7, 11), Paul and those in charge of him left for Rome, arriving in February of 60. He was there, under house arrest, for two years (28:30).

Although the book of Acts may allude to Paul's death (20:22-24, 38; 21:11, 13), neither Acts nor any other document in the New Testament describes it. The early church historian Eusebius wrote that Paul "suffered martyrdom under Nero" in Rome (*Ecclesiastical History* 2.22.2), and he knew a tradition that Paul was beheaded (2.25.5).[11] He also pointed to a tradition that Paul and Peter were killed at the same time (2.25.8). Paul's martyrdom likely occurred in 62, a year that marked a sharp turn in Rome. Early in 62, Nero's administrator S. A. Burrus died, and Nero's moderate adviser Seneca was relieved of his duties. The upper echelons of the empire turned quickly to suspicion and the reestablishment of treason trials. The attention given to treason is particularly to be noted in light of Richard Cassidy's argument that the main charge brought by Roman authorities against Paul was treason, specifically violation of the emperor's "majesty."[12] The mere claim that Jesus was Lord could be considered treasonous.

Where Did Paul Live and Work?

Paul lived and worked in the Roman Empire, primarily in Greco-Roman cities. We can better understand Paul if we know something of the history and culture of those locales.

THE ROMAN EMPIRE

The dominant political reality in the first century was the Roman Empire. It was the soil in which and against which Paul wrote. As Warren Carter has written, "The Roman Empire provides the ever-present political, economic, societal, and religious framework and context for the New Testament's claims, language, structures, personnel, and scenes."[13]

In part because his entire life was lived under the Roman Empire, Paul's world was much larger than his boyhood home of Tarsus.[14] It was larger even than that of the religious and emotional center of the Judean people, Jerusalem. His world in fact included the entire Mediterranean basin. At various times, he lived and worked in Syria, Palestine, Asia Minor (modern-day Turkey), Greece, and Italy. At the time he wrote Romans, he hoped to travel to Spain, in the far west (Rom 15:28). To the Romans, the heart of their vast empire was the Mediterranean Sea,[15] and it is no accident that Paul was often drawn to (and sometimes taken to) cities that were on or near the coasts. At the same time, the Romans were great road-builders who honeycombed the territories they ruled with roads that enabled unprecedented travel.

A Basic Chronology of Paul's Life and Career

Dates	Events	Writings
33	Crucifixion of Jesus	
34	Paul's conversion/call	
35–38	Missionary activity in Arabia (including escape from Damascus and from the ethnarch of Aretas IV)	
	38: First visit to Jerusalem	
38–48	Missionary activity in Syria and Cilicia	
	48, Second visit to Jerusalem (Apostolic Council)	
48–52	Missionary activity in Asia Minor (Galatia), northern Greece (Philippi, Thessalonica, and Beroea), and Achaia (including Corinth)	50–52: writing of 1 Thessalonians
	51–52: Hearing before Gallio	
52–55	Missionary activity centered in Ephesus	Writing of Galatians, 1 Corinthians, portions of 2 Corinthians (Letters C and D; see below, chapter 9), Philemon, perhaps Philippians
55–57	Final missionary activity in Greece (Macedonia and Achaia)	Writing of portions of 2 Corinthians (Letters E, F, G, and H; see below, chapter 9); and Romans (the latter from Corinth)
57–59	Journey to Jerusalem with offering; arrest and imprisonment	
59–60	Journey to Rome as prisoner	
60–62	Imprisonment in Rome	Writing of Philippians, perhaps Philemon
ca. 62	Execution	

The origins of the Roman Empire lay in the city of Rome itself. Originally a village (traditional founding date, 753 BCE) and then a city-state on the Tiber River near Italy's west coast, Rome conquered and incorporated its neighbors as it grew in power both economically and militarily. Its desire to grow soon reached beyond Italy itself, and thus Rome and its great North African rival Carthage fought a series of wars from 264 to 146 BCE. Rome triumphed, thereby gaining control of the central Mediterranean. Its interest had already been drawn to the east. By 171 BCE, Rome's armies were moving into Greece; a century later, they had taken Syria and moved south to Israel. Not long afterward, however, civil war tore apart the Roman world. Julius Caesar, the general who had defeated the Gauls and subdued much of Europe, marched into Rome in 49 BCE in explicit defiance of the order of the Roman Senate. When he tried to become dictator, he was assassinated in 44, and civil war erupted. Forces loyal to Julius Caesar eventually defeated the armies of the Senate. Another war followed in which the former allies who had defeated the Senate, Octavian and Marc Antony, fought each other for supremacy. Octavian, Caesar's great-nephew and adopted son, won and became the first official emperor. He was known as Caesar Augustus (meaning "Most Revered Emperor"). Augustus ruled from 27 BCE to 14 CE. He was succeeded by Tiberius (14–37), who was followed by Caligula (37–41), Claudius (41–54), and Nero (54–68).

Paul almost certainly was born during the reign of Augustus. His experience of being called by God (sometimes called his "**conversion**," a point to which we will return; see chapter 4) probably happened during the reign of Tiberius. He worked as a missionary while Tiberius, Caligula, Claudius, and Nero were emperors. Paul was executed by the Roman state under Nero, as we have seen.

Although various philosophers in the Roman world, such as Panaetius and Cicero, had promoted the ideals of *humanitas* (a recognition that all people indeed are *human* beings) and a universal citizenship in the one *kosmos* (world), so that the later Roman Empire could be viewed as one great city (a cosmopolis; Aelius Aristides, *Oration* 26.36),[16] the everyday social reality was different. The social divisions between people were great. The divisions were many, but among the most significant were those based on citizenship, class, wealth, and gender.

Citizenship was understood in the Roman Empire in ways dramatically different from modern citizenship. People did not become citizens of the empire, or even of the city where they were born, simply by birth. Citizenship could indeed be inherited by birth. It could also be granted because of one's service to the state, including military service, and slaves formally freed by Roman citizens also became citizens. Citizenship had to do with status, therefore, and not mere geographic location or origin. The civil and criminal law for Roman citizens was different from the law for noncitizens, and Roman citizens carried their special legal rights with them wherever they went in the empire.[17]

Distinctions based on class and wealth were intertwined with each other. At the upper levels, Roman society was highly structured, with admission to the senatorial or equestrian orders, for example, closely related to how much wealth a person had amassed, especially based on ownership of land. The Roman Empire was an advanced agrarian society, with land providing the income and power that kept the elites in charge.[18] Subsisting over against that very small (5 percent?) but wealthy minority was the vast majority of people who tilled the land or labored in the cities.[19] That majority included unnumbered masses of slaves. It also included women, who were accorded roles outside the public sphere, usually limited to the home.

MEDITERRANEAN CULTURE

In addition to residing in the Roman Empire, Paul conducted his life and ministry within Mediterranean culture. While there were many subcultures in his world, they were united by common, overarching ways of living in the area often called the **circum-Mediterranean** (lands around the Mediterranean Sea). Two aspects of that common cultural perspective are of special note for our study of Paul: (1) the importance placed on honor and shame; and (2) the significant role of patron-client relationships.

Honor and Shame

The cultures within which Paul operated were **honor** and **shame** cultures. Honor and shame were core values in the Mediterranean worlds of antiquity and still are today. These values are expected in all human interactions.[20]

John Elliott defines honor in this culture as "a claim to worth (on the part of an individual, family, or group) accompanied by the public acknowledgment of, and respect for, that worth."[21] Honor, therefore, has two parts, one internal and one external: "Honor is the value of a person in his or her own eyes (that is, one's claim to worth) *plus* that person's value in the eyes of his or her social group."[22] Bruce Malina likens honor to the credit rating of a contemporary person in a developed nation.[23] Honor is, moreover, a limited good. That is, only so much of it is available; no more honor is available in a given society than already exists. Thus, a person must always be on guard to make sure that someone else is not taking his or her honor.

Honor is either ascribed or acquired. Ascribed honor comes about simply because of who one is (royalty, for example; note the biblical genealogies, which establish this aspect of one's honor) or as a grant from someone else who is honorable. Honor can also be gained by the success of the individual in the societal "game" of life called **challenge and riposte** (described later in this section). Further, honor is gained through beneficence—through giving away rather than keeping the wealth that one has (see the following discussion of patron-client relationships).

Shame is the loss of honor. It occurs when public opinion evaluates the person's deeds as dishonorable or negatively evaluates something that has been done to the person or to (or by) someone who is closely associated with the person (such as a family member).

John Elliott outlines three common elements of the honor-shame framework. First, he notes that "'shame cultures' . . . differ from industrialized 'guilt cultures' in that their members are group-oriented and governed in their attitudes and actions primarily by the opinion and appraisals of significant others."[24] What other people think is fundamental. The first-century circum-Mediterranean person has, therefore, a "**dyadic personality**," meaning the person's sense of self and worth is dependent on others.[25] To be a person is to be related to others or, more specifically, to be embedded in one or more societal groups, such as the most important group, the family.[26]

A second element of the honor-shame network is the nature of interpersonal relationships. Social relations involve constant challenges to and for one's honor rating. Since honor is a finite or limited good, if one person gains honor, someone else necessarily loses honor. A standard way in which honor is gained is by challenging others, calling their honor into question in some way, and winning the challenge. By failing to defend his or her honor successfully, the challenged person is shamed. Another label for the challenge and response is challenge and riposte; *riposte* is a fencing term that indicates a sharp, swift thrust made after stopping the opponent's attack.[27]

Third, while both women and men can bring honor to the family, their roles differ. Female space is the domestic space, the "inside" space. Male space is "external" space, the wider world. Traditionally, women stay at home, while men work in the wider world.[28] The sexual purity of the female is "embedded" in the honor of the male who is responsible for her. That means that violation of her purity lowers the honor rating of the male and, ultimately, of the entire family. In such cultures, rape by those outside the family is a tool of humiliation and shame that shreds the fabric of family life.

Patron-Client Relationships

A second aspect of Mediterranean culture that is of note for the study of Paul is that the cultures in which Paul operated were structured around patron-client relationships.[29] Underlying patronage is the concept, once again, of limited good. Resources—grain, water, money, etc.—are finite. Furthermore, the individual has no intrinsic right to the goods (including services) provided by the government. What are people to do when the resources available to them are inadequate for their needs? They can seek to establish a relationship with a patron, thereby becoming the patron's client. John Pilch and Bruce Malina define a patron as "one who either can obtain for a client something that the client could not obtain personally or can obtain it under better terms than the client might be able to do."[30] The relationship by no means is one-sided, however. It is a reciprocal, albeit asymmetrical, relationship, in which the client owes loyalty (political and otherwise) to the patron and must regularly give honor to the patron. Within this relationship, Bruce Winter explains, "The act of benefiting set up a chain of obligations. The beneficiary had an obligation to respond to the gift with gratitude; profuse expressions of gratitude then placed the benefactor under obligation to do something further for his client."[31] A person in a position to be a patron was expected to act in that manner. To act otherwise would have meant a loss of honor.

The contributions of the patron could take many forms. Perhaps the most common form of patronage was the relationship of a landowner to some (not all) of his tenants.[32] Wealthier patrons—those able to aspire to public office—were expected to build buildings, pave roads, fund theater productions, and underwrite athletic contests. Such people became patrons of the city and often competed intensely for the honor of public office. At the same time, the financial burdens of being so "honored" were heavy. The reward was honor in the form of public recognition: statues, portraits, inscriptions, proclamations, public burials, presents, the best seats at the theater.[33]

The emperor functioned as the human "patron of patrons," sitting on top of the vast system of patronage that enabled the empire to function. As the *princeps*, he was the primary patron or benefactor.

THE GRECO-ROMAN CITY

Paul was an urban missionary. His birthplace and location of upbringing was a city (Tarsus; possibly part of his education took place in Jerusalem), and virtually all of his missionary work was centered in cities (Antioch of Syria, Antioch of Pisidia, Beroea, Thessalonica, Philippi, Corinth, Ephesus, Rome, etc.). His ministry represents a sharp turn from the country and village ministry of Jesus. The change from country to city meant "a great shift in the cultural horizon of Christianity—from a reform impulse within Palestinian Judaism to a Greek-speaking movement based in the cosmopolitan cities of the Greco-Roman world."[34] And although the majority of people lived in rural areas, political and economic power was concentrated in the cities.

The cities in which Paul worked were often hybrids, with characteristics of the Greek city, the Hellenistic city, and the Roman city. The basic model of the cities of Paul's world was the Greek city (*polis*). The city could be governed by an oligarchic/aristocratic minority or a more broadly based democratic assembly; in either structure, the granting of citizenship was tightly controlled. Noncitizens, of course, also lived in the cities—women, children, local men who were not citizens, foreigners, and slaves.

Strictly speaking, the city's boundaries went beyond the city walls to include the surrounding countryside, where many of the citizens farmed. Usually at the center of the Greek city was the marketplace, or *agora*, which had clustered around it the city's major political buildings and religious sanctuaries. Honeycombing the center of the city were *stoas*, which were walkways covered by roofs held up by rows of columns. These covered walkways shielded people from sun and rain and provided legal and business spaces. Of great importance also was the gymnasium, which was the center of intellectual and physical education for youth as well as for adults.[35] It and the *agora* area were the social and business hubs of the Greek city. A theater, in addition, was found in every city of at least moderate size and importance.[36]

Cities were financed by taxes, with income from city-owned mines and farms, and by major gifts expected of the wealthy. Those gifts funded roads, athletic games, theatrical productions, religious ceremonies, and other civic needs, as indicated in our look at patron-client relationships.

In the fourth century BCE, Alexander the Great created an empire that expanded Greek influence far beyond his starting point in northern Greece. Although the spread of his military and political dominance limited the traditional autonomy of the Greek city, it also resulted in the transplanting of the Greek *polis* throughout Asia Minor, the Near East, northern Africa, and beyond. His successors for decades following his death in 323 BCE continued to build new cities based on the Greek model. While they were places of interaction between Greek settlers and local natives, these Hellenistic cities still had at their center the same institutions and buildings typical of the Greek *polis*.

The spread of the Greek city—very much in tune with Alexander's goals—also meant the spread of Greek culture, including Greek philosophy, customs, education, religion, values, and language. Scholars label that process **Hellenization** (from *Hellas*, the Greek word for Greece). The term **Hellenism** refers to the resulting synthesis of Greek thought and life with other cultures. The widespread adoption of a simplified form of the Greek language called *koinē* (common) or Hellenistic Greek immeasurably aided Hellenization. The New Testament is written in that kind of Greek. *Koinē* Greek functioned for centuries, including under the Roman Empire, as the major international language (lingua franca) of the Mediterranean world, much as English is the international language today.

When the political, military, and economic fortunes of Rome grew, Rome established many city colonies built basically according to the Greek model; they also refounded other cities and remodeled many others. The names used to designate the various parts of the city changed, naturally, with the shift from Greek to Latin. Thus, the Greek *agora* became the Latin *forum*. Above all, Roman cities included additional social institutions such as the baths, amphitheater, and temples devoted to the gods of Rome, most notably the trio of Jupiter, Juno, and Minerva. Statues of the emperor and his family were also prominently displayed.[37]

The cities in which Paul carried out his mission were cosmopolitan, including an almost bewildering mixture of peoples, languages, customs, economic levels, and social classes. Although people whose origins were in the same village or region or religion often tried to cluster together in the same way that contemporary immigrant groups do, their assumptions about the way things are and should be were continually challenged. A common response was the formation of associations or clubs that shored up ethnic or religious identity while also providing social and business services. These groups included funeral associations, religious groups, trade associations, and social clubs. In an urban culture that provided a confusing array of options, the associations provided an anchor of identity.

The cities of the Mediterranean world were extremely crowded. Moreover, with much of a city's space devoted to city-owned buildings and plazas, the amount of space available for housing was sharply compressed. The congestion and the

Fig. 3.2 Stone carving of Minerva, Jupiter, and Juno (the Capitoline Triad), from the Sanctuary of Fortuna Primigenia; National Archaeological Museum of Palestrina, Italy.

interweaving of commercial, public, and residential areas made for constant noise, as Juvenal (a first- to second-century Roman poet) humorously reports regarding Rome: "How much sleep, I ask you, can one get in lodgings here? Unbroken nights—and this is the root of the trouble—are a rich man's privilege. The wagons thundering past through those narrow twisting streets, the oaths of draymen caught in a traffic-jam—these alone would suffice to jolt the doziest sea-cow of an Emperor into permanent wakefulness."[38]

Of particular significance for Paul's ministry was the housing pattern in Greco-Roman cities. Almost all urban dwellers resided in one of two kinds of housing: the private house (*domus*) or the apartment building (*insula*). These housing options deeply affected how Paul structured his missionary work. (On housing, see chapter 5.)

How Did Paul Travel?

While travel in the ancient Mediterranean basin seems primitive from the perspective of the twenty-first century, it was in fact more accessible and reliable than it had ever been before. The pages of documents from the first century, including the New Testament, teem with large numbers of travelers. The real surprise regarding Paul is the relatively close contact he maintained with congregations he had founded, despite the barrier of distance. That contact depended on letters and personal visits (see chapter 5). And those contacts depended on the ability to travel.

The **Pax Romana** (the "peace of Rome" imposed by Rome's military might) provided the framework within which travel flourished. The Romans were skilled engineers and prolific road builders. At the height of the empire, they had approximately 186,500 miles of gravel or paved highways in service,[39] and in Asia Minor, they were able to use additional roads left by the Persians.[40] Roman dominance of the Mediterranean Sea itself had earlier reduced the threat of pirates significantly. So while most peasants spent their lives within a narrow geographic area, the empire was crisscrossed in Paul's time not only by Christ-believing missionaries but also by many other kinds of travelers: businesspeople earning a living; shippers transporting their goods (Rome in particular needed massive amounts of grain every day); merchants peddling their products; government officials beginning or ending positions or conducting other official business (one of the largest sources of travelers); soldiers marching to or from an assignment; tourists visiting exotic locations; pilgrims wending their way to the Judean temple in Jerusalem, the great Artemis temple in Ephesus, one of the many shrines to Asclepius (the god of healing), and other holy sites both minor and major; performers and athletes seeking income and recognition at the many athletic games and activities that clustered around them; prisoners being transported (Paul's journey to Rome is a good example; Acts 27:1—28:16); and teachers, philosophers, and students seeking and pronouncing wisdom.

LAND TRAVEL

To knit together their growing empire and give their armies ready access to places of unrest and threat, the Romans built roads. While literally "all roads led to Rome," the roads connected even the remotest region to the rest of the empire.

Paul utilized these roads and utilized them well. While we correctly assume that Paul normally walked while traveling on land, it is not at all impossible that at times he rode an animal or rode in a wagon or other vehicle. By riding, a person could travel between twenty-five and thirty miles a day; by foot, especially on a journey of several days' duration, the pace would be more like fifteen to twenty miles a day.[41] From spring through fall, the relentless Mediterranean sun was a challenge, but during long portions of the winter, snow-blocked mountain passes stopped road travel altogether. Paul appears to have "stayed put" during the unpredictable winter months (1 Cor 16:6); at other times, he also had to be careful of rivers swollen by rain or melting snow (2 Cor 11:26; "danger from rivers"). Problems with robbers on the main roads had been to a certain extent solved by the time of Paul but by no means had vanished altogether (see his reference to bandits in 2 Cor 11:26, as well as the story of the Good Samaritan in Luke 10:29-37, especially v. 30).

The other major challenge of land travel, besides finding food and water, was lodging. Holiday Inn had not yet entered the Mediterranean market! Stories of filthy beds, rabid vermin, exorbitant charges, and dangerous roommates were rampant.[42] Whenever possible, travelers would stay in private homes—of relatives or friends, if they had any in the area, or of people who knew people they knew (see Acts 16:11-15; 17:5; 21:15-16; 28:7, 14). Within a given circle of people, including the church, visitors would often be offered housing, at least for a short time.[43]

Such hospitality was a normal part of Mediterranean life, but it did have limits. The early Christian document entitled *The Didachē* (or *Teaching of the Twelve Apostles*) contains this directive:

> Let everyone who "comes in the Name of the Lord" be received. . . . If he who comes is a traveler, help him as much as you can, but he shall not remain with you more than two days, or, if need be, three. And if he wishes to settle among you and has a craft, let him work for his bread. But if he has no craft provide for him according to your understanding, so that no man shall live among you in idleness because he is a Christian. But if he will not do so, he is making traffic of Christ; beware of such. (XII)

To facilitate proper visits, Paul wrote letters of reference; Rom 16:1-2 is a good example. Paul commends a deacon named Phoebe, asks the recipients of the letter to welcome her and "help her." Note also the many people Paul greets in the rest of the chapter. He did not hesitate to request lodging (1 Cor 16:6-9; Philem 22) or material help for his and others' journeys (Rom 15:24; 1 Cor 16:6; 2 Cor 1:16; see also Titus 3:13 and Acts 15:3),[44] and he acknowledges hospitality extended to him (Rom 16:2, 23).

SEA TRAVEL

It appears that, especially in Acts, Paul traveled by ship whenever he could. When the winds were blowing in the direction the traveler wanted to go, sea travel was much faster than land travel. Under optimal conditions, a person could cover between 110 and 170 miles a day, although 100 miles a day was a more reliable rule of thumb.[45] Thus, a person (perhaps carrying a letter) could travel between Corinth and Rome in about a week if traveling almost entirely by ship. If more land travel and less sea travel were scheduled, the trip would take fifteen days.[46] Although certainly not at the speed of jet aircraft, travel was relatively quick when all factors worked well together.

Sea travel was, however, neither gracious nor highly reliable. With the exception of local passenger ferries, people in antiquity traveled on ships that were carrying goods. Potential passengers would scout out the projected itineraries of the ships in port and make arrangements for the ship that best suited their needs. They then had to wait until the ship sailed—which was not on a preset schedule but when the winds were blowing strongly enough in the right direction. Passengers had to provide their own food and generally their own drinking water, although the latter could be purchased onboard ship. There were no passenger cabins, and most people stayed on deck. In general, traveling west was more difficult than traveling east, but in either direction, storms or lack of wind could play havoc with passengers' plans and their very lives. No wind meant no progress, but high wind and waves could mean shipwreck. Acts 27 provides a vivid description of the actions taken during a storm to avoid the latter fate.

Just as land travel, especially in higher elevations, was limited by winter conditions, so too was sea travel—although the limitations were longer and more

> ### "The Miracle of the Bedbugs"
>
> Travel conditions are illustrated by the following story from The Acts of John, from the latter half of the second century or first half of the third century CE.
>
> 60. And on the first day we arrived at a lonely inn; and while we were trying to find a bed for John we saw a curious thing. There was one bed there lying somewhere not made up; so we spread the cloaks which we were wearing over it, and begged him to lie down on it and take his ease, while all the rest of us slept on the floor. But when he lay down he was troubled by the numerous bugs; and as they became more and more troublesome to him, and it was already midnight, he said to them in the hearing of us all, "I tell you, you bugs, to behave yourselves, one and all; you must leave your home for tonight and be quiet in one place and keep your distance from the servants of God." And while we laughed and went on talking, John went to sleep; but we talked quietly and did not disturb him.
>
> 61. Now as the day was breaking I got up first, and Verus and Andronicus with me; and we saw by the door of the room a mass of bugs collected; and as we were astounded at the great number of them, and all the brethren had woken up because of them, John went on sleeping. And when he woke up we explained to him what we had seen. And he sat up in the bed and looked at them and said to the bugs, "Since you have behaved yourselves and avoided my punishment go (back) to your own place." And when he had said this and had got up from the bed, the bugs came running from the door towards the bed and climbed up its legs and disappeared into the joints. Then John said again, "This creature listened to a man's voice and kept to itself and was quiet and obedient; but we who hear the voice of God disobey his commandments and are irresponsible; how long will this go on?" ("The Acts of John," trans. Knut Schäferdiek, in *New Testament Apocrypha*, ed. Wilhelm Schneemelcher; trans. R. McL. Wilson [Louisville: Westminster John Knox, 1992] 2:193-94)

sharply drawn. The traditional "no travel" time on the Mediterranean was between November 10 and March 10, but the optimum and therefore safest times were from May 26 to September 14.[47] During the no-travel times, the threat of storms and the inability because of clouds to use the stars for navigation kept most ships in harbor.

Paul knew well the uncertainties, indignities, and dangers of travel:

> Three times I was beaten with rods. Once I received a stoning. Three times I was shipwrecked; for a night and a day I was adrift at sea; on frequent journeys, in danger from rivers, danger from bandits, danger from my own people, danger from Gentiles, danger in the city, danger in the wilderness, danger at sea, danger from false brothers and sisters; in toil and hardship, through many a sleepless night, hungry and thirsty, often without food, cold and naked. And, besides other things, I am under daily pressure because of my anxiety for all the churches. (2 Cor 11:25-28).

In spite of such conditions Paul kept moving—almost 10,000 miles altogether, according to Ronald Hock.[48] And already that says something about what kind of person Paul was.

Study Questions

1. In what way is Paul's contact with Gallio and Aretas IV of help in trying to date Paul?
2. Briefly outline the social and economic structure of the Roman Empire.
3. What are honor and shame, and how did they affect people in the first-century Mediterranean world? Do you see any aspects of honor and shame in your world?
4. What are the chief characteristics of the cities in which Paul lived and worked? How do you think these characteristics affected his ministry?

Suggested Reading

Texts

Barrett, C. K. *The New Testament Background: Selected Documents*. New York: Harper & Row, 1961.

Elliott, Neil, and Mark Reasoner, eds. *Documents and Images for the Study of Paul*. Minneapolis: Fortress Press, 2011.

The Roman Empire

Carter, Warren. *The Roman Empire and the New Testament: An Essential Guide*. Nashville: Abingdon, 2006.

Jeffers, James S. *The Greco-Roman World of the New Testament Era: Exploring the Background of Early Christianity*. Downers Grove, IL: InterVarsity, 1999.

Cultural Anthropology of the Circum-Mediterranean

Malina, Bruce J. *The New Testament World: Insights from Cultural Anthropology*. 3rd ed. Louisville: Westminster John Knox, 2001.

Chapter 4

What Kind of Person Was Paul?

Part of the fun—and challenge—of learning to know Paul better is sorting out and putting back together again the stream of religious, cultural, and educational experiences that informed his life and letters. Paul was a Judean, he was a Greco-Roman, he was a leather worker, and he was a Christ-believer. Each identity, however, was more complex than the mere label would signal.

A Judean

Paul was a Judean who was filled with a burning love for his people (see Rom 9:1-5).[1] So he proudly pointed to his heritage: "But whatever anyone dares to boast of—I am speaking as a fool—I also dare to boast of that. Are they Hebrews? So am I. Are they Israelites? So am I. Are they descendants of Abraham? So am I" (2 Cor 11:21b-22).

But simply to state that Paul was a Judean is similar to saying, "Khalid is a Muslim" or "Melissa is a Christian." What kind of Christian is Melissa? Is she Protestant, Catholic, Orthodox? What kind of Muslim is Khalid? Is he Sunni or Shiite? The Judaism into which Paul—and Jesus, for that matter—was born was a Judaism that was struggling mightily to define itself both over against and within its interaction with Greek and Roman thought and life. Jesus had provided his own particular view of Judaism. So did groups such as the Pharisees, **Essenes**, **Sadducees**, and **Zealots**. Often their dislike of each other equaled their disdain

Fig. 4.1 Merchandise is handled in a Roman workshop in this third-century tomb relief. Royal Ontario Museum.

for non-Judeans, with the result that some modern scholars write about Judaisms in the first century.² At the same time there was an overarching unity within Judaism rooted in belief in the one God and dedication to God's gift of the Law (Torah).

In Phil 3:4b-6, Paul makes a key statement of his Judean self-identity. It is intricately intertwined with his group identity. "If anyone else has reason to be confident in the flesh, I have more: circumcised on the eighth day, a member of the people of Israel, of the tribe of Benjamin, a Hebrew born of Hebrews; as to the law, a Pharisee; as to zeal, a persecutor of the church; as to righteousness under the law, blameless." Paul was proud of the identifiers he listed:

- "Circumcised on the eighth day"—Paul was a male; the eighth day was the normal time for Israel's covenant initiation ceremony of **circumcision**.
- "A member of the people of Israel"—Thus, Paul was a member of the ethnic nation and covenant people Israel.
- "Of the tribe of Benjamin"—Paul, as all Judeans, belonged to one of the twelve tribes into which the larger nation of Israel was divided. The first king of Israel, Saul, was from this tribe. Paul was named for him.

- "A Hebrew born of Hebrews"—The phrase could be a bit of rhetorical hyper-identification (compare "I am an American born of Americans"). It may also be a way for Paul to indicate not only ethnic origin but also linguistic ability: Paul can speak Hebrew and/or Aramaic.
- "As to the law, a Pharisee"—Paul here identifies himself in relationship to one of the particular religious groups within first-century Judaism (see below).
- "As to zeal, a persecutor of the church"—See below regarding Paul as one who persecuted Christ-believers, as well as Gal 1:13-15 and 1 Cor 15:9.
- "As to righteousness under the law, blameless"—The word *blameless* (*amemptos*) does not mean "absolutely perfect in relationship to the law" or "fulfilling the law perfectly." It was, rather, a comparative term. The sense in Philippians 3 is that it pointed to "his high socioreligious status in the period immediately prior to his conversion *in relation to other Judeans*."[3]

Paul thus identified himself in his pre-Christ days as a law-abiding member of the people of Israel, whose pride in and zeal for his ancestry and traditions led him actively to oppose the young Christ-movement. More specifically, he identified himself in relation to the sect of the Pharisees (see also Acts 23:6 and 26:5).

A PHARISAIC JUDEAN

During the Judean struggle for identity in the centuries surrounding the birth of Jesus, one of the definitions of Judaism that vied for attention was that of Pharisaic Judaism. The Pharisees apparently began around 150 BCE, when Syria appointed Jonathan as the high priest in Jerusalem.[4] As a response to what they saw as foreign interference in internal Judean religious affairs, a group of priests left the temple in protest and established the community at Qumran, which subsequently produced the Dead Sea Scrolls. A group of laity, to whom the origins of the Pharisaic movement are traced, responded differently: they tried to apply the Mosaic Law to everyday life—"to the field and the kitchen, the bed and the street."[5] As their reputation grew as interpreters of the Law, they gained in political clout and often (although not always) allied themselves with the dominant political group at the right time.[6]

The Pharisaic understanding of Judaism, in addition to commonly held Judean beliefs such as God as creator, was dedicated to four particular emphases: the text, the Law, holiness, and **apocalyptic** expectation.

The Text

The Pharisees were devoted readers and interpreters of the Bible. Over against the Sadducees, however, who argued that only the first five books of the Hebrew Bible (collectively called the Pentateuch) should be considered authoritative, the Pharisees viewed as canonical the Prophets and the Writings as well.

Since Paul quotes and alludes to books from each of the three sections of the Judean Bible,[7] he apparently adheres to the same canon as the Pharisees. He was also able to move from the literal meaning of a passage or concept to a more spiritualized understanding that could be applied to daily life. So, for example, in Rom 12:1, he uses cultic language referring to animal sacrifice to introduce an extended section on living as a Christ-believer: "I appeal to you therefore, brothers and sisters, by the mercies of God, to present your bodies as a living sacrifice, holy and acceptable to God, which is your spiritual worship."[8] He is also able to use Judean sacrificial language (*hilastērion / sacrifice of atonement*; Rom 3:25) and Judean legal language (*apolytrōsis / redemption*; Rom 3:24) when explaining the meaning of Jesus' death.

In addition, Paul uses more discrete methods of biblical interpretation practiced by the Pharisees and their successors, the rabbis. They are discussed in chapter 5.

The Law

Although the Pharisees extended the canon beyond the Law, their desire to help people apply the Law to their lives meant that the Pharisees devoted great energy to the interpretation of the Law. Study of the Law was the path to true wisdom, and observing the Law was the way to righteousness in God's sight. In part because of their uneasiness regarding the way the Temple was being run and who was running it, the Pharisees developed a way of interpreting the Bible that spiritualized it so that even obscure purity laws were reinterpreted to apply to people's daily lives. In addition, they developed oral traditions on how best to understand the written laws. The goal of this oral Law, or unwritten Law, was to fill in the blanks—that is, to explain in more detail what the written Law had left vague.

The purpose of the Pharisees' approach was not to burden people but to give them the assurance that if they were following the oral Law, they were surely following the written Law. Thus, what specifically could a person do on the Sabbath and still keep the Sabbath holy? How far could a person walk, or how much could she carry? How much authority the Pharisees gave to oral tradition in the years before the Temple was destroyed is unclear, but it is likely that early on, the Pharisees proposed that their unwritten laws were authoritative in all areas of life.[9]

It was Paul's zeal for his ancestral traditions, especially the Law, that pushed him to persecute Christ-believers (Gal 1:13-14; 1 Cor 15:9; Phil 3:6). Their inclusion of Judeans and uncircumcised Gentiles at the same table for communal meals, their apparent disregard of Israel's purity laws, and their belief that a crucified and cursed criminal was the Messiah (see Deut 21:23; Gal 3:13) were more than Paul the Pharisee could handle.

It is also in relation to the Law that Paul identified himself in Philippians 3 as a Pharisee. At the same time, since his conversion/call experience had already occurred, he also separated himself from the Pharisees. His views on purity laws and association with Gentiles became sharply different from theirs (see Gal 2:1-16): he determined that fulfilling works of the Law does not justify a person in God's sight, and the laws that prevented Judeans from eating with Gentiles as well as other laws that provided Israel with ethnically based privileges were now passé.

Holiness

With the shift from Temple to daily life as the focus of their interpretation of Judaism, the Pharisees reapplied the concepts of cultic purity and holiness to the conduct of individual Israelites. The basis for their application was Lev 19:2: "You shall be holy, for I the LORD your God am holy." (This text was one to which other Judean groups also referred; see, in addition, Lev 20:7-8, 26; 21:6, 8.) Their attention was directed mainly to laws regarding ritual purity, food, Sabbath observance, and festival observance. By conducting themselves in the ways detailed in the Law and thus living as God wanted them to live, the Pharisees participated in God's holiness and were (themselves) holy.

As a Christ-believer, Paul continued his attention to holiness. For him, God's active presence in the world was the *Holy* Spirit (Rom 5:5; 1 Cor 6:19; 12:3, for example). That Spirit, in turn, makes believers holy at baptism (1 Cor 6:11), so Paul could address the hearers of his letters as "the holy ones" (1 Cor 1:2; 2 Cor 1:1; Rom 1:7; Phil 1:1; translated by the NRSV in each case as "the saints"). He also calls them to *be* holy, to live holy lives (Rom 12:1, for example; see also Rom 6:19 and 22, where the NRSV's "sanctification" can also be translated *holiness / hagiasmos*).[10]

Apocalyptic Expectation

The Pharisees had a clear expectation of resurrection and thus life after death, both of which were denied by their rivals, the Sadducees.[11] The Pharisees anticipated God's early intervention in this world, which would include destruction of all evil, the resurrection of the dead, final judgment, and the establishment of God's kingdom. Similar views were also held by the community at Qumran that produced the Dead Sea Scrolls.[12] Such views are often labeled as apocalyptic. The Greek term lying behind the English word is *apokalypsis* (revelation). It refers to a revealing of God's plan for the end of time, a time that is coming soon but that is impossible precisely to calculate.[13]

Those elements of a future expectation were present in Paul, as well (1 Cor 15:1-58). He clearly anticipated the end of the current eon or age and the beginning of the new (1 Cor 2:6, 8; 10:11; 2 Cor 4:4; Gal 1:4), and he anticipated that the end would come suddenly (1 Thess 5:1-5). His advice on marriage (1 Cor 7:26), celebrating the Lord's Supper (1 Cor 11:32), honoring governmental authority and paying taxes (Rom 13:1-14, noting verses 11b-12a), and resolving disputes within the Christ-believing community (Rom 14:4, 10-12) are based on his conviction that judgment and the final end are coming soon.

At the same time, Paul differed from his Pharisaic roots in two significant ways. First, for Paul, Jesus was the agent of the anticipated future. Second, the final struggle had already begun. The evidence for that was the crucifixion of Jesus. But in addition, since resurrection was to occur only at the end (as per apocalyptic thought), the resurrection of Jesus meant that the future had already broken into the present. The result was that, instead of a clear ending of the old age followed by the coming of the new age, the two ages overlapped. That overlap provided the context within which Christ-believers lived—and struggled to live in the light of the in-breaking age rather than in the darkness of the old age.[14]

How Paul had become a Pharisee is debated, and that returns us to the question of the proper sources to use in studying Paul's life and thought. In Acts 22:3, Paul says, while in Jerusalem, "'I am a Jew, born in Tarsus in Cilicia, but brought up in this city at the feet of Gamaliel, educated strictly according to our ancestral law, being zealous for God, just as all of you are today.'" The Gamaliel in question is Rabbi Gamaliel the Elder, a prominent figure in Pharisaic Judaism (he is also mentioned in Acts 5:34; see the Babylonian Talmud *Sota* 9.15). The Acts passage apparently understands that Paul moved to Jerusalem at an early age and was taught by Gamaliel. For some scholars, the Gamaliel material is to be taken at face value: Paul studied under Gamaliel,[15] and that educational experience was the source of Paul's Pharisaism.

For other scholars, there are good reasons for questioning the historical reliability of the Acts material. Paul himself never refers to Gamaliel, even when listing his credentials in Phil 3:4b-6 and 2 Cor 11:22 as a member of Israel. He even says that at the time of his call, he was unknown by face to the churches of Judea (Gal 1:22). Utilizing the same criteria we used when talking about sources for Paul's life, we encounter another reason for being unsure of the Acts account. The author of Luke-Acts seeks regularly to present Jerusalem as the center of salvation. He therefore tries to link the earliest church with Jerusalem and to show a comparatively smooth and positive transition from Jerusalem to the rest of the (Gentile) Mediterranean world. The fact that the Paul-Gamaliel connection furthers that goal in and of itself makes some scholars suspicious.[16]

It is unlikely, then, that Paul studied under Gamaliel. What we can say, with Roetzel, is that Paul "probably grew up in a Judaism that was strongly Pharisaic and apocalyptic."[17] But it was also a Judaism that was strongly Hellenistic.[18]

A HELLENISTIC JUDEAN

To label Paul a "Hellenistic Judean" is both accurate and insufficient. It is certainly an accurate label, for all first-century Judeans had been Hellenized to one degree or another. As we have already seen in the discussion of the Greco-Roman city, *Hellenization* was the spreading of Greek culture (Hellenism) and language throughout the Mediterranean basin. Paul, for example, was able to write believers in Asia Minor (modern-day Turkey), Greece, and Italy using Greek, and as far as our sources permit us to determine, he spoke with people in his missionary territories in Greek. Greek had spread into Israel as well. Even the names of the educational, social, and religious center for Judeans (synagogue) and the high council in Jerusalem (Sanhedrin) are Greek terms, and at least some Greek was spoken by many people.[19] Among historical-Jesus scholars, for example, the only debate regarding Jesus' language is *how much* Greek he knew.[20]

The process of Hellenization was not only linguistic. It was also cultural, so we turn to Hellenization as it shaped Paul the Judean. Paul grew up in a strongly Hellenized setting, because he grew up in the Judean **diaspora**.[21] The term *diaspora* is a Greek word meaning *dispersion*. It refers to the movement of Judeans out of Palestine, starting with the Assyrian and Babylonian deportations of the eighth and sixth centuries BCE. At times, emigration to other parts of the Mediterranean basin was mandated by military force or sale as slaves. At other times, it was voluntary, as Judeans sought greater economic opportunity. By the time of Paul, the fact of the dispersion was considered normal: far more Judeans lived outside Palestine than within it (a situation paralleled in the twenty-first-century distribution of Jewish people).[22] Judeans lived at various levels of the societies in which they found themselves. For those who wrote, suggests Eric Gruen, the impression they give is of "self-assurance and comfort in the Greek-speaking lands of the Mediterranean."[23]

At the heart of Judean diaspora life was the synagogue. It not only served as the location for worship but also provided space for educational and social activities. Further, it "enabled Judaism to survive the transition from temple to private house of worship and from worship within the Holy Land to worship anywhere that Jews might gather."[24] In addition to his parental residence, the synagogue would have been Paul's original religious "home." It functioned, too, as a beginning point later in his life for missionary work, in part because of the presence of those whom the book of Acts designates as "God-fearers," meaning Gentiles who were attracted to such an extent by Judean religion that they worshipped at the synagogue, studied the Judean Bible, followed at least a minimum of cultic laws, and supported the synagogue with their financial gifts.[25] Although some Gentiles did become full converts (proselytes), more remained God-fearers.[26] They became an

Fig. 4.2 Moses is drawn from the Nile in this fresco from the synagogue at Dura Europos (third century).

initial focus of early missionary outreach (Acts 13:13-16, 26, 42-50; 14:1; 16:14; 17:1-4, 16-17; 18:5-8) and were often first contacted in synagogues.

How did the fact that Paul was a *Hellenistic* Judean show itself? In addition to his use of Hellenistic rhetoric (described in chapter 5), a fundamental answer is that Paul's Bible was almost without exception the Greek translation of the Hebrew Bible. Although he almost certainly spoke Aramaic and likely had knowledge of Hebrew as well, the Bible he used in his missionary work and in his writing was the Greek Bible; the best known Greek Bible is usually called the **Septuagint**. The name comes from a legend that explains the origin of the translation. Seventy (or seventy-two) Hebrew scribes went to Alexandria, Egypt, at the invitation of Pharaoh Ptolemy II Philadelphus (284–247 BCE) to translate the Judean Pentateuch (first five books of the Bible) into Greek for the great library in that city. They worked independently and completed their task in seventy-two days—and their translations were exactly the same![27] The legend has resulted in the name Septuagint (*seventy*) and the abbreviation LXX (seventy in Roman numerals). The translation, in fact, took at least two centuries, was centered in Alexandria, and happened so that Greek-speaking Judeans would have access to their Scriptures. The legend was used by Judeans to assert the divine authority of their Bible, even when it was written in Greek.

Paul as a Judean is a prime example of "both-and." He was both a Pharisaic Judean, who knew and appreciated the "traditions of the fathers" as interpreted by the Pharisees, and a Hellenistic Judean, who grew up and was educated in an environment in which Greek language and values were integrated with and used to express his experience of the God of Israel. Marc Rastoin has therefore emphasized what he labels as Paul's "biculturality"—both Hellenistic and Pharisaic.[28] The Hellenistic side is seen even more clearly when we look at Paul from the broader perspective of the apostle as a Greco-Roman.

A Greco-Roman

We have tried to situate Paul within his native Judaism. That discussion led us to a consideration of Hellenistic Judaism. And our look at *Hellenistic* Judaism, in turn, helps us realize that we need also to understand the apostle Paul as interacting with and reacting to the Greco-Roman world of which he was a part.

What is striking, once we begin that investigation, is that it is difficult to keep separate how much a given part of Paul's approach, thought, or language was Judean in origin, how much was Hellenistic Judean, how much was Greco-Roman, and how much was based on his belief in Christ. The complexity of sorting out such issues is illustrated by the analogy of analyzing a political position taken by a twenty-first-century person. Does taking that position result from an opinion expressed by a grandparent much earlier in one's life, as a result of one's religious beliefs, as a result of education or employment, as a result of one's native language—or a combination of these and other factors? That we cannot always place a given statement of Paul's into one clear-cut category or another is an acknowledgment not only of the complexity of the world in which he lived, but also of the complexity of human life in general. The placement of a given portion of Paul's life into one category rather than another is, therefore, less important than gaining a picture of who Paul was.

EDUCATION AND CITIZENSHIP

We have already explored Paul's educational background in relationship to Judaism. We learned that his way of studying the biblical text was very close, at many points, to that of the Pharisees. At the same time, he had been immersed in the Greek version of Israel's Bible.

In addition to his education specifically as a Judean, Paul had a thoroughly Hellenistic education. The information for that conclusion is not direct. Paul never tells us what schools he attended, under whom he learned, or what subjects he studied. Nevertheless, his letters—their patterns of organization, level of rhetorical sophistication, and use of literary devices—provide us much information about Paul's educational level and likely also his social location.[29]

Rhetorical study of Paul's letters was revived by the 1979 commentary on Galatians by Hans Dieter Betz[30] and has been applied by numerous scholars to Paul's letters.[31] Not only did Paul know how to organize and develop his thoughts by utilizing the best rhetorical techniques of his era, he also showed facility in the use of genres that were learned by people who planned to speak and write in public settings such as law and politics.[32] "The letters themselves," writes Ronald F. Hock, "betray such a command of the Greek language as well as familiarity with the literary and rhetorical conventions of Greek education that only a full and thorough education in Greek on Paul's part makes sense of the evidence."[33]

A good example is Paul's use of diatribe. Diatribe is a way of organizing one's thoughts by debating with an imaginary opponent. The opponent asks questions that set up the teacher-philosopher to respond with the answer the author wants to give. Diatribe, thus, is a way of teaching that proceeds by question and answer.[34] More to the immediate point, Paul's ability to use diatribe points to a level of education far beyond that of basic reading and writing, all the way to at least the level at which students were trained in popular, nontechnical philosophy,[35] although his letters may indicate that he had had even more formal instruction in philosophy. People educated at those levels would have been, at a minimum, at the social level of the **retainer class**—that is, those who served the needs of elites—although it is not impossible that Paul was a member of the urban elite level himself.[36]

Paul's educational level, therefore, pulls him toward the people in his world who had higher social standing. The information in Acts that he was a Roman citizen (16:37-39; 22:25-29) does the same. We have previously seen, however, that crediting Paul with Roman citizenship may dovetail too neatly with Luke's theological goals.[37] In the letters themselves, Paul never referred to his being a citizen, and the fact that he was beaten three times (2 Cor 11:25) would have been highly unusual if he had been a citizen of Rome, since immunity from such treatment was one of the privileges of citizenship (Acts 22:25). It seems in particular odd that he did not refer to his Roman citizenship even when writing to Christ-believers in the capital city of the empire (the letter we call Romans) nor to the Philippians, who lived in a city often called "little Rome."

Is it *possible* that Paul was a Roman citizen? Certainly. But is it probable? No. Our study will proceed on the conclusion that Paul was not a Roman citizen, while acknowledging that the argument is not airtight.[38]

WORK AND SOCIAL LEVEL

Paul, we have seen, was well educated. He was also a craftsman or artisan, someone who worked with his hands. So in 1 Cor 4:12, he wrote, "we grow weary from the work of our own hands," and in 1 Thess 2:9, he reminded his listeners, "You remember our labor and toil, brothers and sisters; we worked night and day, so that we might not burden any of you while we proclaimed to you the gospel of God."[39] Paul himself never said in his letters exactly *what* he did. In Acts 18:1-3, we learn that Paul was a *skēnopoios*, that is, a tentmaker.[40] Scholars almost universally agree that the author of Acts is using a reliable tradition. The military needed many tents, although most of its needs were supplied by its own tentmakers. Civilians needed tents for temporary housing at large, public events such as athletic contests (including the Isthmian Games near Corinth); for market stalls; for land travel; for sea travel, since passengers needed to pitch their tents both to provide a place to sleep and to protect themselves from sun and rain; and to cover the **atria** in their homes. Cities also needed the products of tentmakers, who produced awnings to shade walkways. The tentmaker could use animal hides (leather) as well as cloth, and in some places goat hair. It is quite probable that Paul could make all leather items, ranging from hinges and sandals to tents.[41]

The life of the artisan was hard. Toiling from sunrise to sunset in small, cramped shops,[42] artisans were able to eke out enough income to support themselves and their families—as long as they could work and as long as the economy was reasonably strong. Artisans who built up a good reputation might do better financially, but artisans who moved from city to city, like Paul, probably were not able to do as well.[43]

Artisans, moreover, were not evaluated very positively by the opinion makers in the circum-Mediterranean. The basic criticism of artisans, according to Hock, is that they were viewed as "slavish." The kind of work artisans did was often done by slaves, and whoever had to hunch over their work looked like slaves, whether free or not. They were also criticized for harming their bodies, being uneducated, and producing useless products.[44] Modern people look back at Paul and see an honored figure, but Paul himself understood that—especially over against some of his opponents—he was "last of all," a fool, weak, dishonored, hungry, thirsty, poorly clothed, homeless, and "weary from the work of our own hands" (1 Cor 4:9-12a). Part of the negative evaluation by others was, without question, directly related to his work: "A free man," like Paul, "who took up a trade was viewed as having done something humiliating."[45] Especially in Corinth, members of the young Christ-believing community were embarrassed that their apostle-teacher presented himself as a lowly workman rather than as a professional teacher (1 Cor 1:17; 2 Cor 11:7; 12:11-16).

Paul seems to have been divided in his own mind regarding his work. On the one hand, he could express himself in ways that showed an attitude similar to that of people higher up in the economic and social world. Work was tiring (1 Cor 4:12a; 1 Thess 2:9) and enslaving (1 Cor 9:19), and his particular work did not result in upward mobility (1 Cor 4:12b-13). Indeed, he humbled himself by engaging in the work he did (2 Cor 11:7). On the other hand, he encouraged the believers in Thessalonica to work with their hands (1 Thess 4:10b-12).

Why, then, did he work as a tentmaker, particularly given his high level of education? Why did he not let patrons support him in the way they supported philosophers and teachers? The traditional answer is that Paul, as an educated Pharisee, was conducting his life the way a rabbi should. Rabbis were not to make their living from teaching God's Law but needed to have a trade to support themselves. Many scholars have, therefore, looked at the period of Paul's study under Rabbi Gamaliel as the time when Paul learned his trade.[46] That conclusion rests on the assurance that Paul did in fact study under Gamaliel, a position questioned by many.[47] Moreover, we have no evidence, even if Paul did study with Gamaliel, that Paul was training to become a rabbi, and the earliest evidence for the rabbinic dictum on not making a living from the Torah is dated a century later than Paul.[48] In light of those insights, Hock argued initially that Paul's father taught him the family trade, not Gamaliel.[49]

A different approach to why Paul worked as an artisan—as well as access to his more positive view of working—is gained when we return to why he refused to let others support him. By supporting himself, Paul reached several objectives:

- He maintained his independence to do missionary work where, when, and how he wanted. So he funded himself, even though he had the right to "refrain from working for a living" (1 Cor 9:6; see 9:3-27).
- He thus freed himself from the potential complications of being the client in a **patron-client** relationship. He could indeed accept support from other believers (2 Cor 11:8; Phil 4:10-20), but he was careful, first, not to accept money from believers in the city in which he was working at a given time, and second, to establish when he did accept funding that he was not the client of those who provided the funding (see the careful way he writes to the Philippians in 4:10-20).
- He was able by supporting himself to offer the good news of Jesus free of charge (1 Thess 2:9; 1 Cor 9:12b, 15-18, especially v. 18), thereby gaining a level of credibility that distinguished him from the charlatans who came into a given locale, excited the population with philosophical and/or religious insights, took a collection—and were gone by the next day.
- He was able to move quickly from place to place, wrapping up the few tools needed for his work and easily setting up shop in the next city.
- He used his work to point to Jesus, and he used it as an example of the behavior he wanted to cultivate among believers. We have learned that

Paul's level of education signals a person of some social standing. Being a tentmaker does not. Paul left his former life, which included position and power (Phil 3:4b-6), to embrace the life of the artisan in a move similar to that of the Christ, who became a human being by "taking the form of a slave" (Phil 2:7). Moreover, the same Christ "humbled himself" (Phil 2:8). Paul applies the verb *humble* (*tapeinoō*) to himself, and he clearly understands himself as a person who has voluntarily become a slave (1 Cor 9:19-27, especially v. 19; 2 Cor 11:7-9, especially v. 7; see also his self-designation as a slave in Rom 1:1, Phil 1:1, and Gal 1:10). An important way he does that is by his trade.

It is quite possible that Paul learned his trade *after* his conversion/call experience on Damascus Road, both to embody the radical shift that occurred when Jesus appeared to him and to make his mission possible.[50] The workshop became, in turn, a primary mission site for Paul.[51]

On the complicated question of determining Paul's status within his world, we have found sharp contradictions. In the eyes of circum-Mediterranean societies, Paul had no political or economic power; indeed, his move into the subculture of artisans was a stark example of downward mobility, since his educational level pointed to much higher standing. As an artisan, he had no standing in the broader society and was dishonored (1 Cor 4:10; the NRSV has "in disrepute"). As we have seen, in Corinth and perhaps elsewhere, that societal judgment caused some people in the emerging church to evaluate him negatively. For others within the Christ-believing community, his role as apostle outweighed other considerations, and Paul exercised substantial (although not unchallenged) power. In many ways, Paul is a prime example of status inconsistency.

What Did Paul Look Like?

The bottom line is that we do not know what Paul looked like. Still, it is fun to speculate!

In what he writes, Paul does not present himself in an attractive light: "For they say, 'His letters are weighty and strong, but his bodily presence is weak, and his speech contemptible'" (2 Cor 10:10). How much his opponents are referring to his physical characteristics is unclear; the emphasis may be more on their negative evaluation of his speaking ability (in comparison to theirs!). In Gal 4:13-16, he refers to a physical ailment, which many think is an eye problem. Eye problems that could be seen by others created suspicion and worry that the afflicted person might have an "evil eye" and be able to cast a spell.[52] There is also the matter of his thorn in the flesh (2 Cor 12:7b-9), which may or may not be the same as his eye problem. At the same time, Paul's arduous and extensive travels point to a person of vigorous health whose physical condition permitted him to keep up a grinding schedule for many years.

The only physical description of Paul we have from the first two centuries is found in the *Acts of Paul and Thecla* 2: "And he saw Paul coming, a man small of stature, with a bald head and crooked legs, in a good state of body, with eyebrows meeting and nose somewhat hooked, full of friendliness; for now he appeared like a man, and now he had the face of an angel."[53] To modern Western ears, the description is mixed at best: small, bald head, crooked legs, eyebrows meeting, and a hooked nose are not normal descriptors of a hunk. "A good state of body," "full of friendliness," and "the face of an angel" are much more positive.

Several scholars have taught us to look at the features as code descriptions of Paul's character.[54] Indeed, a person's inner character was thought by ancient Mediterranean people to be reflected in what the person looked like physically, and conversely, what a person looked like provided a window into the person's character.[55] That means, in turn, that what we have in the *Acts of Paul and Thecla* is "a sketch of Paul's 'character' or person,"[56] rather than only a physical description.

So what does this sketch say about Paul?[57] We can look at each trait for clues:

- *Short*. Although being tall was a positive characteristic of generals and warriors, many Greek heroes and civic figures such as Heracles were described as short. So was Caesar Augustus (Suetonius, *The Lives of the Caesars* 2.79.2). A short man who was able to get things done was considered "balanced."
- *Bald head*. While being bald in and of itself was not a positive, the Greek term *psilos* (bald) refers to baldness caused by human action.[58] Might the term refer to shaving his head as part of a religious vow, as seen in Acts 18:18 and 21:24?
- *Crooked legs*. The term refers to being bowlegged. This characteristic signaled that the person could stand firm and was used for soldiers and generals.
- *Eyebrows that met*. A characteristic of warriors and of Caesar Augustus (Suetonius, *The Lives of the Caesars* 2.79.2), eyebrows that met naturally, not as the result of human intervention, were considered manly.
- *Hooked nose*. A hooked nose, or aquiline nose (like an eagle), was another indication of manliness and perhaps of generosity.
- *A good state of body*. Whatever ailments he had, Paul was able to walk many miles in all kinds of terrain.
- *Full of friendliness*. More literally, this descriptor should be translated "full of grace," which suggests a pleasant personality and may also point to God's grace evident in Paul's life.
- *The face of an angel*. The reference is not to the fat little cherubs of Renaissance art but to God's messenger (which is what *aggelos / angel* means in Greek), who comes with a clear mission.

In sum, "the portrait of Paul . . . is first and foremost that of a noble or ideal male."[59]

We have no ability to determine whether the author of the *Acts of Paul and Thecla* had older sources that aided him in describing Paul. What is most probable is that the *Acts of Paul and Thecla* describes what Paul *was like* (to the author and the author's community), rather than what he looked like.

PHILOSOPHY

Paul's relationship to and interaction with the Greco-Roman world of which he was a part are seen also in his interface with the major philosophical movements of his time. While twenty-first-century Westerners tend to think of philosophy as abstract and unconnected with daily living, philosophy was a major way ancient people sought to answer their basic questions on the meaning of life. Indeed, the boundary between religion and philosophy was often hard to maintain.

In addition to the normal life questions posed to all philosophies and religions, thinkers in the first century had other specific issues to address. Those issues were rooted in the Greece of the third century BCE, when traditional religious answers failed in the face of civil war, famine, and the general decline of Greek institutions. Trust in the government evaporated, and many people felt like meaningless bit players in a drama controlled by the Fates or Fortune, a perspective on life that increased with the rise of the vast and impersonal Roman Empire. Attention to study of the physical world, including the human body, waned. By the time of Paul, there was much philosophical and religious ferment as people tried to find their place.[60] Cynicism and Stoicism provided two popular sets of philosophical answers, and both have been studied extensively in relation to Paul.

Cynicism

Diogenes of Sinope (dates vary widely; basically, fourth century BCE) is usually understood to be the founder of Cynicism. He had little interest in developing an overall, comprehensive philosophy, so he turned his attention to how people should behave. He modeled a life that rejected societal convention or law in favor of nature. Living according to nature meant for him a life of asceticism, poverty, begging, berating people, and total shamelessness (contrast the circum-Mediterranean's honor and shame code). At least some of his followers did not hesitate to practice natural bodily functions in public, including eliminating waste and engaging in sexual activities. Such actions resulted in the negative nickname *kynikos* (dog-like; *kyōn* means *dog*), from which the term Cynicism came. The result of living according to nature, he argued, was a life of freedom, self-sufficiency, and boldness to speak the truth—especially about the standard values of society. By the time of Paul, wandering Cynic philosophers took their message from city to city. Their work was primarily urban, as was Paul's. Addressing the social foolishness of their world was their chief mission.[61]

Recent scholarship has identified three areas in which Cynicism may have influenced Paul. First, Cynics developed several forms and genres designed to communicate their views to the masses. Among these are the diatribe (a discussion or debate, often on moral behavior, and also used by the Stoics),[62] the exhortation and the exhortative or paraenetic letter (1 Thessalonians),[63] and the catalog of hardships (2 Cor 11:23-29, for example).[64] Second, Paul's approach and language are at times very similar to that of the Cynics.[65] Thus, the way Paul defends his ministry in Thessalonica (1 Thess 2:1-12) is close at many points to the way Dio Chrysostom (ca. 40–120 CE) describes the ideal Cynic philosopher (32.11-12), including verbal parallels.[66] Third, one strand of the Cynic tradition may provide a model for an important part of Paul's missionary strategy—namely, the use of the leatherworking shop as the location for missionary work.

In contrast, Paul intentionally sought to create communities of believers, rather than isolated, enlightened adherents. He also spent little energy railing against societal norms, since from his perspective, the present world's structures were soon to disappear (1 Cor 7:31), to be replaced by God's rule. That means that the basis for his activities was also substantially different from that of the Cynics, for what Paul says and does is rooted in God's activity in Christ. For that reason, he can boast in his sufferings and rejoice in his self-sufficiency, because they point to God (2 Cor 12:9-10; Phil 4:13).

Stoicism

Zeno of Citium (335–263 BCE) was originally a Cynic but went on to found his own philosophical school, Stoicism. The name derived from his practice of teaching in a colonnaded or columned walkway (*stoa*) in central Athens, where he presented a philosophy that advanced beyond Cynicism by proposing a carefully constructed, unified system in which all reality was understood to be one. According to the Stoics, the world is ruled by divine reason (*Logos*, which can be translated as *word* or *reason*), and God permeates the entire world of nature. In the Stoic system, universal law governs the entire cosmos—a view that provided a worldwide perspective that matched the international thrust of Hellenism as well as the later Roman Empire.

By the time of the writing of the New Testament and later, the chief public interest in Stoicism was in its ethics or way of life. That interest can be seen in the writings of L. Annaeus Seneca (ca. 4 B.C.E.–65 C.E.), Epictetus (ca. 50–150 C.E.), and Marcus Aurelius (120–180 C.E.). Universal law—whether of nature or of virtue—was considered rational, so it could be comprehended and lived out by the wise person, since each person contains a spark of the divine. The goal was harmony with nature, which in turn led to self-sufficiency, contentment, and a kind of tranquility that was independent of outward circumstances. The ideal Stoics accepted their fate without complaint and concentrated their energy on what they could control—their own reactions to whatever happened. At the same time, they had a strong sense of obligation to the entirety of reality, including to the ideal of the universal relatedness of all people (also labeled the unity of humanity).[67]

Stoicism, according to Hans-Josef Klauck, "is accepted generally as the most important point of comparison for Christianity in its earliest development."[68] That statement applies especially to Paul, and it is not insignificant that Paul's hometown of Tarsus was a center of Stoicism (Dio Chrysostom 33.48). As with Cynicism, Stoicism utilized several literary forms that Paul adopted and adapted: the diatribe,[69] lists of virtues and vices,[70] and lists of hardships.[71]

More subtle yet clearly present are passages in which Paul's language and/or thoughts are close to Stoicism. An example early in Romans is Paul's use of a "natural theology" argument for the existence of God, that is, the position that

Fig. 4.3 The Stoa of Attalos in Athens.

observing nature should lead to at least a basic knowledge of the creator God (Rom 1:19-20). In addition, Rom 2:14-15 would fit with Stoic thought on living a virtuous life in harmony with nature. At the same time, Paul counsels Christ-believers to realize that their true citizenship is not in this world, which is passing away, but is in heaven (1 Cor 7:29-31; Phil 3:20). That view has affinities with the Stoic understanding of being a citizen not solely of one city or even one empire but of the whole world (the term *cosmopolitan* expresses that ideal).[72] Abraham Malherbe has argued that in 1 Corinthians 8 and 9, Paul uses Stoic terminology that came from his opponents and counters them by using Stoic categories such as the "weak," the idea that bad people are slaves and that only the wise are free, and the necessity for training that distinguishes between what belongs to a person and what does not.[73] Troels Engberg-Pedersen has worked through Philippians in great detail, concluding that the vocabulary, basic ideas (other than the role of Jesus), and strategy of the letter are "both centrally Stoic and also sufficiently specific to make it highly unlikely that it is anything *but* Stoic."[74]

Epicureanism

Epicurus (341–270 BCE) centered his movement in the garden of his home in Athens. It spread widely and was part of the Roman Empire's philosophical landscape, although it was not as popular as Cynicism and Stoicism. Epicureanism included women and slaves as well as free men; its adherents thought of themselves as friends. Although they did not deny the existence of the gods, Epicureans believed the gods were blissfully uninvolved in human affairs. People should, therefore, anticipate no divine intervention in this life and also no divine judgment in the next, because there was no life after death. Just as the gods were tranquilly detached, so people should be detached from the obligations of civic life.

The Epicurean goal of life was pleasure, but not pleasure as usually defined today or as inaccurately assigned to them by their ancient opponents. Rather, "by pleasure we mean the absence of pain in the body and of trouble in the soul" (Diogenes Laertius 10.131; see also the larger section 10.122-35). Both because of false caricatures of this school of thought and because of their inattention to the gods and to political life, Epicureanism was hounded by charges of immorality, atheism, and civic neglect. Paul likely reflects that attitude in an anti-Epicurean statement in 1 Cor 15:32; he is also pictured in Acts 17:18 as an opponent of Epicureans.

More positively, Epicurean friendship groups were somewhat comparable to the fictive kinship groups of Paul's mission,[75] and the care for its members started by Epicurus has parallels in how Paul tried to care for people in his churches.[76] Opponents of both movements could even lump them together, pointing in particular to their atheism (not worshipping the Roman gods), lack of civic involvement, and supposed immorality (see Lucian, *Alexander the False Prophet* 25 and 38). Paul, for his part, may have consciously tried to distinguish Christ-believers from Epicureans,[77] although his counsel to live quietly with special attention to the sisters and brothers (1 Thess 4:9-12) is reminiscent of Epicurean thought.[78]

Neo-Pythagoreanism

Neo-Pythagoreanism was a philosophical and religious movement that provided part of the matrix in which Paul lived and wrote but does not seem to have influenced him much. Pythagoras founded his school in southern Italy ca. 525–500 BCE. By the time of Paul, the original movement had developed beyond Pythagoras's teachings, declined, and been revived starting in the first century BCE. It taught the transmigration of souls, the need to purify the soul, an ascetic lifestyle, astrology, and the hidden meaning of numbers. The result was a devaluation of the physical body, though there could be strong communal life among its adherents.

Scholars generally limit specific contact between neo-Pythagoreans and the Pauline tradition to the New Testament letters often understood to be written in Paul's name but not by Paul himself. Thus, Eduard Schweizer has suggested that the "philosophy and empty deceit" of Col 2:8, 16-23 may be Pythagorean,[79] and the lists of household duties in Col 3:18—4:1 and Eph 5:22—6:9 are similar to such lists in the Pythagorean tradition.[80] Paul's own listeners, however, likely knew at least the basics of neo-Pythagoreanism.[81]

PERSONAL RELIGION

Paul did not announce the good news of Jesus to people who were nonreligious. There was nowhere in antiquity Paul could go and not encounter religious processions, art, statues, inscriptions, and temples. Local religions, international religions, and political religions abounded, as we will see. Even in the private home, another entity held sway—the domestic cult.

Domestic Cult

In the Greek world, the domestic cult or religion centered on the hearth, where the fire was kept burning. The hearth was the site of extinguishing and relighting the fire each year in a formal ritual, and it also functioned as an altar: at the hearth, prayers were spoken at the start and finish of the day, and small sacrifices were made (especially of wine often mixed with water). Sacrifices provided one way to thank the gods, and they could also be offered to the family's now-dead ancestors. The goddess Hestia was most closely connected with hearth and fire, with Zeus functioning as the divine father of the family.

In the Roman part of the circum-Mediterranean, the domestic cult paid particular attention to certain gods and spirits:

- The *lares familiares* (household gods, who go back to Rome's rural heritage)
- The *Penates* (household gods closely associated with the hearth and food supplies)
- The *genius* of the *pater familias* (guardian spirit of the founder of the family)

Families daily acknowledged the *lares*, with most families dedicating a portion of a room or a cabinet to them and to the *genius*.[82] Such shrines have been discovered in houses at Pompeii and Herculaneum, cities destroyed and buried when the volcano Mt. Vesuvius erupted in 79 CE. Deceased family members were also honored at their graves with food offerings and decorations.[83] The Hestia of Greece was comparable to the Romans' goddess Vesta, although the latter was more important to the Romans than Hestia was to the Greeks. Vesta had a significant function in the public religion as the keeper, through her Vestal virgins, of the city of Rome's sacred fire.[84]

Astrology, Omens, Divination, Oracles, and Magic

The sense of being controlled by invisible powers caused people to do two things. First, they tried to discover their future by astrology (looking for clues in the patterns and relationships of the heavenly bodies), attention to omens (a flashing or streaking star, comet, etc., or the sudden appearance of a bird), divination (looking at the arrangement of the organs in a sacrificed animal, for example; divination could also be used to interpret the past), and oracles (cryptic messages given by the gods to priests and prophets, both male and female).[85] Governments, as well as individuals, coveted whatever information they could gain from these sources.

The second reaction of people to the unseen powers that determined their future was to try to control what they could control or at least to affect the powers. And the particular way they did that was by magic. Over against religions, which petition the deity to do what the believers want, magic tries to force divine

Fig. 4.4 A lararium—the household shrine for honoring the family's ancestral gods—from a home in Herculaneum.

and semidivine powers[86] to do what believers want them to do by the utterance of certain words (spells and curses), the creation of potions or other products, or the performance of rituals that can be carried out only by particular people who are specially trained, called magicians.[87] Non-Judeans often charged Judeans with practicing magic—and some Judeans agreed, claiming that their exceptional magic went back to Solomon (Josephus, *Antiquities* 8.42-49).

In the Pauline literature, magic is listed in Gal 5:20 as a vice to be avoided. (The term is *pharmakeia*; the NRSV translates it as *sorcery*. For *pharmakeia* and related words, see also Rev 9:21; 18:23; 21:8; 22:15.) In Acts, magicians are prominent in two story lines: in Samaria with Simon the magician (8:9-24) and in Cyprus with the Judean magician Elymas (13:4-12). Paul encountered Elymas, and in Ephesus—a traditional center of magic—the gospel Paul proclaims defeats magic and its practitioners (19:11-20). What is important for our study is the recognition that magic was a standard part of the thinking of many people in Paul's world.[88]

Healing Cults

Concern for good health—maintaining it or regaining it—was as large a matter of attention in Paul's world as it is in ours. At different times, various gods were believed to have healing powers, most notably Apollo. In addition, the circum-Mediterranean world was home to the practice of the medical arts, of which today's physicians, nurses, and technicians are descendants. The first key name was Hippocrates (fifth century BCE); the Hippocratic Oath has its origin in the medical school and tradition connected with his name and was centered on the island of Cos, near the modern country of Turkey. Galen of Pergamum (ca. 130–200 CE), the other key name, came after Paul. An acute researcher, he practiced mainly in Pergamum (western Turkey) and Rome. Miraculous healers and miraculous places of healing also were renowned.

The most prominent god of healing, Asclepius, was originally a human being, the son of Apollo and a Thessalonian princess, Coronis. After his death, Asclepius eventually was granted status as a god. The Asclepius temple on Cos did not offer medical care in the narrower sense, but the hundreds of other Asclepius

Fig. 4.5 Votive carving dedicated to Asclepius, god of healing; from Philippi.

temples provided both medical care and alternative therapies that included worship of Asclepius as well as sleeping in the temple complex overnight—or for several years. The hope was that, during sleep, the god would grant the ill person a vision that would lead to relief and, ideally, healing. The best-known such sanctuary is near Epidaurus in southern Greece. The entire complex includes temples, a large theater, baths, wells, gymnasium, stadium, storehouses, and sleeping quarters. Corinth had similar facilities, which gives insight into Paul's warning that Christ-believers not eat in the dining rooms attached to temple complexes (1 Cor 8:10).[89]

Mystery Religions

People also turned in other directions in their quest for protection and meaning. Prominent among the options available was a group of religions usually labeled mystery religions.[90] *Mystery*, or more normally *mysteries*, is a term that comes from antiquity and refers to three aspects of these religions: (1) divine mysteries were revealed to the people who were initiated; (2) the religions' teachings and many ceremonies, especially initiation, were secret and not to be divulged to outsiders; and (3) therefore, the religions remain in many details largely unknown to us.[91] Their secrecy is especially noticeable when we recall the public religions of city and empire, as well as domestic religion. Secrecy was enhanced by initiation rituals that limited the mystery religions to people initiated into a given mystery. The initiation ceremonies, from what we can tell, were elaborate; for example, the initiation process in the cult of Demeter lasted ten days. Meetings in general were secret and often held at night, when reputable people avoided leaving their homes.

Marvin Meyer points out that mystery religions had clear goals: "Commonly originating in ancient tribal and even fertility rituals, these religions emphasized salvation for individuals who decided, through personal choice, to be initiated into the mysteries, and thereby to feel close to each other and to the divine."[92] With the coming of Alexander the Great and the empires that succeeded him, originally local cults and gods were transformed into international mystery religions that offered solidarity with the divine, successful passage through the underworld, and life eternal.

The foundational myths or foundational stories of the various mysteries were not secrets. Thus, the myth in the Eleusinian mystery religion goes all the way back to the seventh or sixth century BCE in the Homeric Hymn to Demeter. The goddess Demeter (or Ceres) had a daughter named Korē (or Persephone). The god of the underworld, Hades (or Pluto), kidnaps Korē and takes her to his world. Demeter searches everywhere on earth for her daughter but cannot find her. Eventually she comes to Eleusis, about fourteen miles west of Athens. Disguised as an old woman, she meets four daughters of the local ruling family, who help her find a job at the palace. As she enters the palace, she engages in various activities that are prototypes for the rituals of the mystery religion. Following a period during which she cares for the royal son, she resumes her search. Out of frustration, she essentially goes on strike, refusing (as the goddess of cereal) to allow grain to grow. The result is a famine that affects both humans and gods. Zeus negotiates an agreement with Hades, to which Demeter assents: Korē will spend four months each year with her husband in the underworld and eight months a year with her mother. The famine ends, and the annual Mediterranean cycle of growth, production, and decay begins again.

The agricultural themes of death and life were applied, in turn, to the lives of those initiated into the mystery, who experienced renewed life in their present existence as well as the promise of life after the end of their physical being. Some mystery religions became popular, as John Stambaugh and David Balch emphasize: "By Roman times, this mystery cult at Eleusis represented a high point of spirituality for the more philosophically inclined, and it was eagerly sought out by all levels of society: Roman emperors, Athenian aristocrats, even freedman and slaves."[93] The expense of the initiation ceremonies did, however, exclude many poorer people. Other prominent mystery religions included the mysteries of Dionysus (Bacchus),[94] the mysteries of Isis,[95] and the mysteries of Mithras.[96]

New Testament scholars have identified some similarities between Paul and the mystery religions:

- In both, the person being initiated is purified and cleansed, with the ceremony of Christ-believing baptism including an experience of death that also looks forward to the new life offered in resurrection (Rom 6:3-5). Related is belief in a dying and rising Christ, which has parallels in the various dying and rising deities of the mystery religions. When developing his views on resurrection, Paul even uses the term *mystery* (*mystērion*; 1 Cor 15:51), and his discussion of dying and rising is close in its basic language to the mysteries of Eleusis (1 Cor 15:36-38).
- While Paul certainly baptized entire households (1 Cor 1:16), often people joined the Christ-believing congregations as individuals (1 Cor 1:14). In a similar fashion, individuals were initiated into the mysteries.
- Christ-believers participated in a sacred meal of bread (body) and wine (blood) that recalled the death of Jesus and that was couched in language reminiscent of, for example, the Mithras and Dionysiac religions.
- Paul's rejection of idolatrous worship in Rom 1:23 seems to show knowledge of Egyptian religion in general and perhaps the Isis cult in particular.[97]

In the latter part of the second century, the great Christian thinker Clement of Alexandria (ca. 150–216) labeled Christianity as itself a mystery religion that had its own "holy mysteries" (*Exhortation to the Greeks*, ch. 12). At the same time, he distinguished between Christian mysteries and the immoral Greco-Roman mysteries (*Exhortation to the Greeks*, ch. 2). By at least the second century, the mystery religions were significant competitors of the Christian movement, with the Mithras cult being a special threat. The often somewhat odd relationship between competitive movements is seen after Paul's lifetime in the adoption by Christians of December 25—the feast day in the Roman calendar for the sun god of

Mithras—as the birthday for Jesus and the use of former Mithraic worship sites as the location of Christian churches.[98]

Did the emerging Christ-believing movement, especially as we experience it in Paul, simply take over mystery religion language and thought? To a large extent, that was the position of the history-of-religions school of thought, which was a dominant force in scholarship from the 1880s to the 1930s. The influence of their approach continued for several more decades.[99] Not only were the language and concepts of the mystery religions and the Christ-movement similar, the latter in fact took over from the mystery religions not only the sacraments of initiation (baptism) and meal (the Lord's Supper) but also the myth of a dying and rising god.

Today scholars are not so sure, in part because the evidence for the mystery religions has been more thoroughly studied and in part because there is greater doubt that the mysteries were as important in the first century as they were earlier and later. It does not appear that a standard element in the mysteries was the belief in immortality by being identified with the fate of the dying-and-rising god, although strands of that belief were present. Also, it seems quite likely that in between the mystery religions and the early Christ movement was the Judaism of the diaspora, which had already commenced before Paul began to use mystery religion categories.[100] Nor does the utilization of a given body of terms mean that Paul also necessarily adopted the theology of the mysteries. As a missionary, Paul used many language "worlds"—business, athletics, and farming are just three. Mystery religion language was current in Paul's world, and he does seem to utilize some of that language (Romans 6; 1 Corinthians 15), but that does not mean he simply took over without reflection the theology of the mysteries. The sheer fact that baptism, the Lord's Supper, and resurrection are part of the story of the historical person Jesus changes significantly the way Paul uses mystery religion language.

Gnosticism

The term ***Gnosticism*** designates a large and somewhat diffuse group of religions that placed great weight on a flash of spiritual insight (*gnōsis / knowledge*) that freed the believer from the shackles of the present material world. With roots in Judaism and often in the philosophy of Plato, Gnosticism operated with the following macro themes:

- The physical world is the tragic product of a limited and low-level god. Details vary wildly, but in general, the highest deity reproduces itself, setting in motion the "birth" of a series of entities or "emanations," usually in male-female pairs, who in turn produce another pair of beings, and so on. Each pair participates in the divine realm, but each pair is less divine than the pair from which it came. Gnostic documents have extensive genealogies that detail the decline in divinity. At the bottom is the creator god, himself the result of a mistake, who thinks he is the only god. Often that god is identified with the god of Israel's Bible, an approach that results in radical reinterpretation of Israel's normal understandings.

- Gnostics understand the physical world as a huge trap that imprisons in material bodies a spark of the divine. The burdens of the flesh enmesh the divine spark in physical existence and cause people to forget their real origin and identity.[101] That state of forgetfulness can be spoken of as sleep. People are asleep in relationship to who they really are.
- The highest god wants to regather all the divine sparks and therefore sends a messenger to awaken the potential believer to his or her true identity by imparting secret knowledge. And so, in the words of Theodotus, a Gnostic of the second century CE, people need to know "who were we? what have we become? where were we? into what place have we been cast? whither are we hastening? from what are we delivered? what is birth? what is rebirth?"[102] Christian Gnostics assigned the messenger role to Jesus, although they denied his incarnation and crucifixion.[103]
- Through the flash of enlightenment, education in Gnosticism, and ritual, the Gnostic believer is freed from the prison of this world and is empowered, after death, to ascend to the highest heaven. The ascent is solely for the divine spark. The rest of the human being is earthly and bound to the earth.[104]

In terms of their daily ethics, their more orthodox Christian opponents divided Gnostics into two camps. The first group, believing that life in the body did not matter, did whatever they wanted to do with their bodies.[105] The other group, fearing the threat the physical body posed to the divine spark trapped in it, closely controlled the body, living ascetically.[106] Gnostic texts discovered in the twentieth century give ample support to asceticism among the Gnostics but little if any support to libertinism (that is, that anything goes). At the same time, for Gnostics, any responsibility to the larger society is simply beside the point.

Could Gnosticism have influenced Paul, or could it have been part of the "against whom" that he wrote? Or does Gnosticism develop too late to have been part of his world? Part of the difficulty in answering those questions is the dating of our source materials. One source of information that has been available since antiquity is that group of Christian authors (often called the church fathers) who understood Gnosticism as a heresy and wrote against it. Prominent names include Irenaeus, Clement of Alexandria, Origen, Hippolytus, and Epiphanius.[107] The first four lived in the second and/or third centuries; the last one lived in the fourth to fifth centuries.

Study of Gnostic documents themselves has become much more precise since the discovery in 1945 near **Nag Hammadi**, Egypt, of a collection of Gnostic and non-Gnostic documents written in Coptic. The discovery has greatly expanded knowledge of the Gnostics and has served to verify much of what Irenaeus said. The collection overall dates from the middle of the fourth century CE, but many of the documents appear to be translations of earlier originals from Greek (and in a smaller number of cases, perhaps from Syriac), with the original writings going back to the second or third century. In addition, scholars argue that in some cases they have been able to "edit out" later Christian alterations and thereby identify

Fig. 4.6 The books containing Gnostic writings buried at Nag Hammadi in the fourth century and discovered in 1946. Institute for Antiquity and Christianity.

a non-Christian Gnostic document.[108] Thus, while the writings themselves are fourth century in origin, at least some of them go back to the second and perhaps even the first centuries and point to a religious movement that arose independently of Christianity.[109]

As far as we can tell, Paul does not quote any Gnostic document. Nor is it safe to assume an organized Gnostic movement prior to the second century. It may be helpful in tandem with German researchers to distinguish between Gnostic*ism*, the full-blown and post-Paul organized movement definitely on the scene in the second century, on the one hand, and Gnosis, which in this usage refers to the general movement that was in the process of developing in the first century but that had not yet coalesced into identifiable religions. That means, in turn, that in order to identify Gnostic or Gnosticizing elements in Paul's opponents or in his responses, it is not necessary to find a specific, formalized Gnostic religion. This study will argue, therefore, that at a number of points, early Gnostics, or proto-Gnostics, were part of the opposition Paul faced.[110] We will see that interaction especially in 1 Corinthians. It is more pronounced in the deuteropauline letters—in particular, Colossians, Ephesians, 1 and 2 Timothy, and Titus.[111] Later Gnostics had a field day reinterpreting Paul in Gnostic directions.[112]

POLITICAL RELIGION

In the world in which Paul lived, religion was not a self-standing phenomenon independent of other institutions. Religion, in fact, was "embedded either in structures of political dominance such as the temples of officially recognized cults put in place by local aristocratic elites (including the imperial cult), or in the household. There was political religion and domestic religion, but not 'religion' *per se.*"[113] A previous section looked at domestic religion. This section explores the official religions connected with governments and their impact on Paul and his people.

Greek and Roman Gods

In the Greco-Roman world, people believed in many gods. At the lowest level of divinity were gods who originally had been human beings but who had become divine because of heroic deeds (Hercules, for example). Next in ascending order were minor gods, such as the goddess of sleep. Significantly higher in rank were the Greek gods of Mt. Olympus, together with their counterparts in other cultures. And at the very top was the supreme god, Zeus (Greece) / Jupiter (Rome). Jupiter was literally the "power behind the throne," from whom power and authority came to the emperor. Jupiter thus provided the legitimacy Roman emperors needed in order to rule.

The Romans continued the Greek practice of building temples inside of which was the sacred statue of the deity being honored. Outside the temple and in front of it priests presided at animal sacrifices. The cults of the major deities were publicly funded, in part because the Romans believed that properly functioning cults ensured that the gods would in turn look favorably on the empire. Conversely, withdrawal of the god's favor could mean the downfall of government.[114]

Roman Political Theology

The need for new political cement to hold together the Roman Empire, the tradition that heroic people could become divine, and examples from the eastern part of the empire where rulers had long been revered as divine came together in the Roman imperial cult.[115] That cult confronted Paul and other early Christ-believers virtually every day of their lives.

Gods of Greece and Rome

Greek Name	Latin Name	Interests
Aphrodite	Venus	Love, beauty
Apollo	Phoebus	Sun, music, poetry
Ares	Mars	War
Artemis	Diana	Chastity, hunting
Athena	Minerva	Wisdom
Hephaestos	Vulcan	Fire, industry
Hera	Juno	Sky, queen, marriage
Hermes	Mercury	Trade, eloquence
Poseidon	Neptune	Sea, earthquake
Zeus	Jupiter	Sky, supreme god

In Rome, the Senate honored Julius Caesar and Caesar Augustus with divine status following their deaths. These emperors (especially Augustus) had brought peace and prosperity to the empire.[116] During his lifetime, Augustus was careful not to claim too much divinity. Altars and temples dedicated to him were limited to a select number of cities in the eastern part of the empire, where such practices had long been common. In Italy, Augustus was more circumspect, but following his death, more and more divine honors were given to the emperors, so that titles such as God, Lord, and Savior became part of the standard imperial propaganda. Even before his death, Augustus put into place the elements that provided the foundation of the imperial cult: devotion to Rome (Roma), to Julius Caesar, and to himself. During the first half of the first century CE (and thus during the lifetimes of Jesus and Paul), the imperial cult spread quickly, especially in the countries of the eastern Mediterranean. Cities and local aristocracies competed fiercely for the right to build the most elaborate imperial temples and to host the most grandiose festivals, and local elites vied to become priests in the imperial cult.[117]

As the imperial cult developed, its temples and altars became the centerpiece of Roman cities, especially new cities and cities that were renovated.[118] Imperial buildings were generally in the center of cities and served as constant reminders of the existence and significance of the empire. The festivals, processions, and games associated with the imperial cult did so as well; often they commemorated the emperor's birthday, military triumphs, the anniversary date of his becoming emperor, or the anniversary of the founding of the cult in a given city. They could also last for days, further embedding the cult in people's civic mind-set. The imperial cult's regularized rituals became part of the rhythm of life and provided relief from the drudgery of daily toil. They also "served as the medium through which the image of the emperor came to represent the network of military, economic, and social relationships of Roman hegemony."[119] In addition, statues of the emperor and his wife, coins with the emperor's face on them, and omnipresent inscriptions on buildings were constant reminders of the source of power in Rome. Even the clothing styles and hairstyles of the imperial family became the rage throughout the empire.[120]

The imperial cult was more than physical objects, however. It also promoted and was sustained by a well-developed ideology that can legitimately be called a theology. The following statements express the heart of Rome's imperial theology:

- *The gods have chosen Rome to rule the world.* Thus, Jupiter proclaims, "For those [the Romans] I set no bounds in space or time; but have given empire without end" (Virgil, *Aeneid* 1.278-79).[121] Juno and Jupiter will "cherish the Romans, lords of the world" (Virgil, *Aeneid* 1.281-82), and Anchises tells his son Aeneas that Rome's task will be "to rule the world . . . , to crown peace with justice, to spare the vanquished and to crush the proud" (Virgil, *Aeneid* 6.855-53).
- *The gods have chosen Rome because of its piety,* that is, its devotion to the gods. The classic statement of that view comes from just prior to the beginning of the actual empire, although during the period when Rome

Fig. 4.7 Bust of Augustus's wife Livia; her severe hairstyle expressed the moral reforms of the Augustan age. The Louvre.

was expanding. In 56 B.C.E., Cicero wrote an essay entitled "On the Soothsayers' Responses." In it he claimed "that Rome's success abroad was due to its morality and religion at home. 'We have surpassed all peoples and nations by *pietas* and *religio* and by the one wisdom, i.e., our realization that everything is ruled and governed by the power of the gods.' And again, 'If we want to compare our affairs with those of others, in regard to other things we will be found to be equal or inferior, but superior in regard to religion, i.e., the worship of the gods' (19)."[122] It was in part for this reason that failure to honor the gods (by Christ-believers, for example) could not be tolerated.[123]

- *Further, the gods have chosen the emperor of Rome to be their patron on earth and the father of the empire.* With the emperor as father, the empire was viewed as one vast family.
- *Rome's military victories and the resulting peace prove that the gods have chosen Rome and its emperors.* The "peace and security" ushered in by Augustus Caesar and protected by his successors even cast the emperors in the role of savior. Much of the imperial theology comes together in a famous inscription from Priene, in Asia Minor. The inscription is dated ca. 9 BCE and honors Augustus. Part of it reads:

Since the Providence which has ordered all things and is deeply interested in our life has set in most perfect order by giving us Augustus, whom she filled with virtue [divine power] that he might benefit mankind, sending him as a savior . . . , both for us and for our descendants, that he might end war and arrange all things, and since he, Caesar, by his appearance . . . [excelled even our anticipations], surpassing all previous benefactors, and not even leaving to posterity any hope of surpassing what he has done, and since the birth of the god Augustus was the beginning for the world of the good tidings . . . that came by reason of him.[124]

- *All people are to submit themselves to Rome's rule.* Given the first three beliefs, Roman political theology concluded that "to submit to Rome was to submit to the will of the gods, and the means of participating in their blessing."[125] Further, military conquest was a justified way for Rome to extend its power.
- *The reign of Augustus marks the beginning of a new Golden Age.* A dominant view in antiquity, enunciated in its classical form by Hesiod (ca. 700 BCE) in his *Works and Days*, is that at the beginning of human history was a Golden Age of peace, enlightenment, productivity, and harmony between nature and people. Following that wonderful beginning, however, Hesiod identified ongoing decline as the world slipped into successively less positive eras—silver, bronze, and iron. As violence increased and people paid less attention to the gods, life became immeasurably harder and nature less productive.

Following the assassination of Julius Caesar, the Roman poet Virgil predicted a ruler who would return humanity and nature to the Golden Age. When later Virgil threw his support to Augustus, the latter was understood to be the fulfillment of the poet's prophecy:

> Now is come the last age of Cumaean song; the great line of the centuries begins anew. . . . And in your consulship . . . shall this glorious age begin, and the mighty months commence their march; under your sway any lingering traces of our guilt shall become void and release the earth from its continual dread. . . . But for you, child, the earth untilled will pour forth its first pretty gifts. . . . Unbidden, the goats will bring home their udders swollen with milk, and the cattle will not fear huge lions. The serpent, too, will perish, and perish will the plant that hides its poison. . . . Every land will bear all fruits. Earth will not suffer the harrow, nor the vine the pruning hook. (Virgil, *Eclogue* 4.4-41)

> Here is Caesar and all the seed of Iulus destined to pass under heaven's spacious sphere. And this in truth is he whom you so

often hear promised you, Augustus Caesar, son of a god, who
will again establish a golden age in Latium amid fields once
ruled by Saturn. (Virgil, *Aeneid* 6.789-94)

Athletic games, monuments, altars, and coins celebrated and advertised the new Golden Age of peace, prosperity, and productivity.[126]

Many scholars in the twenty-first century have come to appreciate the constant message barrage that inundated people regarding the foundations and goodness of the empire and its political and religious structure. A growing number of scholars has also identified many places where Paul (a) utilized the language of Roman imperial theology to express the good news of Jesus and (b) consciously countered Roman propaganda. The chapters on the individual letters will discuss a number of such examples.[127]

The Romans did not require people to abandon their previous religious commitments in favor of the imperial cult. But they did require that people include the cult in their public religious commitments. Prayer in the Jerusalem Temple directed at the well-being of the emperor, for example, was enough to allow the Romans to give Judeans the legal freedom to practice their religion. When Christ-believing groups (whether Judean or Gentile) refused to accommodate the imperial cult, conflict was inevitable. Overall, explains Walter Wagner, "the

Fig. 4.8 Mother Earth reclines in abundance with her children; relief on the Altar of Augustan Peace, dedicated by the Senate in 9 B.C.E.

Empire-emperor cult attempted to establish a common base for devotion and loyalty among the different and competing claims of gods and cults in the Empire. People could hold their many rites and beliefs, yet participation in the imperial cult—no matter how superficial—acknowledged the oneness of the Empire as a community in which there was order and continuity."[128]

A Christ-Believer

Significantly for our study, Paul also became a Christ-believer. This belief began with a conversion or call experience, which as we will see (and contrary to widely held assumptions) did not cause him to change his name. However, the experience did famously cause him to become an apostle with a mission.

CONVERSION AND/OR CALL

Pulsing throughout Paul's being—no matter how we try to parcel out who he was as a Judean and who he was as a Greco-Roman—was the fact that in one of the most famous conversion stories of all time, he came to believe that Jesus was the **Messiah**. That conversion experience moved him from being a persecutor of the emerging community of Christ-believers to being one of its most articulate proponents.

That Paul at one time had persecuted Christ-believers is part of the bedrock of what we know about him. Not only does he tell us he persecuted believers (Gal 1:13-14, 23; Phil 3:6; 1 Cor 15:9), but so does Acts (8:3; 9:1-2; 22:4-5; 26:9-11). Of particular note are these passages:

> You have heard, no doubt, of my earlier life in Judaism. I was violently persecuting the church of God and was trying to destroy it. (Gal 1:13)

> For I am the least of the apostles, unfit to be called an apostle, because I persecuted the church of God. (1 Cor 15:9)

From his own hand, Paul identifies his chief reason for acting as he did: zeal for the traditions of his ancestors (Gal 1:14; Phil 3:6). Given the ongoing attention Paul gives in his letters to the Law of Moses, it is likely that the apparent devaluing of the Law among followers of Jesus was, for Paul, a potentially devastating departure that had to be rooted out.

All of that changed dramatically and suddenly while Paul was traveling to Damascus to persecute those who believed that Jesus was the Messiah.[129] Paul never gives us a detailed account. The most he does is to allude to the Damascus Road events in Gal 1:11-16; 1 Cor 9:1, 15:8; and possibly 2 Cor 4:6. In Acts, however, the event is so important in the story line that its author tells the same basic story three times, with some variations between them (9:1-19; 22:3-16; 26:9-23).[130]

The Acts accounts of Paul's conversion and his allusions to it agree on at least three basic points:

1. The key to Paul's conversion story is the appearance of the crucified Jesus as the resurrected one. Jesus had been killed, but now that same Jesus was alive again. And Paul saw and heard him.
2. The appearance of Jesus was sudden and unexpected, and it was this appearance that brought about Paul's conversion. While scholars at times have argued for some type of psychological preparation that helped lead to his conversion, the biblical texts know nothing about that. Paul was in the process of persecuting Christ-believers, and the resurrected Jesus appeared to him.
3. Through the appearance of the resurrected Jesus, God called Paul to be his apostle. *Call* (*kaleō*) is language used in both testaments of the Christian Bible to designate God's invitation to be part of God's people and to carry out an assignment. Thus, in the Septuagint, God calls the people of Israel, symbolized in the servant (Isa 41:9; 43:1; 48:12; 51:2), to be "a light to the nations" (Isa 42:6; 48:15; 49:1). In addition, God also calls specific individuals, from King Cyrus (Isa 45:1-7) to Paul the apostle (Rom 1:1; 1 Cor 1:1). In Rom 8:30, Paul roots call language in God's prior choice or election as well as in justification. Thus *call*, for Paul, can refer to God's choice of individuals (1 Cor 1:9; Gal 1:6; 1 Thess 2:12); the thought is also expressed through the word *called / klētos*. People who believe in Jesus as the Christ are those who are called (Rom 1:6-7; 8:28; 9:24; 1 Cor 1:2, 24). The unmerited nature of that call is seen in the fact that God's choice of Paul was made even before Paul was born (Gal 1:15). With the call, God also gives the task or mission—in Paul's case, "so that I might proclaim him among the Gentiles" (or "nations"; Gal 1:16; see also Rom 1:5; 11:13).

The implications of this appearance to Paul (which could also be labeled a vision) were many.[131] Some were probably immediately evident to him; others were the result of reflection over the years. Among the implications are the following:

- The initiative that led to the vision was God's. God did the revealing: "But . . . God, who had set me apart before I was born and called me through his grace, was pleased to reveal (Greek: *apokalypsai*) his Son to me, so that I might proclaim him among the Gentiles" (Gal 1:15-16). Jesus appeared to Paul (1 Cor 15:9), not the other way around. Eventually—perhaps immediately—Paul experienced this God-generated appearance as sheer grace (Gal 1:15).
- In the vision, God revealed not only that the accursed, crucified Jesus was somehow alive again, but that God had vindicated and exalted him. The resurrection was God's seal of approval that Jesus is the Son of God (Gal 1:16; 4:4; Rom 1:3, 9; 5:10; 8:3, 29; 1 Cor 1:9; 2 Cor 1:19; 1 Thess 1:10). In addition, Paul understood from the vision that Jesus is Lord (Rom 1:4; 4:24; 5:1; 10:9; 13:14; 15:6; 1 Cor 1:7-9; 8:6; 9:1; 2 Cor 4:5; Gal 6:14; Phil 2:11; 3:8; 1 Thess 1:3).[132]

- If Jesus had been resurrected from the dead, then somehow the end-of-time had broken into the present. Pharisees like Paul believed in resurrection but only at the end of time. A present-tense resurrection meant that normal ways of understanding time had thus been bent—or perhaps even broken. As J. C. Beker has written, "The Christophany [the appearance of the risen Jesus to Paul] then is interpreted by Paul in terms of his prior apocalyptic convictions, and it both modifies and intensifies those convictions radically. It signifies for him primarily the inauguration of the reign of God, which according to God's purpose must embrace his whole creation, that is, both Jews and Gentiles, and for which Paul must prepare the way."[133]
- Further, Paul's understanding of how God operates in the world had been turned upside down. God was to be understood as working through the man Jesus, re-understood as the Christ/Messiah, and through the ritually degrading death of Jesus on the cross. That death, moreover, was to be viewed as somehow effecting the forgiveness of sins (Gal 1:4; 1 Cor 15:3; Rom 5:6-8) and the restoration of a positive relationship with God (2 Cor 5:18-21; Rom 5:10-11). The death of Jesus also, for Paul, sharply redefined the role of the Law of Moses in general, as well as the specifics of circumcision, Temple, and ethnic boundaries.
- The "Christ event," therefore, had universal implications for all people. Somehow Gentiles as well as Judeans were to be included, and taking the message to Gentiles was to be Paul's specific task.

We need to consider two other matters before turning more fully to Paul's understanding of his mission and his role as apostle. The first matter is what Paul's conversion was not. His conversion was not the conversion of a terrible sinner from his immoral ways to a life of righteousness. If anything, it was the opposite and was a conversion from being one who thought he was righteous to being one who realized that he was caught in a matrix of sin from which he could not extract himself. Nor was the conversion Paul's personal decision for Christ. As already mentioned, the initiative was God's, not Paul's.

A second matter is whether conversion is even the proper category to use for describing Paul's experience. We have learned that during the Damascus Road experience, Jesus called Paul to be his apostle. Indeed, the language Paul uses in Gal 1:15-16 to describe that event is close to the language of the call narratives of the prophets Jeremiah (1:4-5) and Isaiah (49:1, 5-6). Many scholars have looked more closely at that part of the event and have suggested that instead of Paul's *conversion*, we should talk about Paul's *call* or *commissioning*.[134]

When we use the word *conversion*, some scholars say, we are implying that Paul has changed religions. There are two problems with that implication. First, when Paul was on Damascus Road, Christianity as a separated-from-Judaism entity did not yet exist; even during the rest of his lifetime, what we call Christianity was in the process of becoming a separate entity, rather than everywhere and in all places being a religion distinct from Judaism. The second problem is that

Paul still worshipped the God of Abraham and Israel, not a new God. Therefore, a good number of scholars have suggested that conversion is not the most helpful label for Paul's experience. Rather, Paul was *called* to a new ministry.

The problem with stopping at the word *call* is that what happened to Paul also transformed him and resulted in new ways of perceiving God, himself, *and* his call. As a result, he can reevaluate his ethnic heritage as *trash* or *rubbish*, not because it is no good, but because "knowing Christ Jesus" as his Lord is of even greater value (Phil 3:4b-9).

Perhaps the best thing is to do what Charles Cousar does and use the awkward expression *call/conversion*. This term ensures that we do not claim too much for Paul's Damascus Road experience but that we do claim enough.[135]

THE APOSTLE'S NAMES

Despite virtually every movie, television show, or skit you may have seen or how many sermons you may have heard, the apostle we are studying did *not* change his name after his conversion/call from Saul to Paul. Most Judeans living in the diaspora had two names: their Judean name (Saul, in this case) and their Greco-Roman name (Paul). Often, the name used outside Judean circles sounded somewhat similar to the Judean name. The situation becomes more complicated if Paul was a citizen, as claimed in Acts 22:25-29 and 23:37 (but never by Paul in the undisputed letters).[136] Roman citizens had three names: the *praenomen* was their personal name, the *nomen* was their clan name, and the *cognomen* was their family name. A fourth kind of name was the *signum*, which was an unofficial or informal name similar to a nickname. Many commentators think Saul was our apostle's Judean name and did not have standing outside Judean circles. Although many scholars argue that Paul (in Latin *Paulus*) was his *cognomen*,[137] others see it as a *signum*.[138]

A key to understanding the functions of Paul's two names (if he had more names, we do not know what they are) is to be attentive to when each name is used. *Saul* is used in Acts, with one exception, when the person being discussed is in a Judean or Judean-Christ-believing context, is referred to from those perspectives, quotes the words of Jesus on Damascus Road, or refers to the ancient king of Israel named Saul. The one exception is the verse that transitions from calling him Saul to calling him Paul, Acts 13:9: "But Saul, also known as Paul, filled with the Holy Spirit, looked intently at him." The setting is a conflict between the apostle and a false prophet in front of the Roman proconsul, a man named Sergius Paulus.[139] The changeover occurs when Paul needs to interact with the imperial order, and from that point on, the narrator calls him Paul. That the change in names does not happen as a result of his conversion/call is indicated by the fact that the first account in Acts of his conversion is in chapter 9, but the name Paul is not used until 13:9.

Paul in his own letters never calls himself Saul. Why not? Probably because every document we have from him is addressed to a Gentile or predominantly Gentile audience. A Latin- or Greek-sounding name would have raised none of the questions a Judean name would have raised. In addition, the Greek word *saulos* had unfortunate meanings the Hebrew term for Saul did not have. In particular, *saulos* could mean the suggestive style of walking used by some prostitutes or devotees of the god Dionysus/Bacchus.[140] In Greek-speaking Judean circles, Saul would have reminded people of Israel's first king; Paul was a member of the same tribe of Benjamin from which Saul had come (1 Samuel 9–10; Phil 3:5). But in Greek-speaking Gentile circles, *Saul* could easily have led to laughter rather than positive recognition.

And if he did have other names as a Roman citizen, why did he not use them? Likely because they would have signaled a status superior to most of his converts, who were in almost all cases not Roman citizens.

So with Saul's/Paul's names, we do not have a situation similar to name changes that sometimes occur when a person converts to Islam. The shift from Saul to Paul is *not* similar to the change from Cassius Clay to Muhammad Ali or from Lisa Najeeb Halaby to Queen Noor of Jordan (Noor al Hussein). The shift in the apostle's case relates rather to the people with whom he was interacting.

AN APOSTLE AND HIS MISSION

Two central results of Paul's conversion/call were, we have seen, his commission to be an apostle and to be an apostle with a mission. The term *apostle* is for Paul a key term. The apostle is God's designated representative. There are precedents within Judaism for such a representative, who had the full authority of the sender.[141] Jewett, while acknowledging that, also points out that Paul's self-understanding as an apostle is quite close to the Greco-Roman world's understanding of the term *ambassador*.[142] Indeed, political ambassadors and special royal messengers can both be designated by the term *apostolos*, and for that matter, Paul also refers to himself using a different term as an ambassador when he uses the verb *presbeuō* ("I am an ambassador"; 2 Cor 5:18-20; see also Eph 6:20). A particular implication is that, since the apostle comes with the full authority of the sender, to reject Paul as apostle is to reject the one who sent him (God, Jesus).[143]

Paul refers to himself many times as an apostle. A good example is Rom 1:1: "Paul, a servant [literally *slave*] of Jesus Christ, called to be an apostle, set apart for the gospel of God" (see also Rom 11:13; 1 Cor 1:1; 4:9 [indirectly]; 9:1-2; 5; 15:9; 2 Cor 2:1; Gal 1:1, 17 [indirectly]; 1 Thess 2:7). In four of the seven undisputed letters, he identifies himself at the beginning as an apostle (Romans; 1 and 2 Corinthians; Galatians). His self-understanding as an apostle lies "in, with, and under" his entire person. "Paul an apostle" is almost for him a mantra.

In part, the significance of the term for him is a result of the fact that there were, indeed, other apostles and that some people doubted his credentials as an apostle (2 Cor 10:12; 11:4-6; 12:11-13). Two examples will need to suffice.

Ironically, Paul does not fit the definition used in the book of Acts when those who first believed in Jesus Christ met to replace the disgraced apostle Judas. Peter outlined the criteria in this way: "'So one of the men who have accompanied us during all the time that the Lord Jesus went in and out among us, beginning from

Did Paul Have a Wife?

Was Paul married? The traditional answer from the fourth century on has been that Paul was a lifelong celibate—someone who had consciously decided never to marry. However, Clement of Alexandria stated that Paul had indeed been married at some point in his life.[144]

What does Paul say? Nothing directly. He never refers to a wife, but such silence is typical in the patriarchal culture of his time. Thus, in Paul's letters, the naming of both wife and husband is a rarity, as in the case of Priscilla (or Prisca, the wife) and Aquila (the husband; Rom 16:3; 1 Cor 16:19). Andronicus and Junia would be another example (Rom 16:7), assuming they are married to each other.

What does Paul imply? A key text is a question he poses to the Corinthians. The context is defense of his standing as an apostle. When he did his original missionary work in Corinth, he refused to exercise his right as an apostle and insist on financial support from the Corinthian believers. Some concluded that he did not claim that right because he was not truly an apostle. But Paul responds with this rhetorical question: "Do we not have the right to be accompanied by a believing wife, as do the other apostles and the brothers of the Lord and Cephas?" (1 Cor 9:5). Does that question imply he at one time had been married? Likely so. The question also implies that his wife was a Christ-believer and therefore would have been just as eligible for support as the wives of others.

By the time Paul writes 1 Corinthians, "Mrs. Paul" was no longer in the picture. While it is theoretically possible they had divorced, if they had taken that route, Paul would not have followed the standards of conduct he himself details in 1 Cor 7:10-11, and his own life would have undermined the directions he gave.[145]

There is other evidence that his wife had died and he was a widower. In 1 Cor 7:8, he writes, "To the unmarried and the widows I say that it is well for them to remain unmarried as I am." Clearly Paul is not married at this point in his life. The term *unmarried* is masculine in Greek; when paired with *widows*, it almost certainly has the meaning of *widowers*. When Paul presents himself as a model of behavior, he identifies himself with those whose spouses have died.

Additional support for Paul's having been married comes from the Judean and Greco-Roman cultures of which he was a part. Not only were male Judeans in general expected to marry and father children, but Pharisees like Paul were specifically directed to marry and have a family. As a teacher of the Law, moreover, his credibility would have easily been attacked if he had not fulfilled those obligations. We have no evidence that such attacks ever occurred. The normal expectation in Greco-Roman cultures was quite similar.

Finally, 1 Cor 7:1-7 contains beautiful and countercultural views on the reciprocity and equality of wife and husband in marriage. Such views may well come from a person who has seen the "inside" of marriage.

the baptism of John until the day when he was taken up from us—one of these must become a witness with us to his resurrection'" (Acts 1:21-22). Paul did not, of course, meet those standards, and Acts is very careful about calling Paul an apostle: there is an indirect reference in 14:4 and a more direct reference in 14:14. Scholars often wonder if 14:14 comes from one of the sources Luke uses.

Paul pointed to a different definition of apostle, which is based on the resurrection appearances of Jesus: "He [Jesus] appeared to Cephas, then to the twelve. . . . Then he appeared to James, then to all the apostles. Last of all, as to one untimely born, he appeared also to me. For I am the least of the apostles, unfit to be called an apostle, because I persecuted the church of God" (1 Cor 15:5, 7-9; see also Gal 1:16). Paul maintained that the basic criterion to be an apostle was an appearance of Jesus to the potential apostle (although not all recipients of such visions became apostles; 1 Cor 15:6). Given his use of call language in tandem with apostle language, his second criterion would certainly have been God's or Jesus Christ's call or commission: "Paul an apostle—sent neither by human commission nor from human authorities, but through Jesus Christ and God the Father, who raised him from the dead" (Gal 1:1; see also 1:15).

The apostle always had a message to announce. God's call to Paul the apostle was to announce the good news, that is, the gospel of Jesus (Rom 1:16). While that good news went first to Judeans, it was meant also for non-Judeans (Rom 1:16). And it was to non-Judeans (called Greeks or Gentiles) that Paul the Judean Pharisee was especially called (Rom 1:5; 11:13; 15:18; 16:26; Gal 1:16; 2:2, 8-9). That call is seen most clearly in two passages: "inasmuch then as I am an apostle to the Gentiles, I glorify my ministry" (Rom 11:13) and "but when God, who had set me apart before I was born and called me through his grace, was pleased to reveal his Son to me, so that I might proclaim him among the Gentiles" (Gal 1:15-16).[146]

Paul's dedication to non-Judeans was not a result of his being a "nice guy" nor the working out of a twenty-first-century desire for inclusivity. Rather, it was a direct implication of God's call to Paul that was rooted in God's centuries-old plan. Indeed, Israel was always meant to be "a light to the nations" (Isa 42:6; see also 49:6). Through Israel's witness, the nations would in the end-time stream into Jerusalem and thus to Jerusalem's God (Isa 2:2-4; 60:3; 66:18; Jer 3:17). But a sort of reverse action was also in Paul's vision. One of the potentially bitter realities of Paul's ministry was the fact that the overwhelming majority of the people of Israel had rejected Jesus as the Messiah (Rom 9:1-5; 10:18-21; 11:7-10). His solution? He believed that his success among non-Judeans would make Israel jealous and thus result in their turning to faith in Jesus (Rom 11:13-15).

Paul functioned, then, as an "eschatological herald"—an announcer or proclaimer that God was in the process through the life, death, and resurrection of Jesus of bringing about the end of the current age (see 1 Cor 7:31, for example). We have already seen that in the resurrection of Jesus, the end of time had broken into the present. Paul announced that radical shift and the end that would soon come. At that point, he was an apocalyptic apostle.

The life of such an apocalyptic figure was a difficult one. As Paul wrote in 1 Cor 4:9-13,

> For I think that God has exhibited us apostles as last of all, as though sentenced to death, because we have become a spectacle to the world, to angels and to mortals. We are fools for the sake of Christ, but you are wise in Christ. We are weak, but you are strong. You are held in honor, but we in disrepute. To the present hour we are hungry and thirsty, we are poorly clothed and beaten and homeless, and we grow weary from the work of our own hands. When reviled, we bless; when persecuted, we endure; when slandered, we speak kindly. We have become like the rubbish of the world, the dregs of all things, to this very day.

The contrast with his former life as a respected Pharisee should not be lost (see Phil 3:3-9). Indeed, Paul tried to conform his life as much as possible to the life Jesus had lived,[147] which resulted for Paul in the same downward movement in social standing identified in Christ (Phil 2:5-11). But his sufferings did not cause him to whine, because he understood their purpose within God's larger plan for the world. His sufferings became, in fact, part of his proclamation (2 Cor 1:5-6; 4:7-12; 6:3-10; 11:23-29; Phil 1:12-14; 3:10; 1 Thess 2:1-2; 3:3-7; see also Rom 8:35). He wrote about his sufferings not to emphasize how great he was because he had suffered, but to show how terribly weak he was. And he could say, "If I must boast, I will boast of the things that show my weakness" (2 Cor 11:30). And further, "So, I will boast all the more gladly of my weaknesses, so that the power of Christ may dwell in me. Therefore I am content with weaknesses, insults, hardships, persecutions, and calamities for the sake of Christ; for whenever I am weak, then I am strong" (2 Cor 12:9b-10; see also 1 Cor 2:1-5).

Thus, for Paul, what he proclaimed and how he lived in light of that proclamation were thoroughly integrated with each other. As Beker has phrased it, "Because the *manner* of God's coming apocalyptic triumph is made manifest in the death and resurrection of Christ, the apostle must therefore communicate in his own apostolic life both the *purpose* of God's intervention in Christ and its *manner*."[148] Christ-believers in general, with Paul as their model, could also boast in *their* sufferings, which produced endurance, character, and hope (Rom 5:3-4).

In this chapter and the preceding one, we have explored when Paul lived, where he lived, how he moved about the Roman Empire, and who he was as a person. We turn in the next chapter to what Paul did—how he carried out his role as apostle among non-Judeans. We will discover that as an apocalyptic apostle, Paul established apocalyptic gatherings or congregations of Christ-believers who were called to take on their own roles as suffering messengers of God's love.

Study Questions

1. Describe the chief characteristics of Paul as a Judean.
2. Describe the chief characteristics of Paul as a Greco-Roman.
3. In what ways do you belong to more than one cultural and social world? How do those different worlds complement each other, and how do they conflict with each other?
4. Summarize the political theology of the Roman Empire. How is that approach similar to and different from the political thinking of the country in which you live?
5. Does it make more sense to talk about Paul's dramatic change in life as a conversion or as a call? How so?

Suggested Reading

Texts

Barrett, C. K. *The New Testament Background: Selected Documents*. New York: Harper & Row, 1961.

Elliott, Neil, and Mark Reasoner, eds. *Documents and Images for the Study of Paul*. Minneapolis: Fortress Press, 2011.

Paul as a Judean

Davies, W. D. *Paul and Rabbinic Judaism: Some Rabbinic Elements in Pauline Theology*. London: SPCK, 1948; reissued, Philadelphia: Fortress Press, 1980.

Neusner, Jacob. *Judaism When Christianity Began: A Survey of Belief and Practice*. Louisville: Westminster John Knox, 2002.

Paul's "Worlds"

Carter, Warren. *The Roman Empire and the New Testament: An Essential Guide*. Nashville: Abingdon, 2006.

Jeffers, James S. *The Greco-Roman World of the New Testament Era: Exploring the Background of Early Christianity*. Downers Grove, IL: InterVarsity, 1999.

Klauck, Hans-Josef. *The Religious Context of Early Christianity: A Guide to Graeco-Roman Religions*. Trans. Brian McNeil. Minneapolis: Fortress Press, 2003.

Stambaugh, John E., and David L. Balch. *The New Testament in Its Social Environment*. Library of Early Christianity. Philadelphia: Westminster, 1986.

Wallace, Richard, and Wynne Williams. *The Three Worlds of Paul of Tarsus*. London: Routledge, 1998.

Paul as a Greco-Roman

Crossan, John Dominic, and Jonathan L. Reed. *In Search of Paul: How Jesus's Apostle Opposed Rome's Empire with God's Kingdom*. New York: HarperSanFrancisco, 2004.

Sampley, J. Paul, ed. *Paul in the Greco-Roman World: A Handbook*. Harrisburg, PA: Trinity Press International, 2003.

Fig. 5.1 The Via Appia (Appian Way) approaching Rome. Photo: Paul Hermans.

Chapter 5

What Did Paul Do?

As we have seen, Paul's mission was to announce the good news of what God had done in Jesus. While the message went first to Judean people, it was also for non-Judeans (Rom 1:16), and to those non-Judeans, Paul had a special mission. That mission, in addition, was understood by Paul to participate in God's long-standing plan that through the witness of Israel, the nations would stream into Jerusalem and to the God of Israel. Of that end-of-time message, Paul was a prominent voice.

But how did Paul carry on that mission? In an era two millennia removed from the electronic social media of the twenty-first century, Paul created a social network of people who believed that Jesus was the Christ. The social network was spread throughout the disparate lands where Paul had done missionary work, and it included people of varying economic and social situations, as well as people whose pre-Christ religious identities ran the gamut of first-century religious possibilities. All, however, were understood by Paul to be "in Christ," and all had some type of relationship with Paul—either directly with him or indirectly through one of the other missionaries who were part of his "team." As a result, Paul envisioned a social network in which believers also had a relationship with each other.[1]

What Was the Heart of Paul's Social Network?

To provide a structure within which his social network could grow, Paul gathered people into worshipping, serving, and supportive groupings known as **churches**. He did that gathering through formal preaching and through conversations in the workplace and home that resulted in relationships that functioned as **fictive** or non-blood-related **families**. He nurtured his Christ-believing social network through personal visits, visits by his coworkers, letters, and a monetary collection.

For Paul, there were macro and micro reasons for gathering believers into identifiable groupings. At the macro or more theoretical level, each congregation he founded became a sign or outpost of God's end-time **justifying** activity that had already broken into the world through the death and resurrection of Jesus. Each individual church was a living demonstration that "*now* is the day of salvation" (2 Cor 6:2), and each community composed of Judeans and Gentiles or Gentiles alone "was a living witness to the eschatological vision he had discovered in Christ."[2] Moreover, that vision stood in sharp contrast to the empire in which he and all believers lived, and as we shall see when we study Paul's letters, the churches he founded composed a network that was a counter to the power and propaganda of Rome.[3]

In working toward his vision, Paul developed a selective process regarding where he did missionary work and where he founded congregations. He wanted to do his missionary work only in new places that did not already have believers: "Thus I make it my ambition to proclaim the good news, not where Christ has already been named, so that I do not build on someone else's foundation" (Rom 15:20). Paul as the first missionary is the one who laid the foundation or planted the church in a given locale (1 Cor 3:9, 11). He also did not try to establish congregations everywhere. Instead of a strategy of moving from a city to the nearest village, and then to the next village after that, he moved normally from one large city to another. He stayed usually in provincial capitals and remained long enough that at least one congregation (or **house church**) was able to function on its own, with leadership adequate for the anticipated changes and challenges after Paul left.[4] Instead of moving into the next town or village, Paul tended to travel on the major commercial routes of his world until he came to another important urban area. In doing that, he was, in essence, planting the flag for God's mission in each province and thus establishing beachheads that were both a sign of God's future and living examples of it.[5]

Because of the sense that these representative congregations "claimed" their province or territory for the mission of God in Christ, Paul could write in Rom 15:19, "From Jerusalem and as far around as Illyricum I have fully proclaimed the good news of Christ." Obviously, he had not preached everywhere, and obviously, only an extreme minority of the population in the eastern part of the Roman Empire had come to believe in Jesus, but his congregations were the first fruits of many more believers to come. Further, as Arland Hultgren suggests, Paul likely in this portion of Romans was not thinking so much of persons as of whole nations.[6]

The congregations were not merely symbols, however. At the micro level, having been launched by Paul each congregation (or house church) became its own mission center. Within the congregations, people worshipped, learned, and served. A word family Paul used to encompass such activities was *to build up* (from *oikodomeō* / *I build* [*up*]). The verb and the related noun for *building* (*oikodomē*) are construction terms. So when advising believers how to act, Paul reminds the Corinthians, "Knowledge puffs up, but love builds up" (1 Cor 8:1; similar in 10:23). Paul gives special attention to how believers experience worship, with the criterion being what builds up. In 1 Corinthians 14, therefore, Paul approaches **speaking in tongues (glossolalia)** from the perspective of what builds up. Those who have that gift (including Paul; 14:18) build up themselves when they speak in tongues (14:4), but the greater good is building up others, both individually (14:3, 17) and corporately as the church (14:4, 6, 12; see also 3:9). So he counsels the Corinthians, "Let all things be done for building up" (14:26), a model that he commends for interactions between Christ-believers (1 Thess 5:11), between believers and nonbelievers (Rom 15:2), and for his own ministry (2 Cor 10:8; 12:19; 13:10). Each congregation, in turn, carried on its mission of proclamation and outreach to nearby villages and cities (1 Thess 1:6-8).

For Paul, then, a fundamental part of his mission was the founding of congregations.

HOUSE CHURCHES

When twenty-first-century people hear the word *church*, they usually think of a building in which worship, classes, and meetings are held, or they think of the church as an institution. The Greek term *ekklēsia*, usually translated as *church*, goes back to at least the fifth century BCE. It was used by Euripides and Herodotus and designated the assembly of the citizens of the Greek city-state (or *polis*). In the **Septuagint**, *ekklēsia* was used to translate the Hebrew noun *qāhāl*. That term could refer to different kinds of assemblies, including a military assembly or army (1 Sam 17:47), but it also was used to refer to Israel when it assembled to hear the word of God (Deut 4:10; 9:10; 10:4; 18:16; 31:30; 1 Kgs 8:14, 22, 55, 65).

Paul applied the term *ekklēsia* to the people he had gathered together who believed his message about Jesus. While, at one level, the term could mean simply a gathering, for Paul the gathering in a given place was, for example, "the church of the Thessalonians in God the Father and the Lord Jesus Christ" (1 Thess 1:1). The gathering, assembly, or church was centered in God the Father (the God of Israel) and in the Lord Jesus Christ, and ultimately each church belonged to God (1 Cor 10:32). At this point, Paul's use of *church* is analogous to the Septuagint's religious use of the term. While it was not fully developed by Paul himself, there is an implicit understanding of the church as something beyond or larger than the single congregation or local gathering. Thus, Paul addresses "the church of God that is in Corinth, to those who are sanctified in Christ Jesus, called to be saints, together with all those who in every place call on the name of our Lord Jesus Christ, both their Lord and ours" (1 Cor 1:2; see also 1 Cor 10:32; 12:28; 2 Cor 1:1; Rom 16:16; negatively, Paul says that he persecuted "the church of God," which also points to more than one gathering; see Gal 1:13; 1 Cor 15:9; Phil 3:6). *Ekklēsia*, therefore, can be used for both the local congregation and the larger concept.[7]

What Christ-believers in Paul's churches did not have was buildings. That is, they had no buildings that were devoted solely to worship, education, and service. Sometime in the second half of the second century, Christians began to dedicate homes as church assembly places; such homes stopped being residences. Eventually, Christians were given permission to build separate, new buildings as churches, with the first basilica being built in 314.

In Paul's mission, believers gathered in private homes. Thus, we read in 1 Cor 16:19 that "Aquila and Prisca, together with the church in their house, greet you warmly in the Lord." *House church* literally in Greek is "the according to their house church," a phrase that Paul uses also in Rom 16:5 and Philem 2; writing in Paul's name, the author of Colossians has the same phrase in 4:15. Paul also refers to other households that may have been house churches (1 Cor 1:16; 16:15; Rom 16:10-11; and possibly Phil 4:22). In sum, a house church is a group of Christ-believers who meet in a private home.

The development of the early church within the context of the household was, in a sense, only natural. Synagogues might remain open to Christ-believers as long as they worshipped in a totally Judean manner, but more peculiarly Christian

Fig. 5.2 The ruins of a spacious private home in Athens. Did Paul's churches meet in such luxurious settings? Photo courtesy of the President and Fellows of Harvard College.

worship, such as the Lord's Supper, could not be conducted there. Eventually, synagogues stopped being open to Christ-believers. Pagan temples were not an option, and rental space involved an expenditure of money that Paul's communities did not have. The private home, in contrast, provided privacy, intimacy, and relative stability.[8] In addition, Greeks and Romans participated in home-based religious activity, so a societal model already existed, at least in part, for Paul's house churches.[9]

The Greek term for *house* or *household* (*oikos*) could mean a number of things: a one-room house or apartment, a house or apartment with several rooms, or a large house. The household could thus be quite intimate, with father, mother, and children, or it could be much more extensive. Within the cities, Paul's major missionary territory, there were two basic kinds of housing: the ***domus*** and the ***insula***. The *domus* was a private home for wealthier and more prominent people. The basic construction pattern was several rooms clustered around a central atrium. The typical *domus* had expensive furnishing and decorations and had an enclosed, columned yard (peristyle) based on earlier Greek models. It was designed to house not only the owner and family, but also household servants. It was also built for social gatherings, so the dining rooms were very important. The Latin name for the dining room was ***triclinium***. A typical *domus* or villa had a *triclinium* of about 36 square meters (387.5 square feet) and an atrium of 55 square meters (592 square feet). The *triclinium* could hold nine or ten people reclining on couches or, without couches, about twenty people. If a gathering could spill into the atrium, up to forty or fifty persons could be accommodated, with thirty to forty being a "comfortable" number.[10]

The *insula* was basically an apartment building.[11] On the ground floor was often a row of shops that faced the street. The shops, which frequently had a mezzanine or back room, also served as home for the shopkeeper and family. The upper floors contained one- and two-room apartments. Some *insulae* had factories on the ground floor, with factory workers living directly above. Most of the apartments had no kitchen or toilet facilities, nor were they big enough to entertain friends. The people who lived in them were largely dependent on public places for their cooking, water gathering, toilet needs, and places to socialize. A room in an *insula* could be a difficult place for people to gather for worship, although some occupants could have larger apartments.

Earlier research identified the *domus* as the primary location for Paul's house churches, but more recent scholarship has argued that apartments in *insulae* likely were used as well.[12] Lampe identifies a minimum of five house churches in Romans 16. From that, he concludes that at least some believers in Rome had enough social status and wealth that they were able to provide more than just a room.

THE CHURCH AS A FICTIVE FAMILY

The location of Pauline churches in the house or household helped Paul to view the gathered believers as a surrogate or substitute family. Or, to use the terminology of cultural anthropology, Paul understood Christ-believers to be a **fictive family** or fictive kin group. According to Hellerman, a surrogate or fictive family "may be defined as a social group whose members are related to one another neither by birth nor by marriage, but who nevertheless (a) employ kinship terminology to describe group relationships and (b) expect family-like behavior to characterize interactions among group members."[13]

The Pauline fictive family was family bound together by common belief in Jesus and the common community life they shared. By entering the church, people became part of a new family or an alternative family, but a real family nevertheless. Paul's fictive family was implicitly set over against local Greco-Roman families that were understood to be the building blocks of society and over against the empire-wide family of all who lived within the Roman Empire's authority and whose head and father was the emperor.[14] Members of the Christ-believing fictive family were called sister and brother (1 Thess 5:26; 1 Cor 1:10-11, 26; 2:1; 3:1; 4:6; 7:24, 29; 10:1; 11:33; 12:1; 14:6, 20, 26, 39; 15:1, 31, 50, 58; 16:15; Rom 8:29; 16:14; Phil 4:1, 21; etc.), and Paul at times referred to himself as the father or mother of his churches and of those he had converted (1 Cor 4:15; Gal 4:19; 1 Thess 2:7, 11).

Since ancient Mediterranean people received their identities mainly from the groups of which they were a part (chief among which was the family), the self-identity that resulted from a new fictive family meant a profound reshuffling of the self-conceptions of believers. One aspect of that shift in identity was the all-important question "Where is honor to be found?" Honor, as one of the core values of Mediterranean cultures,[15] was a special value for the family. Honor also presented a special challenge, as all family members needed to be alert to anything or anyone that might diminish the family's honor. One of the ways to protect or even expand family honor was to attack the honor-rating of another family in the cultural "game" of challenge and riposte.[16]

Paul's view of the fictive family of the church had points of both continuity and discontinuity with the broader culture. He was consistent with the culture of his time in the behavior he expected siblings to exhibit toward each other. Thus, the relationship between blood siblings was extremely close and in many ways central. One sibling was to give to the other in a generous and ungrudging way. The technical term in cultural anthropological study is *familial* (or family) *reciprocity*. It refers to a relationship in which score is not kept, so that the giver does not calculate the cost of the gift to the other sibling, whether the gift is material or a service, nor does the sibling expect to be repaid.[17] Siblings were also understood to be equals.[18]

Paul adopted this basic model from his time, but he also adapted it. First, he applied it to people who were not related to each other by blood. N. T. Wright adds, "For Paul the significance of baptism was that one had come into a new family and had to start behaving as though that was in fact true."[19] Second, Paul urged his listeners to *give* honor to others, rather than keeping or taking it. He directs the Romans to "outdo one another in showing honor," or as Moxnes suggests, "in regard to honor prefer the others to yourselves."[20]

In conclusion, Paul and the post-Paul churches faced three potential problems as a result of the house church and fictive family models:

1. Meeting in separate homes could encourage different house churches to develop different identities and practices, thus working against the unity of the church in a given locale. The divisions Paul addresses in 1 Cor 1:10-17 may in part be related to different house churches.
2. Especially if the setting of a house church was a *domus*, the host could allow social and economic distinctions to spill over from everyday non-church relations into the interactions between members of the house church family. The difficulties Paul addresses in 1 Cor 11:17-22, 33-34 may have arisen in just that way.
3. After Paul's death, the household model (1 Tim 3:15) paved the way for churches to adopt a hierarchical model of authority in which the male bishop, based on the model of the *paterfamilias*, became *the* leader of the congregation (1 Tim 3:1-7).

HOW NONBELIEVERS MIGHT HAVE VIEWED THE CHURCH

As congregations of Christ-believers increased, nonbelievers needed to develop a framework for understanding and evaluating this new phenomenon. Richard Ascough lists four possible models that people may have used to categorize Paul's house churches: synagogues, philosophical schools, the ancient mysteries (often identified as mystery religions), and voluntary associations. All of them could be found in household settings during the first century.[21]

Although Ascough is careful to avoid pigeonholing too quickly each Pauline congregation, he does identify the congregations in Philippi and Thessalonica as similar to voluntary associations, and indeed, for several centuries, scholars have seen in such associations a close analogy to Paul's congregations.[22] In a standard definition, the **voluntary association** is "a group which a man [or woman] joins of his own free will, and which accepts him of its free will, and this mutual acceptance creates certain obligations on both parties."[23] Voluntary associations had existed for centuries by the time Paul's ministry began and were very popular under the Roman Empire, where they were often called *collegia*. Still, the empire was wary of them and went through periods of actively suppressing them. While Kloppenborg has identified three categories of associations (funerary, religious, and professional),[24] associations in practice often had more than one of these functions, as well as providing significant social contacts. As one would anticipate, scholars identify similarities as well as differences between voluntary associations and Paul's churches. See textbox on p. 98 for a brief summary.

The potential danger Christ-believers presented in the eyes of the Roman government was that their associations were different from most associations: they were not trade groups nor athletic clubs nor members of the same ethnic group nor residents necessarily of the same neighborhood. They were united by a belief, and for imperial officials, that pointed to a political group. In a dictatorship, any political group is immediately suspect—let alone one with a universal Father, a universal Lord, and a pan-national identity as a fictive family.[25]

Voluntary Associations and Paul's Churches: A Comparison

Similarities

- Membership voluntary, with associations and churches having roughly same number of members
- Private funding; support by patrons often crucial
- Offered security and stability in an uncertain era
- Concerned about moral behavior, with emphasis on proper sexual expression
- Met in homes of members
- Used family language to refer to themselves
- Strong tendency of members to view each other as equals
- Cut across social and economic lines

Differences

- Associations local; churches local and international[26]
- No physical statue of deity in churches (hard for ancient people to understand)
- Competition for honor in the broader society absent from house churches
- Active evangelization by church members
- With exception of baptism and Lord's Supper, churches lack the sort of sacrifice and other rites typical of voluntary associations
- House church members could not belong to other religious groups

How Did Paul Begin Congregations?

In starting congregations, Paul employed a combination of preaching and conversation.

PREACHING

According to the book of Acts, when Paul entered a new city, his first move was to the synagogue (13:5, 14-53; 14:1; 17:1-4, 10-12, 17; 18:4, 19; 19:8). There he spoke. The account of Paul's work in Thessalonica is a good example of his synagogue-first preaching (Acts 17:1-10), in which he preached not only to Judeans but also to "devout Greeks" (17:4).

By going to the local synagogue, Paul accomplished two tasks: he brought his message to Judeans first, and he also met Gentiles who in Acts are called "God-fearers." They were people who worshipped with **Diaspora** Judeans, selectively followed food laws and other rituals, and contributed financially to the synagogue. They knew the story and stories of Israel, but they had not taken formal steps to convert to Judaism. Such people would have provided Paul an audience prepared for the good news of a universal Judean Messiah with whom they could be united through the non-ethnically based ceremony of baptism.

But is that understanding based on solid historical data, or is it part of Luke's theological desire to show Paul's continuity with Judaism and Jerusalem? Paul himself never talks about preaching in a synagogue—anywhere, including in Thessalonica. In fact, he refers to the Christ-believers in that city as people who have "turned to God from idols, to serve a living and true God" (1 Thess 1:9), a statement he would never direct to Judeans. Paul nowhere uses the word the word *synagogue*, nor, for that matter, do any of the deuteropauline letters. A starting point in the synagogue would also seem to conflict with his primary mission to the Gentiles (Gal 1:16; 2:7-9; Rom 1:5, 13-15; 11:13; 15:15-18). Nevertheless, Paul stated clearly in Romans that his gospel came first to Judeans and after them to the rest of the nations (Rom 1:16; 11:11-12). Certainly, his letters presume a solid understanding of Israel's Bible. In addition to the Judean minority in some congregations, does that level of biblical knowledge point to Gentile God-fearers, who had a pre-Paul knowledge of the texts? Perhaps so. It would have made sense for Paul to have looked for the local Judean community when he arrived in a new city, and most of the cities he targeted had a substantial Judean population; further, there is evidence in 2 Corinthians that he ran afoul of synagogue authorities (11:24, 26). Thus, he had, at least on some occasions, enough contact with people in synagogues to offend some of them.

Where else might Paul have preached? Acts has Paul using the "lecture hall of Tyrannus" for two years during his ministry in Ephesus (19:9-10).[27] Paul also spoke in the *agora* (marketplace/civic center; Acts 17:17) and at the Areopagus, a rock outcropping used in Athens for public debate (17:19-34). Several times in Acts, Paul spoke to governmental officials (13:7-12; 16:25-34; 22:30—23:10; 24:10-21, 24-26; 25:6-12; 26:1-29) and once even to a Jerusalem mob (21:37-22:21). Again, the lack of supporting evidence from Paul's letters raises questions about the reliability of the settings in Acts for Paul's preaching. As Meeks has written, "We must also ask whether the more public settings in Acts may not often reflect some of the author's subtle literary allusions, such as the several hints of Socrates in the encounters in the agora and Areopagus in Athens, or sometimes simply the pattern of the author's day rather than of Paul's."[28]

Furthermore, while waiting for his trial in Rome at what turned out to be the end of his ministry, Paul, according to Acts, was "preaching the kingdom of God and teaching the things about the Lord Jesus Christ" while residing in "his own rented lodgings" (28:30-31).[29] With that statement, we return to the house and the house church as primary settings for Paul's ministry in general but also more specifically for his preaching. We have surveyed already the household as a setting for Paul's work, so in the house, we have a location for his preaching and teaching that is supported by his own words. Stowers notes that "an invitation to teach in someone's house would provide Paul with . . . a sponsor, an audience and credentials. . . . When Paul says 'I baptized the household of Stephanas,' it is probably correct to assume that the preaching which led up to these baptisms occurred not in a marketplace or a gymnasium, but in someone's house."[30]

What is clear is the great significance Paul assigned to proclamation: "If I proclaim the gospel, this gives me no ground for boasting, for an obligation is laid on me, and woe to me if I do not proclaim the gospel! For if I do this of my own will, I have a reward; but if not of my own will, I am entrusted with a commission" (1 Cor 9:16-17; see also 1 Cor 1:18-25; 2 Cor 4:5; and Rom 10:13-17). The message about Jesus had to be spoken, and that was Paul's charge, a charge that had come to him even before birth (Gal 1:15-16) and that was made specific in his call to preach to the uncircumcised (Gal 2:7). Despite his relatively high level of education, he tried to preach in such a way that he did not obscure his message by using "lofty words or wisdom. For I decided to know nothing among you except Jesus Christ, and him crucified" (1 Cor 2:1-2). Indeed, he could even label his preaching "foolishness" (1 Cor 1:21-25)—foolishness, that is, in the eyes of an unbelieving world. Ultimately, though, he could identify in his proclaiming of the good news of Jesus God's power and the work of the Holy Spirit (1 Thess 1:5; Rom 1:16; 15:18-19; see also 1 Cor 4:19-20; 2 Cor 6:7). His own apostolic activity was thus the manifestation of divine power "against the very imperial power that killed Jesus," and his apostolic presence was an invasive power because of the message he announced and embodied.[31] He was able to point, also, to miraculous deeds (likely including healings) as confirmation of his apostolic authority as a preacher of the gospel (2 Cor 12:12; Gal 3:5; Rom 15:18-19).[32]

CONVERSATION

Formal preaching was not the only method Paul used to bring people to Jesus and begin congregations. He also talked with people. While we might well theorize that Paul talked with people while traveling and while shopping in the market, the two places where our sources are clearer is that he used his workplace and the private home as important centers for speaking with people about God's activity and mission.

Earlier, we studied Paul's life as an artisan, more particularly as a tentmaker/leatherworker.[33] The work was tedious and the hours long (1 Cor 4:12; 1 Thess 2:9), but while his fingers might be busy, his tongue was free to talk with other workers and shopkeepers, suppliers, customers, and passersby. In the congested cities in which Paul lived, the high population density, especially in the parts of the city where someone at Paul's economic level could afford to live, meant that people were always around. In a real sense, the urban shop functioned as a sort of ancient neighborhood coffee shop or ice cream parlor where people could wander by, stop in for a few minutes of conversation, or linger to hear a teacher-missionary like Paul expound on the new thing he claimed God had done in Jesus. With families of the workers living behind and above the shop, he also had access to entire families. In addition, the homes of wealthier people were often nearby or even in the same block, with Paul once more having access to whole households.

Given the normal hierarchy of the Greco-Roman family, often when the head of the household converted to belief in Jesus, the entire family did as well. That is exactly what we read in Acts 16:15, 16:31-34, and 18:8, where entire households are baptized; in 1 Cor 1:16, Paul mentions that he had baptized the household of Stephanas. At the same time we have evidence that wives and slaves did convert even when their husband or owner did not (1 Cor 7:12-16; see also 1 Pet 2:18; 3:1-2). Alternatively, the baptism of every household member did not happen automatically, as the case of the slave Onesimus illustrates. According to the letter to Philemon, Onesimus's master, Philemon, had been baptized but not Onesimus. Similarly, Paul is likely not being theoretical when he lays ground rules for the believing husband of a nonbelieving wife and the believing wife of a nonbelieving husband (1 Cor 7:12-16).

While providing a less public setting than a rented building, the *domus* and thus the gathering of Christ-believers in it were not totally private. The *domus* by design was a semipublic building, as seen in the open-air atrium near the front of the building, the banquet space provided in the dining room or rooms, and the morning ritual in which the head of the house would greet his or her clients and be hailed by them.[34]

The crowded buildings and the semi-openness of the *domus* to the public might also speak to worship as part of the oral proclamation by Paul and his coworkers—whether in sermon, conversation, or teaching. Thus, the Lord's Supper, while a meal for the fictive family of the church, was to be conducted in a way that brought honor to the Christ-believing community and exhibited the positive

Fig. 5.3 A thermopolium from Pompeii. At counters like this, usually located between shops, working people could share hot meals and conversation.

sibling relations that were to exist in Christ. The planning and conduct of worship needed to occur with the nonbeliever in mind, as seen in Paul's discussion of the Spirit-directed speaking called *tongues*. Since tongues are an insider experience for believers, Paul would prefer in the community's worship that the emphasis be on **prophecy**, which is the study of a biblical text and Spirit-directed preaching on it (1 Cor 14:22-31).

The house church, once again, proves to be a crucial piece—and place—in Paul's social network. Roger Gehring has summarized its function in this way:

> These houses played an important role in the context of Paul's evangelistic ministry by naturally opening the door to a whole network of relationships. Householders were able to create an immediate audience for Paul by inviting their friends, relatives, and clientele. . . . Within a very short time after becoming a guest in someone's home, Paul had a relatively large number of high-quality contacts for one-on-one conversations and his evangelistic meetings.[35]

Christ-believing households, in turn, became themselves centers of outreach, whether Paul was present or not.[36]

Once congregations were begun and, hopefully, on somewhat steady footing, how did Paul nurture them? How did he keep them going? To those questions we now turn.

How Did Paul Nurture Congregations?

In nurturing the congregations he had begun and thus nurturing the broader network of relationships within the Christ-believing network, Paul engaged in or oversaw four major nurturing activities:

1. He made personal visits to the congregations he had begun.
2. He sent his associates to visit the congregations he had begun.
3. He wrote letters.
4. He took a monetary collection from his basically Gentile congregations to give to the Judean Christ-believers in Jerusalem.

PERSONAL VISITS

While not a "frequent flier" in twenty-first-century terms, Paul was without question a frequent walker and ship passenger. His restless energy not only brought him to places he had never evangelized before, but also caused him to return to congregations he had founded, especially when they were under pressure to believe and act in ways he did not affirm.

Paul seemed to understand the powerful effect his sheer presence could have on a group of believers (despite what his opponents said according to 2 Cor 10:10: "For they say, 'His letters are weighty and strong, but his bodily presence is weak, and his speech contemptible'"). As Elliott observes, Paul's strategy "is to represent himself . . . as an agent of the 'power of God,' distinct from mere practitioners of rhetoric."[37] In writing a letter to people with whom he was especially upset, he wishes he could be present with them: "I wish I were present with you now and could change my tone, for I am perplexed about you" (Gal 4:20). Perhaps it was good that he did not get back to Galatia when he was so upset! And, for that matter, he hopes that before he makes another trip to Corinth, problems might be resolved in a way he deems fitting. If not, he will come with full authority through the power of God (2 Cor 10:1-2; 13:1-4, 10). At the same time, he exercised his power in an ironic way, since he represented a Jesus who was outwardly the quintessentially weak one who was crucified and whose power was manifested in that crucifixion, as well as in the resurrection. Paul wrote that he carried the marks of Jesus branded on his body (Gal 6:17), so that when Paul was present, so was the crucified and resurrected Jesus (2 Cor 4:10). Paul embodied the power in weakness of his Lord.[38]

Paul's preferred style was to deal with problems in person (1 Cor 4:19; 5:3; 16:5-9; at a somewhat greater distance, Phil 1:23-26). That is likely why he prayed that he would be able to be physically present both in congregations he had founded (1 Thess 2:17; 3:10; Phil 1:8; 4:1) and in a group of congregations he hoped would be a springboard to further ministry in Spain (Rom 1:10-11; 15:20-29). At the same time, he knew that his sheer presence did not always solve problems, as he acknowledged in 2 Cor 2:1-2 when referring to his "painful visit" to Corinth. In that personal visit, he clearly did not gain assent. Still, while dealing with challenging situations, Paul also sought more positively to encourage his congregations, to call them to unity, and to promote mutual care (1 Cor 1:10; 12:4-31; 2 Cor 1:3-7; Rom 12:3-8).[39]

VISITS BY HIS ASSOCIATES

Paul could not, of course, be everywhere all the time. Nor did he carry on his missionary work alone. He developed a cadre of associates who not only worked with him while he was evangelizing a given city but also represented him by visiting and nurturing house churches already begun and by extending the mission to smaller communities. Their presence embodied his apostolic aura and authority and was a significant way in which Paul created and sustained the network that supported congregations and individuals.

The actual term *coworker* (*synergos* in Greek; someone who "works with") appears to be a title of some honor for Paul and was reserved for his closest associates. He applied the term to Prisca and Aquila (Rom 16:3-5), Urbanus (Rom 16:9), Timothy (Rom 16:21; 1 Cor 16:10; 1 Thess 3:2), Apollos (1 Cor 3:6-9), Fortunatus, Achaicus, and Stephanas (probably; 1 Cor 16:15-18), Titus (2 Cor 8:23), Epaphroditus (Phil 2:25), Euodia and Syntyche (Phil 4:2-3), Clement (Phil 4:3), Philemon (Philem 1), Aristarchus, Demas, Luke, and Mark (Philem 24). Likely at the same level in Paul's thinking were those to whom he assigned forms of the word *toil* or *labor* (*kopiaō* in Greek): Mary (Rom 16:6) and Persis, Tryphaena, and Tryphosa (Rom 16:12). Early in Paul's ministry, Barnabas was a significant figure (Gal 2:1, 9, 13; Acts 13:1-3), but the two men experienced major

> ## Paul's "Coworkers"
>
> The choice of a general term for those who worked with Paul is difficult to make. *Coworker* is a good descriptive term, but Paul reserved it for a special segment of those who participated in the mission, rather than for all who served. For this book, *associate* has been chosen, because it is a more general term that allows for different levels of involvement and different degrees of relationship with Paul. An analogy is the way contemporaries of Dr. Martin Luther King Jr. use the word *associate* for themselves; it designates those who participated with him in the civil rights movement.

disagreement over eating with Gentile believers and the continuing use of another Christ-believer named Mark (Acts 15:36-41), with the result that Paul and Barnabas went their separate ways. Later in his ministry, Paul does refer positively to Barnabas (1 Cor 9:6).

Paul worked particularly closely with Titus and Timothy. Titus had begun a collection in Corinth that he resumed later, according to 2 Cor 8:6. If 2 Corinthians 8 was originally a separate letter, Titus may have been the one who brought it to Corinth. It is also quite likely that Titus had the difficult task of delivering and interpreting Paul's famous and probably now lost "letter of tears," which was a massive attack on the Corinthians (2 Cor 2:1-11). As Paul moved from one place to another, he was disturbed because Titus did not meet him in Troas to update him, as Paul had expected (2 Cor 2:12-13). But in Macedonia (northern Greece), Titus did find Paul and reported on the dramatic shift that had taken place among the Corinthian believers (7:5-16), caused by Paul's letter but also, no doubt, by Titus's work among them.

Timothy was, together with Silvanus (Silas in Acts), part of Paul's missionary work in Thessalonica (1 Thess 1:1; 3:2, 6; Acts 17:10-15; 18:5; 19:22) and Corinth (1 Cor 4:17; 16:10; 2 Cor 1:1, 19; see Acts 18:1-5). After leaving Thessalonica, Paul was worried about how the new believers there were handling persecution, so he sent Timothy "to strengthen and encourage" them (1 Thess 3:1-3), an embassy that produced positive results (3:6). In 1 Cor 4:17, Timothy is Paul's "beloved," whom Paul has either sent in the past or is sending "to remind you." He is Paul's co-sender of 2 Corinthians (1:1), Philippians (1:1), and Philemon (1), and Paul hoped to send him to Philippi, since, as Paul said, "I have no one like him" (2:19-24).

Paul refers to many others, including a good number of women. Prisca, Euodia, Syntyche, Mary, Tryphaena, and Tryphosa have already been named. Apphia (Philem 2), Junia (Rom 16:7), and Phoebe (Rom 16:1) were all part of Paul's ministry network. Phoebe is of particular note. Not only was she a patron of many people, including Paul, but she also very likely delivered the letter to the Romans and may have read it to them. Without doubt, she would have been in a position to explain the letter to its recipients.

Not only did Paul's network flow from him and his associates to the churches, it also flowed from the churches toward him with information and questions. In 1 Cor 1:11, Paul wrote about the oral reports given to him by Chloe's "people" (her slaves or employees), and in 7:1, he began to address questions they had sent him in written form. (Responses to other questions they posed begin in 8:1, 12:1, and 16:1.) Epaphroditus, no doubt, brought updated information to Paul about Philippi (Phil 2:25-30; 4:18), and obviously in general, Paul knew a great deal about what was happening in the congregations to which he wrote.

Paul had no cell phones or e-mail, but he and his associates created a network that provided emotional support, theological acumen, and responsible challenge in their joint identity and mission as followers of Jesus.[40]

LETTERS

The careful use of associates was just one significant way Paul dealt with the impossibility of being everywhere all the time. A second significant representative of Paul was the letter. Paul's letters were substitutes for his physical presence as an apostle, just as his associates were. Letters in antiquity were designed, in fact, to overcome the geographical and chronological distances between people, so that the letter sought to create the "fiction of personal presence."[41] Paul's letters thus asserted his apostolic authority by re-creating his apostolic presence with the letters' recipients.[42] That sense of presence was aided by the fact that most people had access to the letters aurally, that is, through the ears. The large majority of people could not read, so they experienced the letters by hearing someone else read them aloud. The hearing replicated, to a certain extent, their initial exposure to Paul when he was physically present with them.

Margaret Mitchell, for her part, has little argument with the substitute nature of the letter, but she urges people to avoid a rigid hierarchy in Paul's thinking in which his physical presence was clearly his preferred way of tending his congregations, sending representatives was a distant number two, and writing letters was number three.[43] Rather, she proposes, Paul at times actually preferred the letter format, as is seen by the great length and depth of thought in his letters. In the case of his "painful letter" to the Corinthians (2 Cor 2:4), the letter produced more results than his presence among them would have. And so "the letter . . . was not an inadequate substitute for the more desirable Pauline physical presence, but was in fact deemed by him a superior way to deal with a given situation."[44]

Part of the challenge for Paul's readers in later centuries is that we sorely miss the other side of the conversation. We read Paul's responses to situations and people about whom we know little or nothing. While we do have some reference to correspondence he has received and reports given to him, by and large, reading his letters is like listening to one side of a telephone conversation. We need to look or listen for clues as to what the other conversation partners have said, asked, or done. But conversations his letters certainly are. Or perhaps more exactly, they are the literary deposit of one part of ongoing conversations.

In writing letters, Paul was using a mode of communication that was very popular during his lifetime. Not only did the rise of Rome increase the need for governmental correspondence, it also saw the development of the letter as almost an art form, especially in the hands of sophisticated authors like Cicero and Seneca. Letter writers such as these two men—one who died forty years before Paul's birth (Cicero) and the other a contemporary of Paul (Seneca)—dealt with philosophical and ethical issues that went far beyond business or love letters. To structure their letters, they and others also utilized rhetoric that originally had been used to formulate speeches. Given the popularity of letters, it is no surprise that of the twenty-seven New Testament documents, twenty-one are written more or less in letter format (from Romans to Jude). In addition, Acts contains letters (15:23-29; 23:26-30), and the book of Revelation has within it seven letters (chapters 2–3). The generation of Christ-believers in the last portion of the first century and the initial decades of the second century also used the letter as their dominant genre (see the letters of Ignatius of Antioch, *1 Clement, 2 Clement*, the letter of Polycarp to the Philippians, and the *Epistle of Barnabas*).[45]

In part, the early church used letters because they were a popular and accepted means of communication, but at the same time, letters served the needs of infant and adolescent communities that were not always sure of their identities. They also served the needs of Paul by expanding his ability to "monitor," advise, challenge, and exhort the groups of believers he had established. As Stanley Stowers writes, "Something about the nature of early Christianity made it a movement of letter writers."[46]

Because of the popularity of the letter (and the dry climate of the Mediterranean basin), we have thousands of letters from antiquity. Some of them, particularly the more literary ones, have been known since antiquity. Many others are everyday business and personal letters that have literally been unearthed in modern times from garbage heaps or from the ruins of homes. This large body of letters helps us identify the ways in which Paul's language and rhetoric are both similar to and different from the style of other letter writers of his world.[47]

Genre

A classic debate in Pauline studies is whether the documents we have from Paul are best understood as epistles or as letters. The issue surfaced most strongly following the research of Adolf Deissmann, who compared Paul's documents with the flood of papyrus discoveries that burst into the scholarly world in the latter part of the nineteenth century. He distinguished sharply between two categories of writing:

- *Epistle*. A literary essay in letter format meant for public consumption
- *Letter*. An everyday nonliterary communication meant for private use only

Deissmann argues that all of Paul's documents fit into the letter category that dominated the recently discovered papyrus letters he had studied.[48]

As time went on, more and more scholars questioned Deissmann's classification and the conclusions he drew from it—especially that, as letters (per his definition), Paul's communications were not written at a sophisticated level and may have been composed quickly. The consensus of scholarship today proposes, rather, that Paul's writings exhibit characteristics of both the epistle and the letter, as outlined by Deissmann. They were not meant for general public consumption, so at that level, they were "private" documents. Even so, they were "public" documents within the house churches, to be read to all believers in a given locale (1 Thess 5:27). They were not written for people in general, but for specific churches or individuals with whom Paul had a relationship.[49] Further, study in the last quarter of the twentieth century and until today has emphasized the care and skill with which Paul composed his letters. In this book, we will use *epistle* and *letter* interchangeably.

There is also a certain official nature to the letters of Paul. He writes in his role as an apostle and in that role seeks to exercise his authority. Moreover, as we have learned, the letters were designed to be read in congregational gatherings. Even the one undisputed letter addressed primarily to an individual, Philemon, is also addressed to "Apphia our sister, to Archippus our fellow soldier, and to the church in your [singular] house" (Philem 2). That and other observations have led M. Luther Stirewalt to argue that Paul's letters are much closer to the Greco-Roman world's official administrative letters from rulers and their subordinates than most previous scholars have allowed.[50] Such letters were carried by authorized representatives, read aloud in public settings, interpreted orally, and ideally, put into effect by the listeners.[51] The similarities between the official or formal salutation in Paul's letters and the salutation in official letters from Mediterranean antiquity especially point to official letters as a model for Paul, maintains Stirewalt, even while the warmth of the salutation is reflective of the personal letter.[52]

The letters of Paul, in sum, were hybrids that resist one precise categorization. They presume and assert Paul's authority as an apostle, and they move quickly into sophisticated arguments and biblical interpretation. At the same time, they reveal an intimacy built on common experience and common devotion to the same Lord.[53]

Structure

Paul's usual pattern of organizing his letters has five basic components:

1. *Salutation.* The salutation is the greeting and includes, in order, the name of the sender(s), the name of the person(s) being addressed, and a greeting. In papyrus letters, the greeting is usually *chairein* (greetings; Acts 15:23; 23:26; James 1:1). Paul adopted that form but changed it in two ways (or took over a change earlier Christ-believers may have introduced): he replaced *chairein* with the somewhat similar-sounding and theologically heavy term *charis* (grace) and added the word *eirēnē* (peace), probably from the Hebrew greeting for peace (*shālôm*). The salutation often contains a clue to Paul's argument. In Rom 1:1-7, Paul's use of *apostle, faith*, and *Gentiles* is not casual; he is the apostle called by God

to work about the obedience of faith among the Gentiles. See also Gal 1:1-5 and 1 Cor 1:1-3, where themes to be developed later in the letters are stated at the beginning.

2. *Thanksgiving.* Immediately after the salutation, Paul gives thanks to God for the addressees and/or some other gift of God. The thanksgiving, once again, can give a clue to the basic intent of the letter. To listeners who were taking undue pride in their individual gifts, Paul gives thanks for the grace of God that has been *given* to them (1 Cor 1:4; see also Rom 1:8-14; Phil 1:3-11; and Philem 4-7); in 2 Cor 1:3-4, Paul uses the related structure of a blessing. He omits the thanksgiving in one place: in Galatians. The omission of that standard letter segment indicates his anger at the recipients and would have been heard (or not heard!) by them.[54]

3. *Body of the letter.* This section of the letter contains Paul's major arguments on behalf of the thesis of the letter. There is great variation in how Paul put together the bodies of his letters, since the life situations of his listeners and the issues to be addressed vary widely.[55] In Romans, the body of the letter is at 1:18—11:36.

4. *Ethical section or paraenesis.* Ethical comments can occur almost any place in Paul's letters, but the ethical section is a full section devoted to ethical instruction or **paraenesis** (advice). Paraenetic material is ethical, edifying material and is often associated with moral instruction or preaching. In Romans, the ethical section is 12:1—15:13.[56]

5. *Conclusion.* Paul's letters conclude with one or more of these items: a peace wish, greetings, a laundry list of instructions, and/or a benediction. A good example of a conclusion is 1 Thess 5:12-28.[57]

English-language letters have stereotyped structures, too, although those who write them often use the structure without thinking about it. Why does a twenty-first-century letter begin with "Dear so-and-so," for example? Is it really a term of intimacy—or simply the way the letter begins? Other elements, such as the closing followed by the writer's name, are also highly stereotyped ("Yours truly," or "Sincerely yours," followed by the sender's name), as is the more recent addition of an apology for not writing earlier!

Rhetoric

Despite his protestation that he did not use wise words (1 Cor 2:1-5), Paul's letters illustrate that he knew how to formulate his thoughts by utilizing the methods of Greco-Roman rhetoric. **Rhetoric** is "the disciplined art of persuasion,"[58] and that art had been finely honed by the time Paul began his ministry. He used its insights to produce, as Charles Cousar has described it, "carefully crafted communications, written to persuade readers to think or act in a particular way."[59]

Rhetoric was the center of instruction at the level of education comparable to North American high school—but with the qualification that few people reached that level. Instruction in rhetoric began much earlier in a student's career, certainly by age twelve, and culminated during the period when the student was between sixteen and eighteen years old.[60] Formal attention to rhetoric had developed over several centuries, and students of rhetoric produced handbooks on rhetorical theory and style. Two important handbooks that have survived antiquity are the *Rhetorica ad Alexandrum* (late fourth to early third century B.C.E.) and the *Rhetorica ad Herennium* (late first century B.C.E.).[61] Scholars also wrote handbooks on epistolary theory and styles, two of which are Pseudo-Demetrius's *Epistolary Types* and Pseudo-Libanius's *Epistolary Types*.[62]

While rhetorical theory initially concentrated on oral presentation, the line between speaking and writing was a thin one, in part because reading in antiquity was always done aloud, even when a person was alone when reading. For his part, the theorist Quintilian (ca. 35–100 C.E.) argued that letters to a high degree were written versions of speeches (*Institutio Oratoria* 12.10.53-55).[63] The fact that educated letter writers used the tools of (oral) rhetoric, then, is no surprise. As Witherington concludes, most New Testament letters look very much like rhetorical speeches,[64] and they have what scholars call a "high residual orality."

Attention to and appreciation of good rhetoric was not limited to the elite. As David Aune comments,

> During the first and second centuries A.D., public performances by rhetoricians were in great demand, and they (like contemporary movie stars or rock musicians) received wealth and prestige along with fame. Listening to the public recitation of literary works was also a popular form of entertainment. All levels of the population of the Roman world were exposed to the variety of structures and styles found in the rhetoric, literature, and art that were on public display throughout the Empire.[65]

Speakers and authors of letters meant to be read in public thus created events that all people could comprehend and enjoy, including those with little or no formal education.

It is helpful to realize that, just as Paul moved easily among different cultural and religious contexts, so, too, he did not woodenly adopt one type of rhetoric or one method or school of persuasion. Rather, he selected and modified what was available to him in order best to express the good news of Jesus.[66]

Going back to the work of Aristotle, ancient students of rhetoric divided speeches into three categories, based on how authors wanted to affect their readers. The threefold pattern and its possible application to Paul are found in the textbox on p. 111. The categories were not understood to be straitjackets but were models to be used with flexibility. As an illustration of that fact, in the chart, Ephesians is classified as epideictic, but it also has elements of deliberative rhetoric.

We have already studied Paul's normative way of structuring his letters. Rhetoricians used different labels for the parts of a letter as they envisioned presenting the case to have its greatest possible impact.

- *Exordium*. Essentially the introduction, the *exordium* sets forth the ethos of the speaker (see below) and tries to get the listeners on the side of the speaker.

- *Narratio.* The *narratio* states and clarifies the issue to be discussed.
- *Propositio.* The *propositio* is the thesis of the speech or letter.
- *Probatio* (or *confirmatio*). The *probatio* is the section in which the speaker/author tries to prove the *propositio*.
- *Refutatio.* The *refutatio* attacks arguments of the opponents; the rejected arguments may be anticipated or already actual.
- *Peroratio.* The *peroratio* concludes the speech or letter by summarizing the major arguments and asking for the listeners' assent; the *peroratio* often includes an emotional appeal.[67]

Significant studies that utilize this framework include Betz on Galatians and Jewett on Romans.[68]

Letters and speeches were also to be attentive to the creation of various moods that in turn appealed to different aspects of the listeners' minds and emotions:

- *Ēthos.* An appeal to the character or credibility of the speaker/author. Thus, in 1 Thess 2:1-12, Paul underlined the pastoral way his coworkers and he had worked among the Thessalonians, reminding them of the close relationship they had had in the past.
- *Pathos.* An appeal to the listeners' emotions so that the listeners would agree with the speaker/author not only at an intellectual level but also at a more primal, emotional level. In 1 Cor 1:26-31, Paul reminded the Corinthians that despite their low stations in society, God had called them.[69]
- *Logos.* An appeal to the listeners' reason through the use of logical arguments. In Gal 3:6-14, Paul developed a careful interpretation of passages from Israel's Bible to prove his thesis.

The overall goal was to gain the assent of the entire person.

Forms and Traditions for Constructing His Thoughts

When we go to a lecture or listen to a sermon, we have certain expectations: how long the lecture or sermon will be, what the structure will look like, what the content will cover. We also have expectations of the smaller units that make up a lecture or sermon. If the speaker is a visitor, we look for an opening greeting of some sort ("I want you to know how glad I am to be here"), often followed by an attempt to establish contact with the audience by telling a story of how the speaker arrived or a bit of local color the speaker has noticed. That type of smaller structure is what scholars call a **form**. A form is a pattern of discourse used to enhance communication. It gives us clues as to what the author or speaker is saying and helps us to understand and integrate his or her thinking. To be a form, the material has to have sufficient structure to be recognizable, and it has to be used with some frequency in the literature being studied.

Paul inherited and adapted forms and traditions from his Greco-Roman world, from his Judean world, and from the church. Such materials provided

Types of Rhetoric

Aristotle distinguished three types of rhetorical argument (*Ars rhetorica* 1.3; 1358b). Rhetoricians for centuries continued to use his classification system, and many contemporary scholars think some of the New Testament letters (or portions of them) can be classified according to this system.

Judicial Rhetoric

Other names: Forensic rhetoric, apologetic rhetoric
Original setting: Law court
Goal: Secure justice; convince audience of the rightness or wrongness of a past action
Method: Attack or defense
Time frame: Past
NT example: Galatians: Paul uses judicial rhetoric to defend his ministry to the Gentiles, a ministry independent of the Jerusalem apostles; only Galatians 1–2 are judicial.
NT example: 2 Corinthians 10–13: Paul defends his apostleship against attacks from his opponents.

Deliberative Rhetoric

Other names: Hortatory rhetoric, symbouletic rhetoric
Original setting: Public/political assembly
Goal: Persuade audience to act or not act in certain ways
Method: Persuasion or dissuasion
Time frame: Future
NT example: 2 Thessalonians: The goal of the letter is to dissuade listeners from thinking that the day of the Lord has already come (2:2) or is so near they can quit their jobs (3:6-15).
NT example: 1 Corinthians: The goal of this letter is to answer questions posed by the Corinthians and urge them to behave in the future in ways Paul deems appropriate.

Epideictic Rhetoric

Other names: Demonstrative rhetoric, laudatory rhetoric, display rhetoric
Original setting: Public celebration
Goal: Affirm common beliefs and values and thus gain support for present activities
Method: Praise or blame
Time frame: Present
NT example: Romans: The goal of this letter is to state Paul's understanding of the gospel to believers he does not know but hopes soon to visit. He praises them when their understanding of the gospel fits with his.
NT example: Ephesians: The author praises the Gentile recipients for their inclusion in the people of God and calls on them to live in light of their inclusion.

him preexisting material to use and alter in expressing himself. From his Greco-Roman world, Paul used the following forms:

- *Paraenesis*. Paraenesis is ethical exhortation or instruction about how to live and how not to live. It is usually traditional, reflecting typical ethical commands from the culture as well as adaptations by the church. While 1 Thess 4:1—5:22 is an extended and concentrated paraenetical section, paraenetical material can occur throughout a given letter, as in 1 Corinthians 5, 7, 8, and 10.
    - There are several subdivisions of paraenesis. *Admonitions* are individual paranetical statements strung loosely together, without a common theme (Rom 12:9-21, for example). *Topoi* are extended paraenetical statements dealing with a particular topic or theme (*topos*, the singular, means *place* or *topic*); see Rom 13:1-7 on the believer and the government. *Virtue and vice lists* are lists of virtues to be followed and vices to be avoided; this form is one of the most stereotyped in ancient Greek literature. In Christian circles, the lists were probably used in baptismal instruction for adults. On vices, see, for example, Gal 5:19-21; on virtues, see Gal 5:22-23.
- *Chiasm.* The word *chiasm* comes from the verb *chiazō*, which means *I write a chi*, the Greek letter comparable to the English *x*. The heart of a chiasm is reverse parallelism: two or more terms, phrases, or even ideas are stated and then repeated in reverse order. An example appears in 1 Cor 11:9: "Neither was man created [statement A] for the sake of woman [B], but woman [B'] for the sake of man [A']." Chiasms can be this brief or as long as several chapters (possibly 1 Corinthians 12–14). The form is also quite common in Judean literature.
- *Diatribe.* The diatribe is a structure in which the author debates an imaginary opponent in order to address the audience; it proceeds by question-and-answer format. One of many sections of diatribe in Paul is Rom 3:1-9.
- *Peristaseis. Peristaseis* are hardship catalogs, often used by Stoic and Cynic philosophers to commend themselves or their heroes. Hardships are listed, followed by ways in which the wise man (or apostle, in the case of Paul) endures and overcomes. The classic example is 2 Cor 11:23-28.

Another set of forms comes from Paul's Judean world. Without question, the primary written source for how Paul developed and structured his thoughts was Israel's Bible. Paul had a profound sense of the worth of Scripture. He understood it as holy and prophetic (Rom 1:2; 4:3), the very words of God (3:1-2). Beyond that, since it is the same God who has acted in Jesus who acted in Israel's Scripture, the latter can legitimately be read by Christ-believers in light of their belief that Jesus was Lord (2 Cor 3:12-18), so that even the inclusion of Gentiles by faith is foreseen by the Scripture (Gal 3:8), and texts can be applied to the lives of Paul's congregations (1 Cor 9:8-12). As James Aageson affirms, "For Paul, the biblical text is the revelation of God. It is the *sacred* text."[70]

While over 60 percent of the explicit allusions and quotations from Israel's Bible that Paul makes in his letters are found in Galatians and Romans—two letters concerned most directly with Judean-related issues—Paul's usage of Judean Scripture and his dependence on it for the substructure and vocabulary of his message in general permeate his letters. Silva even suggests that "hardly a paragraph in the Pauline corpus fails to reflect the influence of the Old Testament on the apostle's language and thought."[71] Examples are as varied and widespread as in this selection:

Rom 4:1-25	Gen 15:5-6; 17:5
Rom 3:9-20	Eccles 7:20; Ps 14:1-3; Isa 59:7-8
1 Cor 10:1-13	Exod 13, 14, 16, 32, among others
1 Cor 15:32	Isa 22:13
2 Cor 6:2	Isa 49:8
2 Cor 9:10	Isa 55:10; Hos 10:12
Gal 3:19	Lev 26:46; Deut 5:4-5
Phil 2:10-11	Isa 45:23
Phil 4:18	Exod 29:18; Ezek 20:41
1 Thess 5:13	Jer 6:14.[72]

Diatribe in Paul

Paul uses the diatribe technique in several places in different letters, including 1 Cor 15:29-41; Gal 3:1-9, 19-22; and Rom 2:1-5; 3:1-9; 3:31—4:2a, 6:1-3. Here is a sample from Romans 3, with the questions and answers displayed on separate lines to highlight the diatribe:

> [1] *Then what advantage has the Jew? Or what is the value of circumcision?*
> [2] Much, in every way. For in the first place the Jews were entrusted with the oracles of God.
> [3] *What if some were unfaithful? Will their faithlessness nullify the faithfulness of God?*
> [4] By no means! Although everyone is a liar, let God be proved true, as it is written, "So that you may be justified in your words, and prevail in your judging."
> [5] *But if our injustice serves to confirm the justice of God, what should we say? That God is unjust to inflict wrath on us? (I speak in a human way.)*
> [6] By no means! For then how could God judge the world?
> [7] *But if through my falsehood God's truthfulness abounds to his glory, why am I still being condemned as a sinner?* [8] *And why not say (as some people slander us by saying that we say), "Let us do evil so that good may come"?*
> Their condemnation is deserved!
> [9] *What then? Are we any better off?*
> No, not at all; for we have already charged that all, both Jews and Greeks, are under the power of sin.

From direct quotations to allusions to underlying themes, Paul's letters demonstrate the results of searching Israel's Scriptures in order to understand Jesus and his message—a search undertaken by Paul, certainly, but also by other Christ-believers. To investigate all of Paul's explicit and implicit uses of the Judean Scriptures would result in a restatement of his letters and their content.[73]

Paul's letters show that when he studied Israel's Bible, he utilized the best methods available to him from his Judean heritage, including from the emerging Pharisaic-rabbinic approaches to exegesis and from apocalyptic thought. It is no longer possible to say without qualification that Paul used rabbinic methods that are known chiefly from post–70 CE rabbinic Judaism.[74] But it is possible to identify in Paul approaches that already were developing in the first century:

- *Midrash.* Midrash is a Hebrew term that means *interpretation* or *inquiry*. The basic structure of midrash is twofold: (1) quotation of or allusion to a passage from Israel's Bible; and (2) commentary on the passage, with the commentary and the actual biblical passage often blending into each other. An introduction may also be present ("as it is written"; "Scriptures says"), although such statements are also used simply to introduce a quotation. The goal of midrash is to explain the text so that it is relevant and can speak to the time of the interpreter. Examples are abundant; a good illustration is Rom 10:5-13, which utilizes Lev 18:5; Deut 9:4; 30:12-14; Ps 107:26; Isa 28:16; Joel 2:32 (3:5 in the LXX).[75]
- *Analogy.* The Hebrew term is *gezerah shawah* (similar laws, similar verdicts). It is an exegetical method in which authors connect statements that share the same word(s) or phrase(s) and make their point by interpreting them together. Thus, in Gal 3:10, Paul quotes Deut 27:26: "Cursed is everyone who does not observe and obey all the things written in the book of the law," which leads to his observation in Gal 3:13 that "Christ redeemed us from the curse of the law by becoming a curse for us," which in turn is connected with Deut 21:23, which he quotes: "Cursed is everyone who hangs on a tree." Another good example is Rom 4:1-8, where Paul builds his argument around the word *reckon*, which he adopts from Gen 15:6 and Ps 32:1-2 (31:1-2 in the LXX).
- *Typology.* Typology is a method of interpreting Scripture in which the author shows a correspondence or anti-correspondence between an earlier event or person and a later event or person. Given Paul's understanding of how Christ-believers can appropriate Israel's Bible, it is no surprise that figures and events from Judean Scripture correspond to people and events in the experiences of Jesus and the early church. In addition, the "new" can help the listener to understand the "old" in a symbolic way quite apart from original circumstances.

In Rom 5:12-21, Adam is the negative type "of the one who was to come" (vs. 14), Jesus. In the rest of the passage, Paul contrasts the two universal figures. In 1 Cor 10:1-13, especially verses 1-5, the people of God wandering in the desert under Moses experienced the "type" of baptism and the Lord's Supper, which Paul turns into a warning to the Corinthians. And in Gal 4:21-31, Paul uses typology when discussing the two covenants.

- *Apocalyptic application.* From the Dead Sea Scrolls discovered at Qumran shortly after World War II, we know that a method of textual study important in that Judean apocalyptic group was the *pesher* method. *Pesher* comes from the Hebrew word *pishro* (interpretation); it designates an approach to Israel's Bible in which a passage is quoted and an interpretation is immediately given that applies the passage to the interpreter's community. A good example is the *Commentary on Habakkuk* 12. It quotes Hab 2:17 and applies it (the material in brackets is missing because of a break in the manuscript):

  > *[For the violence done to Lebanon shall overwhelm you, and the destruction of the beasts] shall terrify you, because of the blood of men and the violence done to the land, the city, and all its inhabitants* (ii,17). Interpreted, this saying concerns the Wicked Priest, inasmuch as he shall be paid the reward which he himself tendered to the Poor. For *Lebanon* is the Council of the Community; and the *beasts* are the Simple of Judah who keep the Law.[76]

  Whether or not Paul knew this method from contact with the literature or members of that community, he often used a similar approach in which he applied Israel's Bible to the end-time communities he was founding, just as the Qumran authors thought that the sacred texts were about the eschatological crisis in which they were living. A good illustration of this approach is 2 Cor 6:2: "For he [Isaiah] says, 'At an acceptable time I have listened to you, and on a day of salvation I have helped you.' See, now is the acceptable time; see, now is the day of salvation!" Paul's anticipation of the near end of the present age and the return of Jesus as Lord without question was a crucial filter through which Paul viewed and interpreted the Judean Scriptures.

Finally, some of Paul's forms come from emerging church tradition. While Paul's letters are almost certainly the oldest documents in the New Testament, he was by no means the first Christ-believer to develop materials for use in preaching, teaching, and witnessing, whether oral or written. He inherited from his predecessors and his contemporaries various forms for communicating one aspect or another of the gospel:

- *Confessional statements.* Confessional statements (or creeds) are abbreviated statements of complex beliefs, outlines of the faith that people joining the community needed to understand. As shorthand summaries of the faith, they are in a sense the ancient counterpart of bumper sticker or poster slogans. The briefest confessional formula is only two words in Greek: "Jesus Lord," which in English becomes "Jesus is Lord" (Rom

10:9). Another famous creed is in 1 Cor 15:3-7. Often creeds are introduced by terms such as *deliver, believe*, or *confess*.
- *Baptismal formulas*. Such language refers to baptism and may even quote early baptismal liturgies. Examples are Rom 6:4-5 and Gal 3:27-28.
- *Lord's Supper traditions*. The classic example is the earliest written account of Jesus' last supper with his disciples, in 1 Cor 11:23-25.
- *Blessings and doxologies*. Blessings and doxologies are also liturgical forms; both are directed to God. The blessing typically has the word *blessed*, a reference to God, and a concluding *amen*. So Rom 1:25 says people inappropriately worshipped "the creature rather than the Creator, who is blessed forever! Amen." The doxology is similar, with a reference to God in the Greek dative case, assigning glory (*doxsa*) to God, and a concluding *amen*. In Gal 1:4-5, Paul wrote, "according to the will of our God and Father, to whom be the glory forever and ever. Amen."
- *Hymns and hymnic material*. Pauline material utilized a fair amount of poetry, much of which scholars have identified as liturgical poetry, especially from hymns. The classic example from the undisputed letters is Phil 2:6-11; Col 1:15-20 and 1 Tim 3:16 are the primary examples from the deuteropauline letters. There are many other fragments. Hymnic material often begins with *who*, since the words praise God or Christ "who" acted in certain ways. Such material is usually heavily loaded with theological concepts.
- *Catechetical material*. Catechetical material is material developed for the massive teaching task facing the early church; 1 Thess 4:1-9 is an oft-cited example. The difference between catechetical and paraenetical material is often hard to identify.
- *Words of the Lord*. A number of times, Paul refers to sayings that have come from Jesus. An obvious example is 1 Thess 4:15: "For this we declare to you by the word of the Lord." Whether that word is from the earthly Jesus, the resurrected Jesus, or a prophet speaking in the name of Jesus is unclear. In addition to the Lord's Supper tradition already cited (1 Cor 11:23-25), other examples include 1 Cor 7:10-11 and 9:14.

The forms and traditions serve as road signs. They alert us to matters peculiar to that form and help us to evaluate the material by noting what is standard and what is the special emphasis of our author. The vice lists, to give one illustration, are not meant to detail every bad thing the people in Galatia are doing (Gal 5:19-21) but are lists of everyday vices. Attention to forms and traditions also enables the reader of Paul to remember that he did not operate in a linguistic vacuum but inherited from the world to which he belonged various ways of expressing himself.[77]

Production and Delivery of Paul's Letters

In the actual writing of his letters, Paul obviously did not sit in front of a computer screen and type. Neither, somewhat surprisingly, did he usually sit down with pen and paper when he was composing a letter. What he did do was to use a secretary, a person sometimes called an *amanuensis* (the Latin term).

What evidence do we have that Paul used secretaries? A key bit of data is Rom 16:22, where we read, "I Tertius, the writer of this letter, greet you in the Lord." Although the only such statement in Paul's letters, this kind of statement was fairly common in other written material.[78] It is reasonable to conclude from the statement that Paul knew Tertius (that is, that Tertius was not simply hired from the marketplace), that he was a Christ-believer, since he greets the listeners "in the Lord," and that he was known to at least some of the Roman believers, and so he sends his greetings. His name ("Third") is a typical slave name, and Jewett concludes that Paul's patron Phoebe (Rom 16:1-2) provided Tertius's services to Paul.[79]

The other evidence in Paul's letters for a secretary is found in his statements toward the end of some letters, that there is a change in handwriting and that Paul himself is now writing: "I, Paul, write this greeting with my own hand" (1 Cor 16:21). Similar statements are found in the undisputed letters in Gal 6:11 and Philem 19 (unless in the case of the short letter to Philemon, Paul meant that he has written the entire letter himself) and in two letters whose authorship by Paul is debated (Col 4:18; 2 Thess 3:17).

The secretary was a person employed to write correspondence for another person. The secretary could be a true professional or only a glorified amateur; the secretary could be employed full-time by an individual or government or labor as a freelance secretary working out of the city's marketplace. The skill level of the secretary could also range from minimal competency to the highest proficiency.

An illiterate soldier dictating a letter to his mother, wife, or girlfriend back home would normally have the secretary write the only and final version while the soldier spoke. More important or formal letters, especially when financial resources were available, required greater care. In those cases, the secretary would first write the dictation or basic thoughts onto wooden tablets covered with wax or, perhaps, in parchment notebooks.[80] Better-trained secretaries knew shorthand.[81] They would then rewrite the letter onto papyrus, having cut the paper into sheets and having scored lines onto the paper. Another draft (or even more) was not unusual; E. Randolph Richards envisions exactly that process for the production of Paul's letters.[82] M. Luther Stirewalt draws a different conclusion: "Immediate corrections, parentheses [i.e., explanatory comments], and anacolutha [thoughts that Paul begins but never ends] give evidence that the initial drafts of Paul's epistles were not revised."[83]

How did Paul use his secretaries?[84] Did he dictate word for word, as Cicero did ("I dictated it to Spinthaurus syllable by syllable"; *ad Atticum* 13.25.3)? Did he outline the major ideas and let the secretary puzzle over the exact wording? Or did he give the barest of outlines to the secretary and essentially approve what someone else has written? Given Paul's clear understanding of his role as apostle, it is hard to imagine that he would give a secretary much leeway. Ben Witherington is convinced that, with the possible exception of when he was imprisoned, Paul dictated his letters word for word, and even when his living situation did not allow for that,

> ## Pen, Ink, Paper, and Desk
>
> **Pen**
>
> Reed pen — Standard writing instrument throughout antiquity, from third century B.C.E. on. A secretary used a knife to shape one end to a point and split the point to form a nib (the name for the sharpened and split end of the pen). When the nib started to fray, the extra fibers were rubbed off with a stone. When the nib could not be repaired, the secretary cut if off and formed a new nib.
>
> *Ink*
>
> Black ink — The basic ingredient was soot or ground charcoal; often the carbon deposit from inside a chimney was scraped and processed. The soot was suspended in a solution of gum water that was placed in a ceramic or metal holder. The material was formed into cakes and allowed to dry. The secretary moistened the cake with water in order to write.
>
> Red ink — Used for initial letters and titles; the basic ingredient was red ocher or red iron oxide.
>
> *Paper*
>
> Most readily available paper was made from the papyrus plant, which was slit and laid open. One sheet was placed down with the plant's strong fibers running vertically; a second sheet was placed on top with the fibers running horizontally. A weight placed on the papyrus bound the two sheets together when they dried, or the sheets were put into a press. The very earliest copies of the New Testament are on papyrus, which was the type of paper used by New Testament authors and secretaries.
>
> *Desk*
>
> There would be no desk! Secretaries sat on a bench or stool, more rarely on the floor. They stretched their tunic between their knees to make a somewhat firm surface on which to place the paper.
>
> *Mistakes?*
>
> When secretaries made a mistake, they would erase it with a damp sponge.[85]

Paul closely controlled the content of his letters.[86] One reason to exercise that sort of control is that most secretaries were not educated at the same rhetorical level Paul was. Richards doubts that Paul consistently dictated word for word, but:[87]

> The less literate the writer (or the less important the letter), the more was left to the secretary. Since Paul was literate and considered his letters important,

it is wise to assume that Paul did not give his secretary any freedom to compose. Paul spent a great deal of energy and expense on letters. He was better educated than a secretary, particularly in the Scriptures.... There seems to be no case where he allowed a secretary to compose freely for him.[88]

Another indication of Paul's firm hand in the production of his letters is the level at which they as a group are written. "Since a fairly consistent, medium-level rhetorical sophistication is found in all of Paul's letters," Richards explains, "it is more reasonable to conclude that Paul was the common thread rather than his various secretaries or occasional coauthors."[89]

Having maintained that Paul had control of his own letters, we note in addition that he refers to specific co-senders in 1 Cor 1:1, 2 Cor 1:1, Phil 1:1, 1 Thess 1:1, and Philem 1—five of the seven undisputed letters. Moreover, in Gal 1:2, he includes with himself "all the brothers [and sisters] who are with me" as the ones sending the letter. The tone of the letters, including the preponderance of "I" language (first person singular), signals that Paul is the "real" or final author. At the same time, the listing of co-senders alerts us to the fact that Paul's ministry was not one of isolated contemplation in a monk's cell but one in which he was constantly engaged with people. The listing of co-senders alerts us to the discussion he had with others about the issues he was addressing and almost certainly points to larger and ongoing conversations not only with his coworkers but also with believers in general. Ultimate responsibility for what went out under his name belonged, of course, to Paul.

How were these letters delivered? There was no organized postal service available to the general public. The system of letter carriers begun by Emperor Augustus was used only for the dispatch of governmental communiques. Private individuals had to fend for themselves. Wealthier people could reserve slaves to work as couriers. Other people had to rely on friends, relatives, or business associates who traveled.

No matter who functioned as the carrier of a letter, the odds of a letter reaching its destination were not great. Travel was hazardous, as the biography of Paul shows. Robbery, illness, accidents, and missed connections all could delay or prevent the delivery of a letter. For that reason, wealthier people at times would send two copies of the same letter with two different couriers, if the letter were especially important.

Who delivered Paul's letters? We have some evidence in the New Testament. Stephanas, Fortunatus, and Achaicus likely delivered 1 Corinthians (1 Cor 16:15-18). Titus and an unnamed second believer carried 2 Corinthians 8 (or perhaps a larger letter; 2 Cor 8:16-18). Phoebe probably carried the letter to the Romans (16:1-2). Epaphroditus almost certainly carried back to Philippi Paul's letter to the believers there (Phil 2:25-30), and clearly Paul used the converted slave Onesimus to deliver the letter to Onesimus's master Philemon.

Once received, the letters needed to be read aloud, as only a small minority of people could read. There is a growing consensus among scholars that those who delivered the letters also read them to the recipients, most likely when the local

Christ-believing communities gathered for worship.⁹⁰ That put them in the position of emphasizing by voice tone and gesture crucial points that Paul was making, as well as perhaps indicating that Paul was pulling their legs just a bit. We can only imagine what they could have done with some of Paul's sarcastic remarks, too. In addition, they would have been a resource to answer questions about the communication. As Neil Elliott notes on the oral experience of the recipients,

> The effect of Paul's message *performed orally* would have been to create an atmosphere of effectual energy, an orbit of power. We expect the creation of this "acoustic space" to have been the responsibility of the associate to whom Paul entrusted his letter; thus, Paul would presumably have taken care to prepare this messenger to *perform* the letter as part of his apostolic strategy, for the letter had only done its work once it was performed.⁹¹

THE COLLECTION

A fourth way that Paul built a network of believers was by taking a monetary collection from the basically Gentile congregations of his ministry. The collection was designed to be a gift from them to the Judean Christ-believing congregation/s in Jerusalem. Key passages are Rom 15:25-28; 1 Cor 16:1-4; 2 Corinthians 8 and 9; and Gal 2:10. Paul used different terms to refer to the offering:

- Collection (*logeia*): 1 Cor 16:1
- Service or ministry (*diakonia, diakoneō*): Rom 15:25, 31; 2 Cor 8:20; 2 Cor 9:1, 12, 13
- Fellowship (*koinōnia*): Rom 15:26
- Gift (*charis*): 1 Cor 16:3; 2 Cor 8:6, 7, 19
- Generous gift (*eulogia*): 2 Cor 9:5
- Lavish gift (*hadrotēs*): 2 Cor 8:20

The genesis of the gift was the Apostolic Council, which was an important gathering of church leaders around the year 48. In addition to the basic decision to divide the larger mission into an essentially Judean mission connected with Peter and an essentially Gentile mission connected with Paul (Gal 2:7-9), the Jerusalem leaders had asked Paul to "remember the poor," which indeed he "was eager to do" (Gal 2:10).⁹²

The first literary evidence of Paul's activity in gathering the collection is 1 Cor 16:1-4. He referred to directions he had given to the congregations in Galatia, namely, that believers were to save money each week so that the collection would be ready when he arrived. Then either people from Corinth would go to Jerusalem with the money—together with letters by Paul—or he would go with them. Chapters 8 and 9 in 2 Corinthians contain what are likely two originally separate letters that encouraged believers in Achaia (southern Greece, where Corinth was located) through the example of believers in Macedonia (northern Greece; chapter 8) and that referred to the example of people in Achaia to encourage the believers in Macedonia (chapter 9). Titus is named as the one who has begun and will finish the collection in Corinth (8:6, 16-17, 23); he was to be assisted by other "brothers"

(8:18-19, 22-23; 9:3-5). Finally, in Rom 15:25-28, Paul mentioned the collection for the last time. The same reference to the "poor" is found in verse 26 as it was years earlier in Gal 2:10, and he refers to the positive response from believers in Macedonia and Achaia. We have no evidence of what happened when Paul delivered the offering. The comments in Romans provide the final historical data we have.[93]

Among other possibilities, students of Paul have suggested four reasons why he devoted so many years and so much effort to the collection. They see him motivated by relief for the poor, wanting to teach reciprocal giving, seizing an opportunity to demonstrate the commitment of the Gentile Christ-believers, or desiring to put into action the unity of all believers.

Relief for the Poor

Both the passage containing the original charge (Gal 2:10) and the final reference to the collection by Paul (Rom 15:26) mention the poor. Material relief for economically poor Christ-believers in Jerusalem is an obvious and basic reason for the collection. In addition to Acts 11:27-30, we have other evidence of a famine in Israel ca. 46–48.[94]

Reciprocal Giving

But why should believers who lived so far away help believers whom they did not know, especially since the vast majority of people from whom Paul was soliciting money were themselves living at subsistence level (2 Cor 8:2-4)? Two texts are key. Romans 15:27 reads, "They were pleased to do this [give money for the collection], and indeed they owe it to them [the Judeans]; for if the Gentiles have come to share in their spiritual blessings, they ought also to be of service to them in material things." And in 2 Cor 8:13-14, Paul explained, "It is a question of a fair balance between your present abundance and their need, so that their abundance may be for your need, in order that there may be a fair balance."

Gentile believers have benefited spiritually from believers in Jerusalem, who had shepherded the original message about Jesus and who had overseen at the beginning the spread of that message. As brothers and sisters in the same fictive family, Gentile believers were expected by Paul to share as siblings with Judean believers their relative financial abundance. And that sharing was to be done with no expectation of return. That attitude was what cultural anthropological students of the Bible call "family reciprocity," that is, free giving to others who are siblings.[95] It is no accident that 2 Corinthians 8 begins with Paul addressing the listeners as "brothers and sisters" (vs. 1), nor is it an accident that Paul prefaced his request for funding with a brief discussion of the grace shown to them by Jesus (8:9). The reminder of what God had done in Jesus placed a positive obligation on the Gentile believers to respond, in this case by sharing freely with Judean believers.[96]

Challenge to Jerusalem Authorities

As opposed to the positive view of gift giving outlined in the previous section, Philip Esler looks at a different aspect of gift-giving in antiquity. Any gift (with the possible exception of a family gift) represented a challenge to the recipient's honor, so the recipient had to consider a response carefully. If the response was inadequate or inappropriate, the recipient would be shamed and lose honor. The agreement for Judean and non-Judean believers to share in the Lord's Supper had already been broken in Antioch soon after the agreement had been reached (Gal 2:11-14), and Judean believers more traditional than Paul regarding the inclusion of Gentiles had dogged his ministry (in Galatia, for example). Paul had kept the agreement—and he would live that out when he brought the offering: "Every coin that dropped into Paul's collection bags was a physical reminder that the Jerusalem leaders had breached the Jerusalem agreement."[97] The offering/gift would constitute a challenge to them to live according to the agreement so carefully followed by Paul. Perhaps it was that potential conflict that led to his anxiety about the visit to Jerusalem and his request that Roman believers pray that his "ministry to Jerusalem may be acceptable to the saints" (Rom 15:31).

Symbol of the Unity of Believers

A final position that moves in yet a different direction but resonates with the fictive family and sibling nature of Paul's Christ-believing international community is that, in addition to helping the poor and fulfilling a reciprocal obligation, Paul intended the collection to symbolize the unity of believers.[98] The collection would provide the capstone event of his mission in the eastern part of the Mediterranean, Paul hoped. It would be a signal that that work was done, and he could now turn to Spain in the far western portion of the empire (Rom 15:19, 23-24, 28). The collection thus, insists Wright,

> is itself a massive symbol, a great prophetic sign, blazoned across half a continent, trumpeting the fact that the people of God redefined around Jesus the Messiah is a single family and must live as such, by the principle of practical *agapē* [*love*]. We can only marvel, with boggling minds, at the spectacle of Paul persuading Christians around Greece to part with hard cash on behalf of people they had never met in places they had never visited; at his care to conduct the whole effort with full accountability . . . ; at his travelling for weeks by land and sea, staying in wayside inns and private homes, with the money always there as both motive and risk; and at his full knowledge that, at the end of the day, the church in Jerusalem might well refuse the gift, since it had come precisely from uncircumcised people, and might well be reckoned to be tainted, to have the smell of idolatry still upon it. This project cannot have been a mere whim, a nice idea dreamed up as a token gesture. Paul must have wanted very, very badly to do it; he must have seen it as a major element in his practical strategy for creating and sustaining the one family of God redefined around the Messiah and in the Spirit.[99]

Not only was that family composed of Judean and non-Judean believers as groups, but the process of identifying and strengthening that international family "also strengthened or created inter-city and interregional links among the various Pauline churches. The ecumenical purpose of the collection . . . not only effected unity between Jews and Gentiles, but also unity among the many Gentile churches of Paul's mission."[100] The collection thus functioned as a significant part of the network of communication and interaction Paul built as part of his mission. Or, as Arland Hultgren phrases it, "The unity of all humankind in Christ, which will come into its own at the parousia [the return of Jesus], was thus being initiated at the dawn of the new age."[101]

Study Questions

1. Do you belong to or participate in any fictive families? If so, what are the benefits and the problems of such family groupings? What is your evaluation of Paul's use of the fictive-family model?
2. In what ways might Paul and his message have appeared to threaten the Roman Empire? How does that view of Paul affect your understanding of him?
3. How did Paul nurture his congregations? To what in his approach do you relate positively? To what do you relate negatively?
4. Compare Paul's letters with the ways you nurture your own social network. How are they similar, and how are they different?
5. What role does the collection play in Paul's goal of networking?

Suggested Reading

Introductions to Paul's Letters

Cousar, Charles B. *The Letters of Paul*. IBT. Nashville: Abingdon, 1996.
Puskas, Charles B. Jr. *The Letters of Paul: An Introduction*. Collegeville, MN: Liturgical, 1993.

The Church as a Fictive Family

Hellerman, Joseph. *The Ancient Church as Family*. Minneapolis: Fortress Press, 2001.
Osiek, Carolyn, and Margaret Y. MacDonald, with Janet H. Tulloch. *A Woman's Place: House Churches in Earliest Christianity*. Minneapolis: Fortress Press, 2006.

Literary Forms

Bailey, James L., and Lyle D. Vander Broek. *Literary Forms in the New Testament: A Handbook*. Louisville: Westminster John Knox, 1992.

On Paul in General

Goodacre, Mark. "Paul the Apostle." *The New Testament Gateway*. http://www.ntgateway.com/.

Figures P2 1–6 Funerary portraits from Roman Egypt, second century.

Part Two

What Did Paul Write?

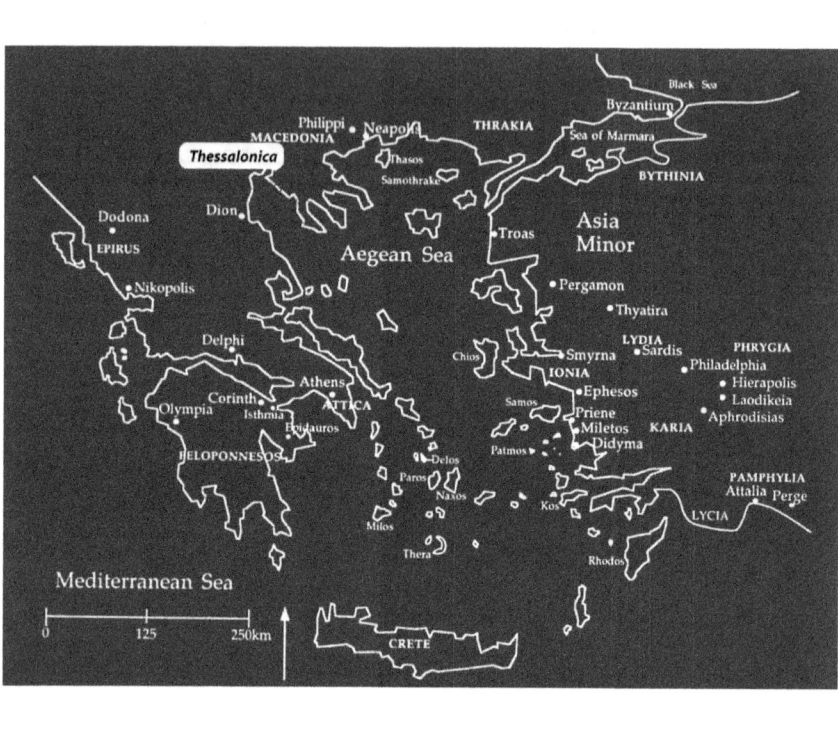

Chapter 6

1 Thessalonians: The End Is Near—but Not Yet

Paraenesis

> Imagine coming in late to a first-century gathering of Christ-believers in the northern Greek city of Thessalonica. As you look for a place to stand or sit in the small apartment, a brother Christ-believer whispers to you that the leader is reading a letter from the missionary who began your congregation, a man named Paul. You are glad that someone is reading the letter, since you cannot read, nor can the vast majority of people in your world. As you begin listening, you know that the letter must be fairly far along when you hear the words "Finally, brothers and sisters, we ask and urge you in the Lord Jesus Christ that, as you learned from us how you ought to live and to please God (as, in fact, you are doing), you should do so more and more" (1 Thess 4:1).

Our imaginary early believer knew that the portion of the letter being read was in the second half of the letter and likely near the end not only when s/he heard the word *finally*, but even more when hearing the words *we ask and urge you*. Those words (especially the word *urge*) signaled to the listeners that Paul was moving into the portion of the letter called the **paraenesis**, or sustained ethical exhortation, the fourth of the five portions of a standard Hellenistic letter. There is, in fact, so much paraenesis in this letter that scholars have actually labeled it a paraenetic letter.[1] Another, related way that it has been classified is as an example of deliberative rhetoric.[2] A glance at the outline for 1 Thessalonians indicates that two of the five chapters are paraenesis. Thus, the word *finally* in 4:1 does not indicate that Paul is at the very end of the letter, but it does indicate that he is switching topics.

But even before we look at the topic he is introducing, we need to stop at the words *brothers and sisters*. In the Greek text, the only word used at that point is *brothers*, the Greek word *adelphoi*. It is a family term and is often used by Paul to remind readers that they are part of the family of God (Paul uses a form of *brother* nineteen times in 1 Thessalonians). The early church was what anthropologists call a fictive family, that is, a family bound together not by common physical descent but in this case bound together through common belief in Jesus and the common life of the community that followed him.[3] Since the Greek has only the masculine word *brothers*, is it legitimate to translate the text as *brothers and sisters*, as the NRSV does? The question we need to ask is this: When Paul uses the masculine word for sibling, does he mean to exclude females, or is his language simply reflective of the world in which he lived, in which a male term could be understood as referring to all people (much as the word *mankind* formerly was understood in North America)? There is no indication that he intends to address men only, so *brothers and sisters* seems to be a legitimate translation.[4]

Also, who is the *we* who "ask and urge"? In 1:1, we learn that the senders of the letter are Paul, Silvanus (Silas), and Timothy.[5] In 4:1, they *ask*, and they *urge* or *exhort* (*parakaloumen*, used by Paul thirty-eight times); *exhort* is the key term for identifying the function of this section. And how do they exhort? They exhort the Thessalonian believers "in the Lord Jesus." For first-century ears, the word *Lord* had many connotations. It could mean simply *sir*, but when used of figures such as Jesus or God, it usually meant much more. For Greek-speaking Judeans, it was a title for God and was used in the Septuagint to translate the holy name Yahweh. In the non-Judean world, people applied the term to divine figures such as Isis and Asclepius and to rulers such as Herod, Agrippa, and Augustus. The term could thus carry political as well as religious meanings. In 1 Thessalonians, Paul uses the term *Lord* (*kyrios*) thirty-three times. In 4:1, he draws his hearers back to their basic commitment—to Jesus as Lord—and to the implications of having him as the ruler of their lives.

And what is the purpose of the exhortation in the Lord Jesus? "That, as you learned from us how you ought to live and to please God (as, in fact, you are doing), you should do so more and more." The word translated as "live" is actually the Greek word for *walk* (*peripateō*). It is a strong ethical term for how one walks one's life, that is, how one lives his or her ethical life as a believer. (Paul uses it eighteen times with that meaning.)

This section of exhortation continues all the way until 5:22. In it, Paul develops four ***topoi***: on sexual behavior (4:3-8), on love for siblings in the Christ-believing family (4:9-12), on the dead in Christ (4:13-18), and on the day of the

Lord (5:1-11). Those sections are followed by a series of miscellaneous exhortations (5:12-22). His first example of how to *walk* as a believer is sexual morality: believers are to control their bodies and, implicitly, channel their sexual desires into their marriages (Paul is more explicit in 1 Cor 7:1-5). His second example of *walk* is *philadelphia* (brotherly and sisterly love). Paul adopts this term from his society and adapts it for his own use. With the one possible exception of 2 Macc 15:14, this word always refers to blood relatives until Christ-believers use it for their fictive family. Paul indicates that God in fact has been their teacher ("you yourselves have been taught by God to love one another"; 4:9), and they have been star pupils ("indeed you do love all the brothers and sisters throughout Macedonia"; 4:10). But he is also concerned about the perception of people outside the believing community. Thus, he gives the somewhat homely advice that they are "to aspire to live quietly, to mind your own affairs, and to work with your hands, as we directed you" (4:11). As we will learn shortly, the believers in Thessalonica have already been persecuted. Paul wants his listeners to avoid drawing unwarranted attention to themselves, which they can accomplish by supporting themselves financially and staying out of trouble. He is also using language that was employed by many philosophers, particularly Epicureans.

The next two *topoi* (4:13-18; 5:1-11) will be discussed in more detail later in this chapter. In 5:12 and 5:14, we see Paul returning to the verbs he used in 4:1, at the beginning of the paraenesis. So in 5:12 we read, "But we appeal to you, brothers and sisters." The word *appeal* is the same Greek word translated in 4:1 as "ask": *erōtōmen*. In 5:14, we encounter once more the verb *urge* (*parakaloumen*), also found in 4:1. Paul is picking up the same verbs used earlier as he begins his final exhortation. In 5:12-13, he deals with respect for those leading the Christ-community and for peace in general among believers. Verses 14-22 give the sense of a laundry list of admonitions that Paul wants to squeeze in before finishing the letter. The whole section is rather choppy. Notice especially the clipped nature of the directives in verses 16-22.

Conclusion to the Letter

Paul concludes his letter in 5:23-28. He first expresses his wish that the God of peace (vs. 23) would sanctify them (that is, make them holy) and keep them until the coming of the Lord Jesus Christ. The basis for Paul's expectation is that "the one who calls you is faithful, and he will do this" (vs. 24; see also 1 Cor 1:9; 10:13; 2 Cor 1:18). In verse 25, Paul asks for the prayers of the Thessalonians. Despite the NRSV's translation of *beloved*, Paul again in Greek uses the term *brothers and sisters*. He repeats that language in verse 26 with his direction that they greet each other with a holy kiss; the kiss most likely was part of the community's worship.

Verse 27 is a formal command that the letter be read to all *the brothers and sisters* (once more missing from the NRSV); notice that the letter shifts here to "I" as the subject and not "we": "I solemnly command you." It may be that at this point Paul has taken the pen from the scribe and has started to write in his own handwriting. This solemn charge is unusual; we do not have it elsewhere in the undisputed letters.[6] Exactly why Paul has the formula is unclear. Finally, in verse 28, he pronounces a concluding blessing or benediction, "The grace of our Lord Jesus Christ be with you."

Historical Situation

Now that we have plunged into the second half of the letter and have begun to identify some of its major themes, we will step back from the text itself to look at why, when, and where Paul wrote this letter.

In 2:2, Paul tells us that before he came to Thessalonica, he had been in the city of Philippi, where he and those with him "had already suffered and been shamefully mistreated." They left that northern Greek city for Thessalonica, which was a hundred miles to the southwest. Paul and his companions would have used the Egnatian Way (*Via Egnatia*), a 530-mile highway built by the Romans. It stretched from the coast of the Adriatic Sea eastward across Greece all the way to Byzantium and united Rome and its eastern provinces both militarily and economically. Thessalonica was the capital of Macedonia. Situated along the Thermaic Gulf and with the Egnatian Way passing through it, Thessalonica was a major trade center and enjoyed status as a free city. That meant that there was no Roman garrison in the city, and it meant that within certain bounds, the city could govern itself. Thessalonica was typical of where Paul preferred to carry out his mission: in large urban areas that had a diverse population.

According to Acts 17:1-3, Paul first went to the city's synagogue, where he began his missionary work. Still, most Christ-believers must originally have been pagan, since in 1 Thess 1:9, Paul reminds them that they had "turned to God from idols, to serve a living and true God." He would not have addressed Judean believers in that way. Paul left the city, likely under duress. In Acts 17:5-9, we have an account of a riot incited by his Judean opponents; the result is that the faithful sent Paul and Silas out of the city (Acts 17:10).[7] Such a sudden departure could easily lead to questions about Paul's sincerity and trustworthiness. How long Paul had been there is unclear. Acts 17:2 says he was in the synagogue on three consecutive sabbaths. That statement does not mean he was there *only* for three sabbath days and the weeks in between, however, and in Phil 4:16, he recalls that the Philippian believers had sent money to him at Thessalonica at least twice, which presumes more than an extremely short stay.

Eventually, Paul ended up at Athens and sent Timothy back to Thessalonica to find out what was going on and to encourage them (1 Thess 3:1-2). According to Acts 18:1-5, Paul meanwhile went to Corinth, where Timothy found him and reported. The good news was that the congregation still loved and respected Paul (1 Thess 3:6). The bad news was that his apostleship was being challenged; some charged him with being a charlatan and with falling into error and uncleanness (2:3-10). Charlatans were well-known figures in antiquity. They were religious or philosophical teachers who came into town, got people excited, gathered a collection—and disappeared with the money. Within that context, Paul's sudden departure took on added significance.[8]

Timothy further reported that the expectation of an imminent return of Jesus had created problems. A crisis occurred when baptized believers died *before* Jesus returned (4:13-18). Apparently, the Thessalonians did not think that any believers would die before the coming of Jesus. Perhaps they even understood baptism as a protection against death. Thus, Paul needed to deal with the misconception that no believer would die before the return of Jesus. In addition, some people had focused so much attention on the next world that they were neglecting life in this world. Some even refused to work, demanding that the rest of the congregation support them (4:11-12; 5:14). It is not hard to imagine the tensions that could simmer and eventually erupt. In response to Timothy's report (and perhaps to a letter from the Thessalonians), Paul writes our letter.

Paul had a close relationship with the Thessalonian congregation (1:2-10; 2:7-11, 18-20; 3:9-10). He even posed and answered this intriguing question: "For what is our hope or joy or crown of boasting before our Lord Jesus at his coming? Is it not you? Yes, you are our glory and joy!" (2:19-20). The close bond may in part have been forged because of persecution: "And you became imitators of us and of the Lord, for in spite of persecution you received the word with joy inspired by the Holy Spirit" (1:6). "For you, brothers and sisters, became imitators of the churches of God in Christ Jesus that are in Judea, for you suffered the same things from your own compatriots as they did from the Jews" (2:14). Nor should that persecution have been a surprise; Paul had warned them about it (3:4). In Acts 17, the opposition came from Thessalonian Judeans who apparently reacted against the success Paul had in attracting Gentiles who had been worshipping with the Judean community (17:4-5). The loss of such Gentiles not only removed numerical and financial support from the synagogue, it also removed the political support of non-Judean patrons who could protect the Judean population. The charge leveled by the Thessalonian crowd against Paul's host Jason, as well as against other Christ-believers, was also political: "They are all acting contrary to the decrees of the emperor, saying that there is another king named Jesus" (Acts 17:7). We may have in that passage a window into an ongoing problem for early believers. While modern North Americans may separate church and state, ancient Mediterraneans did not. To say that "Jesus is lord" had clear political implications (see below on 4:13-18). Some have even wondered if the concern with those who had died (4:13-18) might indicate that believers had been martyred for their beliefs.[9] One further step:

Fig. 6.1 Coin bearing the inscription CAESAR THEOS (lit., "Caesar, God"); from Philippi. Photo courtesy of the President and Fellows of Harvard College.

at this point in the letter the identity of the opponents according to Paul seems to be Gentile Thessalonians, not Judeans (2:14).

Putting together the information Paul gives us with the book of Acts, we have Corinth as the site of writing, somewhere in the years 50–52, but most likely no later than 51. Those dates make 1 Thessalonians the earliest letter of Paul's that we have and thus the earliest document of the New Testament. Paul is unquestionably the author of this letter, and there is almost total agreement among scholars that the letter as we have it is the way Paul wrote it (with the possible exception of 2:14-16, on which see below).

Paul writes this letter, in summary, to do the following:

- To reinforce the identity of the Thessalonians as Christ-believers by emphasizing their identity as members of a fictive family and by separating them from those outside the family
- To encourage them in the difficulties facing them as believers
- To exhort them to live in ways consistent with their new belief
- To answer questions about the return of Jesus and through that to sustain them for the future.

4:13-18

In this earliest of Paul's surviving letters, the apostle looks to the end, specifically to the return of Jesus. While that concern is focused in 4:13-18, it pervades the entire document. Already in 1:10, that theme is noted: "how you turned to God from idols, to serve a living and true God, and to wait for his Son from heaven, whom he raised from the dead—Jesus, who rescues us from the wrath that is coming" (1:9-10). Attention to that return is found in every chapter (1:10; 2:19; 3:13; 4:13-18; and 5:1-11).

Verse 13 says, "But we do not want you to be uninformed, brothers and sisters, about those who have died, so that you may not grieve as others do who have no hope." The issue, once more, appears to be that the believers in Thessalonica expected Jesus to return soon, very soon. They expected that return (the technical term is ***imminent return***) of Jesus so much they thought no Christ-believer would die before Jesus came to earth again. When people in the community did, in fact, die, it created a crisis for those who were still living. Would those who had died be part of the end-time people of God? Would they be resurrected and united with Christ? Or would they simply not exist, since they obviously would not be alive when Jesus returned? "And what about ourselves?" the Thessalonians wondered. "Will we make it if we are not alive when Jesus returns?" In his response, Paul introduces what is probably a new teaching, since "we do not want you to be uninformed" is a standard formula Paul uses for introducing something new (Rom 1:13; 11:25; 1 Cor 10:1; 12:1; 2 Cor 1:8). Perhaps he had not made the matter sufficiently clear, or perhaps he had not had time, since he was forced to leave the city so quickly. The concern is with those who have died, literally in Greek, *the ones sleeping*. *Sleep* was a euphemism widely used in Greco-Roman society to refer to death, but we ought not be confused: the people about whom the Thessalonians are concerned are dead, really dead.

And why does Paul not want them to be ignorant of what he is going to tell them? He does not want them to grieve as do others who have no hope. Apparently, his listeners thought that those who had died would not be included in the end time. Paul argues that their hope is misplaced. What he does in the rest of the section is to outline the hope he sees. Notice that the Thessalonians certainly may grieve. Christ-believers do grieve, but they are to grieve within the context of a hope rooted in Jesus.

Verse 14 continues, "For since we believe that Jesus died and rose again, even so, through Jesus, God will bring with him those who have died." In this verse, Paul provides his first answer to the Thessalonians' dilemma. His first answer is a creed, which is signaled by the words "we believe that." The creed is simple: "Jesus died and rose again."[10] Paul immediately draws implications from that creed: "Even so, through Jesus, God will bring with him those who have died." The resurrection of Jesus affects not only Jesus. It is the beginning of a process that God will complete. And so the argument is this: as Jesus now lives, so will the believers who have died also live in the future.

Verse 15 adds, "For this we declare to you by the word of the Lord, that we who are alive, who are left until the coming of the Lord, will by no means precede those who have died." In this verse, Paul gives his second answer to the Thessalonians' dilemma. That answer is a *word of the Lord*. Whether that word is from the earthly Jesus, the resurrected Jesus, or a Christian prophet speaking in the name of Jesus is unclear. In any event, Paul claims that what he is going to say is a revelation from the Lord Jesus. And that revelation is essentially negative: those who are alive when Jesus returns will *not* precede the ones who have died. The Greek is strongly emphatic: Paul puts the verb into the subjunctive mood and introduces it with a double negative. There is no way that those who are alive when Jesus returns will go ahead of believers who have already died. Paul may also be introducing a subtle note of humor. Literally, the Greek reads, "we, the ones living, the leftovers." The *leftovers* will not go ahead of the ones who have died. There is no disadvantage in having died before Jesus returns.

In this verse, Paul uses the important word ***parousia***. To a certain extent, the word provides a connective link in this letter, since it occurs in 2:19, 3:13, 4:15 (our present verse), and 5:23. When we survey these occurrences, we make several observations:

- In each case, the *parousia* is of the Lord Jesus (Christ) or the Lord (4:15); *parousia* is thus a coming or a being present of the risen Jesus.
- In the three occurrences of the term outside 4:15, some sort of accounting or judgment is implied. So, in 2:19, Paul's basis of boasting at the *parousia* will be the Thessalonians; in 3:13 and 5:23, he writes of being blameless at the *parousia*.
- In 3:13, Jesus is accompanied by the saints (that is, those who believe in him; see also 1 Cor 15:23).

The term itself is a compound word composed of *para*, a preposition that has the connotation of being present with, and *ousa*, a participle that means *being*. The term has roots in various ancient cults, where it referred to the coming of the deity, often in procession. The coming was a revealing of the deity's power, so the deity's devotees responded with a celebration. Thus, on a special cult day, the statue of the deity would be carried with great fanfare in procession into the city. The whole process would be the *parousia*, the *coming*, of the god. The term was also used for the coming in procession of the Roman emperor (in Latin, *adventis*). The *parousia* of Jesus may, in fact, be formulated to contrast with the coming of Caesar, and thus it may well be a term with definite political implications—and it will not be the last such term we find.

In verse 16, Paul writes, "For the Lord himself, with a cry of command, with the archangel's call and with the sound of God's trumpet, will descend from heaven, and the dead in Christ will rise first." The Lord's coming is accompanied by a threefold set of auditions (things people can hear). The basic image comes from Judean apocalyptic thought that Paul has retooled in relationship to Jesus. First is a shout of command; Jesus rules. Second is the archangel's voice (see Rev 4:5; 8:5; 11:19; 16:18). Third is the trumpet of God. The trumpet is a common apocalyptic image, found, for example, in the Dead Sea Scrolls in a document called the *War Scroll*. In that document is an entire section on trumpets (1QM 2.15-3.12). The trumpet was often a sign of God's command (Isa 27:13; Joel 2:1; Zech 9:14; Matt 24:31; 1 Cor 15:51-52; Rev 1:10; 4:1; 8:26, 6, 13; 9:14). Perhaps these sounds are meant to awaken the dead. What is important in this text is that the dead rise first (notice that they were not previously with Jesus).

Verse 17a continues, "Then we who are alive, who are left, will be caught up in the clouds together with them to meet the Lord in the air." Only once the dead in Christ have been raised do the living meet the Lord. The cloud is often in the Bible a symbol of the divine (Exod 16:10; 19:16; Ezek 1:4-28; Dan 7:13). The word for *meet* is in Greek the noun *apantēsis*. It was used to describe the festive and formal meeting of a king or other dignitary who was arriving to visit a city. The official delegation would meet the visitor outside the city and then escort the visitor into the city itself. Thus, "the united community, those who are alive and those who have died and have been raised, will meet the Lord like a delegation of a city that goes out to meet and greet an emperor when he comes to visit."[11] Only in this case, who is the "emperor," the one being met? It is Jesus. And what is this Jesus? He is the *kyrios*, the Lord.

Verse 17b completes the sentence: "and so we will be with the Lord forever." This is one of the most beautiful half verses in the entire Bible. It is also Paul's definition of "heaven" or eternity: simply being with the Lord. "With the Lord" is typically used by Paul to refer to the future relationship of believers and Jesus. When Paul refers to the present relationship with Jesus, he prefers the phrase "in Christ."[12]

Verse 18 says, "Therefore encourage one another with these words." Paul's conclusion reminds us that his concern is less that of giving details of the *parousia* and much more his pastoral concern for his listeners.

5:1-11

In 5:1-11, Paul moves to a different but related topic: *the times and seasons*.

In verse 1, he writes, "But concerning the times and the seasons, brothers and sisters, you do not need to have anything written to you." The word *concerning* often introduces in Paul a new topic (see 1 Thess 4:9 and 13, for example; in 4:13, the Greek term *peri* is translated as *about*). The topic in chapter 5 is the time of the coming day of the Lord: when will that day come? The topic obviously is connected to Paul's concern in chapter 4, where he writes of the *parousia*, the coming of the Lord Jesus.

The reason the Thessalonians do not need more information about the time of the day of the Lord is outlined in verse 2: "For you yourselves know very well that the day of the Lord will come like a thief in the night." The words that follow *that* contain a teaching about which he wants to remind them. They already know what he is going to tell them. He tells them that he knows that they know what he is going to tell them—but he will tell them anyway! This rhetorical device draws attention to his basic message, that "the day of the Lord will come like a thief in the night." The day of the Lord, in Hebrew thought, was the day of judgment. Whereas Israel had traditionally looked forward to the day of judgment when God would reward them and punish their enemies, the prophets reminded Israel that Israel, too, would be judged (Joel 1:15; 2:1-2, 11; Amos 5:18-20). And what about this coming of the day of the Lord? It will come suddenly, writes Paul. Nor is it possible for humanity to hasten it or to avoid it. It simply comes. And it comes without prior announcement, just as the thief gives no notice (see Matt 24:42-43).

Verse 3 continues, "When they say, 'There is peace and security,' then sudden destruction will come upon them, as labor pains come upon a pregnant woman, and there will be no escape!" In this verse, the anonymous "they" proclaim peace and security. Paul probably builds on the words of Jer 6:14, "They have healed the wound of my people lightly, saying 'Peace, peace,' when there is no peace." The Jeremiah text refers to false prophets who counsel relaxation: "Everything is fine. Don't worry." False prophets refuse to live in light of the coming day, even as some in Thessalonica misread the present by misreading the future. But the language of peace and security occurs elsewhere, too, in the propaganda of the Roman Empire. *Pax et securitas* (peace and security) is one of the slogans of the empire. It may well be that Paul is pointing to "the day of the Lord as an event that will shatter the false peace and security" of the Roman Empire.[13]

Let us put together a few of the things we have been discovering. Jesus is what? Lord. And he will return in a way that is called what? *Parousia*. And when the Lord has his *parousia*, the ones who believe in him will do what? Meet him, the technical term for going out to meet a ruler. And when that happens, what is shattered? The peace and security of the Roman Empire. And what was the charge leveled against Christ-believers in Thessalonica (Acts 17:7)? They act contrary to the decrees of Caesar and set up Jesus as king. That is the kind of activity that emperors did not like. Perhaps that is one reason Paul was arrested so frequently: the charge may well have been treason.[14]

136 | Paul: Apostle to the Nations

Fig. 6.2 A statue of Augustus depicted as a divine being; from Thessalonica. Photo courtesy of the President and Fellows of Harvard College.

When people falsely proclaim peace and security, sudden destruction comes—and it comes as a surprise. The analogy Paul draws is to a woman in labor. The image is threefold: it is painful (the old world does not die easily, and the new world does not come easily); it is inevitable (no escape); and it is unpredictable (babies come when they are ready to come). Babies do not come on schedule—any more than the thief of verse 2.

Verse 4 says, "But you, beloved [*brothers and sisters* in Greek], are not in darkness, for that day to surprise you like a thief." Paul applies his views on the day of the Lord to the Thessalonians. Negatively, they are not in darkness. If they were, the thief, who operates at night (vs. 2), could surprise them. But they live in the day (see Rom 13:11-14), as the next verse establishes.

Verse 5 elaborates, "For you are all children of light and children of the day; we are not of the night or of darkness." Here Christ-believers are defined positively: children of light and of day (see also Eph 5:8; John 8:12; 12:36; and the *War Scroll* from Qumran, sometimes called "The War of the Sons of Light against the Sons of Darkness"). In the second half of the verse, Paul turns again to a negative definition; he also shifts from using *you* to using *we*.

Verse 6 exhorts, "So then let us not fall asleep as others do, but let us keep awake and be sober." Paul begins the verse with two concluding conjunctions, literally *therefore therefore*, which is his way of drawing his thoughts to a close and in this case applying his insights to the everyday lives of his listeners. The word for "fall asleep" is a different Greek word from the one he used in chapter 4 for sleeping. The meaning here is to avoid falling physically asleep, and so to stay awake, to be on the watch, because the day of the Lord is coming (and no one knows exactly when, vss. 1-4). The language in this verse is very similar to what Jesus says in Mark 13:33-37, including the same Greek verbs. Mark had not yet been written, so Paul was not dependent on it. But he may have known oral sayings from Jesus, one of which is reflected here (see also Rom 13:11-14).

Verses 7-10 say, "For those who sleep sleep at night, and those who are drunk get drunk at night. But since we belong to the day, let us be sober, and put on the breastplate of faith and love, and for a helmet the hope of salvation. For God has destined us not for wrath but for obtaining salvation through our Lord Jesus Christ, who died for us, so that whether we are awake or asleep we may live with him." In these verses, Paul explains more fully the matter of sleeping. In verse 9, he reminds us that God's plan for humanity is not wrath but salvation, specifically salvation through Jesus Christ. In verse 10, Paul makes two salient theological moves. First, he identifies Jesus as the one *who died for us*. Paul likes that language (Rom 5:6; 8:3; 14:15; 1 Cor 15:3). It is of paramount importance for him that Jesus died and that Jesus died for humanity, *for us*. The Greek word used for *for* is the word *hyper*, which means *on behalf of*, *in the place of*, and thus *for*. Second, Paul answers the question "But what if I am not able to stay awake? What if I do fall asleep?" Paul's answer: it all depends on Jesus. Since he died for humanity, people's place at the day of the Lord depends on him, not on them and not on whether or not they are able to stay awake.

This leads to verse 11: "Therefore encourage one another and build up each other, as indeed you are doing." Paul concludes this topos the same way he concluded the final topos in chapter 4, with the counsel to encourage or comfort each other. In 5:11, he adds the advice that they are to "build up each other." *Building up* comes from the world of construction and is an important missionary term for Paul (1 Cor 3:9; 8:1; 10:23; 14:3-5, 12, 17, 26; 2 Cor 12:19). In his ministry and in the ministry of all believers, he is concerned that the church build up both individuals and the corporate body. And an important part of the building up he does in this section is to remind the Thessalonians that there is no timetable that can predict when the day of the Lord will come. The timing of that day is in God's hands. In addition, he has advised the Thessalonians on *how* they are to live in light of the coming day. The future day is not simply a future hope. That future impinges on the present and, indeed, is in some ways already present in the transformed lives of the Thessalonians (5:4-8).

Chapters 1-3

The bulk of chapter 1 is an extended thanksgiving by Paul for the Thessalonians (1:2-10). He reminds them that God has chosen them (1:4); the way he knows of God's choice is the powerful way in which the gospel came to them (1:5). Paul is particularly thankful that, although their reception of his message resulted in persecution, they still received the message with joy (1:6). That reception, in turn, gives Paul great joy (3:9), so that he can even call the Thessalonians his own personal joy (2:20). The Thessalonians have themselves become examples to other believers (1:7-9). As indicated above, anticipation of the return of Jesus is a fundamental part of the message Paul announced and the Thessalonians believed (1:10).

The section 2:1-12 fulfills two functions: it narrates Paul's history with the Thessalonians, and it defends his apostleship. Verses 3-7 in particular contain Paul's defense against the charge that he was a charlatan. Instead of acting from self-interest and the desire to make money, Paul reminds his listeners, he and those who had worked with him "were gentle among you, like a nurse tenderly caring for her own children" (2:7). Paul cared deeply for the people in the congregation (2:8). He also refreshes their memory about finances: he and his co-missionaries were not like the charlatans who took the money and ran; in fact, they worked long hours to support themselves, so that they would not need to ask the Thessalonians for money (2:9).[15]

Verse 13 begins the second portion of Paul's thanksgiving. He thanks God that the Thessalonians recognized that in his message he was speaking not only his own words but God's word. Verses 14-16 are very difficult verses. They appear to be strongly anti-Judean, as Paul draws a parallel between the persecution the Thessalonians have experienced and the fact that Judeans killed Jesus as they had previously killed the prophets, that they drove "us" out (meaning Paul and his co-missionaries, or Judean Christ-believing missionaries in general?), and that they were hindering Paul and others from taking the good news of Jesus to the nations. For those reasons, God's wrath had overtaken them. Scholars have approached these verses in five basic ways:

1. Yes, the verses are anti-Judean, but they are simply the result of Paul's early, overheated apocalyptic fervor.
2. Yes, the verses are anti-Judean, but the context of Paul's remarks was the persecution of Palestinian followers of Jesus in the late 40s and early 50s; Paul was in the middle of a battle that spilled over into his letter to the Thessalonians.[16] In that battle, Paul used polemical hyperbole (exaggeration) to make his case.[17]
3. Related is the view that Paul was not condemning all Judeans but only those involved in the specific actions of verses 15-16.[18]

4. Paul did not write these verses at all. Verses 14-16 do not fit well in the context of Paul's thought. He uses affectionate language in the earlier verses, only to shift suddenly to the negative language of verses 14-16. Words not found elsewhere in Paul or used only rarely may indicate another author for these verses (*compatriots, kill, drive out, opposed/hostile*). Elsewhere in Paul, *Judean* is used in the contrast of Judean and Gentile, not in the negative way the term is used here. For many scholars who take the position that our verses were added by someone other than Paul, the accusation that Judeans are hostile to the rest of humanity is the key. Hatred of humanity by Judeans was a standard Gentile charge (see Tacitus, *Histories* 5.5). Some also argue that the passage reflects what happened to Judeans following their rebellion against Rome in 66 and the resulting destruction of Jerusalem.[19] For Earl Richard, for example, "the author is post-Pauline and is writing from a Gentile-Christian perspective which one should characterize as anti-Jewish. The plight of the Jew, following the destruction of Jerusalem and later dispersal from Palestine, is seen as the result of divine retribution finally being meted out for centuries of hostility toward God and the whole of humanity."[20]
5. Paul indeed wrote these verses, perhaps using traditions he inherited. The interpretive task is to place the verses within the larger context of his life and theology. Thus, Karl Donfried points out that Paul necessarily alienated some Judean people, because he tried first to bring his own people to Jesus as Messiah. "Through the use of pre-Pauline materials, 1 Thess. 2:13-16 intends both to describe and to reprove the hostility of such Jews against Jesus, the churches in Judea, Paul and the church at Thessalonica."[21] Donfried also questions the standard translation of 2:16: "God's wrath has overtaken them at last." The NRSV lists as other possibilities for "at last" the words *completely* and *forever*. He maintains that the words in question (*eis telos*) should be translated as *until the end*. Thus, the wrath of God has indeed overtaken the Judeans as a group, from Paul's perspective, but there is a terminus. And that terminus is the end of the current age. That view, Donfried argues further, is consonant with what Paul will develop later in Romans 9–11, although in 1 Thessalonians, Paul does not discuss what he does develop in Romans—namely, that on the last day, God's mercy will be revealed to Israel in a new way that will result in Israel's salvation (Rom 11:25-26).[22]

In 2:17, Paul returns to a narration of his history and relationship with the Thessalonians. The aspect of that history highlighted from 2:17 to 3:10 is Paul's desire to see the Thessalonians again and his sending Timothy to encourage them and to find out how they are doing. In 3:11-13, he finally concludes the extended thanksgiving that began in 1:2. He repeats his desire to see them again and concludes this final portion of the thanksgiving with a look toward the coming (*parousia*) of Jesus.

1 Thessalonians: The End Is Near—but Not Yet

I.	Salutation	1:1
II.	Thanksgiving / Narration	1:2—3:13
	A. Thanksgiving / Narration (*Part One*)	1:2-10
	B. Narration / Apostolic Defense	2:1-12
	C. Thanksgiving / Narration (*Part Two*)	2:13-16
	D. Narration / Desire to Visit	2:17—3:10
	E. Thanksgiving / Concluding Wishes (*Part Three*)	3:11-13
III.	Paraenesis	4:1—5:22
	A. Basic Exhortation	4:1-2
	B. Topos on Sexual Behavior	4:3-8
	C. Topos on Love for Siblings in the Fictive Family	4:9-12
	D. Topos on the Dead in Christ	4:13-18
	E. Topos on the Day of the Lord	5:1-11
	F. Miscellaneous Exhortations	5:12-22
IV.	Final Prayers and Greetings	5:23-28
	A. Prayer for Holiness	5:23-24
	B. Request for Prayer	5:25
	C. Final Greeting	5:26
	D. Exhortation to Read the Letter	5:27
	E. Concluding Benediction	5:28

Summary

In 1 Thessalonians, Paul has written a warm, intimate letter that both encourages the recipients by reminding them of who they are and what God in Christ has done for them while at the same time calling them to live today in light of the imminent return of Jesus. That expected return casts a large shadow over the letter, a shadow that we will discover at other points in our journey with Paul.

Study Questions

1. Why did Paul write 1 Thessalonians?
2. What themes in the letter could be interpreted in the first century as placing Paul in opposition to the Roman Empire?
3. What is the imminent return of Jesus, and what is its importance in this letter?
4. How do you think Paul wanted this community of believers to grieve?
5. Describe Paul's view of the *parousia* of Jesus. What similar themes do you see in contemporary music and movies?

Suggested Reading

Donfried, Karl P. "The Theology of 1 Thessalonians." In Karl P. Donfried and I. Howard Marshall, *The Theology of the Shorter Pauline Letters*. Cambridge: Cambridge University Press, 1993. Pp. 1–79.

Furnish, Victor Paul. *1 Thessalonians, 2 Thessalonians*. ANTC. Nashville: Abingdon, 2007.

Gaventa, Beverly Roberts. *First and Second Thessalonians*. IBC. Louisville: Westminster John Knox, 1998.

Malherbe, Abraham J. *The Letters to the Thessalonians*. AB 32B. New York: Doubleday, 2000.

Richard, Earl J. *First and Second Thessalonians*. Sacra Pagina 11. Collegeville, MN: Liturgical, 1995.

Wanamaker, Charles A. *Commentary on 1 and 2 Thessalonians*. NIGTC. Grand Rapids: Eerdmans, 1990.

Witherington, Ben, III. *1 and 2 Thessalonians: A Socio-Rhetorical Commentary*. Grand Rapids: Eerdmans, 2006.

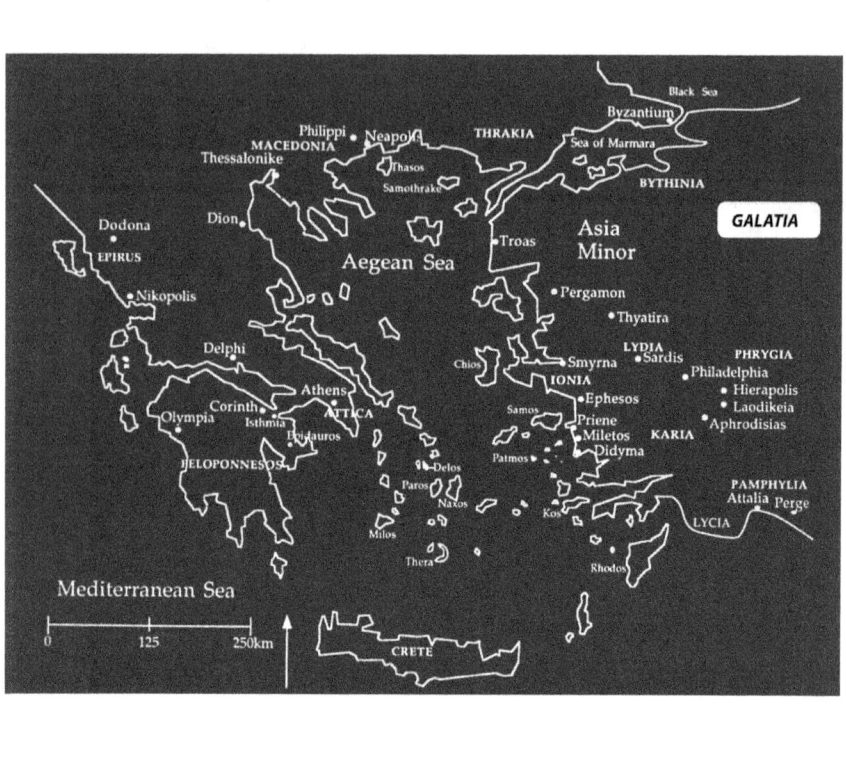

Chapter 7

Galatians: Free to Be Children of God

Why Is Paul So Upset? (1:1—2:21)

> Imagine sitting in a Christ-believing congregation somewhere in the interior of Turkey. There are no pews, and in fact, you are gathered with other Christ-believers in someone's home. Even though you are not well educated, you are well aware of how a letter should be constructed: salutation, thanksgiving, body, exhortation, conclusion. So as the reader begins the letter, you know what to listen for. First the salutation: "Paul an apostle . . . to the churches of Galatia: Grace to you and peace . . . Amen." As the salutation is being read, you anticipate the thanksgiving section. "We had a good relationship with Paul when he was here. I wonder what qualities or actions of ours he will lift up to God for thanks?" What you hear instead is, "I am astonished." The Greek term itself doesn't sound friendly: *thaumazō* (thou-MAH-zoh).

What has caused this expression of astonishment? In this letter, Paul has no thanksgiving, presumably because there was nothing about the Galatians for which he *could* give thanks. Why is he so upset? We do not have to read too far in chapter 1 before we find out.

In 1:6, Paul writes, "I am astonished that you are so quickly deserting the one who called you in the grace of Christ and are turning to a different gospel." "I am astonished" not only expresses Paul's emotion but also is a rhetorical device that indicates his indignation and disgust.[1] "The one who called you in the grace of Christ" could refer to God, who is the one in Paul's writings who usually does the calling (Gal 1:15; 5:8, 13; etc.), but it likely also carries a secondary reference to Paul, who was for the Galatians the agent of God's call. Paul's astonishment is a reaction to an unanticipated move by the Galatian believers. They have deserted Paul and ultimately God by turning to a different gospel, a proclamation of the good news of Jesus so dissimilar to what Paul had taught that the message is indeed another message, another gospel.

Verse 7 continues, "Not that there is another gospel, but there are some who are confusing you and want to pervert the gospel of Christ." Paul denies that there is, really, another gospel. But some have come into the Galatian communities and have sought to pervert the gospel of Christ. Paul's goal in this letter, then, is to confront this perversion of the gospel and bring the Galatians back to the good news of Jesus as Paul himself had announced it. He is so adamant about the truth of his gospel that he pronounces in verses 8 and 9 a double conditional curse: "But even if we or an angel from heaven should proclaim to you a gospel contrary to what we proclaimed to you, let that one be accursed! As we have said before, so now I repeat, if anyone proclaims to you a gospel contrary to what you received, let that one be accursed!" The word *accursed* is the Greek word *anathema*. So Paul's language is strong: if he would proclaim a different "gospel," he should be destroyed (sent to hell); if anyone else proclaims such a "gospel," that one should be destroyed; even if an angel from heaven proclaims that kind of "gospel," that one, too, should be destroyed. He uses no diplomacy in greeting these believers!

That blunt language causes us to reread the salutation. "Paul an apostle—sent neither by human commission nor from human authorities, but through Jesus Christ and God the Father, who raised him from the dead—and all the members of God's family [literally, *all the brothers and sisters*] who are with me, To the churches of Galatia" (1:1-2). At the beginning of 1 Thessalonians, Paul claimed no title or office. Here he does. He is an apostle. The word ***apostle*** (*apostolos*) means "one who is sent with a message." The apostle is an official representative of the one who has sent him or her. To reject the apostle is to reject the sender. To accept the apostle is to accept the sender.[2] Paul is sent by God the father and the Lord Jesus Christ. He is an apostle *not* because someone voted him into that status or because he went to college to become one. He is an apostle because God chose him to be an apostle and revealed Jesus to him (see 1:15-17; Rom 1:1).[3]

Why does Paul show such a concern for his authority? To answer that question, we turn to the thesis of the letter. In 2:15-16, we read, "We ourselves are Jews by birth and not Gentile sinners; yet we know that a person is justified not by the works of the law but through faith in Jesus Christ. And we have come to believe in Christ Jesus, so that we might be justified by faith in Christ, and not by doing the works of the law, because no one will be justified by the works of the law." The issue is how a person is justified.

The words *justify* and *justification* have their home in the law court. The prisoner stands in front of the judge. The prisoner is guilty; of that there is no doubt. The moment comes for the punishment to be announced, but instead of sending the prisoner to prison or death, the judge declares the prisoner innocent and sets the prisoner free. The judge takes away the guilt, and the prisoner is *justified* or made right by the judge. The Greek word for *justification* is the same as the word for *righteousness*: *dikaiosynē*. In Israel's Bible, to be righteous or just meant to hold up one's end of the relationship established by God in the covenant. Justification/righteousness is thus a relational term, used to describe a relationship with God. To say that God is righteous means that God acts to restore or to uphold the relationship with God's people that God has established in the covenant. Humanity has been unrighteous, but God is righteous by restoring people to a positive relationship with God.

But how is that relationship restored? Here is where Paul engages the battle. For Paul, the relationship is restored totally on the basis of Christ's activity (see also Rom 3:21-26). As indicated in the excursus, another way that Gal 2:16 can be translated is, "We know that a person is justified . . . through the faith of Jesus Christ," that is, through his Christ's faithfulness to God and God's will. That translation puts all the weight on Christ's action. Thus, God restores humanity's broken relationship with God through Christ and his death, totally apart from human action. Humanity indeed is invited to believe in Jesus, as verse 16 says. Faith is believing trust that what Paul says God has done in Jesus God has actually done (see the discussion of Abraham in Galatians 3.

Paul's opponents, according to him, teach that a person is justified by the works of the law. The law that is being talked about is clearly the Law of Moses, but what does it mean to be "justified by works of the law"? There are two possibilities. The first possible understanding is that, by "works of the law," Paul meant the boundary markers of Judaism. The rite of male **circumcision** was the basic boundary marker between Judean and non-Judean men. Other boundary markers such as proper Sabbath observance and dietary laws (not eating pork, for example) served to distinguish Judeans and non-Judeans from each other in both the minds of Judean people and the minds of others. The thesis propounded in particular by James D. G. Dunn and Mark D. Nanos is that Paul is objecting to inappropriate trust in such boundary markers—namely, the view that the boundary markers in and of themselves mean that one is in a right relationship with God.[4] The second possible understanding of "works of the law" is the attitude that by keeping the Law of Moses, a person has earned his or her standing with God by having fulfilled what God requires. Although in recent years, scholars have often set the two interpretations over against each other, they ultimately work together, since it is in fulfillment of the Law that a person illustrates that she or he is properly living as a member of the covenant people of God.[5]

Excursus: Faith "in" or Faith "of"

Galatians 2:16 reads in the NRSV, "Yet we know that a person is justified not by the works of the law but through *faith in Jesus Christ*. And we have come to believe in Christ Jesus, so that we might be justified by *faith in Christ*" (italics added). A footnote indicates that in place of the first set of italicized words, one could read, "the faith of Jesus Christ." In the NRSV text, faith is placed *in* Jesus Christ. In the NRSV footnote, Paul would seem to be talking about Jesus Christ's faith. Similarly, in place of the second set of italicized words, according to the footnote, one could read, "the faith of Christ." Why does this confusion exist?

The ambiguity comes from the Greek. In both constructions, there are two sets of nouns: noun *a* (faith) + noun(s) *b* (Jesus Christ or Christ). Noun(s) *b* are in the Greek genitive case. The basic meaning of the genitive is possession. Thus, the English phrase *the girl's computer* would in Greek be *the computer of the girl*. Actually, the word *of* would not occur, but the possessive sense of the word *of* would be indicated by placing *the girl* into the genitive case ("the computer the girl").

The issue in Gal 2:16 is exactly what *kind* of genitive we have. We have two basic options, each of which is grammatically possible:

1. *Objective genitive.* In this understanding, noun(s) *b* receive the implied action of noun *a*. Thus, the action of having faith or believing is directed toward Jesus Christ or Christ. We therefore translate the phrase in this verse as "faith in (Jesus) Christ." The objective genitive understanding is the traditional way of understanding the phrase.

2. *Subjective genitive.* In this understanding, noun(s) *b* function as the implied subject or possessor of noun *a*. Thus, the flow of action is from noun(s) *b* to noun *a*. With that understanding, we translate the words as "the faith of (Jesus) Christ" or "(Jesus) Christ's faith(fulness)." In this usage, "faith" is understood as an act of faithfulness by Jesus to God's will.

We find the same issue in Gal 2:20 and 3:22, Rom 3:22, 26, and Phil 3:9.

Richard Hays has been a strong advocate of the subjective genitive interpretation. For him, the death of Jesus, "in obedience to the will of God, is simultaneously a loving act of faithfulness (*pistis*) to God and the decisive manifestation of God's faithfulness to his covenant promise to Abraham."[6]

James Dunn is a staunch defender of the objective genitive interpretation.[7] His argument makes four points: (1) There is no verbal equivalent in Paul to the subjective genitive understanding. That is, there is nothing like "Christ believed." (2) Outside the disputed phrases themselves, there is no clear reference to Christ's faith. Yet Jesus Christ is clearly presented as the object of faith (Rom 10:9; 1 Cor 12:3; 2 Cor 4:5). (3) When two nouns are in the subjective genitive construction, noun *a* almost always has the definite article *the*. In Greek, noun *a* does not have the definite article in any of the phrases in question. (4) If, in fact, Paul does want to emphasize the faith(fulness) of Jesus, is it not odd that Abraham is Paul's model of faith, rather than Jesus (Galatians 3; Romans 4)?

The final arbiter in each case is context. In Gal 2:16, both occurrences of our phrase could well be translated as "faith/fulness of Christ" in part because of the clear statement also that "we have come to believe in Christ Jesus." That

> statement, in the immediate context of the verse, gives some probability to the interpretation that the disputed phrase has a different nuance. In other verses, the objective genitive is often the preferable way to translate. At the same time, the larger context of the argument that Paul is developing tips the scales in the direction of faith *in* (see Galatians 3).[8]

From a cultural-anthropological perspective, Paul is arguing for what he believes to be the desirable group identity for the Galatian Christ-believing communities, while at the same time arguing against the group identity being pushed by the missionaries who have, from his perspective, invaded Galatia.[9] Paul thought the issues had been resolved at a meeting in Jerusalem often called the Apostolic Council. In that meeting, Titus served as Paul's living audiovisual example of a non-Judean who had come to believe in Jesus and who had become part of the believing community, totally without circumcision (2:3). There was opposition to Paul's position, but he held fast and gained the support of the Jerusalem leaders (2:4-10).[10] The fragile nature of the agreement was illustrated by the Antioch incident (2:11-14). In that congregation, Judean believers and Gentile believers ate together without concern for Judean purity laws; the eating would have included receiving the Lord's Supper.[11] When emissaries connected with James arrived from Jerusalem, Cephas, Paul's own associate Barnabas, and other Judean believers stopped eating with Gentiles. It was at some point after that experience that Paul had worked in Galatia. What he saw developing there in his absence was directly parallel to the confrontations he had already had in Jerusalem and Antioch.

Paul's concern is not Christ-believers versus nonbelieving Judeans. His concern is how Christ-believers are put right with God. His gospel was a Law-less gospel, in the sense that the Law contains no saving or justifying power. The "other gospel" (1:6-7) of his Christ-believing opponents is, apparently, an attempt to add as a requirement the Law of Moses for those who believed in Christ. Without the Law, they taught, people could not be in a righteous relationship with God. Their message seems to have been that Jesus is not enough. Paul's message is true, they said, but only to a point. And the point he neglected to develop is that new Christ-believers must become part of the people of Israel by crossing the boundary between Judean and Gentile. His opponents therefore pushed circumcision and following the Law of Moses as necessary components of their full gospel. Paul had given the Galatians only part of the story. His opponents wanted to give them the rest.

How Does Paul Prove His Thesis? (3:1—4:31)

In seeking to prove his thesis that people are justified not from works of law but through faith in Jesus Christ, Paul turns first to experience. The issue is how the Galatians received the (Holy) Spirit. He begins chapter 3 with a rhetorical insult.

- *Gal. 3:1.* "You foolish Galatians! Who has bewitched you? It was before your eyes that Jesus Christ was publicly exhibited as crucified!" The word for *foolish* (*anoētoi*) could also be translated *stupid*. The term for *bewitched* (*ebaskanen*) is a technical term in Paul's day for casting the evil eye.[12] From Paul's viewpoint, the opponents are evil figures who have attacked his people.
- *3:2.* "The only thing I want to learn from you is this: Did you receive the Spirit by doing the works of the law or by believing what you had heard?" Verses 3-4 contain more insults, with the goal of shaming the Galatians into realizing the error of their thinking.
- *3:3-4.* "Are you so foolish? Having started with the Spirit, are you now ending with the flesh? Did you experience so much for nothing?—if it really was for nothing." The word *flesh* is probably a jab at the opponents, who are urging circumcision of the body; over against that, Paul sets the Spirit. (For more on *flesh*, see the chapter on Romans.) And so he returns to his basic question in verse 5.
- *3:5.* "Well then, does God supply you with the Spirit and work miracles among you by your doing the works of the law, or by your believing what you heard?" The obvious answer (from Paul's perspective, at least!) is this: God works through believing. Therefore, God does not work through doing works of the law.[13]

Paul's second argument for his thesis is Scriptural:

Just as Abraham "believed God, and it was reckoned to him as righteousness,"	(vs. 6)
so, you see, those who believe are the descendants of Abraham.	(vs. 7)
And the scripture, foreseeing that God would justify the Gentiles by faith, declared the gospel beforehand to Abraham, saying, "All the Gentiles shall be blessed in you."	(vs. 8)
For this reason, those who believe are blessed with Abraham who believed.	(vs. 9)

The key figure in verses 6-9, obviously, is Abraham. And who is Abraham? He is a person of belief or faith. And who are the descendants (literally, sons) of Abraham? They, too, are people of faith. But Abraham is much more than a person who happened to believe. Abraham was the first of the Hebrew people. He was the first to be circumcised as part of a covenant with God. That means, too, that Abraham was the first Judean. But what is Abraham, ethnically, in addition to being a Judean? He was before circumcision a Gentile. Abraham is thus a universal figure who comprehends in himself both Judean and Gentile. If Paul can gain Abraham for his side of the argument, he has won the day. That is, if Abraham can be shown to be justified by faith, then that is the way that everyone is justified, since Abraham is, in non-Christ-believing Judean literature of the time, both the quintessential Judean and the representative Gentile convert.[14] In addition to the sort of bridging function Abraham served, Abraham was also viewed in the emerging rabbinic literature as the perfect fulfiller of the Mosaic Law.[15] Thus, Paul is attacking his opponents at their strongest point: Father Abraham, the very first of the covenant people.

When New Testament authors quote a passage from Israel's Scripture, it is helpful to read the quotation in its original setting. The first text Paul quotes (vs. 7) is Gen 15:6. In Genesis, God has promised to make of Abraham a great nation, but so far, Abraham and his wife Sarah are childless. In Gen 15:1-5, God has Abraham gaze at the stars of heaven. Once again, God promises Abraham descendants—in fact, as many as the stars in the sky above. And what does Abraham do, as he hears the promise and tries to count the stars—and as he counts the number of children Sarah and he have, which is not even one? "He believed the Lord; and the Lord reckoned it to him as righteousness." This is the passage Paul quotes to explain how Abraham was made right with God and how any person is made right with God. How does that happen? Through faith. Faith, then, is a looking, a listening, and a believing trust (on Abraham and faith, see also Romans 4). The second passage, from Gen 12:3, contains a promise given to Abraham before he was circumcised (Genesis 17). The promise is that Gentiles would be blessed through Abraham. In our passage, Paul claims to know how that blessing would occur: through faith. So the children of Abraham are those who believe. Thus, being reckoned by faith as righteous is nothing new. It goes back to the very beginning of God's history with the covenant people—and before the Law was given.

In verses 10-14, Paul develops a brief **midrash** on four passages from the Judean Scriptures. He concludes that, through Christ, the blessing pronounced to Abraham centuries earlier could now be given to Gentiles. Thus, the promise of the Spirit, as Paul already argued in 3:6-9, comes through faith. In verses 15-18, Paul uses an example from inheritance law to show that the Mosaic Law was secondary to the covenant with Abraham.

In verses 19-25, Paul leaves for a moment the series of arguments he is developing to say a bit more about the law. In verses 19-20, the view of the law is further compromised:

> Why then the law? It was added because of
> transgressions, until the offspring would come to
> whom the promise had been made; and it was
> ordained through angels by a mediator. (vs. 19)

> Now a mediator involves more than one party; but
> God is one. (vs. 20)

The reason the law was given was because of transgression. It is, says Paul, remedial, temporary, and valid only until "the offspring" (Jesus) arrives. In addition to that, the law was not given directly by God. Rather, it was issued through angels to an intermediary, Moses. Verse 20 revolves around the concept that the oneness of God is preferable to any division. "God is one" is the basic creed of Judaism.

When we reach Romans, we will find Paul saying many positive things about the law—perhaps as a corrective to the more negative view he has in Galatians. At this point, he presents only the negative side, which leads naturally to the question of verse 21: "Is the law then opposed to the promises of God? Certainly not! For if a law had been given that could make alive, then righteousness would indeed come through the law." But Paul's point is that there is no law that can "make alive," for through the law comes God's curse (3:10, 13). In the next verse, Paul refers to the theme of faith: "But the scripture has imprisoned all things under the power of sin, so that what was promised through faith in Jesus Christ might be given to those who believe" (vs. 22).

In verses 23-25, Paul does identify a positive function for the law, albeit a time-limited one:

> Now before faith came, we were imprisoned and
> guarded under the law until faith would be revealed. (vs. 23)
>
> Therefore the law was our disciplinarian until Christ
> came, so that we might be justified by faith. (vs. 24)
>
> But now that faith has come, we are no longer
> subject to a disciplinarian. (vs. 25)

The law is our "disciplinarian" (*paidagōgos*). The term means one who leads (*agō*) a child (*pais*). The disciplinarian was usually a slave, generally one not skilled enough to run the master's business and not strong enough to do hard labor. The disciplinarian accompanied the master's boy to and from school and also watched over the boy's behavior in general. The disciplinarian was not a classroom teacher (the English derivative *pedagogue* is misleading), although he did instruct the boy in morals and "the ways of the world" (see Plutarch, *Moralia* 439F). The disciplinarian had essentially a restraining function (so vs. 23, "we were imprisoned and guarded under the law"). In addition to the restraining function, the second important factor about the disciplinarian is that his work was limited to the boy's legal minority (as long as the boy was under age). Usually, this slave had responsibility for the boy from around age six or seven to the late teens. When the boy became legally an adult, the guardian's function ceased, so Paul uses the example of the disciplinarian to indicate the restraining and limited nature of the law. Note that the law is not a tutor or teacher who leads us to Christ but a disciplinarian until Christ comes.[16] Verse 25 now makes sense. As adult children of God, Christ-believers no longer need the restraining leash of the law.

The reason all of that is true is contained in verse 26: "for in Christ Jesus you are all children of God through faith." With this verse, Paul moves into his fourth proof, which is a proof from church tradition—in particular, baptismal tradition. Notice the address: *you*, the Gentile believers of Galatia. How does it happen that these Gentiles are children (literally in Greek, sons) of God?[17] Is it through works? No, it is by faith. The term *sons/children of God* in Israel's Bible and in Judean literature is usually applied only to Judeans.[18] Paul extends that title of honor to Gentiles on the basis not of an approved Judean method but rather by faith—faith, of course, in Jesus Messiah. Paul thereby gives believers a new identity by defining their status before God: not foreigners in relationship to God but God's own children (see also 4:4-7; Rom 8:14-15).[19] Nor should we fail to notice the familial language: *children of God* (here and in 4:6-7), *children of Abraham* (3:7), *children of the promise* (4:28), and *children of freedom* (4:31). The status previously reserved for Israel is now offered to Gentiles.

Paul gets more specific in verse 27: "As many of you as were baptized into Christ have clothed yourselves with Christ." Paul is specifying how Gentiles have become children of God: by baptism (on baptism, see the following commentary on Romans 6). The act of being baptized is identified with the act of putting on Christ. In the Judean Scriptures, "putting on" is often a symbol of authority, as when one puts on a special garment (so Aaron and his sons, Exod 28:40-43). In our text, believers put on Christ, so that the believer is covered by the one offspring (Christ; Gal 3:16) and made by him into a son/child of God. The new garment reveals who the person really is, just as the father of the prodigal son orders the best robe for his returning son (Luke 15:22). The robe shows the son's true (and renewed) status. The Galatians' real status is seen in who has covered them, Christ.

Verse 28 continues, "There is no longer Jew or Greek, there is no longer slave or free, there is no longer male and female; for all of you are one in Christ Jesus." The result of putting on Christ is unity with him, expressed first in negative terms and then in positive terms. The verse is baptismal in origin, perhaps from a baptismal liturgy. In expressing that unity in a negative way, Paul uses the major divisions that were thought in antiquity to separate people. So, in a saying attributed to Thales, Socrates, and Plato, the speaker gives thanks that "I was born a human being and not a beast, next, a man and not a woman, thirdly, a Greek and not a barbarian" (Diogenes Laertius 1.33; Lactantius, *Div. inst.* 3.19). From the Judean side comes the following prayer of thanksgiving that eventually became part of the synagogue liturgy: "R. Judah says: Three blessings one must say daily: Blessed (art thou), who did not make me a gentile; Blessed (art thou), who did not make me a woman; Blessed (art thou), who did not make me a boor" (*Tosephta, Berakot* 7.18).[20] These sayings are typical of the era, and what Paul says in Galatians contrasts with the going assumptions of the day. On these distinctions, in fact, the basic foundation of Hellenistic culture was built.

Note that Paul's statement here is not "merely" eschatological. It is a statement of fact: "there is no longer" (*ouk eni*). As Betz observes, "It is significant that Paul makes these statements not as utopian ideals or as ethical demands, but as accomplished facts."[21] The divisions between humanity that are given value and significance by the law are declared to be passé. The law was temporary (3:17-25). It and its distinctions are now past. Baptism, then, erases the patterns of classification that were part of the old cultural maps by which people organized life (whether Judean or Gentile).²² Thus, we can make the following observations when we look at what Paul says about these three divisions:

- *Judean–Greek*. The elimination of the advantage of the Judean is a consistent theme in Paul (5:6; 6:15), so that he can even call Christ-believers the true circumcision (Phil 3:3; see also 1 Cor 7:19; Rom 2:25-29; 10:12, and the Abraham discussion in Gal 3:6-18). In his argument, the Judean-Greek division is the most important of the three sets of divisions, although the other two also have significant implications. Bruce Hansen applies theories from ethnic studies to the discussion of the ethnic identity issues surrounding *Judean-Greek*. In the assimilation model, he suggests, when culture A and culture B interact, culture B is assimilated into the dominant culture A, so that A + B = A. Paul, in contrast, proposes what is more in line with the amalgamation model, in which culture A and B form a new identity, so that A + B = C (the new identity, the community of faith). The previous entities are not eliminated but can be taken up into the new identity as long as they do not block the baptismal social solidarity Paul envisions as he seeks to create a new kinship group.²³
- *Slave–free*. Usually slaves were not permitted free association or organization. It is therefore significant that slaves are freely included in the believing community and welcomed into the church.²⁴
- *Male–female*. The pattern Paul uses for the first two pairs ("there is no longer . . . or . . .") is broken in the third pair "(there is no longer . . . and"). The difference may indicate an allusion to Gen 1:27, "male and female he created them." What does Paul mean when he says there is no male and female? Does he long for a return to some sort of pre-creation androgynous state (in which individuals are both male and female)? Does he try to deny the biological differences between the sexes? In other passages, Paul doesn't speak in favor of the elimination of all distinctions between the sexes (1 Corinthians 7; 11:2-16). What he seems to be doing in this verse is to eliminate the value judgments that are assigned to the male–female division. The distinctions still exist in this world, but in Christ, there is equality for believers, for the distinctions have lost their value.

In the final statement of the verse, "for all of you are one in Christ Jesus," Paul moves to the climax of his argument. The result of baptism is that present divisions are declared void, because his listeners are all one in Christ. Just as Christ is not to be divided, so believers themselves are not to be divided from each other (1 Cor 1:10-17). In Christ, all believers are united in a unity that is not only available in the future but also present now, proleptically (ahead of time), in the church.²⁵

In verse 29, Paul returns to the Abraham theme and what he had said in 3:6-7:

"And if you belong to Christ, then you are Abraham's offspring, heirs according to the promise." In 4:1-11, he further explains his language of "heirs" and what it means to be a child of God.²⁶ In 4:12-20, he develops his fifth argument, a narration of his past relationship with the Galatians. He reminds them of their openness to him during his initial visit, concluding with a reminder of the intimate relationship they have—he gave birth to them: "My little children, for whom I am again in the pain of childbirth until Christ is formed in you, I wish I were present with you now and could change my tone, for I am perplexed about you" (vv. 19-20).²⁷

In 4:21-31, Paul concludes his argument with his sixth and final proof, an allegory about the two sons fathered by Abraham. In the allegory, the son of the free woman represents Paul's law-free mission to the Gentiles; the son of the slave woman represents the law-bound mission to the Gentiles.²⁸ He concludes, "So then, friends [in Greek, *brothers and sisters*], we are children, not of the slave but of the free woman" (4:31). The choice the Galatians need to make is between the Law and Christ.

Historical Situation

There is no serious doubt regarding Paul as the author of Galatians. Nor is there any question regarding the literary unity of the letter. What is very much disputed is the location of the recipients of the letter. The letter is addressed to "the churches of Galatia" (1:2; see 3:1). That the recipients lived in Asia Minor (modern-day Turkey) is clear. But the word *Galatia* was used in two ways: to refer to the area in which the ethnic Galatians lived (further north; the territory hypothesis) and to refer to the Roman province created in 25 BCE that encompassed the traditional territory of the Galatians plus areas to the south that did not include ethnic Galatians (the province hypothesis). The province hypothesis creates the possibility of an early date for Galatians, since if addressed to the south, the letter could be connected with Paul's first missionary journey (Acts 13–14). However, Acts 13–14 does not discuss Galatia at all, and the cities that are mentioned are identified by the names of their districts, not the name of the province Galatia (so Antioch in Pisidia, 13:14; Lystra and Derbe in Lycaonia, 14:6). The older argument that the opponents had to be Judeans and that Judeans were found only in the south no longer carries the weight it once did (see the description of opponents later in this chapter).²⁹ A serious question is whether Paul's address to the recipients in 3:1 ("you foolish Galatians") would have worked had it been addressed to people who were not ethnically Galatian (that is, Celtic).³⁰ The ethnic term applied only to people in the north. While there is no consensus on location, the probability is that Paul wrote to the north (central Anatolia), to the area around Ancyra (modern Ankara).³¹ That he mentions no city by name may also point to the north, which was less urbanized than the south.

The circumstances of Paul's initial work in Galatia also provide an argument in favor of the north (territory) hypothesis. In 4:13-14, Paul writes, "You know that it was because of a physical infirmity that I first announced the gospel to you; though my condition put you to the test, you did not scorn or despise me, but welcomed me as an angel of God, as Christ Jesus." Paul usually centered his mission in a major urban area and fanned out to neighboring communities himself and through his associates. He did not follow that pattern according to the information in Galatians. His more typical way of organizing his work would have fit well in the south (province hypothesis), but the fact that he apparently did not intend to do mission work among the Galatians but took advantage of his physical infirmity meant that he did not follow his usual pattern.[32]

Dating is dependent on location of the recipients. Using the province hypothesis, we could date Galatians any time after Paul revisited the southern cities around 50 on his second missionary journey. If Paul wrote to the north, a somewhat later date is likely. Calvin J. Roetzel gives a range of 53–56.[33] Perhaps the date could be sharpened by reference to Acts 19:1, which has Paul going to Ephesus after passing through Galatia and Phrygia. Since in Gal 1:6, Paul says that the Galatians had "so quickly" deserted his gospel, it may be that he wrote them from Ephesus during the period 52–55, probably toward the earlier portion of his stay there.

One other bit of information concerns the collection. At the meeting in Jerusalem that Paul discusses in chapter 2 (almost certainly the Apostolic Council), the Jerusalem leaders "asked only one thing, that we remember the poor, which was actually what I was eager to do" (2:10). The reference is to a monetary collection for the Jerusalem believers, both to provide economic relief and to serve as a sign of unity in the one church of Judean and Gentile believers. Most likely because of his dispute with the Galatians, Paul makes no plans in the letter for gathering such a collection. In 1 Corinthians, we see the plans developing, including a reference to directions he had given to the churches of Galatia (16:1); by the time of 2 Corinthians 8–9, the collection is in full swing. Thus, it is probable that Galatians was written prior to the Corinthian letters. The other factor is the relationship of Galatians to Romans. Since themes enunciated in Galatians are developed more fully and often in a more sophisticated way in Romans, Galatians is universally dated prior to that letter.

PAUL'S OPPONENTS

Who are the people Paul opposes? While members of the congregations have, apparently, agreed with the views Paul opposes, they did not generate those views themselves but adopted them from Christ-believing missionaries who came after Paul left. Often scholars have labeled these opponents "Judaizers" (from Gal 2:14), that is, missionaries who wanted the non-Judean Galatian believers to be circumcised and to follow Judean law. Certainly, they themselves were circumcised (6:13). They have usually been identified as Judean believers who had some connection with Jerusalem. Perhaps they saw themselves as the guardians of the agreement forged at the Apostolic Council (Acts 15 / Gal 2:1-10), an agreement they may have thought Paul was violating. Or perhaps they are related to the "false believers" of 2:4, who likely objected to the agreement. However, Paul charges the Galatians with serving the "elemental spirits" (4:19), and he worries about their tendency to turn freedom in Christ into libertinism (5:13). Those two factors point away from Jerusalem-based Judean believers. It is not impossible that the agitators were Gentile believers who were enamored of the Law and felt that all Gentiles should follow the Law. The fact that they were not Judeans themselves could explain the references to elemental spirits and potential libertinism as well as the apparent disconnect Paul identifies in their teaching between being circumcised and the resulting need to fulfill the precepts of the Law (3:10-14; 6:13).[34] It is not beyond the realm of possibility that they understood circumcision as having a magical protective function that would preserve them from the elemental spirits. As is often the case, Paul gives us just enough information to help us sketch the picture but not enough to fill in the details. But perhaps that is all he knows about them.

The Rhetorical Genre of Galatians

Since the publication of Hans Dieter Betz's commentary on Galatians,[35] the rhetorical genre of Galatians has been hotly debated. Betz argued that Galatians is an extended defense speech, a piece of **judicial rhetoric** intended to defend Paul against his opponents and the Galatians' misguided judgments. Many scholars agree that chapters 1 and 2 are judicial (or apologetic, that is, defending himself) but wonder if that label is correctly assigned to the entire document. Several scholars have argued that the letter is representative of **deliberative rhetoric**, intended to persuade the Galatians.[36] J. Louis Martyn, although agreeing that there is judicial material in Galatians, specifically denies the classification of the letter as deliberative and understands it as an oral sermon that reproclaims the gospel.[37] Perhaps the strength of Betz's judicial argument is seen by Ben Witherington III, who rejects Betz, argues for deliberative rhetoric, and yet produces an outline that is heavily dependent on Betz's analysis.[38]

The outline presented in this book is dependent on Betz's analysis, but that is not to say the entire letter is exclusively apologetic. At a minimum, chapters 1–4, while certainly seeking to persuade the Galatians and thus at that point deliberative, defend Paul, his apostleship, and his gospel. Chapters 5 and 6 may seem to move in another direction, but they can also be seen as defensive.

Paraenesis and the Letter's Conclusion (5:1—6:18)

In chapters 5–6, Paul brings out ethical implications of his understanding of belief in Christ. His move to paraenesis in Galatians is more than his "standard" inclusion of that letter topic. If part of the charge from his opponents is that Gentile believers do not have the ethical guide they need because they are not following the Law of Moses, then Paul must somehow address the charge. Betz argues that the opponents had at that point identified a real problem for the Galatians. Paul had left them with, essentially, only the Spirit as their ethical guide. Once their initial spiritual enthusiasm had passed, problems of improper behavior occurred, and the new believers did not know how to respond. The Law of Moses and its clear directives would have been an attractive solution.[39]

Building from the slave-woman, free-woman allegory of chapter 4, Paul begins his paraenesis by emphasizing the positive nature of the freedom believers have experienced in Christ: "For freedom Christ has set us free. Stand firm, therefore, and do not submit again to a yoke of slavery" (Gal 5:1). In North America, *freedom* signals political freedom, as it did for ancient Greeks and Romans. Interestingly, political freedom in antiquity was closely associated with living under the law of the state; to be free was to be under the law. The vast majority of people, however, could not even dream of political freedom, so certain strands of philosophy, especially Cynicism and Stoicism, turned toward personal freedom. The truly free person was unconcerned with freedom as defined in Greece and Rome. So, the legend goes, when Alexander the Great, the conqueror of the known world, came to the Cynic philosopher Diogenes, Alexander asked him what one favor he would like Alexander to grant. Diogenes replied, "If you could just get out of my light; you're blocking the sun" (Diogenes Laertius 6.38).[40]

Paul rejects both political freedom and radically individual freedom as his focus of concern. His understanding of freedom is, on the contrary, dependent on Israel's Bible. The God of Israel was thought of preeminently as the God who set God's people free from political oppression and servitude as well as from sin. True freedom in Israel's Scriptures was theocentric, that is, based on and in God. It was also rooted in daily life in the Law. For Paul, however, the freedom given by God was not based on the Law of Moses, and the demands of the Judaizers were placing an impossible limitation on the freedom Paul believed Christ had given.

In 5:1, Paul writes a beautifully compact statement indicative of salvation: "For freedom Christ has set us free. Stand firm, therefore, and do not submit again to a yoke of slavery." The subject is Christ—not human activity, the elemental spirits (4:9), or attempts to control the spirits by law or ritual (4:10). So as he moves into the exhortation that follows, Paul does not simply tell the Galatians what they are to do. First, he reminds them of who they *are* because of Christ's relationship with them. Just as God had freed Israel from slavery in Egypt so many centuries earlier, so now Christ has freed the Galatians and in fact all Christ-believers ("us" in the text). While Paul in this verse does not specify from what Christ has freed people, we could certainly think of the boundaries and value judgments introduced by the law (3:28) and the "beggarly elemental spirits" that were thought to control life (4:9). In 5:16-21, Paul provides a laundry list of behaviors from which Christ-believers are to be freed;[41] he summarizes the behaviors as "the desires of the flesh." But the way to be freed was not to place oneself again under the Law.[42] Rather, it was to be led by the Spirit.

For those who are led by the Spirit, "the only thing that counts is faith working through love" (5:6). Another way to translate Paul's Greek is "faith is energized through love." For Paul, God's love energizes believers to work for others. Thus, being freed from the things that hold people back enables them to serve others. But Paul is aware that freedom can be misused, so he writes, "For you were called to freedom, brothers and sisters; only do not use your freedom as an opportunity for self-indulgence, but through love become slaves to one another. For the whole law is summed up in a single commandment, 'You shall love your neighbor as yourself'" (5:13-14).⁴³ The word translated as "self-indulgence" is actually the word *flesh*. Flesh, for Paul, did not refer simply to our bodies. Rather, the term designated persons as they misused the body by placing themselves at the center of existence. That is not what Christ-based freedom is to be.

Paul's answer to the potential problem of misuse of freedom is found in verse 13b: be slaves. How? Through love. The Galatians are both free and captive. They are free from themselves and from trying to save themselves; they are also captives, since they are slaves to God and to other people (Rom 6:15-23).⁴⁴ So Paul can say that the entire Mosaic law is summarized in one commandment—love your neighbor as yourself (Lev 19:18; Matt 19:19; 22:39; Mark 12:31, 33; Luke 10:27; Rom 13:9; James 2:8). He therefore directs them to "live by the Spirit" (5:16; literally, "walk by the Spirit"). The results of such walking are detailed in verses 22-26. The very first "fruit of the Spirit" Paul lists is love. It is the basic "fruit" or product of the Spirit. In a sense, the other fruits listed (joy, peace, patience, kindness, generosity, faithfulness, gentleness, and self-control) are applications of that love in human relationships. In 6:1-2, Paul extends his concern to those in the community who have transgressed. Those who have *not* transgressed are directed not to congratulate themselves on their good morality but rather to reach out to the transgressor.

In verses 11-18, Paul apparently takes the pen from the secretary and in his own hand writes the conclusion to the letter. As we have seen previously, he makes several more disparaging comments about his opponents (vss. 12, 13, 15, 17), in the midst of which he refers again to the cross of Jesus: "May I never boast of anything except the cross of our Lord Jesus Christ, by which the world has been crucified to me, and I to the world" (6:14). For Paul, the world's normal values have been turned upside down by the cross. And it is a "double" cross—a cross for Jesus and a cross for Paul. That double crucifixion results, once more, in freedom. It is freedom from being judged by the world's standards and thus, as in Galatians 5, the freedom to serve. Thus, he pronounces peace on "the Israel of God," a term that probably refers to all people (whether Judean or non-Judean) who trust in Paul's message of freedom.

Summary

Did the letter work? Perhaps we have a bit of data that points toward the letter's effectiveness in moving the Galatians to re-adopt Paul's gospel. In 1 Cor 16:1, he writes, "Now concerning the collection for the saints: you should follow the directions I gave to the churches of Galatia." The letter we have to the Galatians does not mention the collection, so 1 Corinthians must refer to another communication with the Galatians (via letter or messenger), most probably *after* he wrote the document we call Galatians. Thus, despite Paul's often crude language (or because

Galatians: Free to Be Children of God

I.	Salutation	1:1-5
II.	Expression of Astonishment and Confrontation	1:6-10
	A. Reason for Letter	1:6-7
	B. Conditional Curse	1:8-9
	C. Ironic Question and Answer	1:10
III.	Narration / Defense of Apostleship (Statement of Facts)	1:11—2:21
	A. Source of Gospel	1:11-12
	B. Early Ministry	1:13-24
	1. Pre-Christ	1:13-14
	2. Call and Early Mission (Part One)	1:15-17
	3. Early Mission (Part Two)	1:18-24
	C. Conference in Jerusalem	2:1-10
	D. Conflict in Antioch	2:11-14
	E. Thesis of Letter	2:15-21
IV.	Proofs of the Thesis	3:1—4:31
	A. Proof One: Experience	3:1-5
	B. Proof Two: Scripture (Abraham)	3:6-14
	C. Proof Three: Inheritance Law	3:15-18
	D. Discussion of the Place of the Law	3:19-25
	E. Proof Four: Church Tradition	3:26—4:11
	F. Proof Five: Narration of Paul's History with the Galatians	4:12-20
	G. Proof Six: Allegory	4:21-31
V.	Paraenesis	5:1—6:10
	A. Recommendation of Freedom / Warning against Accepting the Law	5:1-12
	B. Warning against the Flesh / Recommendation of the Spirit	5:13-26
	C. Miscellaneous Maxims	6:1-10
VI.	Conclusion	6:11-18

of it?), enough Galatians listened to him that he could take among them the collection for the church in Jerusalem.[45] At the same time, in his letter to Rome, he returns to many of the same themes and seems to modify the harsher approaches he took in Galatians.

In the letter to the Galatians, Paul has pulled out all the rhetorical stops at his disposal to argue his listeners into re-adopting the good news of Jesus he had originally proclaimed. His massive attack on the Judaizers is part of the defense he mounts in maintaining the legitimacy of his law-free gospel and of his call to be apostle.

Study Questions

1. Why is Paul so upset with the Galatians?
2. What does he want them to do, and what does he want them *not* to do?
3. Explain the words *justify / justification* and *make right / righteous / righteousness*. How for Paul does faith figure into the meaning of these words?
4. How does Paul use Abraham in Galatians?
5. What implications do you see in Galatians for Jewish-Christian dialogue—both positive implications and negative ones?
6. How do you see people today living out (or not living out) Paul's assertion that "there is no longer Jew or Greek, there is no longer slave or free, there is no longer male and female"?

Suggested Reading

Betz, Hans Dieter. *Galatians*. Hermeneia. Philadelphia: Fortress Press, 1979.
de Boer, Martinus C. *Galatians: A Commentary*. NTL. Louisville: Westminster John Knox, 2011.
Esler, Philip F. *Galatians*. New Testament Readings. New York: Routledge, 1998.
Martyn, J. Louis. *Galatians*. AB 33A. New York: Doubleday, 1997.
Matera, Frank J. *Galatians*. Sacra Pagina 9. Collegeville, MN: Liturgical, 1992.
Witherington, Ben, III. *Grace in Galatia: A Commentary on St. Paul's Letter to the Galatians*. Grand Rapids: Eerdmans, 1998.

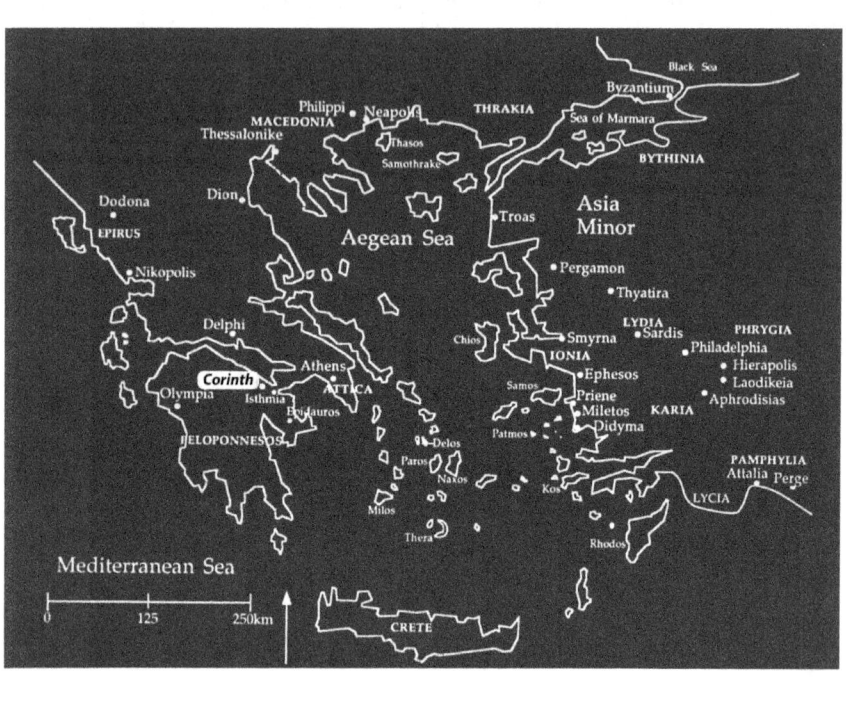

Chapter 8

1 Corinthians: Life in the Body

How Are New Believers to Live?

> Imagine being part of a group of twenty people gathered in the home of a wealthy person. You are there to sing God's praises and to learn. You live in an important city—Corinth, in the province of Achaia.[1] The past few weeks have been exciting but confusing. You recently came to believe that Jesus was God's chosen and sent one. But how are you to live now? The same as before? Freer? Or more restricted? Why, just today your neighbor invited you to go to the health spa connected with the temple of the god Asclepius. Should you go? Your small group of Christ-believers has talked about such questions. Elsewhere in town, other small groups of Christ-believers have come up with their answers, too. Your group leader announces that a letter has come from Paul, the founding missionary of the congregation. Maybe he will have some answers. After a few minutes, you hear these words: "Do you not know that your bodies are members of Christ? . . . For you were bought with a price; therefore glorify God in your body" (1 Cor 6:15a, 20).

Our imaginary first-century follower of Jesus is trying to live her life in the way God wants her to live. But within even the few house churches in Corinth, believers are coming up with different responses on how to live in their multicultural, pluralistic world, and the different views are starting to divide the Corinthian believers from each other. In response, Paul writes the letter we call 1 Corinthians. Together with 2 Corinthians, it forms the most extensive correspondence between Paul and one group of congregations to have survived antiquity. In this correspondence, Paul makes significant theological insights while dealing with the everyday problems his people are facing.[2]

Founding of the Congregation

In the letter itself, Paul makes only general comments about founding the congregation: "I planted, Apollos watered, but God gave the growth" (3:6). Based on Acts 18, Paul came to Corinth in the winter of 50–51 and stayed until the summer of 52, for a total of eighteen months (Acts 18:11). In Acts, we are told that he met fellow Christ-believing tentmakers Priscilla and Aquila, Judean believers recently expelled from Rome. Paul worked with them and supported himself (Acts 18:1-3; 1 Cor 4:12; 9:1-15). According to Acts, Paul spoke in the synagogue to both Judeans and Greeks. When opposition arose, he left the synagogue—only to move his ministry next door to the home of a God-fearer named Titius Justus. Many people believed and were baptized, including two synagogue officials, Crispus and Sosthenes (Acts 18:8, 17; 1 Cor 1:1, 14). Judean opposition remained strong enough, however, that Paul was hauled before the Roman official Gallio (Acts 18:12-17).[3] Shortly thereafter, Paul left Corinth (Acts 18:18).

Why Corinth?

Missionary work in Corinth helped Paul meet his objectives. First, as we have seen previously, Paul liked to set up shop in a large urban area. *Shop* included his practical need to earn a living, which, as a leatherworker, he could do much better in a city than in a village. Corinth, with a population of 70,000 to 80,000, provided that opportunity. In addition, the Isthmian Games (second in importance only to the Olympic Games) were held nearby every other year and, together with the flood of tourists who came to the games, would have provided business for a leatherworker. Other smaller games were also held. The constant flow of goods and people into this port city in general would have created business opportunities for itinerant artisans such as Paul, Priscilla, and Aquila.[4] By locating in this particular city, Paul also gained an important foothold in southern Greece.

Second, Corinth was a vibrant transfer point between the eastern and western portions of the empire, as well as between northern and southern Greece. It was located in the Peloponnesus, a peninsula south of the mainland of Greece and connected to it by a four-mile-wide isthmus. On the east side of the isthmus is the Aegean Sea; on the west is the Adriatic (or Ionian) Sea. Corinth controlled the isthmus and its two ports, Cenchreae and Lechaeum. To avoid the dangerous journey of six days and two hundred miles around the southern end of the peninsula, merchants transporting goods between Italy and Asia often took one of two steps: they would have their ship hauled across land from one port to the other, or they would unload the goods, move them across the isthmus, and reload them onto another ship.[5] Income from the shipping, taxes, and influx of people made Corinth a wealthy city.[6]

Such wealth would have been unthinkable two centuries earlier. During the spread of Roman power, the people of Achaia, led by Corinth, attacked Rome's Greek ally Sparta. The Romans responded in great force, and in 146 BCE, they destroyed the Achaian threat. Because of Corinth's crucial role, the Romans sold the city's inhabitants into slavery, looted the city, and all but destroyed it. In 44 BCE, Julius Caesar ordered the city refounded as a Roman colony with special Roman governing structures and privileges.[7] Original settlers were mainly his own veterans, freed slaves, and artisans and laborers. Settlers from the east quickly supplemented those resettled by Julius Caesar, and the great construction boom they witnessed lasted until the time of Paul. Corinth's trade connections, diverse population with many different origins and associations, and large numbers of visitors would have multiplied the ability of Paul's message to spread.

Third, Corinth served a symbolic function in Paul's strategy. As a Roman colony founded in Greece and as an international transfer point for goods, people, ideas, and religions, Corinth presented unusual opportunities and challenges for proclaiming the good news of Jesus in the multilingual, multiethnic Roman Empire. Barnett identifies in Paul's choice of Corinth a key part to the apostle's strategy: "It can be no accident that Paul positioned himself in Thessalonica, Corinth, and Ephesus, for they were bustling cities and formed a strategic triangle in the Aegean region, enabling the gospel to be spread along the busiest trading routes in the world."[8]

An international population also brought many religions to Corinth. Archaeological excavation and literary remains indicate devotion to Poseidon, Apollo, Hermes, Aphrodite, Asclepius, Dionysus, Demeter, Artemis of Ephesus, Roma, and the emperor. Thus, the Corinthians were exposed to a mix of Greek, Hellenistic-Oriental, and Roman religions.[9] Archaeological evidence may point, in addition, to a synagogue. The evidence is a fragmentary inscription that reads, "Synagogue of the Hebrews." Although initially dated to the time of Paul, the inscription is now assigned to the second century or even the fourth century CE.[10] Literary evidence, however, does point to a substantial Judean population in the refounded Corinth (Philo, *Embassy to Gaius* 281; Acts 18:4).

More disputed is the kind of worship connected with the temple of Aphrodite and with it the reputation of the city. The geographer Strabo called Corinth "the seat of sacred prostitution in the service of Aphrodite" and wrote that a thousand temple prostitutes served the needs of Aphrodite's devotees (Strabo, *Geography* 8.6.20). Harsh words were coined using the city name: "to act like a Corinthian" meant to practice fornication (Aristophanes, Fragment 354); a "Corinthian girl" meant a mistress or prostitute (Plato, *Republic* 404D). Countless commentaries have made much of the city's reputation for sexual excess, but more recently,

Fig. 8.1 An inscription indicating a "synagogue of the Hebrews" in Roman Corinth. Photo courtesy of the President and Fellows of Harvard College.

scholars have questioned the accuracy of the data. Aristophanes and Plato were associated with Athens, Corinth's rival, and Strabo wrote not about the refounded city but the original one; Aristophanes and Plato lived long before "Paul's" Corinth came into existence, and so they wrote about the original Corinth, too. Even regarding the earlier city, scholars doubt the truth of the temple prostitute claims, on both historical and archaeological grounds.[11] Corinth was certainly no model of virtue, but it was no worse than other ancient port-related cities. At the same time, that did mean patterns of behavior that would be offensive to someone of Paul's background and commitments.

Composition of the Congregation

The names of people listed in 1 Cor 16:15-17 and Rom 16:21-23 (the latter lists people in Corinth who are sending greetings to Rome) indicate that the groups of Christ-believers in Corinth included both Judeans and Gentiles, although Gentile names predominate. Paul's reference to circumcised believers (1 Cor 7:18) and his use of Israel's Bible (9:8-10; 10:1-13) point to Judean believers and to Gentiles who had previously become familiar with Judean teaching through association with the synagogue. However, the kinds of issues these early believers were struggling with were issues especially important among Gentiles. A good example is participation in pagan feasts (chapter 10). That particular issue, together with Paul's statement in 12:2 ("when you were pagans"),[12] gives us additional data: some of the believers were Gentiles with no previous connection to Judaism.

The people of the Pauline community in Corinth were also varied in their socioeconomic levels. Paul advises them,

> Consider your own call, brothers and sisters: not many of you were wise by human standards, not many were powerful, not many were of noble birth. But God chose what is foolish in the world to shame the wise; God chose what is weak in the world to shame the strong; God chose what is low and despised in the world, things that are not, to reduce to nothing things that are, so that no one might boast in the presence of God. (1:26-29)

Underneath the rhetorical structure, we can identify two statements about the socioeconomic makeup of the community. First, the majority of the people are not wise, powerful, or of noble birth.[13] But that means, second, that some are. When Paul at a later point in his life was in Corinth, he wrote believers in Rome. Among others in Corinth, Paul brought greetings from "Erastus the city treasurer," literally, the steward (*oikonomos*) of the city (Rom 16:23; see also Acts 19:22; 2 Tim 4:20). That title already indicates a person with a prominent public position, but in addition, an inscription has been found in Corinth with the name *Erastus* in it. The inscription honors an Erastus for having paid for the paving of a square east of the city's theater. The inscription is from the middle of the first century CE and gives Erastus the title of **aedile**. Generally there were two aediles at a time; they handled the city's revenue, streets, and public buildings and were somewhat comparable to contemporary city managers. In distinction from modern officials, however, the aedile had to be wealthy before entering office, which meant that he was the owner of property with cash at his disposal. Are the inscription's Erastus and Paul's Erastus the same? Probably so, since Erastus was not a common name, and we have no evidence of a second Erastus who was an official at Corinth.[14] We also encounter Chloe, who has slaves or employees traveling on her behalf (1:11; while Paul does not specifically identify her as a Christ-believer, she probably was) and Stephanas, the head of a household (1:16). Others of some standing include Crispus (1:14), who probably is the synagogue official of the same name in Acts 18:8.

Fig. 8.2 An inscription found near the theater of Dionysos in Corinth declares that Erastos, a public official, funded the pavement. Photo courtesy of the President and Fellows of Harvard College.

We need to be careful about terms such as *upper class* and *lower class*. In antiquity, the uppermost levels of society, together with their **retainers** (those who directly served the uppermost levels, often called **the elites**) amounted to perhaps 5 percent of the population. Everyone else socially was at the bottom.[15] Within that huge majority at the social bottom, though, there existed wide disparities in economic and educational levels.

Such disparities within this young Pauline community can help us understand some of the dynamics Paul and they faced. As we explore specific texts, we will see the impact of socioeconomic differences on problems regarding the Lord's Supper and meat sacrificed in pagan ceremonies. Perhaps the emphasis some believers placed on knowledge was related to a higher educational level, which in the first century generally meant a higher economic level. Betz and Mitchell may well be correct when they write that "in Corinth the Pauline mission had succeeded—seemingly for the first time—in winning converts from the better educated and cultured circles of a prosperous and cosmopolitan city."[16] At the same time, the educational task must have been daunting. Judeans and God-fearers knew the story of God's dealings with Israel. They also shared a common morality. While their move to being Christ-believers was a significant one, Gentiles with no Judean connections faced a more dramatic need for resocialization, in which they had to learn in light of Christ to view God, the world, and themselves in new ways.[17] The Corinthian believers were not always as able to move beyond their past worldviews as Paul wanted them to, and this provides part of the dynamic of our letter.

One more word about the composition of the congregations. Paul needed places for inquirers and baptized believers to meet. Synagogues and public buildings were rarely open to them. The vast majority of city people lived in apartment buildings that provided little space for gatherings. Wealthier people often lived in a villa (or *domus*) that included a dining room that could accommodate nine or ten people. When the couches were removed and the central courtyard was used, a given villa could handle forty to fifty people, with forty working better.[18] Stephanas (16:15-18) likely provided his villa to the community. Once the community of Christ-believers was larger than one villa could house, it had to meet in multiple places. This structure of "house churches" had at least two results. First, the patterns of socioeconomic distinctions symbolized by the wealthier person's villa could, when care was not taken, determine the interactions between and the practices of believers. Second, meeting in separate homes could encourage different groups to develop different practices, which may be part of what is going on in 1:12.[19]

Why Write Now?

Paul has received oral reports about divisions in the community from Chloe's "people" (slaves or employees; 1 Cor 1:11). The more immediate reason for writing is a letter he has received from Corinth (7:1).[20] But Paul also has received a delegation from Corinth (16:17). It is probable that the three men in the delegation (Stephanas, Fortunatus, and Achaicus) are waiting for Paul's letter to take back with them to Corinth.[21] It is even possible they brought with them the letter referred to in 7:1. With the three men waiting for his reply, Paul dictates 1 Corinthians.

What Issues Does Paul Need to Address?

Although the identity of who is raising which issue is unclear, two issues are of central importance in the letter. The first issue was spiritual elitism. Some Corinthian Christ-believers seemed very interested in the degree of spiritual attainment they had reached. In part reflecting their culture, they focused on Spirit-inspired, ecstatic speaking as the major sign of spiritual attainment. In such speaking, the believer experiences the Spirit overtaking his or her psyche and speaking through the believer's mouth in sounds that have a pattern but are different from any human language. The utterances need, in turn, to be translated and interpreted. Although Paul himself had this "gift of tongues" (14:18, also known as **glossolalia**), he did not want that gift to be understood as *the* gift of the Spirit above other gifts (12:4-11), and he had significant problems with believers who had the gift of glossolalia who thought they were better than others.

Another manifestation of spiritual elitism was overemphasis on wisdom. "Greeks desire wisdom," Paul writes (1:22). The desired wisdom was "insider" wisdom. It can be related in part to educational level, although ultimately the kind of wisdom that was attractive to the Corinthians is knowledge that comes from a sudden flash of insight. That "flash" gave them knowledge of who God was, who they were, what God wanted them to do, liberation from the power of this world, and a share in the heavenly life. *Knowledge*, as understood in Corinth, could be misused when it became another source of inappropriate distinction between believers (and so in 8:1, "knowledge puffs up").

The second issue was denial of life in the present earthly body. Believers were liable to two temptations. First, they could take Paul at his literal word that they were free of the Mosaic Law and conclude that they were free to live ethically in any way they wanted to, totally apart from the law (6:12a). Second, they could also look at the proclamation of Jesus and their resulting baptisms as indicating that there would be no resurrection in the future (15:12) but that in some sense they had already died and been resurrected and therefore were above the ethical restrictions of this world. At one level, some of the Corinthians saw themselves as spiritually "out of this world," with no meaningful ties to it (see Paul's sarcastic words in 4:8). They had lost what for Paul was the important distinction between *already* and *not yet*. "Already" followers of Jesus have a great deal: justification and reconciliation with God, baptism, the gift of the Spirit, the community of believers. But they do "not yet" have everything God will give them: resurrection, unambiguous experience of God, and perfection. Some Corinthians thought they had everything already now.

As a result, members of the community were involved in all sorts of immoral behavior (5:1; 6:15-16) and had been taking each other to secular courts of law (6:1-8). Others apparently mistrusted the physical body and sought rigorously to control it (7:1). Thus, inappropriate spiritualization of present life led to the misuse of individual bodies. The spiritualizing of life in Christ and the development of a spiritual elitism by some also had dire implications for the corporate body of the church. Not only did the claim to be better than others fracture the unity of the church body, so did inappropriate use of theological knowledge (8:1-13). Even the Lord's Supper could be destroyed by insensitivity to the social and economic realities of life in the physical body (11:17-22).

As previously indicated, the potential divisions within the larger Corinthian community may have been exacerbated by the fact that people needed to meet in smaller groups because of space considerations. Traditionally, scholars have read 1:12 as indicating not only smaller house gatherings but four different groups, each organized and with a clearly different understanding of the significance of Jesus and life lived in his name: "What I mean is that each of you says, 'I belong to Paul,' or 'I belong to Apollos,' or 'I belong to Cephas,' or 'I belong to Christ.'" It is quite possible that people are identifying too much with the missionary through whom they came to know Jesus or who had baptized them. That interpretation would explain why Paul expresses his thanks at having baptized only a few people (1:13-17). What about the Christ group? Perhaps that group was composed of

Fig. 8.3 The remains of a spacious dining hall from the sacred precinct of Demeter in Corinth. Diners would have reclined on cushions on the low benches around the walls as servants brought food and wine through the entrances. Photo courtesy of the President and Fellows of Harvard College.

people who saw themselves as more spiritual than others. Or perhaps it was meant to be ironic,[22] to show the absurdity of the first three groups: if you are so excited about who baptized you, why not claim that *Christ* did it?

Although some scholars have identified each of the groups with specific teachings Paul opposed,[23] most are content to admit that he does not distinguish between the teachings of the groups he mentions. In fact, he criticizes and deals with them as a unit. Frequently, all the people Paul opposes or at a minimum those in one group are labeled by modern students as Gnostic.[24] Indeed, what we have identified as the two major issues are often characteristic of what in the second century was called Gnosticism. At the same time, we do not have evidence in 1 Corinthians of the kind of mythological explanations typical of developed Gnosticism, so the most we can say is that Paul's opponents were "proto-Gnostics," people whose positions could easily develop into Gnosticism or whose views could be understood as Gnosticizing.[25] In any event, there are people in Corinth who see the death of Jesus and suffering in general as foolish and who in addition ignore the future resurrection of the body and the weaker sister or brother.

How Does Paul Approach Them?

Scholars frequently identify 1:10 as the thesis of the letter: "Now I appeal to you, brothers and sisters, by the name of our Lord Jesus Christ, that all of you be in agreement and that there be no divisions among you, but that you be united in the same mind and the same purpose." At a first level, then, 1 Corinthians is an extended plea for unity.[26] That means that Paul's interest is in the community life of these believers and not simply in individuals. While in the past, scholars have often assumed that Paul is dealing with a united church that is experiencing signs of a potential split, Betz and Mitchell have raised the possibility that Paul's goal was to unify several individual house churches.[27] In either case, the apostle admonishes and exhorts the Corinthians to live in ways that would express and embody that unity. The overall rhetorical category of the letter is **deliberative**, as Paul seeks to persuade the Corinthians to act in certain practical, everyday ways. A normal type of deliberative speech, in fact, was one that promoted concord or unity.[28] That identification is not to deny the presence of other rhetorical categories (in fact, the mixing of them was common). The argument of 1:10—4:21 and perhaps chapter 9 can be identified as **judicial rhetoric**,[29] and chapter 13 can be classified as **epideictic**.[30]

Paul's purpose in writing was not to encourage unity in the abstract but unity in the concrete circumstances of his hearers' common life in Christ. The specific way he approached those concrete circumstances was to seek to move his hearers to the point of interpreting their individual lives in community in light of the cross of Jesus Christ (1:18-31). Unity was to be a result of living under the authority of the cross, a cross that called them to holy living. The emphasis on the basic message of the cross is so central to 1 Corinthians that Thiselton labels the letter "the reproclamation of grace and the cross to Christian believers," necessitated by the struggle to reverse the listeners' original value systems.[31] The worth of Thiselton's suggestion is that it helps us view 1 Corinthians as something more than an abstract essay on unity and also as something more than miscellaneous responses to various points of dissension. In dealing with unity and points of dissension, Paul was also re-presenting his basic message about Jesus and the cross.

From Where and When Did Paul Write?

The question of where Paul wrote 1 Corinthians is easy to answer. Paul is in Ephesus: "But I will stay in Ephesus until Pentecost" (16:8). Pentecost is in the spring of the year. After he leaves Ephesus, he plans to travel through Macedonia (northern Greece) on his way to Corinth, where he may spend the next winter (16:5-7).

The date when Paul wrote is more difficult to pin down, since the only time reference in the letter is Paul's indication that he was writing before Pentecost—but in what year? Previously, we have placed Paul's initial stay in Corinth to the early 50s, with his appearance before Gallio in 52. Our chronology also showed Paul in Ephesus, with a departure date from there in 55. We thus have a range of 53 to 55 for the writing of 1 Corinthians.[32]

Final Introductory Questions

There are no doubts about the identity of the author of this letter: the author is Paul. Some have raised doubts, however, about whether Paul wrote as a single unified composition the document we call 1 Corinthians. In particular, scholars have identified what appear to be **literary seams** or breaks. A literary seam consists of a block of material that is a clearly defined unit and that seems out of place when compared with the material preceding and following it. Such seams can be indications either of material inserted into a previously existing document or signs of a document put together by an editor from originally independent documents or fragments of documents. The two most frequently mentioned possible seams are at 10:1-22 and 13:1-13. In addition, scholars have identified contradictions within 1 Corinthians or, at a minimum, indications of different writing situations (compare, for example, 1:11 and 11:18; in the former, Paul seems to know more than he indicates in the latter). To explain these phenomena, various scholars have developed theories that identify in 1 Corinthians a combining of originally separate letters.[33]

When we study 2 Corinthians, we will find the evidence for such partition theories in that letter to be much more compelling than similar theories for 1 Corinthians. The sheer variety of partition theories for 1 Corinthians and the fact that major proponents of such theories have sharply altered their theses over time do not inspire confidence. What appear to be instances of unevenness in the letter probably arise from two or perhaps three factors. First, 1 Corinthians is a lengthy document, likely dictated over a fairly long time. Second, Paul has received, as we have seen, different kinds of information at different times and is responding to a lengthy list of individual items. Third, the delegation of Stephanas, Fortunatus, and Achaicus (16:17) may have arrived during the dictation itself, causing Paul to integrate new data or concerns while producing the letter. Moreover, any partition theory has to explain the fact that in the thanksgiving section, Paul—as he does in his thanksgivings in general—outlines what he will discuss later. Thus, 1:4-6 prepare us for the discussion of spiritual gifts in chapters 12–14, and 1:7-8 signals the topics of resurrection and the return of Jesus in chapter 15.[34]

Therefore, the reading of 1 Corinthians that follows assumes a unified document—that is, one letter composed by Paul during an extended period of dictation.

Chapters 1–4

Paul begins 1 Corinthians with a salutation (1:1-3) and a thanksgiving (1:4-9) that are typical Paul, in that he uses these standard features to lay the groundwork for the rest of the letter. Mindful of his listeners' spiritual elitism, Paul sounds the following notes:

- They are "sanctified in Christ Jesus, called to be saints" (vs. 2). The terms *sanctify* and *saint* are based on the Greek word for *holy*. So the Corinthians are made holy. How? "In Christ Jesus." Therefore, they are called to *be* holy. As the letter unfolds, the recipients will learn that holiness has to do with life in the body.
- Paul gives thanks to God not because of the Corinthians' achievements but because of what God has given them. The basic gift is God's grace (vs. 4). The result of that gift is that "in every way" they "have been enriched in him," specifically "in speech and knowledge of every kind" (vs. 5). Therefore, they "are not lacking in any spiritual gift" (vs. 7). God is the one who is faithful, and God has called the Corinthians into the fellowship of Jesus (vs. 9). Thus, all weight is on what God has done for them, rather than on what they have done on their own.
- The day of the Lord Jesus Christ is coming (vs. 8); it is not already here. Thus, the claims of some to perfection and present-tense resurrection are false. The reference to the *day* also prepares us for Paul's return to that theme in 15:50-58.

As indicated earlier, 1:10 is the thesis or proposition of the letter. Paul in 1:11-17 outlines the immediate occasion for his letter: a report from "Chloe's people" that there are divisions among the Corinthians. In response to those divisions,[35] Paul addresses the Corinthians in an interactive way with a series of questions and statements designed to draw them into his instruction. The themes are introduced in verse 17, as Paul concludes a brief defense of his ministry in Corinth: "For Christ did not send me to baptize but to proclaim the gospel, and not with eloquent wisdom, so that the cross of Christ might not be emptied of its power." Paul is the preacher, the proclaimer. How does he carry out that task? "Not with eloquent wisdom," literally, not "with a wisdom of speech" (thus picking up the theme of speech from 1:5). And the reason he does not preach that way is that it would not be consistent with the message of the cross of Christ.

Reading the next passage, we can imagine Paul taking a deep breath before he begins verse 18 and not coming up for air again until he reaches the end of verse 25. In this tightly constructed section, Paul lays out a "theology of the cross," explaining that God is known best not in God's power but in the apparent weakness and powerlessness of the cross of Jesus.[36] From the perspective of those who are not Christ-believers, the cross is both the height of foolishness and the depth of weakness. For Paul, in contrast, the crucifixion of Jesus, ironically, exhibits both the power and the true wisdom of God. "For Jews demand signs and Greeks desire wisdom, but we proclaim Christ crucified, a stumbling block to Jews and foolishness to Gentiles, but to those who are the called, both Jews and Greeks, Christ the power of God and the wisdom of God" (1:22-24). Paul thus sets God's approach against that of those in Corinth who claim to be eloquent and wise.

He applies that insight to the Corinthians themselves in 1:26-31. If the proper standard of evaluation were wisdom, power, and status, they would be excluded, but in fact, God has chosen them in a way that turns upside down humanity's system of hierarchy.

In chapter 2, he turns to himself and his ministry as illustrations of how God works through weakness and lack of human wisdom: "I decided to know nothing among you except Jesus Christ, and him crucified. And I came to you in weakness and in fear and in much trembling" (2:2-3). That message is indeed a message of wisdom (2:6-13)—God's wisdom—but by their actions, the Corinthians have shown that they are not yet mature enough for it (2:14-16). For that reason, Paul confronts them in chapter 3: "And so, brothers and sisters, I could not speak to you as spiritual people, but rather as people of the flesh, as infants in Christ" (3:1).[37] So instead of being already resurrected, as some believed, the Corinthians are thoroughly enmeshed in the flesh, and instead of being mature believers, they are still infants.

In 3:5-15, Paul instructs them on how the church is built. Only God brings about growth (3:7). In verses 16-17, Paul makes sure that the Corinthians understand that the church is something different from the religious associations and social clubs they are used to: "Do you not know that you are God's temple and that God's Spirit dwells in you? If anyone destroys God's temple, God will destroy that person. For God's temple is holy, and you are that temple." The *you* is plural. So "you together, you as the community of Christ-believers are the temple of God" in whom God's Spirit dwells.[38]

In chapter 4, Paul defends his understanding of what an apostle is over against the claims of the Corinthians that they already have all of God's gifts. He ironically—and perhaps a bit sarcastically—points to his own sufferings and to his foolishness and weakness as an apostle (themes from chapter 1 again) as opposed to the greatness and richness the Corinthians think they possess (4:8-13). Paul opposes their theology of glory with his theology of the cross applied to the everyday life of Christ-believers.[39]

Paul does not leave them there. He goes on to admonish them to take him as an example and in their behavior to become imitators of him (4:16).[40]

Chapters 5-7

In chapters 5, 6, and 7, Paul addresses four divisive situations. In each case, he helps the Corinthians draw boundaries by means of their behavior. He is responding to both oral reports (5:1-6:20) and written reports (7:1-40, although some commentators think that already in 6:12, Paul begins addressing what the Corinthians have written him).

Chapter 5 deals with a man who is living with his father's wife, as well as addressing the general question of what to do with immoral people. The specific situation is not incest between a man and his biological mother, most likely, but sexual relations with his stepmother, who is either the widow of the man's deceased father or, less likely, is divorced from him. Such a sexual liaison was prohibited in Judean and Greek cultures. It probably was justified by the man on the basis of a radical separation between life in the Spirit and his existence in the body. Paul asserts every ounce of authority he can in pronouncing judgment on the man and excluding him from the community of believers (5:1-5). His expulsion has two goals: protection of the young Christ-believing community (5:6-13) and eventual salvation of the offender (5:5).

In 6:1-11, Paul discusses another divisive matter: the awkward situation that arises when one believer sues another. His counsel is judgment within the community itself, if judgment is necessary, or, preferably, absorbing the wrong (6:5, 7).

In 6:12-20, Paul returns to sexual morality, this time to relations with a prostitute. As indicated in the NRSV, Paul is probably quoting a slogan in verse 12 and commenting on it: "'All things are lawful for me,' but not all things are beneficial. 'All things are lawful for me,' but I will not be dominated by anything." Although similar slogans can be traced to the philosophical movement of Stoicism, the version of the saying found in 6:12 may be an actual quotation from Paul and/or a misappropriation of what he had said during his eighteen-month stay in Corinth. Theoretically, Christ-believers have been released from the Law of Moses as an absolute set of demands. It appears that some in Corinth have concluded that "anything goes." Paul qualifies the slogan with two comments of his own. First, "Not all things are beneficial" or helpful. And second, "I will not be dominated [mastered] by anything." He gives two examples: food and prostitution. He also introduces the concept of *body / sōma*:[41] "The body is meant not for fornication but for the Lord, and the Lord for the body" (vs. 13b). "Fornication" translates the Greek word *porneia* (sexual immorality). It and related words occur in 5:1, 9, 10, 11; 6:9, 15, 16, 18; 7:2.

If the body is for the Lord and the Lord is for the body, the body must be very important—despite the apparent insistence of some that the body was at best a momentary inconvenience.[42] In verse 14, Paul moves suddenly to resurrection. He does not use the term *body* in that verse, but the clear implication is this: just as God gave Jesus a resurrection body, so God will also give believers resurrection bodies (see 15:20-23 for a more specific statement of that argument).

Paul's discussion is not only future oriented; it is also rooted in the present. And so he says, "Do you not know that your bodies are members of Christ?" (vs.15a). Since the body belongs to the Lord (vs. 14), the individual bodies of the believers are part of the body of Christ (for more on that image read 12:13-31). Therefore, what the individual believer does is not a matter of individual morality but is an action that affects the totality of the community. Consequently, sexual union with a prostitute is forbidden, both for the sake of the individual and for the good of the community (vss. 15b-18). Thus, theoretically, "all things are lawful" in **Torah**-less freedom for Christ-believers, but not all things are helpful to the community and to the individual. Moreover, to become enslaved to a desire is to deny the freedom in Christ that the believer has been given.

Paul concludes his argument with a reference to the cross of Christ: "Or do you not know that your body is a temple of the Holy Spirit within you, which you have from God, and that you are not your own? For you were bought with a price; therefore glorify God in your body" (vss. 19-20). The prostitute, of course, is one who is bought with a price. Believers have been bought, too, but the purchase price for them is the life of Jesus. Because of that purchase price, "*therefore* glorify God in your body." The body—both individual bodies and the body of the Christ-believing community—is not, obviously, unimportant for Paul. Indeed, how one uses the body determines whether or not one gives glory to God. Life in the body is for Paul of extreme importance—which is in part why he argues in chapter 15 for the resurrection of the body.

The final complex of potentially divisive issues in chapters 5–7 is a series of topics, most of which relate to marriage. At the beginning of the chapter, Paul refers to the letter he has received from Corinth: "Now concerning the matters about which you wrote" (7:1a). The words *now concerning / peri de* have generally been taken by students of 1 Corinthians as each in turn introducing a topic from the letter Paul has received (7:1, 25; 8:1; 12:1; 16:1, 12). While that is definitely the case in 7:1, the phrase is used in other Greek letters of Paul's era to indicate a shift in topic or to signal that the author was responding to an oral report, as well as signaling an answer to a letter. Thus, the easily assumed structure that in the first part of the letter Paul is dealing with oral reports and starting at 7:1 he is answering only written questions may be simpler than the reality (for that matter, in 11:18, Paul is still responding to oral reports).

Although the initial portion of chapter 7 has often been understood to be a ringing endorsement of male dominance in marriage as well as of lifelong celibacy, the passage moves in quite different directions. After the introduction to the list of written topics to which he will respond, Paul states, "It is well for a man not to touch a woman." It is significant that the NRSV places that statement in quotation marks to indicate that the editors understand it as a slogan that Paul is quoting from the Corinthians themselves. Some in that community of believers are counseling sexual abstinence, but not Paul. Now indeed, as the chapter continues to develop, "in view of the impending crisis, it is well for you to remain as you are" (7:26). "The impending crisis" is the near end of the world and the suffering and temptations that will accompany it. With that horizon in mind, Paul advises neither to divorce nor to marry—at least the latter is his ideal for single people (vs. 27). There is nothing wrong or sinful in marrying (vs. 28), but because "the appointed time has grown short," any change of status is to be avoided, including the complications of marriage.

In a sense, what Paul says later in the chapter emphasizes the positive opinion he has of marriage at the beginning of the chapter. "Each man should have his own wife and each woman her own husband" (vs. 2) expresses the fundamental principles of monogamy: equality and reciprocity. Those principles, in turn, are expressed in verses 3-5: the husband is duty bound to grant his wife "her conjugal rights," that is, an intimate sexual relationship. In Paul's time, one would have expected the opposite, that the wife was to please the husband, which indeed Paul does advise, but each is to give sexual access to the other. In a world in which men were often reared to seek sexual pleasure outside marriage and to engage in relations with their wives only for the production of legal heirs, the ideal Paul holds up moves marriage to a different level. He goes on in verse 4 to make a statement that any Greco-Roman male would affirm: "the wife does not have authority over her own body, but the husband does." But—utilizing again the principles of equality and reciprocity and going counter to circum-Mediterranean culture—Paul continues, "likewise the husband does not have authority over his own body, but the wife does." Sexual abstinence, in turn, can have a place within marriage (vs. 5), but only under carefully controlled conditions: the couple must agree together, the time of abstinence must be limited, the abstinence must have a purpose, and the couple must plan to reconnect sexually. Instructive, too, is the language with which he introduces abstinence within marriage: "Do not deprive one another." *Deprive* has the basic meaning of *rob* or *steal*; so "do not steal the physical part of marriage from each other."

Further, as noted in chapter 4's textbox "Did Paul Have a Wife?" in the language Paul uses in verse 8, he identifies with those whose spouses have died; he is not talking about lifelong celibacy.

In addition to the eschatological horizon of the rest of the chapter (Jesus is to return soon), Paul operates from two other commitments. First, he states a basic principle regarding social position: "Let each of you lead the life that the Lord has assigned, to which God called you. This is my rule in all the churches. . . . Let each of you remain in the condition in which you were called. In whatever condition you were called, brothers and sisters, there remain with God" (7:17, 20, 24). He initially applies the principle to circumcision and slavery: "Was anyone at the time of his call already circumcised? Let him not seek to remove the marks of circumcision. Was anyone at the time of his call uncircumcised? Let him not seek circumcision" (v. 18). The statement about slavery is less clear. The NRSV expands verse 21: "Were you a slave when called? Do not be concerned about it. Even if you can gain your freedom, make use of your present condition now more than ever." The major alternative is indicated in a footnote in the NRSV (in italics): "Even if you can gain your freedom, *avail yourself of the opportunity.*" The ambiguity comes from the Greek. A very literal translation reads, "But if indeed you are able to become free, rather use." The first translation implies that a person ought not to change his or her status as a slave; the second implies that a slave should take the opportunity to become free. Bartchy has argued that neither is the case, since gaining freedom or accepting it was generally not up to the slave. He argues that what Paul is saying is that a freed slave was to "use" the new identity in Christ to which the person had been called (vs. 17) to glorify God; *that* status was more fundamental than any status the culture could give.[43]

Second, Paul has obvious concerns in chapter 7 with how believers use their bodies. That concern is consistent with the rest of the letter to Corinth.

8:1—11:1

In 8:11—11:1, Paul comments twice on a problem that seems remote to us: food sacrificed to idols. The problem was, however, a very real one for the Corinthians, and the principles Paul worked out in addressing it are instructive.

In ancient Greco-Roman cities, the only meat that could be purchased had been offered to pagan gods. Part of it was eaten in sacred meals, and the rest was sold in the market. Persons who believed in Jesus were faced with a dilemma. If they ate meat, did they by that action show support for the gods or indicate that they believed in them? And if they did not eat such meat, how could they participate in the social and economic life of the city? What, for example, should Christ-believing businesspeople do when meat was placed in front of them at a dinner party? Poorer people—the large majority of the population—did not need to think things through in so refined a way, because usually they could not afford meat anyway. The only time they ate meat was when it was distributed at a public festival. And at that point, the same questions arose.[44]

In approaching the topic of food offered to idols, Paul uses a simple structure, which is an example of **chiasm**, or reverse parallelism:

A. Food offered to idols (8:1-13)
B. Positive example: Paul himself (9:1-27)
B^1. Negative example: the generation that wandered in the wilderness (10:1-13)
A^1. Food offered to idols (10:14—11:1)

In 8:1, Paul identifies the topic: "now concerning food sacrificed to idols." He immediately quotes what is probably a slogan being used by some of the Corinthians: "We know that 'all of us possess knowledge.'" Knowledge, of course, was both a special interest and a special claim of Corinthian believers. Paul qualifies that slogan much as he did the slogan of 6:12. "Knowledge," Paul writes, "puffs up, but love builds up." Against the spiritual elitists who merely want to be puffed up with their knowledge, Paul places a force that builds, and builds solidly, the concept of love. The love that he writes about and to which he will turn again in chapter 13 is not physical or romantic love, family love, or friendship love. Greek has a different word for each of those kinds of love. The word Paul chooses is *agapē*, which is a love directed to the other and the needs of the other. Paul's ethic is a love ethic, as indicated later in the chapter. But before he reaches that point in his presentation, he reminds us that the one who loves God is known by God (8:3). That is, knowing is not nearly as important as *being known* by God.

In 8:4, Paul enunciates what he as well as many of the Corinthians believe is the right knowledge: idols do not exist, and the only God is the God of Israel. With that basic theological knowledge, believers in Christ are free to eat whatever food is presented them, because they know that there is no reality behind the idols. But not everyone has that correct theological knowledge (vs. 7), so Paul is concerned that the Corinthians not misuse their knowledge to harm others who lack the same level of insight (vss. 9-12). Paul limits the ethical freedom of the Corinthians by love for the sister or brother in Christ: "Therefore, if food is a cause of their falling, I will never eat meat, so that I may not cause one of them to fall" (vs. 13). Thus, a love ethic does not mean that believers can act in any way they want. Freedom is limited by love for the other. In chapter 9, Paul presents himself as a positive example of one who limits his freedom for the sake of the ministry to which he is called. Specifically, he has put aside his right as an apostle to financial support, so that no obstacle would be placed in the way of the good news of Jesus (9:3-7, 12, 18).

In 10:1-13, Paul places a negative example over against his positive example. The negative example is the generation of the people of Israel that escaped slavery in Egypt (the book of Exodus). Even though they had experienced in dramatic ways God's saving activities (1 Cor 10:1-4), they earned God's wrath because they turned from God to worship an idol, the golden calf (Exodus 32), as well as engaging in other excesses. Through that negative example, Paul warns the Corinthians to be wary of the temptation to worship idols.

That leads to his second discussion of food offered to idols (10:14—11:1). In a view that the syncretistic world of the first century could not appreciate, Paul argues that participation in the Lord's Supper and participation in the worship of idols are mutually exclusive (vss. 15-22). In verses 25-30, he applies his insights to three specific situations:

- "Eat whatever is sold in the meat market without raising any question on the ground of conscience" (vs. 25).
- "If an unbeliever invites you to a meal and you are disposed to go, eat whatever is set before you without raising any question on the ground of conscience" (vs. 27).
- "But if someone says to you, 'This has been offered in sacrifice,' then do not eat it, out of consideration for the one who informed you, and for the sake of conscience—I mean the other's conscience, not your own" (vss. 28-29).

He states the basis for those directives in verse 23: "'All things are lawful,' but not all things are beneficial. 'All things are lawful,' but not all things build up." Much of this language has already occurred in 6:12. In chapter 10, Paul applies it in this way: believers know that idols do not exist, so they are free to eat food that has been part of a pagan ceremony. But behavior that is theologically correct ("'all of us possess knowledge'"; 8:1) can be misinterpreted and therefore be harmful and not build up others. As a missionary, Paul is keenly aware of how easy it is to tear people down and how hard it is to build them up. He concludes this section of advice and instruction with a call to imitate him, as he imitates Christ, specifically in acting in ways that work for the salvation of others (10:31—11:1).

11:2-34

In the fourth section of advice and instruction, Paul delves into two more issues that have potential for dividing the Corinthian community: gender-related dress and roles (11:2-16) and the Lord's Supper (11:17-34). The first issue is very complicated. Paul tells both women and men what to wear, and he draws a comparison between Christ as the head of every male, the husband as the head of his wife, and God as the head of Christ (11:3).

Two keys may help open the interpretive lock to this section. The first key is the suggestion of Robin Scroggs that the word used here as *head* or *authority* (*kephalē*) actually should be understood as *source*.[45] He points to many examples of the use of *kephalē* as meaning *source*, such as the source of a river. In addition, in verses 8 and 12, Paul discusses the relationship of female and male in terms of origin or source.

The second interpretive key is the recognition that women are to have their heads covered while they are praying or prophesying. The word for *unveiled* in verses 5 and 13 can refer to loose or unbound hair. By loosening her hair in public, a woman was, in essence, confessing to adultery. The result was that, technically speaking, her head should be shaved (Num 5:18 / LXX; see the strange discussion in 1 Cor 11:6). A woman's loose hair outside the privacy of the home was a sign of uncleanness and ritual defilement. Given that perspective, Paul naturally advised women to wear their hair bound up when praying and prophesying. And note that the women are praying and prophesying; that is, they are leading worship in the Christ-believing community (a "right" for which Paul does not need to argue; he simply assumes it). The issue is only how the female leader should present herself.

Males are under the opposite restriction: they must have their heads *un*covered. Why? In the Greco-Roman world, men normally did not cover their heads, but to indicate piety, especially during prayer and sacrifice, they lifted their togas over the backs of their heads. Augustus Caesar is often represented that way in statues when he is depicted in his priestly role. Paul wants to separate Christ-believing male leaders from their pagan male counterparts. So both women and men are under restrictions regarding how best to present themselves when leading the community in worship.

In verse 17, which starts his instruction on the Lord's Supper, Paul begins with a negative evaluation: "Now in the following instructions I do not commend you, because when you come together it is not for the better but for the worse." The "coming together" is for worship and the eating of the Lord's Supper. What are they doing that has Paul so upset?

Basically, the Corinthians are celebrating the Lord's Supper in such a way that they are denying the very body of Christ that the Supper is meant to embody and sustain (vs. 29). The delicate question of how to follow Jesus and still remain in the Greco-Roman world—the same kind of issue that elsewhere in 1 Corinthians has been engaged regarding knowledge, sexual behavior, and food sacrificed to idols—underlies the specifics of the problem. In Greco-Roman culture, dinner parties or banquets were often organized around socioeconomic distinctions. Seating was assigned to honor those with whom the host felt the closest relationship. The farther away from the host, the less honored the guest was. Even the menu varied, with the social equals of the host eating the best food, while others were given more modest fare. The problem could also in part have been physical. A wealthy host would have received into his or her *domus* or villa all members of the Christ-believing community, but given the space limitations of even expensive homes, the host would have been able to entertain in the dining room only a portion of the congregation—likely those of the same socioeconomic level as the host—while excluding poorer people and slaves.[46]

The Corinthians have apparently brought the graphic socioeconomic distinctions of their culture into the celebration of the central meal of the church: "For when the time comes to eat, each of you goes ahead with your own supper, and one goes hungry and another becomes drunk" (vs. 21). In the potluck meal that included their celebration of the Lord's Supper, people brought food to share. Given the composition of the congregation some people could afford to bring more and better food, while others could bring little. In addition, the people who could control their schedules arrived before those working for others, including slaves, could arrive. Instead of waiting for the needy to come, the earlier arrivals ate what they had brought, leaving nothing to share. That attitude denied what the Lord's Supper was about, so Paul can say in verse 20, "When you come together, it is not really to eat the Lord's supper." Their insistence on maintaining society's distinctions was destroying both the meal and their corporate life as Christ's body (vss. 2, 29).

In response, Paul not only refuses to commend or praise them (vs. 22), he also reminds them of the words of Jesus that instituted the meal (vss. 23-26). There are five elements in what Paul reports:

1. He is handing on a tradition received from the Lord. The words *received* and *handed on* are technical terms for the reception and transmission of a tradition.
2. The tradition originates in the final meal Jesus had with his disciples, "on the night when he was betrayed," that is, the night when Judas Iscariot

led officials to the Garden of Gethsemane, where Jesus was arrested (Matt 26:47-56; Mark 13:43-52; Luke 22:47-54; John 18:1-12).
3. The tradition includes two actions by Jesus. The first is his taking a loaf of bread, giving thanks, breaking it, and interpreting the bread in relationship to himself: "This is my body that is for you. Do this in remembrance of me."
4. The second action is Jesus' saying over the cup, "This cup is the new covenant in my blood. Do this, as often as you drink it, in remembrance of me."
5. The tradition—or Paul—interprets the actions of the meal as repeated by Christ-believers to be the proclamation of the death of Jesus until he comes again.[47]

In the next paragraph, he applies to the Corinthians insights from this earliest written account of the Lord's Supper.[48] Casual eating of the Lord's Supper is dangerous: anyone who eats it in that way will have to answer to God (vs. 27). For that reason, appropriate self-examination is needed before taking part in the meal (vs. 28), and indeed judgment results for those "who eat and drink without discerning the body" (vs. 29). Over the centuries, the discerning of the body has often been understood to refer to a proper understanding of the presence of Christ in the meal, but within the context of Paul's advice, it also refers to the ability to identify in the community of believers itself the body (of Christ; on body, see also 12:12-31). And in that community, societal distinctions are not to carry the weight they do in the wider society.

Thus, in a somewhat different but still related way, 11:17-34 deals with the same theme of "life in the body" that has run throughout the letter. The difference is that in this case, Paul's interest is in how individual bodies of Christ-believers live as members of the corporate body of the church. Chapter 12, in its own way, will continue to deal with significant aspects of that theme.

Chapters 12–14

In a manner similar to the structure he used in 8:1—11:1, Paul divides the central topic of his fifth section of advice and instruction into two parts: 12:1-31a and 14:1-40 both address the divisive issue of spiritual gifts. In between those two sections is an extended example of how to live (12:31b—13:13).

The specific issue regarding spiritual gifts that Paul needs to address is the weight some in the community have assigned to certain of the spiritual gifts and how that weighted evaluation causes divisions. In verses 4-6, Paul begins his response with a long, carefully constructed sentence:

Now there are varieties of gifts, but the same Spirit;
and there are varieties of services,[49] but the same Lord;
and there are varieties of activities, but it is the same God who activates all of them in everyone.

Paul's point is this: the source of all spiritual gifts, services, and activities is the same. Therefore recipients of a specific gift or ministry need to recall that God provides the gift or ministry, not the persons themselves; for that reason, it is inappropriate to claim that one manifestation of the Spirit is better than another. Indeed, "To each is given the manifestation of the Spirit for the common good" (vs. 7). The gifts or ministries are not the private preserves of individual believers but are given to specific persons in order that they be used for the entire community.

In verses 8-10, Paul details some of those specific gifts. It is of note that the first two gifts are wisdom and knowledge, which were favorites of the Corinthians. While there appears to be a certain democratization of the gifts, it is not without purpose that "various kinds of tongues" and "the interpretation of tongues" are at the bottom of the list—the very opposite of the Corinthians' ranking. "Tongues," as we have seen previously, refers to the gift of the Spirit in which the Spirit speaks through the mouth of the believer in words that are not immediately understandable and must therefore be interpreted. It is that gift that the Corinthians have evaluated more highly than other gifts.[50] The way Paul structures verses 8-10 is a subtle reminder that no one person has all the gifts, and verse 11 summarizes the Spirit's initiative in choosing who receives which gift: "All these are activated by one and the same Spirit, who allots to each one individually just as the Spirit chooses."

The need for the differently gifted members of the church to share their Spirit-given gifts with each other is pictured by Paul through use of the somewhat humorous image of the body:[51] "For just as the body is one and has many members, and all the members of the body, though many, are one body, so it is with Christ. . . . Indeed, the body does not consist of one member but of many" (vss. 12, 14). Therefore, the foot cannot withdraw from the body because it is not a hand, nor the ear because it is not the eye (vss. 15-16). Indeed, what if the whole body were an eye or an ear (vs. 17)? It could not function. And so, "there are many members, yet one body" (vs. 20).

In verse 27, Paul applies the body image to the followers of Jesus: "Now you are the body of Christ and individually members of it." Paul thus uses again the body language that has been so prominent in this letter. Here he uses *body* in a corporate way: the individual bodies of believers together with each other are the earthly, present-tense collective *body of Christ*. The members of the body are different and unique, yet all are needed and united in the one body.[52]

In verses 28-30, Paul outlines another list of gifts (notice again where speaking in tongues appears). But in vs. 31, he promises to show them "a still more excellent way."

The "still more excellent way" Paul talks about in chapter 13 is the way of love. The Greek word for love is the same word we encountered earlier, *agapē*. *Agapē* is self-giving love that does not base its love on how lovable the one being loved is. In verses 1-3, Paul qualifies all other qualities on the basis of that love:

> If I speak in the tongues of mortals and of angels, but do not have love, I am a noisy gong or a clanging cymbal. And if I have prophetic powers, and

understand all mysteries and all knowledge, and if I have all faith, so as to remove mountains, but do not have love, I am nothing. If I give away all my possessions, and if I hand over my body so that I may boast, but do not have love, I gain nothing.

In verse 1, Paul meets head-on those who overevaluate speaking in tongues. "Speaking in the tongues of angels" is another way to talk about glossolalia. Without love—love that is patient, kind, not envious or boastful or arrogant or rude (vss. 4-5)—speaking in tongues is merely noise. In verse 2, Paul qualifies the insight and knowledge so important to his listeners, and in verse 3, the asceticism attractive to some (see 7:1). All of these gifts, important as they are, will eventually end. But "love never ends" (vs. 8). How then should Christ-believers use their gifts? As expressions of love. And that love is based on God's love shown in the self-giving love of Christ, who died for people not because they were good but because he loved them (Rom 5:6, 8).

In chapter 14, Paul returns to the specific gift of speaking in tongues. He evaluates that gift highly and indicates that he himself speaks in tongues (vs. 18). But he is also aware of the potentially divisive nature of speaking in tongues. The gift he emphasizes is that of **prophecy**, which is the application of God's word to life today. He contrasts the two gifts in verse 4: "Those who speak in a tongue build up themselves, but those who prophesy build up the church." Once more, Paul mentions the theme of building up (8:1, 10; 10:23; also 14:5). There is nothing wrong with being eager for spiritual gifts, but the purpose of excelling in them is to build up the church (vss. 12, 26).

A much-disputed passage runs from verse 33b through the end of verse 36 and is printed in the NRSV in parentheses. It says women are to be silent in the churches and are not to speak, as the law has indeed taught. It is possible that, since Mediterranean women usually did not have the right to speak in an assembly, they may have been abusing that right granted to them by Paul. For many interpreters, the conflict between 14:33b-36 and the leadership role of women in chapter 11 is, however, so great that there seems no way to reconcile the two passages, in part because no similar passage is found elsewhere in the undisputed letters. Might the section be an **interpolation**? The following reasons are cited to support that possibility:

- The theology is different from elsewhere in the undisputed letters.
- There is a concentration in the passage of unusual language.[53]
- The verses disturb the flow of the passage's argument.
- Part of the manuscript tradition puts verses 34-35 after verse 40, indicating confusion in antiquity as to the place of these verses.
- The section views women in a way quite close to the deuteropauline 1 Tim 2:11-12.
- It is hard to imagine Paul appealing to the law the way verse 34 does.

The conclusion that the section is an interpolation is held by a wide range of scholars.[54]

Chapter 15

In chapter 15, Paul begins his final section of advice and instruction. The topic is resurrection. Some in the church, it appears, believed that they had already been raised, probably at their baptisms. For them, any talk of a *future* resurrection seemed strange.[55]

Paul sets up the topic by quoting a **creed**, or confession of faith: "For I handed on to you as of first importance what I in turn had received" (vs. 3a). We already saw when we looked at 11:23 that the language of *handing on* and *receiving* is used for the transfer of formal tradition from one person to another. In this case, the tradition is a creed: "that Christ died for our sins in accordance with the scriptures, and that he was buried, and that he was raised on the third day in accordance with the scriptures, and that he appeared to Cephas, then to the twelve" (vss. 3b-5). To this creed that predated him, Paul adds an expanded list of resurrection witnesses in verses 6-8.

There are two foci in this creed. First, Jesus died and was buried. Jesus was dead. He was not a victim of a coma or drug-induced sleep. Second, this same Jesus was raised on the third day. Paul does not argue for the truth of that statement; he simply asserts it by means of the creed. The **Pharisees** also believed in a resurrection that would occur at the end of time. Paul, according to his own dictation, was a member of that group (Phil 3:5). Since he as a Pharisee believed in an end-time resurrection and since Jesus had already been resurrected, the end-time must in some fashion be present in the world already now. The Corinthians most likely built their view on that basic observation. What they did not recognize was the other part of Paul's approach: the not yet. *Already* Jesus has been raised, but believers have *not yet* been raised. For all but Jesus, resurrection is a future-time concept.

The difficulties some people had with Paul's view of resurrection were compounded by Paul's understanding that Christ was raised *from the dead*. "Now if Christ is proclaimed as raised from the dead, how can some of you say there is no resurrection of the dead?" (vs. 12). The Greek reads more literally, "Now if Christ is proclaimed as raised from *dead ones*." So *dead* is not some abstract concept but the totality of dead humanity. Out of all those who have died, out of all of those whose dynamic bodies have become corpses, only Christ has been resurrected. This may well be part of what some Corinthians do not like. First, they do not like the idea that only Christ has been raised. What about them? Have they not already been raised? ("No," says Paul.) Furthermore, they do not like resurrection of a dead person. They do not want Jesus to have a resurrection *body*, and they do not want resurrection bodies either. For them, the body was not important, and they could not imagine life eternal with a body, of all things.[56]

In verses 13-19, Paul lays out the problems for the message about Christ if there is no resurrection from the dead. He also ties closely together the resurrection of Jesus and the resurrection of believers.

In verse 20, Paul begins his response. He introduces two major ideas: first, that Christ is the first fruits, and second, that there will be a final victory:

> But in fact Christ has been raised from the dead, the first fruits of those who have died. For since death came through a human being, the resurrection of the dead has also come through a human being; for as all die in Adam, so all will be made alive in Christ. But each in his own order: Christ the first fruits, then at his coming those who belong to Christ. Then comes the end, when he hands over the kingdom to God the Father, after he has destroyed every ruler and every authority and power. For he must reign until he has put all his enemies under his feet. The last enemy to be destroyed is death. (vss. 20-26)

Christ is the first fruits. First fruit is an agricultural concept that goes far back in Israel's history. At the time of the annual harvest, the first part of the harvest was to be offered to God.[57] Thus, the first fruits represented the whole harvest. So Jesus is the first fruit. First fruits promise or provide a sort of down payment that, in fact, there will be later fruit. In that sense, the resurrection of Christ, for Paul, is a kind of down payment that indeed believers will be raised. And when will they be resurrected? Verse 23 says, "at his coming." So once more, we are at the *parousia*, the return of Jesus, the day of the Lord (1 Thess 4:13—5:11). Thus, there is an order to time: Christ's resurrection, then ongoing human life, then the return of Christ, and then the resurrection of believers. So obviously, the Corinthians have not been resurrected yet.

And what else will happen when Jesus returns? The final victory will occur "after he has destroyed every ruler and every authority and power" (vs. 24). And "the last enemy to be destroyed is death" (vs. 26). This is the future and final triumph of God.

In verses 35-49, Paul highlights the *dis*continuity between present bodies and resurrected bodies. The present bodies are physical. They decay, wear out, and perish. Resurrected bodies, in contrast, are spiritual bodies. They do not decay, wear out, or perish. And above all, in their new resurrected bodies, believers are conformed to the image of "the man of heaven" (vs. 49), who is, of course, Jesus.

What is a "spiritual" body, the language Paul uses in this section? A spiritual body is a body that is ruled by the Spirit. That is, as opposed to present life in the body, in which people continually struggle between being ruled by the Spirit and being ruled by the forces of evil, the resurrected body is governed totally by God's Spirit and therefore is a spiritual body.[58]

Paul concludes his response with further reflections on the resurrected body and the final end:

> What I am saying, brothers and sisters, is this: flesh and blood cannot inherit the kingdom of God, nor does the perishable inherit the imperishable. Listen, I will tell you a mystery! We will not all die, but we will all be changed, in a moment, in the twinkling of an eye, at the last trumpet. For the trumpet will sound, and the dead will be raised imperishable, and we will be changed. For this perishable body must put on imperishability, and this mortal body must put on immortality. When this perishable body puts on imperishability, and this mortal body puts on immortality, then the saying that is written will

be fulfilled: "Death has been swallowed up in victory." "Where, O death, is your victory? Where, O death, is your sting?" (vss. 50-55)

The trumpet will sound (just as in 1 Thess 4:16), the dead will be raised with their perfected, imperishable resurrection bodies, and those still alive when Jesus returns will suddenly be changed to have the same perfected, imperishable bodies as those who have already died. Paul uses here the word *immortality*. He is not talking about the immortality of the soul, but rather that the body will become immortal, nondying, nondecaying. When that happens, the victory will have been won, and the last enemy, death, will have been destroyed.

The inability of believers to comprehend the incomplete nature of their present life helped, at least in part, to lead to the arrogance and condescension they displayed in relationship to believers who had gifts different from theirs. The endtime has not yet arrived.[59] Christ-believers are certainly to live in light of its coming, but they are not to pretend that they already are fully living in it.

Chapter 16

In chapter 16, Paul concludes his lengthy communication in typical fashion: greetings, brief topics, and exhortations. He opens the final chapter with directions for gathering money for "the collection for the saints" (vss. 1-4). Paul for some years had been raising money among the essentially Gentile congregations as an offering to be given to the Judean church in Jerusalem. The offering was designed to do two things: relieve physical suffering among members of the Jerusalem church and serve as a tangible symbol of the unity in the one church of Gentile and Judean followers of Jesus (Rom 15:25-28, 31; 2 Corinthians 8–9; Gal 2:10; Acts 11:29-30).[60] Having provided that forward look regarding the collection, Paul moves to travel plans (vss. 5-12). First his own: he plans to come again to Corinth, but that stay needs to be postponed because of plans for Macedonia (northern Greece) and Ephesus (western Turkey). In verses 10-12, he turns to the travel plans of Timothy and Apollos.

Verses 13-14 contain an exhortation: "Keep alert, stand firm in your faith, be courageous, be strong. Let all that you do be done in love." Verse 14 picks up the dynamic for ethical behavior, love, which Paul has developed earlier in the letter. He follows with a commendation of the household of Stephanas and acknowledges his arrival together with Fortunatus and Achaicus (vss. 15-18). Greetings follow (vss. 19-20). Aquila and Prisca and the believers meeting in their home send greetings, as do in general the churches in that part of the world.

In verse 21, Paul takes the pen from the secretary to write a greeting in his own handwriting (he does the same thing at Gal 6:11 and Philem 19). Next, he states a brief curse formula on the one who does not love the Lord, which leads to the exclamation and hope, "Our Lord, come!" (vs. 22; in Aramaic, not Greek). A final wish for the grace of the Lord Jesus and Paul's expression of love for the Corinthians conclude the letter (vss. 23-24).

1 Corinthians: Life in the Body

I.	Salutation	1:1-3
II.	Thanksgiving	1:4-9
III.	Body	1:10—15:28
	A. Thesis	1:10
	B. Advice and Instruction: Section 1	1:11—4:21
	1. Narration: Reason for Writing and Paul's Defense	1:11-17
	2. Instruction: True Wisdom (the Cross)	1:18—2:16
	3. Confrontation and Instruction: Building the Church	3:1-23
	4. Instruction, Confrontation, and Admonition: Proper Behavior	4:1-21
	C. Advice and Instruction: Section 2	5:1—7:40
	1. Divisive Issue 1: Sexual Immorality (Relations with Father's Wife)	5:1-13
	2. Divisive Issue 2: Lawsuits between Christ-Believers	6:1-11
	3. Divisive Issue 3: Sexual Immorality (Relations with Prostitute)	6:12-20
	4. Divisive Issue 4: Marital Relationships	7:1-40
	a. Instruction to the Married	7:1-7
	b. Instruction to the Unmarried and Widows	7:8-9
	c. Instruction to Those Considering Divorce	7:10-16
	d. Statement of Basic Principle: Maintain Current Status	7:17-24

Summary

In 1 Corinthians, Paul addresses life in the body—both the individual body and the corporate body. For Paul, the physical body is not a "throwaway," a dispensable shell of no importance to the "real" person. For Paul, it is in the body that one glorifies—or does not glorify—God. Behavior in the body in this life is therefore of great significance for him, so he comments on many aspects of individual behavior. One of the reasons that life in the body carries such weight for Paul is that he firmly believes in the resurrection of a transformed body. Paul does not, however, understand the individual to be isolated from other people. Persons who believe in Jesus find, according to Paul, that their individual bodies are also part of a corporate body, the church, a body that is not to be divided by factions, egos, or claims to superiority. All such behaviors and attitudes are to be abandoned in light of the cross of Jesus as the individual and the church seek to live in love.

		e.	Instruction: Application of Basic Principle to Various Relationships	7:25-40
	D.	Advice and Instruction: Section 3		8:1—11:1
		1.	Divisive Issue (Part A): Food Sacrificed to Idols	8:1-13
		2.	Positive Example: Paul's Use of Freedom	9:1-27
		3.	Negative Example: Wilderness Generation's Worship of Idols	10:1-13
		4.	Divisive Issue (Part B): Food Sacrificed to Idols	10:14—11:1
	E.	Advice and Instruction: Section 4		11:2-34
		1.	Divisive Issue 1: Gender-Related Dress and Roles	11:2-16
		2.	Divisive Issue 2: Eating the Lord's Supper	11:17-34
	F.	Advice and Instruction: Section 5		12:1—14:40
		1.	Divisive Issue (Part A): Spiritual Gifts	12:1-31a
		2.	Positive Example: Love	12:23b—13:13
		3.	Divisive Issue (Part B): Spiritual Gifts	14:1-40
	G.	Advice and Instruction: Section 6		15:1-58
		1.	Introduction: Creed	15:1-11
		2.	Divisive Issue: Denial of Resurrection from the Dead	15:12-19
		3.	Paul's Response	15:20-58
IV.	Conclusion			16:1-24
	A.	Instruction on the Collection		16:1-4
	B.	Plans for Future Visits: Paul, Timothy, Apollos		16:5-12
	C.	Exhortation		16:13-14
	D.	Commendation of the Household of Stephanas		16:15-18
	E.	Greetings and Conclusion		16:19-24

Study Questions

1. What made Corinth an attractive place for Paul to do mission work?
2. How is the description of Corinth in this chapter similar to or different from where you live or go to school?
3. What is the socioeconomic mix of Christ-believers in Corinth? What possibilities and what difficulties does that mix present?
4. What are the basic problems among believers in Corinth that Paul needs to face? What are his responses?
5. What is the thesis of the letter, and how does Paul seek to bring that thesis into effect?
6. List the ways Paul uses in 1 Corinthians the term *body*. What for Paul is the significance of the body in the present life and in the resurrection?

Suggested Reading

Collins, Raymond F. *First Corinthians*. Sacra Pagina 7. Collegeville, MN: Liturgical, 1999.
Fitzmyer, Joseph A. *First Corinthians: A New Translation with Introduction and Commentary*. AB 32. New Haven: Yale University Press, 2008.
Hays, Richard B. *First Corinthians*. Interpretation. Louisville: John Knox, 1997.
Murphy-O'Connor, Jerome. *St. Paul's Corinth: Texts and Archaeology*. 3rd ed. Collegeville, MN: Liturgical, 2002.
Thiselton, Anthony C. *The First Epistle to the Corinthians: A Commentary on the Greek Text*. NIGTC. Grand Rapids: Eerdmans, 2000.
Witherington, Ben, III. *Conflict and Community in Corinth: A Socio-Rhetorical Commentary on 1 and 2 Corinthians*. Grand Rapids: Eerdmans, 1995.

Websites

American School of Classical Studies at Athens. "Excavations in Ancient Corinth." http://www.ascsa.edu.gr/index.php/excavationcorinth/about-the-corinth-excavations/.
Clarkson, J. Shannon. "Paul's Letter to the Corinthians." *Conflict and Community in the Corinthian Church*. United Methodist Women's Division. http://gbgm-umc.org/umw/corinthians/.
Corinth Computer Project. http://corinth.sas.upenn.edu/corinth.html. Virtual movies of the ancient city of Corinth.
"Greece: Corinth." BiblePlaces.com. http://www.bibleplaces.com/. Pictures and text from *Pictorial Library of Bible Lands*. In drop-down menu on left side, move to Greece, then Corinth.
Papakyriakou/Anagnostou, Ellen. "Corinth." *Ancient Greek Cities*. http://www.sikyon.com/Korinth/korinth_eg.html.

Chapter 9

2 Corinthians: Treasure in Clay Jars

Where Do We See God's Power?

In response to the missionary conversation and preaching of the apostle Paul, you were baptized some months ago. It was a glorious event. You felt the Spirit's surge of power then and for weeks afterward. Your belief in Jesus as the Christ is still solid, but you wonder why God's power is not evident in your life in more obvious ways that can be seen by others. Because of that concern, your ears immediately pick up Paul's remarks as his latest letter is read in the assembly of believers: "We have this treasure in clay jars, so that it may be made clear that this extraordinary power belongs to God and does not come from us" (2 Cor 4:7). You know all about clay jars. You store olive oil and wine in them at home, see them in most shops and all corner snack bars, and see pieces of broken jars everywhere you walk. Clay jars are wonderful objects in which to store things, but they do crack and can break—just like you. But God gives the treasure of the good news of Jesus to you, a very breakable yet usable clay jar. And that reminds you that the power is God's and is hidden to unseeing eyes.

Fig. 9.1 The *bēma*, the ceremonial platform used on civic events for addressing the people, from the Corinthian forum. Photo courtesy of the President and Fellows of Harvard College.

The twenty-first-century reader might think 1 Corinthians should have resolved all problems among the Christ-believers in Corinth. Unfortunately, by the time of 2 Corinthians, the circumstances confronted by Paul were even more complex and difficult than before, with rival missionaries creating at least part of the new problem.

To investigate how Paul deals with the new situation, we will need to do some detective work on 2 Corinthians. Our letter may, in fact, be a composite document created when someone placed together two or more originally separate letters. Once we have explored the possibilities, we will discover a Paul who is battling—sometimes brilliantly—for his apostolic life.

Seams

In the previous chapter, we saw that a **literary seam** in a document consists of "a block of material that is a clearly defined unit and seems out of place when compared with the material preceding and following it. Such seams can be either indications of material inserted into a previously existing document or signs of a document put together by an editor from originally independent documents or fragments of documents."[1] Readers of 2 Corinthians have identified several places that may indicate such seams: between chapters 1–9 as a unit and chapters 10–13 as a unit; between 2:13 and 2:14; between chapters 8 and 9; and between 6:14—7:1 and the material on either side of it. Our discussion will begin with the seam that involves the entire content of 2 Corinthians. Each of the other three seams deals with progressively smaller amounts of text.

BETWEEN CHAPTERS 1–9 AND 10–13

As Victor Paul Furnish writes, "Any thoughtful reader of canonical 2 Cor[inthians] will be struck at once by the abrupt shift—not only in subject matter but also in tone and style—between chaps. 9 and 10."[2] The shift is even more obvious when chapters 10–13 as a unit are compared with chapters 1–9 as a unit.

In chapters 1–7, Paul looks back at the beginning of fresh agitation against him. He traces that opposition up to his complete reconciliation with the congregation, so chapter 7 ends, "I rejoice, because I have complete confidence in you" (7:16). Then follow two chapters that appeal for money.

In chapters 10–13, the situation seems quite different. In those chapters, Paul's battle with his opponents is at its height. The following passage is illustrative of his approach in 10–13: "And what I do I will also continue to do, in order to deny an opportunity to those who want an opportunity to be recognized as our equals in what they boast about. For such boasters are false apostles, deceitful workers, disguising themselves as apostles of Christ. And no wonder! Even Satan disguises himself as an angel of light" (11:12-14). (2 Cor. 10:7-12 is another good example of the heated battle in which Paul finds himself.)

Reading 7:4 and 11:19-21 in tandem provides an additional striking juxtaposition of passages that illustrates the contrasts between the tone of chapters 1–9 and the tone of chapters 10–13. In 7:4, Paul addresses the Corinthians in this way: "I often boast about you; I have great pride in you; I am filled with consolation; I am overjoyed in all our affliction." But in 11:19-21a, the bitter irony fairly drips from his pen: "For you gladly put up with fools, being wise yourselves! For you put up with it when someone makes slaves of you, or preys upon you, or takes advantage of you, or puts on airs, or gives you a slap in the face. To my shame, I must say, we were too weak for that!"

As these examples illustrate, different things are going on in the two sections that are now chapters 1–9 and 10–13. It is also hard to imagine that Paul consciously follows two chapters (8 and 9) in which he appeals for money with four chapters of harsh rhetoric (10–13). That is not a good way to raise money![3]

In addition, each set of chapters contains different travel plans. Paul threatens, in 12:14 and 13:1, 10, to come to Corinth soon for a third and potentially harsh visit. In 1:15-16 and 2:1-2, however, he gives no indication that he is planning to come soon and in fact has postponed a visit.

A final indication that the two sections are likely originally separate letters involves the choice of pronouns. In 1–9, Paul generally uses the first person plural (*we*), but in 10–13, he uses the first person singular (*I*).

BETWEEN 2:13 AND 2:14

Another potential seam is found at 2:13-14. In 2:12-13, Paul writes, "When I came to Troas to proclaim the good news of Christ, a door was opened for me in the Lord; but my mind could not rest because I did not find my brother Titus there. So I said farewell to them and went on to Macedonia." Verse 14 goes on, "But thanks be to God, who in Christ always leads us in triumphal procession." Even granting the presence of the word *but*, there seems to be no logical connection between Paul's comments on not finding Titus and the thanksgiving expressed to God, since obviously Paul was not thankful that he did not find Titus.

If we instead reread 2:12-13 and immediately move ahead to 7:5-7, we discover an interesting result: "For even when we came into Macedonia, our bodies had no rest, but we were afflicted in every way—disputes without and fears within. But God, who consoles the downcast, consoled us by the arrival of Titus, and not only by his coming, but also by the consolation with which he was consoled about you, as he told us of your longing, your mourning, your zeal for me, so that I rejoiced still more." The material in 7:5-7 appears to be a direct continuation of 2:12-13.

Those two sections are separated, however, by a sustained defense of Paul's apostleship (2:14—7:4). The subject matter of the defense is similar to the topic of chapters 10–13, but the critical point found in 10–13 has not yet been reached in 2–7. Therefore, 2:14—7:4 was apparently written when Paul had heard of new agitation against him in Corinth but while he still trusted in the loyalty of the Corinthians. Moreover, in 2:14—7:4, Paul is in the middle of a problem, but in the material that concludes with 2:13, he is writing of a *past* problem. Thus, the material about Titus seems to have been interrupted by an originally separate letter or portion of a letter (2:14—7:4 or, more exactly, 2:14—6:13 and 7:2-4).[4]

BETWEEN 6:14—7:1 AND WHAT SURROUNDS IT

Surrounding 6:14—7:1, there appears again to be a break in the flow of thought. In 6:11-13, Paul makes an affectionate appeal to his listeners: "We have spoken frankly to you Corinthians; our heart is wide open to you. There is no restriction in our affections, but only in yours. In return—I speak as to children—open wide your hearts also." The very next words are these: "Do not be mismatched with unbelievers. For what partnership is there between righteousness and lawlessness? Or what fellowship is there between light and darkness?" (6:14). Without transition, the text moves from the warm statements of 6:11-13 to the harsh directive of 6:14.

However, 7:2-4 connects directly with the language, concern, and tone of 6:11-13: "Make room in your hearts for us; we have wronged no one, we have corrupted no one, we have taken advantage of no one. . . . I often boast about you." The reader could jump from 6:13 to 7:2 without losing a beat. To many scholars, it seems clear that 6:13 and 7:2 originally belonged together, with 6:14—7:1 separating them. Nor do 6:14—7:1 tie in well with the language of reconciliation found in the rest of this larger section of 2 Corinthians.[5]

The short section 6:14—7:1 exhibits strong non-Pauline characteristics. It contains eight words that occur nowhere else in the New Testament, let alone elsewhere in Paul.[6] Furthermore, "as God said" (6:16) is not the way Paul elsewhere introduces quotations from Israel's Bible. And the implication drawn from the quotation in 7:1, "let us cleanse ourselves from every defilement," is unique in Paul in its presupposition that believers *can* cleanse themselves. Since the early 1950s, scholars have identified close ties between the language and content of this section and the theology of the **Dead Sea Scrolls** found at **Qumran**.[7] In the case of the other material identified by supposed seams, there is no question but that the material originates with Paul. In the case of 6:14—7:1, substantial questions have been raised regarding whether the apostle authored this material at all.

BETWEEN CHAPTERS 8 AND 9

Chapters 8 and 9 both deal with a collection Paul was taking among the (basically) Gentile congregations he had founded. The collection was for the Judean congregation in Jerusalem, and it had two goals: it was designed to relieve suffering among Christ-believers in Jerusalem, and it was meant to be an expression of the unity in the one church of both Judean believers and Gentile believers.[8]

While the general topic of both chapters is the same, the details suggest different time periods. In chapter 8, Paul writes a short personal letter of recommendation for Titus, who is being sent to Corinth to continue gathering the monetary gift. Paul uses the example of the Macedonian believers (northern Greece) to spur on the Corinthians (southern Greece) in their giving (8:1-4). But in chapter 9, Paul uses the Corinthian example to encourage the Macedonians (9:2)! Chapter 9 therefore gives the impression of being composed at a point different from chapter 8—probably later, since in chapter 8, the Corinthians need to be encouraged to be ready, whereas in 9:2, they are eager. And in 9:2, the Macedonians have to be encouraged to give, whereas in 8:1-4, their giving is spontaneous.

A final jog occurs at the transition from chapter 8 to chapter 9: "Now it is not necessary for me to write you about the ministry to the saints" (9:1). ("Ministry to the saints" equals the collection.) Given the current placement of chapters 8 and 9, it is not necessary to write them about the topic, because he already did that in chapter 8! Chapter 9 begins, however, as though chapter 8 is unknown, which increases the possibility of two originally distinct communications.

Furthermore, George A. Kennedy has argued that chapters 1–7 are complete rhetorically, with all announced topics fully explored.[9] Hans Dieter Betz, for his part, has written an entire commentary based on chapters 8 and 9 as separate originally from 1–7, as well as separate from each other.[10] According to this view, chapter 8 is addressed to Corinth; it is an advisory letter similar to ancient official letters of recommendation. Chapter 9 is addressed to believers in Achaia and is a deliberative letter encouraging them to fulfill their promised contribution.

For Ralph Martin, however, the disjunctions between the two chapters are best explained simply by a break in Paul's dictation. Paul's train of thought was interrupted at the end of chapter 8, and he began at a slightly different point in chapter 9.[11]

CONCLUSION

However one seeks to account for these apparent seams, the observations that lie behind their identification still exist. The problems, as Furnish says, "cannot be dismissed as imaginary."[12] So we turn next to the various explanations scholars have developed to account for the seams.

Proposed Solutions

Solutions offered by biblical scholars include the idea that 2 Corinthians was originally two letters (chapters 1–9 and 10–13), that it was the same two letters written in the reverse order, that it comprises several fragments, and that it was a unified document written in the canonical order. Before arriving at any conclusions about these theories, we will look at the strengths and weaknesses of each.

TWO LETTERS: 1–9 AND 10–13

Already in 1776, J. S. Semler proposed that 2 Corinthians is composed of two letters by Paul: chapters 1–9 are from an early letter by Paul, and chapters 10–13 are from a later letter by him. That is also the basic position of twentieth-century works by F. F. Bruce, C. K. Barrett, Victor Paul Furnish, and Ralph Martin.[13] Margaret Thrall's position is a modification of this basic proposal; she identifies three communications: 1–8, 9, and 10–13.[14]

Proposals concerning the Composition of 2 Corinthians

Two Letters	Chaps. 1–9
	Chaps. 10–13
or	Chaps. 10–13
	Chaps. 1–9
(or Three)	Chaps. 1–8
	Chap. 9
	Chaps. 10–13
Several fragments	2:14—6:13 + 7:2-4 (Apostolic Defense Letter)
	10:1—13:10 (Letter of Tears)
	1:1—2:13, 7:5-16, 13:11-13 (Letter of Reconciliation)
	Chapter 8 (collection letter)
	Chapter 9 (collection letter)
	6:14—7:1 (non-Pauline interpolation)
Unified document	1:1—13:13

Furnish provides a good paradigm for understanding this first position. He maintains that the break between 2:13 and 2:14 is not as sharp as others have decided it is. He argues that 6:14—7:1 is non-Pauline, although he thinks Paul put it in himself. Martin, in contrast, argues that Paul wrote 6:14—7:1, although he qualifies his view by suggesting that during a break in his dictation, Paul read either a tract from Qumran or a tract that resembled the theology of Qumran. Desiring to warn the Corinthians that they were identifying too much with the unbelieving world, he used thoughts from the hypothetical tract as the basis for 6:14—7:1. Although Thrall wavers a bit, she concludes that Paul did write 6:14—7:1; the unusual language in that section comes from Paul's use of baptismal motifs. But for all three, 6:14—7:1 is part of the unified section composed of chapters 1–9 (for Thrall, 1—8). Back to Furnish: while he appreciates the arguments for two separate collection letters (chapter 8 and chapter 9), he concludes that these arguments can be overcome. Chapters 1–9 are a unity.

What writing circumstances does Furnish envision for chapters 1–9? Paul had written 1 Corinthians. Chapters 1–9 of 2 Corinthians look back on Paul's second, painful visit to Corinth, to which he had responded by writing his **Letter of Tears** (references to which are at 2:3-4, 9; 7:8, 12). That letter has not survived. Paul wrote from Macedonia shortly after Titus arrived with news from Corinth: the Letter of Tears had worked (7:5-16), but problems remained. Paul was confident, so he sent Titus back to finish the collection.

Furnish concurs with the reasons already listed for separating 10–13 from 1–9. What accounts for the withering tone of 10–13? "It is clear that the situation has substantially deteriorated"[15] since Paul wrote 1–9. Titus may have misread the situation, or Paul may have overly optimistically interpreted his report. Most likely, new information has reached Paul (perhaps from Titus, who delivered chapters 1–9), and he either learns for the first time or realizes in new ways that rival apostles have invaded the congregation.[16]

Why, on this theory, were the two letters subsequently joined? Furnish envisions two possibilities. One is that an editor identified that the two letters dealt with the same complex of issues and were close in date, so the editor joined the letters by adding the shorter to the longer (or the later to the earlier). A second possibility is that an editor found one letter with the opening or conclusion damaged or missing entirely, and the editor created one complete letter by combining the two originally separate documents. Furnish projects a date for this editing of 96–125, because 2 Corinthians appears not to be known by the author of *1 Clement* (96 CE) but was without doubt circulating by the time of Marcion in the second century.

This version of the two-letter hypothesis has clear strengths:

- *Simplicity.* Only two letters need to be combined.
- *Canonical order.* It retains the chapters in the order in which we have them.

It also has potential weaknesses:

- It downplays or ignores the seams identified within chapters 1–9.
- It has to theorize a situation to account for the break between 1–9 and 10–13. We have no direct statement by Paul regarding new or renewed problems in Corinth.
- It has to suppose the loss of a closing at the end of 9 and a salutation at the beginning of 10.

TWO LETTERS: 10–13 AND 1–9

Another version of the two-letter hypothesis reverses the order of chapters 1–9 and 10–13. This theory goes back to Adolf Hausrath, who in 1870 proposed that chapters 10–13 were part of the Letter of Tears. That theory has found assent in the work of Alfred Plummer and Hans-Josef Klauck.[17] According to this view, the reconciliation toward which chapters 1–9 move and actually reach is best explained by understanding 1–9 as a letter that followed Paul's attack on the Corinthians in the Letter of Tears (chs. 10–13). Since the Letter of Tears worked, Paul was able to approach the Corinthians much more graciously in 1–9.

At the center of this position is the content of 10–13, whose sharply worded rhetorical flourishes seem to fit well the harshly written and blunt letter to which Paul refers in 2:3-4, 9 and 7:8, 12. Other data are also used in support of this position. For example, some statements in 10–13 look forward, whereas comparable statements in 1–9 look backward. In 1:23, Paul writes, "It was to spare you that I did not come again to Corinth," whereas in 13:2, he says, "If I come again, I will not be lenient." From these statements, it is not hard to imagine 13:2 preceding 1:23. Moreover, in 3:1 and 5:12, Paul is charged with commending himself, and many statements in 10–13 could be interpreted as self-commendation.[18]

Other data in support of dating 10–13 earlier include Paul's statement of his goal in 10:16 that "we may proclaim the good news in lands beyond you." From Rom 15:22-29, we know that Paul's next major projected missionary move was going to be to Rome and then Spain. Chapters 10–13 were probably written by Paul from Macedonia (11:9), and it would be odd for Paul to refer to Rome and Spain as *beyond* Corinth.[19] If, however, Paul were in Ephesus, as many proponents of the Letter of Tears hypothesis argue, then the reference to "lands beyond you" would make sense.[20] But he was in Ephesus before Macedonia, so 10–13 was written before 1–9.

There are also weighty reasons for concluding that chapters 10–13 are not part of the Letter of Tears. One is that the Letter of Tears was written when Paul had decided not to make another painful visit (2:1, 4), but Paul in 12:14 and 13:1-2 mentions coming again. Also, 12:18 refers to the trip of Titus, who by then had been to Corinth and reported back to Paul. That must mean that chapters 10–13 were written after the Letter of Tears, since Titus is the one who delivered it. He has now returned. A third reason is that the Letter of Tears dealt with the disciplining of one person, but chapters 10–13 do not contain that action, nor does Paul in those chapters mention the incident that created the need for discipline.[21]

Furthermore, the Letter of Tears referred, according to Paul, to a change in travel plans, but those plans are absent from 10–13. Finally, if 10–13 is the Letter of Tears that changed the Corinthians' attitude toward Paul, why does he still need to defend his apostleship in 1–9?

This version of the two-letter hypothesis has the following strengths:

- *Simplicity*—we need to imagine only two letters being edited and combined.
- It explains the literary data without a need to posit fresh agitation.
- It provides plausible explanations for the differences between the two parts of the document.

It has these weaknesses:

- Rearrangement of the canonical order of the chapters, which helps to raise the question of why the negative section is placed last, if that is not its order of writing.
- There are various arguments against chapters 10–13 being the Letter of Tears.
- It has to suppose the loss of a closing at the end of chapter 9 and a salutation at the beginning of chapter 10.

SEVERAL FRAGMENTS

The third thesis maintains that 2 Corinthians is composed of several fragments, all but one of which were written by Paul. The most prominent and widely followed version is that of Günther Bornkamm, who arranges the letter fragments in the following order:

- Working with the seams between 2:13 and 2:14, between 6:13 and 6:14, and between 7:1 and 7:2, he argues that 2:14—6:13 and 7:2-4 together make up an Apostolic Defense Letter Paul wrote to Corinth. The letter did not have the effect Paul desired.
- Thus, he subsequently made his painful visit to the city.
- In response to his painful visit, he wrote his Letter of Tears, 10:1—13:10. Some time later, Titus reported to Paul that this letter had worked.
- Paul followed with his Letter of Reconciliation, which is the material in chapters 1–7 not already identified as part of the Apostolic Defense Letter (6:14—7:1 is omitted from both letters; see below), as well as the conclusion to the entire document. This letter is composed of 1:1—2:13, 7:5-16, and 13:11-13.
- Titus returned to Corinth yet again, taking a collection letter, chapter 8.
- Paul later wrote a second collection letter, chapter 9.[22]
- That leaves 6:14—7:1, which Bornkamm sees as a later non-Pauline insertion.[23]

When and why would such a patchwork be composed? Bornkamm argues that the composition of what we call 2 Corinthians took place in Corinth about the same time as the writing of Acts and the Pastoral Epistles (1–2 Timothy and Titus), so that the fragments would not be lost. He notes that documents and authors of the end of the first century and the beginning of the second (*1 Clement*, Ignatius of Antioch, and Polycarp) frequently quote 1 Corinthians but never 2 Corinthians. That phenomenon may well indicate that 2 Corinthians was not pieced together until the end of the first century. The Letter of Tears was placed last, since warnings of heresy are frequently placed at the end of early Christian literature. Such warnings are often related to the end-times, so the placement points to Paul's opponents as end-time false prophets.[24]

Bornkamm's theory has been quite popular and is followed to one degree or another by Dieter Georgi, Hans Dieter Betz, and Helmut Koester.[25] Bultmann argued for a variation in which 2:14—6:13 and 7:2-4 belong with chapters 10–13 as part of the Letter of Tears.[26]

Major strengths of the several-fragments theory include the following:

- It seeks to explain all seams.
- It accounts for the uniquenesses of the various portions of the document.

Its most significant weaknesses are these:

- It is complex. The beginnings and endings of several letters have been altered or omitted, and the fragments are out of chronological sequence.
- The process that produced such a hybrid document is difficult to conceive.

A UNIFIED DOCUMENT WRITTEN IN CANONICAL ORDER (1:1—13:13)

The final major scholarly position on the composition of 2 Corinthians is that Paul wrote it exactly the way we have it. The chief proponents of the unified position are Werner Kümmel, Paul Barnett, Udo Schnelle, and Ben Witherington.[27]

In support of this view, the proponents of a unified document assert that differences between chapters 10–13 and 1–9 are overly emphasized. There are, after all, several places in chapters 1–7 where Paul defends himself even if he does not use the heavy-handed language of 10–13.[28] Further, Paul Barnett argues that chapters 10–13 properly conclude the letter composed of chapters 1–13 by gathering up previously mentioned themes and making a final emotional appeal.[29]

Fragment theories assume that the end and beginning of several letters have been omitted. Scholars who hold to a unified document question the plausibility of such wholesale editing. They also question the weight to be placed on proposed seams: what appear to be significant shifts in topic are, in fact, digressions in Paul's thinking.[30] Thus, Udo Schnelle points to the verbal links between 7:4, which is supposedly from one letter, and 7:5-16, which is supposedly from another.[31] Frederick Danker, affirmed by Ben Witherington, understands chapters 8 and 9 as a unit, with chapter 8 giving details regarding the collection and chapter 9 outlining the motivation for it.[32] On the seam between 2:13 and 2:14, Werner Kümmel turns to a psychological argument: when Paul mentions Titus in 2:13, he is so thrilled at recalling him that he immediately turns to a doxology, from which it takes him until 7:5-16 to recover and return to his theme.[33]

Scholars who hold to a unified composition spend much time studying 6:14—7:1. We have already seen the positions of scholars who understand chapters 1–9 as a unity: Furnish thinks the section is non-Pauline but included by Paul, Martin sees Paul being influenced by a Qumran or Qumran-like document, and Thrall thinks the unusual language in the section is baptismal. In his support of unified composition, Barnett understands the section as an admonition by Paul to the Corinthians to separate themselves from pagan temple worship. Indeed, he sees the section as the climax of Paul's defense of his apostolate.[34] While not so sure of that, Neyrey still sees Paul in 6:14—7:1 erecting "a formidable boundary to fence in and protect the holy people of God."[35]

A frequent position taken by those who argue for a unified 2 Corinthians is that the jogs or seams are the result of interruptions in the dictation process.[36]

There is no manuscript evidence that any part of 2 Corinthians ever circulated independently or as part of a separate letter. So, for example, we have no manuscript that contains only chapters 10–13; or that has only 1:1—2:13, 7:5-16, and 13:11-13.

The thesis of a unified composition has two major strengths:

- It takes the canonical order at face value.
- It is simpler than the other proposals.

At the same time, the unified proposal presents serious difficulties:

- It ignores or underplays the seams in the text.
- It frequently resorts to special pleading to explain the differences, such as the psychological explanation for the seam at 2:13/2:14 and the reliance on interrupted dictation.[37]

CONCLUSION AND PROPOSAL

From our study, we can draw the following conclusions:

- The literary seams are real, not imagined.
- Arguments for the unity of chapters 1–9 and 10–13 seem weak and do not explain the shift in tone from chapter 9 to chapter 10.
- Chapters 10–13 do not fit the limited data we have on the Letter of Tears. That letter, while possibly found in part in 10–13, is more probably lost.
- There is a growing consensus that the proper order is 1–9 followed by 10–13; the proposal found in the textbox "Paul's Correspondence with Corinth" builds on that consensus.
- Therefore, it seems likely that fresh trouble broke out after the writing of chapters 1–7 (and perhaps 8–9).
- The text at 6:14—7:1 is an interpolation.

The textboxes on pages 200 and 204 tries to express in brief the historical outline being proposed here. Although it builds on the work of Bornkamm, it is somewhat different from it. The task of the reader is to determine which proposal presented in this chapter best explains the texts themselves.

Time and Place

While specific dates are at best educated guesses, one important set of parameters can be gleaned. In 1 Cor 16:1-4, Paul gives instructions to the Corinthians to begin collecting their money for the Jerusalem gift. In 2 Corinthians 8 and 9, the process in both northern and southern Greece, including Corinth, is much more fully developed. Finally, in Rom 15:25-27, Paul has the money and is ready to go to Jerusalem. Thus, the series of letters in 2 Corinthians is properly to be placed between 1 Corinthians and Romans. That gives us 55–56 as the dates for the events in Corinth and Paul's literary responses in 2 Corinthians. By the summer or fall of 56, Paul was again in Corinth; during that stay, he wrote Romans. In the spring of 57, he left for Jerusalem.[38]

Paul's Correspondence with Corinth

1. Paul writes to Corinth sometime in 51–54: that letter, Letter A, is now lost (see 1 Cor 5:9).
2. Paul sends Timothy to Corinth for the collection.
3. After Timothy leaves, in 54, Paul receives a letter and oral reports from Corinth; he writes Letter B, our 1 Corinthians.
4. Paul writes his Apostolic Defense Letter, Letter C, portions of which we have in 2 Cor. 2:14—6:13 and 7:2-4.
5. Paul makes his painful visit to Corinth in the spring of 55.
6. Paul writes his Letter of Tears, Letter D, now lost (see 2 Cor 2:3-4, 9; 7:8, 12), in the spring or summer of 55.
7. Paul sends Titus to Corinth.
8. Paul meets Titus in Macedonia. Good news!
9. Paul writes the Letter of Reconciliation, Letter E, portions of which survive as 2 Cor. 1:1—2:13, 7:5-16, and maybe also 13:11-13.
10. Paul receives bad news of fresh agitation; he writes Letter F (chapters 10–13).
11. Paul writes Letter G (chapter 8) and Letter H (chapter 9); probably two separate letters).
12. Paul arrives in Corinth in the summer or fall of 56 and stays the winter. During that time, he writes Romans.
13. Paul leaves Corinth for Jerusalem in the spring of 57.
14a. Paul edits together parts of Letters C and E through H to make our 2 Corinthians in the late 50s or early 60s; *or, more likely,*
14b. A later editor edits these letters together (and interpolates the non-Pauline 6:14—7:1) to make our 2 Corinthians in approximately 85–90.

Paul's location(s) when writing are equally ambiguous, although there is some data. For Letter C (1 Cor 16:8-9), he is probably still in Ephesus. Letter D likely was penned there as well. By the time of Letter E (2 Cor 7:5-7), Paul is in Macedonia; Letter F is probably written from there, too (11:9 may point to that conclusion). Letter G gives the impression of being written in Macedonia (8:1), as does Letter H (9:2, 4).

Genre

George Kennedy has written that 2 Corinthians "provides the most extended piece of **judicial rhetoric** in the New Testament."[39] Chapters 8 and 9 are deliberative, as Paul gives directions for the future process of gathering the collection, but even they have a judicial function "as part of Paul's defense by showing his aboveboard handling of money matters."[40] But the rest of 2 Corinthians is largely judicial, as is indicated in the outline, in which the term *defense* points to an imaginary courtroom setting (that is, judicial) in which Paul needs to defend his actions. In 12:19, he specifically says that that is what he is doing. The more specific type of writing represented by 2 Corinthians can be labeled an ***apologia***, that is, an apology or defense, in this case for his apostleship.

As is typical of judicial rhetoric, 2 Corinthians has a strong interest in the past. The letter therefore has several sections devoted to narrating Paul's understanding of previous events (1:8—2:13; 7:5-16; several statements in 10:1—13:10). Furthermore, 2 Corinthians exhibits judicial rhetoric's typical interest in ***logos***, ***ēthos***, and ***pathos***. *Logos* refers to logical deductive argumentation (8:9) and use of examples (Moses; 3:7-18). *Ēthos* refers to the need of speakers/authors to establish their character, especially over against and superior to that of their opponents. In chapters 1–7, Paul establishes in a relatively gentle way his character and thus his right to address the Corinthians (Letters E and C). In chapters 10–13 (Letter F), he carries on the comparison in a much more strident fashion that moves into *pathos*, which is the attempt to gain agreement with one's position by arousing the listeners' emotions. The "fool's speech" (11:1—12:13) is a good example of *pathos*, as are the emotional statements at 6:11-13 and 7:2-4. In the "fool's speech," Paul uses every rhetorical device at hand, especially irony and sarcasm. The placement of such material at the end of the document also serves an important rhetorical purpose, whether placed there by Paul or an editor: "The best and most emotional harangue is saved for last since the audience is more apt to remember what they heard last."[41]

The goal is defense of his apostleship, certainly, but Paul through that defense wants to reestablish a positive relationship with the Corinthians and win them back to his understanding of the faith.

Crises and Opponents

After Paul wrote 1 Corinthians, Judean Christ-believing missionaries came to Corinth.[42] Their message found a ready hearing among the Corinthian

Christ-believers and directly challenged Paul's mission and gospel. Paul's initial response (Letter C) was firm yet still confident that the Corinthians would react positively to him. While the exact reasons for his next visit to Corinth are unclear, Paul made a disastrous visit, the so-called painful visit. His comments indicate how difficult it was for him (2:1, 5-11; 7:12); he was treated badly, probably in a public setting within the congregation (2:3, 5; 7:12). At the center of the misbehavior was one member of the community. After his retreat from Corinth, Paul wrote the Letter of Tears (Letter D). When Titus reported that the letter had worked, Paul wrote Letter E, which reveals that the person who had caused trouble during the painful visit had been disciplined by his fellow believers (2:5-11; 7:12). Paul also had to defend himself regarding his travel plans, which had been rearranged during the previous difficulties.[43] The changes had made him appear untrustworthy.

Finally, a fresh and more successful invasion of non-Pauline missionaries not only resurrected earlier problems but brought them to a critically dangerous new level. Paul's counterattack is the brilliant piece of bitter irony in 10:1—13:10 (Letter F).

The attacks by Paul's opponents were comprehensive and potentially devastating (see textbox "Attacks against Paul"). The charges—and his defense—indicate that the charges made at least some sense to the Corinthians. In general, the charges revolve around sharply different understandings of leadership, apostleship, and ministry. Paul's opponents and a significant number of the Corinthians look toward their society's model of the leader as one who holds great honor, spiritual gifts, and rhetorical abilities, all of which give him power. Good references witness to the leader's success and reliability, and acceptance of support by patrons illustrates that the leader-apostle understands his place vis-à-vis wealthier members of the community and fits the model of other teachers:[44] "The opponents believe that apostles should be impressive figures who are successful and demonstrate

---

Attacks against Paul

- Paul's letters (1:13) and his gospel (4:3) are unclear, and he vacillates (1:17).
- He lacks letters of recommendation (3:1; 4:2).
- He enriches himself financially, especially through the collection for Jerusalem (7:2; 12:14-18).
- Only in his letters is he bold; in person, he is weak (10:1, 10), and he is an ineffective speaker (10:10; 11:6).
- He acts (literally, *walks*) according to the flesh (10:2).
- He is inferior to the super-apostles (11:5; 12:11).
- His apostleship is so weak he will not allow himself to be supported by the congregation (11:7-11; 12:13).
- In fact, he is not a legitimate apostle (12:12).
- Christ does not speak through him (13:3).

Paul's Opponents as Defined by Themselves—and by Paul

They carry with them written recommendations, testimonials to their mighty deeds (3:1).	Paul's "letter of recommendation" is the Corinthians themselves (3:2-3).
In general, they boast of their accomplishments as a way to gain authority over the Corinthians (11:12-13, 18).	Paul counters with his own "foolish" boasting, especially his weaknesses (11:16-18; 11:30-32).
They claim to be apostles endowed with charismatic gifts (11:5, 13; 12:11).	Paul derisively calls them "super-apostles" (11:5; 12:11).
They claim to have a strong public presence and sophisticated rhetorical skill (10:10; 11:6). At that point, they were similar to other wandering Hellenistic teachers who attracted attention by ostentatious speech and prodigious deeds (12:12).[45]	Paul claims to be "untrained in speech, but not in knowledge" (11:6); the letter shows how well trained "in speech" he really is.
They boast of their descent and standing: Hebrews, Israelites, descendants of Abraham, and ministers of Christ (11:22).	Paul claims those titles, too, but argues that he is a better minister because of his sufferings (11:22-29).
Although they emphasize their Judean descent, they do not, in 2 Corinthians, promote circumcision or Torah-observance (and thus should not be identified with the Judaizers of Galatia nor be understood as sent from the Jerusalem apostles).[46]	Paul points to his own visions and revelations, especially a heavenly journey, against which he sets his weaknesses, including his "thorn in the flesh" (12:1-10).
They boast of visions (12:1).	
(From Paul's perspective) they proclaim another Jesus, a different Spirit, and a different gospel from what he proclaims (11:4).	
It is possible that (seen from Paul's perspective) they have the same confusion about the "not yet" of final salvation that Paul dealt with in 1 Corinthians (2 Cor 5:7).	
They accept money to support themselves in their apostolic work, understanding that as an apostolic right they need to exercise (11:20; also 2:17).	Contrast Paul, who accepted support from churches outside Corinth so that he could preach to the Corinthians without cost (11:7-10).[47]

the power of God in their lives by means of this manner of life, this bearing and demeanor."[48]

Paul's response is manifold, but at the center of his response, he argues that "apostles show God's power by enduring trials and hardships (i.e. being 'weak') with faith and, in the process, bring others to the gospel."[49] Thus, the keys to Paul's understanding of apostleship and ministry are weakness and suffering (4:7—5:10; 6:4-10; 11:29-33; 12:10), but weakness and suffering tied in with and based on the weakness and suffering of Jesus (4:10-12; 5:15, 21; 8:9).[50]

Who are the people who bring these charges against Paul and who bring such sharply divergent views of leadership and ministry? They are probably different from the opponents of 1 Corinthians, since they seem to have arrived in Corinth only recently with their letters of introduction (2 Cor 3:1; 11:4). From 2 Corinthians, we can conclude that they were Greek-speaking Judean Christ-believing itinerant missionaries who came to Corinth from somewhere else (10:12-18; compare 11:4). It is possible that these people found easy acceptance among Paul's earlier opponents, but we do not know that for sure.

The Letter Fragments in 2 Corinthians, in Sequence

Letter C (Apostolic Defense Letter)		2:14–6:13		7:2-4				
Letter D (Letter of Tears, Now Lost)								
Letter E (Letter of Reconciliation)	1:1–2:13				7:5-16			13:11-13 (?)
Letter F								Chaps. 10–13
Letter G						Ch. 8		
Letter H							Ch. 9	
Interpolation			6:14–7:1					
Final editing (after Paul's death)	1:1–2:13	2:14–6:13	6:14–7:1	7:2-4	7:5-16	Ch. 8	Ch. 9	Chaps. 10–13 13:11-13

Reading through 2 Corinthians, Fragment by Fragment

The brief commentary that follows explores the canonical 2 Corinthians by discussing the meaning of the letter fragments contained within it, according to the chronology laid out above, and how they work in the present canonical arrangement. For clarity, the preceding textbox shows to which stage in Paul's correspondence with the Corinthians the parts of the present letter belong; the subsequent textboxes show how each original letter fragment, as reconstructed here, fits into the outline of our 2 Corinthians.

(See also the outline of the whole letter on pages 206–7.)

1:1—2:13

**Letter E: Letter of Reconciliation
(1:1—2:13, 7:5-16, perhaps 13:11-13)**

I.	Salutation	1:1-2
II.	Benediction Addressed to God	1:3-7
III.	Body	1:8—13:10
	A. Narration: Basis for Paul's Defense	1:8—2:13
	1. Paul's Experience in Asia	1:8-11
	2. Paul's Experience in Corinth	1:12—2:13
	a. Paul's Boast: The Corinthians	1:12-14
	b. Paul's Explanation, Part 1	1:15-22
	c. Paul's Explanation, Part 2	1:23—2:4
	d. Paul's Counsel: Forgive	2:5-11
	e. Corinthians' Response to Letter of Tears	2:12-13
	[Resumed at 7:5]	

The passage at 1:1—2:13 originally comes from Letter E, a letter of reconciliation, and was written following Titus's report to Paul that Paul's Letter of Tears had resulted in repentance by the Corinthians. Within the overall document of 2 Corinthians, the section provides the salutation, benediction, and beginning of the body of the letter.

The salutation in 1:1-2 is organized in typical Pauline fashion: sender to recipient, greetings. Paul immediately reminds his listeners that he is "an apostle of Christ Jesus by the will of God" (1:1). He is no self-appointed leader. The letter is sent primarily to Corinth but also to "all the saints throughout Achaia," the province of which Corinth was the capital (Achaia is mentioned again in 9:2 and 11:10).

Instead of the more normal thanksgiving, 2 Corinthians continues with a benediction addressed to "the God and Father of our Lord Jesus Christ" (2:3; for similar opening benedictions, see Eph 1:3; 1 Pet 1:3). We have seen that Paul's thanksgivings state, sometimes subtly, the major themes of the letter. In verses 3-7, Paul introduces the topic that will dominate 2 Corinthians, the legitimacy of his conflict-riddled ministry. He outlines three keys to his ministry: (1) whenever there is affliction, God provides consolation; (2) consolation in turn enables him to console others; and (3) both the sufferings and the consolation of Christ are abundant in Paul (vss. 4-5). The benediction also sounds a note that will indeed be

2 Corinthians: Treasure in Clay Jars

This outline follows the sequence of our 2 Corinthians and identifies each component part according to the proposal discussed above.[51]

Letter E: Letter of Reconciliation (1:1—2:13; 7:5-16; perhaps 13:11-13)

I.	Salutation	1:1-2
II.	Benediction Addressed to God	1:3-7
III.	Body	1:8—13:10
	A. Narration: Basis for Paul's Defense	1:8—2:13
	1. Paul's Experience in Asia	1:8-11
	2. Paul's Experience in Corinth	1:12—2:13
	a. Paul's Boast: The Corinthians	1:12-14
	b. Paul's Explanation, Part 1	1:15-22
	c. Paul's Explanation, Part 2	1:23—2:4
	d. Paul's Counsel: Forgive	2:5-11
	e. Corinthians' Response to Letter of Tears (Resumed at 7:5)	2:12-13

Letter C: Apostolic Defense Letter (2:14—6:13; 7:2-4)

	B. Thesis: not peddlers but sincere proclaimers	2:14-17
	C. Paul's First Defense	3:1—6:13
	1. Paul's Letter of Recommendation	3:1-3
	2. Paul's Ministry of a New Covenant	3:4—5:21
	a. Source of Competency	3:4-6
	b. Contrast between Two Glories	3:7-18
	c. Content of Paul's Proclamation	4:1-6
	d. Paul's Suffering Ministry	4:7—5:10
	e. Paul's Ministry of Reconciliation	5:11-21
	3. Paul's Self-Commendation	6:1-10
	4. Emotional Conclusion (Resumed at 7:2)	6:11-13

Interpolation (6:14—7:1)

	D. Ethical Aside	6:14—7:1
	1. Call for Separation from Unbelievers	6:14-16a
	2. Scriptural Support	6:16b-18
	3. Conclusion	7:1

Letter C, Resumed

	E. Emotional Appeal and Transition (Resumption of III.C.4 above, 6:11-13)	7:2-4

Letter E, Resumed

	F. Narration: Basis for Paul's Second Defense (resumption of III.A.2.e above, 2:12-13)	7:5-16

Letter G (8:1-24)

	G. Appeal to the Corinthians to Participate in the Collection	8:1-24
	1. Example: Generosity of the Macedonians	8:1-6

2.	Thesis: Prime Directive	8:7-8
3.	Argument in Support of Thesis	8:9-15
4.	Recommendation of Titus and the Brothers	8:16-23
5.	Concluding Emotional Appeal	8:24

Letter H (9:1-15)

H. Appeal to the People of Achaia to Participate in the Collection — 9:1-15
    1. Identification of the Topic — 9:1
    2. *Captatio benevolentiae* — 9:2
    3. Sending of the Brothers — 9:3-5
    4. Reasons for Giving — 9:6-14
    5. Emotional Conclusion: Prayer of Thanksgiving — 9:15

Letter F (10:1—13:10 [11-13])

I. Paul's Third Defense — 10:1—13:10
    1. Appeal for Obedience and Statement of Charge — 10:1-6
    2. Sarcastic Restatement of Charge — 10:7-11
    3. Sarcastic Comparison with Opponents — 10:12-18
    4. The Fool's Speech: Refutation of Charge — 11:1—12:13
        a. Introduction — 11:1-15
            1. Paul's Jealousy — 11:1-4
            2. Self-Comparison with Opponents — 11:5-6
            3. Defense of Paul's Financial Independence — 11:7-11
            4. Charges against Opponents — 11:12-15
        b. Paul's "Foolish" Boast 1: Weakness — 11:16-33
            1. Sarcastic Introduction — 11:16-21a
            2. Paul's Qualifications as Member of Israel — 11:21b-22
            3. Paul's Qualifications as a Minister — 11:23-33
        c. Paul's "Foolish" Boast 2: Visions and Revelations — 12:1-10
            1. Boast of a Heavenly Journey — 12:1-7a
            2. Boast Qualified by Suffering — 12:7b-9a
            3. Result: Boast of Weaknesses — 12:9b-10
        d. Conclusion — 12:11-13
    5. Renewal of the Appeal — 12:14—13:10
        a. Announcement of Third Visit — 12:14a
        b. Defense regarding Finances — 12:14b-18
        c. Statement of Fears regarding Third Visit — 12:19-21
        d. Warning regarding Application of Apostolic Authority — 13:1-10

Letter E, Resumed (Perhaps)

IV. Epistolary Conclusion — 13:11-13

challenged later in 2 Corinthians but that is dominant in Letter E: "our hope for you is unshaken" (vs. 7).

From 1:8 to 2:13, Paul provides an autobiographical narrative that becomes the basis for his defense. He begins with his ministry in Asia (today called Asia Minor), tying it to the previous section by the word *affliction* (1:8; 2:4; compare *punishment* in 2:6). The motif of the suffering apostle is thus the first example of what his ministry has been and rhetorically serves to create sympathy for him.[52] In verse 12, he turns to his history with Corinth. The overarching theme he states is how straightforwardly and honestly he has dealt with them. He begins with a twofold affirmation: "This is our boast, the testimony of our conscience." Boasting—both positive and negative—will be a theme throughout the larger letter (1:14; 5:12; 7:4, 14; 8:24; 9:2, 3; 10:8, 13, 15, 16, 17; 11:10, 12, 16, 17, 18, 21, 30; 12:1, 5, 6, 9). And what is his boast and testimony? "We have behaved in the world with frankness and godly sincerity, not by earthly wisdom but by the grace of God—and all the more toward you" (1:12). Over against (implicitly) his opponents who operate with *earthly wisdom*, Paul relies on the grace of God. And his defense is that he and those with him have behaved "with frankness and godly sincerity." *Frankness* (*haplotēs*) means "simplicity" and refers to open and honest communication that has integrity. The subsection concludes with a dual boast: "On the day of the Lord Jesus we are your boast even as you are our boast." Paul's fate and that of the Corinthians are inextricably bound together.

In 1:15-22, Paul begins to explain his travel plans. Yes, indeed, he had planned to come to Corinth. But, he explains in 1:23—2:4, he had had good reason to cancel the trip: "it was to spare you that I did not come again to Corinth" (1:23). He wanted to avoid another painful visit (2:1) and thus a repetition of the circumstances that led him to write the Letter of Tears (2:3-4, Letter D). In 2:5-11, Paul recasts the painful visit: the one who caused Paul pain in reality caused pain for everyone in the community (2:5). But that person has now been disciplined and should be forgiven (2:6-8). Paul also introduces the response of the Corinthians to his Letter of Tears by tracing his dis-ease at not hearing from Titus how the Corinthians had reacted (2:12-13). The story is resumed at 7:5.

2:14—6:13

The next section is from what is probably the earliest fragment we have, Letter C, Paul's Apostolic Defense Letter. The thesis or proposition of the letter is contained in 2:14-17: "For we are not peddlers of God's word like so many; but in Christ we speak as persons of sincerity, as persons sent from God and standing in his presence" (2:17).

The rest of this section is Paul's defense, which has four parts: his letter of recommendation, his ministry of a new covenant, his self-commendation, and an emotional conclusion. As opposed to his opponents, first of all, who carry with them letters of introduction from other ministry sites, Paul claims that "you yourselves are our letter, written on our hearts, to be known and read by all" (3:2). Most of the section is devoted not to that topic but to testimony about his ministry

> ### Letter C: Apostolic Defense Letter (2:14—6:13; 7:2-4)
>
> | | | |
> |---|---|---|
> | B. | Thesis: Not Peddlers but Sincere Proclaimers | 2:14-17 |
> | C. | Paul's First Defense | 3:1—6:13 |
> | | 1. Paul's Letter of Recommendation | 3:1-3 |
> | | 2. Paul's Ministry of a New Covenant | 3:4—5:21 |
> | | a. Source of Competency | 3:4-6 |
> | | b. Contrast between Two Glories | 3:7-18 |
> | | c. Content of Paul's Proclamation | 4:1-6 |
> | | d. Paul's Suffering Ministry | 4:7—5:10 |
> | | e. Paul's Ministry of Reconciliation | 5:11-21 |
> | | 3. Paul's Self-Commendation | 6:1-10 |
> | | 4. Emotional Conclusion [Resumed at 7:2] | 6:11-13 |

itself. He begins with a disclaimer: "Not that we are competent of ourselves to claim anything as coming from us; our competence is from God" (3:5). And what God has done is to make Paul and his coworkers "competent to be ministers of a new covenant, not of letter but of spirit" (3:6). That new covenant is sharply contrasted with what Paul labels "the ministry of death" (3:7), which rather clearly refers to the Mosaic ministry, "chiseled in letters on stone tablets" (3:7). Certainly, as a member of the people of Israel, Paul has no difficulty recognizing that God's glory was present in that ministry, symbolized in the brilliant shining of Moses' face when he came down from Mt. Sinai with the Law (Exod 34:30), but at the same time, he identifies a greater glory in the ministry of the Spirit and the ministry of justification (3:8-9). Indeed, apart from Christ, people's minds are hardened when they hear the old covenant read (3:14). The discussion may be a comment on his opponents, who claim impeccable credentials as people of Israel (11:22).

In 4:1-6, Paul outlines the content of his proclamation, but in typical Paul fashion, he also outlines what he is *not* about. Positively, he engages in his ministry by God's mercy; therefore, negatively, he does not lose heart or become discouraged (4:1). Still working from a negative starting point, Paul and his coworkers "have renounced the shameful things that one hides; we refuse to practice cunning or to falsify God's word" (4:2a). But positively, "by the open statement of the truth we commend ourselves to the conscience of everyone in the sight of God" (4:2b). And what is his "open statement of the truth"? Again, he begins by stating what he is not about: "For we do not proclaim ourselves" (4:5a), once more obliquely contrasting himself with those who *do* proclaim themselves. Over against that kind of ministry, Paul and his team "proclaim Jesus Christ as Lord and ourselves as your slaves for Jesus' sake" (4:5b).

Does that proclamation mean that Paul goes from one success to another success and that his ministry is an unopposed "triumphal procession" (2:14)?[53] No. Paul in fact develops in 4:7—5:10 the everyday result of his proclamation of

Jesus Christ as Lord. And that everyday result is suffering. First, Paul reminds his listeners that the treasure of God's glory and of the good news of Jesus is given not to perfect people with no problems. Rather, "we have this treasure in clay jars" (4:7a). As we saw at the beginning of the chapter, clay jars were everyday items well known to people in Paul's world. They were both functional and breakable. Thus, Paul does not claim superhuman or super-apostle status. He and those with him are clay jars, finite, limited human beings to whom God has given a great gift. And why does God entrust so great a gift to so breakable a container? "So that it may be made clear that this extraordinary power belongs to God and does not come from us" (4:7b).

The second move that Paul makes in his discussion of his suffering ministry is to outline in a rhetorically effective way the sufferings he regularly experiences (4:8-12). There are two foci in these verses. First, while Paul openly acknowledges the suffering he has endured, he does not feel abandoned by God, nor does he contemplate giving up. Second, it is in the very suffering ("carrying in the body the death of Jesus") that he is able to live out and proclaim the life of Jesus. Thus, he closely links his suffering and that of Jesus while at the same time understanding his own suffering as a witness to Jesus and the life he offers.[54] That understanding of his ministry is absolutely counter to the opponents' understanding of ministry. Their understanding is encapsulated in the phrase *theology of glory*. Paul's view of ministry is summarized in the words *theology of the cross*: God is known and God's power is evident not in an unbroken chain of successes but in the hardships endured by the apostle, just as Jesus endured hardships and death.[55]

Fig. 9.2 Amphores, clay jugs crafted for the transportation of wine or olive oil, here stacked as for shipping. Bodrum Castle, Turkey; photo: Ad Meskens.

The third step that Paul takes in 4:7—5:10 is to look forward to the resurrection of the body and to understand that future as providing power to serve in the present (4:13—5:10). He is sure of his resurrection as well as that of the Corinthians (4:14). The result is that he does not lose heart (4:16), "for this slight momentary affliction is preparing us for an eternal weight of glory beyond all measure." In 5:1-5, he contrasts the "earthly tent" of life in the present mortal body with the life of the resurrected body, in which the person will be further clothed. The down payment or guarantee is the presence in believers of the Spirit (5:5; 1:22). The outcome is that "we are always confident" (5:6).

The final point Paul develops in the discussion of his new covenant ministry is one particular aspect of that ministry: it is a ministry of reconciliation (5:11-21). He restates the basis for his ministry and thus his work with the Corinthians: "For the love of Christ urges us on,[56] because we are convinced that one has died for all; therefore all have died" (5:14). Paul makes two important statements in this verse. First, Christ's love is the dominant force in the life of believers. Second, Paul enunciates the basic principle of belief in Christ and thus of ministry in his name: "one has died for all." The word translated as *for* is *hyper*, a preposition that means *on behalf of, in the place of*. And because that one has died, all (believers) have also died. While that death is not explained further here, Paul in Rom 6:3-11 talks about baptism as a death—a baptism into Christ's death and a death to sin. In 2 Cor 5:15a, Paul restates the basic principle that Christ died *on behalf of*: "And he died for all." The result is that the living ones (recall that in vs. 14, believers first died) live not for themselves but for him (5:15b). Thus, life has a new direction or orientation for the Christ-believer.

The result is eminently practical: "From now on, therefore, we regard no one from a human point of view" (5:16). "From a human point of view" is literally *according to the flesh* (Greek *kata sarka*); thus, Paul regards no one in a merely human way or from a merely human perspective. The proper perspective is that of the one who died for them (5:15). And if that seems impossible, Paul reminds them that in Christ, believers have been made new creatures, new people: "So if anyone is in Christ, there is a new creation: everything old has passed away; see, everything has become new!" (5:17). And how does that happen? "All this is from God" (5:18a). And who is God? God is the one "who reconciled us to himself through Christ" (5:18b). The flow of the reconciliation is from God to humanity. God, not humanity, does the reconciling. And not only has God reconciled humanity to God, God in addition "has given us the ministry of reconciliation" (5:18c), "entrusting the message of reconciliation to us" (5:19). The result is being called to be God's ambassadors: "So we are ambassadors for Christ, since God is making his appeal through us" (5:20a). The term used for "ambassadors" (actually in Greek the verb *presbeuō*) is the term used in the Greek-speaking part of the Roman Empire for official representatives, including the representatives of Caesar. As such an ambassador, Paul calls on his listeners to be reconciled to God (5:21b).

The third part of Paul's defense is his self-commendation in 6:1-10. He lists thirty-seven different ways in which he is to be commended (6:4-10). Of particular note is the way he begins: namely, with a laundry list of suffering, including beatings, riots, hard work, sleepless nights, and hunger. At the same time, he is able to list positive ways in which to commend himself, including love, truthful speech, and the power of God. He concludes with a series of conflicting self-views: honor and dishonor, sorrowful yet always rejoicing, poor yet making many rich.[57]

The rhetorical crescendo reached at the end of Paul's list in 6:5-10 is carried forward into the fourth portion of his defense, an emotional conclusion and appeal to the Corinthians (6:11-12). The conclusion itself does not end at this point, however, because 6:14—7:1 has been added to the document.

INTERPOLATION IN 6:14—7:1

Interpolation (6:14—7:1)

D. Ethical Aside	6:14—7:1
1. Call for Separation from Unbelievers	6:14-16a
2. Scriptural Support	6:16b-18
3. Conclusion	7:1

Although it seems doubtful that 6:14—7:1 is by Paul, it is part of 2 Corinthians and as such functions as an ethical aside. The initial section, 6:14-16b, calls for the listeners to separate themselves from unbelievers. "Do not be mismatched with unbelievers" (6:14) is the basic directive. The best way to make sense of the section within its current placement, as we have seen previously, is to view it as a paraenesis by "Paul" for the holy people of God to separate themselves from the corrupting culture, particularly pagan worship. The opening concludes with this reason for their behavior: "For we are the temple of the living God" (6:16b; see also 1 Cor 3:16-17, 19). The middle section of the aside provides scriptural support for the directive in 6:14-16a, and the author concludes, "Let us cleanse ourselves from every defilement of body and of spirit, making holiness perfect in the fear of God" (7:1).

7:2-16

The first three verses of the next portion of the letter continue Letter C (Apostolic Defense Letter) by resuming the theme of "room in your hearts" from 6:13. Paul continues his appeal: "We have wronged no one, we have corrupted no one, we have taken advantage of no one" (7:2). He concludes with a strong statement of confidence in the Corinthians—as well as once more reminding them of affliction: "I often boast about you; I have great pride in you; I am filled with consolation; I am overjoyed in all our affliction" (7:4).

Verse 5 resumes the other letter that earlier broke off, Letter E (Letter of Reconciliation). Paul narrates the basis for his second defense and states that defense.

> **Resumption of Letters C and E**
>
> **Letter C, Resumed**
> E. Emotional Appeal and Transition 7:2-4
>   (Resumption of 6:11-13)
>
> **Letter E, Resumed**
> F. Narration: Basis for Paul's Second Defense 7:5-16
>   (Resumption of 2:12-13)

Paul had sent his Letter of Tears; while impatiently waiting for Titus to report to him on the effect of the letter Paul went to Macedonia, where finally Titus found him and reported (7:5-16). In 7:5-7, Paul returns to the travel narrative, including the basic message from Titus. In verses 8-13a, Paul, on the basis of the good news from Titus, defends the Letter of Tears. He concludes his thoughts with statements of confidence about both Titus and the Corinthians themselves (7:13b-16).

8:1-24

> **Letter G (8:1-24)**
>
> G. Appeal to the Corinthians to Participate in the
>   Collection 8:1-24
>   1. Example: Generosity of the Macedonians 8:1-6
>   2. Thesis: Prime Directive 8:7-8
>   3. Argument in Support of Thesis 8:9-15
>   4. Recommendation of Titus and the Brothers 8:16-23
>   5. Concluding Emotional Appeal 8:24

In the composition of 2 Corinthians, the conclusion of chapter 7 prepares the listeners for chapter 8: based on the "complete confidence" Paul has in the Corinthians (7:16), he moves in chapter 8 into an appeal to them to participate in the collection. As is normal in deliberative rhetoric, Paul uses an example to encourage the Corinthians to give. In this case, the example is that of the Macedonians, who despite affliction, have responded with overflowing generosity (8:3).[58] Their response is an example of power in weakness.

The chief directive is in 8:7-8. In verse 7, Paul compliments the Corinthians on their desire to excel, knowing that they will "excel also in this generous undertaking" (8:7; "generous undertaking" translates the Greek word *charis*, often translated *grace*). Verse 8 makes an intriguing rhetorical move. Paul claims that he is not commanding them but rather is "testing the genuineness of your love against the earnestness of others" (8:8). Taking part in the collection becomes, then, a matter of honor for the Corinthians. But in addition to that dynamic for giving, he uses an important example to support his directive: "the generous act" (the Greek word again is *charis*) of Jesus, who "though he was rich, yet for your sakes he became poor, so that by his poverty you might become rich" (8:9).[59] On that basis, Paul gives his advice: complete the collection in accord with their means (8:10-11). Such giving results in a "fair balance" (8:13) or equality between the material abundance of the Corinthians and the need of the church in Jerusalem (8:14).

Verses 16-23 constitute a recommendation of Titus and the brothers who will be coming to Corinth to complete the work of the collection. A somewhat emotional appeal concludes this letter fragment, as Paul calls on the Corinthians to show proof of their love and proof that his boasting about them is based in reality (8:24).

9:1-15

> ### Letter H (9:1-15)
>
> H. Appeal to the People of Achaia to Participate in the Collection — 9:1-15
> 1. Identification of the Topic — 9:1
> 2. *Captatio benevolentiae* — 9:2
> 3. Sending of the Brothers — 9:3-5
> 4. Reasons for Giving — 9:6-14
> 5. Emotional Conclusion: Prayer of Thanksgiving — 9:15

Chapter 9 is another appeal related to the collection, but this time to Christ-believers in Achaia as a whole and not just to the city of Corinth. Verse 1 identifies the topic at hand but also is a disclaimer: "Now it is not necessary for me to write you about the ministry to the saints." Within the flow of the larger document called 2 Corinthians, the verse, as we have seen previously, appears a bit odd, coming on the heels of chapter 8.

Verse 2 utilizes once again the theme of eagerness, which was a constant refrain in chapter 8 (8:11, 12, 19). Paul has been using the eagerness of the Achaians to encourage the people of Macedonia (9:2). Rhetorically, the verse is what scholars call *captatio benevolentiae*, that is, a "capturing" of the listeners by praising them. Paul compliments them on their eagerness. Now, according to 9:3, he will take advantage of it! Negatively, however, he will be sending "the brothers" to finish the collection so that the Achaians and Paul will not be humiliated when they come—that is, they will not lose honor (9:4). Verse 5 contains Paul's directive: the brothers will come before Paul, finish collecting the gift, and have it ready when Paul arrives.

In verses 6-14, Paul details various reasons for giving. The appeal concludes with a prayer of thanksgiving designed to remind the Achaians of what God has already done for them and thus implicitly to encourage them to give in return: "Thanks be to God for his indescribable gift!" (9:15).

10:1—13:13

Letter F (10:1—13:10 [11-13])

I.	Paul's Third Defense	10:1—13:10
	1. Appeal for Obedience and Statement of Charge	10:1-6
	2. Sarcastic Restatement of Charge	10:7-11
	3. Sarcastic Comparison with Opponents	10:12-18
	4. The Fool's Speech: Refutation of Charge	11:1—12:13
	a. Introduction	11:1-15
	1. Paul's Jealousy	11:1-4
	2. Self-Comparison with Opponents	11:5-6
	3. Defense of Paul's Financial Independence	11:7-11
	4. Charges against Opponents	11:12-15
	b. Paul's "Foolish" Boast 1: Weakness	11:16-33
	1. Sarcastic Introduction	11:16-21a
	2. Paul's Qualifications as Member of Israel	11:21b-22
	3. Paul's Qualifications as a Minister	11:23-33
	c. Paul's "Foolish" Boast 2: Visions and Revelations	12:1-10
	1. Boast of a Heavenly Journey	12:1-7a
	2. Boast Qualified by Suffering	12:7b-9a
	3. Result: Boast of Weaknesses	12:9b-10
	d. Conclusion	12:11-13
	5. Renewal of the Appeal	12:14—13:10
	a. Announcement of Third Visit	12:14a
	b. Defense regarding Finances	12:14b-18
	c. Statement of Fears regarding Third Visit	12:19-21
	d. Warning regarding Application of Apostolic Authority	13:1-10

Chapters 10–13, in our outline, are Letter F, Paul's third defense. Although it is unlikely that it is the Letter of Tears, the section is blunt and hard-hitting. It begins with an appeal for obedience, together with the statement of a charge or indictment being made against him (10:1-6). The charge is that he is humble when face-to-face with them but bold toward them when away (10:1b). It is the same charge he faces in verse 10: "For they say, 'His letters are weighty and strong, but his bodily presence is weak, and his speech contemptible.'" Paul surrounds the first statement of the charge with an appeal for obedience so that he will *not* need to be bold when present again with the Corinthians.

In verses 7-11, Paul responds to the charge.[60] First, he boasts of belonging to Christ and of the authority given to him by the Lord. He is not ashamed of that authority. While verse 10 specifically restates the charge made against Paul by his opponents, verse 11 contains his very firm response: "Let such people understand that what we say by letter when absent, we will also do when present."

Having stated and responded to one of the charges being made against him, Paul in verses 12-18 sarcastically compares himself with his opponents in Corinth. He sharply comments on their propensity for comparing themselves with others. Paul would not do that, of course (although that is exactly what he is doing!). He would not dare to compare himself with them or dare to put himself into the same category (vs. 12). He, however, knows the limits (vss. 13-17) beyond which his boasting should not go (again, implicitly, his opponents do *not* know what the proper limits of boasting are), and just as important, he knows the limits God has set for his missionary work. Thus, "we were not overstepping our limits when we reached you; we were the first to come all the way to you with the good news of Christ" (vs. 14). Therefore, he and his coworkers have done their missionary work in such a way that they have no need of "boasting of work already done in someone else's sphere of action," because they have stayed out of the territory of other missionaries (vs. 16; see the statement of his operating principle in Rom 15:20). His opponents have not done that. From Paul's perspective, they have invaded his missionary territory and sought to corrupt it. Finally in this subsection, he points out that self-commendation (implicitly what his opponents are doing) does not count for anything. What does count is the Lord's commendation (10:18).

From 11:1 to 12:13, Paul uses the literary device of the fool's speech to organize his thoughts. His words in 11:1-15 introduce the speech, with verse 1 signaling what he proposes to do: "I wish you would bear with me in a little foolishness. Do bear with me!" Paul goes on to state his "divine jealousy" (11:2) for them, using the analogy of marriage: "I promised you in marriage to one husband, to present you as a chaste virgin to Christ" (11:2). Likely building on the image of Yahweh betrothed to Israel, according to the Judean Scriptures (Isa 54:5-6; 62:5; Ezekiel 16; Hos 2:19-20), Paul pictures himself as "the elder male of the family whose role it is to betroth the virgin church to Christ."[61] He is fearful, though, that they will lose their "sincere and pure devotion to Christ" (11:3). They may be deceived,[62] and in fact, they already easily enough accept another Jesus, a different spirit, and a different gospel from the ones Paul proclaimed (11:4). That those who purvey such false teaching are his opponents Paul makes explicit in verse 5 by comparing himself with them: "I think that I am not in the least inferior to these super-apostles." And why is he not inferior? "I may be untrained in speech, but not in knowledge" (11:6).[63]

Paul in verses 7-11 defends his financial independence from the Corinthians. The background for this issue is the patron-client relationships that honeycombed first-century societies. People in need of housing, food, other necessities, or favors had no "right" to them in the modern democratic sense. What people in need could do was to align themselves with a wealthier or more highly placed person who could provide what was needed or serve as a broker for what was lacking. That person was the patron of the needier person, the client. This patron, in turn, functioned as the client of someone higher up in the economic and/or social scale, and such relationships continued all the way to the emperor, who was the patron of all. The client, at whatever level, owed the patron loyalty.[64] Paul sought when possible financially to support himself when doing missionary work, although at times he needed to accept financial assistance. Thus, in 11:9, he refers to funds received from believers in Macedonia, but he maintained his apostolic independence by proclaiming the gospel in Corinth free of charge, thus declining to become the client of potential Corinthian patrons. And indeed that independence is a boast of his (11:11), ostensibly over against the opponents, who did place themselves into the client position by accepting money for their work.

In verses 12-15, Paul levels serious charges against his opponents. As opposed to 10:12, where Paul ironically declines to classify himself with the opponents, here he turns things in the opposite direction: "And what I do I will also continue to do, in order to deny an opportunity to those who want an opportunity to be recognized as our equals in what they boast about." He labels them as "false apostles, deceitful workers, disguising themselves as apostles of Christ" (11:13), whose "end will match their deeds" (11:15).

In verse 16, Paul resumes in a more obvious way the persona of the fool that he had announced in verse 1. The entire section (11:16-33) is devoted to Paul's first "foolish" boast. He begins by identifying once more his role as fool: "I repeat, let no one think that I am a fool; but if you do, then accept me as a fool, so that I too may boast a little" (11:16). But before boasting, he castigates the Corinthians with some of the harshest language of the entire letter: "For you gladly put up with fools, being wise yourselves! For you put up with it when someone makes slaves of you, or preys upon you, or takes advantage of you, or puts on airs, or gives you a slap in the face. To my shame, I must say, we were too weak for that!" (11:19-21a). We can only imagine the voice tones of the person reading these sentences to the Corinthians. The acid almost eats through the paper! The opponents, of course, are the real fools, and they are the ones who enslave, prey upon, take advantage of, lord it over, and slap the Corinthians.

In the rest of chapter 11, Paul turns to the specifics of the opponents' boasts—and his.[65] Of what do they boast? They boast that they are Hebrews, Israelites, and descendants of Abraham. Paul's answer to each of their boasts: "So am I" (11:22). He thus has honorable origins. They also boast that they are ministers of Christ (11:23). To that boast, Paul provides a much longer answer: "Are they ministers of Christ? I am talking like a madman—I am a better one: with far greater labors, far more imprisonments, with countless floggings, and often near death" (11:23). He goes on to list in some detail the suffering he has experienced: whippings, beatings, a stoning, shipwrecks, hard work, sleepless nights, hunger, thirst, cold, and nakedness (11:24-29). What qualifies him as a minister of Christ is the suffering he has endured. To the eyes of the world and the eyes of his opponents (and, regrettably for Paul, most likely the eyes of the Corinthians), such suffering has shown that he is weak. And as if to underscore that view, he relates his thoroughly dishonorable escape from Damascus: lowered in a basket that was let down through a window in the city wall (11:32-33). Yet exactly in those signs of weakness he boasts and claims his credentials as a minister of Christ (11:30).

Paul's "fool" continues in chapter 12 with another boast, this time related to "visions and revelations of the Lord" (12:1). Although Paul tells in the third person the story of a vision in which, in Christ, a person "fourteen years ago was caught up to the third heaven" (vs. 2), he is no doubt writing about his own experience (note vss. 6b-7a). Writing of oneself in the third person is a well-known rhetorical device in antiquity; in this case, it detaches Paul from the vision itself in order to maintain the focus on his primary criterion as an apostle, the criterion of weakness.[66] What he really wants to boast about are his weaknesses (12:5). He prefers not to boast as others boast but, on the contrary, simply have people evaluate him on "what is seen in me or heard from me" (12:6) in his role as an apostle, including his weaknesses.

As a way to keep him from exalting himself because of his visionary experience, "a thorn was given me in the flesh, a messenger of Satan to torment me, to keep me from being too elated" (12:7). The exact nature of this "thorn in the flesh" has been the subject of lengthy debate.[67] Many scholars seek to identify a physical ailment as the thorn in the flesh. Patricia Nisbet, for example, identifies an eye disorder sometimes called acute ophthalmia. The thorn, in that interpretation, would be "intermittent or encroaching blindness."[68] Alan Hisey and James Beck try to trace Paul's thorn to a hemorrhage that perhaps took place during the Damascus Road experience of Acts (9:1-9; 23:3-11; 26:9-18) and may be related to the visionary experience at the beginning of 2 Corinthians 12.[69] Such a hemorrhage could leave the intellect unaffected while creating problems in seeing, walking, and writing. Paul himself, while not designating the exact nature of the problem, does discuss in Galatians a physical problem that created the condition for his proclamation in Galatia (probably forcing him to stop traveling). That condition must have been obvious to others and perhaps offensive to them: "Though my condition put you to the test, you did not scorn or despise me, but welcomed me as an angel of God, as Christ Jesus" (Gal 4:14). Consequently, some have pointed to malaria or epilepsy.[70] Paul gives no data about the nature of a physical ailment, which is why the theories can vary so widely. Still, the sheer image of "thorn in the flesh" points to something that regularly causes Paul personal pain and difficulty.

Others identify the thorn as a figure of speech used by Paul to describe his opponents.[71] Jerry McCant shifts attention from Paul's opponents to the Corinthians themselves, who have rejected Paul's apostleship.[72] Whether "a messenger [Greek: *aggelos*; English: *angel*] of Satan" could clearly refer to a group of people is at least questionable.[73] Robert Price and J. W. Bowker represent those who trace the heavenly journey of 2 Corinthians 12 and the thorn in the flesh to Jewish mysticism, especially *Merkabah* mysticism, which is based on Ezekiel's vision of the throne of God.[74] Those who take such heavenly journeys are susceptible to angels or demons who seek to block their journey. While intriguing, this interpretation moves Paul's prayers and God's denial of relief to the heavenly sphere rather than the earthly, which is where Paul struggles.[75]

Paul prayed three times to have the thorn removed, but the Lord said to him, "My grace is sufficient for you, for power is made perfect in weakness" (12:9a). Thus, even when Paul allows himself to write of his heavenly journey, he qualifies what he says by the criterion of weakness. And "so, I will boast all the more gladly of my weaknesses" (12:9b). The reason he will boast of his weakness is "so that the power of Christ may dwell in me" (12:9c). The interplay of power and weakness in Paul's thought is directly counter to that of his opponents.

In verses 11-13, Paul concludes his fool's speech with another sarcastic barrage: "I am not at all inferior to these super-apostles," he writes, "even though I am nothing" (12:11). With reference once more to the issue of financial independence (previously addressed in 11:7-11), Paul finishes his speech: "How have you been worse off than the other churches, except that I myself did not burden you? Forgive me this wrong!"

In 12:14, Paul returns to and renews the appeal for obedience he introduced at 10:1-6. In verse 14a, he announces his third visit; from verse 14b through verse 18, he once more defends the financial management of both his ministry in Corinth and the collection for Jerusalem. But financial charges are not his only fear in returning to Corinth. In general, "I fear that when I come, I may find you not as I wish, and that you may find me not as you wish" (12:20). Nevertheless, in 13:1-10, he reasserts his apostolic authority. Again he refers to his upcoming third visit (13:1) and in a complex sentence issues this warning: "I warned those who sinned previously and all the others, and I warn them now while absent, as I did when present on my second visit, that if I come again, I will not be lenient" (13:2). For one last time in this letter, Paul works with the interplay between weakness and power (13:3-4), but the Corinthians should not be fooled—Paul will deal with them in a power-filled way. His final counsel is that they examine themselves (13:5-9), with the goal that he will not need to be so judgmental when he comes (13:10). Thus, Letter F concludes on a note much less harsh than much of the earlier content of the letter, but still with a clear assertion of Paul's apostolic authority.

13:11-13

Letter E, Resumed (Perhaps)

Epistolary Conclusion   13:11-13

The letter ends with a typical epistolary conclusion (perhaps originally from Letter E). A brief list of final imperatives ("put things in order, listen to my appeal, agree with one another, live in peace") is followed by the promise of God's presence ("and the God of love and peace will be with you," 13:11). Paul ends with greetings, including the holy kiss (13:12) and a benediction (13:13).

Effect and Summary

Did the communications work? That is an interesting question—in answer to which we have nothing from the Corinthians themselves to tell us. There is, of course, the sheer fact that the Corinthians preserved his letters. In addition, in Rom 15:26, which Paul wrote from Corinth after he wrote 2 Corinthians, he informs the Romans, "Macedonia and Achaia have been pleased to share their resources with the poor among the saints at Jerusalem." Thus, the data we do have point to ultimate success for Paul's letters to Corinth.

Taken as a whole, 2 Corinthians lays out Paul's understanding of his apostolic ministry from the inside. He tells us what he considers important, and what he considers important is the opposite of what his opponents think counts. For Paul, the center of ministry is the cross of Jesus. That same cross is exhibited in the suffering ministry of those called to serve in the name of Jesus. Therefore, to return to a key word in the benediction of chapter 1, affliction is not the sign of an unfaithful minister but is an indication of ministry that is consonant with the ministry of Jesus.

Study Questions

1. Which theory or theories about the compositional history of 2 Corinthians make the most sense to you? And which make the least sense? What are the reasons for your conclusion?
2. How does Paul use the image of the clay jar to talk about his ministry? In what ways might that language and its understanding of the human situation be helpful to people in general?
3. Contrast Paul's views on leadership with the views of his opponents. Where do you see similar discussions going on in your world?
4. What is Paul's self-understanding as a suffering apostle? How does he use it to legitimize his ministry?
5. Paul boasts of his weaknesses. What sense does that make, and how does Paul use that boasting in his ministry?
6. How could Paul have handled the problems in 2 Corinthians differently?

Suggested Reading

Barnett, Paul. *The Second Epistle to the Corinthians*. NICNT. Grand Rapids: Eerdmans, 1997.
Danker, Frederick W. *II Corinthians*. ACNT. Minneapolis: Augsburg, 1989.
Furnish, Victor Paul. *II Corinthians*. AB 32A. Garden City, NY: Doubleday, 1984.
Martin, Ralph P. *2 Corinthians*. WBC 40. Waco: Word, 1986.

Chapter 9: 2 Corinthians: Treasure in Clay Jars | 221

Matera, Frank J. *II Corinthians: A Commentary*. NTL. Louisville: Westminster John Knox, 2003.
Thrall, Margaret E. *The Second Epistle to the Corinthians*. ICC. 2 vols. Edinburgh: T & T Clark, 1994, 2000.
Wan, Sze-kar. *Power in Weakness: The Second Letter of Paul to the Corinthians*. NTC. Harrisburg, PA: Trinity Press International, 2000.
Witherington, Ben, III. *Conflict and Community in Corinth: A Socio-Rhetorical Commentary on 1 and 2 Corinthians*. Grand Rapids: Eerdmans, 1995.

Chapter 10

Romans: God Justifies the Ungodly

Not Ashamed of the Gospel

Imagine living in the crowded, dirty, exciting capital of the empire, the city of Rome. As a decade-long believer in Christ, you have heard of the missionary Paul, but you have never met him. You learned at work yesterday that the congregation had received a letter from him, so you rush to the weekly worship gathering to hear it read. The letter starts out well enough: "Paul, a servant of Jesus Christ, called to be an apostle" (Rom 1:1). Soon he indicates that he wants to proclaim the gospel in Rome (1:15). And then he explains why he wants to do that: "For I am not ashamed of the gospel; it is the power of God for salvation to everyone who has faith, to the Jew first and also to the Greek" (1:16). Why does he say he is not ashamed, what exactly is this gospel, and how does he view faith? You would ask similar questions of any Christ-believing teacher, but you have heard that Paul is soft on the Law and on ethical behavior.

Introducing Paul and His Gospel

As is typical of Paul, he places his theological cards on the table in the opening section of the letter (1:1-17). Because these lines are filled with information about the way Paul understands himself, his mission, and the Roman congregation he addresses, they deserve particular attention at the start of our discussion of the letter.

The salutation (1:1-7) is structured in typical fashion: sender (Paul) to recipients ("to all God's beloved in Rome"), greetings ("grace to you and peace"). What is not typical is the dramatic way in which Paul expands his self-identification. Since he is writing to a congregation he did not found, he needs to introduce himself and his gospel in ways unnecessary in his other letters. Paul says four things about himself in verse 1:

1. His name is Paul, which was his legal name outside Judean circles.
2. He is "a servant of Jesus Christ." The Greek word *doulos*, often translated "servant," is better translated with its more literal meaning, *slave*. The people of Israel often thought of themselves as slaves of God, with *slave of God* a title of **honor** for Moses, Joshua, David, and the prophets (2 Kgs 18:12; Judg 2:8; 2 Sam 7:5; Jer 7:25, for example). In addition, as Robert Jewett has reminded us,[1] Romans was written to the capital city of the Roman Empire. That empire was run by a vast bureaucracy, much of which was composed of slaves. On their tombstones, they proudly proclaimed that they were the "slaves of Caesar." Who is Paul, then? He also is a slave, but a slave of Christ. In writing to a city whose population was composed of 25 to 40 percent slaves,[2] Paul's language was particularly appropriate. What Paul is doing is to introduce himself with the proper credentials as the representative not of Caesar but of Christ Jesus. And he declares that Jesus is the Messiah, the Christ, terms with royal meaning, as they designate the anointed king of Israel who is to be the ruler of all kings (Pss 72:8-11; 89:27; Isa 11:1-4). Such language sets up the political-religious contrast between Caesar and Christ.[3]
3. Paul is "called to be an apostle." Paul did not appoint himself to be an apostle. God called him (see Gal 1:1, 11-12; Acts 9, 22, 26).
4. Paul says he was "set apart for the gospel of God," meaning God had called him to a particular task (see also Gal 1:15-16). The particular task was to announce the "gospel of God." *Gospel* (*euaggelion*) literally means *good news*. The word was used in imperial propaganda. So the citizens of Priene, in the province of Asia, proclaimed concerning Caesar Augustus in 9 BCE: "Not only has he surpassed earlier benefactors of humanity, but he leaves no hope to those of the future that they might surpass him. The god's [birthday] was for the world the beginning of the good news [plural of *euaggelion / gospel*] that he brought."[4] As Helmut Koester has reminded us, such inscriptions "result from the religio-political propaganda of Augustus in which the rule of peace, initiated by Augustus'

victories and benefactions, is celebrated and proclaimed as the beginning of a new age. *This* usage of the term *euaggelion* is new in the Greco-Roman world. It elevates this term and equips it with a particular dignity."[5] Over against that use of the word *gospel*, Paul almost certainly chose the word, which he uses over fifty times, to indicate that the good news of Jesus was different from and opposed to the good news of the emperor. In a more general way, Paul likely used *gospel* because what he had experienced in Jesus was such wonderful good news that it made everything else that claimed to be good news seem insignificant.

Paul continues his self-identification in the following verses by more closely identifying *the gospel of God* for which he has been set apart. He makes four points:

1. God promised the gospel in the scriptures of the people of Israel, especially through God's prophets (vs. 2).
2. This gospel from God is about God's Son, Jesus (vs. 3).
3. To outline his understanding of God's Son, Paul uses language he adopted from other Judean believers: "who was descended from David according to the flesh and was declared to be Son of God with power according to the spirit of holiness by resurrection from the dead" (vss. 3-4). Virtually every phrase represents language or theological understanding not found elsewhere in Paul, which is why scholars think Paul adopted the language from others.[6] Who would be concerned to identify Jesus as the son of David? (Other) Judean believers, so the words in 1:3b-4b are identified as part of an early Judean Christ-believing creed utilized by Paul.

   But why would Paul be concerned to quote such material? In 49 CE, the Emperor Claudius had expelled from Rome all Judeans. That order would have included Judean believers as well as non-Christ-believing Judeans, since the empire did not yet make such distinctions. At the time they were expelled, Judean believers were the largest ethnic group in the Roman churches and were the leaders. Once they left, Gentile believers naturally assumed leadership and continued to bring in new Gentile believers. After the expulsion order was lifted in 54 CE, Judeans began to return to Rome. Judean believers found that their churches had changed. Gentile believers were now the majority. Some practices and beliefs were different (see 14:1—15:6). In that situation, Paul signaled to Judean believers that he knew their traditions and could be trusted. At the same time, he added to the end of the borrowed material his own favorite way of designating Jesus, the word *Lord* (*kyrios*), which was popular among Gentile believers.
4. It is through the gospel about the Son that Paul is connected with the Romans. His call is to "bring about the obedience of faith among all the Gentiles" (*ethnē*; vs. 5), and the majority of the believers in Rome are Gentiles (vs. 6). Another valid and perhaps more precise way to translate *ethnē* in verse 5 is *nations*. *Gentiles* works especially when Paul is writing

about non-Judeans in distinction from Judeans (Rom 2:14; 3:29; 1 Cor 1:23; Gal 2:12, 14-15). But the word also has a corporate meaning, in which case it refers to the nations in a collective way as the nations of the world. Arland Hultgren suggests that Paul uses the term that way when he quotes the Septuagint (Rom 4:17, quoting Gen 17:5; Rom 10:19, quoting Deut 2:21; and Gal 3:8b, quoting Gen 12:3).[7] He also identifies that meaning in Rom 1:5; thus, Paul's task is "to bring about the obedience of faith among all the nations."[8] Translating *ethnē* in this and similar contexts as *nations* fits Paul's otherwise odd perspective that he had finished his work in the eastern part of the empire, even though the overwhelming majority of people had still never heard of Jesus. What he had done was to preach and establish congregations in representative cities in the east, having won "obedience from the nations" (15:18).[9]

We also should not pass too quickly the phrase *the obedience of faith* in verse 5. Discussions of Paul often center on his theme of believing—and rightfully so. But for Paul, believing is more than intellectual assent. It means complete trust in God, to such an extent that the believer also obeys God. To have faith means to use hands, heart, feet, indeed one's total life, in obedient service to God (see also 5:19; 6:16; 6:26; 12:1).[10] In 15:18, Paul returns specifically to obedience when he boasts about "what Christ has accomplished through me to win obedience from the Gentiles." Thus, already in the salutation, Paul is addressing an important issue: what does he have to say about ethical behavior (see the question posed in 3:8)? He is also redrawing "the boundaries which marked out the people of God,"[11] since the obedience of faith is extended to the Gentiles.

In verse 6, the Romans "are called to belong to Jesus Christ," and in verse 7, they "are called to be saints." Although they do not have the same call as Paul, they are still called by God. The call in verse 7 points to the boundary-shattering aspect of Paul's ministry. The Roman (basically Gentile) believers are called to be saints, the Greek word *hagioi* (literally, *holy ones*). In the scriptures of Israel, the saints or holy ones are not the morally perfect. Rather, they are the elect, the chosen ones, those who are holy because of their relationship with God (Deut 7:6 and 14:2 are clear expressions of this view). In calling the believers in Rome saints or holy ones, Paul is applying one of the important titles for the people of God in Israel's Scriptures to Christ-believing Gentiles and Judeans. To these holy ones, Paul finally concludes his salutation by wishing them grace and peace.

The thanksgiving and the narration connected to it lay out more of the letter's themes. In verse 8, Paul gives thanks "because your faith is proclaimed throughout the world." He not only compliments the Romans, he also raises faith as an important matter. In verses 9-10, he supports his thanksgiving by indicating that, "without ceasing," he prays for the Romans, requesting that he might be able to come to them. That statement moves into a brief narration of his history with the Romans—or, rather, his nonhistory. He longs to see them, "so that I may share with you some spiritual gift to strengthen you" (vs. 11). That statement indicates an assertion of authority (he is, after all, the apostle to the nations), but Paul quickly modifies his assertion: "or rather so that we may be mutually encouraged by each other's faith, both yours and mine" (vs. 12). But he has made his rhetorical point. He tells them again of his longtime yearning to see them (vs. 13). What has prevented him? He does not say. Perhaps the edict of Claudius has kept him out. Perhaps the passive verb in verse 13 ("but thus far [I] have been prevented") indicates a "divine passive," in which God is the implied actor (see also 15:22).

Whatever the details of his inability to come to Rome, Paul's eagerness to proclaim the gospel in Rome is clear (vs. 15), because he is "a debtor both to Greeks and to barbarians, both to the wise and to the foolish" (vs. 14). He owed all people the good news (gospel) of Jesus.

And it is that gospel to which he turns in verse 16. He says he is "not ashamed of the gospel." Why might he be ashamed of the gospel? Three possibilities seem most pertinent. First, a key question at the final judgment is whether or not people will be able to stand in God's presence (Isa 1:29; 28:16 [LXX]; 50:7; Ps 25:2, 20, etc.). Will they be honored or **shamed**? Paul knows that the good news of Jesus will stand with him, so just as Paul will not be shamed at the future judgment, he will not be ashamed now. Second, the cross of Jesus and the message streaming from that cross are, in Paul's world, very much shame filled. In fact, dying on a cross was probably the most dishonorable way to die. Staking one's life and future on such a shame-filled death was no way to win societal honor. By his statement, Paul acknowledges that and also turns upside down the normal way that honor and shame were reckoned. Third, one group at Rome may well have said that Paul's message *was* shameful, because he taught that Gentiles could be the recipients of God's salvation apart from obeying the Law of Moses.[12] The reason he is not ashamed is that this gospel about Jesus "is the power of God for salvation to everyone who has faith, to the Jew first and also to the Greek" (vs. 15).[13] The gospel, then, is the powerful way God saves. And it is powerful to the person who has faith—thus, the theme stated already in the salutation and thanksgiving is stated again in the thesis of the letter. That believer can be Judean or Gentile, but notice "to the Judean first." Paul maintains the priority of salvation history for the people of Israel, but he also extends it to the Gentile (or Greek). That theme will become the focus of chapters 9–11.

How is it that the gospel, this message proclaimed by human beings, is God's power for salvation? The answer is in verse 17: "For in it the righteousness of God is revealed through faith for faith; as it is written, 'The one who is righteous will live by faith.'" In the message proclaimed by Paul, the **righteousness** of God is revealed; it exercises its authority. But what is the righteousness of God? To understand that term, we should take five steps.

First, the word *righteousness* belongs to a word family that Paul frequently uses. The word translated *righteousness* is the Greek word *dikaiosynē*; a related noun, less used in Paul,[14] is *dikaiōsis* (translated "justification" in Rom. 4:25; 5:18). The adjective is *dikaios* ("righteous"), and the verb is *dikaioō* (literally, "I make righteous"). The same complex of words indicates justice. Thus, "righteousness of God" also means "justice of God," and "I make righteous" can also be translated "I justify."[15]

Second, the righteousness of God since antiquity has been understood in forensic terms, that is, the language of a law court. The image is that of a prisoner who stands in court to be sentenced. The prisoner is guilty. About that there is no question. The time for sentencing comes, but instead of condemning the prisoner, the judge declares the guilty prisoner innocent and sets the person free. God's righteous-making or justifying activity, in this model, is viewed as the removal of the sinner's sin and guilt and the declaration of the sinner's innocence because of the death and resurrection of Jesus.[16]

Third, C. E. B. Cranfield, Ernst Käsemann, and James D. G. Dunn[17] have reminded us that the language world of *righteousness* and related terms is also language of the covenant. To be just or righteous is to uphold the covenantal relationship. Thus, righteousness is a relational term. To speak of God as being righteous or just, therefore, means that God acts to restore or to uphold the covenant. So what God is doing when God is being righteous is to restore humanity to a positive relationship with God's self.

And it is God who must restore the relationship, because humanity has broken the covenant with God. Christ is the way in which God does the restoration. God thereby makes humanity righteous or just.

Righteousness intimately connected with Jesus as Christ represents, as the work by E. P. Sanders indicates,[18] a major shift from the perspective with which Paul grew up as part of the people of Israel. To be righteous in the literature of Israel meant to obey the Law and to repent of transgression. To be righteous in Paul means to be justified by Christ: "Most succinctly, righteousness in Judaism is a term which implies the *maintenance of status* among the group of the elect; in Paul it is a *transfer term*."[19]

Fourth, the construction *righteousness of God* has been understood in two different ways, depending on how the relationship between the two nouns is understood. The word *God* is in the Greek genitive case, which basically indicates possession (English adds the word *of* to bring out the possessive sense). Greek has two basic ways of understanding the genitive, in part resulting in the following two views:[20]

1. The classical Protestant view was that the term should be understood as an objective genitive, which means the noun in the genitive case (*God*) receives the implied action of the other noun. Thus, as in Luther, for example, this is the righteousness that is valid before God; it is God's gift to humanity and is the righteousness that "counts" in God's eyes. By means of that righteousness, the sinner is judged to be righteous. This view relies heavily on the forensic model. Others, both Protestant and Roman Catholic, have modified this first position to talk about a genitive of origin: the righteousness proceeds from God to humanity.

2. The second basic position is that we have in *righteousness of God* a subjective genitive, which means the righteousness belongs to God; it is God's righteousness (that is, God is the "subject" of the righteousness). This view was especially developed in the twentieth century by Ernst Käsemann.[21]

For him, the gift aspect of God's righteousness is inseparable from the Giver of the gift. So when the gospel is proclaimed, God is present in God's righteousness to justify or make right those who believe.

Fifth, Käsemann helps us expand the concept of the *righteousness of God* beyond a focus solely on individuals. Paul's concern, he argues, is much more than solely a concern for the individual, but rather the righteousness of God "is God's sovereignty over the world revealing itself eschatologically in Jesus."[22] That is, in the proclamation and activity of the righteousness of God, God is in the process of reclaiming the world, which for Käsemann is part of Paul's apocalyptic perspective. Further, justification turns the justified person toward the world God is reclaiming. God's power-filled gift obligates the believer to obedience (1:5 again) and also makes that obedience possible, as the believer is called to witness to God's justice/righteousness in the world.[23]

All of this is revealed "through faith for faith" (1:16, NRSV), or literally, "from faith into faith." The phrase is read in two ways: (1) It indicates that righteousness proceeds from the faithful response of the believer but that the process is ongoing as well. Faith is not a one-point-in-time action but a continuing one. (2) The phrase indicates a movement from *God's* faithfulness or *Christ's* faithfulness to humanity's faith response.[24] As support for his assertion that righteousness is based on faith, Paul turns to the prophet Habakkuk: "As it is written, 'The one who is righteous will live by faith'" (1:17b). The Greek words are in a somewhat different order from the NRSV and are more accurately translated as "The one who is righteous by faith will live." The words *by faith* define how a person is made *righteous*.[25]

In the rest of the letter, Paul will explore the implications of 1:1-17. His approach can be challenging. Keck contends, "Romans is the Everest of the Pauline range. Scaling its heights proves to be a challenge few students of Paul can refuse because, like Everest, it is there."[26] And the climb is well worth the effort. Luther suggests that Romans "is in truth the most important document in the New Testament, the gospel in its purest expression. . . . It is the soul's daily bread, and can never be read too often, or studied too much. . . . It is a brilliant light, almost enough to illumine the whole Bible."[27]

Why Did Paul Write to the Romans?

To attempt to understand why Paul wrote Romans, we need to step back into the history of the Christ-believing community in Rome and answer three prior questions:

1. How was the community founded?
2. How did the edict of Claudius affect the community?
3. What kinds of people made up the community to whom Paul wrote?

Answers to those questions provide the necessary background for developing theories about why he wrote to the Romans.

THE CHRIST-BELIEVING COMMUNITY IN ROME

We have little data on the founding of the community. An old tradition has Peter founding the church in Rome in the early 40s. But Paul in Romans, in the earliest evidence from a believer for the existence of the community in Rome, says nothing about Peter.[28] The earliest documents produced by Roman Christ-believers do not talk about Peter either as the founding missionary or as the first bishop of the congregation (*1 Clement* and *The Shepherd of Hermas*). The origins of the community are probably to be sought in the large Judean population living in Rome. By the time of Paul, between forty and fifty thousand Judeans lived there, and synagogues have been found in several quarters of the city.[29] After Rome took control of Judea, there was continual close contact between Rome and the Judean homeland. It is likely that belief in Christ was brought to Rome by Judean Christ-believing merchants, believers from elsewhere who relocated in Rome, or a missionary about whom we have no record. In part because Paul refers to a lengthy period of wanting to come to Rome (1:10, 13; 15:22), scholars look toward the decade of the 40s as the period when belief in Christ was introduced to that city.

In our discussion of 1:3-4, we have already explored the impact of the edict of Emperor Claudius. The changed demographic and theological situations no doubt created tensions between Gentile believers and Judean believers. The statement by Suetonius regarding the edict may possibly point to other, earlier tensions: "Since

Fig. 10.1 The emperor Claudius; bronze bust from about 50 c.e., from the National Archaeological Museum, Madrid.

the Jews constantly made disturbances at the instigation of Chrestus [*impulsore Chresto*], he [Claudius] expelled them from Rome."³⁰ Scholars consider it probable that the text refers to Jesus Christ and the message about him, which apparently created tensions within the Judean community. The statement also gives indirect evidence of the presence of Christ-believers in Rome prior to 49, a presence that is confirmed by Acts 18:2. The Christ-believing community in Rome was thus composed of both Gentiles and Judeans. To go beyond that to project percentages is speculation.

Given what we have seen regarding housing patterns and house churches, it is also probable that the Christ-believing community was divided into an unknown number of house groups. Indeed, in chapter 16, Paul greets five different groups (vss. 5, 10, 11, 14, 15) and perhaps others. An open question is how isolated or cooperative the various groups were. Although we do not know for sure, it is probable that by the time Paul wrote our letter, the Christ-believers in Rome had separated from the synagogue.³¹

WHY PAUL WROTE: SIX THEORIES

We are now able to turn more specifically to the reasons why Paul wrote our letter. We will look at six theories.

To Prepare for a Trip to Spain

One reason is clearly stated in the text of Romans (15:22-32): Paul planned a new missionary thrust in Spain, and he hoped that Rome and the Roman believers would become the launching pad and financial support for that new work.³² Jewett has developed a related position with his argument that Romans is essentially an ambassadorial letter, advocating a cooperative mission to evangelize Spain on behalf of the power of God. The theological argumentation of Romans outlines the gospel to be proclaimed, and the ethical portions show how the gospel is to be lived.³³

To Resolve Misunderstandings

Although Paul had not visited Rome, he was at least somewhat known by reputation to believers there. When Judeans were expelled from Rome, the Judean believers took refuge by and large in the eastern part of the empire. There they first heard about Paul. Some of them, like Prisca and Aquila, met Paul and even worked with him. Others knew him only by reputation, and not everything they heard was positive, for they ran into missionaries who opposed Paul and caused others to misunderstand him.

Evidence of such a misunderstanding is found in 3:8: "And why not say (as some people slander us by saying that we say), 'Let us do evil so that good may come'? Their condemnation is deserved!" The view of himself that Paul rejects in 3:8 is that anything goes for the law-free Christ-believer. As the outline of the letter indicates, Paul spent much space dealing with that misunderstanding (6:1—8:39). A second misunderstanding he needed to resolve had to do with the place of Israel in God's salvation scheme (3:1-4), a misunderstanding he addresses in chapters 9–11.

What Peter Stuhlmacher sees Paul doing in Romans, in part, is trying to beat his opponents to the theological punch. That is, by his letter, Paul is trying to keep his opponents from gaining a foothold in Rome before he can travel there. If they gain control, his missionary plans, including the mission to Spain, will be seriously endangered. So indeed he must lay out his basic theological understandings. He is in a battle for the future of his work for Christ.[34]

To Heal Divisions

A standard theory for why Paul wrote Romans is that he was seeking to heal divisions within the Roman Christ-believing community. Among scholars, the opinions on who is upset with whom and the nature of the problem vary:

- *Raise status of Judean believers.* The problem that the letter deals with is that of the relationship between the Gentile believers, who are now the majority, and the returning Judean believers, who have become a minority. Romans, according to Wolfgang Wiefel, "was written to assist the Gentile Christian majority, who are the primary addressees of the letter, to live together with the Jewish Christians in one congregation, thereby putting to an end their quarrels about status."[35] So in a society marked by hostility toward Judeans, Paul wants to raise the status of Judean believers in the eyes of Gentile believers.
- *Raise status of Gentile believers.* Francis Watson argues that Paul's discussions of law, works, grace, faith, and election are attempts to legitimate the validity of Gentile Christ-believing communities in which the Law was not observed. Thus, Paul is trying to elevate the position of Gentile believers in the eyes of Judean believers. Paul hopes by his letter to persuade the Judean believers to recognize the legitimacy of the Gentile congregation(s) and to join with the Gentiles in worship, thus ending their own relationship as Judean believers with the synagogue.[36]
- *Raise both.* Wright is certain that the Edict of Claudius and the return of Judean believers to Rome were at the heart of the difficulties: "When the Jews returned to Rome in 54 upon Claudius's death, we may properly assume that the (Gentile) church leadership would not exactly be delirious with excitement."[37] Wright then puts together two scenes from Paul's missionary life: his desire to use Rome as a base for mission in Spain, as he had used Antioch previously, and his memories of problems in Antioch, where Judean believers thought they were superior to Gentile believers. The problem in Rome, according to Wright, is a mirror of the problem in Antioch. How could Paul avoid marginalizing or isolating Judean believers while at the same time avoiding the claims to Judean superiority he had had to encounter in Antioch?[38]
- *Offer a new identity.* Related is the position of Philip F. Esler, who asserts that Paul is attempting to exercise leadership over the Judean and

non-Judean believers by seeking to reinforce the fundamental common identity that they (and he) share in relation to God and Christ. Paul seeks to create a unity between Judean and Greek ethnic subgroups that will overcome the previously existing hostility between them. He does that by proposing a new, overarching identity in Christ that will become a sort of supra-identity that allows the subgroups to retain their original ethnic identities.[39]

To Rehearse for Jerusalem Trip

In 15:30-31, Paul requests with emotion, "I appeal to you, brothers and sisters, by our Lord Jesus Christ and by the love of the Spirit, to join me in earnest prayer to God on my behalf, that I may be rescued from the unbelievers in Judea, and that my ministry to Jerusalem may be acceptable to the saints." Some scholars have concluded that Paul is trying to do two things with his letter: (1) indirectly appeal to those in Rome who have significant contacts in Jerusalem to use them on Paul's behalf; and (2) rehearse with the Romans the approach he will take when he arrives in Jerusalem.

To Create a Timeless Treatise or Circular Letter

One frequent understanding of Romans moves in a totally different direction. Romans is viewed either as a timeless treatise or a circular letter that was sent to many believing communities, not only to Rome. In either case, Romans is seen as a sort of mini-systematic theology of Paul.[40] In that view, any attention to delineating an exact historical situation is misplaced energy.

This theory seems to fit the data of Romans the least. Although it has a long history, it is today a decidedly minority position, in part because of the connections we have seen between Paul and believers in Rome. It also misunderstands how Paul does theology: not in isolation with the goal of formulating a well-rounded system but in response to specific contexts, even in the case of Romans. Certainly, Romans does contain much theology that has been very important over the centuries, but it does not deal with everything in an encyclopedic way.[41]

For Multiple Reasons

Perhaps the best that can be done is to acknowledge with A. J. M. Wedderburn that no one reason is the sole reason Paul wrote. So Wedderburn argues that the complexity of the letter leads to the identification of multiple purposes; hence the title of his study, *The Reasons for Romans*.[42] A summary of the reasons Paul wrote is contained in the textbox.

As to whom Paul needs to raise in the eyes of others, Wright's position answers the most questions: the tightrope Paul is walking in Romans is one on which his balancing pole needs continually—and carefully—to swing between the Judean believers' side and the Gentile believers' side so that neither is made to feel inferior or superior to the other. "Or is God the God of Jews only? Is he not the God of Gentiles also? Yes, of Gentiles also" (3:29).

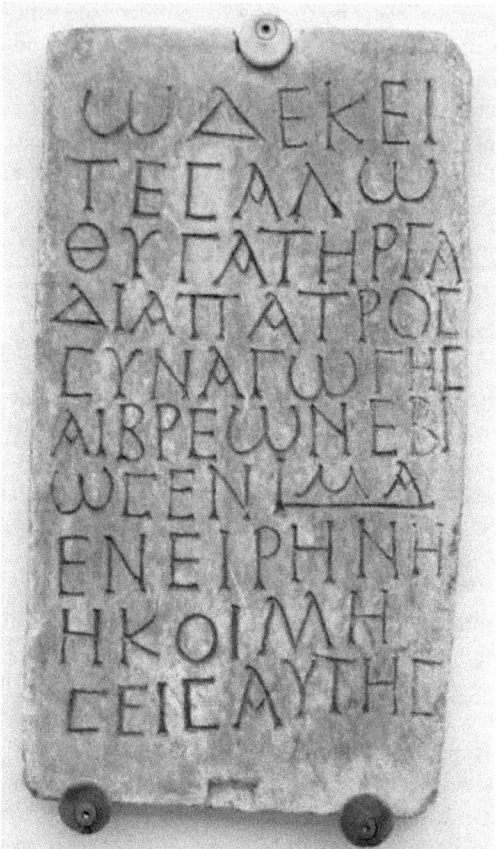

Fig. 10.2 A third-century c.e. funeral inscription for Salo, daughter of Gadias, "father of the synagogue of the Hebrews," one of a number of ancient synagogues in the imperial capital.

What Genre(s) Did Paul Use?

Romans is a real letter with multiple purposes. Of the three subgenres of rhetoric we have studied (**judicial, deliberative**, and **epideictic**), epideictic is the best match for the majority of the document.[43] Epideictic rhetoric affirms common beliefs and values and uses that affirmation to gain support. It frequently uses praise and/or blame. The rhetorical goal of Romans is to commend Paul's understanding of the gospel to a community he does not yet know but hopes soon to visit. As we have seen, he commends the Romans, and he certainly seeks their

> ### Why Did Paul Write Romans?
>
> - To prepare the Romans for his visit to them.
> - To ask them to help support his new missionary work in Spain.
> - To gain acceptance for his understanding of the gospel.
> - To resolve any misgivings about his understanding of the gospel and to prevent inroads by missionaries who disagreed with him.
> - To heal divisions between Judean believers and Gentile believers.
> - To ask for prayers for his trip to Jerusalem and possibly intercession with Jerusalem believers.

support for the Jerusalem trip and the Spanish mission. These rhetorical considerations are close, also, to Jewett's designation of Romans as an ambassadorial letter.

A style of argumentation Paul often uses in Romans is diatribe.[44] In this method of teaching, the teacher-philosopher raises objections to his opinions which the students have made—or might make in the future (or privately with their friends!). The class session proceeds on a question-and-answer or statement-and-response basis in which potential objections to the teacher's position are surfaced and answered. The flow of the teaching was similar to a comedy team in which one person is the straight man who sets up the other comedian; the straight man or woman in the diatribe is known as the interlocutor. Good examples of the diatribe style are found in 3:1-4 and 6:1-2. A result of this kind of argument is that Paul does not always move directly from point A to point B, but in between will deal with various aspects of the issue, as objections and questions are raised.

In terms of literary integrity, the only substantial questions regarding the original form of Romans have to do with chapter 16. There are two questions: First, is chapter 16 part of Paul's original letter to Rome, or is it a later, separate letter of recommendation appended to chapters 1–15? Second, are verses 25-27 an addition, whether or not chapter 16 is original? Those questions will be explored in the later discussion of chapter 16.

Where and When Did Paul Write?

As we saw when we studied 2 Corinthians, Paul wrote Romans during his final stay in Corinth during the fall and winter of 56–57. By the spring of 57, he was on his way to Jerusalem. Other dates, of course, are proposed, and it is not at all impossible that Paul wrote Romans a year earlier or a year later.[45]

The place of writing is Corinth or, more exactly perhaps, Cenchreae (16:1). Cenchreae was one of the harbor towns associated with Corinth and was seven miles from the city.

1:18—3:20

In our study of the opening of Paul's letter, we saw that Paul stated the thesis in 1:16-17. As a negative proof of the thesis (or as an indication of the need for the truth stated in the thesis), Paul develops in 1:18—3:20 a section in which he alleges that humanity is universally sinful and therefore deserving of the wrath of God. God's wrath is not, in the Bible, the same thing as anger or being peeved, however. To understand the concept of the wrath of God, we need to consider three points:

1. The basic characteristic of God in the Bible is that God is *holy*—that is, separate, special, and distinct from humanity. Psalm 99, for example, refers to God's holiness several times (vss. 3, 5, 9). The heavenly creatures in Isaiah also continually praise God's holiness: "And one called to another and said: "Holy, holy, holy is the LORD of hosts; the whole earth is full of his glory" (Isa 6:3).
2. Wrath is the reaction of God to what is sin, to what is unholy (see Rom 2:5).
3. According to Fitzmyer, wrath is Paul's "inherited way of expressing the inevitability of evil finding its own retribution."[46] That is, when God's laws are broken, an inevitable response begins. Wrath, in a sense, "protects" or participates in God's holiness. When humanity crosses the line—when humanity sins—wrath comes into play. Wrath, then, is reflexive. When humanity crosses the boundaries God has set, humanity brings upon itself the corresponding punishment.

Why, in Romans 1, does God express wrath? Paul's answer is in 1:19-20: God had revealed enough of God's self that people should have known better than to act as they did. The result? "They are without excuse." And who are "they"? Probably Gentiles. Gentiles might respond to Paul, "God never gave *us* the Law of Moses. How did we know what we were supposed to do?" Paul's response was that all people are responsible for their actions, since God has shown enough of who God is in the created world that people should have known that God existed and honored God as God.

But that is not how people acted (1:21-23). They worshipped everything except God, thus breaking the first commandment from Exod 20:3, "You shall have no other gods before me." So Paul charges, "they exchanged the truth about God for a lie and worshiped and served the creature rather than the Creator" (1:25). Certainly, in Paul's world, there were many different gods, but his analysis cuts even more deeply. The "creature" humanity serves, from Paul's perspective, is often humanity itself. People put themselves, rather than God, at the center of life.[47]

How does the wrath of God work itself out? In Romans 1, there is nothing about fire coming from heaven to incinerate everyone who sins. Rather, Paul gives a strange answer: "Therefore [because of confusing Creator and creature] God gave them up in the lusts of their hearts to impurity, to the degrading of their bodies among themselves" (1:24). Achtemeier writes:

> The wrath which God visits on sinful humanity consists in simply letting humanity have its own way. . . . In a move that our contemporary world shows is perhaps the most terrifying thing God could do, God punishes sin by letting us have control over our own destinies. . . . The way God in his wrath delivers humanity over to the just punishment of sin is to become permissive. He withdraws the gracious power of his absolute lordship and allows other lordships to prevail.[48]

The specific sins in 1:26-32, therefore, are the result of the basic sin and thus the working out of humanity's non-God-related desires. They also show, from Paul's perspective, how sin has reversed the order of what God has created.[49]

As we have seen, most likely in 1:18-32, Paul is referring specifically to Gentile sinners. He caps his denunciation of sin with these words, "They know God's decree, that those who practice such things deserve to die—yet they not only do them but even applaud others who practice them" (1:32). The listeners hear 1:32 and sit on the edge of their seats: "Off with their heads!" But then Paul reverses directions: "Therefore you have no excuse, whoever you are, when you judge others; for in passing judgment on another you condemn yourself, because you, the judge, are doing the very same things" (2:1). Paul probably turns in 2:1 to his Judean Christ-believing listeners, but in a more general way, he turns to all listeners as they sit in judgment. In relationship to those who belong to the people of Israel, Paul maintains that, although they have the law and circumcision, they are ultimately no better off than the Gentiles, for they do not practice the law. So in 2:17-24, Paul condemns the Judean who relies on and boasts in the Law without practicing the Law, and in a move that would have been impossible for most Law-abiding Judeans of his day, Paul relativizes the value of circumcision (2:25-29), so that "real circumcision is a matter of the heart—it is spiritual and not literal" (2:29).

The way chapter 2 concludes leads to the questions at the beginning of chapter 3: "Then what advantage has the Jew? Or what is the value of circumcision?" (3:1). The listener might well expect that Paul would say, "There is no advantage. There is no value." But Paul has led us down a rhetorical pathway that takes a sharp turn, for his basic answer is, "Much in every way" (3:2). He has also introduced one of the questions he will answer later: Has God been unfaithful to the people of Israel? In verse 8, he introduces a second question, one that likely is a misunderstanding of his view of the law and ethical behavior: "And why not say (as some people slander us by saying that we say), 'Let us do evil so that good may come'?" Paul does not answer that question at this point, but he will deal with it later (6:1—8:39; 12:1—15:13).

For now, he returns to his basic concern in 1:18—3:20, that of the universal sinfulness of humanity. Who, then, sins? Paul's answer: everyone. To be a sinner for Paul means less one who commits individual acts of sinful behavior and more one whose basic life orientation is misdirected. The condition of being sinful is thus more profound than we might think.[50] So he concludes, "There is no one who is righteous, not even one" (3:10), and, "All, both Jews and Greeks, are under the power of sin" (3:9).

3:21—5:21

Given that the relationship between God and humanity has been broken by humanity (1:18—3:20), how is that relationship restored? As Paul begins his answer in 3:20, he takes us back to 1:16-17 by reintroducing the righteousness of God. Over against humanity's sin, God has revealed God's righteousness. It "is attested by the law and the prophets" (compare 1:2), but it is "the righteousness of God through faith in Jesus Christ for all who believe" (3:21).[51] Thus, righteousness comes through Jesus and belief in him.

In seeking to lay out the meaning of Christ's death, Paul uses three images: **justification, redemption,** and **sacrifice**. We have already investigated justification and **righteousness**. God is righteous by restoring humanity's relationship with God through the cross of Jesus. So those who believe "are now justified by his grace as a gift" (vs. 24). **Grace** is God's unmerited love.

The second image Paul uses is redemption (vs. 24b). The original home of this language was slavery. To redeem a slave was to free the slave in a religious ceremony, usually by paying money. There is a strong sense in this term of paying the price or ransoming the slave. In Israel's Bible, the major action of redemption is the freeing of God's people from being slaves in Egypt (see Deut 7:8, for example). Paul reapplies that language to help explain what has happened in Jesus.[52]

The third image in chapter 3 for what has happened in Jesus is sacrifice: Jesus is the one "whom God put forward as a sacrifice of atonement by his blood, effective through faith" (vs. 25). The connection with faith occurs again. But what is a "sacrifice of **atonement**"? We need to take five quick steps involving Greek and some references to Israel's Scriptures.

- First, "sacrifice of atonement" (NRSV) is the translation of a single Greek word, *hilastērion*.
- *Hilastērion* is another word from Israel's Scriptures and usually means *the lid of the ark of the covenant*.
- *Covenant* in this case refers to the two tablets on which the law given to Moses was written. *Ark* refers to the portable chest or box in which the tablets were kept. It indicated God's presence with Israel, both during the wandering in the wilderness and during the time of Solomon's temple in Jerusalem.
- The lid of the ark of the covenant is, then, the lid that sits on top of the ark (see Exod 25:10-22; note that *lid* is often translated in the NRSV as *mercy seat*, with a note to the alternative translation, *the cover*).
- Two important things happen at the ark and its lid. First, that is where God meets humanity. Thus, in Exod 25:21-22, God says, "You shall put the mercy seat [lid] on the top of the ark. . . . There I will meet with you, and from above the mercy seat [lid], . . . I will speak with you of all that I will give you in commandment for the people of Israel." The other important action at the lid of the ark is that it was sprinkled with blood on the Day of Atonement (Lev 15:15).

So what does it mean to say that Jesus is the "sacrifice of atonement"? It means, first, that Jesus is where God and humanity meet. And second, just as the sacrificial blood of animals kept the Mosaic covenant in force, so the sacrificial blood of Jesus renews the first covenant, gives it new meaning, and works the forgiveness of sins (3:25-26).[53] That Jesus has died for humanity is a constant theme in Paul's writings (Rom 5:6, 8; 14:15; 2 Cor 5:14, 15, 21; Gal 1:4; 2:20; 1 Thess 5:10).

In light of what Paul has developed in verses 21-26, any boasting of achievement is, simply, excluded (vs. 27). The reason is "that a person is justified by faith apart from works prescribed by the law" (vs. 28; see the textbox, "'Works of the Law' and the New Perspective on Paul"). That method of justification applies to all people equally, whether part of the people of Israel or not (vs. 30).

As an extensive proof of that claim, in chapter 4, Paul turns once more to Abraham (see Galatians 3). After eliminating works (achievement) as the ground for Abraham's justification (4:2), Paul turns, as he did in Galatians 3, to Gen 15:6. As we saw in the discussion of the Genesis passage,[60] Abraham is made right with God through faith. Thus, God has from the very beginning operated on the basis of righteousness through faith. In verses 4-5, Paul underlines the total gift nature of faith and righteousness: "To one who without works trusts him who justifies the ungodly, such faith is reckoned as righteousness" (vs. 5). That God justifies the *un*godly runs counter to normal understandings of what it is to be just/righteous in God's sight (see also 5:6).

Later in chapter 4, Paul gives further attention to God's promise that Abraham would be the father of many nations (vss. 17-18). But Abraham had no outward guarantee of God's promise. He had no proof that God would come through. So Abraham "hoped against hope" (vs. 18), for his own body was dead in terms of the ability to reproduce, as was Sarah's (vs. 19). But Abraham never wavered (vs. 20). Why not? He was "fully convinced that God was able to do what he had promised" (vs. 21), and "Therefore his faith 'was reckoned to him as righteousness'" (vs. 22).

The beginning of chapter 5 draws present-tense implications from justification: "Therefore, since we are justified by faith, we have peace with God through our Lord Jesus Christ." Justified people also boast (contrast the exclusion of the wrong kind of boasting in 3:27). They boast in the hope of sharing the glory of God (vs. 2), and they boast in their sufferings (vs. 3), knowing that hope will not disappoint them (in Greek, does not shame them).

In verses 6-11, Paul looks both to the past and to the future. First to the past: Christ died (vs. 6). When? "While we were still weak." And for whom did he die? "For the ungodly," the same theme as in 4:5. Note the use in 5:6 of the preposition *hyper* (on behalf of), which he also uses in 1 Thess 5:10; 2 Cor 5:14. Thus, Christ's death is not for the perfect nor the good but, in fact, for sinners (5:8). The past-tense results of his death are justification by his blood (vs. 9) and reconciliation to God (vs. 10). Paul also looks to the future: we will be saved (vss. 9, 10). The verb *save* is normatively in Paul reserved for future time. So in verse 9, Paul and his

> ## "Works of the Law" and the New Perspective on Paul
>
> Rom 3:28 maintains, "A person is justified by faith apart from works prescribed by the law," and 3:20 states, "'No human being will be justified in his sight' by deeds prescribed by the law." In both cases, the more literal phrase is *works of the law* (*ergōn nomou*). The interpretation of that phrase took a significant new turn in 1977 with the publication by E. P. Sanders of *Paul and Palestinian Judaism*.[54] He argued that the Judaism of the time of Jesus and Paul was best called "covenantal nomism," which means the law of Moses was understood by Judean people to be a way to keep the covenant going, but not a way to establish the covenant or to "get right" with God. That basic view resulted in other conclusions:
>
> - Ancient Judaism was a religion of grace; a person did not get in by fulfilling the law.
> - Ancient Judaism was not a religion of legalism and works-righteousness.
> - *Works of the law* refers to the identity markers of Judaism, the chief of which are circumcision, food laws, and Sabbath observance. James Dunn has in particular picked up that insight and coined "the New Perspective on Paul" as the name for this view of Paul's thought.[55]
>
> Starting around 2000, a massive critique came forward, signaled by the work of Charles Talbert.[56] The work of E. P. Sanders, James D. G. Dunn, and other proponents of the New Perspective sent scholars back to the primary, ancient Judean sources, where they found in text after text, they asserted, the view that keeping the law of Moses does in fact result in salvation. So Brendan Byrne concludes, "There is a genuine historical context for what appears to be an opposition in Romans between righteousness by faith and a quest for righteousness through performance of the law."[57] Even if one were to agree with Sanders that such texts say only that to stay inside the covenant, one must keep the Law, does that not make the Law essential for salvation? Hultgren elaborates: "One must take Paul as an important witness to first-century views concerning the law, and there one finds evidence that, for this former Pharisee, Torah observance had been the way of righteousness in the community he knew (Rom 9:31; 10:5; Phil 3:9). Moreover, those practices were not simply 'boundary markers' of Jewish identity—which they were—but, at least for some, a basis for justification and final salvation as well."[58]
>
> It is possible, at least to a certain extent, to bring the two views together, as we sought to do in chapter 7,[59] and as Hultgren has done. In fulfilling the Law, a person illustrated that she or he was properly living (and thus was righteous) as a member of the covenant people of God (thus living within the identity markers of Judaism). The questions for Paul were whether that fulfillment was sufficient for the Judean and whether it was required of the Gentile.

listeners will be saved from God's wrath (future tense), and in verse 10, they will be saved by Jesus' life (future tense). For Paul, believers have not already been saved. Justified, yes. Reconciled, yes. But not yet saved. His care in talking about salvation as a future phenomenon is part of his larger framework of "already but not yet."[61]

In verses 12-21, Paul contrasts Adam and Christ. Just as Adam is understood to be the human being who stands at the beginning and whose actions determine the fate of humanity (Genesis 1–2), so Jesus Christ is understood to be the one who stands at the beginning of a new humanity and whose actions determine those who follow him. Of the several themes Paul develops in 5:12-21, one that is prominent is obedience (compare 1:5, "to bring about the obedience of faith"). Adam in 5:19 was disobedient (*parakoē*); Jesus was obedient (*hypakoē*). Jesus' obedience is what enables the obedience of those who follow him. The result is that humanity in Christ is freed from the power of death.

6:1—8:39

In chapter 6, Paul proposes that Christ-believers are also freed from the power of sin. He begins with questions typical of diatribe: "What then are we to say? Should we continue in sin in order that grace may abound?" In other words, if God responds to sin with grace, why not just keep on sinning? (See also 6:15.) Paul thereby restates the misunderstanding he identified in 3:8. He responds to the

Adam and Christ in Romans 5

Adam		Christ	
vs. 15:	trespass	vs. 15:	free gift
	many died		grace and free gift abounded
	through the one man's trespass		in the grace of the one man
vs. 16:	effect of the one man's sin	vs. 16:	free gift
	judgment		free gift
	following one trespass		following many trespasses
	brought condemnation		brings justification
vs. 17:	because of the one man's trespass		[through the one man, Jesus Christ]
	death exercised dominion		those who receive the abundance of grace and the free gift of righteousness will exercise dominion
	through that one		through the one man, Jesus Christ
vs. 18:	one man's trespass		one man's act of righteousness
	led to condemnation for all		leads to justification and life for all
vs. 19:	by the one man's disobedience		by the one man's obedience
	the many were made sinners		the many will be made righteous
vs. 21:	sin exercised dominion in death		grace might also exercise dominion through justification

questions with his own brief statement and two more questions: "By no means! How can we who died to sin go on living in it? Do you not know that all of us who have been baptized into Christ Jesus were baptized into his death?" (6:3). The baptism of the believers united them with the fate of their Lord. Those baptized enter *into* the life of Christ Jesus, become part of the body of Christ, and are identified with Christ (but without in any way *becoming* Christ).

In 6:4, Paul repeats his assertion about the identity of believers with the death of Jesus: "Therefore we have been buried with him by baptism into death." At the same time, he connects that death-identity with the resurrection of Jesus: "so that, just as Christ was raised from the dead by the glory of the Father, so we too might walk in newness of life" (6:4).[62] The identification of the believer is therefore not with the death of Jesus alone but also with the saving power of that death expressed in the resurrection. That saving power works so that the believer is able to "walk in newness of life." As we saw in our study of 1 Thessalonians, *walk* is a strong ethical term for how one walks one's life, that is, how one lives his or her ethical life as a believer. So, in answer to the questions posed in 6:1, the one who believes in Jesus does not remain in sin but walks in new ways.[63]

Paul continues his discussion of freedom from sin by presenting in verses 12-21 this model: everyone is in slavery; everyone has a lord. The only choice is to whom one will be obedient: sin, which leads to death, or God in Christ, which leads to righteousness (vs. 16). Paul uses the death of the believer in baptism as the centerpiece for his position that the believer is freed also from the power of the law (7:1-6). The listener might think that the law is only a negative for Paul, but he concludes that "the law is holy, and the commandment is holy and just and good" (vs. 12). One of the functions of law is to identify what is within bounds and what is outside bounds. That identification causes people to desire what is outside the boundaries: "sin, seizing an opportunity in the commandment, produced in me all kinds of covetousness" (vs. 8) and "deceived me and through it killed me" (vs. 11). So it is not the law that is at fault, but sin.

Sin is thus more than individual misdeeds. For Paul, sin also means a condition of humanity. And as we have seen, it means broken relationships: with God (1:18, 21-25) and with other people (1:26-32). In Romans 7, Paul writes about a third relationship that is broken by sin: the one people individually have with themselves. When people are separated from God, they are also divided within themselves. So Paul looks back at what his life was like outside a relationship with God in Christ: "I do not understand my own actions. For I do not do what I want, but I do the very thing I hate. . . . For I do not do the good I want, but the evil I do not want is what I do" (7:15, 19).[64]

Why is that the case? It is the case, for Paul, because when people are separated from God, they are controlled by sin (vs. 17). Sin, in addition to individual misdeeds, is also a power, a force in the world that works outside people as well as inside of them. Humanity falls prey to sin and finds itself trapped in it. As a power, sin overtakes the life of the individual and rules that life in such a way that the individual's positive will is overridden and controlled by sin (or, better expressed, by *sin* with a capital *S* = *Sin*). Does that absolve people of responsibility for their own actions? Not for Paul, since people have individually bought into the realm of Sin by displacing God at the center of life and trying to place themselves there (1:18-25). People have welcomed the power of Sin—and then been overwhelmed by it.[65] So in 5:12, Paul writes, "Death came through sin, and so death spread to all because all have sinned."

The result of this for Paul is internal division: "I can will what is right, but I cannot do it" (7:18b; see the textbox "Flesh and Body"). There is no way that he can work his way out of this dilemma. And that leads him to the shout of desperation, "Who will rescue me from this body of death?" (vs. 24). The answer for Paul is Jesus Christ (vs. 25), an answer he states even more explicitly in chapter 8: "There is therefore now no condemnation for those who are in Christ Jesus. . . . By sending his own Son in the likeness of sinful flesh, and to deal with sin, he condemned sin in the flesh, so that the just requirement of the law might be fulfilled in us, who walk not according to the flesh but according to the Spirit" (8:1, 3-4).

In addition to his emphasis on the work of Christ, Paul has introduced the Spirit. For Paul the **Spirit** (or **Holy Spirit**) was God's end-time power, seen already both in the resurrection of Jesus from the dead and in the present activity of God in the community of believers. It was imparted to believers through baptism, and it made them into the body of Christ (12:3-8). The Spirit is also the power that stands over against the flesh (8:4-11) and provides believers a new center for their lives. Thus, "all who are led by the Spirit of God are children of God" (8:14). *Children* is in Greek the word *sons / huioi*. In the Judean Scriptures, *sons of God* refers to the people of Israel (for example, Deut 14:1).[66] Just as God adopted Israel in the past, now God has adopted those who are led by the Spirit,

---

Flesh and Body

Although Paul is not totally consistent in his use of terms, he normally distinguishes between *flesh* and *body*. *Body* for him means the entire person. The body comes from God and belongs to God, and it is in the body that the believer brings glory to God (1 Cor 6:19-20). *Body* is so important for Paul that he cannot conceive of a resurrection existence without some sort of body (1 Cor 15:44-49). The term is thus a positive one for Paul.

Flesh also refers to the entire person, but with the special meaning of referring to people in their weakness or fallenness. *Flesh* almost always has a negative sense. So when Paul wants a shorthand term for the person/body who has fallen into sin, he uses *flesh*. When flesh is elevated and becomes the focus of a person's life, then that life is misdirected and opposed to God. Such a life serves the flesh and thinks in terms of the flesh (Rom 8:6, 12). For that reason, "those who are in the flesh cannot please God" (8:8). The believer, by contrast, is not in the flesh but in the Spirit (8:9): that is, the Christ-believer is not ruled by the flesh (the body as misused) but by the Spirit.

whether or not they are part of the original people of God. So the person adopted in baptism is able to call God *Father* (vs. 15).

In verse 17, Paul draws implications for the identity of believers as children of God. If they are God's adopted children, they are also God's heirs. Paul builds quite a crescendo: "children, heirs, heirs of God, joint heirs of Christ." Everything seems to be moving in a positive direction. But then the progression stops dead: "if, in fact, we suffer with him so that we may also be glorified with him." Being an heir with Christ means being an heir not only of future glory but also of present suffering. So Paul calls his listeners to identify with the suffering in the world and *of* the world (8:18-30), a world subjected to decay but awaiting redemption and restoration.

The conclusion of the chapter recapitulates the main points of the argument and makes an emotional appeal for consent and commitment.[67] Paul organizes the material in diatribe fashion. Verse 31a is the introductory question. Verse 31b begins the first rhetorical exchange: "If God is for us, who is against us?" Paul responds with another question. God gave God's own son; there is nothing else that God will withhold (vs. 32). The second rhetorical exchange is in verse 33. The question: "Who will bring any charge against God's elect?" Answer: "It is God who justifies." The implication of this exchange can best be understood when put together with the third rhetorical exchange, in vs. 34. The question: "Who is to condemn?" Answer: "It is Christ Jesus, who died, yes, who was raised, who is at the right hand of God, who indeed intercedes for us." The basic point of verses 33 and 34 is the same. The only ones who could condemn the believers are the very ones who protect them. No matter what charge is brought, God is still the one who justifies. No matter what condemnation is attempted, Christ Jesus is the one who intercedes. The fourth rhetorical exchange (vss. 35-39) begins with the question "Who will separate us from the love of Christ?" The word *separate* also means in Greek to *divorce* (*chōrizō*). What will divorce believers from Christ's love? Paul gives an extensive list of life factors and cosmic forces that potentially could threaten that relationship, but he concludes that none of those things "will be able to separate us from the love of God in Christ Jesus our Lord" (8:39). These verses bring to a conclusion the themes that were stated in 5:1-11 at the beginning of this lengthy section of Romans.

9:1—11:36

An opinion that was registered already at the beginning of chapter 3 but that Paul has not yet dealt with is the view that God has rejected the people of Israel. Given the ways Paul has relativized the importance of the law (of Moses) and circumcision, and given his emphasis that justification through Jesus Christ is the way that God justifies all people, it is not hard to comprehend why some might have thought that Paul saw God rejecting Israel. Do God's promises of old still count, or have they now been nullified because of the new promise in Jesus? And if the gospel is what Paul says it is, why have his own people rejected it? Paul agonizes over those questions in chapters 9–11.

As an indication of his own anguish over Israel, Paul begins the section with a lament (9:1-5) that is reminiscent of the lament of Moses over the people of Israel (Exod 32:32): "For I could wish that I myself were accursed and cut off from Christ for the sake of my own people, my kindred according to the flesh" (Rom 9:3). At the end of chapter 8, Paul confidently concluded that nothing could separate believers from God's love in Christ. But in 9:3, he would forfeit that love and in essence undo his baptism if it would mean that his own people would believe.

Yet the word of God—that is, God's promise—has not in fact failed (vs. 6). For that matter, not all of those descended from Israel and Abraham are truly their descendants (vss. 6-7). The promise, somewhat ironically, belongs not to those who are physical descendants only but to those who are true descendants of the promise (vss. 7-8). Paul proceeds to defend God's right to elect and reject whom God chooses (vss. 9-21). Thus, God has included the Gentiles, who have obtained righteousness through faith (vss. 22-33). Israel, however, failed because it sought righteousness based on the law (vs. 32a).[68] Christ and his cross remain for them a stumbling stone (vs. 32b).

Israel's zeal, therefore, was in fact misdirected (10:2): "For, being ignorant of the righteousness that comes from God, and seeking to establish their own, they have not submitted to God's righteousness" (10:3). While the words appear initially to be accusatory, Hofius has argued that what Paul says is an indication of his ongoing anguish over Israel.[69] In part, what Israel as a group has not understood is that "Christ is the end of the law so that there may be righteousness for everyone who believes" (10:4).[70] In the following verses, Paul contrasts the righteousness

Fig. 10.3 The stadium at Olympia, Greece, where footraces were run. Paul relies on the metaphor of a footrace to describe the current situation of Judean and Gentiles. Photo courtesy of the President and Fellows of Harvard College.

that comes from the law and righteousness that comes from faith (vss. 5-10). In verses 11-17, Paul continues to emphasize the importance of the message and the significance of believing it. In the remainder of the chapter, Paul removes from his own people any excuse: they have heard the message, but they have rejected it (vss. 18-21).

That leads to a natural and obvious question: "I ask, then, has God rejected his people?" (11:1a). The listener expects Paul to say, "Yes, God has rejected them." But instead Paul shouts, "By no means!" (vs. 1b). How can he say that? He points to himself: he is an Israelite, so obviously God has not rejected Israel as a group. Paul goes on to develop a theme from the Scriptures of Israel, the theme of the remnant. A remnant has been elected by God's grace (vss. 2-6). What about the rest? Their hearts were hardened so that the message would go from Israel to the Gentiles, and the Gentiles would be saved (vss. 7-12). But their salvation has, in turn, another goal: "so as to make Israel jealous" (vs. 11b).[71] God's saving action for the Gentiles, however, is not one in which the Gentiles should take pride, so Paul turns directly to the Gentiles (vss. 13-24). God is able to prune the Gentiles out just as easily as God has grafted them in.

In verses 25-26a, Paul resumes the theme of hardening and states his concluding thesis: "I want you to understand this mystery: a hardening has come upon part of Israel, until the full number of the Gentiles has come in. And so all Israel will be saved." The word *mystery* does not refer to a whodunit novel but to the divine secrets now being revealed, namely, God's eternal purpose to include Gentiles *and* Israel. Who is all Israel? While some would point to every last person in the people of Israel,[72] others such as J. A. T. Robinson think the passage applies not to individual people but to groups: "All that Paul is actually saying is that no groups as such will ultimately be excluded."[73] So also Hofius, who points out that the term *all Israel* in the Judean Scriptures is a collective designation for the people as a whole, without connoting numerical completeness.[74]

And how will "all Israel" be included? According to verse 26b, through the deliverer, who implicitly is Jesus. At his return, Christ removes the hardening of Israel. By removing ungodliness (vs. 26b) and forgiving Israel's sins (vs. 27), God in Christ extends to Israel the justification of the ungodly already given to the Gentiles.[75] Thus, ultimately, God will redeem God's promise to Israel, "for the gifts and the calling of God are irrevocable" (vs. 29). So can God be trusted? Yes; God will keep the promise to Israel. And perhaps as an indication of how hard he has struggled, Paul moves in verses 33-36 to a doxology that celebrates the ultimate unknowability of God.

12:1—15:13

As we have seen, one of the misunderstandings of Paul's work was that his gospel provided no basis for ethical action. He has answered that objection in part in chapter 6 in his discussion of baptism, but indeed, the bulk of chapters 1–11 deals with what God has done. "What God has done" is often in biblical theology called the **indicative**. Chapters 12–15 turn in a different direction: the daily response of the believer to what God has done (the **paraenesis**). Directives to act in certain ways are labeled the **imperative**. The pattern of indicative first and then imperative is significant. First, Paul states God's actions for humanity. Only then does he draw out the implications. The indicative-imperative pattern is frequent in the Bible. We may think of the Ten Commandments as entirely imperatives (that is, commands), but they begin with a ringing statement of indicative: "'I am the LORD your God, who brought you out of the land of Egypt, out of the house of slavery'" (Exod 20:2). God first reminds the people of what God has done; only in light of that prior activity does God call on the covenant people to live in certain ways.

The indicative-imperative pattern alerts us in Rom 12:1a to the important word *therefore*: "I appeal to you therefore, brothers and sisters, by the mercies of God." The *therefore* refers at one level to the discussion just concluded (chapters 9–11), but more broadly, it refers to the entire sweep of God's righteous-making *mercies* detailed in chapters 1–11. God, then, has given humanity many gifts. A natural conclusion for people of the first century would be to express their thanks by making a sacrifice. But since the gifts that have been given are so overwhelming, there is only one possible gift that can be given in response: the offering of one's entire self to God. And that is what Paul tells the Romans: "I appeal to you therefore, brothers and sisters, by the mercies of God, to present your bodies as a living sacrifice, holy and acceptable to God, which is your spiritual worship" (12:1).[76]

In tandem with verse 1 is verse 2: "Do not be conformed to this world, but be transformed by the renewing of your minds, so that you may discern what is the will of God—what is good and acceptable and perfect." The not conforming and the being transformed are not, ultimately, human activities. In Greek, they are passive verbs: do not *be conformed*, but *be transformed*. The passive voice of the verbs indicates divine action. God renews the minds of believers and makes them able to discern God's will. The verbs and the pronoun *you* are all plural: the discerning is done in community as believers together seek to discern God's will. But Paul also remembers 1:18—3:20, so the commands in verse 2 are in the present tense, which in Greek indicates ongoing action. The nonconforming and the being transformed need to happen over and over again.

The remainder of the section outlines how life in the community of believers is to be lived. Sober self-assessment is needed as believers seek to live together as the one body of Christ (vss. 3-8; see also 1 Cor 12:4-31) and as they seek to express love to others (vss. 9-21) and give honor to others, especially the lowly (vss. 10, 16). In 13:1-7, Paul turns to life within the governmental structures of the world. The position he enunciates is similar to the most widespread Hellenistic philosophical understanding of government in the first century.[77] God has instituted the governing authorities, and the task of Paul's listeners is to obey them. The specific reason for the counsel he gives is probably contained in the directives to pay taxes and duties (vss. 6-7). Tax protests and problems were known in Rome around this time,[78] and Paul may be interested in keeping believers out of trouble—especially Judean believers, in light of previous expulsions.[79] Judean fellow-believers had only recently been allowed to return to Rome, and there was no reason to attract undue attention from the authorities. Also, for that matter, submission to the government should only be temporary: the end is coming soon (vss. 11-14).[80] The fact that the first few years of Nero's reign were much more stable and beneficent than his later years and that he had not yet turned against Christ-believers gave Paul the space to write as he does. Cassidy also points out that Paul had yet to endure a lengthy Roman imprisonment.[81]

Meanwhile, believers are to love (vs. 8). Loving others is for Paul the primary way a believer lives the transformed life of living sacrifice. The final dynamic for action is the nearness of the end: "The night is far gone, the day is at hand. Let us then cast off the works of darkness and put on the armor of light; let us conduct ourselves becomingly as in the day" (vs. 12; similar language is used in Eph 6:11-17). *The day* refers to the day of the Lord, the time of judgment and full life with the Lord (1 Thess 4:13-18). The believer is to act as though already living in that final day.

The final topic in the paraenesis of Romans is the proper relationship between the weak and the strong. The underlying issue is disagreement over food rules and holy days. Some members of the community (probably some Judean believers but likely including others) abstained from certain foods and observed holy days not observed by the whole Christ-believing community. They were probably the "weak." Paul's advice? "Welcome those who are weak in faith, but not for the purpose of quarreling over opinions" (14:1). In the matters under discussion, people can agree to disagree: "Let all be fully convinced in their own minds" (vs. 5), as long as people do what they do (or do not do) as a result of their commitment to the Lord (vs. 6).[82]

Moreover, the "strong" (probably those who agree with Paul) are to support and carry the weak: "We who are strong ought to put up with the failings of the weak, and not to please ourselves" (15:1). The first concern is the other believer. And what is the basis for his listeners not trying to please themselves? "For Christ did not please himself" (vs. 3). Christ is the model for the behavior of believers (see also Phil 2:5-11).

15:13—16:23 [25-27]

Paul begins the concluding section of his letter with a restatement of his call (15:16) and his mission (vss. 19-23), including his plans for Spain and for taking the collection to Jerusalem (vss. 24-33). At the head of the section, though, stands his expression of confidence in the Romans, as well as a brief defense of his boldness in writing them (vss. 14-15). He also reiterates from 1:5 his emphasis on obedience among the nations (vs. 18), which may in part be a final reference to the seriousness with which his mission has approached people outside Israel.

Chapter 16 has four functions: commendation of Phoebe, greetings from Paul, warning against false teachers, and greetings from Paul's associates. In verses 1-2, Paul commends Phoebe. She is a deacon of the congregation in Cenchreae, one of Corinth's ports. On the assumption that chapter 16 is part of the original letter to Rome (see below), Phoebe is most likely the person who is carrying the letter. It is also quite possible that she was to read it aloud to Rome's Christ-believers.

In verses 3-16, Paul greets many people in Rome. He not only thereby greets them at the personal level, he also signals to his listeners that he knows a good number of people in their midst whom they can ask about him. Paul concludes his own remarks with a warning against "those who cause dissensions and offenses" (vs. 17) and a brief benediction (vs. 20). Paul brings his letter to a close in verses 21-23 with greetings from Timothy and Paul's relatives; the scribe Tertius; Gaius, who has hosted Paul and the church (apparently in Corinth); and Erastus, the city treasurer (again, apparently in Corinth).[83]

But is chapter 16 even part of the letter to the Romans? The following major arguments have been offered *against* chapter 16 belonging originally to chapters 1–15:

- It is unlikely Paul would have known twenty-six people in Rome.
- In 1 Cor 16:19, Prisca and Aquila are in Asia, probably the city of Ephesus. What are they now doing in Rome?
- In verse 5, Paul greets Epaenetus, who was from Asia.
- The warning in verses 17-18 seems presumptuous to a community of believers he did not know.
- The manuscript evidence is split, with some manuscripts ending Romans at 15:33 and even at 14:23.[84]
- Chapter 16 could well be a letter commending Phoebe to the church in Ephesus, not in Rome, and could have been sent to Ephesus together with the letter to Rome (chapters 1–15).

On the other side are arguments *for* including 16 as part of the original document:

- Exactly because Paul had not been to Rome, he greeted everyone he knew.
- Paul knew that many people in Rome because some people he had met in the eastern part of the Mediterranean basin had moved to Rome or were visiting (Epaenetus), while others had returned to Rome after the death of Claudius (Prisca and Aquila).
- It is quite normal for Paul to include warnings about heresy toward the end of a letter. By including the warning, he separates himself from false teachers.
- Manuscript evidence is strongest for 16 as part of the original letter.[85] It is likely that the shortened forms were adaptations to remove the specific references to Rome so that all churches might more immediately apply

the text to themselves. The fourteen-chapter form was probably created by Marcion (second century) to eliminate Paul's positive statement about Israel's Bible in 15:4.

On balance, 16:1-23 appears to be part of the original letter to Rome.

Summary

In addition to establishing a relationship with the Roman believers in preparation for his projected visit and mission to Spain (a mission that never occurred), Paul has held two complexes of thought in tension. On the one hand, he has sought to maintain the priority of Israel in God's plan of salvation, but on the other hand, he has tried to argue, in part using the Scriptures of Israel, that the only way any person is justified before God is through God's justifying activity comprehended by faith. Thus, Paul argues for a universal sinfulness of humanity that is matched—indeed, overwhelmed—by God's grace.[86] It is, in the final analysis, the ungodly who are justified.

Romans: God Justifies the Ungodly[87]

I.	Salutation	1:1-7
II.	Thanksgiving and Narration	1:8-15
	A. Thanksgiving	1:8-10
	B. Explanation of Prayer/Narration of History with the Romans	1:11-15
III.	Body	1:16—11:36
	A. Thesis	1:16-17
	B. Negative Proof: Universal Revelation of the Wrath of God on All People	1:18—3:20
	1. Negative Proof 1: Revelation in Creation as Ground for Accusation of Idolatry	1:18-23
	2. Negative Proof 2: Judgment in the Present: Wrong Behavior	1:24-32
	3. Negative Proof 3: Judgment in the Future	2:1-29
	a. Impartial Judgment according to Deeds	2:1-11
	b. Relativizing of Importance of Law and Circumcision	2:12-29
	c. Advantage of the Judean	3:1-8
	(1) Misunderstanding 1: God Is Unfaithful to God's People	

		(2) Misunderstanding 2: Christ-Believers Fail to Strive to Do Good	
	d.	All People Sin	3:9-20
C.	Positive Proof: Universal Revelation of the Righteousness of God for All People		3:21—5:21
	1.	Positive Proof 1: Revelation of Christ as the Ground of Making Humanity Righteous	3:21-26
	2.	Positive Proof 2: Justification (Being Made Righteous) in the Present: Faith	3:27—4:25
	a.	Exclusion of Boasting	3:27-31
	b.	Example: Faithful Abraham	4:1-25
	3.	Positive Proof 3: Salvation in the Future	5:1-21
	a.	Transition: Present-Tense Results of Justification	5:1-5
	b.	Future Salvation Rooted in Christ's Death for the Ungodly	5:6-11
	c.	Contrasting Realms of Adam and Christ	5:12-21
D.	Implications of Righteousness for Life in the Present		6:1—8:39
	1.	Implication 1: Dead to Sin by Baptism	6:1-14
	2.	Implication 2: Change of Lordship	6:15-23
	3.	Implication 3: Freed from Law through a New "Marriage"	7:1-6
	4.	Implication 4: Contrast with Life before Christ	7:7-25
	a.	Defense of the Law	7:7-13
	b.	Defense and Cry of the "I"	7:14-25
	5.	Implication 5: Life in Christ/in the Spirit	8:1-39
	a.	Life according to the Flesh vs. Life according to the Spirit	8:1-11
	b.	Result of Living according to the Spirit: Adoption	8:12-17
	c.	Result of Living according to the Spirit: Suffering in Hope	8:13-30
	d.	Result of Living according to the Spirit: Victory in Christ	8:31-39
E.	Justification as the Election of Israel and Gentiles		9:1—11:36
	1.	Paul's Lament over Israel	9:1-5
	2.	Defense of God's Sovereignty to Elect and Reject	9:6-29
	3.	Definition of Righteousness in Relationship to the Law	9:30—10:4
	4.	God's Offer of Salvation through Preaching	10:5-21
	a.	Nearness of the Word	10:5-13
	b.	Need for Proclamation	10:14-17
	c.	Rejection and Acceptance of the Gospel	10:18-21
	5.	Eschatological Salvation of Israel and Gentiles	11:1-36
	a.	Answer to Question: God Has Not Rejected God's People; See the Remnant	11:1-10

			b.	Answer to Question: God Has a Hidden Purpose for Israel's Stumbling	11:11-24
			c.	Mystery of Israel's Salvation	11:25-32
			d.	Doxology	11:33-36
IV.	Paraenesis (Righteousness in Daily Life)				12:1—15:13
	A.	Thesis			12:1-2
	B.	Directive: Sober Assessment and Use of Gifts			12:3-8
	C.	Admonition: Guidelines for Genuine Love			12:9-21
	D.	Topos: Relationship to Government			13:1-7
	E.	General Directive: Love and Law			13:8-10
	F.	Eschatological Horizon for Daily Life			13:11-14
	G.	Exhortation on the Weak and the Strong			14:1—15:13
		1.	Guidelines for Mutual Acceptance		14:1-12
		2.	Guidelines for Mutual Upbuilding		14:13-23
		3.	Example of Christ		15:1-6
		4.	Concluding Exhortation		15:7-13
V.	Conclusion				15:14—16:23 [25-27]
	A.	Restatement of Paul's Call and Mission			15:14-21
	B.	Travel Plans			15:22-33
		1.	Appeal for Support for Mission to Spain		15:22-24
		2.	Plans to Take Collection to Jerusalem		15:25-29
		3.	Appeal for Prayer Regarding Jerusalem Trip		15:30-33
	C.	Recommendation of Phoebe			16:1-2
	D.	Apostolic Greetings			16:3-16
	E.	Warning against False Teachers			16:17-20
	F.	Greetings from Associates of Paul			16:21-23
	[G.	Concluding Benediction			16:25-27]

Study Questions

1. What does the phrase *obedience of faith* mean for Paul? How do you think it does or does not fit his overall understanding of belief in Christ?
2. Explain in your own words what this statement means: God justifies the person who lives by faith.
3. What does *righteousness* mean in Romans?
4. What do you think is the main reason Paul wrote the letter to the Romans?
5. What, according to Paul, is humanity's basic sin? Do you experience the power of sin in the way he describes it? How so?
6. Which of Paul's images that seek to explain the meaning of the death of Jesus (Romans 3 and 5) work best for you?
7. What is Paul's take on the place of Israel in God's salvation plans?

Suggested Reading

Achtemeier, Paul. *Romans.* Interpretation. Richmond: John Knox, 1985.
Donfried, Karl P., ed. *The Romans Debate.* Revised and expanded ed. Peabody, MA: Hendrickson, 1991.
Dunn, James D. G. *Romans 1–8* and *Romans 9–16.* WBC 38A and 38B. Dallas: Word, 1988.
Fitzmyer, Joseph A. *Romans.* AB 33. New York: Doubleday, 1993.
Hultgren, Arland J. *Paul's Letter to the Romans: A Commentary.* Grand Rapids: Eerdmans, 2011.
Jewett, Robert. *Romans: A Commentary.* Hermeneia. Minneapolis: Fortress Press, 2007.
Stuhlmacher, Peter. *Paul's Letter to the Romans: A Commentary.* Trans. Scott J. Hafemann. Louisville: Westminster John Knox, 1994.

DVD Course

Taylor, Walter F., Jr. "Romans: Living Faithfully." SELECT DVD (12 sessions; 6 hours; includes Study Guide), 2008.

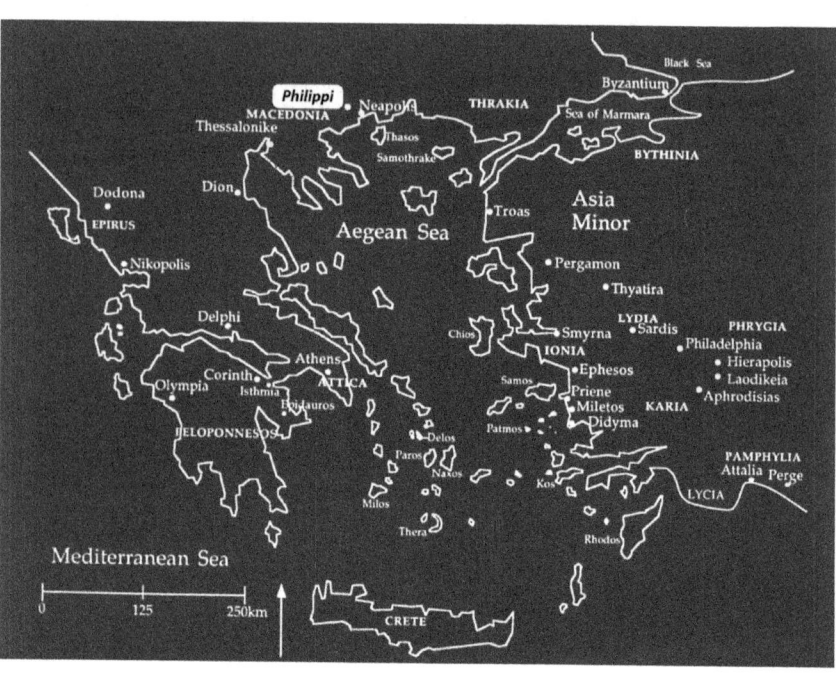

Chapter 11

Philippians: Citizenship in Heaven

A New Home

You are a first-century Christ-believer living in Philippi, a northern Greek city where many gods are worshipped. On your way to this week's time for worship and education, you happen to notice the beautiful buildings dedicated to Egyptian deities. Even more, the temples to the deified emperors Julius, Augustus, and Claudius catch your eye. In your city, often called "little Rome," you also glance for the thousandth time at the many inscriptions honoring the emperors. After you crowd into the home of a believer, you are pleased when the leader reads a new letter from Paul. But you have to wonder what he means when he writes, "Our citizenship is in heaven, and it is from there that we are expecting a Savior, the Lord Jesus Christ" (3:20).[1]

The City of Philippi

Our imaginary believer lived in a city that had a special relationship with Rome. Philippi was located on the Via Egnatia, the main road linking Rome with the eastern part of its growing territory. Near Philippi in 42 BCE, **Octavian** (later called **Augustus**) and **Antony** defeated the assassins of **Julius Caesar**. Philippi was reconstituted as a Roman colony, and many discharged army veterans were given land there. In 31 BCE, Octavian, in turn, defeated Antony. As a result, another five hundred Roman soldiers settled in Philippi. The city was renamed *Colonia Iulia Augusta Philippensis* and was given the *ius Italicum*, a special privilege that meant it was governed by Roman law. Physically, too, the city was modeled on Rome: road patterns and architecture copied the capital city. The colony was even given the nickname "little Rome." While the archaeological site provides evidence of a number of religions, the **imperial cult** was dominant during the first century CE—and thus during the ministry of Paul.[2]

Founding of the Congregation

Philippi was Paul's first missionary stop in Europe, in 48–49 or 49–50. From 1 Thess 2:2 and Phil 1:30, we learn that Paul was mistreated by nonbelievers. The names of the converts in Phil 4:2 and, at a secondary level, the names and life situations of converts in Acts 16:14-40 imply that the congregation was essentially Gentile.[3] The prominent role of women in Acts 16 is consonant with what we know of Philippian society and is consistent with the two women mentioned in Phil 4:2.[4]

Over the years, Paul had had a close relationship with the congregation. While he was working in Thessalonica and Corinth, the Philippians had provided him financial assistance (4:15-16; 2 Cor 11:8-9). As we have seen, his refusal to accept monetary gifts from Corinth had caused a rift between Paul and the Corinthians.[5] Philippians may in part have been written to deal with the problems created when Paul *did* accept such a gift.

Reasons for Writing

Recently, the Philippians had sent another monetary gift to Paul. The gift had been brought by Epaphroditus, who became ill either while with Paul or on the way. He has now recovered and is apparently to take Paul's letter back to Philippi (2:25-30). Paul takes the opportunity to tell his supporters how things are with him (1:12-14, 18c-26) and to indicate that he will soon send Timothy (2:19-24). Paul also warns the community about opponents (3:2, 18-19) and needs to address a conflict between two women (4:2-3).

Furthermore, Paul must deal with the generosity of the Philippians (4:10-20). That is different from simply thanking them. He must carefully maintain his independence as an **apostle** as he seeks to avoid becoming their **client**. Paul is thus seeking to reverse his culture's mind-set: namely, that a gift from a superior to an inferior (a person who cannot respond with a gift of at least equal value) establishes a **patron**-client relationship in which the patron to one degree or another controls the client.

In addition to maintaining his independence, Paul is also trying to help the Philippians—those living in "little Rome"—to redefine themselves in relationship to the ideology of the Roman Empire. To that end he takes five important steps.

1. He identifies his suffering as a prisoner in imperial custody with their suffering (1:30), thus reminding them that the Roman imperial government is creating difficulties for them because of their belief in Jesus.
2. In 2:9-11, he writes of a Jesus whose name is above every name, to whom every creature will kneel (including, presumably, the emperor), and who is "Lord" (*kyrios*), a title claimed by the emperor. This same Jesus, of course, was crucified by the empire (2:8)—and Paul may well be in custody in the capital city of that empire when he writes this letter.
3. Paul tells them that the proper citizenship or commonwealth of believers is not to be found in Rome or Rome's colony Philippi but in heaven, from which believers expect "a Savior, the Lord Jesus Christ" (3:20; savior / *sōtēr* is another title for the emperor).
4. Paul writes in 2:14-15 and 3:18-19 "against influential pagans [the emperor and other leaders of the empire] whose sexual conduct is reprehensible."[6]
5. Paul states the thesis of the letter in 1:27-30. The fundamental principle is at the beginning: "Live your life (*politeuesthe*) in a manner worthy of the gospel of Christ" (1:27). The verb *politeuesthe* has buried in it the Greek word *polis*, which means *city*. Thus, the word Paul uses for *live your life* is a political term. It is no accident that he employs it when writing to the imperially charged city of Philippi, urging believers there to reject Rome's understanding of reality and further to embrace Paul's.

Finally, in addition to dealing with the monetary gift and redefining the Philippians, Paul counsels unity: "I will know that you are standing firm in one spirit, striving side by side with one mind for the faith of the gospel" (1:27c); "Make my joy complete: be of the same mind, having the same love, being in full accord and of one mind.... Let each of you look not to your own interests, but to the interests of others" (2:2, 4); "I urge Euodia and I urge Syntyche to be of the same mind in the Lord" (4:2).

How Many Letters Do We Have?

Many scholars have theorized that our Philippians is a composite document composed of two or more originally discrete letters combined by a later editor. To be able to interpret Philippians adequately, we need to determine as closely as possible when and under what circumstances Paul wrote the different portions of the letter. Scholars note four factors:

1. *Literary seams.* The most obvious potential **literary seam** occurs between 3:1 and 3:2. Verse 1 says, "Finally, my brothers and sisters, rejoice in the Lord. To write the same things to you is not troublesome to me, and for

you it is a safeguard." Verse 2 says, "Beware of the dogs, beware of the evil workers, beware of those who mutilate the flesh!" The shift seems abrupt, and the language of verse 2 unusually harsh. In addition, 4:4 ties in well with 3:1a. Might 3:2 (or 3:1b)—4:3 be an insertion of another letter? (Others would say 3:2—4:9.)

2. *False stops.* Already in 2:23, Paul alludes to his travel plans, which frequently are listed near the end of his letters. And, indeed, a few verses later, he writes, "finally, my brothers and sisters" (3:1a)—only to continue writing for two more chapters. Does 3:1a signal the end of an originally separate letter? Paul, moreover, uses *finally* another time (4:8).

3. *Sequencing.* It seems ungracious that, in the letter, Paul waits all the way until 4:10-20 to thank the Philippians for their monetary gift. It also seems strange that he has waited so long to write them at all. Perhaps 4:10-20 is part of an earlier letter.

4. *Opponents and conflict.* Some scholars point out that Paul exhibits differing attitudes toward opponents and congregational troublemakers. In chapters 1 and 2, he speaks of them only in vague terms (1:28; 2:15), but in chapters 3 and 4, he becomes more specific (3:2; 4:2). Thus, in the supposed first letter, there is no conflict (4:10-20); in the second, Paul responds to rivalry that he does not consider threatening (1:1—3:1; 4:4-7; 4:21-23); and in the third letter, he meets head-on what he has learned is a very explosive situation (3:2—4:3; 4:8-9). Do these sources of difficulty indicate different stages in Paul's correspondence with Philippi?[7]

Although two-letter theories have been proposed,[8] the most common partition theories divide Philippians into three letters, here named for convenience Letters A, B, and C.

A. 4:10-20 — Written soon after Epaphroditus arrived with the gift

B. 1:1—3:1; 4:4-7; 4:21-23 — Written to report Paul's situation and outline a worthy, joy-filled life

C. 3:2—4:3; 4:8-9 — Written to warn against opponents, perhaps newly arrived, and to correct behavior

There are innumerable variations of the three-letter hypothesis, but there is widespread agreement among partition scholars that 4:10-20 is a separate letter and the earliest surviving communication from Paul to Philippi.[9]

Arguments for a unified letter are in part counterarguments to partition theories:

- *Literary seams.* The language in 3:2 certainly appears sharp, but it is not without preparation. Already in 1:28, Paul writes about the destruction of opponents, and in 3:1b, he indicates he is writing about things he has already discussed with them. Moreover, the term *dogs* may best be viewed as ironical. Paul is writing against believers who want the male followers of Jesus to be **circumcised**. Circumcised people at times label as "dogs" those who were uncircumcised and outside the **covenant**. Paul applies that label to the opponents in a biting way.[10] Elsewhere, moreover, Paul does shift gears rather abruptly (Rom 16:17; 1 Cor 15:58), so Duane Watson can maintain that the shift at 3:2 is well within what was conventional in first-century **rhetoric**.[11] John Fitzgerald, who proposes that Philippians is a friendship letter, suggests, finally, that in such letters, "the ridiculing of one's enemies is but the natural antithesis to the praising of one's friends."[12] Important, too, is how one in 3:2 translates the Greek verb *blepete*. The NRSV translates it, "*Beware of* the dogs, evil workers, and those who mutilate the flesh." G. D. Kilpatrick suggests *look at* and *consider* as ways to translate the verb,[13] and G. W. Peterman argues for *consider* or *see*, thus softening the contrast.[14] In sum, the seams are neither as numerous nor as pronounced as, for example, the seams in 2 Corinthians.

- *False stops*. It is not the case that travel plans occur only at the end of a letter.[15] Nor does *finally* in 3:1 and 4:8 inevitably point to the end of a document: the two words translated as *finally / to loipon* can also mean *beyond that, in addition*,[16] or *furthermore*.[17]
- *Sequencing*. The assumption that Paul should have thanked the Philippians earlier in the letter may be a North Atlantic, culturally bound assumption.[18] But is Paul even giving thanks in 4:10-20 (see comments below on the text)? He needs to deal with the gift, but he carefully places it toward the end of the document.
- *Opponents and conflict*. The argument based on opponents stumbles if Paul is dealing with different opponents at different points in the (one) letter, rather than changing his attitude over a period of time.

Apart from responses to the letter fragment theories, the two major arguments for the literary unity of Philippians come from two types of evidence: (1) the common themes and vocabulary found throughout the **canonical** document in general and (2) the themes from the thanksgiving and thesis that are found elsewhere in the letter:

- *Common themes and vocabulary*. The commonality of themes and vocabulary is not a matter of simple repetition of words; it is also a matter of the core concepts of the letter. Thus, suffering because of one's relationship with Christ is found in 1:7, 17, and 29; that suffering will be reversed by the return of Christ (3:20-21), who has himself suffered (2:8). And Christ's ability to return at the end of time (3:20-21) is predicated on his having been exalted (2:9-11). The call for unity is also found in different parts of the document: it pervades chapter 2, although it is concentrated in 2:1-5; it is also the chief goal of the behavior Paul urges for Euodia and Syntyche in 4:2-3. The linkages extend to specific vocabulary, especially between the Christ hymn and the end of chapter 3: *humble / tapeinoō*

(2:8) and *humiliation / tapeinōsis* (3:21); *form / schēma* (2:7) and *transform / metaschēmatizō* (3:21); *form / morphē* (2:6, 7) and *conformed / symmorphos* (3:21); Lord Jesus Christ (2:11 and 3:20); *in heaven / epouranios* (2:10) and *heaven / ouranos* (3:20); *every / pasa* (2:11) and *all things / ta panta*, derived from *pas* (3:21). An indication of a unified letter is Paul's constant refrain of the related words *rejoice / chairō* (1:18; 2:17; 2:18; 2:28; 3:1; 4:4 [twice]) and *joy / chara* (1:4; 1:25; 2:2; 2:29; 4:1). And while there is a concentration in chapter 2 on following examples (Christ, 2:5-11; Timothy, 2:20-22; Epaphroditus, 2:25-30), that theme is also present in chapter 3 (Paul and others, 3:17). Finally, Paul urges his listeners to be united, to be of the same mind (2:2; 2:5; 3:15; 4:2, while 3:19 has the opposite). In each case, the verb is *phroneō* (I think; I have a mind-set).

- *Themes from the thanksgiving and thesis.* We have seen, when studying other letters, that Paul often in his thanksgiving states themes he will develop later in the letter. We observe that same pattern in Philippians. Moreover, the thesis (or *propositio*) in 1:27-30 contains terms that are relatively rare but are found later in the letter:

1:27	*politeuesthe* (live your life)	3:20	*politeuma* (citizenship)
	stēkete (standing firm)	4:1	*stēkete* (stand firm)
	synathlountes (striving with)	4:3	*synēthlēsan* (labored)[19]

The number of common themes and words found throughout the letter strongly points to a unified document. Our study of Philippians will proceed on the basis of one letter.[20]

What Does Paul Want from the Philippians? The Question of Genre

The opening line of the letter's thesis statement reads, "Live your life in a manner worthy of the gospel of Christ" (1:27). That statement helps us identify the dominant rhetoric of the letter: it is primarily **deliberative**.[22] Such rhetoric, we have learned, is concerned with future behavior. The particular behavior about which Paul writes in Philippians is unity among believers (2:2; 2:5; 3:15; 4:2).

More specifically in terms of genre, a popular thesis is that Philippians is a letter of friendship. The letter of friendship was one of the basic kinds of ancient letters,[23] and Philippians exhibits many of the themes found in such letters.[24] Thus, Philippians shows a deep and warm relationship between Paul and the congregation (1:3-8), with emphases on unity and fellowship (*koinōnia*; 1:5; 2:1; 3:10; 4:14-15).[25]

Where and When Did Paul Write?

The final answer to the question of where and when Paul wrote is that we do not know. But to start with what is more definite, Paul tells us that he is in custody (1:7, 13, 14, 17)—literally, that he is in chains (the NRSV uses each time the word

Connections between Thanksgiving and Rest of the Letter

Thanksgiving	Elsewhere in Philippians
Joy (1:4)	Joy (1:25; 2:2; 2:29; 4:1) Rejoice (1:18; 2:17; 2:18; 2:28; 3:1; 4:4 [twice]); 4:10)
Their "sharing in the gospel from the first day until now" (1:5)	Financial gift (4:10-20)[21] Sharing his distress (4:14) In early days of the gospel shared with him (4:15)
"The one who began a good work among you will bring it to completion by the day of Jesus Christ" (1:6)	From heaven expecting a Savior, the Lord Jesus Christ (3:20) "I can boast on the day of Christ" (2:16)
"You hold me in your heart, for all of you share in God's grace with me" (1:7)	"Whom I love and long for, my joy and crown" (4:1)
"That your love may overflow more and more" (1:9)	"Live your life in a manner worthy of the gospel of Christ" (1:27); "consolation from love" (2:1); "be of the same mind, having the same love" (2:2)
"So in the day of Christ you may be pure and blameless" (1:10)	From heaven expecting a Savior, who "will transform the body of our humiliation that it may be conformed to the body of his glory" (3:20-21)

imprisonment, which softens Paul's stark language).[26] He is able to interpret his incarceration in a positive way, however, since he has used that opportunity to witness to the whole Praetorium (or Praetorian Guard; 1:12-13). He thinks he will be released, even though there is a possibility of death (1:20; 2:17). Still, he hopes to come to Philippi (1:26; 2:24). The letter also reveals that messengers have carried a number of communications between Philippi and Paul.

But what geographical setting from Paul's career fits this information? The three cities in competition are Rome, Caesarea, and Ephesus. Rome is the traditional site assigned by church authors, and it has been affirmed by many modern scholars as well. The second answer is that Paul was in Caesarea (also known as Caesarea Maritima), on the coast of Israel; few scholars look any more to that city. The third answer—and one that has been increasingly popular—is Ephesus, which was on the west coast of modern-day Turkey (the ancient province of Asia).

Factors that work in favor of Rome include the following:

- The word *praetorium* (Latin) / *praitōrion* (Greek) had two meanings: the headquarters of the governor of an imperial province or the emperor's elite guard. In 1:13, Paul uses the term, translated by the NRSV as *imperial guard*. That guard was centered in Rome, and in Acts 28:16, 30, Paul is in Rome for two years under house arrest, guarded by a soldier. Cassidy and others maintain that 1:13 must refer to people rather than a building, since Paul writes, "throughout the whole *praitōrion* and to all the rest." *To all the rest* logically refers to people, which makes it likely that *praitōrion* does, too.[27]
- In addition, in 4:22, Paul writes, "All the saints greet you, especially those of Caesar's household" (RSV). *Caesar's household* refers to the emperor's slaves, servants, and freedmen. While members of Caesar's household could be found anywhere, they were concentrated in Rome. Cassidy emphasizes Paul's word *especially*, which could be a sign of encouragement to the Philippians; perhaps "those of Caesar's household" can work for Paul's release.[28]
- The Roman imprisonment in Acts lasted two years (28:30), which allows time for the various contacts between Philippi and Paul.

There are, however, arguments against Rome as the site of writing:

- According to Rom 15:24, 28, Paul wanted to go to Spain (far west of the Mediterranean world) after he came to Rome. How can those plans be put together with the trip to Philippi (east of Rome) that Paul projects in Phil 1:26 and 2:24, if he is in fact in Rome (center)? The counter to that is that travel plans can change, especially when a person is in custody.
- Philippians gives us the sense of a lively exchange of letters. Is that really possible, given the distance of 700 to 1,200 miles between Rome and Philippi (the distance varies with the route taken)? Udo Schnelle points out the relative nature of the argument: the route by sea took around two weeks; the land route with some sea travel took about four weeks. A two-year imprisonment in Rome would give enough time for several such trips.[29]

The major competitor for the writing site is Ephesus, based on the following arguments:

- Paul spent substantial time in Ephesus. Even though he never says directly that he was in custody there, he does refer to significant difficulties in Ephesus and in that province (1 Cor 15:32a; 2 Cor 1:8-9). We know from his own hand that he was in custody many times before Caesarea and Rome (2 Cor 6:5; 11:23), and there is some probability that Paul had one or more periods of incarceration while in Ephesus, so his being in chains (Phil 1:7, 13, 14, 17) could fit Ephesus.
- Geographically, Ephesus works better than Rome or Caesarea for repeated travel between Paul's location and Philippi. By sea or a combination of

sea and land, the distance is approximately four hundred miles, with a travel time of seven to nine days.
- A setting in Ephesus fits with Paul's hopes of visiting Philippi soon and of going after that to Rome and Spain.

People use two main arguments against Ephesus as the place of writing:

- The strongest argument is the lack of direct evidence for custody there.
- What about the reference to the *praetorium*? How might that term apply to Ephesus? Whether or not the governor's residence in the province of Asia could properly be called a *praetorium*, as some have maintained, is the subject of debate, as is inscriptional evidence for the praetorian guard (or a single member of it) in Ephesus. F. F. Bruce shifts for these reasons from his earlier support for Ephesus.[30]

In this case, the traditional site seems to be the best choice, with Ephesus next, and Caesarea the least likely site for Paul's writing of Philippians. The lack of clear reference in the New Testament to an Ephesian imprisonment and the questions surrounding the legitimacy of the word *praetorium* in Ephesus tip the scales to Rome.[31] The explorations by Gordon Fee, Peter O'Brien, Ben Witherington, and John T. Fitzgerald, all of whom argue for Rome, are supplemented by Cassidy, who seeks to connect Paul's situation when he writes Philippians with the capital charge of *maiestas* (treason), which was a particular danger under Nero.[32]

The two chief implications of location are the date of the letter and its setting. If the letter was sent from Caesarea, Paul wrote between 56 and 58 or between 58 and 60. If he wrote from Ephesus, the letter was written earlier, between 52 and 56, probably between 55 and 56.[33] If he wrote from Rome, Paul wrote between 60 and 62, placing it in the latter stages of his life. If he is in Rome, the many references to Roman imperial symbols and propaganda make even more sense than they would otherwise.

Opponents

The struggle to identify the people Paul wants to counter is the source of much **exegetical** grief. Already in 1973, Gunther listed eighteen theories on the identity of the opponents—just in Philippians 3![34] Studies that take all passages in Philippians dealing with opponents as referring to one group fail to distinguish the different settings and ways in which Paul writes. There appear to be three sets of opponents: Judean-Christ-believing missionaries, local believers, and persecutors of the Philippians.

JUDEAN CHRIST-BELIEVING MISSIONARIES

In 3:2, Paul warns the Philippians about "the dogs, the evil workers, those who mutilate the flesh." The word *dogs* likely refers to Judean believers who require Gentiles to be circumcised. *Workers* signals that they are missionaries. The phrase *those who mutilate the flesh* translates two Greek words, *tēn katatomēn* (the mutilation).

Mutilation is a combination of two words that together mean *cut down(ward)*. That term is set in opposition to 3:3, where Paul claims, "For it is we who are the circumcision." **Circumcision**, another compound word, means *cut around*. Thus, circumcision is cutting around the penis to remove the foreskin, but mutilation is cutting down in order to castrate. With the latter term, Paul denigrates the opponents. Whether or not they required anything else besides circumcision, we cannot tell. Although the language of 3:2 is sharp, the sense of the passage is that these people have not been successful in Philippi.

LOCAL BELIEVERS

A second group of opponents is composed of certain believers in the city in which Paul is imprisoned. On the one hand, they preach "from envy and rivalry, out of selfish ambition, not sincerely" (1:15, 17). Yet they still proclaim Christ. Paul's positive statement about them distinguishes them from the opponents of 3:2. Perhaps they are ashamed of his chains—a normal reaction in antiquity.[35] There is no indication that they bothered the majority of Philippian believers.

PERSECUTORS OF THE PHILIPPIANS

In 1:28, Paul encourages the Philippians: you "are in no way intimidated by the opponents. For them this is evidence of their destruction, but of your salvation." Paul gives us one other clue regarding these opponents. In 1:30 he writes, "since you are having the same struggle that you saw I had and now hear that I still have." And what struggle does he have? He is in chains because of his proclamation of Christ. Thus, these opponents are nonbelievers, and since they have the authority to keep Paul in chains and to threaten death, they are almost certainly Roman authorities or Rome in general.

That understanding may help us when we turn to 3:18-19: "For many live as enemies of the cross of Christ. . . . Their end is destruction; their god is the belly; and their glory is in their shame; their minds are set on earthly things." Some commentators have argued that Paul is pointing to false believers or former Christ-believers. Others have suggested that Paul is simply talking about opponents in general. Only in 1:28 and 3:19, however, do we find in Philippians the word *destruction*; salvation language is also found both in 1:28 and 3:20, so that the two sections seem to have a relationship with each other. Cassidy has argued that 1:28 and 3:18-19 both refer to the debauchery of Emperor **Nero** and those around him.[36] Paul rejects their perspective and posits a way of living in a commonwealth (*politeuma*) different from that of Rome (3:20-21). Thus, the Philippians are to live in such a way that they will be "without blemish in the midst of a crooked and perverse generation" (2:15).

1:1-26

Paul structures the **salutation** the same way as he has done elsewhere: sender–to recipients–greeting. What is unusual is twofold. First, this is the only time other than Rom 1:1 when Paul in a salutation calls himself a slave (NRSV: *servant*) of Christ Jesus (more exactly, Paul and Timothy are "slaves of Christ Jesus"). Paul is writing to "little Rome," whose population included many present and former slaves of Caesar. Perhaps that has encouraged Paul to identify Timothy and himself as slaves.[37] Second, for the only time in the undisputed letters, Paul uses the word *episkopos* (bishop), here in the plural.[38] In classical Greek and in the **Septuagint**, the term means *overseer*. In our text, it is joined with the term *diakonos*, which can be translated *deacon*; it too is in the plural. Do we have what exists at a later date: a bishop in charge of the community, assisted by deacons? Probably not. The exact responsibilities of these people are unclear. The most we can say is that they are leaders.

In verses 3-11, Paul includes another standard letter element, the thanksgiving. Although the salutation was from both Timothy and Paul, the thanksgiving uses only singular verbs and pronouns (*I, me, my*). The intimacy between Paul and the Philippians is immediately evident in his language of joy and sharing. Thus, the mode of his thanksgiving is joy, and his specific reason for giving thanks is their "sharing in the gospel from the first day until now."[39] In verses 6-8, he details the reasons he is able to pray. One reason is that he is confident that God will complete on "the day of Jesus Christ" the good work begun in Philippi (v. 6). Also, he can pray because of his confidence in the Philippians. Finally, he is able to pray because of his longing for them (v. 8).

In verses 12-26, Paul brings his listeners up-to-date on his situation. He focuses on the implications of his incarceration, of which there are three. First, being in custody has enabled him "to spread the gospel" (v. 12). Second, his being in chains has emboldened most believers in the city where he is incarcerated "to speak the word with greater boldness and without fear" (v. 14). But third, some believers have taken advantage of his situation (vv. 15, 17), perhaps in part because of embarrassment at his chains.

In the second half of the narration of his current situation, Paul outlines a dilemma: is it better to stay and serve or depart (that is, die) and be with Christ? At the personal level, Paul is honest: his "desire is to depart and be with Christ" (1:23), for being with Christ means an even deeper fellowship with the risen Lord. But his own desires are not the final arbiter; the needs of the gospel are. Thus, "to remain in the flesh is more necessary for you" (1:24), because it will mean "fruitful labor" (1:22). Paul thereby gives an example of the kind of behavior he will call for in 2:4—considering the needs of others (which the Philippian believers already have done for Paul; 4:10-20). Fundamental, too, is his concern for **honor**, albeit honor redefined by the gospel: "It is my eager expectation and hope that I will not be put to **shame** in any way" (1:20a). To be shamed, in the **circum-Mediterranean**, is to lose one's standing or honor-rating.[40] Paul is confident that he will not be ashamed, "but that by my speaking with all boldness, Christ will be exalted now as always in my body, whether by life or by death" (1:20b).[41]

1:27-30

Paul's thesis statement is in 1:27-30. He makes three main points. "Live your life in a manner worthy of the gospel of Christ" (1:27). *Live your life* means literally *to be a citizen; to live like a citizen*. Instead of using his standard language for ethical living (*I walk*), Paul adopts a political term—indeed, the word *political* is related to this Greek verb *politeuomai*. Both come from the Greek word for *city: polis*. People were proud of being citizens of Philippi, and there is at least a possibility that some of the Philippian Christ-believers had Roman citizenship. Everyone, however, would have understood the reference to being a citizen. Paul uses the related noun *commonwealth / politeuma* in 3:20. He calls on his listeners to live as citizens not of Rome but of the commonwealth that is in heaven. And they are to do that in such a way that they honor the gospel, the good news, of Christ.

He calls on the Philippians to stand "firm in one spirit, striving side by side with one mind for the faith of the gospel" (1:27). Standing is an image Paul uses elsewhere (1 Cor 16:13; Rom 11:20; Gal 5:1). It is in part a military image. After the battle is over, who will remain standing? The way Paul wants the Philippians to stand is in unity: one spirit and one mind. And he trusts that they will live that way whether he is able to come or whether he is absent (a typical friendship theme).

He also trusts that they will not be intimidated by their opponents (v. 28). In a sense, verses 29-30 show how Paul's thesis can be true. It is true because God has graciously granted them not only belief but also suffering. Suffering and struggle were not at the top of the list of what Paul's culture valued. Rather, the Greco-Roman world revolved around the core values of honor and shame.[42] Paul reverses those values in his counsel to live as citizens of a commonwealth from heaven. What in the broader society is seen as shameful is now, within the community of Christ-believers, an indicator of honor. The pattern of that shameful activity of suffering will be illumined in chapter 2 by the example of the Christ. It is also seen in the chains of Paul.

2:1-30

From 2:1 through 4:3, Paul supports his thesis by stating a basic principle, followed by four appeals. The basic principle is found in 2:1-4. The primary directive is "make my joy complete." Why are the Philippians to do that? "In order that you might be of the same mind" (2:2), literally, *think the same thing* or *have the same mind-set*. And how are they to do that? By "having the same love, being in full accord, being of one mind, doing nothing from selfish ambition or conceit, but in humility regarding others as better than yourselves, each looking not to his/her own interests but those of others" (2:2-4).[43]

The basic principle becomes, in turn, the transition to the first appeal, the Christ hymn in verses 6-11. So 2:5 reads, "Let the same mind be in you that was in Christ Jesus." Thus, Christ Jesus will become Paul's first (and primary) example of proper behavior. Examples are quite common in deliberative documents, and Paul pulls out all the stops with his first example. He also uses an extended poem, quite likely a hymn.[44]

The poem is divided into two stanzas: verses 6-8 and 9-11. Stanza one begins with the relative pronoun *who*, which links it to verse 5:[45] "He [*who*, in Greek] was in the form of God" (v. 6). *Form* (Greek: *morphē*) refers to what can be perceived by the senses. So from what can be seen, heard, and felt, the form of Christ Jesus was that of God. But *form* carries a deeper connotation. It points also to that which inwardly corresponds to the outward, so that being in this form indicates participation in the reality or essence of the form. So to say that Christ was in the form of God means he shared God's glory and was in essence God. Further, this one "did not regard equality with God as something to be exploited." The phrase *something to be exploited* translates a rare Greek word, *harpagmos*; in fact, this is its only New Testament occurrence. R. W. Hoover has done detailed study of not only the word itself but what it means when it occurs with the verb *regard*. He suggests that the entire phrase, together with the surrounding words, should be translated, "He did not regard being equal with God as something to take advantage of," or "He did not regard being equal with God as something to use for his own advantage."[46] Hoover further maintains that every time the two words are used together, the reference is to something the person already has, so the issue is not trying to reach something not yet attained but how to use what one has. Thus, being "in the form of God" and having "equality with God" were not to be clung to, but were to be voluntarily given up for humanity (v. 7). For that reason, the NRSV's translation of verse 6 needs to be questioned: "who, *though* he was in the form of God." The Greek says simply, "who, being in the form of God." C. F. D. Moule has argued that the phrase is best translated, "Precisely *because* he was in the form of God."[47]

Joseph Hellerman looks at the Christ hymn from a social perspective.[48] He starts with the *cursus honorum* (course of honor), which was the formalized sequence of public offices a Roman aristocrat was to follow as he advanced in his career. At each stage, the upwardly mobile young man gained new rights: at one point, he could wear this kind of toga; at another point, a different kind; he would have special seats in the theater; he would sit at particular places in private banquets. Lower-class people developed their own sequence of offices, whether in government or in voluntary associations. Just as much of society today imitates people at the higher economic and social levels, so they did also in antiquity. In the case of Philippi, Hellerman maintains, the concern for such honor ratings and status was, if anything, greater than usual, because the elites in Philippi were Roman and the city was a Roman colony. He argues that Paul took the *cursus honorum* and turned it upside down. Thus, Paul portrays Christ descending rather than ascending; Hellerman's name for this descending is the *cursus pudorum*, meaning *course of ignominy* or *course of shame*.

Hellerman identifies three levels of degradation or shame in the hymn. Verse 6 is the first level, in which he sees Paul beginning to deconstruct Roman social norms and reconstruct norms for the new Christ-believing community.

Hellerman notes in particular the contrast between the Roman need for glory and honor and Jesus' shame. The second level of degradation is stated in verse 7a, he "emptied himself." Thus, he did not exploit his divine form (v. 6) but pursued a dramatic "course of status reversal."[49] The goal of public life was to increase one's status, to move up in the system. Christ does the opposite. He takes "the form [*morphē*] of a slave, being born in human likeness." But what does it mean to say that he was born "in human likeness"? Was he not a true human being? A key to understanding verse 7 is Rom 8:3: "By sending his own Son in the likeness of sinful flesh, and to deal with sin, he [God] condemned sin in the flesh." For Paul, there is a thin line between Jesus—who is certainly a full human being—and the rest of humanity: Jesus does not sin; he is in "the *likeness* of sinful flesh," but not sinful flesh itself.

Fig. 11.1 A coin of Augustus and Julius Caesar highlights Philippi's status as a Roman colony. Photo courtesy of the President and Fellows of Harvard College.

For Hellerman, verses 7b-8 are the third level of degradation. Christ, "being found in human form" (v. 7d), "humbled himself" (v. 8a).[50] Paul has already used the word *humility* (v. 3). The word family for *humility/humble* means "lower, make low," and "to cause someone to lose prestige or status, . . . humiliate, abase."[51] To lose status is to be shamed. Nowhere in Paul's society was such loss of status a virtue. The three other times Paul uses the verb *humble*, he applies it to himself (2 Cor 11:7; 12:21; Phil 4:12), and he also designates himself with the adjective *humble* (2 Cor 10:1). Paul, too, is a model of self-humbling, expressed in his current situation of being in chains.

The two main active verbs in the first half of the hymn are *emptied* (v. 7) and *humbled* (v. 8). Both verbs are followed by *himself.* How does Christ humble himself? By becoming "obedient to the point of death—even death on a cross" (vv. 8b-8c).[52] In Rom 5:19, the obedience of Jesus is set over against the disobedience of Adam. Here Jesus is obedient to God all the way to death. The death of Jesus is the ultimate humbling of himself and the point of most radical obedience. Christ reaches the nadir of his humiliation by dying on a cross.

With the dramatic little word *therefore*, the focus of the hymn shifts in verse 9, and the hymn enters its second stanza. In stanza one, Christ has been the subject of the verbs. In verses 9-11, God (the Father) is now the subject of the verbs and acts to exalt Jesus. The exaltation reverses the status degradation of the crucifixion and shows that Rome's power is not ultimate. God also gives Christ a name: "the name that is above every name" is probably the word *Lord* (Greek: *kyrios*, one of the titles of the emperor), although a few commentators think the name is *Jesus* (v. 10a). Most respond to the latter view by pointing out that he had the name of Jesus simply by being born, so the "name that is above every name" must be something else. In the Septuagint, *Lord* is used for the personal name of the God of Israel, Yahweh. Thus in Isa 42:8, we read, "I am the Lord [Greek: *kyrios*], that is my name; my glory I give to no other." That is the name God has given to Jesus (Phil 2:11).

In verse 10, the power of the name is picked up again, with specific reference to the name of Jesus. At that name, every knee shall bow.[53] It is significant that *Jesus* is used here. There is, in fact, no personal name used in the first half of the hymn, but in the second half, the half that deals with exaltation, the personal name of the earthly human being is used. Thus, the now-exalted Lord is clearly the same one who walked the roads of Galilee. Whether or not the whole hymn is based on Isaiah, the parallels to Isa 45:18-25 are obvious: "I am the Lord, and there is no other" (v. 18); "There is no other god besides me" (v. 21); "Turn to me and be saved, all the ends of the earth!" (v. 22); "By myself I have sworn . . . 'To me every knee will bow, every tongue will swear'" (v. 23). In Isaiah 45, God is speaking. The hymn makes bold assertions by applying the passage to Jesus.

What "every tongue should confess" is "that Jesus Christ is Lord" (Phil 2:11). We have seen previously that the earliest **confession** or **creed** of the church was "Jesus is Lord."[54] Here it is also the climax of the hymn, which in Greek literally reads "Lord (is) Jesus Christ." By placing *Lord* first, the hymn gives that term special emphasis. Jesus, not Nero, is Lord. Hellerman says that this title, *Lord*, was a direct challenge to the emperor and trumps all other titles and honors. The way Jesus reaches that status, of course, is the direct opposite of the *cursus honorum* and the direct opposite of the emperor's greed for honor.[55] And all of that happens "to the glory of God the Father." The Father's glory is not diminished but is actually enhanced when the Son is honored.

What are the implications of having this "same mind be in you that was in Christ Jesus" (v. 5)? Being a follower of the Jesus whose career is outlined in this hymn means rejecting the status definitions of Greco-Roman society and its ways of seeking honor, and it means being prepared to suffer the consequences—including death like that of Jesus or incarceration like Paul's. "The commonwealth of heaven" (3:20) thus has a definition of status and honor diametrically opposed to that of Rome.

In verse 12, Paul begins to apply the Christ hymn to the Philippians. Just as Christ was obedient to death, Paul expects them to be obedient. What does he want them to do? "Work out your own salvation with fear and trembling." *Work out* and *your own* are plural—salvation is to be worked out in a Christ-believing community in which people work together. Lest the listeners think salvation depends on them, however, Paul reminds them in verse 13 that *God* is the one working in them. As opposed to the generation of Israel that wandered in the desert (and complained), the Philippians are to act differently (v. 14; see Num 11:1-6; 14:1-4; 20:2; 21:4-5). The goal is that they will be "without blemish in the midst of a crooked and perverse generation" (v. 15).

The second appeal consists of the example of two believers, Timothy and Epaphroditus. Paul hopes to send Timothy to them in the near future. He had

Shame and Glory in Phil 2:6-11

Literal translation by author in italics.

Stanza 1: Shame (Status Degradation)

v. 6a	Original status of glory	*who, being in the form of God*
v. 6b	Christ Jesus chooses path of shame	*did not consider being equal with God something to exploit*
v. 7	Shame-filled degradation #1	*but emptied himself*
v. 7a		*having taken the form of a slave*
v. 7b		*having been born in the likeness*
v. 7c		*of human beings*
vv. 7d-8	Shame-filled degradation #2	*and having been found in form as a human being*
v. 7d		*he humbled himself*
v. 8a		*having become obedient until death*
v. 8b		
v. 8c	Total degradation	*even death on a cross*

Stanza 2: Glory (Status Restoration—and More)

v. 9a	Transition	*Therefore*
v. 9a	Act of restoration #1	*also God highly exalted him*
v. 9bc	Act of restoration #2	*and gave to him the name that is above every name*
vv. 10-11	Results of restoration	
v. 10a	Glory (honor) of the name	
v. 10b, c	Result #1	*every knee should bow, in heaven and on the earth and underneath the earth*
v. 11	Result #2	*and every tongue confess that Lord is Jesus Christ to the glory of God the Father in order that at the name of Jesus*

been involved in the initial missionary work in Philippi and would represent Paul well. The worth of Epaphroditus in Paul's eyes is indicated by what he calls him: "my brother and co-worker and fellow soldier, your messenger [literally, *apostle*], and minister to my need" (v. 25). When Epaphroditus comes, they should welcome and honor him (v. 29), for he almost died for the work of Christ (v. 30).

3:1—4:1

In 3:1, Paul transitions into his third appeal, which is both negative and positive. We have seen that the use of *dogs* is ironical, since it is a term applied by the people of Israel to those who are not circumcised. These opponents (the "dogs") most likely are Judean-Christ-believing missionaries who required Gentiles to be circumcised. Over against their *mutilation / katatomē* of the flesh, Paul sets his own understanding of circumcision (*peritomē*): "For it is we who are the circumcision" (v. 3), that is, the ones "who worship in the Spirit of God and boast in Christ Jesus and have no confidence in the flesh" (v. 3). The mention of "confidence in the flesh" leads Paul to state that he, too, has "reason for confidence in the flesh" (v. 4), that is, in the signs of ethnic identity as part of Israel. "So you want to list your credentials? I have my credentials too—and they are impeccable," he seems to say. And then he goes on to list them in verses 5-6: "circumcised on the eighth day, a member of the people of Israel, of the tribe of Benjamin, a Hebrew born of Hebrews; as to the law, a Pharisee; as to zeal, a persecutor of the church; as to righteousness under the law, blameless." There is no other Judean Christ-believing missionary with credentials better than Paul's.[56]

But Paul has totally reevaluated those ethnic boundary markers in light of his experience of Christ: "Yet whatever gains I had, these I have come to regard as loss because of Christ" (v. 7). It is not that Paul decided that they were bad, but that there was something better: "the surpassing value of knowing Christ Jesus my Lord" (v. 8). And that "surpassing value" had given him a vocation with important parallels to Christ's life. And so, "for his sake I have suffered the loss of all things, and I regard them as rubbish, in order that I may gain Christ and be found in him" (v. 8).[57] Among the "all things" he has lost would have been the status and privileges indicated by his credentials in verses 5-6. He also anticipates further identity with the death of Jesus, as well as his resurrection (vv. 10-11). And the way Paul identifies with the saving activity of Christ is through justification, his realization that he does not have "a righteousness of my own that comes from the law, but one that comes through faith in Christ, the righteousness from God based on faith" (v. 9).

In verses 12-16, Paul cautions against the perspective that he has already attained resurrection or perfection. The need for striving is seen in the athletic imagery of verse 14: "I press on toward the goal for the prize of the heavenly call of God in Christ Jesus." The word for *goal*, *skopos*, refers to the marker at the finish line. Runners run toward that marker as they race; the marker keeps them on track. Paul runs toward a goal, too, and that goal keeps him on track for the prize (see also 1 Cor 9:24). In this case, however, others do not lose because Paul hopes to finish; the same prize is available to all.

In the final section of his extended third appeal, Paul again mixes positive and negative examples. He begins with a call to imitate his own positive example. Elsewhere, too, Paul calls on believers to imitate him insofar as he imitates Christ (1 Thess 1:6; 1 Cor 4:16-17; 11:1; see also 1 Thess 2:14; Gal 4:12). The Philippians are also to imitate those who walk in the same way that Paul and others walk (the NRSV translates *walk* as *live*). Those positive examples are highlighted by the negative example of those who live (literally, walk) "as enemies of the cross of Christ" (Phil 3:18).

Over against the negative example of the enemies of the cross, Paul enunciates the positive orientation of believers: "But our citizenship is in heaven" (3:20). An interpretive key is the word translated as *citizenship*. In Greek, it is *politeuma*, and it belongs to the same word family as the key verb in the letter's thesis, *politeuomai* (1:27): "live your life in a manner worthy of the gospel of Christ." A better translation than *citizenship* is the word *commonwealth*, which often was used for a colony of foreigners or relocated veterans.[58] That language has a certain sharpness in a letter written to a Roman colony. The proper commonwealth of believers is thus not found in Rome or its colony Philippi, so believers are to live as citizens of their commonwealth in heaven. Further, from that commonwealth, believers expect "a Savior, the Lord Jesus Christ" (v. 20). As opposed to earthly emperors who claim to be savior, Paul sets "the Lord Jesus Christ," the same language used in 2:11. And this savior does what no earthly emperor could do: "he will transform the body of our humiliation that it may be conformed to the body of his glory" (v. 21). *Humiliation* connects us again to the Christ hymn (2:8); being conformed in the future "to the body of his glory" is a counterpart to "becoming like him in his death" (v.10; despite the different translations, the same basic Greek word for *conform* is found in both verses). In 3:21, the view is of the end-time body that will share the glory of the resurrected body of Jesus. Thus, the ultimate pattern for the believer is the same as for Christ in the hymn of chapter 2: humiliation followed by exaltation. In 4:1, Paul concludes his call to imitation with the directive to "stand firm in the Lord." With that language, he yet again restates a theme from the thesis (1:27).

4:2-23

Verses 2-3 contain a final and brief appeal. Paul twice uses the verb *urge*, and the sense is of turning first to one person and then to the other. It is highly unusual for Paul to name people with whom he is upset; that may point to the seriousness of the disagreement between the two women. What the disagreement is he does not say, but it is likely that the two women are prominent in the congregation, for he identifies them as coworkers and as having struggled beside him in the work of the gospel. The one other time he uses *struggle with* is in the thesis, in 1:27 (*synathleō*), and it is a term of honor. A public dispute between them would set a bad example.

Starting with verse 4, Paul summarizes the argument (the technical term is *peroratio*). His first summary statement is expressed in the language of joy and peace (vv. 4-7). Rejoicing, of course, has been a theme in many parts of the letter.[59] Such rejoicing, for Paul, is independent of one's changeable circumstances in life, for it is a rejoicing "in the Lord always." "The Lord is near" (v. 5) is difficult to interpret. Most commentators understand the statement **eschatologically**: the return of the Lord Jesus is chronologically near. It could also be read spatially: the Lord is near in the sense of being available to hear the prayers of believers (v. 6). In any event, the ability to pray to God enables the Philippians to put aside their—and Paul's—very real worries. The result is that the peace of God will guard their hearts and minds (v. 7).

The second summary statement (vv. 8-9) uses language frequently found in popular philosophy of Paul's time, especially in Stoicism. At many points in Paul's writings, scholars identify Stoic influence, especially in his ethical material.[60] That is not to say he adopted the Stoic system. He exercised real care in what he did and did not use from elsewhere, but he did not cut himself off from the best thought of his day. He concludes the brief section with another call to imitate him, as well as with a repetition of the theme of peace.

The final major section of the letter is both an acknowledgment of the gift given Paul by the Philippians and a concluding emotional appeal. It also deals with the delicate arena of finances. As we have seen, Paul's financial relationship with the Philippian congregation is unique. He has accepted financial support from the Philippians (Phil 4:15-16; 2 Cor 11:8-9), and the acceptance of such support has raised the question of Paul's exact relationship with them: are they in some way his patrons, and would they seek to use that relationship to control him?

Many scholars continue to insist that Paul is giving thanks to the Philippians in 4:10-20.[61] Others have noted the lack of standard "thanks-giving" language. Thus, a number of scholars have agreed with the observation of Martin Dibelius that Paul's section is a "thankless thanks."[62] John Reumann has suggested another option by looking at Philippians from the perspective of patron-client relationships and ancient concepts of friendship. In that system, the relationship between two people (or groups) was viewed as a mutual relationship where one favor demanded another.[63] Paul had brought the message of Jesus to the Philippians, and they had responded by supporting him. The gift during his imprisonment created problems, however. What could he give in return? Reumann expresses the dilemma this way: "Had he brought this on, he had to ask himself, by appearing to be in need (v. 11)? Was he seeking gifts for himself (as some in Philippi might have been whispering in the house churches there)?"[64]

Reumann sees Paul "trying to extricate himself from the Philippians' own Greco-Roman cultural understanding of friendship" by doing two things.[65] First, he insists that he is independent of the Philippians and doing fine without them (vv. 11-13). Second, he turns the direction of his thoughts away from the Philippians-Paul relationship to God (vv. 18b-20). Thus, he expresses his appreciation, but he avoids putting himself in a subservient relationship by directly expressing his

Philippians: Citizenship in Heaven[68]

I. Salutation	1:1-2
II. Thanksgiving	1:3-11
A. Thanksgiving Proper	1:3-5
B. Reasons Paul Is Able to Pray	1:6-8
C. Prayer of Intercession	1:9-11
III. Narration: Paul's Imprisonment and the Spread of the Gospel	1:12-26
A. Imprisonment: Ironic Spread of the Gospel but Varying Reactions of Local Believers	1:12-18b
B. Paul's Dilemma: Stay or Depart	1:18c-26
IV. Thesis: Live as Citizens in a Way Worthy of the Gospel of Christ	1:27-30
V. Argument in Support of the Thesis	2:1-4:3
A. Statement of Basic Principle	2:1-4
B. Appeal 1: The Example of Christ	2:5-18
1. Introduction and Quotation of Christ Hymn	2:5-11
2. Application of the Example	2:12-18
C. Appeal 2: The Example of Believers	2:19-30
1. The Example of Timothy	2:19-24
2. The Example of Epaphroditus	2:25-30
D. Appeal 3: The Negative Example of the Dogs and the Positive Example of Paul	3:1—4:1
1. Transition	3:1
2. Warning against the Negative Example of the Dogs	3:2
3. Counterexample of Paul	3:3-16
4. Call to Imitate the Positive Examples	3:17—4:1
a. Call to Imitate	3:17
b. Contrast with Enemies of the Cross	3:18-19
c. Statement of Believers' Positive Orientation (Based on Thesis)	3:20-21
d. Conclusion of Call	4:1
E. Appeal 4: Believers to Agree	4:2-3
VI. Summary of the Argument	4:4-20
A. General Summary	4:4-9
1. Summary in Terms of Joy and Peace	4:4-7
2. Summary in Terms of Virtues	4:8-9
B. Appeal to Emotions/Acknowledgment of Gift	4:10-20
VII. Conclusion	4:21-23

thanks, and he also avoids being put into the patron's position. Finally, Reumann presents the standard scholarly understanding of Greco-Roman friendship according to which true friends, in fact, did not need to say "thank you."[66]

Paul concludes with greetings. Noteworthy is the phrase "those of the emperor's household." The reference is to imperially owned slaves and freedmen, who were comparable to civil servants and ran much of the empire's day-to-day bureaucracy.[67]

Summary

In writing to Philippi, Paul pens a warm, intimate letter in which he directs the Philippians to "live your life in a manner worthy of the gospel of Christ." In writing to believers in "little Rome," he uses language with strong political implications to urge them to live in unity and to realize that their true commonwealth and Lord come from heaven, not Rome. His extensive use of examples, including the central role he gives to the example of Christ, provides much of the dynamic for the behavior he is urging.

Study Questions

1. What to you are the three most important reasons Paul wrote the Christ-believers in Philippi?
2. How significant are other people as models of behavior? How and why did Paul rely so heavily on models (or examples) when urging his listeners to act the way he wanted them to act?
3. What are the most important elements in the Christ hymn in chapter 2? What "moves" does Christ make, according to the hymn?
4. How did Paul want the members of his community to behave in relationship to each other?
5. What problems were created when Paul accepted a financial gift from the Philippians? How did he deal with the problems?
6. How was Paul able, in a difficult situation, to express joy?

Suggested Reading

Cousar, Charles B. *Philippians and Philemon: A Commentary*. NTL. Louisville: Westminster John Knox, 2009.

Fee, Gordon D. *Paul's Letter to the Philippians*. NICNT. Grand Rapids: Eerdmans, 1995.

Hawthorne, Gerald F. *Philippians*. Revised and expanded by Ralph P. Martin. WBC 43 Rev. ed. Nashville: Thomas Nelson, 2004.

O'Brien, Peter T. *The Epistle to the Philippians: A Commentary on the Greek Text*. NIGTC. Grand Rapids: Eerdmans, 1991.

Reumann, John. *Philippians*. Anchor Yale Bible 33B. New Haven: Yale University Press, 2008.
Thurston, Bonnie B., and Judith Ryan. *Philippians and Philemon*. Sacra Pagina 10. Collegeville, MN: Liturgical, 2004.
Witherington, Ben III. *Friendship and Finances in Philippi: The Letter of Paul to the Philippians*. The New Testament in Context. Valley Forge, PA: Trinity Press International, 1994.
———. *Paul's Letter to the Philippians: A Socio-Rhetorical Commentary*. Grand Rapids: Eerdmans, 2011.

Websites

Hayes, Holly. "Philippi." *Sacred Destinations*. http://www.sacred-destinations.com/greece/philippi.htm. History, links, and other information about ancient Philippi in Greece.
Lendering, Jona. "Philippi." Livius.org. http://www.livius.org/phi-php/philippi/philippi.html. History with pictures and many links.
Martin, Michael. *New Testament Maps and Artifacts*. http://ntimages.net/. To see pictures of Philippi, click on Greece, then Philippi.
Paola, Justin D. *A Visual Compendium of Roman Emperors*. http://www.roman-emperors.com/.
"Philippi." BiblePlaces.com. http://www.bibleplaces.com/philippi.htm. Several photos with descriptions.

Chapter 12

Philemon: Life in the Christ-Believing Family

How Did People Live in the Family?

> As a Christ-believer with a modest income and a small apartment, you have always appreciated Philemon's generosity. He regularly makes his large home available for worship, and he has financially helped several believers. So you have no problem identifying with the new letter from Paul when the apostle compliments Philemon: "The hearts of the saints have been refreshed through you, my brother" (Philem v. 7).[1] But then Paul goes on to talk about Onesimus, a slave of Philemon's who had disappeared but who has now come to believe in Christ. Paul tells Philemon to accept Onesimus "no longer as a slave but more than a slave, a beloved brother" (v. 16). At that point, you glance at Philemon. What is going through his mind? And what does Paul want?

The Story behind the Letter

Norman R. Petersen's classic book on Philemon has taught us that we must understand the story of Philemon, Onesimus, and Paul and their interaction if we want to understand the letter.[2]

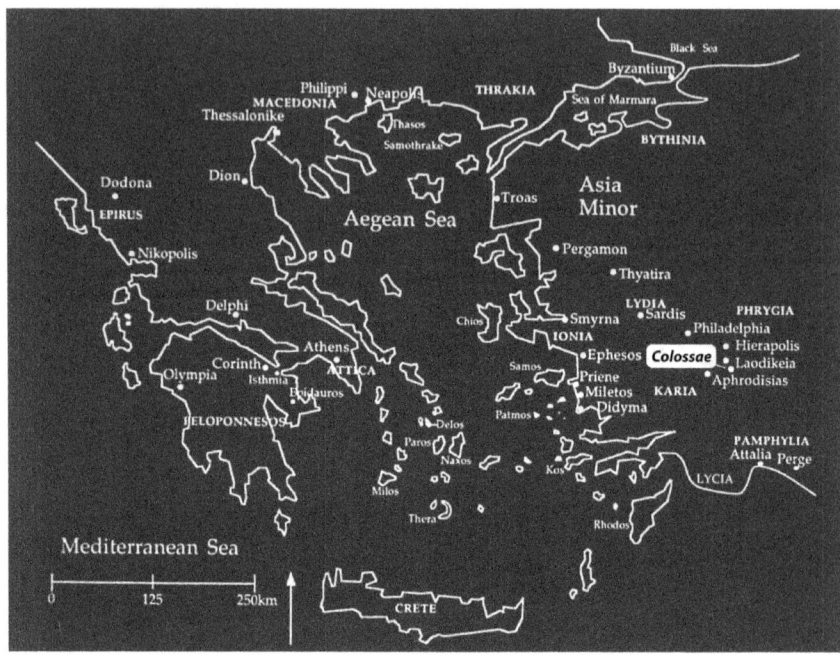

THE PLAYERS

The story of this letter involves three main players or actors:

1. Paul
2. Onesimus, a slave who has left his owner and is with Paul
3. Philemon, the primary person to whom the letter is addressed (v. 1), the person for whom the letter is named, and the owner of Onesimus

Although the traditional view that Paul is the author of Colossians is today much disputed, it is of note that an Onesimus is mentioned in that letter as a member of the Colossian congregation (Col 4:9). In addition, Archippus is named both in Col 4:17 and Philem 2. Thus, Onesimus's home was most likely in **Colossae**, a city 110 miles east of Ephesus in what today is Turkey.

Philemon appears to be relatively wealthy, since he is a slave owner and has a house that not only has a guest room (v. 22) but also is large enough to hold the local congregation (v. 2). (Owning a slave does not, in and of itself, indicate wealth.) Since Philemon was Onesimus's owner, he probably lived in Colossae.[3] At a minimum, Philemon had been converted by the Pauline mission,[4] but Paul's language in verse 19c signals that Paul likely was the missionary through whom Philemon had come to believe in Jesus: "I say nothing about your owing me even your own self."[5] Since we have no evidence that Paul had ever been in Colossae, perhaps Philemon and Paul had met in Ephesus during Paul's lengthy ministry there. Philemon was close to Paul, with Paul calling him *beloved* (v. 1, *agapētos*; the NRSV has "dear friend"). Paul also identifies Philemon as an active believer, who is Paul's "co-worker" (v. 1) and "partner" (v. 17). He is almost certainly the leader of the house church that met in his home.

THE PLOT

Paul is somewhere in custody. Onesimus has left his owner, Philemon, and has made contact with Paul. Under Paul's tutelage, Onesimus has come to believe in Jesus. Paul writes Philemon a letter that, apparently, Onesimus is to take to Philemon.

Two major theories seek to explain how the plot fits together. In the first (or traditional) theory, Onesimus has stolen from Philemon (v. 18) and fled from him. Onesimus is thus a fugitive (Latin: *fugitivus*). Onesimus is arrested and thrown into the same facility as Paul, where Paul converts him. By Roman law, Paul must return Onesimus to his owner. Our letter of Philemon is a "cover" letter by Paul to Onesimus's master to reintroduce Onesimus as now a believer.

The second theory is that Onesimus is not a fugitive but a slave who experienced some form of disagreement with his master. Onesimus did something inappropriate or stupid or was perceived as having done something that caused Philemon financial loss (v. 18). Whether that loss was misappropriation of money, robbery, or simply the loss of Onesimus's services is unclear. He has not been arrested but has sought out Paul on purpose as a third party; the technical Latin name is *amicus domini* (friend of the master).[6] Onesimus's hope is that Paul will intervene with Paul's beloved friend Philemon on behalf of Onesimus, seeking to resolve the problem to Onesimus's advantage.[7] During the conversations between Paul and Onesimus, Onesimus comes to believe in Jesus as the Christ. Paul and he also grow very close (v. 12), and Onesimus, who is not in custody, helps Paul in his imprisonment (vv. 11, 13). Paul writes the letter, then, to accompany Onesimus when he returns to Philemon. As an *amicus domini*, Paul both intercedes for Onesimus and introduces him as a new believer.

The second theory seems to fit better the content of the letter. It is difficult to imagine that Onesimus would have been arrested and happen to be held in the same facility as Paul—and remain there long enough to be converted. Usually, runaway slaves were returned to their owners as soon as possible. Paul as a prisoner had no authority to return any runaway slave to anyone. A runaway slave was liable to severe beating and even death, but Paul does not address such potential punishments. Nor, for that matter, does the letter explicitly say that Onesimus has run away. The extremely careful way Paul phrases his thoughts also points to the *amicus domini* interpretation.[8]

Genre

The Letter to Philemon has aspects of both a private letter and a more public communication. On the one hand, as Charles Puskas has emphasized, Philemon shares more characteristics with ancient personal correspondence than any other New Testament letter.[9] Among those characteristics is the fact that almost the entire letter is addressed to *you* (singular), and the letter has an intensely personal tone. On the other hand, the letter is addressed not only to Philemon but also to Apphia, Archippus, and "the church in your house" (v. 2; *your* is singular and almost certainly designates Philemon). Moreover, the greeting is extended to *you* (plural; v. 3), and the letter ends by addressing the whole church: "The grace of the Lord Jesus Christ be with your spirit" (v. 25; *your* is plural). The letter thus has a public aspect, too, as it is to be heard not only by Philemon but also by the gathered believing community.

In terms of genre, scholars have sometimes understood Philemon to be a letter of recommendation.[10] More in line with the "story" underlying the letter is the view that Philemon is a letter of petition,[11] a letter of mediation,[12] or a letter of intercession.[13] The rhetorical function of Philemon as a letter of intercession is a bit more obvious: it belongs to **deliberative rhetoric**,[14] as it seeks to persuade Philemon to act in the future in specific new ways. The letter exhibits the three major divisions of deliberative rhetoric as found in Aristotle, Cicero, and Quintilian: the exordium, which praises the recipients with the goal of winning their approval (vv. 4-7); the body or proof, which tries to persuade the recipients about a future course of action (vv. 8-16); and the peroration, which is a summary and emotional appeal (vv. 17-22).

But what does Paul want Philemon to do? One clear directive is to prepare a guest room for Paul (v. 22). Beyond that, Paul wants Philemon to accept Onesimus (v. 16). Philemon, in fact, is to welcome him as he would welcome Paul (v. 17). Verses 13-14 imply that Paul would like Philemon to return Onesimus to Paul so that Onesimus could aid Paul in his imprisonment and mission. What is murkier is the meaning of verse 21: "Confident of your obedience, I am writing to you, knowing that you will do even more than I say." What is the "even more"? And how does it connect with receiving Onesimus as a beloved brother in the flesh as well as in the Lord? To answer those questions moves us into the exegesis of the letter (see the commentary later in this chapter).

Location and Date

The only direct statement regarding location is that Paul is in custody (v. 1). But where? The letter itself contains no geographical reference. The only possible information comes from the names common to Philemon and Colossians, which locate Onesimus and Philemon in Colossae.

Three sites are most frequently mentioned as the place where Paul was in custody: Caesarea, Rome, and Ephesus. Caesarea, however, has been explored less and less as a possible location, so that Rome and Ephesus remain the two live possibilities. Ancient church tradition is united in assigning Philemon to Rome. The great distance between Rome and Colossae fits well with Onesimus as a fugitive slave: that is, he fled far from his master and sought to disappear in the masses that populated Rome. And certainly from Acts, we know that Paul was in custody in Rome (28:16-30). If from Rome, Paul wrote Philemon sometime between 60 and 62.[15]

The distance between Rome and Colossae is, however, substantial. If Onesimus were a slave seeking out Paul as an *amicus domini*, would he have sought an intermediary so far away? And what of Paul's request that Philemon prepare a guest room for him (v. 22) both in terms of distance and in terms of Paul's plans to go west from Rome, not east (Rom 15:23-29)? Onesimus could reach Ephesus in a week or less, which would also increase the feasibility of his returning to his master and possibly being sent back to Paul—to say nothing of the greater likelihood that Paul would be able to use Philemon's guest room. If Ephesus were the site of writing, the date would be in the range of 52–55, perhaps toward the end of the period. The major weakness of Ephesus as Paul's location is that we have at most an allusion to imprisonment in the area of Ephesus (2 Cor 1:8), although we ought not live in the illusion that we have data on every incarceration of Paul's (2 Cor 11:23).[16] Nevertheless, Ephesus is an increasingly popular choice for the site of writing.[17]

James D. G. Dunn, among others, finds it difficult to make a decision. "Fortunately, however," he writes, "the exposition of the letter depends only marginally on the conclusion regarding its place of writing, so that to that extent the issue can be left open."[18] While realizing the tentative nature of the information available, the present study will operate with the hypothesis that Paul wrote Philemon while in Ephesus at some time during the years 52–55.

Verses 1-7

Verses 1-3 constitute a typical Pauline salutation: senders (v. 1a) to recipients (vv. 1b-2) and the actual greeting (vv. 3), composed of the standard two Pauline elements of **grace** and *peace*. What is not typical is Paul's self-designation. Here he identifies himself neither as an apostle nor as a slave of Christ Jesus but as "a prisoner of Christ Jesus." Cassidy argues that this self-description is central to Paul's appeal, an observation sustained by four references to imprisonment in the first thirteen verses (vv. 1, 9, 10, 13).[22] The word for *prisoner / desmios* in verses 1 and 9 is literally *one who is chained*, and in verses 10 and 13, Paul specifically writes about his chains (*desmois*); the NRSV translates the word as *imprisonment*. *Chains* could mean being chained to one or more soldiers during the night or even the day, being chained to a wall, or wearing extremely heavy chains that allowed movement if the person was strong enough.[23] It is all the more remarkable, then, that Paul does not identify himself as a prisoner of Rome or of the emperor, but as a prisoner *of Christ Jesus*. By that, he means he is in chains because of his witness to Christ.

Timothy is called "brother," language that will become important later in the letter. Philemon is labeled "our dear friend and co-worker" (v. 1). *Coworker* is

A Note on Slavery

A brief look at slavery in Greco-Roman antiquity can help us better understand the dynamics of the letter.[19] The following statements summarize our state of knowledge about slavery during this place and time:

- In urban areas, one-third to one-half of the population was composed of slaves.
- Many slaves had important positions, including in the bureaucracy of the empire.
- Slaves could own property, and some were wealthy.
- Urban slaves and slaves working in homes had some possibility of being educated.
- Such slaves were usually considered part of the master's household.
- Such slaves had realistic expectation of being freed by age thirty; many were freed earlier (especially likely for a woman whose owner wanted to marry her).
- Slavery had nothing to do with race.
- Many slaves shared language, culture, and religion with their masters.
- Slaves came from nations conquered by the Romans, people kidnapped by pirates, children born to slaves, and people who sold themselves or their children into slavery to pay debts or secure a better life.
- In general, urban slaves fared better than rural slaves, especially field hands.

While we need to be careful not to gloss over the very real abuses done to slaves and their lack of legal rights, it is of note that slavery in Paul's world was often substantially different from the slavery that existed until the 1860s in the United States. Glancy's work, however, is a substantial reminder that the ancient slave's body was subject to all sorts of misuse.[20]

While over time, slavery was questioned by philosophical schools or rejected in principle by groups such as the people at Qumran and the Therapeutae of Egypt, overall there was little questioning of the propriety of slavery. For Paul, slavery, as all institutions, was part of this world that was passing away (1 Cor 7:31). Moreover, Paul sharply challenged the value judgments people assigned to slave and free (1 Cor 7:21-24; 12:13; Gal 3:28; and Philemon itself). In addition, the new relationship that Onesimus and Philemon had as brothers "in the Lord" undercut the basis of slavery and led the church to agree that believers in such a relationship were also brothers "in the flesh," that is, in the world (Philem 16). Marshall concludes that "the fuller implication of Paul's teaching here is that the Christian faith is incompatible with the ownership of slaves. Paul himself may not have come to this realization, but he had charted a route which leads to this destination."[21]

a special term of honor Paul uses for those who have labored closely with him.[24] *Dear friend* translates the Greek word *agapētos* (beloved), which will surface again in verse 16 as a reason for Philemon to act positively toward Onesimus, since the latter has become a *beloved* brother—just as Paul has loved Philemon. Apphia is called simply "sister," a word frequently used to designate a female believer. Most commentators regard her as Philemon's wife, but the text is not explicit. Archippus is given the title of "fellow soldier," a term used elsewhere in Paul only in Phil 2:25.

Verses 4-7 contain the thanksgiving section, which we have learned is a normal part of Paul's letters. In terms of deliberative rhetoric, the section functions also as the exordium, which seeks to gain a positive hearing from the recipient and seeks to pull him onto Paul's side. The primary recipient is Philemon; the *you* and *your* of verses 4-7 are singular, not plural. Paul thanks God for Philemon because of the reports he has received about him (v. 5). Verse 6 introduces a specific prayer request that revolves around the word *koinōnia*, "sharing," also translated as *fellowship* or *participation*. The request is that the common faith that Philemon shares with other believers may become even more effective than it already is. Paul concludes the thanksgiving with another compliment, naming the benefits that Philemon has already provided: "I have indeed received much joy and encouragement from your love, because the hearts of the saints have been refreshed through you, my brother" (v. 7). This is the second time Paul has mentioned Philemon's love (v. 5 is the other), and he will use it again in verse 9 as the basis of his appeal to Philemon. Note, once again, that Philemon is called "brother," a theme that will continue to inform the rest of the letter.[25]

Verses 8-16

In verse 8, Paul moves into the body of the letter. Verses 8 and 9 are an intriguing disclaimer: Paul has the authority to command Philemon to do his duty (vs. 8),[26] but instead of doing that, he appeals to him "on the basis of love"—the same love for which he has already complimented Philemon in verses 4 and 7. Paul lays aside his authority and in part plays with the concept of duty. As the head of the household, Philemon would be expected to fulfill his duty by punishing Onesimus. That is the honorable thing to do. Paul appeals to him to fulfill his duty in a different way, just as Paul has put aside his right to command Philemon.[27] At the same time, even though Paul does not in this letter claim his authority as an apostle, he does claim a more personal authority: he is an old man, and he is an old man who is a prisoner of Christ Jesus. As an old man in Mediterranean culture, he is in a position that Philemon should respect. From the perspective of a Christ-believer, Philemon should respect him even more because the old man Paul is a prisoner of Christ.[28] The language reflects both Paul's cultural status and the emotional weight of his imprisonment.

Verses 10-14 contain the appeal. The NRSV loses the careful way Paul has constructed his thoughts, which is seen in this more literal translation: "I am appealing to you for my child, whom I begot in chains, Onesimus [in English, literally *Useful*] who formerly to you was useless but now to you and to me is useful" (vss. 10-11). *Child*, of course, is a family term, as is *brother* (for more on family, see the comments on v. 19). It is only in verse 10 that Paul introduces the name Onesimus (in fact, it is the only time that word occurs in the letter). Rhetorically, Paul has identified Onesimus as his child, one whom Paul fathered while bound in chains in the sense of being the converting missionary. Only at that point does he introduce the slave's name. And as soon as he does that, he constructs a play on words. Before believing in Christ, "Useful" (Onesimus) was in fact useless to Philemon. But now that he has come to believe, he is finally really useful both to Philemon and to Paul (v. 11).[29]

Paul has more to say about Onesimus. Paul is sending him back to Philemon.[30] But in sending him back, Paul is sending his "own heart," literally the word *bowels* (v. 12; also vv. 7, 20). The intestines or bowels were viewed as the location of strong emotions, so sending Onesimus back is no cavalier decision. Paul thus raises the emotional quotient of his request, which he continues in verses 13 and 14. During his period in chains, Paul preferred retaining the services of Onesimus, who would in a sense take Philemon's place, but he does not want to do anything without Philemon's permission, "in order that your good deed might be voluntary and not something forced" (v. 14). So Paul has now put aside his own desire to keep Onesimus with him, and he has earlier put aside his authority as an apostle. It is now Philemon's turn to do something, and it is a matter of honor that Philemon respond.[31]

In verses 15-16, Paul ties his request to God's will and finally says (in part) what he wants Philemon to do. In verse 15, Paul speculates a bit: "Perhaps this is the reason he was separated from you for a while." The verb *was separated* is passive; that is, the subject (*he*) is being acted upon. Who is doing the acting? The sentence does not say, but a typical use of the passive by Judean and Christ-believing authors was to indicate God's action. Ultimately, then, the dynamic behind Onesimus's leaving may have been God's will (Paul carefully avoids language such as *he ran away*). And what would be the purpose of God's will in separating them? Paul suggests, "So that you might have him back forever" (v. 15). At one level, that looks like the typical interpretation of slave owners in the United States: Paul is returning the slave to his master. But he goes on to qualify his statement sharply and to state what he wants Philemon to do. Having Onesimus back forever means having him "no longer as a slave but more than a slave, a beloved brother—especially to me but how much more to you, both in the flesh and in the Lord" (v. 16). Treating Onesimus as "a beloved brother" should occur not only "in the Lord"—say, for example, during worship—but also "in the flesh," in everyday life.

Verses 17-25

In verses 17-25, Paul summarizes his position and appeals to Philemon's emotions. He labels Philemon and himself partners (v. 17). Philemon has been active in Paul's ministry. The second step is that Philemon (Paul's partner) should welcome

Onesimus in the same way he would welcome Paul. And who is Paul? Philemon's partner. Thus, just as Philemon and Paul are partners, so is Onesimus. That, too, alters the master-slave relationship.

Also of note in this verse and the next two is the business language Paul uses. Only now does he begin to address the financial aspects of the Philemon-Onesimus relationship. Rhetorically, Paul may have wanted to wait until later in the letter to broach this delicate topic. In dealing with Philemon's potential objection—namely, Onesimus had in some way cost him money—Paul takes a strong stand. First, he promises to pay whatever loss Onesimus has caused: "If he has wronged you in any way, or owes you anything, charge that to my account" (v. 18). In verse 19a, Paul reemphasizes his promise: "I, Paul, am writing this with my own hand: I will repay it." While some commentators think Paul is indicating that he has written the whole letter by hand, most think that, at this point, he takes the pen from the secretary and begins writing. He does two things: he signs his name, and in his own handwriting, he restates his guarantee.[32]

Paul also takes another step. He reminds Philemon of what he owes Paul: "I say nothing about your owing me even your own self" (v. 19b). Philemon owes Paul his life as a Christ-believer. Thus, if Philemon wants to talk about debt, fine. Philemon also owes a debt.

Two closely related concepts come together in Philemon: kinship and obligation. Concerning kinship, Timothy is called a brother (v. 1), Apphia is called a sister (v. 2), Philemon is twice directly addressed as brother (vv. 7, 20), and Onesimus is to be received as a beloved brother (v. 16). That language of familial relationship is not a casual address by Paul but establishes the family framework of his letter. In Paul's view, the church is what social-science students of the Bible call a **fictive family** or a fictive kin group. By entering the entity called the church, people become part of a new family. It is a fictive family because it is not joined by blood ties, but it is a real family nevertheless. Not only are the members of this fictive kin group called sister and brother, but also Paul at times refers to himself as the father or mother of his churches or of people he has converted (1 Cor 4:15; Gal 4:19; 1 Thess 2:7, 11).[33]

The primary group for people in the ancient circum-Mediterranean was the kin group. Life within that group provides the origin of the second concept of note, obligation. Within the family, members felt obligated to help each other. Even more, members of the same in-group—in our case, the fictive kin group of the church—were felt to owe each other a debt of gratitude. In a very particular way, that debt of interpersonal obligation within the family of the church is seen in Paul's letter to Philemon.

Rhetorically, the letter revolves around the concept of debt. First, there is the debt of the slave himself (v. 18); for this, Paul uses the business term *owe / opheilō*. The second debt, as we have learned, is in verse 19: Philemon *owes / prosopheilō* Paul. But there is also a third debt, and that is the debt—or, as Norman Petersen calls it, the obligation—that Philemon has "to *be* a brother to the brothers and sisters in the Lord. Upon conversion and entry into the sibling relationship that obtains among the children of God, one becomes a brother or a sister, and behaving as such becomes a responsibility."[34] Now that his slave Onesimus has become a Christ-follower, Philemon has a new relationship with him. It is a more complicated one, for not only is Philemon now the master of Onesimus, he is also the brother of Onesimus (vv. 15-16). Receiving Onesimus as a brother "in the Lord" was probably a lot easier than receiving him as a brother "in the flesh." And that fact raised dramatically the stakes for Philemon: "If Philemon refuses to accept a brother as a brother, then Philemon's status in the brotherhood is at stake, for *he* has not shown himself to be a brother."[35] Philemon has a debt of obligation to the entire family "to receive Onesimus for and as what he had become, not for and as what he had been."[36] And on what basis does Paul exhort Philemon? On the basis of love (*agapē*; v. 9), which, within Mediterranean culture, included the willingness to pay one's debt of interpersonal obligation.[37]

Verse 20 continues the theme of family as Paul addresses Philemon as *brother*. He also once more plays with the meaning of the name Onesimus: "Yes, brother, let me have this benefit from you in the Lord! Refresh my heart in Christ." The verb *to have benefit of* is the verb from which the name Onesimus comes. Paul repeats, too, the word *refresh*, which he used in verse 7. Also as in verse 7, the NRSV's *heart* is the word *bowels*, the seat of the emotions. Obviously, Paul is summarizing his appeal.

In verse 21, Paul states his confidence in Philemon. Paul has experienced Philemon as a coworker and brother in the past, so now he feels he knows what Philemon will do. Interesting is the word *obedience*. Paul does not demand obedience, but he expects it. Paul concludes the verse, "I am writing to you, knowing that you will do even more than I say." Paul believes Philemon will not just meet the minimum standards of this pass-fail system, but will go beyond them. What specifically does Paul want Philemon to do? At a minimum, Philemon is told (implicitly) to do two things: (1) refrain from punishing Onesimus; and (2) if you keep him as a slave, live with him in a radically different relationship based on your common faith in Christ. But what is the "more" to which Paul refers? Many scholars see a reference to manumission, so that Paul wants Philemon not to delay in manumitting Onesimus because he sought out Paul,[38] but to free Onesimus now, thus treating him "no longer as a slave," and return him as a free person to Paul.[39] The final decision is Philemon's, albeit within the framework of the believing community that meets in his house.

Verse 22 contains Paul's request for a guest room. The request is a signal to Philemon that Paul does hope to be released from custody and will learn firsthand what Philemon decides to do with Onesimus. Verses 23 and 24 contain personal greetings from four of Paul's associates, one of whom is a fellow prisoner, Epaphras. The letter concludes in verse 25 with a brief benediction.

Did the letter succeed? We do not know for sure. Most commentators think Philemon responded positively to Paul's letter. Otherwise, they argue, it is hard to see why the church preserved the letter. The reference to an Onesimus in Col 4:9 may be proof, too, that Philemon not only accepted Onesimus but freed him. Even

Philemon: Life in the Christ-Believing Family

I.	Salutation	vss. 1-3
II.	Exordium/Thanksgiving	vss. 4-7
	A. Statement of Thanksgiving	vs. 4a
	B. When Thanks Is Given	vs. 4b[42]
	C. Reason for Thanksgiving	vs. 5
	D. Specific Prayer Request	vs. 6
	E. Benefits Paul and the Saints Have Received from Recipient	vs. 7
III.	Body	vss. 8-16
	A. Statement of Paul's Authority	vss. 8-9
	1. Statement of Authority to Command	vs. 8
	2. Dismissal of Authority to Command in Favor of an Appeal	vs. 9
	a. Basis for Appeal	vs. 9a
	b. Paul's Personal Authority	vs. 9b
	B. The Appeal	vss. 10-14
	1. Statement of the Appeal	vs. 10a
	2. Identification of the Person for Whom Paul Is Appealing	vss. 10b-14
	a. Identification 1: Child	vs. 10b
	b. Identification 2: Paul Begat	vs. 10c
	c. Identification 3: Name of Person	vss. 10d-11[43]
	d. Identification 4: Paul Sends Person, Calls Him His "Bowels"	vs. 12
	e. Identification 5: Paul Desires to Keep Him; Reason; Why Writing Instead	vss. 13-14
	C. Possible Basis for Appeal: God's Will	vss. 15-16
	1. Introduction of Divine Reason for Separation	vs. 15a
	2. Goals of the Separation	vss. 15b-16
	a. Goal 1: Have Him Forever	vs. 15b
	b. Goal 2: Brother	vs. 16
IV.	Peroration (Summary and Emotional Appeal)	vss. 17-22
	A. Restatement of the Appeal	vs. 17
	B. Answer to Possible Objection	vss. 18-19
	1. Offer to Repay Losses Caused by Onesimus	vs. 18
	2. Assurance of Offer to Repay Losses	vs. 19a
	3. Reminder of What Recipient Owes Paul	vs. 19b
	C. Emotional Appeal	vs. 20
	D. Statement of Confidence in Response of Recipient	vs. 21
	E. Request for Lodging	vs. 22
V.	Conclusion	vss. 23-25
	A. Greetings from Other Believers	vss. 23-24
	B. Benediction	vs. 25

if Paul did not write Colossians, it would be passing strange to refer to Onesimus in the way Colossians does if he had not been freed, since the ancient recipients of Colossians would have known Onesimus. Finally, Ignatius of Antioch refers to a bishop of Ephesus named Onesimus (Ign. *Eph.* 1.3, 2.1, 6.2). While it is possible that he refers to the Onesimus of Philemon, it is more likely that the person simply had the same name (it was quite common) or was even named for Philemon's Onesimus. In any event, Ignatius writes sometime between 110 and 117, a good sixty years after Paul's letter.

Summary

In writing to the slave owner Philemon, Paul presents a rhetorically sophisticated argument as an *amicus domini* requesting that Philemon accept as a brother in Christ his slave Onesimus. The letter revolves around the concepts of debt and obligation. It also places over against each other two institutions[40] or two families[41]: the culturally normal Greco-Roman household, with its institution of slavery, and the church, a fictive family in the process of being defined. In his intervention for Onesimus, Paul outlines some of the basics of life in the Christ-believing community, which is a family of siblings.

Study Questions

1. Which possible "story line" underlying this letter makes the most sense to you? Why?
2. How does Paul use the concept of debt?
3. What do you think Paul wants Philemon to do regarding Onesimus?

Suggested Reading

Barth, Markus, and Helmut Blanke. *The Letter to Philemon*. Eerdmans Critical Commentary. Grand Rapids: Eerdmans, 2000.
Dunn, James D. G. *The Epistles to the Colossians and to Philemon*. NIGTC. Grand Rapids: Eerdmans, 1996.
Fitzmyer, Joseph A. *The Letter to Philemon*. AB 34C. New York: Doubleday, 2000.
Osiek, Carolyn. *Philippians; Philemon*. ANTC. Nashville: Abingdon, 2000.
Petersen, Norman R. *Rediscovering Paul: Philemon and the Sociology of Paul's Narrative World*. Philadelphia: Fortress Press, 1985.
Thurston, Bonnie B., and Judith Ryan. *Philippians and Philemon*. Sacra Pagina 10. Collegeville, MN: Liturgical, 2004.
Wilson, Robert M. *A Critical and Exegetical Commentary on Colossians and Philemon*. ICC 38b. London: T & T Clark, 2005.

Chapter 13

How Did People Develop What Paul Wrote?

The purpose of this chapter is to survey the Pauline tradition in the generations immediately following Paul, in order to see how Paul and his thought were utilized as the church continued to develop. Six letters in the New Testament that are associated with the name of Paul are understood in this book to have been written in his name by someone else after his death. Such writings were common in antiquity and were viewed as ways both to honor the original author or founding figure (in our case Paul) and to update him for a new time and place.[1] The six such Pauline letters are 2 Thessalonians, Colossians, Ephesians, 1 Timothy, 2 Timothy, and Titus. They are *Pauline* in the sense that they seek to continue Paul's heritage, but they are not Pauline in the sense that Paul was their author, and for that reason they are sometimes called "deuteropauline" (*deutero-* meaning "secondary") or "pseudopauline." After considering those New Testament letters, we will also look briefly at other documents and movements in which Paul figures prominently: the New Testament book of Acts, the writings of Ignatius of Antioch, those of Marcion, Gnosticism, the *Acts of Paul and Thecla*, and the Pseudo-Clementinian literature.

Richard Pervo identifies both the importance of the **deuteropauline** letters in the New Testament for Paul's ongoing significance and the variety of that material: "The most important fact communicated by the existence of pseudo-Pauline letters is that the apostle continued to have authority. They would not otherwise exist.... Investigation of these letters will also demonstrate that a single form of

290 | Paul: Apostle to the Nations

Fig. 13.1 The apostle Paul is depicted as a miracle worker, suffering no harm as he throws a poisonous snake into the fire after being shipwrecked on Malta (Acts 28:1-6). Twelfth-century fresco from Canterbury Cathedral.

Deutero-Pauline thought, with appropriate developments within that framework, cannot be traced."[2] Therefore, we will consider how each piece of deuteropauline and other material illuminates the apostle from different perspectives.

The Eschatological Paul (2 Thessalonians)

The situation to which 2 Thessalonians is addressed has two foci. First, there is reference to persecution. We do not know the content of the suffering that has faced the recipients, but the author is able to boast about the recipients because of the way they have maintained the faith "during all your persecutions and the afflictions that you are enduring" (1:4).

Second, a false teacher has apparently referred to oral or written statements of Paul to support the teacher's view that the Day of the Lord has already arrived:

"As to the coming [*parousia*] of our Lord Jesus Christ and our being gathered together to him, we beg you brothers and sisters, not to be quickly shaken in mind or alarmed, either by spirit or by word or by letter, as though from us, to the effect that the day of the Lord is already here" (2:1-2). This **realized eschatology** has sharply affected the daily life of some believers, who are refusing to work in light of the end (3:6-15), so the author has to be blunt: "Anyone unwilling to work should not eat" (3:10).

In response to the situation of the recipients, the author of 2 Thessalonians develops in 2:1-12 a timetable that lists specific events that need to occur before the coming of the Day of the Lord. Whereas in 1 Thess 4:13-18 and 1 Cor 15:20-58, Jesus could return suddenly at any moment, that cannot happen in 2 Thessalonians, in part because the author wants to dampen the kind of "eschatological excitement" that has led to the belief that the coming of Jesus either has already in some way happened or will occur imminently. The chief solution the author proposes is a division of the present and future into periods, each of which needs to happen in order before the return of Jesus. First come "the rebellion" and the revealing of "the lawless one" (in Greek, *the man of lawlessness*). Ultimately, he takes God's seat in the temple (presumably in Jerusalem) and declares himself to be God, but for the moment, he is being restrained. At the same time, "the mystery of lawlessness is already at work" (vs. 7), which no doubt speaks to the persecution the believers are enduring. Once the restraint is removed, the lawless one will be revealed, and then the Lord Jesus will destroy him. The author reminds the listeners that previously he had taught all of this to them (vs. 5). Since the lawless one has not yet been revealed and has not yet taken over the temple, the Day of the Lord is clearly not at hand.

Thus, while the section implicitly encourages people to pay attention to the various steps that have yet to occur, it functions to relax the sense of a soon-to-happen return of Jesus. Or to put it in other language, the sense in the undisputed letters, particularly 1 Thessalonians, that the end cannot be calculated—for example, "the day of the Lord will come like a thief in the night" (1 Thess 5:2-3)—becomes in 2 Thessalonians a prediction of the end. As Beker has phrased it in reference to the Paul of the seven undisputed letters, "For Paul Christian hope is *a matter of prophecy and not of prediction*. The incalculability of the hope is for Paul one of its essential marks."[3] In 2 Thessalonians, believers can plot the end according to the timetable of chapter 2.[4] Thus, while the language of apocalyptic is used, the end is far off in the future.

Another striking characteristic of 2 Thessalonians is its emphasis on judgment. The persecutions and afflictions of the recipients (1:4) are "evidence of the righteous judgment of God, . . . intended to make you worthy of the kingdom of God, for which you are also suffering" (1:5). Even more, God will punish those who are harming the Thessalonians; thus, "it is indeed just of God to repay with affliction those who afflict you" (1:6). Similarly, when Jesus returns, he will inflict "vengeance on those who do not know God and on those who do not obey the gospel of our Lord Jesus. These will suffer the punishment of eternal destruction"

(1:8-9; see also 2:8). The result is that Jesus is seen as the judge.[5] The perspectives found in 2 Thessalonians are not themes in the undisputed letters.

Apart from eschatological concerns, Paul's role and theology seem to move in other new directions. In 1 Thessalonians, Paul urges believers "to stand firm in the Lord" (3:8). In 2 Thess 2:15, they are to "stand firm and hold fast to the traditions that you were taught by us, either by word of mouth or by our letter." Paul's teaching is viewed as a tradition to which believers should adhere, which in turn puts him more strongly into a position of great authority that allows him to issue orders (3:6, 10, 12, 14-15). Thus, Paul's labor as an artisan is not so much an example of his service to the gospel he proclaims as it is a moral example of how believers should live (3:6-9, 12).

Proposed dates for the letter depend, of course, on conclusions about authorship. For people who hold to authorship by someone other than Paul himself, dates range from approximately 70 to 100 CE. Persecution, while a possibility for Christ-believers at any time, appears to have increased in the latter part of the first century, which in turn could well have spurred greater attention to questions of when the end would come as well as the meaning of the sufferings believers were enduring.[6]

The Universal Paul (Colossians, Ephesians)

We will look at Colossians and Ephesians together, in part because approximately a third of Colossians is repeated in Ephesians, and about one-half of the sentences in Ephesians contain language clearly from Colossians.[7] We will center on three areas in which the two related epistles show a further development of the thought and person of Paul known from the undisputed letters.

The first area of interest is a shift in expectation regarding the near return of Jesus. The documents do not exhibit the kind of imminent expectation of the end that we have seen in the undisputed letters. The soon-to-come Day of the Lord has disappeared as an active dynamic for living the Christ-believing life, and it no longer provides the impetus for Paul's mission. Thus, God "has rescued us from the power of darkness and transferred us into the kingdom of his beloved Son" (Col 1:13), a view that fits the understanding that the believer not only has died with Christ in baptism (Rom 6:4) but has also been resurrected with him: "When you were buried with him in baptism, you were also raised with him through faith in the power of God, . . . And when you were dead in trespasses and the uncircumcision of your flesh, God made you alive together with him" (Col 2:12-13).[8] Indeed, in Colossians, the basis for ethical action is not life to be lived in light of the coming return of Jesus, but in the present experience of resurrection: "So if you have been raised with Christ, seek the things that are above, where Christ is" (3:1).

The reference to *above* is even more pronounced in Ephesians and signals a shift from chronological interests in the nearness of the end to spatial categories such as above and below. So in Eph 2:5-6, the author writes that God "made us alive together with Christ—by grace you have been saved—and raised us up with him and seated us with him in the heavenly places in Christ Jesus"; see also 1:20-22. The present-tense experience of salvation is also stated in the phrase "by grace you have been saved" (repeated in 3:8), which is quite different from the future tenses for *save* Paul almost always uses in the undisputed letters.[9] To return to the matter of space, even alienation from Christ can be phrased in spatial terms (2:12-13, 17-19), and the cosmic nature of the church, to which we will turn momentarily, is likewise a spatial concept.

The line that we saw in the undisputed letters between *already* and *not yet* does still exist, but it is drawn at a different point. Much more *already* has been realized in Colossians and Ephesians, and there is less that has *not yet* been given to believers.

Another indication of the shift away from expectation of a near end is the existence in both letters of *Haustafeln* (tables of household duties). These lists specify the proper behavior for believers in certain relationships: wives and husbands, children and parents, slaves and masters (Col 3:18—4:1; Eph 5:21—6:9). In a world that was not passing away nearly as quickly as Paul had expected, believers had to develop patterns for living in the world over the long term. More specific directives needed to be spelled out to guide believers. These lists of duties also fostered a kind of respectability in the broader society for the followers of Jesus, since the basic duties are similar to those of ethical thinkers in the Greco-Roman world, although for believers, the duties are rooted in love (*agapē*) and in Christ's activity for humanity.

Fig. 13.2 Slaves being led to the slave market; stone relief from Miletus, second or third century C.E. Photo: G. Dall'Orto.

Our second area of interest is the understanding of the church. The basic shift from the undisputed letters is that in Colossians and Ephesians, the church is thought of less as the local congregation and more as a cosmic entity. The house church of the undisputed letters is hardly in view. So in Ephesians, the church is the sphere of activity of the cosmic Christ that unites all believers on earth and in the heavenly places, with special reference to the inclusion of the Gentiles (2:11-22). The church has a crucial role in God's plan, for it is "through the church" that "the wisdom of God in its rich variety might now be made known to the rulers and authorities in the heavenly places" (3:10), and it is in the church that God is glorified (3:21). The church as church becomes the focus of much more attention than in the undisputed letters.

In tandem with the basic cosmic-wide or universe-wide conception of the church is the perspective that the church is the body of Christ of which Christ himself, who is now in heaven, is the head (Col 1:18; 2:19; Eph 1:22-23; 4:15-16). That is a striking change from Rom 12:3-8 and 1 Cor 12:12-31, where Paul uses the image of the church as the body of Christ but never identifies Christ as the head in the hierarchical way that Colossians and Ephesians do. Pervo likens the image to that of the emperor: "In a metaphor that would become enduring, Christ as king rules over a hierarchical pyramid, like the Roman emperor."[10] An important difference is that Christ rules from heaven (Col 3:1), and in Col 1:15-20, the cosmic nature of Christ is expressed in the clearest language. Not only is he the agent of creation, and "all things have been created through him and for him" (1:16), but also it is "in him" that "all things hold together" (1:17; see also 2:3, 10, 15; 3:1). And in one of the most theologically lofty assertions about Christ in the New Testament, he is the one in whom "the whole fullness of deity dwells bodily" (2:9). Moreover, in Eph 1:23, the church "is his [Christ's] body, the fullness of him who fills all in all," and in 5:23-33, the church is Christ's bride, which is a statement of the intimate relationship of believers as a corporate entity with the Lord.

The third area of significant development in relationship to the undisputed letters is the understanding of Paul himself. Just as the church is viewed as a universal entity, so Paul is seen as the universal apostle. Gone is the need seen in the undisputed letters for him to argue for and defend his apostleship; it is replaced with a view of his apostolic office that includes sufferings, surely, but that views his work as part of the revealing of God's eternal mysteries (so Col 1:24—2:5, especially 1:25-27; also 4:3). In Ephesians, too, Paul reveals the mystery of God's will (1:9; 3:1-6, 9; 6:19), which is the unity in the one church of Judeans and Gentiles (2:11-22) and not the mystery of the cross of Jesus (1 Cor 2:2; overall 1:18—2:5). The dominance of the church is also seen in Colossians, where Paul is a *minister / servant / diakonos* of the church (1:24-25), rather than a *minister / servant / diakonos* of God (2 Cor 6:4) or a *minister / servant / diakonos* of a new covenant (2 Cor 3:6).

Remarkable is the emphasis on his sufferings as an apostle, beyond even what Paul himself said. Thus, in Col 1:24, the apostle claims, "I am now rejoicing in my sufferings for your sake, and in my flesh I am completing what is lacking in

Christ's afflictions for the sake of his body, that is, the church." The sense seems to be that while Christ's sufferings were vicarious, that is, for others, so too are the apostle's sufferings, a concept that is not found in the undisputed letters, let alone any indication that Paul had to complete what Christ had not finished. It is noteworthy that Paul's suffering is for the church rather than, for example, the gospel (Phil 1:2; 1 Thess 2:1-2). Colossians appeals to the listeners' emotions by its attention to Paul's sufferings (the literary device of **pathos**). He toils and struggles with every ounce of energy (1:29), even while in prison and in chains (4:3, 18). Colossians 4:18 in particular leaves the listeners with the final image of the apostle suffering for them ("Remember my chains"), as does Eph 6:20 ("I am an ambassador in chains"). Related statements are made in Eph 3:1, 13; 4:1.

There is a strong sense of looking backwards in Colossians and Ephesians that begins with the idealization of Paul's suffering. In addition, Paul is part of the "holy apostles and prophets" to whom "the mystery of Christ" has been revealed (Eph 3:5), and "built upon the foundation of the apostles and prophets" is the "household of God," the church (2:19-20). Such a view seems different and later when compared with 1 Cor 3:11, where Paul insists that "no other foundation can anyone lay than that which is laid, which is Jesus Christ." In fact, as Christiaan Beker has stressed, both letters present "a Paul of 'blessed memory,'"[11] who even seems to acknowledge that he is addressing people who will never know him (Col 2:1-5).

Dates for Colossians range from as early as 60, if possibly written by an associate of Paul's while he was still alive, to the early 90s of the first century. Dates for Ephesians go from 75 to as late as 100.[12]

The Ecclesiastical Paul (Acts, 1–2 Timothy, Titus, Ignatius of Antioch)

In the book of Acts, the Pastoral Epistles, and the letters of Ignatius of Antioch, Paul is understood to be an iconic figure of the institutional church. He is placed into the church's hierarchy, where he guarantees the church's tradition and doctrine and where he becomes a focal point for church unity.

ACTS

We have already discussed the difficulties of using the New Testament book of Acts to reconstruct the life and thought of Paul.[13] Together with other post-Paul documents, the eschatology of Paul as developed in the book of Acts is substantially different from that of the undisputed letters. As Philipp Vielhauer wrote many years ago, in Acts "the eschatology [of Paul] disappears. . . . Eschatology has been removed from the center of Pauline faith to the end and has become a 'section on the last things.'"[14] In tandem with the deemphasis on eschatology is a heightened emphasis on the church as an institution, which is illustrated by the sheer existence of a book that outlines the spread of the church. The church is realizing that it has a long-range future, for which it must prepare itself. Together with the attention given to the church's growth, Acts shows a minimum of church dissension and disagreement as the message about Jesus spreads quickly. The kinds of difficulties Paul encountered in Galatia or in Corinth are largely absent from Acts.

Of particular interest is how Acts describes the person of Paul. While his theology may be missing from Acts, his person is definitely not. Paul, in fact, is not only the chief human actor in the second half of the book, he is also really the hero of the story in chapters 13–28. Beker phrases it this way: "The mission 'to the ends of the earth' (1:8) refers unmistakably to him [Paul], since he . . . almost single-handedly carries the gospel in ever-widening missionary conquests from Antioch to Rome,"[15] even though, as seen earlier, Paul for the author of Luke was not an apostle and was subordinated to the original apostles.[16]

Paul's subordination to his apostolic predecessors in Jerusalem as well as to James the brother of Jesus is illustrated also by the fact that in the speeches of Acts, each of the Christ-believing speakers has the same theology.[17] Moreover, the church as pictured in Acts has one theology and one Jerusalem-centered mission, under which Paul's mission to the Gentiles is subsumed. Paul also becomes the representative of a church that is declared to be no threat to the empire (16:39; 18:14-15; 26:31). Although the book concludes with Paul's being in house custody, his real relationship with Rome is hidden. He becomes a representative figure for the nonthreatening and urbane religion Acts wants to represent.[18]

Fig. 13.3 Paul is depicted arguing with Judeans in Damascus (see Acts 9:22) in a Byzantine mosaic from the Palatine Chapel in Palermo.

Finally, when reading the New Testament in the order in which the books are arranged in the **canon**, it is important to realize that Acts not only precedes all the letters of Paul, but also serves to introduce Paul to the reader before the letters are ever reached. As Crossan and Reed express it, "You meet the Lukan Paul of the Acts of the Apostles before you meet the Pauline or historical Paul of his own letters. In other words, Paul gets colored Lukan."[19] In this history of the early church, written somewhere between 70 and 90,[20] Paul thus becomes an ecclesiastical figure rather than the intense apocalyptic apostle.

THE PASTORAL EPISTLES

Since antiquity, 1 Timothy, 2 Timothy, and Titus have been understood as a unit, because their vocabulary, writing style, and concerns are so similar. For three centuries, they have been called the "Pastoral Epistles." Ironically, the letters never use the word *pastor*, but they do pay significant attention to the qualifications good church leaders need. Understood by the large majority of scholars as having been written by someone other than the historical Paul, they are addressed to Paul's associates Timothy and Titus. In 1 Timothy and Titus, there is a strong interest in church organization, while 2 Timothy is cast in the genre of a farewell letter.

As with other documents in the Pauline tradition written by someone other than Paul, the theology of the Pastorals differs from that of the undisputed letters. Jesus is straightforwardly called God (Titus 2:13), although never *son of God*. Nor for that matter is the cross specifically mentioned. What is important, however, is the *appearance* or *manifestation* of Jesus, expressed in the Greek word *epiphaneia* (epiphany) and the related verb (for his first appearance, see 2 Tim 1:10; Titus 2:11; 3:4; for his return, see 1 Tim 6:14; 2 Tim 4:1, 8; Titus 2:13). While *kyrios / lord* is used, as it is in the undisputed letters, the word *savior / sōtēr* is much more significant in the Pastorals (in the undisputed letters only in Phil 3:20). As with the other documents surveyed so far in this chapter, the sense of an imminent expectation of the return of Jesus has been relinquished, and there are clear elements of a realized eschatology (that is, more of the *already* is present than in the undisputed letters). Salvation has already been given (2 Tim 1:9-10; Titus 3:5), so the believer can "take hold of" eternal life now (1 Tim 6:12, 19). The interest in church order, with bishop, deacon, elder, and widow as offices, also signals that the author expects the world to be around for the longer term.[21] At the same time, there is a future aspect to salvation, too (1 Tim 4:16; 2 Tim 2:10-11; 4:18; Titus 1:2; 2:13; 3:7), even though there is nothing comparable to the imminent expectation of Rom 13:11-14 or 1 Thess 4:13—5:11.

The figure of Paul in these letters has three major aspects. First, he is a sinner. Jesus came into the world to save sinners (1 Tim 1:15-16), of whom Paul is the "foremost." That theme resonates, of course, with other letters (1 Cor 15:9; Eph 3:8). Second, Paul is *the* apostle, not just an apostle (1 Tim 2:7; 2 Tim 1:11). He is the major authority figure of the three letters, who guarantees and interprets the tradition (1 Tim 4:1-16), instruction (1 Tim 3:14), deposit of truth (1 Tim 6:20; 2 Tim 1:12, 14), and doctrine (Titus 1:9; 2:1). For that reason, his associates and he have no need for debate with the opponents; opponents are simply to be avoided (2 Tim 2:14; 16; 1 Tim 4:7; 6:20). The perspective of the letters is defensive or, in the insightful model of Margaret MacDonald, "community-protecting."[22] Third, he is the model of the perfect martyr for other believers who will have to testify (2 Tim 1:11-12; 2:8-10; 3:10-11; 4:6-8, 17). Particularly in the second two components of the reconstruction of Paul in the Pastorals, the view looks backward to a figure who has been gone for a good number of years.

One final word: women in the undisputed letters lead worship (1 Cor 11:5-6);[23] they serve as patrons, including of Paul, and prepare for the next steps in his mission (Rom 16:1-2); they are important missionaries and associates of his (Rom 16:3-4, 6, 12, 13, 15); and at least one is an apostle (Rom 16:7). In the Pastorals, however, they are to keep silent and not lead worship (1 Tim 2:8-15), and the author is quite concerned to bring the widows in the congregation until control (1 Tim 5:3-16). Women are not always viewed in the most positive light (2 Tim 3:6). The Pastorals represent a clear shift from the undisputed letters. There is nothing comparable to Paul's statement in Gal 3:28 that gender differences have no value in evaluating members of the body of Christ.[24]

Estimates of dates for the writing of these letters vary from the 90s to early 100s, 100–125, or 120–125.[25]

IGNATIUS OF ANTIOCH

A final person in this section who identifies in Paul an iconic figure and, in this case, a model to imitate is Ignatius, the bishop of Antioch. Sentenced to die in the capital city of the empire, Ignatius wrote seven letters while he was traveling from Antioch to Rome. The dating of his letters falls somewhere in the first half of the second century; the traditional dates assigned to his writing are 110–117, but more recently, scholars have worked with dates ranging from 105–110,[26] 130–140,[27] and 125–150.[28]

In two of the letters, Ignatius names Paul and clearly idealizes him. In writing to Christians in Ephesus, he declares, "You are a passageway for those slain for God; you are fellow initiates with Paul, the holy one who received a testimony and proved worthy of all fortune. When I attain to God, may I be found in his footsteps, this one who mentions you in every epistle in Christ Jesus" (Ign. *Eph.* 12.2).[29] Paul is "holy" and "worthy," and Ignatius hopes to imitate him ("be found in his footsteps"), which refers to Paul's martyrdom. The other time Ignatius mentions Paul is in tandem with Peter: "I am not enjoining you as Peter and Paul did. They were apostles, I am condemned; they were free, until now I have been a slave" (Ign. *Rom.* 4.3). Even though he is the bishop of Antioch and will soon be a martyr, Ignatius does not claim to have the authority to command the Romans as did the apostles. Peter and Paul remain above him in the ecclesiastical hierarchy. (For more on his view of the apostles, see Ign. *Trall.* 3.1, 3.)

Ignatius clearly knew several of Paul's letters. He used 1 Corinthians frequently, even though he most likely would have had no manuscripts with him to consult. He utilizes Ephesians, even if not as often, and probably 1 and 2 Timothy;

> ### The Word *Christian*
>
> According to the book of Acts, it was in Syrian Antioch that the disciples of Jesus were first called "Christians" (11:26). We have no evidence to confirm such an early use, however; Paul certainly does not use the noun. It is used, however, by the early second-century bishop Ignatius, who refers to *Christianity* in his letters (Ign. *Magn.* 10:1, 3; Ign. *Rom.* 3:3; Ign. *Phld.* 6:1). Without question, we can use the word *Jew* instead of *Judean* for documents, people, and movements dated around the year 200; if the documents, people, and movements have given up hope of rebuilding the temple, we can use the word *Jew* as early as 135. For the complex questions involved in the discussion of "Jewish Christianity," see note 55.

it is also possible that he used Romans and 2 Corinthians.[30] Among the themes in Ignatius's letters that are clearly based on Paul's thought, unity and imitation/ martyrdom are the two most significant.

For Ignatius, unity within the church is paramount, so he lauds the Ephesians "who have always agreed with the apostles by the power of Jesus Christ" (Ign. *Eph.* 11.2). His particular way of grounding unity is more in tune with 1–2 Timothy than with the undisputed letters, as he emphasizes the centrality of the bishop, as well as the roles of the presbyters and deacons (Ign. *Eph.* 3.2, 4.1-2; *Magn.* 6.1-2, 7.1; *Trall.* 2.1-3, 7.1-2; *Phld.* 3.2; *Smyrn.* 8.1-2, 9.1): "So too let everyone respect the deacons like Jesus Christ, and also the bishop, who is the image of the Father; and let them respect the presbyters like the council of God and the band of the apostles. Apart from these a gathering cannot be called a church" (Ign. *Trall.* 3.1).[31]

The letters of Ignatius have many references to imitation and the related concept of discipleship. Imitation in the first place is to be imitation of the crucifixion of Jesus (Ign. *Smyrn.* 1.1; *Rom.* 6.3), as Ignatius is hoping to do. If martyrdom is not a possibility, the believer is called to imitate Jesus by being in unity with the bishop (see the previous paragraph). Ignatius is also driven to imitate Paul's sacrifice, suffering, and unworthiness, all of which are the ways in which Paul imitates Christ (Phil 1:21, 23). For both Paul and Ignatius, Christ and his cross are at the center, and the death of the believer is viewed not only as a future possibility but also as a present reality through the death that occurred in baptism (Rom 6:6, 8). In addition, both men spoke specifically of being poured out as a libation or sacrifice (Ign. *Rom.* 2.2; Paul, Phil 2:17).[32]

Thus, Ignatius has provided a firm place for Paul in the church's hierarchy and has taken him as both a hero and a model.

The Radical Paul (Marcion)

Paul was a hero for an energetic and divisive figure named Marcion, as Paul was for others we have studied, but Marcion's interpretation of Paul moved in very different directions. A native of a port city on the Black Sea, Marcion was almost certainly a Christian from birth and was a wealthy ship owner. Little is known of his biography, but as an adult and because he was a Christian, he relocated to Rome and sought to move the leaders of the Christian community there to accept his understanding of the faith. They did not agree with him, and he began to establish congregations that spread into many parts of the Roman Empire by the time of his death around 160; his approximate date of birth was 85. Nothing that he wrote has survived, and what we do have about him from antiquity is written by people who sharply disagreed with him.

From his reading of Paul, Marcion determined that Paul saw a radical contrast between the gospel of love found in Paul's letters and the law and covenant of Israel's Bible. The God of Jesus, then, must have been other than the God of creation and law. That contrast, Marcion believed, had been softened by the church, which saw basic continuity between what would become the two testaments (in Christian thought, the Old Testament and the New Testament); an example was the teaching that Old Testament prophecy had been fulfilled in Jesus. As of yet, a New Testament canon did not exist, but Marcion proposed that the authoritative writings for Christians should be limited to the letters of the true apostle, Paul (in this order: Galatians, 1 Corinthians, 2 Corinthians, Romans, 1 Thessalonians, 2 Thessalonians, Laodiceans [equals Ephesians], Colossians, Philippians, and Philemon[33]) and the Gospel of Luke. While he may have inherited a list of Paul's letters with Galatians mentioned first, Galatians most clearly fit the pattern of Marcion's thought. The material from the letters was edited, however, to fit even more closely his perspective. Thus, references to Abraham as the forefather of believers (Galatians 3 and Romans 4), positive statements about Israel (most of Romans 9–11), and Christ as the agent of creation (Col 1:15b-16) were eliminated. The editing was more thorough in the case of Luke, where positive use of Israel's Bible, including fulfillment of prophecies in Christ, Christ as the Son of the Creator God, and the birth narrative of Jesus, were excised.[34]

One of the important writings of Marcion's that has not survived was entitled *Antitheses*, which included a list of statements contrasting the God of the Old Testament / Law and the God of the New Testament / Gospel. In Adolf von Harnack's attempt to reconstruct the *Antitheses*,[35] statements 7 and 20 read as follows:

> 7. The prophet of the God of Creation, when the people was engaged in battle, climbed to the mountain peak and extended his hands to God, imploring that he kill as many as possible in the battle. [cf. Exod. 17:8ff.]. But our Lord, the good, extended his hands [on the cross] not to kill men, but to save them.
> ...
> 20. Cursing characterizes the Law; blessing, the faith.

Actual practices of Marcion's churches were similar to those of the emerging "catholic" churches, but often with a significant difference. The structure of the priestly hierarchy was similar, but Marcionites ordained women. People came into the Marcionite church through baptism, but at their baptism, they committed themselves to celibacy as a way to counter the desire of the creator God for people to "be fruitful and multiply" (Gen 1:28). The Eucharist was held in Marcionite churches, but there is some evidence that they used water rather than wine.[36]

While the Marcionite challenge likely had a major role in forcing the emerging catholic churches to develop a canon of authoritative readings, Marcion was actively opposed by church authors. Depending on how early Marcion is dated and how late the Pastoral Epistles are dated, the latter may in part have been written against him. Irenaeus and Tertullian were just two of the eloquent opponents of Marcion and were also representative of those who wrote against him even after his death. In sum, Marcion presented a radical Paul, but he exaggerated Paul's radicality to the point of denying that Paul believed in the God of Israel. In the classic assessment of von Harnack, "Marcion was the only Gentile Christian who understood Paul, and even he misunderstood him."[37]

The Spiritualized Paul (Gnosticism)

In our investigation of the basics of Gnosticism,[38] we have already looked at its overarching themes. We discovered that while Paul did not quote any Gnostic document, he at times needed to counter the views of Gnostics or Proto-Gnostics, especially in 1 Corinthians. The need to oppose Gnostic views increased with the deuteropauline letters of Colossians, Ephesians, 1–2 Timothy, and Titus, with 1 Tim 6:20-21 quite likely the earliest evidence from a Christ-believing author that some followers of Christ considered Gnosticism a heresy.

It is somewhat ironic, then, that many Gnostics were so fascinated with Paul that "some of the most enthusiastic interest shown early on in Paul's teaching was that of Gnostic Christians, who considered Paul a kindred spirit and an articulate guide to spiritual truth."[39] Or as Elaine Pagels has put it, Gnostic writers "dare to

---

"Catholicity" and "Orthodoxy"

Historians refer to the "catholic" church and to early "orthodoxy." Those words were used as early as the second century, for example by Irenaeus of Lyons. "Catholic" comes from the Greek *katholikē*, an adjective formed from the phrase *kath' holon*, literally "according to the whole." *Katholikē* thus means "universal," and referring to the "catholic church" originally meant asserting that all Christians belonged to one universal church. Different individuals and different churches claimed to be Christian, however, even when they held different and sometimes contradictory beliefs. Thus, Irenaeus and others who used the term were claiming that only those Christians who held to "right belief" or *orthodoxy* were "true" Christians—a claim that others would have contested. This early language of "catholicity" and "orthodoxy" should be distinguished from contemporary references to the Roman Catholic or Greek Orthodox churches today.

claim his letters as a primary source of *gnostic* theology."[40] Such a claim was especially true for a creative Gnostic thinker named Valentinus and for his followers, so we will concentrate on them. In a chain of tradition, they maintained that a certain Theudas had been a disciple of Paul's and that Valentinus had studied with Theudas (Clement of Alexandria, *Stromata* 7.17). The key to that chain of tradition was that Valentinian Gnostics claimed Paul had taught them his secret way of interpreting Scripture. Paul, they argued, had taught during his lifetime in two ways. To the general class of believers, he taught the gospel of the cross, but to the elect, he taught a spiritualized Christ that in turn sharply affected how each group read the church's authoritative writings—in our case, especially the writings of Paul. The Gnostic was to avoid the literal level of Scripture interpretation in favor of a pneumatic or symbolic interpretation. What to do, then, with the Pastoral Epistles and their attack on Gnosticism? The Valentinian response was simple and a foreshadowing of scholarship still 1,500 years in the future: Paul did not write 1–2 Timothy and Titus. Thus, the Paul of the other letters ascribed to him could be the chief apostle and the ideal believer for Valentinian Gnostics.[41]

About Valentinus himself, little is known. He was educated in Alexandria, Egypt, but spent most of his adult life in Rome (approximately 135–165), after which he moved to Cyprus.[42] A brilliant exegete, he and his followers identified in Paul's writings new meanings, especially when they removed passages from their original contexts. Illustrative of the passages that guided them are these:

- "For I know that nothing good dwells ... in my flesh" (Rom 7:18).
- "Who will rescue me from this body of death?" (Rom 7:24).
- "You are not in the flesh; you are in the Spirit" (Rom 8:9).
- "I punish my body and enslave it" (1 Cor 9:27).
- "Flesh and blood cannot inherit the kingdom of God" (1 Cor 15:50).
- "The god of this world has blinded the minds of the unbelievers" (2 Cor 4:4).
- The descending and ascending redeemer (Phil 2:6-11).

Pagels lists from other scholars evidence in Valentinian material for these documents associated in antiquity with the name of Paul: Romans, 1–2 Corinthians, Galatians, Ephesians, Philippians, Colossians, 1–2 Thessalonians, and Hebrews.[43]

One of the most noteworthy of the Valentinian documents found at **Nag Hammadi** is the *Gospel of Truth*, which may have been written by Valentinus himself. It is not a gospel in the genre of the New Testament gospels but is more a sermon that primarily aims to "drive home the fact that the Father has redeemed the elect from their illusory existence."[44] The material world will disappear totally (I, *3* 25.1-10), but that positive development is already seen in the fact that "his children are perfect and worthy of his name, for he is the Father" (I, *3* 43.20).[45] In developing his thoughts, the author uses Romans, 1–2 Corinthians, Ephesians, Colossians, and Hebrews.[46]

A significant example from Nag Hammadi both of the Valentinian understanding of resurrection and of Valentinian reliance on Paul is *The Treatise on Resurrection*, also known as the *Epistle to Rheginos*. This document utilizes Paul to turn a New Testament text in the opposite direction of what appears to be its original intent. The people pictured in 2 Tim 2:18 as Paul's opponents "have swerved from the truth by claiming that the resurrection has already taken place," but that is exactly the view of resurrection proposed by the Nag Hammadi treatise:

> The Savior swallowed up death ... for he put aside the world which is perishing. He transformed [himself] into an imperishable Aeon and raised himself up, having swallowed the visible by the invisible, and he gave us the way of our immortality. Then, indeed, as the Apostle said (Romans 8:17, Ephesians 2:5-6), "We suffered with him, and we arose with him, and we went to heaven with him." ... This is the spiritual resurrection. (I, *4* 45.14-40)

Other Valentinian material from Nag Hammadi directly connected with Pauline material includes *The Prayer of the Apostle Paul* and *The Apocalypse of Paul*. The former is a brief document that uses Ephesians and Colossians. The latter collapses together a fuller description of the revelation Paul experienced on Damascus Road when the resurrected Jesus appeared to him (Gal 1:15-17) with the heavenly vision Paul described in 2 Cor 12:1-5.

Examples of Gnostic use of Paul could easily be multiplied; another good illustration is the use of terminology from 1 Corinthians to put people into three categories, as seen in *The Tripartite Tractate* from Nag Hammadi. Nevertheless, the evidence just discussed demonstrates the significance of Paul's thought for Gnostics in general and the Valentinians in particular. As Nicholas Perrin phrases it, "For Valentinus and his followers, Paul was 'the' apostle."[47]

The Ascetic Paul (*The Acts of Paul and Thecla*)

For many people in the early centuries of this era, what was most significant about Paul was that he was an **ascetic** believer who kept his body very much under control and encouraged others to do the same, especially regarding sexual behavior. Our paradigmatic text for this view of Paul is one part of a larger document, the *Acts of Paul*, which was composed of a collection of documents that almost certainly originally circulated independently. The three parts of the larger *Acts of Paul* are *The Martyrdom of Paul*, a letter dubbed *3 Corinthians*, and our focus, the *Acts of Paul and Thecla*.

Andrew Gregory places the composition of the individual units in the late second or early third century,[48] whereas Richard Pervo envisions that the larger document already had been put together sometime between 170 and 175.[49] The one piece of external evidence is the negative comment directed against the material on Paul and Thecla by Tertullian in his treatise *De Baptismo* 17.5 around the year 200. The author or editor of the larger work was a native of Asia Minor; the

Acts he produced was considered canonical in the Syrian and Armenian churches. He and/or his sources used Acts, Paul's letters, gospel traditions, and likely other sources, including oral ones, in producing the document.[50]

The story line of the *Acts of Paul and Thecla* is complicated, in part because materials that apparently had different origins were not always edited together smoothly. In Iconium, a young engaged woman named Thecla, listening from an adjacent building, hears Paul preaching about purity and virginity. Enthralled by his preaching, she decides for a life of perpetual virginity, despite the protests of her fiancé and her mother. Paul is arrested, Thecla visits him at night, and both are suspected of adultery (untrue, of course). Paul is beaten and sent from the city, but Thecla is sentenced to be burned. She escapes not only that governmental attempt on her life but several others elsewhere, being rescued each time by God's miraculous intervention and supported at first by many women and then, as the story unfolds, by all women. One of the dramatic complications is that she longs to be again with Paul but is kept from finding him. When they are reunited and she updates Paul on her wanderings and her ministry, he tells her, "Go and teach the word of God!" (41).

Although the character of Thecla is well worth further study, our focus is on the Paul who converts her and to whom she is (chastely) devoted. Building on the New Testament passages in which Paul's own discipline and asceticism are highlighted (1 Cor 9:26-27), as well as his celibacy (1 Cor 7:7-8), the *Acts* sharpen his asceticism even more. In his statement of blessings, Paul announces:

> Blessed are they who have kept the flesh pure, for they shall become a temple of God. Blessed are the continent, for to them will God speak. . . .
> Blessed are they who have wives as if they had them not, for they shall be heirs of God. . . . Blessed are the bodies of the virgins, for they shall be well pleasing to God, and shall not lose the reward of their purity. (5-6)

Therefore, the charge against Paul—based both on this teaching and on the actions of Thecla and many other women in the story—is that "he deprives young men of wives and maidens of husbands, saying: 'Otherwise there is no resurrection for you, except ye remain chaste and do not defile the flesh, but keep it pure'" (12).

In the Roman Empire (as within any patriarchal structure), the family was considered the basic building block of society and thus of the empire itself. Constant virginity was a radical protest against the social order, with the potential of undermining it. It was a subversive tactic and so recognized, as the responses of the authorities in the *Acts of Paul and Thecla* amply illustrate. Or in the words of Richard Pervo, the message of this Paul "has a strongly anti-establishment edge, rejecting the established forms of authority, notably the emperor, and its institutions, particularly the family."[51] In terms of the Thecla of the *Acts of Paul and Thecla*, one might view her as the radical realization of Gal 3:28 ("there is no longer male and female") and the embodiment of the "old wives' tales" against which Timothy is warned (1 Tim 4:7) and of the female activity Timothy is directed to control or oppose (1 Tim 2:11-15; 4:3; 5:14-15).[52] Both ascetic figures—Thecla and Paul— were highly attractive to many believers.

The Apostate Paul (The Pseudo-Clementines)

The final figure of Paul drawn by believers moves in a very different direction. No longer is Paul a hero or *the* apostle. In our last group of writings, he is an apostate and the enemy.

The Pseudo-Clementine writings include several different documents assembled in the fourth century under the name of Clement of Rome but going back in origin to at least 250 CE and likely up to a century earlier. They tell the fictitious story of Clement, a seeker after truth, who is converted and travels with Peter. Clement has also been separated from his scattered family, so in a popular genre of the time, the romantic novel of separation and reunion, the material is organized around his search for his family.⁵³ By far the longest documents are the *Recognitions*, which contain the story of the dispersal and reunion of Clement's family, and the *Homilies*, which claim to be sermons delivered by the apostle Peter. The two documents agree verbatim in a number of places, with most scholars concluding they shared a common source (rather than one copying the other). The theoretical source dates to the early 200s and is Jewish Christian. There may be other sources, especially a sort of church history that was produced around 150.⁵⁴ The other Pseudo-Clementine document of relevance for the literature's view of Paul is the *Epistle of Peter to James*, a purported letter from Peter to James, the brother of Jesus and head of the Jerusalem church.

Often the Pseudo-Clementinian literature is associated with a Jewish Christian group called the Ebionites. They traced themselves to the Jerusalem mother church and saw themselves as its proper descendants. Whether or not the label *Ebionite* is entirely appropriate for the Pseudo-Clementines, they do seem to represent the same wider strand of tradition that promoted a Jewish Christianity that relied on the Law of Moses.⁵⁵

Irenaeus, a second- to third-century bishop who wrote against what he considered heresies, had this to say about the Ebionites:

> Those who are called Ebionites agree that the world was made by God. . . . They use the Gospel according to Matthew only, and repudiate the Apostle Paul, maintaining that he was an apostate from the law. As to the prophetical writings, they endeavour to expound them in a somewhat singular manner: they practise circumcision, persevere in the observance of those customs which are enjoined by the law, and are so Judaic in their style of life, that they even adore Jerusalem as if it were the house of God. (*Against Heresies* I.26.2)⁵⁶

In the *Recognitions*, Paul is presented even more negatively, although never specifically named. In the flow of the narrative, James has brought a number of Judeans to the brink of baptism (I.66-69), and then danger arises: "And when matters were at that point that they should come and be baptized, some one of our enemies, entering the temple . . . began to cry out" (I.70). The enemy is Saul (Paul), who creates chaos in the temple. Amid the shouting of both sides, he grabs a firebrand from the altar, hits people with it, and is followed by others who do the same. During the resulting mayhem, "that enemy attacked James, and threw him headlong from the top of the steps; and supposing him to be dead, he cared not to inflict further violence upon him." The identification of the enemy with Saul is confirmed in I.71, where the enemy is commissioned to go to Damascus to "make havoc among the faithful."[57] Saul is never rehabilitated in the document; that is, he is never described in positive terms as a Christian.

The *Letter of Peter to James* functions as a cover letter for the *Homilies*. Once more, the unnamed Saul/Paul is the enemy: "For some from among the Gentiles have rejected my lawful preaching and have preferred a lawless and absurd doctrine of the man who is my enemy.... For to do such a thing means to act contrary to the law of God which was made known by Moses and was confirmed by our Lord in its everlasting continuance" (2.3, 5).[58] The attack on Paul reaches its height in the *Homilies*, where Simon the Magician (or Simon Magus) is a stand-in for Paul. Simon was considered the first heretic, and he had a major confrontation with Peter (Acts 8:9-24). Thus, "if pious men had understood this mystery, they would never have gone astray, but even now they should have known that Simon, who now enthralls all men, is a fellow-worker of error and deceit" (II.15). In II.18, Paul is an enemy and a deceiver, so Peter needs to follow him "as light upon darkness, as knowledge upon ignorance, as healing upon disease" (II.17). Finally, Paul's appeal to a commissioning by Christ on Damascus Road is a false claim: "If then, our Jesus appeared to you in a vision, made Himself known to you, and spoke to you, it was as one who is enraged with an adversary; ... But can any one be rendered fit for instruction through apparitions?" (XVII.19). Thus, Paul's very call and the basis for his ministry are seriously undermined. The lines are clearly drawn, and Paul is, instead of *the* apostle, *the* heretic.

Conclusion

My goal in placing the Pseudo-Clementines last was not to end with a negative view of Paul but to reiterate, after our journey with the apostle of antiquity, the fact that he was a controversial figure not only during his lifetime but for centuries after—and no doubt will be into the future. Each of the documents, movements, and individuals studied in this chapter picked up one or more strands of the Paul we have come to know in the undisputed epistles. Even the Pseudo-Clementinian literature has an understanding of Paul that is consistent with his Law-free understanding of how humanity is made right with God. The other figures, movements, and literature explored in this chapter illustrate the brilliance of Paul as a seminal thinker, whose life and writings inspired people in a multitude of interpretive directions. From a historical perspective, this chapters has started with the documents that are more in harmony with the Paul of the undisputed letters and has moved to interpretations that are increasingly dissonant when compared with the theology and person revealed in the seven pillar epistles.

Many others during the past two millennia have studied Paul and used him as a basis for their thought. Significant names include Irenaeus, Augustine, Martin

Luther, John Calvin, F. C. Baur, Albert Schweitzer, Rudolf Bultmann, and Ernst Käsemann. Nor has the study of Paul slowed down among New Testament scholars or thinkers, with European political philosophers such as Giorgio Agamben also mining Paul for insights.[59] Whether beloved, tolerated, or vilified, Paul's life and theology continue to attract, challenge, and offend people as he tries to make sense of human life lived in a world given to empire but already invaded by God.

Study Questions

1. Which piece of literature or individual surveyed in this chapter do you think provides a picture of Paul and his thought that most closely approximates what you have learned about him from the New Testament?
2. Which piece of literature or individual surveyed in this chapter do you think provides a picture of Paul and his thought that differs most from what you have learned about him from the New Testament?
3. Which view of Paul from this chapter is most challenging to you? Which view is most inviting?
4. The *Acts of Paul and Thecla* and the Pastoral Epistles express very different views of Paul and women. How would you explain the fact that these two sets of documents were able to claim Paul as their authority and yet reach such dissimilar conclusions?
5. What most surprised you about the views of Paul outlined in this chapter?

Suggested Reading

General
de Boer, Martinus. "Images of Paul in the Post-Apostolic Period." *CBQ* 42 (1980): 359–80.
Pervo, Richard I. *The Making of Paul: Constructions of the Apostle in Early Christianity*. Minneapolis: Fortress Press, 2010.

2 Thessalonians
Donfried, Karl P. "The Theology of 2 Thessalonians." In *The Theology of the Shorter Pauline Letters*, ed. Karl P. Donfried and I. Howard Marshall, 81–113. Cambridge: Cambridge University Press, 1993.
Fee, Gordon D. *The First and Second Letters to the Thessalonians*. NICNT. Grand Rapids: Eerdmans, 2009.
Krodel, Gerhard. "2 Thessalonians." In *The Deutero-Pauline Letters: Ephesians, Colossians, 2 Thessalonians, 1–2 Timothy, Titus*, ed. Gerhard Krodel, 39–58. Proclamation Commentaries. Rev. ed. Minneapolis: Fortress Press, 1993.
Malherbe, Abraham J. *The Letters to the Thessalonians*. AB 32B. New York: Doubleday, 2000.

Richard, Earl J. *First and Second Thessalonians.* Sacra Pagina 11. Collegeville, MN: Liturgical, 1995.
Wanamaker, Charles A. *The Epistles to the Thessalonians.* NIGTC. Grand Rapids: Eerdmans, 1990.

Colossians

Barth, Markus, and Helmut Blanke. *Colossians.* AB 34B. Garden City: Doubleday, 1994.
Dunn, James D. G. *The Epistles to the Colossians and to Philemon.* NITGC. Grand Rapids: Eerdmans, 1996.
Hultgren, Arland J. "Colossians." In *The Deutero-Pauline Letters: Ephesians, Colossians, 2 Thessalonians, 1–2 Timothy, Titus,* ed. Gerhard Krodel, 24–38. Rev. ed. Minneapolis: Fortress Press, 1993.
MacDonald, Margaret Y. *Colossians and Ephesians.* Sacra Pagina 17. Collegeville, MN: Liturgical, 2000.
Sumney, Jerry L. *Colossians: A Commentary.* NTL. Louisville: Westminster John Knox, 2008.
Wilson, Robert M. *Colossians and Philemon.* ICC. Edinburgh: T & T Clark, 2005.

Ephesians

Best, Ernest. *Ephesians.* ICC. Edinburgh: T & T Clark, 1998.
Lincoln, Andrew T. *Ephesians.* WBC 42. Waco: Word, 1990.
MacDonald, Margaret Y. *Colossians and Ephesians.* Sacra Pagina 17. Collegeville, MN: Liturgical, 2000.
Schnackenburg, Rudolf. *Ephesians: A Commentary.* Trans. Helen Heron. Edinburgh: T & T Clark, 1991.
Taylor, Walter F. Jr. *Ephesians.* ACNT. Minneapolis: Augsburg, 1985.

Acts

Fitzmyer, Joseph A. *The Acts of the Apostles.* AB 31. New York: Doubleday, 1998.
Haenchen, Ernst. *The Acts of the Apostles: A Commentary.* Trans. Bernard Noble and Gerald Shinn. Philadelphia: Westminster, 1971.
Pervo, Richard I. *Acts: A Commentary.* Hermeneia. Minneapolis: Fortress Press, 2009.
———. *Luke's Story of Paul.* Minneapolis: Fortress Press, 1990.

1 Timothy, 2 Timothy, Titus

Collins, Raymond F. *1 & 2 Timothy and Titus.* NTL. Louisville: Westminster John Knox, 2002.
Fiore, Benjamin. *The Pastoral Epistles: First Timothy, Second Timothy, Titus.* Sacra Pagina 12. Collegeville, MN: Liturgical, 2007.
Hultgren, Arland J. "The Pastoral Epistles." In *The Cambridge Companion to St Paul,* ed. James D. G. Dunn, 141–55. Cambridge: Cambridge University Press, 2003.
Johnson, Luke Timothy. *The First and Second Letters to Timothy.* AB 35A. New York: Doubleday, 2001.
Quinn, Jerome D. *The Letter to Titus.* AB 35. Garden City: Doubleday, 1990.
Quinn, Jerome D., and William C. Wacker. *The First and Second Letters to Timothy.* Eerdmans Critical Commentary. Grand Rapids: Eerdmans, 1999.

Taylor, Walter F., Jr. "1–2 Timothy, Titus." In *The Deutero-Pauline Letters: Ephesians, Colossians, 2 Thessalonians, 1–2 Timothy, Titus*, ed. Gerhard Krodel, 59–93. Rev. ed. Minneapolis: Fortress Press, 1993.

Ignatius of Antioch

Foster, Paul. "The Epistles of Ignatius of Antioch." In *The Writings of the Apostolic Fathers*, ed. Paul Foster, 81–107. London: T & T Clark, 2007.

Jefford, Clayton N., with Kenneth J. Harder and Louis D. Amezaga Jr. *Reading the Apostolic Fathers: An Introduction*. Peabody, MA: Hendrickson, 1996. Pp. 53–71.

Schoedel, William R. "Ignatius, Epistles of." *ABD* 3:384–87.

———. *Ignatius of Antioch: A Commentary on the Seven Letters of Ignatius*. Hermeneia. Philadelphia: Fortress Press, 1985.

Marcion

Clabeaux, John J. "Marcion." *ABD* 4:514–16.

Harnack, Adolf von. *Marcion: The Gospel of the Alien God*. Trans. John E. Steely and Lyle D. Bierma. Durham, NC: Labyrinth, 1990.

Hoffmann, R. Joseph. *Marcion: On the Restitution of Christianity: An Essay on the Development of Radical Paulinist Theology in the Second Century*. AAR Academy Series 46. Chico, CA: Scholars, 1984.

Moll, Sebastian. *The Arch-Heretic Marcion*. WUNT 250. Tübingen: Mohr Siebeck, 2010.

Gnosticism (in Relationship to Paul)

Pagels, Elaine H. *The Gnostic Paul: Gnostic Exegesis of the Pauline Letters*. Philadelphia: Fortress Press, 1975.

Perrin, Nicholas. "Paul and Valentinian Interpretation." In *Paul and the Second Century*, ed. Michael F. Bird and Joseph R. Dodson, 126–39. London: T & T Clark, 2011.

The *Acts of Paul and Thecla*

Barrier, Jeremy W. *The Acts of Paul and Thecla: A Critical Introduction and Commentary*. WUNT 2.270. Tübingen: Mohr Siebeck, 2009.

Klauck, Hans-Josef. *The Apocryphal Acts of the Apostles: An Introduction*. Trans. Brian McNeil. Waco, TX: Baylor University Press, 2008.

MacDonald, Dennis R. "Thekla, Acts of." *ABD* 6:443–44.

Matthews, Shelly. "Thinking of Thecla: Issues in Feminist Historiography." *JFSR* 17 (2002): 39–65.

The Pseudo-Clementines

Irmscher, Johannes, and Georg Strecker. "The Pseudo-Clementines." In *New Testament Apocrypha*, ed. Edgar Hennecke and Wilhelm Schneemelcher; English trans. ed. R. M. Wilson, 2:483–541. Rev. ed. Louisville: Westminster John Knox, 1992.

Jones, F. Stanley. "Clementines, Pseudo-." *ABD* 1:1061–62.

Segal, Alan F. "Jewish Christianity." In *Eusebius, Christianity, and Judaism*, ed. Harold W. Attridge and Gohei Hata, 326–51. Detroit: Wayne State University Press, 1992.

Glossary

admonition individual paraenetical statement; in the plural, refers to such statements strung loosely together without a common theme

aedile city official who handled revenue, streets, and public buildings; contributed much of own money for the upkeep of the city

amanuensis secretary; scribe

analogy the Hebrew term is *gezerah shawah*; an exegetical method in which authors connect biblical statements that share the same word(s) or phrase(s) and make their point by interpreting them together

Antony, Marc Roman politician and general; Octavian and he defeated the assassins of Julius Caesar; Octavian in turn defeated Antony in 31 B.C.E.

apocalyptic understanding that God will soon end the present evil age

apologia apology or defense

apostle one who is sent with a message; especially for designated representatives of Christ understood to be sent by him; Paul was an apostle

ascetic / asceticism disciplining oneself to minimize bodily pleasures, such as sexual expression, alcohol consumption, or eating; self-denial

atonement effect of Jesus' death in reconciling God and humanity

atrium; plural, atria   room near the front of a Roman house with open roof at the center

Augustus   The "revered one": title given by the Senate to Octavian, the first Roman emperor; sole ruler from 27 B.C.E. to 14 C.E.

call   God's invitation to be a follower of Jesus; more narrowly, invitation to a specific ministry

canon   a list of authoritative writings

canonical   belonging to a canon

captatio benevolentiae   literary device: "capturing" listeners by praising them

catechetical   referring to the teaching ministry of the church, which is called catechesis

challenge and riposte   in honor-and-shame cultures, public verbal exchanges in which the winner gains honor from the loser

chiasm   reverse parallelism

Christ   Messiah promised in Israel's Bible; to be a descendant of King David of Israel; some Judeans believed he would come to restore to the people of Israel their previous glory; others anticipated a powerful spokesperson for God; in the New Testament, identified with Jesus; same as **Messiah**

church   (a) local gathering of Christ-believers designed for worship, service, and mutual support; (b) collective terms for individual churches seen as one entity, as in "the worldwide church" or "the church in Macedonia"

circumcise; circumcision   surgical removal of the foreskin of a male's penis; sign of the covenant God made with Israel

circum-Mediterranean   lands around the Mediterranean Sea

confession / confessional statement   abbreviated statement of complex beliefs; same as **creed**

covenant   in the Bible, an agreement between God and the people of Israel in which God would protect and lead Israel and Israel would worship God and follow God's Law

creed   abbreviated statement of complex beliefs; same as **confessional statement**

cultural anthropology   the social-scientific study of human culture

Dead Sea Scrolls   a collection of Judean writings, many of which are apocalyptic; discovered starting in 1947 at Qumran; produced ca. 150 B.C.E. to 70 C.E.

deliberative rhetoric   type of rhetoric designed to persuade or dissuade; focus is on the future

deuteropauline describing letters ascribed to Paul but that scholars believe were written after his death by others wanting to update him for a new place and time; Ephesians, Colossians, 2 Thessalonians, 1 and 2 Timothy, and Titus

diaspora dispersion; designates the phenomenon of Judeans living outside Israel

diatribe literary device in which the author or speaker debates an imaginary opponent

domus private home for wealthier people

doxology ascribing glory (Greek: *doxa*) to God

dyadic personality orientation in which a person's sense of self and worth is dependent on others

elites those at the uppermost levels of the population

epideictic rhetoric type of rhetoric designed to praise or blame; focus is on the present

epistle a letter

eschatology; eschatological the study of end-time events and life after death

Essenes a Judean sect active during the lifetimes of Jesus and Paul; often identified as the authors of the Dead Sea Scrolls

ethos a sort of rhetorical appeal to the character or credibility of a speaker or author

exegesis; exegetical scholarly, scientific study of the Bible

feminist study a method of Bible study that challenges patriarchal values in the texts and/or patriarchal interpretations of texts

fictive family a surrogate family united not by blood but by common commitments

form a pattern of discourse used to enhance communication

Gentile a non-Judean.

glossolalia ecstatic speech inspired by the Holy Spirit; the Spirit speaks through the believer's mouth in sounds that have a pattern but are different from any known human language; also known as **speaking in tongues**

Gnosticism dualistic religions that taught that the divine sparks within people could be saved through secret knowledge from the evil world in which they were trapped

gospel good news about what God has done for humanity through Jesus Christ

grace God's unmerited love

Haustafel; plural, Haustafeln "table(s) of household duties," listing family responsibilities

Hellenism the synthesis of Greek thought and life with other cultures

Hellenization the spread of Greek culture and language

historical study the systematic, scientific investigation of the past

Holy Spirit God's end-time power understood by Christ-believers to be active in the present

honor claim to worth and social acknowledgment of that worth

house church a group of Christ-believers who meet in a private home (apartment or *domus*)

imminent return belief that Jesus would return soon as triumphant Lord of the universe

imperative directive to act in certain ways; command, especially from God

imperial cult the official religion of the Roman Empire; adherence to its deities was thought to be necessary for the survival of the Empire

indicative statement of what God has done

insula apartment building, often with shops or factories on the first floor and apartments above; also, a house or block of houses surrounded on all sides by streets or alleys

interpolation later insertion into a text by someone other than the author

Judean translation of *Ioudaios*; used to designate an ancient person who had ancestral connections with Judea and/or the official religion of Judea

judicial rhetoric type of rhetoric designed to attack or defend; focus is on the past

Julius Caesar Roman statesman and general whose military conquests led to his becoming dictator; his assassination led to a series of wars that resulted in the first Roman emperor, his adopted son, Octavian

justification God's action in Jesus Christ to put humanity into a positive relationship with God

justify to put into a right relationship with

letter a written message, addressed to individuals or to communities

literary seam a block of material that is clearly defined and seems out of place when compared with the surrounding material; may indicate an insertion or a document put together by an editor from originally independent documents or fragments of documents

literary study   method of Bible study that approaches the Bible as literature; more narrowly, study of the Bible using modern literary theory

logos   "word"; in rhetoric, an appeal to the listeners' or readers' reason by means of logical arguments

Messiah   future leader promised in Israel's Bible; to be a descendant of King David of Israel; some Judeans believed he would come to restore to the people of Israel their previous glory; others anticipated a powerful spokesperson for God; in the New Testament, identified with Jesus; same as **Christ**

midrash   Hebrew term for *interpretation*; a method for commenting on a biblical text

Nag Hammadi   location in Egypt where a library of Coptic Gnostic books was found in 1945

narrative criticism   study of biblical narrative that uses modern literary theory

Nero   Roman emperor from 54 to 68, during whose reign Paul wrote several of his letters; probably also the emperor when Paul was executed by the Romans

Octavian   the first Roman emperor; sole ruler from 27 B.C.E. to 14 C.E.; also known by the title Augustus

paraenesis   advice, especially ethical; Paul often includes a paraenetical section in his letters

parousia   Greek word for *presence*; usually refers to the return of Jesus at the end of time (his second coming); also refers to the presence of Paul in a community of believers

Pastoral Epistles   1–2 Timothy and Titus

pathos   an appeal to the listeners' or readers' emotions

patron-client   significant relationship between a social superior (patron) and a social inferior (client); the patron provides benefits to the client, who responds with political support and displays of honor; present throughout Mediterranean cultures

Pax Romana   "peace of Rome"; Roman imperial propaganda term for the political, military, and economic rule Rome imposed on other nations

peristaseis   lists of hardships

pesher   from the Hebrew for *interpretation*; a method of interpreting the Bible in which a passage is quoted and applied directly to the interpreter's community

Pharisee   one of the most important Judean sects during the first century; assigned high value to living according to the Law of Moses; Paul was a Pharisee

pillar epistles letters certainly written by Paul: Romans, 1–2 Corinthians, Galatians, Philippians, 1 Thessalonians, Philemon

political study investigation of the New Testament by paying special attention to the governmental and military realities of life under the Roman Empire

princeps "first in order" or "first citizen"; an official title of the Roman emperor

prophecy study of a biblical text and preaching on it

pseudonymity writing in the name of another person

Qumran archaeological site where the Dead Sea Scrolls were found

realized eschatology the idea that the end of time has already arrived or that its benefits are available in the present

redemption buying back, especially a slave or prisoner of war; a way to describe what Jesus has done for humanity in relation to sin and death

resurrection rising of Jesus from the dead; rising of dead at the last judgment

retainer class/retainers those who directly served the elites (retainers)

rhetoric the art of persuasion; used to structure speeches and letters

rhetorical study study of the Bible using insights from ancient rhetoric

righteous / righteousness the state of being in a positive relationship with God

sacrifice offering of a person, animal, plant, wine, or other object to honor or assuage a deity

Sadducees Judean sect of the first century; closely associated with the Temple in Jerusalem and its sacrifices

salutation opening section of an ancient letter; usual format is sender to recipient, greetings

Septuagint Greek translation of the Hebrew Bible used at the time of Jesus and Paul; often abbreviated LXX

shame absence of honor

sin thinking and acting in ways that break humanity's relationship with God and other people

social history historical work that describes and analyzes the social matrix of ancient literature, history, and archaeology

social-scientific study method of investigating the Bible by using models and tools developed in the social sciences

sociological study in biblical study, the utilization of sociological theory in the study of a text; also known as sociological exegesis

speaking in tongues ecstatic speech inspired by the Holy Spirit; the Spirit speaks through the believer's mouth in sounds that have a pattern but are different from any known human language; also known as **glossolalia**

Spirit God's end-time power understood by Christ-believers to be active in the present

theological study investigation of the Bible's understanding of God's activity, including the God-human relationship

topos; plural, topoi an extended paraenetical statement on a particular topic or theme

Torah the first five books of Israel's Bible; also used to designate the Law of God as known through Israel's Bible

triclinium dining room in a *domus*, with seating on three sides of the room

typology a method of interpreting Scripture in which the author shows a correspondence or anti-correspondence between an earlier event or person and a later event or person

undisputed letters of Paul letters certainly written by Paul: Romans, 1–2 Corinthians, Galatians, Philippians, 1 Thessalonians, Philemon

voluntary association a group that people join of their own will and whom the group accepts

Zealots anti-Roman Judeans who advocated armed conflict to drive out the Romans

Abbreviations

Abbreviations for books of the Bible follow The SBL Handbook of Style.

AAR	American Academy of Religion
AB	Anchor Bible
ABD	*Anchor Bible Dictionary*
ABRL	Anchor Bible Reference Library
ACNT	Augsburg Commentaries on the New Testament
AGSU	Arbeiten zur Geschichte des Antiken Judentums und des Urchristentums
ANRW	*Aufstieg und Niedergang der römischen Welt: Geschichte und Kultur Roms im Spiegel der neueren Forschung.* Ed. H. Temporini and W. Haase. Berlin, 1972-
ANTC	Abingdon New Testament Commentaries
BA	*Biblical Archaeologist*
BAR	*Biblical Archaeology Review*
BBR	*Bulletin for Biblical Research*
BDAG	*Greek-English Lexicon of the New Testament and Other Early Christian Literature.* Ed. F. W. Danker, W. Bauer, W. F. Arndt, and F. W. Gingrich. 3rd ed. Chicago, 1999

BHT	Beiträge zur historischen Theologie
Bib	*Biblica*
BJRL	*Bulletin of the John Rylands (University) Library of Manchester*
BTB	Biblical Theology Bulletin
BZAW	Beihefte zur Zeitschrift für die alttestamentliche Wissenschaft
BZNW	Beihefte zur Zeitschrift für die neutestamentliche Wissenschaft
CBQ	*Catholic Biblical Quarterly*
ConBNT	Coniectanea biblica: New Testament Series
CurTM	*Currents in Theology and Mission*
DNTB	Dictionary of New Testament Background
DPL	Dictionary of Paul and His Letters
EDNT	Exegetical Dictionary of the New Testament
EKKNT	Evangelisch-katholischer Kommentar zum Neuen Testament
EPRO	Etudes préliminaires aux religions orientales dans l'empire romain
ExpTim	*Expository Times*
FF	Foundations and Facets
GBS	Guides to Biblical Scholarship
GNS	Good News Studies
HNT	Handbuch zum Neuen Testament
HNTC	Harper's New Testament Commentaries
HTR	*Harvard Theological Review*
HTS	Harvard Theological Studies
HUT	Hermeneutische Untersuchungen zur Theologie
HvTSt	*Hervormde teologiese studies*
IBC	Interpretation: A Bible Commentary for Teaching and Preaching
IBT	Interpreting Biblical Texts
ICC	International Critical Commentary
Int	*Interpretation*
JAAR	*Journal of the American Academy of Religion*
JBL	*Journal of Biblical Literature*
JBR	*Journal of Bible and Religion*
JFSR	*Journal of Feminist Studies in Religion*
JRE	*Journal of Religious Ethics*

JSNT	*Journal for the Study of the New Testament*
JSNTSup	Journal for the Study of the New Testament: Supplement Series
JSS	*Journal of Semitic Studies*
JTS	*Journal of Theological Studies*
LCL	Loeb Classical Library
LSJ	Liddell, H. G., R. Scott, H. S. Jones, *A Greek-English Lexicon*. 9th ed. with revised supplement. Oxford: Oxford University Press, 1996.
LXX	Septuagint
NCB	New Century Bible
NEchtB	Neue Echter Bibel
NIB	*The New Interpreter's Bible*
NIBCNT	New International Biblical Commentary on the New Testament
NICNT	New International Commentary on the New Testament
NIDB	*The New Interpreter's Dictionary of the Bible*
NIDNTT	*New International Dictionary of New Testament Theology*
NIGTC	New International Greek Testament Commentary
NIV	New International Version
NovT	*Novum Testamentum*
NovTSup	Supplements to Novum Testamentum
NRSV	New Revised Standard Version
NT	New Testament
NTC	New Testament in Context
NTL	New Testament Library
NTS	*New Testament Studies*
OBT	Overtures in Biblical Theology
PSB	*Princeton Seminary Bulletin*
SBLDS	Society of Biblical Literature Dissertation Series
SBLRBS	Society of Biblical Literature Resources for Biblical Study
SBLSBS	Society of Biblical Literature Sources for Biblical Study
SBLSP	Society of Biblical Literature Seminar Papers
SBLSymS	Society of Biblical Literature Symposium Series
SBT	Studies in Biblical Theology
SNTSMS	Society for New Testament Studies Monograph Series
SR	*Studies in Religion/Sciences religieuse*

SUNT   Studien zur Umwelt des Neuen Testaments
TDNT   *Theological Dictionary of the New Testament*
THKNT   Theologischer Handkommentar zum Neuen Testament
TSR   *Trinity Seminary Review*
TynBul *Tyndale Bulletin*
VCSup   *Vigiliae christianae* Supplement
WBC   Word Biblical Commentary
WTJ   *Westminster Theological Journal*
WUNT   Wissenschaftliche Untersuchungen zum Neuen Testament
WW   *Word and World*
ZNW   *Zeitschrift für die neutestamentliche Wissenschaft und die Kunde der älteren Kirche*

Notes

INTRODUCTION

1. From *Martin Luther: Selections from His Writings*, ed. John Dillenberger (New York: Doubleday, 1961), 19.

2. Leander E. Keck and Victor Paul Furnish, *The Pauline Letters* (IBT; Nashville: Abingdon, 1984), 12–13.

3. For a collection of these and other texts, see *The Writings of St. Paul: Annotated Texts, Reception and Criticism*, ed. Wayne A. Meeks and John T. Fitzgerald (2nd ed.; New York: Norton, 2007).

4. Philip F. Esler, *Conflict and Identity in Romans: The Social Setting of Paul's Letter* (Minneapolis: Fortress Press, 2003), 62–68. Others who agree with Esler include Bruce J. Malina and Richard L. Rohrbaugh, *Social-Science Commentary on the Gospel of John* (Minneapolis: Fortress Press, 1998), 44–46; John J. Pilch, *Cultural Dictionary of the Bible* (Collegeville, MN: Liturgical Press, 1999), 98–104; Richard A. Horsley, *Galilee: History, Politics, People* (Valley Forge, PA: Trinity Press International, 1995).

5. See Graham Harvey, *The True Israel: Uses of the Names Jew, Hebrew and Israel in Ancient Jewish and Early Christian Literature* (AGSU 35; Leiden: Brill, 1996), 11–20; and so Louis H. Feldman translates *Ioudaios* as *Judean* (Feldman, trans. and commentator, *Flavius Josephus: Judean Antiquities 1–4* [Flavius Josephus 3; Leiden: Brill, 2000], xiii).

6. For a counterargument, see Anders Runesson, "Inventing Christian Identity: Paul, Ignatius, and Theodosius," in *Exploring Early Christian Identity*, ed. Bengt Holmberg, 59–92 (WUNT 226; Tübingen: Mohr Siebeck, 2008). For a balanced discussion of both sides of the debate, see Joshua D. Garroway, "*Ioudaios*," in *The Jewish Annotated New Testament*, ed. Amy-Jill Levine and Marc Zvi Brettler, 524–26 (Oxford: Oxford University Press, 2011).

7. John H. Elliott, *1 Peter: A New Translation with Introduction and Commentary* (AB 37B; New York: Doubleday, 2000), 789–94.

8. For others who reach similar conclusions, see Esler, *Conflict and Identity in Romans*, 12–13; and Rikard Roitto, "Act as a Christ-Believer, as a Household Member or as Both?" in

Identity Formation in the New Testament, ed. Bengt Holmberg and Mikael Winninge (WUNT 227; Tübingen: Mohr Siebeck, 2008), 141, n. 1. Joseph H. Hellerman affirms the difficulties in using *Christian* and *Christianity* but continues to use them because the alternatives seem awkward. *The Ancient Church as Family* (Minneapolis: Fortress Press, 2001), 231, n. 2.

9. Elisabeth Schüssler Fiorenza, *In Memory of Her: A Feminist Theological Reconstruction of Christian Origins* (rev. ed.; New York: Crossroad, 1983).

10. Mary Daly, *Beyond God the Father: Toward a Philosophy of Women's Liberation* (Boston: Beacon, 1993).

11. Robin Scroggs, *Paul for a New Day* (Philadelphia: Fortress Press, 1977), 1.

12. This observation is not meant to deny that the Gospel writers and others, including Paul, used earlier sources, some perhaps written. Rather, it is meant to indicate that Paul's letters are the earliest-dated documents in the New Testament.

13. Giorgio Agamben, *The Time That Remains: A Commentary on the Letter to the Romans*, trans. Patricia Dailey (Stanford, CA: Stanford University Press, 2005); Alain Badiou, *Saint Paul: The Foundation of Universalism*, trans. Ray Brassier (Stanford, CA: Stanford University Press, 2003).

14. Calvin Roetzel, *Paul: The Man and the Myth* (Minneapolis: Fortress Press), 69.

CHAPTER 1

1. Carl R. Holladay, "Contemporary Methods of Reading the Bible," in *NIB* 1.130; see the rest of his discussion on historical study, 1.128–36.

2. Unless noted otherwise, Bible translations are from the New Revised Standard Version.

3. See the comments by Elisabeth Schüssler Fiorenza, *Revelation: Vision of a Just World* (Proclamation Commentaries; Minneapolis: Fortress Press, 1991), 1–6, 15–16. Earlier scholars had raised similar questions. See, for example, Rudolf Bultmann, "Is Exegesis without Presuppositions Possible?" in *Existence and Faith: Shorter Writings of Rudolf Bultmann*, ed. Schubert M. Ogden, 89–96 (New York: World, 1960).

4. What N. Clayton Croy calls "the dump-truck fallacy." *Prima Scriptura: An Introduction to New Testament Interpretation* (Grand Rapids: Baker Academic, 2011), 67–68.

5. Leander E. Keck and Victor Paul Furnish, *The Pauline Letters* (IBT; Nashville: Abingdon, 1984), 30.

6. Closely related is postcolonial study. For an introduction, see the essays in *The Colonized Apostle: Paul in Postcolonial Eyes*, ed. Christopher D. Stanley (Minneapolis: Fortress Press, 2011).

7. See S. Scott Bartchy, "Slavery (Greco-Roman)," *ABD* 6:65–73.

8. Excellent examples of such study include Bengt Holmberg, *Paul and Power: The Structure of Authority in the Primitive Church as Reflected in the Pauline Epistles* (Philadelphia: Fortress Press, 1980); and John H. Schütz, *Paul and the Anatomy of Apostolic Authority* (SNTSMS 26; Cambridge: Cambridge University Press, 1975; with new introduction by Wayne A. Meeks, Louisville: Westminster John Knox, 2007). The model use of sociological exegesis is John H. Elliott, *A Home for the Homeless: A Sociological Exegesis of 1 Peter, Its Situation and Strategy* (Philadelphia: Fortress Press, 1981; with a new introduction, Minneapolis: Fortress Press, 1990). See also the pioneering work of Wayne A. Meeks, *The First Urban Christians: The Social World of the Apostle Paul* (2nd ed.; New Haven: Yale, 2003).

9. Dale F. Eickelman, *The Middle East: An Anthropological Approach* (2nd ed.; Englewood Cliffs, NJ: Prentice Hall, 1989), 17.

10. John H. Elliott, "Disgraced yet Graced: The Gospel according to 1 Peter in the Key of Honor and Shame," *BTB* 25 (1995): 168.

11. Bruce J. Malina, *The New Testament World: Insights from Cultural Anthropology* (3rd ed.; Louisville: Westminster John Knox, 2001), 30.

12. On the relationship between social-scientific and historical study, see Walter F. Taylor Jr., "Cultural Anthropology as a Tool for Studying the New Testament—Part II," *TSR* 18 (1997): 77; and John H. Elliott, *What Is Social-Scientific Criticism?* (GBS; Minneapolis: Fortress Press, 1993), 107–9. Note the pithy statement of Luke Timothy Johnson: "The social analysis

of the NT is not a fad; it is a better way of doing history." *The Writings of the New Testament: An Interpretation* (3rd ed.; Minneapolis: Fortress Press, 2010), 8.

13. The term *listeners/readers* is chosen consciously. Very few people in antiquity could read, so written texts were composed with the idea that they would be read aloud. For that reason, rhetorical techniques originally developed for oral presentations were easily adapted for written documents. "Since Paul's epistles were to be read in the churches, it is logical to assume that they were fashioned like speeches." Duane F. Watson, "Rhetorical Criticism, New Testament," *Dictionary of Biblical Interpretation*, ed. John H. Hayes (Nashville: Abingdon, 1999), 2.402.

14. Johnson, *The Writings of the New Testament*, 548.

15. Chaim Perelman and Lucie Olbrechts-Tyteca, *The New Rhetoric: A Treatise on Argumentation* (Notre Dame, IN: University of Notre Dame, 1969).

16. Aristotle, *The Art of Rhetoric (Ars Rhetorica)*, trans. J. H. Freese (LCL; Cambridge, MA: Harvard University Press, 1926); *The Poetics*, trans. Stephen Halliwell (LCL; Cambridge, MA: Harvard University Press, 1995). Anaximenes, *Rhetorica ad Alexandrum*, trans. H. Rackham (LCL; Cambridge, MA: Harvard University Press, 1937). Cicero, *De inventione*, trans. H. M. Hubbell (LCL; Cambridge, MA: Harvard University Press, 1949). (Disputed authorship), *Rhetorica ad Herennium*, trans. Harry Caplan (LCL; Cambridge, MA: Harvard University Press, 1954). Quintilian, *Institutio Oratoria*, trans. H. E. Butler (LCL; 4 vols.; Cambridge, MA: Harvard University Press, 1920–22). Translations from Greek and Latin authors, unless noted otherwise, are from the LCL.

17. Burton L. Mack, *Rhetoric and the New Testament* (GBS; Minneapolis: Fortress Press, 1990), 28.

18. Holladay, "Contemporary Methods of Reading the Bible," 1.136.

19. Ibid., 1.137.

20. Mark Allan Powell, *What Is Narrative Criticism?* (GBS; Minneapolis: Fortress Press, 1990), 5. For a comparison of literary and historical methods of study, see 6–10.

21. Mark Allan Powell, "Narrative Criticism," in *Hearing the New Testament: Strategies for Interpretation*, ed. Joel B. Green (2nd ed.; Grand Rapids: Eerdmans, 2010), 240.

22. For definitions and examples, see Powell, *What Is Narrative Criticism?*; Powell, "Narrative Criticism," in *Hearing the New Testament*; and Mark Allan Powell, "Narrative Criticism," *Dictionary of Biblical Interpretation*, ed. John H. Hayes, 2.201–4 (Nashville: Abingdon, 1999).

23. Norman R. Petersen, *Rediscovering Paul: Philemon and the Sociology of Paul's Narrative World* (Philadelphia: Fortress Press, 1985).

24. Ben Witherington III, *Paul's Narrative Thought World: The Tapestry of Tragedy and Triumph* (Louisville: Westminster John Knox, 1994).

25. Holladay, "Contemporary Methods of Reading the Bible," 1.147.

26. I am frequently asked, "If positive roles for women have always been present in the New Testament texts, why didn't people identify them until the second half of the twentieth century?" My answer: "Because people weren't asking the right questions."

27. On Moses, see 2 Kgs 18:12; on Joshua, Judg 2:8; on David, 2 Sam 7:5 and Pss 78:70 and 89:3; on the prophets, Amos 3:7 and Zech 1:6.

CHAPTER 2

1. Romans through 2 Thessalonians are all addressed to congregations; the order is, roughly, from the longest to the shortest. The same principle is followed from 1 Timothy through Philemon, but those four letters are addressed to individuals. On the formation of the canon (list of authoritative writings) of the New Testament, see R. T. Beckwith, "Canon of the Bible," *Dictionary of Biblical Interpretation*, ed. John H. Hayes, 1:161–64 (Nashville: Abingdon, 1999); Harry Y. Gamble, "Canon: New Testament," *ABD* 1:852–61; Lee Martin McDonald, "Canon of the New Testament," *NIDB* 1:536–47; and Bruce M. Metzger, *The Canon of the New Testament: Its Origin, Development, and Significance* (Oxford: Oxford University Press, 1997). Some translations of the Bible list Paul as the author of Hebrews, but his name does not appear in the document, and Paul as author of Hebrews has been denied for centuries.

2. They might also think of pen names: Mary Ann (Marian) Evans published her work under the name George Eliot, and Samuel Clemens under the name Mark Twain.

3. John L. White, *Light from Ancient Letters* (FF; Philadelphia: Fortress Press, 1986), 189–90. Lewis R. Donelson develops in detail the characteristic features of Greco-Roman psuedepigraphic letters in his *Pseudepigraphy and Ethical Argument in the Pastoral Epistles* (HUT 22; Tübingen: Mohr Siebeck, 1986), 23–54.

4. William Sanday and Arthur C. Headlam, *The Epistle to the Romans* (ICC; Edinburgh: T & T Clark, 1895; 5th ed., 1902; reprint ed., 1971), lv.

5. Klaus Beyer, *Semitische Syntax im Neuen Testament* I.1 (SUNT I,1; Göttingen: Vandenhoeck & Ruprecht, 1962), 232, 295, 298. He calls these constructions "Grecisms."

6. For doubts about these criteria and the results they yield, see Luke Timothy Johnson, *The Writings of the New Testament* (3rd ed.; Minneapolis: Fortress Press, 2010), 240–42.

7. See the list in Gerhard Krodel, *Acts* (Proclamation Commentaries; Philadelphia: Fortress Press, 1981), 103–11.

8. Bart D. Ehrman, *The New Testament: A Historical Introduction to the Early Christian Writings* (5th ed.; New York: Oxford University Press, 2012), 309.

9. For a brief discussion of the issues, see Mark Allan Powell, *What Are They Saying about Acts?* (Mahwah, NJ: Paulist, 1991), 30–32. The classic article is Martin Dibelius, "The Speeches in Acts and Ancient Historiography," in *Studies in Luke-Acts*, ed. Leander Keck and J. Louis Martyn, 138–91 (reprint ed., Philadelphia: Fortress Press, 1980).

10. John Knox, *Chapters in a Life of Paul* (rev. ed.; Douglas R. A. Hare, ed.; Macon, GA: Mercer, 1987), 78.

11. On the manifestly non-Paul speech to the philosophers in Athens (Acts 17:16-34), see Philipp Vielhauer, "On the 'Paulinism' of Acts," in *Studies in Luke-Acts*, ed. Leander Keck and J. Louis Martyn, 33–50 (reprint ed.; Philadelphia: Fortress Press, 1980).

12. Vernon K. Robbins argues that the shift to "we" is simply a stylistic device and does not necessarily signal that the author took part in the "we" events. *Sea Voyages and Beyond: Emerging Strategies in Socio-rhetorical Interpretation* (Emory Studies in Early Christianity; Dorset, UK: Deo, 2010), chs. 1 and 2.

13. Powell, *What Are They Saying about Acts?*, 90. For a discussion of the historical trustworthiness of Acts, see 80–95.

14. The authors and documents mentioned in this section will be discussed in greater detail in chapter 13.

15. Marion L. Soards is quite blunt: "This is *bad* method! One cannot simply take a secondary source (here, Acts) and derive from it a framework into which a primary source (here, Galatians) must be made to fit." *The Apostle Paul: An Introduction to His Writings and Teaching* (Mahwah, NJ: Paulist, 1987), 9.

CHAPTER 3

1. Most older lives of Paul take this approach; see also Rainer Riesner, *Paul's Early Period: Chronology, Mission Strategy, Theology*, trans. Doug Stott (Grand Rapids: Eerdmans, 1998).

2. Gerd Lüdemann represents perhaps the most thoroughgoing attempt at this approach. *Paul, Apostle to the Gentiles: Studies in Chronology*, trans. F. Stanley Jones (Philadelphia: Fortress Press, 1984).

3. John Knox enunciated a principle followed by many who take the third position: "We may, with proper caution, use Acts to supplement the autobiographical data of the letters, but never to correct them." *Chapters in a Life of Paul* (rev. ed.; Macon, GA: Mercer, 1987), 19.

4. During Paul's ministry the country of Greece did not exist; the term *Greece* is thus geographical, not political.

5. From C. K. Barrett, *The New Testament Background: Selected Documents* (New York: Harper & Row, 1961), 48–49.

6. So F. J. Foakes-Jackson and K. Lake, eds., *The Beginnings of Christianity Part I: The Acts of the Apostles*, 5:462–63 (London: Macmillan, 1920-33; repr. ed.; Grand Rapids: Baker, 1979).

7. Robert Jewett, *A Chronology of Paul's Life* (Philadelphia: Fortress Press, 1979), 39.

8. So also Charles B. Puskas Jr., *The Letters of Paul: An Introduction* (Collegeville, MN: Liturgical Press, 1993), 21; Jewett, *A Chronology of Paul's Life*, 38–40; and Lüdemann, *Paul, Apostle to the Gentiles*, 163–64. Crossan and Reed argue that the Gallio reference is not historical; they also conclude that it is impossible to develop a precise chronology of Paul's life. John Dominic Crossan and Jonathan L. Reed, *In Search of Paul: How Jesus's Apostle Opposed Rome's Empire with God's Kingdom* (New York: HarperSanFrancisco, 2004), 230.

9. See the discussion in Thomas E. Phillips, *Paul, His Letters, and Acts* (Library of Pauline Studies; Peabody, MA: Hendrickson, 2009), 81–82.

10. The chronology that follows takes his conversion/call as the reference point.

11. The traditional site of the martyrdom is on the Via Ostiense. It was identified first by a shrine erected by believers. Under Emperor Constantine, a small church was consecrated in 324 and was followed in 395 by a larger church. Following a fire in 1823, the current church, St. Paul's Outside the Walls, was built. Archaeologists excavated from 2002 to 2007 the space underneath the main altar. The space contains a sarcophagus (stone tomb) that dates to at least 390 and has traditionally been identified as the final resting place for Paul's body.

12. Richard J. Cassidy, *Paul in Chains: Roman Imprisonment and the Letters of St. Paul* (New York: Crossroad, 2001), 55–67, 144–62. Klaus Haacker ("Paul's Life and Work," in *The Cambridge Companion to St Paul*, ed. James D. G. Dunn [Cambridge: Cambridge University Press, 2003], 20) thinks Paul may have died in 64 during Nero's persecution of Christians following the great fire in Rome, as do Crossan and Reed, *In Search of Paul*, 400–402. For a detailed study of Paul's death, see Harry W. Tajra, *The Martyrdom of St. Paul: Historical and Judicial Context, Traditions, and Legends* (WUNT 2.67; Tübingen: Mohr Siebeck, 1994).

13. Warren Carter, *The Roman Empire and the New Testament: An Essential Guide* (Nashville: Abingdon, 2006), 1.

14. On Tarsus, see Udo Schnelle, *Apostle Paul: His Life and Theology*, trans. M. Eugene Boring (Grand Rapids: Baker Academic, 2005), 58–60; and W. Ward Gasque, "Tarsus," *ABD* 6:333–34.

15. For a detailed study of the Mediterranean world, see Peregrine Horden and Nicholas Purcell, *The Corrupting Sea: A Study of Mediterranean History* (Oxford: Blackwell, 2000).

16. See Walter F. Taylor Jr., "Unity/Unity of Humanity," *ABD* 6:746–53, especially 748.

17. See Peter Garnsey, *Social Status and Legal Privilege in the Roman Empire* (Oxford: Oxford University Press, 1970); and A. N. Sherwin-White, *Roman Society and Roman Law in the New Testament* (Oxford: Clarendon, 1963). For an overview of citizenship in antiquity, see James S. Jeffers, *The Greco-Roman World of the New Testament Era: Exploring the Background of Early Christianity* (Downers Grove, IL: InterVarsity, 1999), 197–210; Jeffers assumes that Paul was a Roman citizen.

18. Gerhard Lenski and Jean Lenski, *Human Societies: An Introduction to Macrosociology* (5th ed.; New York: McGraw-Hill, 1987).

19. On social class and status, see Jeffers, *The Greco-Roman World*, 180–96.

20. John J. Pilch and Bruce J. Malina, eds., *Handbook of Biblical Social Values* (Peabody, MA: Hendrickson, 1998), xix. See further David D. Gilmore, "Anthropology of the Mediterranean Area," *Annual Review of Anthropology* 11 (1982): 175–205; David D. Gilmore, ed., *Honor and Shame and the Unity of the Mediterranean* (American Anthropological Association Special Publication 22; Washington, DC: American Anthropological Association, 1987); Jean G. Peristiany, ed., *Honour and Shame: The Values of Mediterranean Society* (London: Weidenfeld & Nicolson, 1965; Chicago: University of Chicago, 1966); David A. deSilva, *Honor, Patronage, Kinship and Purity: Unlocking New Testament Culture* (Downers Grove, IL: IVP Academic, 2000), 23–93. On xxxi, Pilch and Malina provide a chart on "Value Orientation Profiles" comparing various persons and groups from the first-century circum-Mediterranean as well as the United States; on xxxii–xxxix, they compare and contrast many features of U.S. and Mediterranean societies.

21. John H. Elliott, "Disgraced yet Graced: The Gospel according to 1 Peter in the Key of Honor and Shame," *BTB* 25 (1995): 168.

22. Bruce J. Malina, *The New Testament World: Insights from Cultural Anthropology* (3rd ed.; Louisville: Westminster/John Knox, 2001), 30.

23. Ibid., 31–32. Another way to formulate the concern for honor is the language of one's "face" and of gaining or losing face.

24. Elliott, "Disgraced yet Graced," 168.

25. On Paul as a dyadic personality, see Bruce J. Malina and Jerome H. Neyrey, *Portraits of Paul: An Archaeology of Ancient Personality* (Louisville: Westminster John Knox, 1996).

26. As Philip F. Esler phrases the matter, "Everyone finds a place in society by being embedded in one or more groups, such as the family, which is by far the most important, and in craft associations, religious cults or even military units." *The First Christians in Their Social Worlds: Social-Scientific Approaches to New Testament Interpretation* (London: Routledge, 1994), 29.

27. Another term for the larger phenomenon is "agonistic culture," *agōn* being the Greek word for *struggle* or *fight*.

28. An excellent illustration of the inside-outside phenomenon, as well as honor-shame values in general, is provided in Elizabeth Warnock Fernea, *Guests of the Sheik* (Garden City, NY: Doubleday, 1965). The author recounts her experience as an American living a secluded, veiled life in an Iraqi village. On the cultural ideal that women should be at home and on the gender division of labor, see Bruce J. Malina, *Windows on the World of Jesus: Time Travel to Ancient Judea* (Louisville: Westminster John Knox, 1993), 71–78.

29. For a study of Paul in relationship to patron-client relations and honor-shame values, see Walter F. Taylor Jr., "Obligation: Paul's Foundation for Ethics." *TSR* 19, no. 2 (Fall/Winter 1997): 91–112; *Josephinum Journal of Theology* 5, no. 1 (Winter/Spring 1998): 5–25 (different versions of the same article).

30. Pilch and Malina, *Handbook of Biblical Social Values*, 37.

31. Bruce W. Winter, *Seek the Welfare of the City: Christians as Benefactors and Citizens* (First-Century Christians in the Graeco-Roman World; Grand Rapids: Eerdmans; Carlisle, U.K.: Paternoster, 1994), 46. The following studies are particularly helpful: John K. Chow, *Patronage and Power: A Study of Social Networks in Corinth* (JSNTSup 75; Sheffield: JSOT, 1992); S. N. Eisenstadt and L. Roniger, *Patrons, Clients and Friends: Interpersonal Relations and the Structure of Trust in Society* (Cambridge: Cambridge University Press, 1984); John H. Elliott, "Patronage and Clientism in Early Christian Society: A Short Reading Guide," *Forum* 3 (1987): 39–48; A. Wallace-Hadrill, ed., *Patronage in Ancient Society* (London/New York: Routledge & Kegan Paul, 1990); deSilva, *Honor, Patronage, Kinship and Purity*, 95–156.

32. Pilch and Malina, *Handbook of Biblical Social Values*, 153; Halvor Moxnes, "Patron-Client Relations and the New Community in Luke-Acts," in *The Social World of Luke-Acts: Models for Interpretation*, ed. Jerome H. Neyrey (Peabody, MA: Hendrickson, 1991), 244–46, 248–49.

33. Moxnes, "Patron-Client Relations," 250.

34. John E. Stambaugh and David L. Balch, *The New Testament in Its Social Environment* (Library of Early Christianity; Philadelphia: Westminster, 1986), 54.

35. Ibid., 121–22.

36. The second-century traveler and author Pausanias had clear criteria for what constituted a city (or at least clear criteria for what did *not* constitute a city!): "From Chaeroneia it is twenty stades to Panopeus, a city of the Phocians, if one can give the name of city to those who possess no government offices, no gymnasium, no theatre, no market-place, no water descending to a fountain, but live in bare shelters just like mountain cabins, right on a ravine" (Pausanias, *Description of Greece* 4.1). See also the much earlier criteria listed by Aristotle, *Politics* 7.1328b2-23. For a helpful discussion of the *polis* from the perspective of the elites, see Malina and Neyrey, *Portraits of Paul*, 17–18, 20–21.

37. For more information on the preindustrial city and on the Roman Empire as an advanced form of a preindustrial agrarian society, see Walter F. Taylor Jr., "Cultural Anthropology as a Tool for Studying the New Testament: Part I," *TSR* 18, no. 1 (Summer 1996): 21–24.

38. Juvenal, *Satire III*, lines 235–37, in Juvenal, *The Sixteen Satires*, trans. Peter Green (Baltimore: Penguin, 1967), 95; also in *Juvenal and Persius*, trans. G. G. Ramsay (London: William

Heinemann, 1930), 48–51. For information about where Christ-believers lived in Rome, see Peter Lampe, *From Paul to Valentinus: Christians at Rome in the First Two Centuries*, trans. Michael Steinhauer; ed. Marshall D. Johnson (Minneapolis: Fortress Press, 2003), especially 19–66.

39. Robert J. Forbes, *Studies in Ancient Technology* (Leiden: Brill, 1955), 2:138.

40. On Roman roads, see Victor W. von Hagen, *The Roads That Led to Rome* (London: Weidenfeld & Nicolson, 1967); and Raymond Chevallier, *Roman Roads*, trans. N. H. Field (Berkeley: University of California Press, 1976).

41. Riesner, *Paul's Early Period*, 309–11. Raymond E. Brown doubts that Paul could have afforded any travel mode other than his own feet. *An Introduction to the New Testament* (ABRL; New York: Doubleday, 1997), 460–61.

42. Richard Wallace and Wynne Williams, *The Three Worlds of Paul of Tarsus* (London: Routledge, 1998), 26.

43. Such visits helped to create the social network that enabled the Christian church to grow and develop. See L. Michael White, ed., *Semeia 56: Social Networks in the Early Christian Environment: Issues and Methods for Social History* (Atlanta: Scholars Press, 1992).

44. The verb common to the last six passages is *propempō*, which means "to assist someone in making a journey, *send on one's way* with food, money, by arranging for companions, means of travel, etc." (BDAG, 873)

45. Riesner, *Paul's Early Period*, 314; Jeffers, *The Greco-Roman World*, 37. On sea travel in general, see Lionel Casson, *The Ancient Mariners: Seafarers and Sea Fighters of the Mediterranean in Ancient Times* (2nd ed.; Princeton: Princeton University Press, 1991); Casson, *Ships and Seamanship in the Ancient World* (Princeton: Princeton University Press, 1986); and Casson, *Travel in the Ancient World* (London: Allen & Unwin, 1974).

46. Riesner, *Paul's Early Period*, 316.

47. Blake Leyerle, "Communication and Travel," in *The Early Christian World*, ed. Philip F. Esler (London: Routledge, 2000), 1:469. F. F. Bruce, "Travel and Communication: The New Testament World," *ABD* 6:649.

48. Ronald F. Hock, *The Social Context of Paul's Ministry: Tentmaking and Apostleship* (Philadelphia: Fortress Press, 1980), 27.

CHAPTER 4

1. Hultgren writes concerning 9:1-5, "This little section reveals the inner, personal feelings of Paul more than any other in his Letter to the Romans. It exudes with ethnic and religious pride that he has for his Jewish heritage. . . . Few of his time could have known and loved the Jewish tradition more than he." Arland J. Hultgren, *Paul's Letter to the Romans: A Commentary* (Grand Rapids: Eerdmans, 2011), 355.

2. Jacob Neusner, "Preface," in *Judaisms and Their Messiahs at the Turn of the Christian Era*, ed. Jacob Neusner, William S. Green, and Ernest Frerichs (Cambridge: Cambridge University Press, 1987), xi–xiii.

3. Philip F. Esler, *Conflict and Identity in Romans: The Social Setting of Paul's Letter* (Minneapolis: Fortress Press, 2003), 233.

4. The approach to the Pharisees taken here is basically that of Jacob Neusner, who has painstakingly applied to the ancient materials on Pharisaic Judaism the same historical-critical method used in the study of biblical texts. From among Neusner's many works, see especially *The Rabbinic Traditions about the Pharisees before 70* (3 vols.; Leiden: Brill, 1971; Atlanta: Scholars Press, 1999); *From Politics to Piety: The Emergence of Pharisaic Judaism* (Englewood Cliffs, NJ: Prentice-Hall, 1973); and *Judaism When Christianity Began: A Survey of Belief and Practice* (Louisville: Westminster John Knox, 2002). The major point of divergence from Neusner is his understanding of the Pharisees' political involvement. He posits early political activity that was squelched under Herod the Great and continued to be squelched under the Romans during the lifetimes of Jesus and Paul. Thus, the Pharisees' attention turned mainly to Law and ritual. To others, especially Ellis Rivkin, the Pharisees were very much politically active. Ellis Rivkin, *A Hidden Revolution: The Pharisees' Search for the Kingdom Within* (Nashville: Abingdon, 1978).

Rivkin even sees them as political revolutionaries. Information from the first-century Judean author Josephus indicates a politically active movement that was popular with the mass of people, although (or perhaps because) the Pharisees did not wield much actual power (*War* 2.111-66; *Antiquities* 18.11-25). On the lack of evidence for the Pharisees and the resulting problems for interpretation, see Anthony J. Saldarini, "Pharisees," *ABD* 5:289.

5. Neusner, *From Politics to Piety*, 89.
6. See Saldarini, "Pharisees," 5:291–94.
7. On the wide range of Paul's citations, see James W. Aageson, *Written Also for Our Sake: Paul and the Art of Biblical Interpretation* (Louisville: Westminster John Knox, 1993); and Richard B. Hays, *Echoes of Scripture in the Letters of Paul* (New Haven: Yale University Press, 1989).
8. For more on the entire passage, see Walter F. Taylor Jr., "Obligation: Paul's Foundation for Ethics," *TSR* 19, no. 2 (Fall/Winter 1997): 91–112; also in *Josephinum Journal of Theology* 5, no. 1 (Winter/Spring 1998): 5–25. "*Spiritual* worship" is not an accurate translation; better would be "logical worship" or "reasonable worship" (the Greek term is *logikē*). There is also Hellenistic influence in his use of cultic language.
9. Rivkin sees the oral tradition of the Pharisees—what he calls the Unwritten Law—"as the core of Pharisaism." *A Hidden Revolution*, 72.
10. On Paul's concern for purity and pollution, see Jerome H. Neyrey, *Paul, In Other Words: A Cultural Reading of His Letters* (Louisville: Westminster John Knox, 1990), 219–20.
11. On their conflict regarding the resurrection, see Acts 23:6-10.
12. Calvin Roetzel reminds us that apocalyptic thought was more widespread than Qumran and Pharisaism and that the exact amount of influence on Paul from each is impossible to determine. *Paul: The Man and the Myth* (Minneapolis: Fortress Press, 1999), 37–38. On Pharisees as apocalyptic, see also Bart E. Ehrman, *The New Testament: A Historical Introduction to the Early Christian Writings* (5th ed.; Oxford: Oxford University Press, 2012), 314.
13. On apocalyptic, see Christopher Rowland, "Apocalypticism," *NIDB* 1:190–95; Adela Yarbro Collins, "Apocalypses and Apocalypticism: Early Christian," *ABD* 1:288–92; John J. Collins, "Apocalypses and Apocalypticism: Early Jewish Apocalypticism," *ABD* 1:282–88; Paul D. Hanson, ed., *Visionaries and Their Apocalypses* (Philadelphia: Fortress Press, 1983).
14. Among the many scholars who view apocalyptic as an important key to understanding Paul, two are especially significant: Ernst Käsemann (an important essay is "'The Righteousness of God' in Paul," in his *New Testament Questions of Today* [Philadelphia: Fortress Press, 1969], 168–82); and J. Christiaan Beker (one benchmark book of his is *Paul's Apocalyptic Gospel: The Coming Triumph of God* [Philadelphia: Fortress, 1992]).
15. For example, Johnson envisions Paul coming to Jerusalem as a young adult. Luke Timothy Johnson, *The Writings of the New Testament* (3rd ed.; Minneapolis: Fortress Press, 2010), 232. W. C. Van Unnik sees Paul in Jerusalem from early childhood on. *Tarsus or Jerusalem: The City of Paul's Youth*, trans. C. Ogg (London: Epworth, 1962), 55.
16. Roetzel, *Paul*, 2, 11–12; John Knox, *Chapters in a Life of Paul* (rev. ed.; Macon, GA: Mercer University Press, 1987), 21; J. Andrew Overman, "*Kata Nomon Pharisaios*: A Short History of Paul's Pharisaism," in *Pauline Conversations in Context: Essays in Honor of Calvin J. Roetzel*, ed. Janice Capel Anderson, Philip Sellew, and Claudia Setzer (JSNTSup 221; London: Sheffield Academic, 2002), 189. Crossan and Reed refer to Paul's "Jerusalem education as a Lukan upgrading of Paul's status and as part of his theme that everything starts from Jerusalem." John Dominic Crossan and Jonathan L. Reed, *In Search of Paul: How Jesus's Apostle Opposed Rome's Empire with God's Kingdom* (New York: HarperSanFrancisco, 2004), 5.
17. Roetzel, *Paul*, 3.
18. For important interpretations of Paul that see him almost totally within a Pharisaic/rabbinic framework, see W. D. Davies, *Paul and Rabbinic Judaism: Some Rabbinic Elements in Pauline Theology* (London: SPCK, 1948; reissued, Philadelphia: Fortress Press, 1980); and Pinchas Lapide and Peter Stuhlmacher, *Paul, Rabbi and Apostle*, trans. Lawrence W. Denef (Minneapolis: Augsburg, 1984).

19. A. W. Argyle, "Greek among the Jews of Palestine in New Testament Times," *NTS* 20 (1973/74): 87–89; Joseph A. Fitzmyer, "The Languages of Palestine in the First Century A.D.," *CBQ* 32 (1970): 501–31.

20. Joseph A. Fitzmyer, "Did Jesus Speak Greek?" *BAR* 18 (September/October 1992): 58–63.

21. Johnson reminds us that diaspora Judaism and Hellenistic Judaism are not necessarily the same thing. *The Writings of the New Testament*, 65. His reminder is appropriate, but the diaspora Judaism that Paul encountered and of which he himself was a part was thoroughly Hellenized.

22. Johnson points to 5 million Judeans living outside Palestine in the first century and 2 million living within. *The Writings of the New Testament*, 66. Non-Palestinian Judeans did not necessarily evaluate their living locale negatively. Eric S. Gruen argues that "Jews of the Second Temple period did not perceive themselves as victims of a diaspora." *Diaspora: Jews amidst Greek and Romans* (Cambridge: Harvard University Press, 2002), 135.

23. Gruen, *Diaspora*, 212.

24. Eric M. Meyers, "Synagogue: Introductory Survey," *ABD* 6:259. More specifically on diaspora synagogues, see Rachel Hachlili, "Synagogue: Diaspora Synagogues," *ABD* 6:260–63.

25. On the positive evaluation of Judean religion held by many Gentiles, see Josephus, *Against Apion* 2.282-86.

26. The two terms used for them in Acts are *sebomenoi* (worshipping, devout) and *phoboumenoi (ton theon)* (fearing [God]). See Kirsopp Lake, "Proselytes and God-Fearers," in F. J. Foakes-Jackson and K. Lake, eds., *The Beginnings of Christianity Part I: The Acts of the Apostles*, 5:74–96 (London: Macmillan, 1920–33; repr. ed.; Grand Rapids: Baker, 1979).

27. Anyone who has taken Greek I knows that this story *has* to be a legend! The story is found in *The Letter of Aristeas* in *The Old Testament Pseudepigrapha*, ed. James H. Charlesworth (Garden City, NY: Doubleday, 1985), 2:7–34; Philo, *The Life of Moses* 2.25-44; and Josephus, *Antiquities* 12.2. For a brief introduction to the letter, see Leonard Greenspoon, "Aristeas, Letter of," *NIDB* 1:260–61.

28. Marc Rastoin, *Tarse et Jérusalem: La Double Culture de l'Apôtre Paul en Galates 3,6–4,7* (Analecta Biblica: Rome: Pontifical Biblical Institute, 2003).

29. On the relationship between the two, see Abraham J. Malherbe, *Social Aspects of Early Christianity* (2nd ed., enlarged; Philadelphia: Fortress Press, 1983), 29–59; Jerome H. Neyrey, "The Social Location of Paul: Education as the Key," in *Fabrics of Discourse: Essays in Honor of Vernon K. Robbins*, ed. David B. Gowler, L. Gregory Bloomquist, and Duane F. Watson, 126–64 (Harrisburg, PA: Trinity Press International, 2003); Ronald F. Hock, "Paul and Greco-Roman Education," in *Paul in the Greco-Roman World: A Handbook*, ed. J. Paul Sampley, 198–227 (Harrisburg, PA: Trinity Press International, 2003). Hock provides a succinct summary of scholarship on Greco-Roman education, 198–208; on education itself, see John T. Townsend, "Education (Greco-Roman)," *ABD* 2:312–17; and Neyrey, "The Social Location of Paul," 158–60 and the literature cited there.

30. Hans Dieter Betz, *Galatians: A Commentary on Paul's Letter to the Galatians* (Hermeneia; Philadelphia: Fortress Press, 1979); Betz, "The Literary Composition and Function of Paul's Letter to the Galatians," *NTS* 21 (1974–75): 353–73.

31. Neyrey, "The Social Location of Paul," 133–40.

32. For examples, see ibid., 140–49.

33. Hock, "Paul and Greco-Roman Education," 198. Scribes, it should be noted, were not educated at the sophisticated level evidenced in Paul's letters. Neyrey, "The Social Location of Paul," 133. Thus, the content, arrangement, and rhetorical strategies of the letters cannot be attributed to the scribes who took Paul's dictation.

34. See James L. Bailey and Lyle D. Vander Broek, *Literary Forms in the New Testament: A Handbook* (Louisville: Westminster John Knox, 1992), 38–42.

35. Neyrey, "The Social Location of Paul," 150, utilizing Stanley K. Stowers, *The Diatribe and Paul's Letter to the Romans* (SBLDS 57; Chico, CA: Scholars, 1981). See also Hock, "Paul

and Greco-Roman Education," 209. Neyrey goes on to argue that the way Paul uses lists of virtues and vices, catalogs of hardships, Stoic terminology and argument, polemical arguments against Epicureans, and standard topics from common philosophy argues for formal education in philosophy (150–57). On Paul's knowledge of philosophical language and issues, see Abraham J. Malherbe, *Paul and the Popular Philosophers* (Minneapolis: Fortress Press, 1989); F. Gerald Downing, *Cynics, Paul, and the Pauline Churches: Cynics and Christian Origins II* (London: Routledge, 1998); and Troels Engberg-Pedersen, *Paul and the Stoics* (Louisville: Westminster John Knox, 2000). For more examples from Paul's writings of his high level of education, see Hock, "Paul and Greco-Roman Education," 208–15, and the discussions of Paul's letters, below, in the chapters dealing with individual letters.

36. See Neyrey, "The Social Location of Paul," 160. In Lenski's description of the Roman Empire as an advanced agrarian society, the top 1 to 2 percent of the population consisted of the ruling and governing class, with another 5 percent composed of the retainers (household servants, personal assistants, professional soldiers, higher governmental officials). Lenski and Lenski, *Human Societies*; and Gerhard E. Lenski, *Power and Privilege: A Theory of Social Stratification* (Chapel Hill: University of North Carolina Press, 1984).

37. See the discussion of Luke's theology in chapter 2.

38. For more on the issue of citizenship, see Roetzel, *Paul*, 19–22, and Udo Schnelle, *Apostle Paul: His Life and Theology*, trans. M. Eugene Boring (Grand Rapids: Baker Academic, 2005), 60–62.

39. For other references to his work, see 1 Cor 9:6; 2 Cor 6:5; 11:27; see also 2 Thess 3:7-9 and Acts 20:34.

40. See the extensive discussion in BDAG, 928–29.

41. Ronald F. Hock, *The Social Context*, 20–21; Hock, "The Problem of Paul's Social Class: Further Reflections," in *Paul's World*, ed. Stanley E. Porter (Pauline Studies 4; Leiden: Brill, 2008), 10. For discussions of tentmaking in general and of Paul as tentmaker, see Schnelle, *Apostle Paul*, 62–63; and Peter Lampe, *From Paul to Valentinus: Christians at Rome in the First Two Centuries*, trans. Michael Steinhauer; ed. Marshall D. Johnson (Minneapolis: Fortress Press, 2003), 187–95. The basic study is by Hock (*The Social Context*), updated by him in "The Problem of Paul's Social Class," 7–18.

42. Lampe estimates that in Corinth the shops in one street were 3 feet 3 inches wide and 4 feet 4 inches deep. *From Paul to Valentinus*, 192. Hock points also to somewhat larger shops. *The Social Context*, 32–33.

43. Hock, *The Social Context*, 35. On working conditions for artisans, see Hock, 31–35; and Jerome Murphy-O'Connor, *St. Paul's Corinth: Texts and Archaeology* (3rd ed.; Collegeville, MN: Liturgical Press, 2002), 196–97.

44. From Hock, *The Social Context*, 35–36.

45. Ibid., 36.

46. Hock surveys this position. Ibid., 22.

47. See above, p. 57, 61.

48. Hock, *The Social Context*, 22–23.

49. Ibid., 23–24. He has since changed his mind; see next note.

50. Murphy-O'Connor argues that Paul learned his trade during his three years in Damascus after he had returned from Arabia (Gal 1:17-18). *St. Paul's Corinth*, 192. Hock has modified his earlier position that Paul learned tentmaking from his father; he now concludes that Paul learned his trade after leaving his hometown of Tarsus. "The Problem of Paul's Social Class."

51. See ch. 5.

52. See below, p. 148.

53. Wilhlem Schneemelcher, "The Acts of Paul," in *New Testament Apocrypha*, ed. Wilhelm Schneemelcher, trans. ed. Robert M. Wilson (rev. ed.; Louisville: Westminster John Knox, 1992), 2:239.

54. Abraham J. Malherbe, "A Physical Description of Paul," in his *Paul and the Popular Philosophers* (Minneapolis: Fortress Press, 1989), 165–70; Bruce J. Malina and Jerome H. Neyrey,

"Physiognomics and Personality: Looking at Paul in *The Acts of Paul*," in their *Portraits of Paul: An Archaeology of Ancient Personality* (Louisville: Westminster John Knox, 1996), 100–152.

55. The technical name for that understanding is physiognomics, which "is the study of human character on the basis of how people look and act." Malina and Neyrey, "Physiognomics and Personality," 109.

56. Ibid., 128.

57. For the following, see ibid., 130–48; Malherbe, "A Physical Description of Paul," 167–70.

58. See LSJ.

59. Malina and Neyrey, "Physiognomics and Personality," 146; for more, see 146–48.

60. For more, see Calvin J. Roetzel, *The Letters of Paul: Conversations in Context* (5th ed.; Louisville: Westminster John Knox, 2009), 42; and Luther H. Martin, "Graeco-Roman Philosophy and Religion," in *The Early Christian World*, ed. Philip F. Esler (London: Routledge, 2000), 1:61–62.

61. See, for example, Epictetus 3.22.23-25. Resources on Cynicism include Abraham J. Malherbe, *The Cynic Epistles: A Study Edition* (Atlanta: Scholars, 1977); Ronald F. Hock, "Cynics," *ABD* 1:1221–26; Donald R. Dudley, *A History of Cynicism: From Diogenes to the 6th Century AD* (2nd ed.; London: Bristol Classical, 1998); Hans-Josef Klauck, *The Religious Context of Early Christianity: A Guide to Graeco-Roman Religions*, trans. Brian McNeil (Minneapolis: Fortress Press, 2003), 377–85; and N. Clayton Croy, "Stoicism and Cynicism," in *Encyclopedia of the Historical Jesus*, ed. Craig A. Evans, 606–609 (New York: Routledge, 2008).

62. See above, p. 59, and in the chapter on Romans, below. Other philosophical traditions used the diatribe as well. In addition to Bailey and Vander Broek, *Literary Forms* see Stanley K. Stowers, "Diatribe," in *ABD* 2:190–93.

63. See Benjamin Fiore, *The Function of Personal Example in the Socratic and Pastoral Epistles* (Analecta Biblica 105; Rome: Biblical Institute Press, 1986), 10–21; Malherbe, *Paul and the Popular Philosophers*, 49–66; Malherbe, "Hellenistic Moralists and the New Testament," *ANRW* 2/26, no. 1, 278–93; Bailey and Vander Broek, *Literary Forms*, 62–65.

64. For more, see John T. Fitzgerald, *Cracks in an Earthen Vessel: An Examination of the Catalogs of Hardships in the Corinthian Correspondence* (SBLDS 99; Atlanta: Scholars Press, 1988); and David E. Fredrickson, "Paul, Hardships, and Suffering," in *Paul in the Greco-Roman World*, 172–97.

65. So Malherbe, *Paul and the Thessalonians*; Malherbe, *Paul and the Popular Philosophers*; Downing, *Cynics, Paul, and the Pauline Churches*.

66. Malherbe, *Paul and the Popular Philosophers*, 35–48.

67. See Taylor, "Unity/Unity of Humanity," *ABD* 6:746–53, esp. 748; and Harold C. Baldry, *Unity of Mankind in Greek Thought* (Cambridge: Cambridge University Press, 1965). On Stoicism, including Stoic views of pantheism and the cyclical destruction of the world by fire, see J. M. Rist, *Stoic Philosophy* (Cambridge: Cambridge University Press, 1969); Thomas Schmeller, "Stoics, Stoicism," in *ABD* 6:210–14; Paul Oskar Kristeller, *Greek Philosophers of the Hellenistic Age*, trans. Gregory Woods (New York: Columbia University Press, 1993), 22–35 (on Zeno); Christopher Forbes, "Epictetus," in *DNTB*, 321–24; Thomas N. Habinek, "Seneca," *DNTB*, 1098–99; Johan C. Thom, "Stoicism," *DNTB*, 1139–42.

68. Klauck, *The Religious Context*, 335. Note that in Acts 17:18, Paul debates with Stoic and Epicurean philosophers.

69. Already discussed under Cynicism and used by both Cynics and Stoics; in Paul, examples are Rom 1:18—2:11; 3:1-20; 8:31-39; 1 Cor 9:1-27; 15:29-49.

70. A real favorite of the Stoics; in Paul, see Gal 5:19-23. For vices only, see Rom 1:29-31; 13:13; 1 Cor 5:10-11; 6:9-10; 2 Cor 12:20-21. For virtues only, see 2 Cor 6:6-7a; Phil 4:8.

71. In Paul, see 1 Cor 4:9-13; 2 Cor 4:8-12; 6:4-10; 12:10.

72. Taylor, "Unity/Unity of Humanity," 748.

73. Abraham J. Malherbe, "Determinism and Free Will: The Argument of 1 Corinthians 8 and 9," in *Paul in His Hellenistic Context*, ed. Troels Engberg-Pedersen (Minneapolis: Fortress Press, 1995), 231–55.

74. Troels Engberg-Pedersen, "Stoicism in Philippians," in Engberg-Pedersen, *Paul in His Hellenistic Context*, 279. The entire chapter is pp. 256–90. See also his *Paul and the Stoics*, 81–130.
75. On which see below, p. 95–97.
76. Malherbe, *Paul and the Thessalonians*, 40–43, 84–87, 101–6; Clarence E. Glad, *Paul and Philodemus: Adaptability in Epicurean and Early Christian Psychagogy* (NovTSup 81; Leiden: Brill, 1995).
77. Malherbe, *Paul and the Thessalonians*, 104.
78. Basic discussions of Epicurus and Epicureanism include the following: J. M. Rist, *Epicurus: An Introduction* (Cambridge: Cambridge University Press), 1972; Elizabeth Asmis, "Epicureanism," *ABD* 2:559–61; Kristeller, *Greek Philosophers*, 5–21; N. Clayton Croy, "Epicureanism," *DNTB*, 325–27; Klauck, *The Religious Context*, 385–400; Brett S. Provance, "Epicurus, Epicureanism," in *NIDB* 2:284–86.
79. Eduard Schweizer, *The Letter to the Colossians: A Commentary*, trans. Andrew Chester (Minneapolis: Augsburg, 1982), 129–33, 151, 157.
80. David L. Balch, "Household Ethical Codes in Peripatetic, Neopythagorean, and Early Christian Moralists," *SBLSP* 11 (1977): 397–404; Balch, "Neopythagorean Moralists and the New Testament Household Codes," *ANRW* (1992) 2/26, no. 1, 380–411. On parallels scholars have identified between Jesus and the neo-Pythagorean teacher Apollonius of Tyana, see N. Clayton Croy, "Neo-Pythagoreanism," *DNTB*, 740–41 and the bibliography on 742.
81. For more on neo-Pythagoreanism, see Johan C. Thom, "Pythagoreanism," *ABD* 5:562–65, and Croy, "Neo-Pythagoreanism," 739–42.
82. On household shrines, see David L. Balch, "Rich Pompeiian Houses, Shops for Rent, and the Huge Apartment Building in Herculaneum as Typical Spaces for Pauline House Churches," *JSNT* 27 (2004): 37–40.
83. On the care of the dead, see Klauck, *The Religious Context*, 68–80.
84. On the domestic cult, see W. K. Lacey, *The Family in Classical Greece* (Ithaca, NY: Cornell University Press, 1968); Daniel P. Harmon, "The Family Festivals of Rome," *ANRW* 2/16, no. 2, 1592–1603; David G. Orr, "Roman Domestic Religion: The Evidence of the Household Shrines," *ANRW* 2/16, no. 2, 1557–91; Jane F. Gardner and Thomas Wiedemann, eds., *The Roman Household: A Sourcebook* (London: Routledge, 1991); Suzanne Dixon, *The Roman Family* (Baltimore: Johns Hopkins University Press, 1992); Klauck, *The Religious Context*, 55–63.
85. For more, see Klauck, *The Religious Context*, 177–209, 231–49.
86. In addition to belief in various gods, ancient people usually believed in intermediate beings who ranked between the gods and human beings. The intermediate beings were called *daimones*, or *demons*; in the New Testament, the term is more often *daimonia* (plural), and the singular is *daimonion*.
87. For a discussion of magic, see Klauck, *The Religious Context*, 209-31; on the distinction between magic and religion, see 217–18.
88. Additional resources on magic include Edwin M. Yamauchi, "Magic in the Biblical World," *TynBul* 34 (1983): 169–200; Fritz Graf, *Magic in the Ancient World*, trans. Franklin Philip (Cambridge: Harvard University Press, 1997); Marvin W. Meyer and Paul Mirecki, eds., *Ancient Magic and Ritual Power* (Boston: Brill, 2001); Sarah Iles Johnston, "Magic," in *Religions of the Ancient World: A Guide*, ed. Sarah Iles Johnston, 139–52 (Cambridge: Belknap, 2004).
89. For more on healing, especially Asclepius, see Klauck, *The Religious Context*, 154–68.
90. Johnston prefers labeling the mysteries as cults rather than religions, because the mysteries "were optional supplements to civic religions, rather than competing alternatives." *Religions of the Ancient World*, 99.
91. Parades, processions, and some sacrifices were public events.
92. Marvin W. Meyer, "Mystery Religions," *ABD* 4:941.
93. John E. Stambaugh and David L. Balch, *The New Testament in Its Social Environment* (Library of Early Christianity; Philadelphia: Westminster, 1986), 133. For more on the Demeter cult, see George E. Mylonas, *Eleusis and the Eleusinian Mysteries* (Princeton: Princeton University Press, 1961); Richard Reitzenstein, *Hellenistic Mystery-Religions: Their Basic Ideas and*

Significance, trans. John E. Steely (Pittsburgh: Pickwick, 1978); Luther H. Martin, *Hellenistic Religions: An Introduction* (New York: Oxford University Press, 1987), 62–72; Larry J. Alderink, "The Eleusinian Mysteries in Roman Imperial Times," *ANRW* 2/18, no. 2, 1457–98; and Klauck, *The Religious Context*, 90–106. On mystery religions in general, see Marvin W. Meyer, "Mystery Religions," *ABD* 4:941–45; Meyer, "Mysteries," *DNTB*, 720–25; Hugh Bowden, *Mystery Cults of the Ancient World* (Princeton, NJ: Princeton University Press, 2010). For texts, see Barrett, *New Testament Background*, 120–34; and Marvin W. Meyer, *The Ancient Mysteries: A Sourcebook* (Sacred Texts of the Mystery Religions of the Ancient Mediterranean World; San Francisco: Harper & Row, 1987; paper ed., 1999).

94. Introductions to the Dionysiac mysteries include Walter F. Otto, *Dionysus: Myth and Cult* (Bloomington: Indiana University Press, 1965); Martin, *Hellenistic Religions*, 91–98; and Klauck, *The Religious Context*, 106–17.

95. On the Isis mysteries, see R. E. Witt, *Isis in the Ancient World* (Baltimore: Johns Hopkins University Press, 1971; paperback ed., 1997; also issued as *Isis in the Graeco-Roman World* [London: Thames and Hudson, 1971]); Sharon Kelly Heyob, *The Cult of Isis among Women in the Graeco-Roman World* (EPRO 51; Leiden: Brill, 1975); Martin, *Hellenistic Religions*, 16–34, 72–81; and Klauck, *The Religious Context*, 128–39.

96. Resources on Mithraism include Franz Cumont, *The Mysteries of Mithras*, trans. Thomas J. McCormack (New York: Dover, 1956); M. J. Vermaseren, *Mithras: The Secret God*, trans. Therese and Vincent Megaw (London: Chatto and Windus, 1963); Martin, *Hellenistic Religions*, 113–18; Klauck, *The Religious Context*, 139–49.

97. Robert Jewett, *Romans: A Commentary* (Hermeneia; Minneapolis: Fortress Press, 2007), 161–62; Witt, *Isis in the Graeco-Roman World* and *Isis in the Ancient World*, 255–57. For other possible parallels to language from the Isis cult, see Witt, 263, 266–68 (in either volume).

98. The church of San Clemente in Rome is a good example.

99. Prominent names are Richard Reitzenstein, *Hellenistic Mystery-Religions*; Wilhelm Bousset, *Kyrios Christos: A History of the Belief in Christ from the Beginnings of Christianity to Irenaeus*, trans. John E. Steely (repr. ed.; Nashville: Abingdon, 1970); Rudolf Bultmann, *Theology of the New Testament*, trans. Kendrick Grobel (New York: Scribner's Sons, 1951–55), 1:187–352.

100. Klauck, *The Religious Context*, 152.

101. On the creation of humanity according to an important Gnostic document, see the *Apocryphon of John* from Nag Hammadi (for translations, see notes 104 and 112, below). Klauck (467–70) and Pearson (61–69) summarize the document. Klauck, *The Religious Context*, 467–70; Birger A. Pearson, *Ancient Gnosticism: Traditions and Literature* (Minneapolis: Fortress Press, 2007).

102. Clement of Alexandria, *Excerpta ex Theodoto* 78.2, in Werner Foerster, *Gnosis: A Selection of Gnostic Texts*, trans. R. McL. Wilson; Vol. I. *Patristic Evidence* (Oxford: Clarendon Press, 1972), 230.

103. On the view of a "redeemed redeemer," see Klauck, *The Religious Context*, 474. Although prominent at certain points in the twentieth century, this position is no longer widely held. Besides Jesus, other revealers include Adam, Seth, and Sophia/Wisdom.

104. See "The Hymn of the Pearl," available in Foerster, *Gnosis*, 355–58; Bentley Layton, *The Gnostic Scriptures* (Garden City, NY: Doubleday, 1987), 366–75; Willis Barnstone and Marvin Meyer, eds., *The Gnostic Bible* (Boston: New Seeds, 2006), 386–94.

105. So Paul about his Corinthian opponents, who may have been influenced by Gnostic thought: "All things are lawful to me" (1 Cor 6:12). Carpocrates and his son Epiphanes are often cited as examples of Gnostic libertinism (Iraenaeus, *Against Heresies*, 1.6.3-4; 1.25.4).

106. For example, the *Apocryphon of John* II, *1* 25.23-27.11.

107. Collected in Foerster, *Gnosis*.

108. Pearson, *Ancient Gnosticism*, 11, 61–69, 211–18), on the *Apocryphon of John*, *Eugnostos the Blessed*, and *Sophia of Jesus Christ*.

109. On theories that seek to explain the origins of Gnosticism, see Klauck, *The Religious Context*, 455–61; Edwin M. Yamauchi, "Gnosticism," in *DNTB*, 416–17.

110. The position taken here is to be distinguished from the work of Walter Schmithals, who found a Gnostic behind every exegetical bush. See, for example, his *Gnosticism in Corinth: An Investigation of the Letters to the Corinthians*, trans. John E. Steely (Nashville: Abingdon, 1971); and *Paul and the Gnostics*, trans. John E. Steely (Nashville: Abingdon, 1972).

111. 1 Tim 6:20-21 may well be the earliest evidence for Gnosticism understood as a Christian heresy.

112. Elaine H. Pagels, *The Gnostic Paul: Gnostic Exegesis of the Pauline Letters* (Philadelphia: Fortress Press, 1975). For helpful introductions to Gnosticism, see the following: Kurt Rudolph, *Gnosis: The Nature and History of Gnosticism*, trans. R. M. Wilson (San Francisco: Harper & Row, 1983); Birger A. Pearson, "Nag Hammadi," *ABD* 4:982–93; Kurt Rudolph, "Gnosticism," *ABD* 2:1033–40;Yamauchi, "Gnosticism," 414–18; Klauck, *The Religious Context*, 429–503; and Pheme Perkins, "Gnosticism," *NIDB* 2:81–84. Pearson, *Ancient Gnosticism*, is especially helpful for introductions to collections and documents. For collections of texts, see Foerster, *Gnosis*; Layton, *The Gnostic Scriptures*; Barrett, *New Testament Background*, 92–119; James M. Robinson, general ed., *The Nag Hammadi Library in English* (4th rev. ed.; Leiden: Brill, 1996); Barnstone and Meyer, *The Gnostic Bible*; and Marvin W. Meyer, ed., *The Nag Hammadi Scriptures* (New York: HarperOne, 2007).

113. Philip F. Esler, "The Mediterranean Context of Early Christianity," in *The Early Christian World*, ed. Philip F. Esler (London: Routledge, 2000), 1:5. On religion as embedded, see also Bruce J. Malina, "'Religion' in the World of Paul: A Preliminary Sketch," *BTB* 16 (1986): 92–101.

114. On the gods of Greece and Rome as well as the imperial cult, see W. K. C. Guthrie, *The Greeks and Their Gods* (Boston: Beacon, 1971); D. P. Harmon, "The Public Festivals of Rome," *ANRW* 2/116, no. 2, 1440–68; H. J. Rose, *Religion in Greece and Rome* (New York: HarperCollins College Division, 1979); J. R. Fears, "The Cult of Jupiter and Roman Imperial Ideology."*ANRW* 2/17, no. 1, 3–141; Burkhard Gladigow, "Roman Religion,"*ABD* 5:809–16; Klauck, *The Religious Context*, 313–27; and Neil Elliott and Mark Reasoner, eds., *Documents and Images for the Study of Paul* (Minneapolis: Fortress Press, 2011), 119–73.

115. On the Hellenistic background of ruler cults, see Klauck, *The Religious Context*, 250–88.

116. "Peace and prosperity" came, of course, to those who acquiesced to Rome's growing power, especially to the elite. Opposition to the empire was substantial, and the lives of unnumbered people were significantly altered by the empire's policies. See Richard A. Horsley, "Introduction," in *Paul and the Roman Imperial Order*, ed. by Richard A. Horsley, 6–19 (Harrisburg, PA: Trinity Press International, 2004).

117. S. R. F. Price, "Rituals and Power," in *Paul and Empire: Religion and Power in Roman Imperial Society*, ed. Richard A. Horsley, 55–56 (Harrisburg, PA: Trinity Press International, 1997); Paul Zanker, "The Power of Images," in Horsley, *Paul and Empire*, 76–82. On the importance of competition within a given city for the rapid spread of the cult, see Zanker, "The Power of Images," 79.

118. Price, "Rituals and Power," 61–64.

119. Neil Elliott, "The Apostle Paul's Self-Presentation as Anti-Imperial Performance," in Horsley, *Paul and the Roman Imperial Order*, 70.

120. Zanker, "The Power of Images," 75–76.

121. Quotations and references from Virgil are from *Virgil: Eclogues, Georgics, Aeneid I–VI*, trans. H. Rushton Fairclough; rev. G. P. Goold (LCL; Cambridge, MA: Harvard University Press, 1999).

122. Crossan and Reed, *In Search of Paul*, 58.

123. See Neil Elliott, "PIETAS: Piety and the Scandal of an Irreligious Race," in his *The Arrogance of Nations: Reading Romans in the Shadow of Empire* (Paul in Critical Contexts; Minneapolis: Fortress Press, 2008), 121–42.

124. From M. Eugene Boring, Klaus Berger, and Carsten Colpe, eds., *Hellenistic Commentary to the New Testament* (Nashville: Abingdon, 1995), 169. "Good tidings" translates the Greek term for *gospels* (*euaggeliōn*).

125. Warren Carter, *The Roman Empire and the New Testament: An Essential Guide* (Nashville: Abingdon, 2006), 83.

126. For more detail, see Robert Jewett, "The Corruption and Redemption of Creation: Reading Rom 8:18-23 within the Imperial Context," in Horsley, *Paul and the Roman Imperial Order*, 25–46, and the literature cited there. On Augustus and the Golden Age, see also Crossan and Reed, *In Search of Paul*, 135–44. The power of the symbols and mythology of the Roman Empire should not be underestimated; see Edward Champlin, *Nero* (Cambridge, MA: Belknap, 2003), esp. 92–96.

127. On Paul's response, see Dieter Georgi, "Who Is the True Prophet?", in Horsley, *Paul and Empire*, 36–46. Significant resources on Roman imperial theology and its relationship to Paul include Klaus Wengst, *Pax Romana*, trans. John Bowden (Philadelphia: Fortress Press, 1987); Neil Elliott, *Liberating Paul: The Justice of God and the Politics of the Apostle* (Maryknoll, NY: Orbis, 1994; Minneapolis: Fortress Press, 2006); Horsley, *Paul and Empire*; Horsley, *Paul and the Roman Imperial Order*; Crossan and Reed, *In Search of Paul*, who emphasize especially the inscriptions and art works that illustrate imperial theology; Neil Elliott, *The Arrogance of Nations*; and David R. Wallace, *The Gospel of God: Romans as Paul's Aeneid* (Eugene, OR: Pickwick, 2008).

128. Walter H. Wagner, *After the Apostles: Christianity in the Second Century* (Minneapolis: Fortress Press, 1994), 59.

129. On the reasons why Paul wanted to go to Damascus, see James D. G. Dunn, *Beginning from Jerusalem*, vol. 2 of *Christianity in the Making* (Grand Rapids: Eerdmans, 2009), 346–48.

130. On the variations, see Ehrman, *The New Testament*, 316 (box 20.4); and J. M. Everts, "Conversion and Call of Paul," *DPL*, 158–59.

131. On the appearances of Jesus from a cultural anthropological perspective, see John J. Pilch, "Appearances of the Risen Jesus in Cultural Context," *BTB* 28 (1998): 52–60; Pilch, "Paul's Ecstatic Trance Experience near Damascus in Acts of the Apostles," *HvTSt* 58 (2002): 690–707. In 2 Cor 12:1-5, Paul speaks of a different kind of visionary experience (or alternate state of consciousness), probably referring to himself.

132. Moyer V. Hubbard argues that in four of his allusions to the Damascus Road experience, Paul utilizes key terms from his Christology: Lord (1 Cor 9:1); Messiah/Christ (1 Cor 15:8); God's son (Gal 2:16); image of God (2 Cor 4:4-6). *Christianity in the Greco-Roman World: A Narrative Introduction* (Peabody, MA: Hendrickson, 2010), 56.

133. J. Christiaan Beker, *Paul's Apocalyptic Gospel: The Coming Triumph of God* (Philadelphia: Fortress Press, 1982), 57.

134. A groundbreaking study was Krister Stendahl, *Paul among Jews and Gentiles* (Philadelphia: Fortress Press, 1976), 7–23. Roetzel has developed the additional thesis that often an emphasis on conversion has sought to denigrate Judaism. *Paul*, 44–45.

135. Charles Cousar, *The Letters of Paul* (IBT; Nashville: Abingdon, 1996), 19, n. 6. Dunn distinguishes between the two kinds of language but tries to retain both: "Of course we should not think of Saul as converting from one religion to another (Judaism to Christianity). . . . Nevertheless we can hardly avoid speaking of Paul's experience as a conversion. . . . We have no reason . . . to set the two categories in contrast or antithesis. 'Conversion' is more the language of the historian of religion; 'commissioning' is the language of Paul's self-understanding. But the two can easily cohabit the same space." *Beginning from Jerusalem*, 353–54. For more on the Damascus Road experience and its significance, see Schnelle, *Apostle Paul*, 87–102; and Seyoon Kim, *The Origin of Paul's Gospel* (WUNT 2nd ser., 4; 2nd ed.; Tübingen: Mohr Siebeck, 1984). On conversion in antiquity from a social-scientific perspective, see Zeba A. Crook, *Reconceptualising Conversion: Patronage, Loyalty, and Conversion in the Religions of the Ancient Mediterranean* (BZNW 130; Berlin: de Gruyter, 2004).

136. On the question of Paul's citizenship, see above, pp. 30–31, 59–60.

137. C. E. B. Cranfield, *A Critical and Exegetical Commentary on the Epistle to the Romans* (ICC; Edinburgh: T &T Clark, 1975, 1979), 1:49, for example.

138. Jewett, *Romans*, 99; Ben Witherington III, *Conflict and Community in Corinth: A Socio-Rhetorical Commentary on 1 and 2 Corinthians* (Grand Rapids: Eerdmans, 1994), 15, n. 12. On both theories, see T. J. Leary, "Paul's Improper Name," *NTS* 38 (1992): 467–68.

139. Scholars long ago rejected the theory that the apostle Paul adopted the proconsul's name.

140. LSJ, "*saulos*"; also Leary, "Paul's Improper Name," 468.

141. Scholars often point to the Hebrew term *shāliaḥ* as providing part of the term's nuance. The *shāliaḥ* was authorized to negotiate business deals and to sign contracts, which the sender then had to fulfill. The question is whether the evidence we have for the *shāliaḥ* is early enough to help in understanding the term *apostle*. On the *shāliaḥ*, see Dietrich Müller, "Apostle," in *NIDNTT* 1:127–28, 132–34; Jan Adolf Bühner, "*apostolos*," in *EDNT* 1:143, 145; Karl Heinrich Rengstorf, "*apostellō, apostolos*, . . ." in *TDNT* 1:413.

142. Jewett, *Romans*, 101.

143. On the concept of apostle, see Müller, *NIDNTT* 1:126–37; Rengstorf, *TDNT* 1:398–447; Bühner, *EDNT* 1:142–46; Hans Dieter Betz, "Apostle," *ABD* 1:309-11; Paul W. Barnett, "Apostle," in *DPL*, 45-51; Terence Donaldson, "Apostle," *NIDB* 1:205-7; C. K. Barrett, *The Signs of an Apostle* (London: Epworth, 1970). These resources deal with the understanding of the Twelve as apostles as well as other issues beyond the scope of this study.

144. Eusebius, *Ecclesiastical History* 3.30, quoting Clement of Alexandria, *Stromata* 3.

145. Jeremias thought it probable that Paul's wife had died prior to Paul's Damascus Road experience. Joachim Jeremias, "War Paulus Witwer?" *ZNW* 25 (1926): 312.

146. For an eloquent formulation of Paul's call and role, see N. T. Wright, *Paul: In Fresh Perspective* (Minneapolis: Fortress Press, 2005), 157.

147. See further Michael J. Gorman, *Cruciformity: Paul's Narrative Spirituality of the Cross* (Grand Rapids: Eerdmans, 2001).

148. Beker, *Paul's Apocalyptic Gospel*, 57.

CHAPTER 5

1. On social network theory, see J. Boissevain and J. C. Mitchell, eds., *Network Analysis: Studies in Human Interaction* (The Hague: Mouton, 1973); Robert A. Atkins Jr., *Egalitarian Community: Ethnography and Exegesis* (Tuscaloosa: University of Alabama Press, 1991); Bruce J. Malina, "Early Christian Groups: Using Small Group Formation Theory to Explain Christian Organizations," in *Modelling Early Christianity: Social-Scientific Studies of the New Testament in Its Context*, ed. Philip F. Esler, 96–113 (London: Routledge, 1995); and especially L. Michael White, ed., *Social Networks in the Early Christian Environment: Issues and Methods for Social History* (Semeia 56; Atlanta: Scholars, 1992).

2. Donald Senior and Carroll Stuhlmueller, *The Biblical Foundations for Mission* (Maryknoll, NY: Orbis, 1983), 185.

3. See, in general, Richard A. Horsley, ed., *Paul and Empire: Religion and Power in Roman Imperial Society* (Harrisburg, PA: Trinity Press International, 1997), especially part IV, "Building an Alternative Society." On Paul's message as counterimperial, see N. T. Wright, "Paul's Gospel and Caesar's Empire," in *Paul and Politics: Ekklesia, Israel, Imperium, Interpretation*, ed. Richard A. Horsley (Harrisburg, PA: Trinity Press International), 160–83; Neil Elliott, "The Apostle Paul's Self-Presentation as Anti-Imperial Performance," in *Paul and the Roman Imperial Order*, ed. Richard A. Horsley, 67–88 (Harrisburg, PA: Trinity Press International, 2004); and Neil Elliott, *The Arrogance of Nations: Reading Romans in the Shadow of Empire* (Minneapolis: Fortress Press, 2008).

4. The problems that arose among believers in Galatia and Corinth indicate that Paul's evaluation of the ability of congregations to function on their own may at times have been too optimistic. At other times, he was forced to end his ministry abruptly and leave before he wanted to; see 1 Thess 2:1-2 on his time in Philippi and 1 Thess 2:13-20 on his time in Thessalonica.

5. Günther Bornkamm wrote that Philippi stands for Macedonia, Thessalonica for Macedonia and Achaia, Corinth for Achaia, and Ephesus for Asia. *Paul*, trans. D. M. G. Stalker (New York: Harper & Row, 1971), 53–54.

6. Arland J. Hultgren, "The Scriptural Foundations for Paul's Mission to the Gentiles," in *Paul and His Theology*, ed. Stanley E. Porter (Pauline Studies 3; Leiden: Brill, 2006), 27.

7. For studies of the word *ekklēsia*, see *"ekklēsia,"* BDAG 303–4; K. L. Schmidt, *"ekklēsia,"* *TDNT* 3:501–36; Jürgen Roloff, *"ekklēsia,"* *EDNT* 1.410–15; Lothar Coenen, "Church, synagogue," *NIDNTT* 1:291–307. For statements that envision a worldwide or *kosmos*-wide church (that is, earthly and heavenly), see the deuteropauline documents Colossians (1:18, 24) and Ephesians (1:22-23; 3:8-10, 20-21; 5:23-32).

8. Roger W. Gehring points also to the role of the household in the ministry of Jesus and his disciples. *House Church and Mission: The Importance of Household Structures in Early Christianity* (Peabody, MA: Hendrickson, 2004), 28–61.

9. See above, ch. 4.

10. Jerome Murphy-O'Connor, *St. Paul's Corinth: Texts and Archaeology* (3rd ed.; Collegeville, MN: Liturgical Press, 2002), 178–82; Murphy-O'Connor, "The Corinth That Saint Paul Saw," *Biblical Archaeologist* 47 (1984): 147–59; Gehring, *House Church and Mission*, 140–41 (and the literature cited there), 290; Peter Oakes, *Reading Romans in Pompeii: Paul's Letter at Ground Level* (Minneapolis: Fortress Press), 81; see his book for detailed arguments on the kinds of people who would have comprised house churches.

11. The term *insula* is also used to refer to a square or rectangular block that could contain apartment buildings, a *domus* or two, shops, and/or factories.

12. So Peter Lampe, *From Paul to Valentinus: Christians at Rome in the First Two Centuries*, trans. Michael Steinhauser (Minneapolis: Fortress Press, 2003). For a survey and discussion on the shift in scholarship, see David L. Balch, "Rich Pompeiian Houses, Shops for Rent, and the Huge Apartment Building in Herculaneum as Typical Spaces for Pauline House Churches," *JSNT* 27 (2004): 27–46. Gehring, *House Church and Mission*, 148–49, argues against house churches in the tenements (*insulae*), as the spaces there were too small. The literature on house churches is voluminous. Among the many resources are Floyd Filson, "The Significance of the Early House Churches," *JBL* 58 (1939): 105–12; Vincent P. Branick, *The House Church in the Writings of Paul* (Zacchaeus Studies: New Testament; Wilmington, DE: Michael Glazier, 1982); David L. Balch, "Paul, Families, and Households," in *Paul in the Greco-Roman World: A Handbook*, ed. J. Paul Sampley, 258–92 (Harrisburg, PA: Trinity Press International, 2003); Carolyn Osiek and Margaret Y. MacDonald, with Janet H. Tulloch, *A Woman's Place: House Churches in Earliest Christianity* (Minneapolis: Fortress Press, 2006). Gehring provides a history of research on the house church (1–26) and has an extensive section on "The Use of Houses in Pauline Missional Outreach" (119–228).

13. Joseph Hellerman, *The Ancient Church as Family* (Minneapolis: Fortress Press, 2001), 4. On potential origins of the fictive kinship idea, including the thought of Jesus, see 59–91 and his *Jesus and the People of God: Reconfiguring Ethnic Identity* (Sheffield: Sheffield Phoenix, 2007). For introductions to fictive kinship, see David M. Bossman, "Paul's Fictive Kinship Movement," *BTB* 26 (1996): 163–71; S. Scott Bartchy, "Undermining Ancient Patriarchy: The Apostle Paul's Vision of a Society of Siblings," *BTB* 29 (1999): 68–78; and Walter F. Taylor Jr., "The Lord's Supper as a Meal of Siblings," in *Raising Up a Faithful Exegete: Essays in Honor of Richard D. Nelson*, ed. K. L. Noll and Brooks Schramm, 325–39 (Winona Lake, IN: Eisenbrauns, 2010). On kinship and marriage in antiquity, see Bruce J. Malina, *The New Testament World: Insights from Cultural Anthropology* (3rd ed.; Louisville: Westminster John Knox, 2001), 134–60; and Halvor Moxnes, ed., *Constructing Early Christian Families: Family as Social Reality and Metaphor* (London: Routledge & Kegan Paul, 1997).

14. On the emperor and Paul as each *paterfamilias*, see Stephan J. Joubert, "Managing the Household: Paul as *paterfamilias* of the Christian Household Group in Corinth," in Esler, *Modelling Early Christianity*, 213–23.

15. See above, ch. 3.

16. See above, ch. 3.

17. For more, see Aasgaard's summary of what it meant in the ancient Mediterranean area to be a sibling. Reidar Aasgaard, "'Brotherly Advice': Christian Siblingship and New Testament Paraenesis," in *Early Christian Paraenesis in Context*, ed. James Starr and Troels Engberg-Pedersen (BZNW 125; Berlin: de Gruyter, 2004), 244. Hellerman provides a similar list of responsibilities. Hellerman, *The Ancient Church*, 43–50. For more on reciprocity in the Pauline communities, see these articles by Walter F. Taylor Jr.: "Obligation: Paul's Foundation for Ethics," *TSR* 19.2 (Fall/Winter 1997): 91–112 (another version is published in *Josephinum Journal of Theology* 5, no. 1 [Winter/Spring 1998]: 5–25); "Reciprocity, Siblings, and Paul: Why Act Ethically?" *Lutheran Theological Journal* (Adelaide, South Australia) 39, nos. 2–3 (August and December 2005): 181–95; and "The Lord's Supper."

18. Elisabeth Schüssler Fiorenza, "The Study of Women in Early Christianity: Some Methodological Considerations," in *Critical History and Biblical Faith: New Testament Perspectives*, ed. Thomas J. Ryan, 46–49 (Villanova, PA: Villanova University, 1979); Schüssler Fiorenza, *In Memory of Her* (London: SCM, 1983), 147–51. Bartchy has raised questions about applying the language of equality to family life. "Undermining Ancient Patriarchy," 77.

19. N. T. Wright, *Paul: In Fresh Perspective* (Minneapolis: Fortress Press, 2005), 165.

20. Halvor Moxnes, "The Quest for Honor and the Unity of the Community in Romans 12 and in the Orations of Dio Chrysostom," in *Paul in His Hellenistic Context*, ed. Troels Engberg-Pedersen (Minneapolis: Fortress Press, 1995), 225; see also Taylor, "Obligation," 100–101. For the application of similar insights to Philippians and 1 Corinthians, see Bartchy, "Undermining Ancient Patriarchy," 71–72.

21. Richard S. Ascough, *What Are They Saying about the Formation of Pauline Churches?* (New York: Paulist, 1998), 9.

22. Ibid., 97–98. For a history of the scholarship on voluntary associations and the early church, see 71–94. Already in the second and third centuries, Christians and non-Christians saw the similarities between churches and voluntary associations (79, 84).

23. Ibid., 75, quoting C. H. Roberts, T. C. Skeat, and A. D. Nock, "The Guild of Zeus Hypsistos," *HTR* 29 (1936): 75.

24. John S. Kloppenborg, "*Collegia* and *Thiasoi*: Issues in Function, Taxonomy and Membership," in *Voluntary Associations in the Graeco-Roman World*, ed. John S. Kloppenborg and Steven G. Wilson (London: Routledge, 1996), 18. See also John E. Stambaugh and David L. Balch, *The New Testament in Its Social Environment* (Library of Early Christianity; Philadelphia: Westminster, 1986), 125–26. Funerary associations provided a decent burial for their members and at times also honored the deceased on the anniversaries of their deaths.

25. In addition to the resources already cited, see E. A. Judge, *The Social Pattern of Christian Groups in the First Century: Some Prolegomena to the Study of New Testament Ideas of Social Obligation* (London: Tyndale, 1969); Philip Harland, *Associations, Synagogues, and Congregations: Claiming a Place in Ancient Mediterranean Society* (Minneapolis: Fortress Press, 2003); John S. Kloppenborg, "Associations in the Ancient World," in *The Historical Jesus in Context*, ed. Amy-Jill Levine, Dale C. Allison, and John Dominic Crossan, 323–38 (Princeton, NJ: Princeton University Press, 2006); Alicia Batten, "The Moral World of Greco-Roman Associations," in *SR* 36 (2007): 133–49.

26. For Robert L. Wilken, this difference makes early churches more like philosophical schools than associations; ultimately, he identifies the church as a combination of the two. See his "Collegia, Philosophical Schools and Theology," in *The Catacombs and the Colosseum: The Roman Empire as the Setting of Primitive Christianity*, ed. Stephen Benko and John J. O'Rourke, 268–91 (Valley Forge, PA: Judson, 1971); and *The Christians as the Romans Saw Them* (New Haven: Yale University Press, 1984).

27. The term may also refer to a "guild" hall or meeting place for a *collegium*; see Wayne A. Meeks, *The First Urban Christians: The Social World of the Apostle* (2nd ed.; New Haven: Yale University Press, 2003), 223, n. 44.

28. Ibid., 26.

29. The second translation is from BDAG.
30. Stanley K. Stowers, "Social Status, Public Speaking and Private Teaching: The Circumstances of Paul's Preaching Activity," *NovT* 26 (1984): 68.
31. Elliott, "The Apostle Paul's Self-Presentation," 72, 68; see Rom 1:15-16.
32. For a re-created outline of the basic structure of Paul's preaching, see Calvin J. Roetzel, *Paul: The Man and the Myth* (Minneapolis: Fortress Press, 1999), 66, based in part on the work of C. H. Dodd.
33. See above, pp. 60–62.
34. Michele George, "Domestic Architecture and Household Relations: Pompeii and Roman Ephesos," *JSNT* 27 (2004): 7–25; also Balch, "Rich Pompeiian Houses," 28–29.
35. Gehring, *House Church and Mission*, 188.
36. Ibid., 188–89, 293.
37. Elliott, "The Apostle Paul's Self-Presentation," 73; see 1 Cor 4:20-21.
38. For more, see ibid., 82–83.
39. On "apostolic *parousia*" (that is, apostolic presence) as a discrete literary unit, see Robert W. Funk, "The Apostolic *Parousia*: Form and Significance," in *Christian History and Interpretation: Studies Presented to John Knox*, ed. W. R. Farmer, C. F. D. Moule, and R. R. Niebuhr, 249–68 (Cambridge: Cambridge University Press, 1967), with modifications suggested by L. Ann Jervis, *The Purpose of Romans: A Comparative Letter Structure Investigation* (JSNTSup 55 [Sheffield: Sheffield Academic, 1991], 455. Acts records a number of nurturing visits by Paul to congregations he had founded (14:21-23; 15:36, 41; 16:1-5; 18:23; 20:1-3a).
40. On Paul's network of associates, see the series "Paul's Social Network: Brothers and Sisters in Faith," published in Collegeville, MN, by Liturgical Press: Richard S. Ascough, *Lydia: Paul's Cosmopolitan Hostess*, 2009; Joan Cecilia Campbell, *Phoebe: Patron and Emissary*, 2009; Patrick J. Hartin, *Apollos: Paul's Partner or Rival?*, 2009; Marie Noël Keller, *Priscilla and Aquila: Paul's Coworkers in Christ Jesus*, 2010; Karl Allen Kuhn, *Luke: The Elite Evangelist*, 2010; Bruce J. Malina, *Timothy: Paul's Closest Associate*, 2008; John J. Pilch, *Stephen: Paul and the Hellenist Israelites*, 2008; Ken Stenstrup, *Titus: Honoring the Gospel of God*, 2010; Michael Trainor, *Epaphras: Paul's Educator at Colossae*, 2008.
41. Stanley K. Stowers, "Greek and Latin Letters," *ABD* 4:290.
42. See Funk, "The Apostolic *Parousia*."
43. So ibid., 258.
44. Margaret Mitchell, "New Testament Envoys in the Context of Greco-Roman Diplomatic and Epistolary Conventions: The Example of Timothy and Titus," *JBL* 111 (1992): 642. One indication of the significance of the letters for Paul is their length. D. A. Carson and Douglas J. Moo remark, "Cicero wrote 776 letters, ranging in length from 22 to 2,530 words; Seneca 124 letters, from 149 to 4,134 words in length; Paul averages 1,300 words in length, and Romans has 7,114," *An Introduction to the New Testament* (2nd ed.; Grand Rapids: Zondervan, 2005), 332–34.
45. Stanley K. Stowers points to more than 9,000 Christian letters from antiquity. *Letter Writing in Greco-Roman Antiquity* (Library of Early Christianity; Philadelphia: Westminster Press, 1986), 15.
46. Ibid.
47. On letters in antiquity, see William G. Doty, *Letters in Primitive Christianity* (GBS: NT; Philadelphia: Fortress Press, 1973); Stowers, *Letter Writing*; Stowers, *ABD* 4:290–93.
48. Adolf Deissmann, "Prolegomena to the Biblical Letters and Epistles," in his *Bible Studies*, trans. Alexander Grieve, 1–59 (Edinburgh: T & T Clark, 1901; repr. ed., Peabody, MA: Hendrickson, 1988), esp. 42–49; Deissmann, *Paul: A Study in Social and Religious History*, trans. William E. Wilson (New York: Harper, 1957), 9–15.
49. Even in the case of Romans, note in chapter 16 all the people Paul knows.
50. M. Luther Stirewalt Jr., *Paul, the Letter Writer* (Grand Rapids: Eerdmans, 2003).
51. Ibid., 8, 19.

52. Ibid., 33–34, 37, 46. See also Sean A. Adams, "Paul's Letter Opening and Greek Epistolography: A Matter of Relationship," in *Paul and the Ancient Letter Form*, ed. Stanley E. Porter and Sean A. Adams, 33–55 (Leiden: Brill, 2010).

53. For descriptions of the wide variety of letters authored in Paul's world, see Stowers, *Letter Writing*, 49–173; David E. Aune, *The New Testament in Its Literary Environment* (Library of Early Christianity; Philadelphia: Westminster, 1987), 160–72; Hans-Josef Klauck, *Ancient Letters and the New Testament: A Guide to Context and Exegesis* (Waco, TX: Baylor University Press, 2006), 9–42, 67–297. For a collection of letters, see John L. White, *Light from Ancient Letters* (FF: NT; Philadelphia: Fortress Press, 1986).

54. For more on thanksgivings, see Paul Schubert, *Form and Function of the Pauline Thanksgivings* (BZNW 20; Berlin: Töpelmann, 1939); Peter T. O'Brien, *Introductory Thanksgivings in the Letters of Paul* (NovTSup 49; Leiden: Brill, 1977).

55. On the body of the letter, see John L. White, *The Form and Function of the Body of the Greek Letter: A Study of the Letter-Body in the Non-Literary Papyri and in Paul the Apostle* (SBLDS 2; Missoula, MT: Scholars, 1972).

56. On ethical instruction, see Abraham J. Malherbe, *Moral Exhortation: A Greco-Roman Source Book* (Philadelphia: Westminster, 1986).

57. For more on the conclusions to Paul's letters, see Jeffrey A. D. Weima, *Neglected Endings: The Significance of the Pauline Letter Closings* (JSNTSup 101; Sheffield: Sheffield Academic Press, 1994). On the fivefold structure as an expansion of the usual structure of ancient letters, see Charles B. Puskas, Jr., *The Letters of Paul: An Introduction* (Collegeville, MN: Liturgical, 1993), 7–8. For more on the basic divisions of Paul's letters, see Calvin J. Roetzel, *The Letters of Paul: Conversations in Context* (5th ed.; Louisville: Westminster John Knox, 2009), 59–72; Roetzel, *Paul*, 81–92.

58. Charles B. Cousar, *The Letters of Paul* (IBT; Nashville: Abingdon, 1996), 36.

59. Ibid., 23.

60. D. L. Stamps, "Rhetoric," *DNTB*, 956; Ben Witherington III, *New Testament Rhetoric: An Introductory Guide to the Art of Persuasion in and of the New Testament* (Eugene, OR: Cascade, 2009), 120–21. For an outline of twentieth-century study of rhetoric, see Burton L. Mack, *Rhetoric and the New Testament* (GBS: NT; Minneapolis: Fortress Press, 1990), 14–21, and for application of rhetoric to the New Testament, see George A. Kennedy, *New Testament Interpretation through Rhetorical Criticism* (Chapel Hill: University of North Carolina Press, 1984).

61. Aristotle, *Rhetorica ad Alexandrum*, trans. H. Rackham (LCL; Cambridge, MA: Harvard University Press, 1937); *Rhetorica ad Herennium*, trans. Harry Caplan (LCL; Cambridge, MA: Harvard University Press, 1954). For brief surveys of the history of ancient rhetoric, see Stamps, "Rhetoric," 953–56; Witherington, *New Testament Rhetoric*, 10–16; G. W. Hansen, "Rhetorical Criticism," *DPL*, 822–26; Mack, *Rhetoric and the New Testament*, 25–48. For a collection of essays on the history, theory, and application of rhetoric both inside and outside the New Testament, see *Handbook of Classical Rhetoric in the Hellenistic Period, 330 B.C.–A.D. 400*, ed. Stanley E. Porter (Leiden: Brill, 2001). On the history of the application of ancient rhetoric to the study of the New Testament, see Klauck, *Ancient Letters*, 221–27; and R. Dean Anderson Jr., *Ancient Rhetorical Theory and Paul* (Leuven: Peeters, 1999).

62. J. A. Weima, "Epistolary Theory," *DNTB*, 327–28; see also Abraham J. Malberbe, "Ancient Epistolary Theorists," *Ohio Journal of Religious Studies* 5 (1977): 3–77; and Malberbe, *Ancient Epistolary Theorists* (Atlanta: Scholars, 1988).

63. Donald A. Russell, ed. and trans., *The Orator's Education; Institutio Oratoria* (LCL; 5 vols.; Cambridge, MA: Harvard University Press, 2001).

64. Witherington, *New Testament Rhetoric*, 5.

65. Aune, *The New Testament in Its Literary Environment*, 12–13.

66. Roetzel, *Paul*, 80. For reservations about the use of rhetoric to study ancient letters, see Weima, "Epistolary Theory," 329; and Carson and Moo, *An Introduction to the New Testament*, 333–34.

67. Based on Quintilian, *Institutio Oratoria* 3.9.1-6.

68. Hans Dieter Betz, *Galatians* (Hermeneia; Philadelphia: Fortress Press, 1979); Robert Jewett, *Romans: A Commentary* (Hermeneia; Minneapolis: Fortress Press, 2007).
69. For more on pathos, see Thomas H. Olbricht and Jerry L. Sumney, eds., *Paul and Pathos* (SBLSymS 16; Atlanta: Society of Biblical Literature, 2001).
70. James W. Aageson, *Written Also for Our Sake: Paul and the Art of Biblical Interpretation* (Louisville: Westminster John Knox, 1993), 130.
71. Moisés Silva, "Old Testament in Paul," *DPL*, 634.
72. For a listing of citations in Paul from Israel's Bible, see ibid., 631. For students who use the Nestle-Aland *Novum Testamentum Graece*, the back of the volume contains IV. *Loci Citati vel Allegati* (citations and allusions); A. *Ex Vetere Testamento*; page numbers vary depending on the printing; the information is readily available to the English reader. For a listing of Paul's quotations from Israel's Bible, see Steve Moyise, *Paul and Scripture: Studying the New Testament Use of the Old Testament* (Grand Rapids: Baker Academic, 2010), 131–32.
73. For exactly that approach, see Moyise, *Paul and Scripture*; in a briefer format, Steve Moyise, *The Old Testament in the New: An Introduction* (Continuum Biblical Studies Series; London: Continuum, 2001), 75–97. Gorman outlines the framework of Paul's vision of God's activity as based on Isaiah 40–66. Michael J. Gorman, *Apostle of the Crucified Lord: A Theological Introduction to Paul and His Letters* (Grand Rapids: Eerdmans, 2004), 63–65; see also J. Ross Wagner, "Isaiah in Romans and Galatians," in *Isaiah in the New Testament*, ed. Steve Moyise and Maarten J. J. Menken, 117–32 (London: T & T Clark, 2005).
74. See Richard B. Hays, *Echoes of Scripture in the Letters of Paul* (New Haven: Yale University Press, 1989), 10–14.
75. Resources on midrash include Gary G. Porton, *Understanding Rabbinic Midrash: Texts and Commentary* (Hoboken, NJ: KTAV, 1985); and Jacob Neusner, *What Is Midrash?* (GBS; Philadelphia: Fortress Press, 1987).
76. Geza Vermes, *The Dead Sea Scrolls in English* (4th ed.; Sheffield: Sheffield Academic Press, 1995), 346.
77. James L. Bailey and Lyle D. Vander Broek have provided a very helpful resource for form criticism. *Literary Forms in the New Testament: A Handbook* (Louisville: Westminster John Knox, 1992).
78. E. Randolph Richards, *The Secretary in the Letters of Paul* (WUNT 2.42; Tübingen: Mohr Siebeck, 1991), 169–71.
79. Jewett, *Romans*, 978–79.
80. E. Randolph Richards, *Paul and First-Century Letter Writing: Secretaries, Composition and Collection* (Downers Grove, IL: InterVarsity, 2004), 55–57.
81. Richards, *The Secretary*, 26–43. He does not think Paul always had access to a secretary with this skill, although Tertius may have been such a person. *First-Century Letter Writing*, 30–31 and n. 57, p. 31. For more on Greek shorthand, see 68–73.
82. Richards, *First-Century Letter Writing*, 91.
83. Stirewalt, *Paul, the Letter Writer*, 24. The bracketed material was added by the author of this textbook.
84. On the range of possibilities, see Richards, *First-Century Letter Writing*, 64–80.
85. For further information on ancient writing, see R. J. Forbes, *Studies in Ancient Technology*, vol. 3 (Leiden: Brill, 1955); André Lemaire, "Writing and Writing Materials," *ABD* 6:999–1008; Christopher A. Rollston, "Writing and Writing Materials," *NIDB* 5:937–38; John L. White, *Light from Ancient Letters*, FF: NT (Philadelphia: Fortress Press, 1986), pp. 213–20; R. J. Williams, "Writing," *IDB* 4:909–21.
86. Ben Witherington III, *Conflict and Community in Corinth: A Socio-Rhetorical Commentary on 1 and 2 Corinthians* (Grand Rapids: Eerdmans, 1995), 37–38.
87. Richards, *The Secretary*, 26–43.
88. David B. Capes, Rodney Reeves, and E. Randolph Richards, *Rediscovering Paul: An Introduction to His World, Letters and Theology* (Downers Grove, IL: IVP Academic, 2007), 70–71.
89. Richards, *First-Century Letter Writing*, 90–91.

90. Stirewalt, *Paul, the Letter Writer*, 14–16.
91. Elliott, "The Apostle Paul's Self-Presentation," 72.
92. It is of note that Acts 15 does not refer to a collection Jerusalem's leaders directed Paul to make. An earlier passage in Acts does mention the need for aid in light of famine (11:27-30).
93. For a discussion of major theories on what happened when Paul arrived with the offering, see Arland J. Hultgren, *Paul's Letter to the Romans: A Commentary* (Grand Rapids: Eerdmans, 2011), 563.
94. Ibid., 558, n. 64.
95. See above, p. 96.
96. On obligation as the basis for interaction with others, see on Philemon below (chapter 12); Taylor, "Obligation"; and Taylor, "Reciprocity, Siblings, and Paul." For a different understanding of how reciprocity and obligation affected Paul's view of the collection, see Stephan Joubert, *Paul as Benefactor: Reciprocity, Strategy and Theological Reflection in Paul's Collection* (WUNT 2.124; Tübingen: Mohr Siebeck, 2000). For the position that Paul's model is an alternative to the patron-client system, see Steven J. Friesen, "Paul and Economics: The Jerusalem Collection as an Alternative to Patronage," in *Paul Unbound: Other Perspectives on the Apostle*, ed. Mark D. Given, 27–54 (Peabody, MA: Hendrickson, 2010).
97. Philip F. Esler, *Conflict and Identity in Romans: The Social Setting of Paul's Letter* (Minneapolis: Fortress Press, 2003), 130; see also 359.
98. David J. Downs prefers different language: the collection is an "ecumenical offering." *The Offering of the Gentiles: Paul's Collection for Jerusalem in Its Chronological, Cultural, and Cultic Contexts* (WUNT 2.248; Tübingen: Mohr Siebeck, 2008), 15, 72. Others who identify the collection as a symbol of unity are Keith F. Nickle, *The Collection: A Study in Paul's Strategy* (SBT 48; London: SCM, 1966), 111–29; and Dieter Georgi, *Remembering the Poor: The History of Paul's Collection for Jerusalem* (Nashville: Abingdon, 1992), 33–42.
99. Wright, *Paul*, 167.
100. Downs, *The Offering of the Gentiles*, 72.
101. Hultgren, "Scriptural Foundations," 44. See also Walter F. Taylor Jr., "Unity/Unity of Humanity," *ABD* 6:746–53.

CHAPTER 6

1. David E. Aune, *The New Testament in Its Literary Environment* (Library of Early Christianity 8; Philadelphia: Westminster, 1987), 203, 206; Luke Timothy Johnson, *The Writings of the New Testament: An Interpretation* (3rd ed.; Minneapolis: Fortress Press, 2010), 251.
2. See above, chapter 5, on deliberative rhetoric; also George A. Kennedy, *New Testament Interpretation through Rhetorical Criticism* (Chapel Hill: University of North Carolina, 1984), 142; and Charles B. Puskas Jr., *The Letters of Paul: An Introduction* (GNS; Collegeville, MN: Liturgical, 1993), 113. Abraham J. Malherbe uses similar language when he styles 1 Thessalonians as an "admonishing letter" or an "encouraging letter." *Ancient Epistolary Theorists* (Atlanta: Scholars, 1988).
3. See S. Scott Bartchy, "Undermining Ancient Patriarchy: The Apostle Paul's Vision of a Society of Siblings," *BTB* 29 (1999): 68–78; Halvor Moxnes, ed., *Constructing Early Christian Families: Family as Social Reality and Metaphor* (London: Routledge, 1997), esp. chs. 8, 10; and Joseph H. Hellerman, *The Ancient Church as Family* (Minneapolis: Fortress Press, 2001). On the Thessalonian church as a voluntary association, see Richard S. Ascough, *Paul's Macedonian Associations: The Social Context of Philippians and 1 Thessalonians* (WUNT 2.161; Tübingen: Mohr Siebeck, 2003).
4. Note that while the NRSV does often translate *adelphoi* as *brothers and sisters*, it also translates the word as *believer, one, another, beloved,* and *comrades*, which lose any familial connection.
5. Paul is without question the main figure of the three, and his point of view is clearly the dominant one (see, for example, 2:1-11, 18; 3:1).

6. In Col 4:16, there is a direction to have the letter read by the original recipients and then to have it taken to the Laodiceans, but the language is not nearly as formal as in 1 Thessalonians. See also Rev 1:3 and 22:18-19, although the language is not the same.

7. On the relationship of 1 Thessalonians and the account in Acts of Paul's ministry in Thessalonica, see Karl P. Donfried, "The Theology of 1 Thessalonians," in Karl P. Donfried and I. H. Marshall, *The Theology of the Shorter Pauline Letters* (New Testament Theology; Cambridge: Cambridge University Press, 1993), 7–9, 66–72.

8. See the description in Aelius Aristides of a hypocritical Cynic in *Discourses* 4, quoted in *Hellenistic Commentary to the New Testament*, ed. M. Eugene Boring, Klaus Berger, and Carsten Colpe (Nashville: Abingdon, 1995), 491.

9. Karl P. Donfried, "The Cults of Thessalonica and the Thessalonian Correspondence," *NTS* 31 (1985): 349–51. For others who take the same position, see Rainer Riesner, *Paul's Early Period: Chronology, Mission Strategy, Theology*, trans. Doug Stott (Grand Rapids: Eerdmans, 1998), 386, nn. 22–24. Robert Jewett and Karl P. Donfried relate the difficulties of the Thessalonian Christ-believers to the cult of Cabirus so prominent in first-century Thessalonica. Jewett, *The Thessalonian Correspondence: Pauline Rhetoric and Millenarian Piety* (Philadelphia: Fortress Press, 1986), 126–32; Donfried, "The Cults of Thessalonica." Archaeological and literary evidence point not only to the Cabirus cult but also to worship of Oriental deities such as Isis, Osiris, and Serapis, as well as the Roman gods and the emperor. Thus, it is possible to see the opponents in 2:14 as Gentiles.

10. The likelihood that Paul is quoting a creed is strengthened by the verb for *rose* (*anestē*). This occurrence is the only time in the undisputed letters that Paul uses the verb for Jesus.

11. Helmut Koester, "Imperial Ideology and Paul's Eschatology in 1 Thessalonians," in *Paul and Empire: Religion and Power in Roman Imperial Society*, ed. Richard A. Horsley (Harrisburg, Pa: Trinity Press International, 1997), 160.

12. Some interpreters have used 4:17 to develop the doctrine called "the rapture." In that teaching, Jesus secretly returns to earth *prior to* the end and raptures or snatches all true believers from this earth so that they will not suffer during the period preceding the final end of the world. Notice in 1 Thessalonians that Paul's concern is with what happens at the very end, at the resurrection. There also is nothing in the text about the suffering of any who are left behind, and the audible events make it hard to imagine the scene as anything other than public. Furthermore, Paul and his fellow believers have not been raptured from suffering, nor does he expect they will be. As Christ-believers, they in fact participate in suffering (3:4; Rom 8:18; 1 Cor 7:26).

13. Koester, "Imperial Ideology and Paul's Eschatology," 162.

14. See Richard J. Cassidy, *Paul in Chains: Roman Imprisonment and the Letters of St. Paul* (New York: Crossroad, 2001). For more on the relationship between 1 Thessalonians and imperial thought, see Peter Oakes, "Re-mapping the Universe: Paul and the Emperor in 1 Thessalonians and Philippians," *JSNT* 27 (2005): 301–22; Warren Carter, *The Roman Empire and the New Testament: An Essential Guide* (Nashville: Abingdon, 2006), 53–56.

15. On the relationship of chapter 2 to Hellenistic philosophers, see the studies by Abraham J. Malherbe: "'Gentle as a Nurse': The Stoic Background to 1 Thess. II," *NovT* 12 (1970): 203–17; Malherbe, *Paul and the Thessalonians: The Philosophic Tradition of Pastoral Care* (Philadelphia: Fortress Press, 1987).

16. Charles A. Wanamaker, *The Epistles to the Thessalonians: A Commentary on the Greek Text* (NIGTC; Grand Rapids: Eerdmans, 1990), 113.

17. Carol J. Schlueter, *Filling Up the Measure: Polemical Hyperbole in I Thessalonians 2:14-16* (JSNTSup 98; Sheffield: JSOT Press, 1994).

18. F. D. Gilliard, "The Problem of the Antisemitic Comma between 1 Thessalonians 2.14 and 15," *NTS* 35 (1989): 481–502.

19. Birger Pearson, "1 Thessalonians 2:13-16: A Deutero-Pauline Interpolation," *HTR* 64 (1971): 79–91.

20. Earl J. Richard, *First and Second Thessalonians* (Sacra Pagina 11; Collegeville, MN: Liturgical, 1995), 127.

21. Donfried, "The Theology of 1 Thessalonians," 69; and Donfried, "Paul and Judaism. 1 Thessalonians 2:13-16 as a Text Case," *Int* 38 (1984): 242–53.

22. On the theory that 2:14 refers to Gentiles rather than Judeans, see n. 9 above.

CHAPTER 7

1. Hans Dieter Betz, *Galatians: A Commentary on Paul's Letter to the Churches in Galatia* (Hermeneia; Philadelphia: Fortress Press, 1979), 47; see n. 39.

2. Cynics used similar language for themselves: "The true cynic . . . must know that he has been sent by Zeus to men, partly as a messenger, in order to show them that in questions of good and evil they have gone astray, and are seeking the true nature of the good and the evil where it is not, but where it is they never think." Epictetus, *Discourses* 3.22.23.

3. The salutation concludes with vss. 3-4: "Grace to you and peace from God our Father and the Lord Jesus Christ, who gave himself for our sins to set us free from the present evil age, according to the will of our God and Father, to whom be the glory forever and ever. Amen." The language of "the present evil age" in 1:4 is apocalyptic language. The opposite of "the present evil age" is, in Galatians, "the new creation" (Gal 6:15; also 2 Cor 5:17). As J. Louis Martyn observes, "As 'the present evil age' stands near the opening of Galatians, so 'the new creation' plays a weighty role at the close, clear indications that the motif of apocalyptic discontinuity is central to Paul's understanding of the gospel in this letter." "The Apocalyptic Gospel in Galatians," *Int* 54 (2000): 253.

4. James D. G. Dunn, *The Theology of Paul the Apostle* (Grand Rapids: Eerdmans, 1998); Mark D. Nanos, *The Mystery of Romans: The Jewish Context of Paul's Letter* (Minneapolis: Fortress Press, 1996).

5. Charles Talbert, "Paul, Judaism, and the Revisionists," *CBQ* 63 (2001): 1–22; Brendan Byrne, "Interpreting Romans Theologically in a Post-'New Perspective' Perspective," *HTR* 94 (2001): 227–41; Byrne, "Interpreting Romans: The New Perspective and Beyond," *Int* 58 (2004): 241–52. For a similar perspective, see also Bruce W. Longenecker, *The Triumph of Abraham's God: The Transformation of Identity in Galatians* (Nashville: Abingdon, 1998).

6. Richard B. Hays, "*PISTIS* and Pauline Christology: What Is at Stake?" SBLSP, ed. Eugene H. Lovering Jr. (Atlanta: Scholars, 1991), 715. See especially his dissertation, *The Faith of Jesus Christ: An Investigation of the Narrative Substructure of Galatians 3:1–4:11* (SBLDS 56; Chico, CA: Scholars, 1983). Others who agree with Hays's position include George Howard, "On the 'Faith of Christ,'" HTR 60 (1967): 459–65; Howard, "The Faith of Christ," *ExpTim* 85 (1974) 212–15; Morna D. Hooker, "*Pistis Christou*," *NTS* 35 (1989): 321–42; Leander E. Keck, "'Jesus' in Romans," *JBL* 108 (1989): 443–60; Stanley K. Stowers, "*Ek pisteo[macron]s* and *tēs pisteōs* in Romans 3:30," *JBL* 108 (1989) 665–74; Frank J. Matera, *Galatians* (Sacra Pagina ; Collegeville, MN: Liturgical, 1992); Charles B. Cousar, *The Letters of Paul* (IBT: Nashville: Abingdon, 1996); and J. Louis Martyn, *Galatians: A New Translation with Introduction and Commentary* (AB 33A; New York: Doubleday, 1997).

7. James D. G. Dunn, "Once More, *PISTIS CHRISTOU*," SBLSP, ed. Eugene H. Lovering Jr., 730–44 (Atlanta: Scholars, 1991). Other scholars who retain the objective genitive interpretation include C. E. B. Cranfield, A Critical and Exegetical Commentary on the Epistle to the Romans (ICC; 2 vols.; Edinburgh: T & T Clark, 1975, 1979); Joseph A. Fitzmyer, Ernst Käsemann, *Commentary on Romans*, trans. Geoffrey W. Bromiley (Grand Rapids: Eerdmans, 1980); Arland J. Hultgren, "The *Pistis Christou* Formulations in Paul," *NovT* 22 (1980) 264–83; Joseph A. Fitzmyer, *Paul and His Theology: A Brief Sketch* (2nd ed.; Englewood Cliffs, NJ: Prentice Hall, 1989); Ulrich Wilckens, *Der Brief an die Römer* (EKK 6; Neukirchen-Vluyn: Neukirchener, 2010); Hultgren, *Paul's Letter to the Romans: A Commentary* (Grand Rapids: Eerdmans, 2011), esp. 623–61.

8. Theologically, scholars such as Hays (see note 9) and Martyn emphasize, in their utilization of the subjective genitive reading, God's action over against humanity's response. They are quite concerned that human faith not be seen as a new "work" by which people seek to save themselves. See J. Louis Martyn, *Galatians: A New Translation with Introduction and Commentary*

(AB 33A; New York: Doubleday, 1997); and Martyn, "The Apocalyptic Gospel in Galatians," 246–66. What they do not factor in is that, for Paul, the believing response itself is a gift of God's Spirit (Gal 5:22). On Gal 5:22, Marion L. Soards explains, "The apostle is saying that *faith itself* is a product of God's Spirit, not something that humans generate. It is not the case that God has acted in Christ, and now, if humans respond to that act with faith, they are saved. Rather, Paul says that part of what God has done in Jesus Christ is to create saving faith in human beings." *The Apostle Paul: An Introduction to His Writings and Teaching* (New York: Paulist, 1987), 64.

9. See the comments by Philip F. Esler, *Galatians* (New Testament Readings; London: Routledge, 1998), 37–38. On 40–53, Esler outlines and applies insights from social-identity theory.

10. For more on the Apostolic Council, see Günther Bornkamm, *Paul*, trans. D. M. G. Stalker (New York: Harper & Row, 1971), 31–42.

11. For more on the difficulties of "mixed table fellowship," see Philip F. Esler, *Galatians*, 93–116.

12. See Jerome H. Neyrey, *Paul, in Other Words: A Cultural Reading of His Letters* (Louisville: Westminster John Knox, 1990), 186–206; John H. Elliott, "Paul, Galatians, and the Evil Eye," *CurTM* 17 (1990): 262–73.

13. In Betz's interpretation, Paul has moved us into a courtroom. The defendant and defense attorney are Paul. The accusers are the Judaizers (Paul's opponents). The jury is composed of the Galatian Christ-believers.

14. Philo, *De Migratione Abrahami*; *De Virtutibus* 39.211-19; *Jubilees* 11.16-17; Josephus, *Antiquitates Judaicae* 1.55 (LCL); *Genesis Rabbah* 30.8, 38.13, 39.1, 48.2, 48.8, 48.9; Babylonian Talmud *Sukka* 49; *Mekilta Neziqin* 18.9-36.

15. Mishna *Qiddušin* 4.14; *2 Apocalypse of Baruch* 57.2; *Canticles Rabbah* 8. See also the comments by Samuel Sandmel, *Philo's Place in Judaism* (augmented ed.; New York: KTAV, 1971), 95.

16. For more on the disciplinarian, consult Ben Witherington III, *Grace in Galatia: A Commentary on Paul's Letter to the Galatians* (Grand Rapids: Eerdmans, 1998), 264–67. This fifth-century-BCE comment by Xenophon is instructive: "When a boy ceases to be a child, and begins to be a lad, others release him from his moral tutor and his schoolmaster: he is then no longer under a ruler and is allowed to go his own way" (*Constitution of the Lacedaemonians* 3.1).

17. Carolyn Osiek stresses that *son* has important implications for being able to inherit and ought not be abandoned too quickly in translation. "Galatians," *The Women's Bible Commentary*, ed. Carol A. Newsom and Sharon H. Ringe (expanded ed.; Louisville: Westminster John Knox, 1998), 424.

18. Exod 4:22-23; Deut 14:1-2; Hos 11:1; see also Sir 36:17 and 3 Macc 6:28.

19. According to Brendan Byrne, the designation in particular refers to the ideal Israel of the end-time. *"Sons of God"—"Seed of Abraham": A Study of the Idea of Sonship of God of All Christians in Paul against the Jewish Background* (Rome: Biblical Institute Press, 1979), 62–63.

20. Rabbi Judah dates from the middle of the second century. Another form occurs in which "slave" replaces "boor" (see Jerusalem Talmud, *Berakot* 13b).

21. Betz, *Galatians*, 189.

22. See the comments by Neyrey, *Paul*, 66–68; on 134, he relates baptism to the "liminal" state that occurs in rituals of status transformation such as baptism. Elisabeth Schüssler Fiorenza sees dramatic ongoing results of the liminal state. "The Praxis of Coequal Discipleship," in *Paul and Empire: Religion and Power in Roman Imperial Society*, ed. Richard A. Horsley, (Harrisburg, PA: Trinity Press International, 1997), 224–41.

23. Bruce Hansen, *"All of You Are One": The Social Vision of Galatians 3.28, 1 Corinthians 12.13 and Colossians 3.11* (Library of New Testament Studies 409; New York: T & T Clark, 2010), esp. 67–106.

24. On slavery, see 1 Cor 7:14-24 and the basic studies by S. Scott Bartchy, *First-Century Slavery and the Interpretation of 1 Corinthians 7:21* (Eugene, OR: Wipf & Stock, 2002); Bartchy, "Slavery (Greco-Roman)," *ABD* 6:65–73.

25. A natural question is "all of you are one" *what* in Christ Jesus? Does Paul imply a noun that should follow the word *one*? One theory is that what is implied is *man/human*—that is, there is one human (*anthrōpos*) in Christ, referring to the idea of Christ as the *one man* in Romans 5 and 1 Corinthians 15. This understanding has the advantage of providing a masculine noun to go with the masculine adjective *one*. Someone familiar with the rest of Paul's writing might easily supply *body*, so there is "one body in Christ Jesus" (see Rom 12:5; 1 Cor 12:12-13). The grammatical problem is that *body* in Greek is neuter, while the word for *one* in Gal 3:28 is masculine. Or one could conclude that no implied noun is meant; believers are simply *one*. For more on the unity of humanity, see Walter F. Taylor Jr., *The Unity of Mankind in Antiquity and in Paul* (Ann Arbor, MI: University Microfilms, 1981); Taylor, "Unity/Unity of Humanity," *ABD* 6:746–53.

26. Martyn identifies in 4:3-5 "the theological center of the entire letter." *Galatians*, 388. He styles God's action outlined in these verses as an apocalyptic invasion in which God has liberated humanity from the powers of this present evil age. "The Apocalyptic Gospel," 255.

27. For an illuminating discussion of Paul's use of feminine imagery for himself, see Beverly Roberts Gaventa, "The Maternity of Paul," in her *Our Mother Saint Paul* (Louisville: Westminster John Knox, 2007), 29–39.

28. This interpretation, based on Martyn, *Galatians*, 431–66, replaces the traditional interpretation that the child of the slave represents Judeans and the child of the free woman represents Christ-believers.

29. And, for that matter, Esler (*Galatians*, 31) argues that there probably were Judeans in the territory of Galatia.

30. For David L. Barr, that is the point: Paul means to insult the Hellenized people of the south by calling them "Galatians." *New Testament Story: An Introduction* (3rd ed.; Belmont, CA: Wadsworth, 2002), 117–18.

31. Among the scholars who argue for the territory hypothesis are Betz, *Galatians*; Raymond E. Brown, *An Introduction to the New Testament* (ABRL; New York: Doubleday, 1997); Bart D. Ehrman, *The New Testament: A Historical Introduction to the Early Christian Writings*, 5th ed. (Oxford: Oxford University Press, 2012); Charles B. Puskas Jr., *The Letters of Paul: An Introduction* (Collegeville, MN: Liturgical, 1993); Philip R. Esler, *Galatians* (New Testament Readings; New York: Routledge, 1998); Soards, *The Apostle Paul*; Martyn, Galatians; and Werner G. Kümmel, *Introduction to the New Testament*, trans. Howeard C. Kee (rev. English ed.; Nashville: Abingdon, 1975). Those who find the province hypothesis more probable include Rainer Riesner, *Paul's Early Period: Chronology, Mission Strategy, Theology*, trans. Doug Stott (Grand Rapids: Eerdmans, 1998); Barr, *New Testament Story*; Witherington, *Grace in Galatia*; and Matera, *Galatians*.

32. In 3:15, Paul says the Galatians would have torn out their eyes for him; in 6:11, he takes the pen from the secretary and writes, "See what large letters I make when I am writing in my own hand!" Are those two statements enough to conclude that Paul had some sort of eye problem and that was what interrupted his journey?

33. Calvin Roetzel, *Paul: The Man and the Myth* (Minneapolis: Fortress Press, 1999), 212, n. 77.

34. On various theories regarding the identity of the opponents, see Hans Dieter Betz, "Galatians, Epistle to the," *ABD* 2:874; and J. C. O'Neill, "Galatians, Letter to the," *Dictionary of Biblical Interpretation*, ed. John H. Hayes, 1:428 (Nashville: Abingdon, 1999).

35. Betz, *Galatians*.

36. On Galatians as deliberative, see Jerome Murphy-O'Connor, *Paul the Letter-Writer: His World, His Options, His Skills* (Collegeville, MN: Liturgical, 1995), 6; George A. Kennedy, *New Testament Interpretation through Rhetorical Criticism* (Chapel Hill: University of North Carolina, 1984),144–45; J. Smit, "The Letter of Paul to the Galatians: A Deliberative Speech," *NTS* 35 (1989): 1–26; and Frank J. Matera, *Galatians* (Sacra Pagina 9; Collegeville, MN: Liturgical, 1992), 11.

37. Martyn, *Galatians*, 21–23. In a similar vein, Martinus C. de Boer thinks Galatians is an "intensely apocalyptic sermon." *Galatians: A Commentary* (NTL; Louisville: Westminster John Knox, 2011), 71.

38. Witherington, *Grace in Galatia*, 25–35.

39. Betz, *Galatians*, 8–9.

40. On freedom in antiquity, see Hans Dieter Betz, *Paul's Concept of Freedom in the Context of Hellenistic Discussions about the Possibilities of Human Freedom* (Protocol Series of the Colloquies of the Center for Hermeneutical Studies in Hellenistic and Modern Culture 26; Berkeley: Center for Hermeneutical Studies in Hellenistic and Modern Culture, 1977).

41. On the source of such lists in Hellenism, see the discussion of "Forms and Traditions," pp. 110–11. A good example of such lists is found in Diogenes Laertius, *Lives of Eminent Philosophers*, "Zeno," 7.

42. Notice the negative and graphic statements about circumcision in these two chapters (5:2, 4, 6, 12; 6:13-14). Verse 6:17 may also allude to circumcision (Paul carries the true marks of Jesus; the opponents, implicitly, have only the marks from their circumcision).

43. Note Paul's positive use of *Law*. For Paul, the full meaning of the Law can be found only in Christ. Thus, the Law still functions as a norm for believers but only as interpreted through the life, death, and resurrection of Jesus.

44. See Luther's classic statement: "A Christian is a perfectly free lord of all, subject to none. A Christian is a perfectly dutiful servant of all, subject to all." "The Freedom of a Christian," in *Luther's Works*, ed. Harold J. Grimm (Philadelphia: Muhlenberg, 1957), 31:344.

45. Martyn has an extensive discussion on the relationship between Galatians and the collection. *Galatians*, 222–28.

CHAPTER 8

1. Greece did not exist as a political entity in the first century CE. Achaia was the southern province in what had been Greece, and Macedonia was the northern province.

2. Not all of Paul's correspondence with Corinth has survived. In 1 Cor 5:9, he refers to a letter earlier than 1 Corinthians that no longer exists. We have no correspondence from Corinth to Paul.

3. See the earlier discussion on the Gallio inscription, pp. 36–37.

4. On economic and other benefits, see Anthony C. Thiselton, *The First Epistle to the Corinthians: A Commentary on the Greek Text* (NIGTC; Grand Rapids: Eerdmans, 2000), 10–11; and Victor Paul Furnish, "Corinth in Paul's Time: What Can Archaeology Tell Us," *BAR* 14 (1988): 23–25. On the archaeology of Corinth, see Jerome Murphy-O'Connor, *St. Paul's Corinth: Texts and Archaeology* (3rd ed.; Collegeville, MN: Liturgical, 2002); Murphy-O'Connor, "The Corinth That Saint Paul Saw," *BA* 47 (1984): 147–59; Murphy-O'Connor, "Corinth," *ABD* 1:1134–39; Furnish, "Corinth in Paul's Time," 14–27; Donald W. Engels, *Roman Corinth: An Alternative Model for the Classical City* (Chicago: University of Chicago Press, 1990); and Sherman E. Johnson, *Paul the Apostle and His Cities* (Wilmington, DE: Glazier, 1987), 94–105.

5. The canal that today joins the two seas was not finished until 1893.

6. So Strabo, *Geography* 8.6.20, writing in 7 BCE. On Corinth's economic status, see Furnish, "Corinth in Paul's Time," 17–19.

7. Richard Wallace and Wynne Williams discuss Roman colonies in *The Three Worlds of Paul of Tarsus* (London: Routledge, 1998), 87–91.

8. Paul Barnett, *The Second Epistle to the Corinthians* (NICNT; Grand Rapids: Eerdmans, 1997), 4.

9. See Daniel N. Schowalter and Steven J. Friesen, eds., *Urban Religion in Roman Corinth: Interdisciplinary Approaches* (HTS 53; Cambridge: Harvard University Press, 2005).

10. Raymond F. Collins, *First Corinthians* (Sacra Pagina 7; Collegeville, MN: Liturgical, 1999), 22; Furnish, "Corinth in Paul's Time," 16; Murphy-O'Connor, *St. Paul's Corinth*, 78–79.

11. Hans Conzelmann, *1 Corinthians*, trans. James W. Leitch (Hermeneia; Philadelphia: Fortress Press, 1975), 12, n. 97.

12. The Greek is *ethnē*, which can also be translated "Gentiles" or "nations."

13. That is exactly why Celsus, writing in the second century CE, condemns Christians. Origen, *Against Celsus* 3.44, 59, 64.

14. Justin J. Meggitt states the opposing view in "The Social Status of Erastus (Rom. 16:23)," *NovT* 38 (1996): 218–23.

15. Gerhard E. Lenski, *Power and Privilege: A Theory of Social Stratification* (New York: McGraw-Hill, 1966), 219, 243–45, 248–85; Walter F. Taylor Jr., "Cultural Anthropology as a Tool for Studying the New Testament—Part I," *TSR* 18 (1996): 22. For a summary discussion of theories regarding the social classes of early believers, see Walter F. Taylor Jr., "Sociological Exegesis: Introduction to a New Way to Study the Bible—Part II," *TSR* 12 (1990): 29–34. For a discussion of the social composition of Pauline and post-Pauline communities, see Ekkehard W. Stegemann and Wolfgang Stegemann, *The Jesus Movement: A Social History of Its First Century*, trans. O. C. Dean Jr. (Minneapolis: Fortress Press, 1999), 288–316.

16. Hans Dieter Betz and Margaret M. Mitchell, "Corinthians, First Epistle to the," *ABD* 1:1146.

17. Richard B. Hays, *First Corinthians* (Interpretation; Louisville: John Knox, 1997), 4, 11–12. On the concept of resocialization, see Ben Witherington III, *Conflict and Community in Corinth: A Socio-Rhetorical Commentary on 1 and 2 Corinthians* (Grand Rapids: Eerdmans, 1995), 8–9 and n. 21.

18. Murphy-O'Connor, *St. Paul's Corinth*, 178–82.

19. See pp. 96–97.

20. For an outline of the correspondence between Paul and Corinth, see chapter 9.

21. Collins, *First Corinthians*, 4.

22. Betz and Mitchell, "Corinthians," *ABD* 1:1141.

23. For example, John Drane, *Introducing the New Testament* (3rd ed.; Minneapolis: Fortress Press, 2011), 323–25. For a critique of that position, see Werner Georg Kümmel, *Introduction to the New Testament*, trans. Howard C. Kee (rev. English ed.; Nashville: Abingdon, 1975), 272–74.

24. The staunchest defender of that position is Walter Schmithals, *Gnosticism in Corinth*, trans. John E. Steely (Nashville: Abingdon, 1971); and Schmithals, "The *Corpus Paulinum* and Gnosis," in *The New Testament and Gnosis*, ed. A. H. B. Logan and A. J. M. Wedderburn, 107–24 (Edinburgh: T & T Clark, 1983). See also Kümmel, *Introduction to the New Testament*, 274–75.

25. See above, pp. 73–75. Elaine H. Pagels investigates how later Gnostics used Paul's letters. *The Gnostic Paul: Gnostic Exegesis of the Pauline Letters* (Philadelphia: Fortress, 1975).

26. Margaret M. Mitchell, *Paul and the Rhetoric of Reconciliation: An Exegetical Investigation of the Language and Composition of 1 Corinthians* (HUT 28; Tübingen: Mohr Siebeck, 1991).

27. Betz and Mitchell, "Corinthians," *ABD* 1:1141.

28. Collins, *First Corinthians*, 19; Mitchell, *Paul and the Rhetoric of Reconciliation*, 20–64.

29. Charles B. Puskas Jr., *The Letters of Paul: An Introduction* (Collegeville, MN: Liturgical, 1993), 62–63.

30. Witherington, *Conflict and Community in Corinth*, 46. For similarities between 1 Corinthians and letters of morality, friendship, and recommendation, see Collins, *First Corinthians*, 6–10.

31. Thiselton, *The First Epistle to the Corinthians*, 334.

32. So, too, Hays, *First Corinthians*, 5. Collins says as early as 53–54 and certainly before 57 (*First Corinthians*, 23–24); Kümmel argues for spring of 54–55 (*Introduction to the New Testament*, 279); Thiselton, for 54–55 (*The First Epistle to the Corinthians*, 32).

33. See especially Johannes Weiss, *Der erste Korintherbrief* (9th ed.; repr.; Göttingen: Vandenhoeck & Ruprecht, 1970); and Schmithals, *Gnosticism in Corinth*. Udo Schnelle summarizes partition theories and arguments in *The History and Theology of the New Testament Writings*, trans. M. Eugene Boring (Minneapolis: Fortress Press, 1998), 62–64.

34. Important arguments for the literary unity of 1 Corinthians are made by John C. Hurd, *The Origin of I Corinthians* (new ed.; Macon, GA: Mercer University Press, 1983); and Mitchell, *Paul and the Rhetoric of Reconciliation*.

35. On them, see above under Section F.

36. Charles B. Cousar gives a fine exposition of what theology of the cross means. *A Theology of the Cross: The Death of Jesus in the Pauline Letters* (OBT; Minneapolis: Fortress Press, 1990), esp. 1–9.

37. For more on flesh, see this book's chapter 10, on Romans.

38. Jerome H. Neyrey argues that Paul transferred Israel's sense of sacred space (the temple in Jerusalem) to the Christian community. *Paul in Other Words: A Cultural Reading of His Letters* (Louisville: Westminster John Knox, 1990), 50.

39. Ronald F. Hock argues that Paul's work as a leatherworker was an indication to the Corinthians that he was weak, that is, socially inferior. *The Social Context of Paul's Ministry: Tentmaking and Apostleship* (Philadelphia: Fortress Press, 1980), 60.

40. Elsewhere, Paul uses similar language: 1 Cor 11:1; Phil 3:17; 4:9; 1 Thess 1:6.

41. On the flesh-body distinction, see chapter 10, on Romans.

42. At this point, the Corinthians were heirs to a major strand of Greek tradition in which the mortal, physical body was seen as separable from the immortal soul. The tradition goes back at least to Socrates, as contained in Plato (*Phaedo* 64C-E, 70-77, 105E, 114C), and included a sharp antithesis between the physical and the spiritual. Gnosticism was based on that antithesis. In Paul's thought, the body and soul were not set in opposition to each other, which meant that when the body ceases functioning, so does the soul. On body-soul thought in Paul, see Walter F. Taylor Jr., "Humanity, NT View of," *ABD* 3:323.

43. S. Scott Bartchy, *First-Century Slavery and the Interpretation of 1 Corinthians 7:21* (Eugene, OR: Wipf & Stock, 2002), 155–59. On the fact that the slave's body was at the disposal of others, see Jennifer A. Glancy, *Slavery in Early Christianity* (Minneapolis: Fortress Press, 2006).

44. On the availability of meat and meals that took place in the temple of Asclepius, see Murphy-O'Connor, *St. Paul's Corinth*, 186–91; on the sociological issues, see Gerd Theissen, *The Social Setting of Pauline Christianity: Essays on Corinth*, trans. John H. Schütz (Philadelphia: Fortress Press, 1982), 125–32. For an explanation of animal sacrifice, see John E. Stambaugh and David L. Balch, *The New Testament in Its Social Environment* (Library of Early Christianity; Philadelphia: Westminster, 1986), 128–29.

45. Robin Scroggs, "Paul and the Eschatological Woman," *JAAR* 40 (1972): 283–303; Scroggs, "Paul and the Eschatological Woman: Revisited," *JAAR* 42 (1974): 532–37.

46. On 1 Cor 11:17-34 and meals in antiquity, see Theissen, *The Social Setting of Pauline Christianity*, 145–74; and Stegemann and Stegemann, *The Jesus Movement*, 283–84.

47. In 10:16-17, Paul emphasizes the participation (*koinōnia*) in the blood and body of Christ that comes through the cup and the bread.

48. The accounts in Matthew 26:26-29, Mark 14:22-25, and Luke 22:19-20 were written later than 1 Corinthians.

49. A better way to translate *diakoniōn* might be *ministries*.

50. On the gift of tongues as a form of trance, see Neyrey, *Paul in Other Words*, 28–29.

51. In the Hellenistic world, the body was a common metaphor for the city, used to explain the interdependence of the city's inhabitants. The most famous example is the fable of Menenius Agrippa in Livy, *History of Rome*, 2.32.9-12.

52. On the possible relationship between Paul's use of the body-parts image and the offerings to the gods of replicas of various body parts, see Murphy-O'Connor, *St. Paul's Corinth*, 190–91.

53. See Conzelmann, *1 Corinthians*, 246.

54. In addition to Conzelmann, also Gordon D. Fee, *The First Epistle to the Corinthians* (NICNT; Grand Rapids: Eerdmans, 1987), 699–705; Richard B. Hays, *First Corinthians* (Interpretation; Louisville: John Knox, 1997), 248. See them for other theories as well.

55. See Charles B. Cousar, *A Theology of the Cross*, 93, n. 6, for a good summary of the opponents' position.

56. J. Christiaan Beker writes, "In terms of their theology, then, a resurrection of the dead (that is, a resurrection of dead bodies) is both disgusting (because the body is inimical to salvation) and superfluous, and unnecessary (because our present spiritual union with Christ constitutes the redemption of our true self)." *The Triumph of God: The Essence of Paul's Thought* (Minneapolis: Fortress Press, 1990), 72.

57. Exod 23:16, 19; Lev 23:10; Num 18:8, 12.

58. See Thiselton, *The First Epistle to the Corinthians*, 1276–81; and N. T. Wright, *The Resurrection of the Son of God*, vol. 3, *Christian Origins and the Question of God* (Minneapolis: Fortress Press, 2003), 348–52.

59. On the relationship between their beliefs and their actions, see Neyrey, *Paul in Other Words*, 140–41.

60. See above, chapter 5, pp. 120–23.

CHAPTER 9

1. See p. 170.

2. Victor Paul Furnish, *II Corinthians* (AB 32A; Garden City, NY: Doubleday, 1984), 30.

3. See the comments by Furnish, *II Corinthians*, 31; Margaret E. Thrall, *The Second Epistle to the Corinthians* (ICC; Edinburgh: T & T Clark, 1994), 1:6.

4. Charles B. Puskas Jr. seeks to account for the different tones and the break in narrative by means of rhetorical analysis. *The Letters of Paul: An Introduction* (GNS; Collegeville, MN: Liturgical, 1993), 57. Ralph P. Martin points to linguistic connections between 7:4 and 7:5-16. *2 Corinthians* (WBC 40; Waco: Word, 1986), xliii.

5. Attempts to identify 6:14—7:1 with the lost letter of 1 Cor 5:9 are intriguing. There we read, "I wrote to you in my letter not to associate with sexually immoral persons"; 2 Cor 6:14—7:1 calls for separation from unbelievers. But the 1 Corinthians passage goes on, "Not at all meaning the immoral of this world, or the greedy and robbers, or idolaters, since you would then need to go out of the world. But now I am writing to you not to associate with anyone who bears the name of brother or sister who is sexually immoral or greedy, or is an idolater, reviler, drunkard, or robber. Do not even eat with such a one" (1 Cor 5:10-11). Paul's concern in 1 Corinthians is separation from corrupt believers, not separation from unbelievers. The latter is the concern of 2 Cor 6:14—7:1.

6. *Mismatched* and *partnership* (6:14); *agreement* and *Beliar* (6:15); *agreement* (a different Greek word from 6:15) and *walk among* (6:16); *welcome* (6:17); *defilement* (7:1). In addition, *Almighty* (6:18) and *cleanse* (7:1) do not occur elsewhere in the undisputed letters of Paul.

7. See Joseph A. Fitzmyer, "Qumran and the Interpolated Paragraph in 2 Corinthians 6:14-17," *CBQ* 23 (1961): 271–80; Hans Dieter Betz, "2 Cor 6:14—7:1: An Anti-Pauline Fragment?" *JBL* 92 (1973): 88–108; and Betz, "Corinthians, Second Epistle to the," *ABD* 1:1150. Betz sees the origin of the section in Judean Christianity, perhaps even among Paul's opponents. As Szekar Wan writes, "The unqualified dualistic language of light and darkness, believers versus unbelievers, God and idols, cleanliness and defilement, and finally body and spirit does not find a place in Paul, but is much more characteristic of the Qumran sectarians." *Power in Weakness: The Second Letter of Paul to the Corinthians* (NTC; Harrisburg, PA: Trinity Press International, 2000), 98.

8. See pp. 120–23.

9. George A. Kennedy, *New Testament Interpretation through Rhetorical Criticism* (Chapel Hill: University of North Carolina Press, 1984), 91–92.

10. Hans Dieter Betz, *2 Corinthians 8 and 9* (Hermeneia; Philadelphia: Fortress Press, 1985).

11. Martin, *2 Corinthians*, xliii.

12. Furnish, *II Corinthians*, 34. On the history of scholarship see Victor Paul Furnish, "Corinthians, Second Letter to the," in *Dictionary of Biblical Interpretation*, ed. John H. Hayes, 1:224–26 (Nashville: Abingdon, 1999); and Betz, *2 Corinthians 8 and 9*, 3–36.

13. Johann Salomo Semler, *Paraphrasis II. Epistulae ad Corinthos. Accessit Latina vetus translatio et lectionum varietas* (Halle: C. H. Hemmerde, 1776); F. F. Bruce, *1 and 2 Corinthians* (rev. ed.; NCB; Grand Rapids: Eerdmans, 1980); C. K. Barrett, *2 Corinthians* (HNTC; New York: Harper & Row, 1973); Furnish, *II Corinthians*; Martin, *2 Corinthians*.

14. Thrall, *The Second Epistle to the Corinthians*.

15. Furnish, *II Corinthians*, 45.

16. Raymond E. Brown discusses and dismisses the theory that chapters 10–13 are an addendum written in response to new and disturbing news from Corinth and included by Paul after he had written 1–9 but before he had sent it. *An Introduction to the New Testament* (ABRL; New York: Doubleday, 1997), 550. The Achilles heel of that position is why, then, Paul does not refer to the new information that occasioned his writing the addendum.

17. Adolf Hausrath, *Der Vier-Capitel-Brief des Paulus an die Korinther* (Heidelberg: Fr. Bassermann, 1870); Alfred Plummer, *A Critical and Exegetical Commentary on the Second Epistle of St. Paul to the Corinthians* (ICC 47; Edinburgh: T & T Clark, 1915); Hans-Joseph Klauck, *2. Korintherbrief* (NEchtB; Würzburg: Echter, 1986). The identification of 10–13 as part of the Letter of Tears is also common among those who hold to multiple fragments. See, for example, Günther Bornkamm, *Paul*, trans. D. M. G. Stalker (New York: Harper & Row, 1971); and Hans Dieter Betz, "Corinthians, Second Epistle to the," *ABD* 1:1149.

18. Another example deals with money. In 12:16-18, Paul needs to address the concern that he is not financially reliable, but in chapter 8, that does not seem to be an issue, in part because of the way the collection will be handled. Scholars have seen 12:16-18 as representing an earlier problem that, by the time of chapter 8, Paul has solved.

19. The direction would be from north (Macedonia) to south (Corinth) to sharply west and north (Rome).

20. The direction would be from east (Ephesus) to west (Corinth) to further west and north (Rome).

21. To argue that the disciplinary action and precipitating incident were contained in the portion of the Letter of Tears that is now lost is no argument at all. One could argue that *anything* is in what is no longer available to us to check. We can evaluate only what does in fact exist.

22. This view is upheld by Keith F. Nickle, *The Collection: A Study in Paul's Strategy* (SBT; Naperville, IL: Allenson, 1966); and Barrett, *2 Corinthians*. Betz, *2 Corinthians 8–9*, has written an entire commentary based on chapters 8 and 9 as separate originally from 1–7, as well as separate from each other. According to this view, chapter 8 is addressed to Corinth; it is an advisory letter similar to ancient official letters of recommendation. Chapter 9 is addressed to believers in Achaia and is a deliberative letter encouraging them to fulfill their promised contribution.

23. Günther Bornkamm, *Die Vorgeschichte des sogenannten zweiten Korintherbriefes* (Heidelberg: Winter, 1961); also in his *Geschichte und Glaube II: Gesammelte Aufsätze* (Munich: Kaiser, 1971), IV:162–94. English summaries are available in Bornkamm, "The History of the Origin of the So-Called Second Letter to the Corinthians," *NTS* 8 (1962): 258–63; and Bornkamm, *Paul*, 244–46.

24. David Trobisch contends that Paul himself composed 2 Corinthians from his own letter fragments at the same time he edited 1 Corinthians, Romans, and Galatians. *Paul's Letter Collection: Tracing the Origins* (Minneapolis: Fortress Press, 1994). Romans 16 functioned as the cover letter to the collection.

25. Dieter Georgi, *The Opponents of Paul in Second Corinthians: A Study of Religious Propaganda in Late Antiquity* (Philadelphia: Fortress Press, 1986), 11–14; Betz, "Corinthians, Second Epistle to the"; Helmut Koester, *Introduction to the New Testament* (2nd ed.; New York: de Gruyter, 1995–2000), 2:53, 131–35.

26. Rudolf Bultmann, *The Second Letter to the Corinthians*, trans. Roy A. Harrisville (Minneapolis: Augsburg, 1985).

27. Werner Georg Kümmel, *Introduction to the New Testament*, trans. Howard C. Kee (rev. English ed.; Nashville: Abingdon, 1975); Paul Barnett, *The Second Epistle to the Corinthians* (Grand Rapids: Eerdmans, 1995); Udo Schnelle, *The History and Theology of the New Testament*

Writings, trans. M. Eugene Boring (Minneapolis: Fortress Press, 1998); Ben Witherington III, *Conflict and Community in Corinth: A Socio-Rhetorical Commentary on 1 and 2 Corinthians* (Grand Rapids: Eerdmans, 1995).

28. See, for example, Ben Witherington III, *Conflict and Community in Corinth*, 351.

29. Paul Barnett, *The Second Epistle to the Corinthians*, 18. Young and Ford use a similar model. Frances Young and David F. Ford, *Meaning and Truth in 2 Corinthians* (Grand Rapids: Eerdmans, 1987), 27–59. By design, the earlier portion of the letter was composed to be calmer, gentler, and friendlier—again in tandem with the rhetorical standards of Paul's time.

30. John Drane, *Introducing the New Testament* (Minneapolis: Fortress Press, 2001), 333, for example. Udo Schnelle argues for thematic connections that bind 2:14—7:14 and 1:1—2:13. *The History and Theology of the New Testament Writings*, 83.

31. Schnelle, *The History and Theology of the New Testament Writings*, 83.

32. Frederick W. Danker, *II Corinthians* (ACNT; Minneapolis: Augsburg, 1989), 19; Witherington, *Conflict and Community in Corinth*, 331.

33. Kümmel, *Introduction to the New Testament*, 291. With all due respect, this argument is not the strongest argument Kümmel ever developed.

34. Barnett, *The Second Epistle to the Corinthians*, 23–24, 341. He is unable to explain why Paul used the word *Beliar/Belial*. Gordon D. Fee seeks to be more specific: the narrower issue is taking part in cultic meals held in pagan temples. "II Corinthians vi.14-vii.1 and Food Offered to Idols," *NTS* 23 (1977): 140–61.

35. Jerome H. Neyrey, *Paul in Other Words: A Cultural Reading of His Letters* (Louisville: Westminster John Knox, 1990), 83.

36. Kümmel, *Introduction to the New Testament*, 292. So Martin admits that there is an awkward transition from 8:24 to 9:1, but he agrees with F. F. Bruce that there was a short break in dictation between those two chapters. Martin, *2 Corinthians*, xliii. Hans Lietzmann asserted that Paul had a sleepless night between concluding his dictation of chapter 9 and beginning his dictation of chapter 10. *An die Korinther I/II* (HNT 9; 5th ed.; Tübingen: Mohr Siebeck, 1969), 139. Christian Wolff contends that Paul meant chapters 8–9 to be the conclusion of the letter but added chapters 10–13 to 1–9 after receiving disturbing news from Corinth. *Der zweite Brief des Paulus an die Korinther* (THKNT 8; Berlin: Evangelische Verlagsanstalt, 1989), 193–94. Danker takes a similar position in *II Corinthians*, 147. This position is close to the two-letter hypothesis (with chapters 1–9 and 10–13 being the two letters) and seeks also to account for the positive conclusion to the letter in 13:11-13. Schnelle, *The History and Theology of the New Testament Writings*, 87.

37. As Marion L. Soards alleges, "Anyone who has ever dictated a letter and been interrupted while doing so will find this explanation weak, for it is a simple matter to turn to the secretary and say, 'Now where was I before I was interrupted?'" *The Apostle Paul: An Introduction to His Writings and Teaching* (New York: Paulist, 1987), 85. A modification of the unified-composition theory is that chapters 1–9 are the work of Paul's scribe, who did the actual writing from Paul's dictation, while chapters 10–13 are the work of Paul himself. So G. Adolf Deissmann, *Light from the Ancient East: The New Testament Illustrated by Recently Discovered Texts of the Graeco-Roman World*, trans. L. R. M. Strachan (rev. ed.; New York: Doran, 1927), 166–67, n. 7. There is no data to support his position, nor did Deissmann have the advantage of more recent work on the relationship between the author and the scribe. See E. Randolph Richards, *The Secretary in the Letters of Paul* (WUNT 2.42; Tübingen: Mohr Siebeck), 1991.

38. Again, the dates are probable, not absolute.

39. Kennedy, *New Testament Interpretation through Rhetorical Criticism*, 86.

40. Witherington, *Conflict and Community in Corinth*, 333, n. 23.

41. Ibid., 335.

42. It is also possible they did not come until after Letter E.

43. In 1 Cor 16:5-9, Paul plans to go to Macedonia and then on to Corinth; in 2 Cor. 1:16, he indicates that those plans had changed to Corinth first, then Macedonia, Corinth again, and Judea. Yet he followed neither plan and has to defend himself in 1:15-24.

44. See Witherington, *Conflict and Community in Corinth*, 348–49.
45. Georgi, *The Opponents of Paul in 2 Corinthians*, identifies them as "divine men" (*theioi andres*) who understand themselves as successors to Jesus and Moses, both of whom were charismatic miracle workers.
46. Paul uses neither *nomos* (law) nor *peritomē* (circumcision) in 2 Corinthians. Barrett argues, in part based on Romans, that the opponents indeed *were* Judaizers (*The Second Epistle to the Corinthians*, 35–36). Kümmel identifies them as Palestinians who have joined the Gnostic opponents whom Kümmel identifies in 1 Corinthians; he thus sees a "Gnostic-Palestinian-Jewish-Christian anti-Pauline opposition" (*Introduction to the New Testament*, 286). Against these positions is the fact that absent from 2 Corinthians is the sort of polemic against Judaizers that we find in Galatians as well as the polemic against gnosticizing thoughts we find in 1 Corinthians. Thrall thinks Paul's opponents were part of the Petrine mission to the Judeans (*The Second Epistle to the Corinthians*, 2:941). Ironically for her view, there is no mention of Peter in 2 Corinthians.
47. The understanding of the opponents presented in this section is influenced by Jerry L. Sumney, *"Servants of Satan," "False Brothers" and Other Opponents of Paul* (JSNTSup 188; Sheffield: Sheffield Academic, 1999), 79–133.
48. Ibid., 101.
49. Ibid., 102.
50. For a parallel between Paul and Cynicism on the public style of apostle and philosopher, see ibid., 132–33.
51. The outline is designed to show both the individual letter fragments and how they fit into the edited letter as we have it. Kennedy has insightful comments regarding the rhetorical structure of 2 Corinthians: *New Testament Interpretation through Rhetorical Criticism*, 87–96. For helpful outlines, see Puskas, *The Letters of Paul*, 65–68; and Betz, *2 Corinthians 8 and 9*, 38–41, 88–90.
52. Kennedy identifies a combination of *ethos* and *pathos*: *New Testament Interpretation through Rhetorical Criticism*, 87.
53. On the subtle way in which Paul uses the image of the triumphal procession, see Neil Elliott, "The Apostle Paul's Self-Presentation as Anti-Imperial Performance," in *Paul and the Roman Imperial Order*, ed. Richard A. Horsley (Harrisburg, PA: Trinity Press International, 2004), 75–77.
54. As Puskas writes, "In his person, the apostle seems to embody the gospel of the cross": *The Letters of Paul*, 68.
55. See the helpful section on 4:7-15 by Charles Cousar, *A Theology of the Cross: The Death of Jesus in the Pauline Letters* (OBT; Minneapolis: Fortress Press, 1990), 149–57.
56. Not the RSV's "controls us."
57. Kennedy points out the dramatic power derived from the variety of images Paul uses, especially when the section is experienced aurally rather than only visually; *New Testament Interpretation through Rhetorical Criticism*, 91.
58. Affliction is a thread that runs through the first eight chapters of 2 Corinthians: 1:4, 6, 8; 2:4; 4:8, 17; 6:4; 7:4, 5; 8:2, 13. The noun is *thlipsis*; the verb is *thlibō*.
59. Witherington suggests another motivation. Contributing to the collection allows the Corinthians to fulfill their desire to be benefactors but still keeps them from being Paul's personal patrons;*Conflict and Community in Corinth*, 331.
60. The sarcasm, bitter irony, and parody in chapters 10–13 are typical of similar defenses (or "apologies") in the Socratic philosophical tradition. The basic study is Hans Dieter Betz, *Der Apostel Paulus und die sokratische Tradition: Eine exegetische Untersuchung zu seiner "Apologie" 2 Kor 10–13* (BHT 45; Tübingen: Mohr Siebeck, 1972).
61. Neyrey, *Paul in Other Words*, 209.
62. The deception of Eve by the serpent is implied; see 1 Tim 2:13. In Rom 5:12-21, Paul traces the origin of sin back to Adam, not Eve.

63. Of course, the letter itself proves that Paul has a good depth of rhetorical sophistication or technique. His statement at the beginning of 11:6 is similar to the persona in television and movies of the "poor country lawyer" who always outwits the big-city attorney.

64. Loyalty could include voting for the patron for public office, running errands for the patron, and being part of the patron's entourage. On the patron-client relationship, see Walter F. Taylor Jr., "Cultural Anthropology as a Tool for Studying the New Testament—Part II," *TSR* 18 (1997): 71–73, and the literature cited there; see also pp. 43–44 above.

65. Bruce J. Malina and Jerome H. Neyrey identify 11:21—12:10 as an encomium, which is a speech of praise. *Portraits of Paul: An Archaeology of Ancient Personality* (Louisville: Westminster John Knox, 1996), 55–63. "This literary and speech pattern covers a person's origins, formation, accomplishments, comparisons (with the origins, formation, and accomplishments of others)." Ibid., 60.

66. Danker, *II Corinthians*, 188. On altered states of consciousness, see John J. Pilch, "Paul's Ecstatic Trance Experience near Damascus in Acts of the Apostles," *HvTSt* 58 (2002): 690–707; Pilch, "The Transfiguration of Jesus: An Experience of Alternate Reality," in *Modelling Early Christianity: Social-Scientific Studies of the New Testament in Its Context*, ed. Philip F. Esler, 47–64 (London: Routledge, 1995); and Bruce J. Malina and John J. Pilch, *Social-Science Commentary on the Letters of Paul* (Minneapolis: Fortress Press, 2006), 331–33, which contains a "reading scenario" on altered states of consciousness.

67. As Robert M. Price wrote in a study on this topic, "it has been a thorn in the side to exegetes as well." "'Punished in Paradise' (An Exegetical Theory on II Corinthians 12:1-10)," *JSNT* 7 (1980): 35. For a helpful survey of theories, see Thrall, *The Second Epistle to the Corinthians*, 2:809–18; she opts for migraine headaches.

68. Patricia Nisbet, "The Thorn in the Flesh," *ExpTim* 80 (1969): 126.

69. Alan Hisey and James S. P. Beck, "Paul's 'Thorn in the Flesh': A Paragnosis," *JBR* 29 (1961): 125–29.

70. See references in Furnish, *II Corinthians*, 549.

71. Terence Y. Mullins, "Paul's Thorn in the Flesh," *JBL* 76 (1957): 302–303.

72. Jerry W. McCant, "Paul's Thorn of Rejected Apostleship," *NTS* 34 (1988): 550–72.

73. Barnett decides for the anti-Paul opponents, even while acknowledging the paucity of data: *The Second Epistle to the Corinthians*, 570. Although the thorn is an angel of Satan, the ultimate origin of the thorn is probably God (thus the "divine passive" in 12:7, "a thorn in the flesh *was given* to me," with the passive being a standard way to avoid the name of God). On Satan as being in the service of God, see Bultmann, *The Second Letter to the Corinthians*, 225. In Israel's Bible, the Satan can indeed function as God's agent (Job 2:6-7 is the classic text). Danker identifies a joke here: Satan should be happy that Paul is elated with pride, for that would allow Satan to do his work; by afflicting Paul with the thorn in the flesh, Satan in effect is providing Paul the antidote to the pride that might otherwise bring him down. *II Corinthians*, 193.

74. Price, "'Punished in Paradise,'" 34–35; J. W. Bowker, "'Merkabah' Visions and the Visions of Paul," *JSS* 16 (1971): 157–73.

75. Furnish, *II Corinthians*, 548.

CHAPTER 10

1. Robert Jewett, "Romans as an Ambassadorial Letter," *Int* 36 (1982): 13; Jewett, *Romans: A Commentary* (Hermeneia; Minneapolis: Fortress Press, 2007), 46–49.

2. James S. Jeffers, *Conflict at Rome: Social Order and Hierarchy in Early Christianity* (Minneapolis: Fortress Press, 1991), 101. On slavery as a metaphor for salvation, see Dale B. Martin, *Slavery as Salvation: The Metaphor of Slavery in Pauline Christianity* (New Haven: Yale University Press, 1990). On the hardnosed realities of slavery, see Jennifer A. Glancy, *Slavery in Early Christianity* (Oxford: Oxford University Press, 2002).

3. Jewett, "Romans as an Ambassadorial Letter," 100–101.

4. As translated in Christopher Bryan, *A Preface to Romans: Notes on the Epistle in Its Literary and Cultural Setting* (Oxford: Oxford University Press, 2000), 37–38.

5. Helmut Koester, *Ancient Christian Gospels: Their History and Development* (Philadelphia: Trinity Press International, 1990), 4.

6. "Descended from David": Paul nowhere else writes of Jesus as the son of David; "according to the flesh" is normatively in Paul a negative phrase, used to designate the human body as separated from God; "declared to be Son of God" implies that Jesus became Son of God at a certain point in time, whereas in Gal 4:4 Paul implies an eternal or pre-birth status for Jesus as God's Son; "the spirit of holiness" is a somewhat awkward way to express what Paul elsewhere labels simply as the "holy spirit."

7. Arland J. Hultgren, "The Scriptural Foundations for Paul's Mission to the Gentiles," in *Paul and His Theology*, ed. Stanley E. Porter (Pauline Studies 3; Leiden: Brill, 2006), 23–25.

8. Arland J. Hultgren, *Paul's Letter to the Romans: A Commentary* (Grand Rapids: Eerdmans, 2011), 50–51. See also the discussions in James M. Scott, *Paul and the Nations: The Old Testament and Jewish Background of Paul's Mission to the Nations with Special Reference to the Destination of Galatians* (WUNT 84; Tübingen: Mohr Siebeck, 1995), 58–134; and Ksenija Magda, *Paul's Territoriality and Mission Strategy: Searching for the Geographical Awareness Paradigm behind Romans* (WUNT 2.226; Tübingen: Mohr Siebeck, 2009), 187–92.

9. See also above, chapter 5.

10. Paul utilizes the "three zones" of the human being as identified in Mediterranean cultural anthropology: heart-eyes, mouth-ears, and hands-feet. The three zones describe and symbolize the entire person. See Bruce J. Malina and John J. Pilch, *Social-Science Commentary on the Letters of Paul* (Minneapolis: Fortress Press, 2006), 405, on "Three-Zone Personality."

11. Don B. Garlington, "The Obedience of Faith in the Letter to the Romans: Part I," *WTJ* 52 (1990): 202. See also these works by Garlington: *"The Obedience of Faith": A Pauline Phrase in Historical Context* (WUNT 2.38; Tübingen: Mohr Siebeck, 1991); and *Faith, Obedience, and Perseverance: Aspects of Paul's Letter to the Romans* (WUNT 79; Tübingen: Mohr Siebeck, 1994).

12. A. J. M. Wedderburn, *The Reasons for Romans* (Minneapolis: Fortress Press, 1991), 104; and Peter Stuhlmacher, *Paul's Letter to the Romans: A Commentary*, trans. Scott J. Hafemann (Louisville: Westminster John Knox, 1994), 28. Wedderburn argues that the listeners will learn, as the book unfolds, that God according to Paul does behave righteously from a Jewish perspective.

13. On the power-filled nature of Paul's proclamation, see also 1 Cor 1:18; 1:23-24; 2:4.

14. Only in Rom 4:25 and 5:18.

15. The bibliography on righteousness is extremely large. Fundamental works include Ernst Käsemann, "'The Righteousness of God' in Paul," in *New Testament Questions of Today*, trans. W. J. Montague (Philadelphia: Fortress Press, 1969), 168–82; J. A. Ziesler, *The Meaning of Righteousness in Paul* (SNTSMS 20; Cambridge: Cambridge University Press, 1972); John Reumann, *"Righteousness" in the New Testament* (Philadelphia: Fortress Press, 1982); Reumann, "Righteousness (NT)," *ABD* 5:745–73.

16. See also the discussion of Galatians in ch. 7.

17. C. E. B. Cranfield, *The Epistle to the Romans* (ICC; Edinburgh: T & T Clark, 1975), 1:94; Käsemann, *"'The Righteousness of God' in Paul,"* 172; James D. G. Dunn, *Romans 1–8* (WBC 38A; Dallas: Word, 1988), 40–42.

18. E. P. Sanders, *Paul and Palestinian Judaism: A Comparison of Patterns of Religion* (Philadelphia: Fortress Press, 1977).

19. Ibid., 544.

20. The grammatical issues are the same as in the case of "faith in" or "faith of," which was discussed in ch. 7 with relation to Galatians. See also the discussion by Hultgren, *Paul's Letter to the Romans*, 605–15.

21. Käsemann, "'The Righteousness of God' in Paul."

22. Ibid., 180. Käsemann's apocalyptic understanding of righteousness is in part a corrective to the work of his teacher Rudolf Bultmann, who sought to remove the apocalyptic nature of the early Christian message by interpreting the New Testament within the framework of

individualistic existentialism. Bultmann, *Theology of the New Testament*, trans. Kendrick Grobel (2 vol. in 1; New York: Scribner's, 1951, 1955).

23. N. T. Wright highlights how the way Paul uses *justice* is yet another challenge to the Roman Empire: "Paul was coming to Rome with the gospel message of Jesus the Jewish Messiah, the Lord of the world, claiming that through this message God's justice was unveiled once and for all. Rome prided itself on being, as it were, the capital of Justice, the source from which Justice would flow throughout the world.... If justice is wanted, it will be found not in the *euaggelion* that announces Caesar as Lord but in the *euaggelion* of Jesus." He goes on to talk about the relatively recent rise of *Iustitia* to the level of a goddess. N. T. Wright, "Paul's Gospel and Caesar's Empire," in *Paul and Politics: Ekklesia, Israel, Imperium, Interpretation*, ed. Richard A. Horsley (Harrisburg, PA: Trinity Press International, 2000), 171–72.

24. God's faithfulness: Dunn, *Romans 1–8*, 44; Marion L. Soards, *The Apostle Paul: An Introduction to his Writings and Teaching* (New York: Paulist, 1987), 104. Christ's faithfulness: N. T. Wright, "Romans and the Theology of Paul," in *Pauline Theology*, vol. III, *Romans*, ed. David M. Hay and E. Elizabeth Johnson (Minneapolis: Fortress Press, 1995), 65; Luke Timothy Johnson, *The Writings of the New Testament* (3rd ed.; Minneapolis: Fortress Press, 2010), 307.

25. Cranfield, *Romans*, 1:102; Hultgren, *Paul's Letter to the Romans*, 78–79.

26. Leander E. Keck, "Romans in the Pulpit: Form and Formulation in Romans 5:1-11," in *Listening to the Word*, ed. Gail R. O'Day and Thomas G. Long (Nashville: Abingdon Press, 1993), 77.

27. From *Martin Luther: Selections from His Writings*, ed. John Dillenberger (New York: Doubleday, 1961), 19.

28. Paul does mention Peter in Gal 2:7-8 and Cephas, Peter's Aramaic name, in 1 Cor 1:12; 3:22; 9:5; 15:5; and Gal 1:18; 2:9; 2:11; 2:14.

29. James S. Jeffers, *Conflict at Rome*, 10. Seven of the nine synagogues that have been located (out of the eleven known) were located in Transtiberinum (modern Trastevere).

30. Suetonius, *Claudius* 25.4, trans. J. C. Rolf (LCL 38; repr. ed.; Cambridge, MA: Harvard University Press, 1992), 52–53.

31. Peter Lampe, *From Paul to Valentinus: Christians at Rome in the First Two Centuries*, trans. Michael Steinhauser (Minneapolis: Fortress Press, 2003), 11–16.

32. Werner Georg Kümmel, *Introduction to the New Testament*, trans. Howard C. Kee (rev. English ed.; Nashville: Abingdon, 1975), 312; Cranfield, *Romans* 1:22–23. Cranfield also emphasizes the fifth theory. Ibid., 2:814–23.

33. Jewett, "Romans as an Ambassadorial Letter," 5–20.

34. Stuhlmacher, *Paul's Letter to the Romans*, 6.

35. Wolfgang Wiefel, "The Jewish Community in Ancient Rome and the Origins of Roman Christianity," in *The Romans Debate*, ed. Karl P. Donfried (rev. ed.; Peabody, MA: Hendrickson, 1991), 96.

36. Francis Watson, *Paul, Judaism and the Gentiles: A Sociological Approach* (Cambridge: Cambridge University Press, 1986).

37. Wright, "Romans and the Theology of Paul," 35.

38. Ibid. Bryan modifies the ethnic basis of the division, so that the law-oriented group was "mostly but not necessarily all of Jewish descent" and the group that resented the claims of the former group was "mostly but not necessarily all of gentile origin." *A Preface to Romans*, 27.

39. Philip F. Esler, *Conflict and Identity in Romans: The Social Setting of Paul's Letter* (Minneapolis: Fortress Press, 2003).

40. Two representatives of this approach are Manson and Bornkamm. The titles of their articles reveal their approaches: T. W. Manson, "St. Paul's Letter to the Romans—and Others," in Donfried, *The Romans Debate*, 3–15; Günther Bornkamm, "The Letter to the Romans as Paul's Last Will and Testament," in Donfried, *The Romans Debate*, 16–28.

41. Important aspects of his theology are missing if indeed Romans is his theological testament or systematic theology. There is no teaching about the church, the Lord's Supper, or his sufferings as an apostle. More typical of the current view of Romans and of Paul are the opinions

of Arland J. Hultgren, *Paul's Gospel and Mission: The Outlook from His Letter to the Romans* (Philadelphia: Fortress Press, 1985). He writes bluntly, "To speak of a 'Pauline theology' is an anachronism. . . . He was not a theologian who worked apart from particular contexts; he did not set out to produce a 'timeless' theology" (2). Paul was certainly a theologian, according to Hultgren, but a theologian similar to Luther. That is, he was working in a context to which he needed to respond and which he tried to shape, but he had no sense of creating a well-rounded system.

42. Joseph A. Fitzmyer, *Romans* (AB 33; New York: Doubleday, 1993), goes in a similar direction.

43. See Wilhelm Wuellner, "Paul's Rhetoric of Argumentation in Romans," in Donfried, *The Romans Debate*, 139–41. So, too, George A. Kennedy, *New Testament Interpretation through Rhetorical Criticism* (Chapel Hill: University of North Carolina Press, 1984), 152.

44. See chapter 5 above.

45. Paul J. Achtemeier estimates a date sometime between 55 and 64. *Romans* (Interpretation; Atlanta: John Knox, 1985). Barrett estimates January–March 55; Dunn's first choice is late 55 to early 56; his second choice is late 56 to early 57. Fitzmyer suggests winter of 57–58; Puskas says winter of late 56 or early 57; Stuhlmacher estimates spring of 56; Jewett suggests it was dictated during the winter of 56–57 and sent in the spring of 57; and Hultgren estimates 55–58. (For sources see previous notes.)

46. Fitzmyer, *Romans*, 272.

47. As Johnson puts it, "At root, sin is the disposition that strives to establish one's own existence and value apart from the claims of the Creator God." Johnson, *The Writings of the New Testament*, 309.

48. Achtemeier, *Romans*, 40.

49. Much current debate regarding the appropriateness of same-gender sexual expression revolves around Romans 1:26-28. Representative literature includes the following: David L. Balch, ed., *Homosexuality, Science, and the "Plain Sense" of Scripture* (Grand Rapids: Eerdmans, 2000); L. William Countryman, *Dirt, Greed, and Sex: Sexual Ethics in the New Testament and Their Implications for Today* (Philadelphia: Fortress Press, 1988); Victor Paul Furnish, *The Moral Teaching of Paul: Selected Issues* (2nd ed.; Nashville: Abingdon, 1985); Robert A. J. Gagnon, *The Bible and Homosexual Practice: Texts and Hermeneutics* (Nashville: Abingdon, 2001); Richard B. Hays, "Relations Natural and Unnatural: A Response to John Boswell's Exegesis of Romans 1," *JRE* 14 (1986): 184–215; Arland J. Hultgren and Walter F. Taylor Jr., *Background Essay on Biblical Texts for 'Journey Together Faithfully, Part Two: The Church and Homosexuality'* (Chicago: Evangelical Lutheran Church in America, 2003); Jeffrey Siker, ed., *Homosexuality in the Church: Both Sides of the Debate* (Louisville: Westminster John Knox, 1994).

50. For more on sin, see the comments below on Romans 7.

51. On the two interpretations ("faith in Jesus Christ" and "faith of Jesus Christ"), see the excursus "Faith 'In' or Faith 'Of,'" in chapter 7, above.

52. Trying to figure out to whom the price is paid presses the image too far (paid to God? to the devil?).

53. Many scholars have argued that Rom 3:24-26 is a confessional statement, perhaps a liturgical fragment from Greek-speaking Judean Christianity, that was taken over by Paul. See John Reumann, "The Gospel of the Righteousness of God: Pauline Reinterpretation in Romans 3:21-31," *Int* 4 (1966): 432–52.

54. Sanders, *Paul and Palestinian Judaism*.

55. James D. G. Dunn, *The New Perspective on Paul* (rev. ed.; Grand Rapids: Eerdmans, 2007).

56. Charles H. Talbert, "Paul, Judaism, and the Revisionists," *CBQ* 63 (2001): 1–22.

57. Brendan Byrne, "Interpreting Romans: The New Perspective and Beyond," *Int* 58 (2004): 248.

58. Hultgren, *Paul's Letter to the Romans: A Commentary*, 172.

59. See ch. 7. Other significant contributions to the discussion include Brendan Byrne, "Interpreting Romans Theologically in a Post–'New Perspective' Perspective," *HTR* 94 (2001):

227–41; A. Andrew Das, *Paul, the Law, and the Covenant* (Peabody, MA: Hendrickson, 2001); Donald A. Hagner, "Paul and Judaism: The Jewish Matrix of Early Christianity: Issues in the Current Debate," *BBR* 3 (1993): 111–30; Seyoon Kim, *Paul and the New Perspective: Second Thoughts on the Origin of Paul's Gospel* (Grand Rapids: Eerdmans, 2002); Mark M. Mattison, *The Paul Page* (www.thepaulpage.com); Francis Watson, *Paul, Judaism, and the Gentiles: Beyond the New Perspective* (rev. ed.; Grand Rapids: Eerdmans, 2007); Stephen Westerholm, *Perspectives Old and New on Paul: The "Lutheran" Paul and His Critics* (Grand Rapids: Eerdmans, 2004); N. T. Wright, *Justification: God's Plan and Paul's Vision* (Downers Grove, IL: InterVarsity, 2009).

60. See ch. 7 above.

61. For other examples of holding things for the future, see Rom 6:5, 8; 8:11; 10:9.

62. Paul does not say, as some of the Corinthians might have said, "So too we were resurrected." He continues to reserve resurrection of believers for the future (6:5).

63. As Dunn has written, "The object of conversion-initiation is not a better kind of death in the future, but a new quality of life in the here and now." *Romans 1–8*, 330. Candidates for baptism, Neyrey writes, "leave one world, cross a boundary, and enter another world." Jerome H. Neyrey, *Paul, in Other Words: A Cultural Reading of His Letters* (Louisville: Westminster John Knox, 1990), 88. On the kinship implications of baptism, see Bruce J. Malina and Jerome H. Neyrey, *Portraits of Paul: An Archaeology of Ancient Personality* (Louisville: Westminster John Knox, 1996), 192–93.

64. The bibliography on the exact identity of the "I" in Romans 7 is enormous. Basic resources include the following: J. Lambrecht, *The Wretched 'I' and Its Liberation: Paul in Romans 7 and 8* (Louvain: Peeters, 1992); Werner Kümmel, *Man in the New Testament*, trans. John J. Vincent (London: Epworth, 1963), 49–61. See also the comments by Gerd Theissen, *Psychological Aspects of Pauline Theology*, trans. John P. Galvin (Philadelphia: Fortress Press, 1983), 201; James D. G. Dunn, *The Theology of Paul the Apostle* (Grand Rapids: Eerdmans, 1998), 472–77; Hultgren, *Paul's Letter to the Romans*, 681–91.

65. In some ways for Paul, sin and its power are similar to alcoholism or other addictions. At first, people willingly drink the alcoholic beverage. But soon they compulsively reach for alcohol and ultimately find that it controls their lives. On sin as violation of rules, on the one hand, and corruption and disease, on the other, see Neyrey, *Paul, in Other Words*, 48, 154–55.

66. It is often necessary to look at older translations such as the Revised Standard Version in order to see the masculine translation *son(s)*.

67. A. H. Snyman, "Style and the Rhetorical Situation of Romans 8:31-39," *NTS* 34 (1988): 228.

68. On the athletic imagery in chapters 9–11, see Calvin J. Roetzel, *Paul: The Man and the Myth* (Minneapolis: Fortress Press, 1999), 127–31.

69. Otfried Hofius, "'All Israel Will Be Saved': Divine Salvation and Israel's Deliverance in Romans 9–11," *PSB*, supplementary issue 1 (1990): 26–27.

70. Debate over the translation and meaning of 10:4 continues unabated. The first reading is what the NRSV has: "Christ is the end [*telos*] of the law." In this interpretation, there are two mutually exclusive possibilities: Christ and the Law. Dunn, as a figure representative of Käsemann and many others, maintains that the context demands that the primary reference of the term be to end in the sense of termination. There are alternatives in this text: Christ or the Law (so, too, Hultgren, *Paul's Letter to the Romans*, 383–84). The law that is ended is the Law as misunderstood in terms of *works* (9:32), that is, misunderstood as a means of establishing righteousness as the special prerogative of Israel. The role of Law as a badge of election is over. James D. G. Dunn, *Romans 9–16* (WBC 38B; Dallas: Word, 1988), 597–98. Stuhlmacher approaches the question from the vantage point of the final judgment: "Everything depends for Paul on the fact that in the final judgment it is not the Law, but the messiah, Jesus, ... who has the decisive word before God." *Paul's Letter to the Romans*, 155–56. The other interpretation translates *telos* as *goal*, so that Christ is the fulfillment or completion of the Law in the sense that he is its ultimate goal. Thus, Bryan cites Rom 3:31, 7:7-14, 8:3-4, 13:8-10, and the Scripture passages that follow in chapter 10 as proof that Paul does not eliminate the Law. *A Preface to Romans*, 171–72; see

also Jewett, *Romans*, 619. But, with E. P. Sanders, we can identify Paul's double-sided approach: the Law is ended as the way of establishing one's relationship with God, but the Law still has a function as a guide to ethical behavior. Sanders, *Paul and Palestinian Judaism*, 543, 550.

71. Jealousy is desire for what properly belongs to someone; envy is desire for what belongs to another.

72. Roy A. Harrisville, *Romans* (ACNT; Minneapolis: Augsburg, 1980), 184; Jewett, *Romans*, 701–702.

73. John A. T. Robinson, *Wrestling with Romans* (Philadelphia: Westminster, 1979), 131. Also taking the same position are Nils Dahl, *Studies in Paul* (Minneapolis: Augsburg, 1977), 153; William Sanday and Arthur C. Headlam, *A Critical and Exegetical Commentary on the Epistle to the Romans* (ICC; Edinburgh: T & T Clark, 1895; repr. ed., 1971), 335–36; C. K. Barrett, *The Epistle to the Romans* (2nd ed.; London: Black, 1991), 223–24. On "all Israel" as a corporate reference, see Hultgren, *Paul's Letter to the Romans*, 419–20.

74. Hofius, "'All Israel Will Be Saved,'" 35.

75. A time-honored theory is that of two covenants: the Gentiles are saved by faith in Christ; Israel is saved by traditional covenantal faithfulness. The result is two religions and two chosen people, which is the position taken by Peter Richardson, *Israel in the Apostolic Church* (SNTSMS 10; Cambridge: Cambridge University Press, 1969); Krister Stendahl, *Paul among Jews and Gentiles and Other Essays* (Philadelphia: Fortress Press, 1976); and others. E. Elizabeth Johnson presents a strong critique of that position in *The Function of Apocalyptic and Wisdom Traditions in Romans 9–11* (SBLDS 109; Atlanta: Scholars, 1989), 176–205. As she writes, "For all its attractiveness in the context of interreligious dialogue, the claim that Paul holds such a 'two-covenant' position is historically and exegetically indefensible." "Romans 9–11: The Faithfulness and Impartiality of God," in *Pauline Theology*, vol. III: *Romans*, ed. David M. Hay and E. Elizabeth Johnson (Minneapolis: Fortress Press, 1995), 214, n. 12. See also Fitzmyer, *Romans*, 619–20.

76. For more on this passage, see Walter F. Taylor Jr., "Obligation: Paul's Foundation for Ethics," *TSR* 19 (1997): 91–112; a slightly different version is in *Josephinum Journal of Theology* 5 (1998): 5–25. In addition to insights on obligation, the comments on "spiritual worship" (see Rom 12:1) are a needed corrective to an unfortunate translation in the NRSV. Ibid., *TSR*, 96–97; *Josephinum Journal of Theology*, 10–11.

77. August Strobel, "Zum Verständnis von Röm 13," *ZNW* 47 (1956): 67–93. See also Ernst Käsemann, "Principles of the Interpretation of Romans 13," in his *New Testament Questions of Today*, 196–216.

78. Tacitus, *Annals* 13.50-51; also in Suetonius, *Nero* 10.1. See Stuhlmacher, *Paul's Letter to the Romans*, 200–201.

79. Neil Elliott, "Romans 13:1-7 in the Context of Imperial Propaganda," in *Paul and Empire: Religion and Power in Roman Imperial Society*, ed. Richard A. Horsley (Harrisburg, PA: Trinity Press International, 1997), 188, 191. On the need to avoid contact with governmental authorities, see Stuhlmacher, *Paul's Letter to the Romans*, 191–92.

80. At the same time, Paul's labeling of the government as "God's servant for your good" (vs. 4) raises the question about the government that is not acting as God's servant nor acting for the good of its population. Would resistance or revolt be acceptable or even advisable under those circumstances? Paul does not address that question, but he lays the foundation for a positive response.

81. Richard J. Cassidy, *Paul in Chains: Roman Imprisonment and the Letters of St. Paul* (New York: Crossroad, 2001), 34.

82. He says that even though he is convinced that all foods are ritually clean (Rom 14:14, 20).

83. On Erastus, see ch. 8.

84. Romans appears in ancient manuscripts in the following three ways: as chs. 1–14 plus what is now 16:25-27; as chs. 1–15 plus 16:25-27; and as 1:1—16:23 (sometimes with 16:25-27). The evidence for the fourteen-chapter Romans is especially weak. In addition, chapter 15 so clearly continues the discussion of chapter 14 that almost all debate centers only on 16 as

possibly not original. The verses in 16:25-27 are found at several places in the manuscripts. The way those verses are formulated is evaluated by most scholars as non-Pauline. Perhaps Marcion was the author; they may also be an early liturgical addition to aid in reading during worship.

85. See especially the study by Harry Y. Gamble, *The Textual History of the Letter to the Romans* (Grand Rapids: Eerdmans, 1977).

86. For more on the unity of humanity in Paul, see Walter F. Taylor Jr., "Unity/Unity of Humanity," *ABD* 6:746-52.

87. In the preparation of this outline, the following outlines of Romans have been particularly helpful: Ernst Käsemann, *Commentary on Romans*, ix-xi; Robert Jewett, "Following the Argument of Romans," *WW* 6 (1986): 386-89; Gerd Theissen, "Letter to the Romans" (unpublished lecture, University of Heidelberg, summer semester 1989).

CHAPTER 11

1. For an introduction to the imperial cult, see Donald L. Jones, "Roman Imperial Cult," *ABD* 5:806-809; Philip A. Harland, "Emperor Worship," *NIDB* 2:255-57.

2. On the history and archaeology of Philippi, see Charalambos Bakirtzis and Helmut Koester, eds., *Philippi at the Time of Paul and after His Death* (Harrisburg, PA: Trinity Press International, 1998).

3. Acts 16:13 implies that there were not enough Judean men in Philippi to form a synagogue, nor is there archaeological evidence of a synagogue during Paul's lifetime. In addition, there are no quotations in the letter from the Judean Scriptures.

4. See Lilian Portefaix, *Sisters Rejoice: Paul's Letter to the Philippians and Luke-Acts as Received by First-Century Philippian Women* (ConBNT 20; Stockholm: Almqvist and Wiksell, 1988); and Ben Witherington III, *Women in the Earliest Churches* (Cambridge: Cambridge University Press, 1988), 111-13.

5. See above, ch. 9.

6. Richard J. Cassidy, *Paul in Chains: Roman Imprisonment and the Letters of St. Paul* (New York: Crossroad, 2001), 165.

7. Another possible argument for a composite letter comes from Polycarp, who lived in the middle part of the second century. He refers to Paul's letters to the Philippians (Pol. *Phil.* 3.2). That could mean the canonical letter plus one or more others or originally independent letters that have been combined into the present document. However, at 11.3, Polycarp uses the singular *epistle* when referring to Philippians.

8. Letter A = 3:1b—4:20 (written soon after Epaphroditus arrived with the gift); Letter B = 1:1—3:1a, 4:21-23 (written after Epaphroditus recovered). The proponents of two letters include Edgar J. Goodspeed, *An Introduction to the New Testament* (Chicago: University of Chicago Press, 1937); and Leander E. Keck, "The Letter of Paul to the Philippians," in *The Interpreter's One-Volume Commentary on the Bible*, ed. Charles M. Laymon (Nashville: Abingdon, 1971), 845-55.

9. The proponents of three letters include F. W. Beare, *The Epistle to the Philippians* (HNTC; New York: 1959); Günther Bornkamm, "Der Philipperbrief als paulinische Briefsammlung," in *Neotestamentica et Patristica: Eine Freundesgabe, Oscar Cullmann zu seinem 60. Geburtstag überreicht* (NovTSup6; Leiden: Brill, 1962), 192-202; R. H. Fuller, *The Foundations of New Testament Christology* (New York: Scribner, 1965); Helmut Koester, "The Purpose of the Polemic of a Pauline Fragment (Philippians III)," *NTS* 8 (1961-62): 317-32; Eduard Lohse, *The Formation of the New Testament*, trans. M. Eugene Boring (Nashville: Abingdon, 1981); Willi Marxsen, *Introduction to the New Testament*, trans. G. Buswell (Philadelphia: Fortress Press, 1968); Charles B. Puskas, Jr., *The Letters of Paul: An Introduction* (GNS 25; Collegeville, MN: Liturgical, 1993); John Reumann, *Philippians* (Anchor Yale Bible 33B; New Haven: Yale University Press, 2008); and Walter Schmithals, *Paul and the Gnostics*, trans. J. E. Steely (Nashville: Abingdon, 1972).

10. So Peter T. O'Brien, *The Epistle to the Philippians: A Commentary on the Greek Text* (NIGTC; Grand Rapids: Eerdmans, 1991), 14. See Isa 56:10-11; Matt 7:6; and Mark 7:27.

11. Duane F. Watson, "A Rhetorical Analysis of Philippians and Its Implications for the Unity Question," *NovT* 30 (1988): 86-87.

12. John T. Fitzgerald, "Philippians, Epistle to the," *ABD* 5.321.
13. G. D. Kilpatrick, "*BLEPETE*, Phil 3,2," in *In Memoriam Paul Kahle*, ed. Matthew Black and Georg Fohrer (BZAW 103; Berlin: Töpelmann, 1968), 146–48.
14. G. W. Peterman, *Paul's Gift from Philippi: Conventions of Gift-Exchange and Christian Giving* (SNTSMS 92; Cambridge: Cambridge University Press, 1997), 17–18.
15. See 1 Cor 4:17-21. Galatians 4:12-20 and 1 Thess 2:17—3:10 contain reports of travel already completed.
16. BDAG, 602. On 603, BDAG does note that the term can be used "as a transition to something new (Phil 3:1), especially when it comes near the end of a literary work *finally*." That meaning is also listed for 4:8.
17. Peterman, *Paul's Gift from Philippi*, 18.
18. Ibid., n. 62.
19. Both words belong to the same root word, *synathleō*.
20. Others who decide for a unified document include David E. Aune, *The New Testament in Its Literary Environment* (Library of Early Christianity; Philadelphia: Westminster, 1987); W. J. Dalton, "The Integrity of Philippians," *Bib* 60 (1979): 97-102; Gordon D. Fee, *Paul's Letter to the Philippians* (NICNT; Grand Rapids: Eerdmans, 1995); Luke Timothy Johnson, *The Writings of the New Testament* (3rd ed.; Minneapolis: Fortress Press, 2010); Werner G. Kümmel, *Introduction to the New Testament*, trans. Howard C. Kee (rev. English ed.; Nashville: Abingdon, 1975); O'Brien, *The Epistle to the Philippians*; Peterman, *Paul's Gift from Philippi*; T. E. Pollard, "The Integrity of Philippians," *NTS* 13 (1966–67): 57–66; Udo Schnelle, *The History and Theology of the New Testament Writings*, trans. M. Eugene Boring (Minneapolis: Fortress Press, 1998); Marion L. Soards, *The Apostle Paul: An Introduction to His Writings and Teaching* (New York: Paulist, 1987); Ben Witherington III, *Friendship and Finances in Philippi: The Letter of Paul to the Philippians* (The New Testament in Context; Valley Forge, PA: Trinity Press International, 1994); and Witherington, *Paul's Letter to the Philippians: A Socio-Rhetorical Commentary* (Grand Rapids: Eerdmans, 2011).
21. O'Brien argues that the parallels between 1:3-11 and 4:10-20 are so strong the two sections form an *inclusion* that brackets the entire document (p. 18).
22. Among others, Duane F. Watson, "A Rhetorical Analysis of Philippians and Its Implications for the Unity Question," *NovT* 30 (1988): 57–88; and L. Gregory Bloomquist, *The Function of Suffering in Philippians* (JSNTSup78; Sheffield: JSOT Press, 1993).
23. So Pseudo-Demetrius in his handbook, the text and translation of which can be found in Abraham J. Malherbe, *Ancient Epistolary Theorists* (SBLSBS 19; Atlanta: Scholars, 1988), 30–41; and the prolific writer Cicero, *Epistulae ad Familiares* 2.4.1. The classic work on friendship was Aristotle, *Nicomachean Ethics* 8 and 9. See the collection of essays in John H. Fitzgerald, ed., *Greco-Roman Perspectives on Friendship* (SBLRBS 34; Atlanta: Scholars, 1997).
24. Fitzgerald provides a convenient summary in *ABD* 5:320; see also his more extensive work, "Philippians in the Light of Some Ancient Discussions of Friendship," in *Friendship, Flattery, and Frankness of Speech: Studies on Friendship in the New Testament World*, ed. John T. Fitzgerald, 141–60 (NovTSup 82; Leiden: Brill, 1996). Reumann sees elements of the friendship theme in Philippians but not the genre of the "friendly letter": "Philippians, Especially Chapter 4, as a 'Letter of Friendship': Observations on a Checkered History of Scholarship," in Fitzgerald, *Friendship, Flattery, and Frankness of Speech*, 83–106; Reumann, *Philippians*, 678–85. Ben Witherington III also denies that Philippians is a friendship letter; he styles it a family letter. Witherington, *Paul's Letter to the Philippians*, 17–21.
25. And thus in all three hypothetical fragments.
26. Prison in the Roman world was not designed to be a place of long-term punishment. On the meaning of custody in antiquity, see B. M. Rapske, "Prison, Prisoner," *DNTB*, 827–30, and Cassidy, *Paul in Chains*. Paul's very life, including adequate food, depended on believers such as Epaphroditus.
27. Cassidy, *Paul in Chains*, 127.
28. Ibid., 128–29.

29. Schnelle, *History and Theology*, 133. O'Brien refers to forty days in either direction, and Ben Witherington III estimates four to seven weeks, but the point is the same. O'Brien, *Epistle to the Philippians*, 25; Witherington, *Friendship and Finances*, 25.

30. See O'Brien, *Epistle to the Philippians*, 22; Fee, *Paul's Letter to the Philippians*, 35, including nn. 86 and 87; and F. F. Bruce, *Philippians* (NIBCNT 11; Peabody, MA: Hendrickson, 1989), 11–12.

31. An Ephesian setting for the writing of Philippians tends to be supported by scholars who identify two or more letters buried in the canonical Philippians.

32. Cassidy, *Paul in Chains*, 131, 141–62.

33. Charles B. Cousar argues for Ephesus between 52 and 55. *Philippians and Philemon: A Commentary* (NTL; Louisville: Westminster John Knox, 2009).

34. John J. Gunther, *St. Paul's Opponents and Their Background: A Study of Apocalyptic and Jewish Sectarian Teachings* (NovTSup 35; Leiden: Brill, 1973), 2.

35. Cassidy, *Paul in Chains*, 132–35; Craig S. Wansink, *Chained in Christ: The Experience and Rhetoric of Paul's Imprisonments* (JSNTSup 130; Sheffield: Sheffield Academic, 1996), 48, 59. Imprisonment was a test for friends. Cassidy, *Paul in Chains*, 48.

36. Cassidy, *Paul in Chains*, 173–74, 191–94. Paul J. Achtemeier, Joel B. Green, and Marianne Meye Thompson see the language as referring to Judaizers. *Introducing the New Testament: Its Literature and Theology* (Grand Rapids: Eerdmans, 2001), 397–98.

37. In addition, in 2:7, Christ Jesus is identified as having taken "the form of a slave."

38. Elsewhere in the Pauline literature, it is used in 1 Tim 3:2 and Titus 1:7, but only in the singular.

39. Paul uses various forms of the word *fellowship / sharing / koinōnia* throughout the letter (1:5; 2:1; 3:10; 4:14-15). The word *gospel* occurs nine times in Philippians—the highest rate per page of any of his letters (1:5, 7, 12, 16, 27 [twice]; 2:22; 4:3, 15). It is also of note that *gospel* occurs twice in the letter's thesis statement (1:27).

40. See the discussion earlier in ch. 3, above.

41. Notice once more in Paul the emphasis on life in the body; see the parallel statement in 1 Cor 6:20. What Paul does not seem to indicate is any sense of death as escape from the trials of this world, especially through suicide, a thought that was common among ancient thinkers. See the examples from Plato, *Apology* 40 CD; Aeschylus, *Prometheus* 747, 750–51; and Sophocles, *Antigone* 463–64, quoted in *Hellenistic Commentary to the New Testament*, ed. M. Eugene Boring, Klaus Berger, and Carsten Colpe (Nashville: Abingdon, 1995), 479. Prisoners did choose suicide. Wansink, *Chained in Christ*, 119–24; see also Cassidy, *Paul in Chains*, 42, 53. It is difficult, however, to reconcile the letter's constant theme of joy with a serious contemplation of suicide. Ultimately, the reference to suicide is most likely a rhetorical device to highlight choosing the good of the community over personal gain; so, too, N. Clayton Croy, "'To Die Is Gain' (Philippians 1:19-26): Does Paul Contemplate Suicide?" *JBL* 122 (2003): 517–31.

42. The word *struggle* is an athletic term. Paul likes athletic metaphors, perhaps in part because they help him stress that being a Christ-follower requires strenuous and ongoing effort. Sports were popular in antiquity, and Philippi, like other cities, held athletic contests as forms of entertainment. Athletic language is found in Philippians also in 2:16 and 3:12-14. On athletic imagery, see Victor C. Pfitzner, *Paul and the Agōn Motif: Traditional Athletic Imagery in the Pauline Literature* (NovTSup 16; Leiden: Brill, 1967); and N. Clayton Croy, *Endurance in Suffering: Hebrews 12.1-13 in Its Rhetorical, Religious, and Philosophical Context* (SNTSMS 98; Cambridge: Cambridge University Press, 1998), 37–76.

43. Author's modification of the NRSV. *Humility / tapeinophrosynē* ties the introductory section with the first example, since in verse 8 Christ "humbled himself" (*etapeinōsen heauton*). Humility and thinking that the other person is better cut sharply against the grain of first-century culture, which is based on clear distinctions between people. For parallels to verse 4, see 1 Cor 10:24, 33; 13:5; Rom 15:1-3.

44. The interpretative literature—and the variety of opinions expressed in it about authorship, structure, and background—are enormous. A benchmark summary is Ralph P. Martin,

Carmen Christi: Philippians 2:5-11 in Recent Interpretation (2nd ed.; Grand Rapids: Eerdmans, 1983), reissued with a preface on interpretation since 1983 as *A Hymn of Christ: Philippians 2:5-11 in Recent Interpretation and in the Setting of Early Christian Worship* (3rd ed.; Downers Grove, IL: InterVarsity, 1997).

45. Often hymnic material begins with a relative pronoun, which makes sense, as many Christian hymns praise God or Christ, "who ...." See Col 1:15 and 1 Tim 3:16; in each case the NRSV has hidden the word *who*.

46. R. W. Hoover, "The HARPAGMOS Enigma: A Philological Solution," *HTR* 64 (1971): 118. See also N. T. Wright, "*Harpagmos* and the Meaning of Philippians 2:5-11," *JTS* 37 (1986): 321–52.

47. C. F. D. Moule, "The Manhood of Jesus in the NT," in *Christ, Faith and History*, ed. S. W. Sykes and J. P. Clayton (Cambridge: Cambridge University Press, 1972), 97.

48. Joseph Hellerman, *Reconstructing Honor in Roman Philippi: Carmen Christi as Cursus Pudorum* (SNTSMS 132; New York: Cambridge University Press, 2005).

49. Ben Witherington III, *Friendship and Finances*, 67.

50. In this case, the word for *form* is *schēma*, which refers to the way something appears to our senses. So from what could be seen and experienced, Jesus certainly was in form a human being.

51. BDAG, 1990.

52. Scholars who argue that Paul utilized a hymn written by someone else usually also maintain that Paul added the words "even death on a cross."

53. Notice that the passage reads "the name of Jesus," not "the name Jesus." The name *of* Jesus is *Lord*.

54. Rom 10:9; 1 Cor 12:3; 2 Cor 4:5.

55. Hellerman, *Reconstructing Honor*, 151–53. For more on the contrast between Christ and the emperor, see Peter Oakes, *Philippians: From People to Letter* (SNTSMS 110; Cambridge: Cambridge University Press, 2001), 129–74.

56. To be blameless means Paul lived in conformity with the law as interpreted by his fellow Pharisees; it does not mean he was sinless or perfect. For another set of credentials, see 2 Cor 11:21—12:13. On Paul as a persecutor of the church, see Acts 8:3; 9:1, 21; 22:4, 19; 26:10-11; 1 Cor 15:9.

57. Fred B. Craddock points out that Paul does not say Judaism was no good: "Paul does not say Judaism is worthless, that it is refuse ... that intrinsically that way of life is of no value. What he is describing is his consuming desire to know Jesus Christ, to be in Christ ... and for the surpassing worth of that, he *counts* gain as loss.... Paul does not toss away junk to gain Christ; he tosses away that which was of tremendous value to him." Craddock, *Philippians* (Interpretation; Atlanta: John Knox, 1985), 58.

58. BDAG, 845.

59. *Joy* appears in 1:4; 1:25; 2:2; 2:29; 4:1. *Rejoice* appears in 1:18; 2:17; 2:18; 2:28; 3:1; 4:4 (twice).

60. See, for example, Troels Engberg-Pedersen, *Paul and the Stoics* (Louisville: Westminster John Knox, 2000). See above, chapter 4.

61. So, for example, O'Brien, *Epistle to the Philippians*, and Witherington, *Friendship and Finances*.

62. Martin Dibelius, *A Fresh Approach to the New Testament and Early Christian Literature* (New York: Scribner, 1936), 164.

63. John Reumann, "Philippians and the Culture of Friendship," *TSR* 19 (1997): 74–76. G. W. Peterman suggests that friendship and patronage are simply different manifestations of such social reciprocity (*Paul's Gift from Philippi*, 3–4). On friendship themes in this section, see John T. Fitzgerald, "Paul and Friendship," in *Paul in the Greco-Roman World: A Handbook*, ed. J. Paul Sampley (Harrisburg, PA: Trinity Press International, 2003), 332–34.

64. Reumann, "Philippians and the Culture of Friendship," 76.

65. Ibid., 77.

66. Ibid.; Reumann, *Philippians*, 686–88. In addition, a "thank you" often puts an end to a reciprocal relationship. Bruce J. Malina and John J. Pilch, *Social-Science Commentary on the Letters of Paul* (Minneapolis: Fortress Press, 2006), 318.

67. On the emperor's household, see P. R. C. Weaver, *Familia Caesaris: A Social Study of the Emperor's Freedmen and Slaves* (Cambridge: Cambridge University Press, 1972).

68. This outline uses the basic structure provided by Witherington, *Friendship and Finances*, ix–x, 18. Another helpful resource is Watson, "A Rhetorical Analysis of Philippians," 57–88.

CHAPTER 12

1. Note that Philemon has only verse numbers, since it is not divided into chapters.

2. Norman R. Petersen, *Rediscovering Paul: Philemon and the Sociology of Paul's Narrative World* (Philadelphia: Fortress Press, 1985; paperback ed.; Eugene, OR: Wipf & Stock, 2008).

3. See James D. G. Dunn, *The Epistles to the Colossians and to Philemon* (NIGTC; Grand Rapids: Eerdmans, 1996), 300; Joseph A. Fitzmyer, *The Letter to Philemon* (AB 34C; New York: Doubleday, 2000), 12; Eduard Lohse, *Colossians and Philemon*, trans. William R. Poehlmann and Robert J. Karris (Hermeneia; Philadelphia: Fortress Press, 1971), 186; Peter T. O'Brien, *Colossians, Philemon* (WBC 44; Waco, TX: Word, 1982), 265–66.

4. Perhaps through the work of Paul's subordinate Epaphras, who worked in Colossae (Col 1:7-8).

5. It is of note, however, that Paul does not call Philemon his child, as he does Onesimus (v. 10).

6. See S. Scott Bartchy, "Philemon, Epistle to," *ABD* 5:307–309; I. Howard Marshall, *The Theology of the Shorter Pauline Letters* (New Testament Theology; Cambridge: Cambridge University Press), 177–79; Dunn, *The Epistles to the Colossians and to Philemon*, 301–306; Carolyn Osiek, *Philippians, Philemon* (ANTC; Nashville: Abingdon, 2000), 128–29.

7. An important example of such intervention that is quoted in almost all commentaries is the letter from Pliny the Younger to Sabinianus, in which Pliny intervenes for a freed slave. *Epistle* 9.21, quoted in Dunn, *The Epistles to the Colossians and to Philemon*, 304–305; Lohse, *Colossians and Philemon*, 196–97, n. 2; and Fitzmyer, *Letter to Philemon*, 21–22. Pliny's *Epistle* 9.24 indicates that *Epistle* 9.21 worked. Evidence for the practice supposed in the *amicus domini* interpretation comes also from a first-century Roman legal expert, Proculus, who is quoted in the *Digest* of Justinian, 21.1.17.4 (available in Fitzmyer, *Letter to Philemon*, 20).

8. So Bruce J. Malina and John J. Pilch, *Social-Science Commentary on the Letters of Paul* (Minneapolis: Fortress Press, 2006), 326–27. Jennifer A. Glancy holds to the runaway-slave interpretation. *Slavery in Early Christianity* (Minneapolis: Fortress Press, 2006), 91. Allen Dwight Callahan denies that Onesimus was a slave at all; the only reference to his slavery is in verse 16, which has been misunderstood for centuries. Rather, Onesimus and Philemon are biological brothers who are estranged from each other. Callahan has found little agreement among other scholars, in part because of the technical Greek question regarding how to read the word *as* (Greek: *hōs*) in verse 16; grammatically, the word cannot bear the interpretation Callahan gives it. Callahan, "Paul's Epistle to Philemon: Toward an Alternative Argumentum," *HTR* 86 (1995): 357–76; Callahan, *Embassy of Onesimus: The Letter of Paul to Philemon* (New Testament in Context; Valley Forge, PA: Trinity Press International, 1997); see Fitzmyer, *Letter to Philemon*, 19.

9. Charles B. Puskas, *The Letters of Paul: An Introduction* (GNS; Collegeville, MN: Liturgical, 1993), 94.

10. David E. Aune, *The New Testament in Its Literary Environment* (Library of Early Christianity; Philadelphia: Westminster, 1987), 203; Chan-Hie Kim, *Form and Structure of the Familiar Greek Letter of Recommendation* (SBLDS 4; Missoula, MT: Scholars, 1972), 123–28. Fitzmyer specifically rejects this categorization. *Letter to Philemon*, 24. For J. Albert Harrill, the letter is a "'journeyman apprentice' contract"; in it, Paul "asks Philemon to let Onesimus be apprenticed to Paul for service in the gospel." *Slaves in the New Testament: Literary, Social, and Moral Dimensions* (Minneapolis: Fortress Press, 2006), 14.

11. Fitzmyer, *Letter to Philemon*, 7 and 24.

12. Stanley K. Stowers, *Letter Writing in Greco-Roman Antiquity* (Library of Early Christianity; Philadelphia: Westminster, 1986), 153–65.

13. Bartchy, "Philemon, Epistle to," 305.

14. Aune, *The New Testament in Its Literary Environment*, 211; Bartchy, "Philemon, Letter to," 306; F. Forrester Church, "Rhetorical Structure and Design in Paul's Letter to Philemon," *HTR* 71 (1978): 17–33; Puskas, *Letters of Paul*, 96.

15. Assigning Philemon to Rome: the Marcionite *Prologue to Philemon*, which refers to Paul: "He composes a private [?] letter to Philemon on behalf of Onesimus his servant, but he writes to him from prison in Rome"; translated in Fitzmyer, *The Letter to Philemon*, 9, with reference to D. de Bruyne, "Prologues bibliques d'origine marcionite," *Revue Bénédictine* 24 (1907) 1–16; also available in John Knox, Marcion and the New Testament: An Essay in the Early History of the Canon (Chicago: University of Chicago Press, 1942), 170–71. Another example is John Chrysostom, *In Ep. ad Philemonem Commentarius*; in J. Migne, *Patrologia Graeca*, 62.701-20. Scholars who decide for Rome include Markus Barth and Helmut Blanke, *The Letter to Philemon: A New Translation with Notes and Commentary* (The Eerdmans Critical Commentary; Grand Rapids; Eerdmans, 2000), albeit without great confidence; F. F. Bruce, *The Epistle to the Colossians, to Philemon, and to the Ephesians* (NICNT; Grand Rapids: Eerdmans, 1984); G. B. Caird, *Paul's Letters from Prison (Ephesians, Philippians, Colossians, Philemon) in the Revised Standard Version; Introduction and Commentary* (Oxford: Oxford University Press, 1976; reprint ed., 1981); C. H. Dodd, "The Mind of Paul: Change and Development," *BJRL* 18 (1934): 69–110; reprinted in his *New Testament Studies* (Manchester: Manchester University, 1953), 83–128; C. F. D. Moule, *The Epistles of Paul the Apostle to the Colossians and to Philemon* (The Cambridge Greek Testament Commentary; Cambridge: Cambridge University Press, 1968); Peter T. O'Brien, *Colossians, Philemon* (WBC 44; Waco, TX: Word Books, 1982); Udo Schnelle, *The History and Theology of the New Testament Writings*, trans. M. Eugene Boring (Minneapolis: Fortress Press, 1998).

16. The Marcionite *Prologue to Colossians* says Paul was in custody in Ephesus when he wrote Colossians (the text is in Knox, *Marcion and the New Testament*, 170–71). What is important for our purposes is not whether Paul actually wrote Colossians but that an early tradition knows of an imprisonment in Ephesus.

17. Scholars who conclude for Ephesus include Fitzmyer, *The Letter to Philemon*; Lohse, *Colossians and Philemon*; Osiek, *Philippians, Philemon*; Puskas, *The Letters of Paul*; Peter Stuhlmacher, *Der Brief an Philemon* (EKKNT 18; Neukirchen-Vluyn: Neukirchener Verlag, 1975); Sara C. Winter, "Paul's Letter to Philemon," NTS 33 (12987): 1–15.

18. Dunn, *Epistles to the Colossians and to Philemon*, 308; similarly Ralph P. Martin, *Ephesians, Colossians, and Philemon* (Interpretation; Atlanta: John Knox, 1991), 138.

19. There are many fine studies of slavery. Good orientation resources include S. Scott Bartchy, "Slavery (Greco-Roman)," *ABD* 6:65–73; S. Scott Bartchy, *First-Century Slavery and the Interpretation of 1 Corinthians 7:21* (Eugene, OR: Wipf & Stock, 2002); K. R. Bradley, *Slaves and Masters in the Roman Empire: A Study in Social Control* (New York: Oxford University Press, 1987); M. I. Finley, *Ancient Slavery and Modern Ideology* (New York: Viking, 1980); Bruce W. Winter, *Seek the Welfare of the City: Christians as Benefactors and Citizens* (First-Century Christians in the Graeco-Roman World; Grand Rapids: Eerdmans, 1994), 152–59 (on manumission and voluntary slavery).

20. Glancy, *Slavery in Early Christianity*.

21. Marshall, *The Theology of the Shorter Pauline Letters*, 190.

22. Richard J. Cassidy, *Paul in Chains: Roman Imprisonment and the Letters of St. Paul* (New York: Crossroad, 2001), 68, 73. In verse 23, Paul also refers to Epaphras as "my fellow prisoner in Christ Jesus." On coworkers, see chapter 5 of this book.

23. Ibid., 76.

24. Rom 16:3, 9, 21; 2 Cor 8:23; Phil 2:25; 4:3; 1 Thess 3:2; Philem 24. On coworkers, see chapter 5, above.

25. There are many words in the thanksgiving that Paul will use later: *love, beloved* (vv. 5, 7, 9, 16); *prayers* (vv. 4, 22); *sharing / partnership* (vv. 6, 17); *the good* (vv. 6, 14); *hearts* (literally, the word *bowels*; vv. 7, 12, 20); *refresh* (vv. 7, 20); the direct address form of the word *brother* (vv. 7, 20).

26. The word for *duty* (*to anēkon*) is a standard term in philosophical literature, especially in Stoicism.

27. See Lohse, *Colossians and Philemon*, 200. For more on duty and obligation, see the comments on v. 19.

28. In antiquity, people often talked about the "seven ages" of the human being. The lists vary, but commonly, the "old man" was the second oldest, from ages fifty to fifty-six, although in some classifications the "old man" was the last age period and designated people in their sixties.

29. Another level of wordplay may be going on, too. In the Greek spoken at the time of Paul, the word *useful* (*chrēstos*), two forms of which are used in verse 11, was pronounced the same way as the word *Christ* (*christos*). Perhaps the play is this: "Formerly he was useless/Christ-less to you, but now he is indeed useful/with Christ." See Lohse, *Colossians and Philemon*, 200.

30. Literally, Paul writes, "I sent him back to you." The sense seems to be this: while Paul is writing, he plans to send Onesimus to Philemon with the letter. When Philemon receives and reads the letter, the action of having sent Onesimus will be in the past, so Paul writes, "I sent him."

31. See Church, "Rhetorical Structure and Design," 27.

32. Elsewhere, too, Paul takes up the pen toward the end of the document (Gal 6:11; 1 Cor 16:21).

33. On the church as a fictive family, see Joseph H. Hellerman, *The Ancient Church as Family* (Minneapolis: Fortress Press, 2001); Halvor Moxnes, ed., *Constructing Early Christian Families: Family as Social Reality and Metaphor* (London: Routledge, 1997); S. Scott Bartchy, "Undermining Ancient Patriarchy: The Apostle Paul's Vision of a Society of Siblings," *BTB* 29 (1999): 68–78; and ch. 5, above.

34. Petersen, *Rediscovering Paul*, 76.

35. Ibid., 78.

36. Ibid., 295.

37. Walter F. Taylor Jr., "Obligation: Paul's Foundation for Ethics," *TSR* 19 (1997): 91–112, published in a different version in *Josephinum Journal of Theology* 5, no. 1 (1998): 5–25.

38. Bartchy, "Philemon," 5:308.

39. With varying degrees of certainty, Fitzmyer, *Paul's Letter to Philemon*, 32; Marshall, *The Theology of the Shorter Pauline Letters*, 179–80; O'Brien, *Colossians, Philemon*, 267.

40. Petersen, *Rediscovering Paul*, 23.

41. Lloyd A. Lewis, "An African American Appraisal of the Philemon-Paul-Onesimus Triangle," in *Stony the Road We Trod: African American Biblical Interpretation*, ed. Cain Hope Felder (Minneapolis: Fortress Press, 1991), 240.

42. In Greek, the actual statement of thanksgiving ("I give thanks") is stated first; the description of when thanks is given ("always remembering you in my prayers") comes second.

43. The Greek word order in verse 10 differs from the NRSV: "I am appealing to you for my child, whom I begot in chains, Onesimus" (author's literal translation). Verse 11 more closely identifies Onesimus by means of a wordplay on his name.

CHAPTER 13

1. See ch. 2 above. It is not the purpose of this chapter to enter into the various arguments regarding authorship but to build on the conclusion in ch. 2 regarding the authorship of these letters.

2. Richard I. Pervo, *The Making of Paul: Constructions of the Apostle in Early Christianity* (Minneapolis: Fortress Press, 2010), 63.

3. J. Christiaan Beker, *The Triumph of God: The Essence of Paul's Thought* (Minneapolis: Fortress Press, 1990), 34. The italicized material is from Beker. As Brown puts it, the Thessalonians "can relax because the apocalyptic signs that must precede the coming of that day have not yet

occurred." Raymond E. Brown, *An Introduction to the New Testament* (New York: Doubleday, 1997), 590.

4. The identity of the restraining agent is the source of much exegetical grief. In 2:6, the language is *to katechon* (what is restraining); the term is in the neuter gender. Thus, one theory has been that the restraining agent is the gospel (*to euaggelion*, a neuter noun) or even the Roman Empire. But in 2:7, the term that is used is *ho katechōn* (the restrainer); the noun is masculine and has been understood to refer to God, Christ, or Paul. If the "man of lawlessness" is the emperor, then perhaps *the restrainer* is Roman law that tries to keep the emperor under control. On this complex of issues, see Charles A. Wanamaker, *The Epistles to the Thessalonians* (NIGTC; Grand Rapids: Eerdmans, 1990), 250–52; Karl P. Donfried, "The Theology of 2 Thessalonians," in *The Theology of the Shorter Pauline Letters*, ed. Karl P. Donfried and I. Howard Marshall, 93–94 (Cambridge: Cambridge University Press, 1993); Earl J. Richard, *First and Second Thessalonians* (Sacra Pagina 11; Collegeville, MN: Liturgical, 1995), 337–40; Abraham J. Malherbe, *The Letters to the Thessalonians* (AB 32B; New York: Doubleday, 2000), 422–24.

5. For Charles B. Puskas Jr., the theme of divine retribution against the persecutors of believers is a definite sign of the post-Paul generation. *The Letters of Paul: An Introduction* (GNS; Collegeville, MN: Liturgical, 1993), 108–109.

6. On the history of scholarship on 2 Thessalonians, see F. W. Hughes, "Thessalonians, First and Second Letters to the," in *Dictionary of Biblical Interpretation*, ed. John H. Hayes, 2:568–72 (Nashville: Abingdon, 1999).

7. Walter F. Taylor Jr., *Ephesians* (ACNT; Minneapolis: Augsburg, 1985), 11–13; Andrew T. Lincoln, *Ephesians* (WBC 42; Dallas: Word, 1990), xlvii–lvi. For a discussion about the authorship of Ephesians, see chapter 2 above. Ernest Best maintains that the use of Colossians by the author of Ephesians is not as certain as many scholars assume. *Ephesians* (ICC; Edinburgh: T & T Clark, 1998), 20–25, 36–40. Clinton E. Arnold is sure that Ephesians did not use Colossians. *Ephesians* (Zondervan Exegetical Commentary on the New Testament; Grand Rapids: Zondervan, 2010). Ephesians also uses several other New Testament documents. Taylor, *Ephesians*, 13; Lincoln, *Ephesians*, lvi–lviii.

8. In Rom 6:4, Paul exercises great care *not* to say that the believer has already been resurrected. Christ has been raised from the dead, but believers have not; they are to "walk in newness of life."

9. See above, chapter 10 on Romans.

10. Pervo, *The Making of Paul*, 67.

11. J. Christiaan Beker, *Heirs of Paul: Paul's Legacy in the New Testament and in the Church Today* (Minneapolis: Fortress Press, 1991), 68, 72; see also Pervo, *The Making of Paul*, 70.

12. On the history of the interpretation of Colossians and Ephesians, see J. B. MacLean, "Colossians, Letter to the," *Dictionary of Biblical Interpretation*, 1:206–210; and W. F. Taylor, "Ephesians, Letter to the," *Dictionary of Biblical Interpretation*, 1:336–40.

13. Note especially the charts in ch. 2.

14. Philipp Vielhauer, "On the 'Paulinism' of Acts," in *The Writings of St. Paul*, ed. Wayne A. Meeks (1st ed.; New York: Norton, 1972), 174. Hans Conzelmann carried that insight further by arguing that Luke replaced the primitive Christian view of the imminent end with a theology of saving history. *The Theology of St. Luke*, trans. Geoffrey Buswell (New York: Harper, 1960). Ernst Käsemann, in distinction from Hans Conzelmann, maintained that the real theme of Luke is that the church is in fact in the middle of time and is representative of what he labeled early catholicism (which for Käsemann was not a positive term). "Paul and Early Catholicism," in his *New Testament Questions of Today*, trans. W. J. Montague (Philadelphia: Fortress Press, 1969), 236–51.

15. Beker, *Heirs of Paul*, 50.

16. Chapter 2 above.

17. The type of "natural theology" and benign view of Greco-Roman idols evidenced in Paul's Areopagus speech (Acts 17:22-31) are especially dissonant with the Paul of the undisputed letters.

18. Pervo, *The Making of Paul*, 153.
19. John Dominic Crossan and Jonathan L. Reed, *In Search of Paul: How Jesus's Apostle Opposed Rome's Empire with God's Kingdom* (New York: HarperSanFrancisco, 2004), 105.
20. Richard L. Pervo suggests a substantially later date of 110–120. *Acts: A Commentary* (Hermeneia; Minneapolis: Fortress Press, 2009).
21. For more on church organization in the Pastorals, see Walter F. Taylor Jr., "1–2 Timothy, Titus," in *The Deutero-Pauline Letters: Ephesians, Colossians, 2 Thessalonians, 1-2 Timothy, Titus*, ed. Gerhard Krodel, 80–86 (Proclamation Commentaries; rev. ed.; Minneapolis: Fortress Press, 1993); Taylor, "1 Timothy 3:1-7. The Public Side of Ministry," *TSR* 14 (1992): 5–17; Raymond E. Collins, *1 & 2 Timothy and Titus: A Commentary* (NTL; Louisville: Westminster John Knox, 2002), 326–32.
22. Margaret Y. MacDonald, *The Pauline Churches: A Socio-historical Study of Institutionalization in the Pauline and Deutero-Pauline Writings* (SNTSMS 60; Cambridge: Cambridge University Press, 1988), 159–234.
23. The dispute over head covering or hairstyle is simply that: a dispute over how a woman who prays or prophesies (preaches) in the believing community is to present herself. There is no question about a woman's ability to lead worship; that is simply assumed.
24. For an overview of the Pastorals' perspective on women, see Collins, *1 & 2 Timothy and Titus*, 72–75.
25. Taylor, "1–2 Timothy, Titus," 77; David E. Aune, *The New Testament in Its Literary Environment* (Early Christian Library; Philadelphia: Westminster, 1987), 204; Pervo, *The Making of Paul*, 83, respectively. On the history of the interpretation of the Pastoral Epistles, see Ernest Best, "Pastoral Letters," in *Dictionary of Biblical Interpretation* 2:242–47.
26. Clayton N. Jefford, with Kenneth J. Harder and Louis D. Amezaga Jr., *Reading the Apostolic Fathers: An Introduction* (Peabody, MA: Hendrickson, 1996), 59.
27. Pervo, *The Making of Paul*, 134–35.
28. Paul Foster, "The Epistles of Ignatius of Antioch," in *The Writings of the Apostolic Fathers*, ed. Paul Foster, 84–89 (London: T & T Clark, 2007).
29. Quotations of Ignatius come from *The Apostolic Fathers*, ed. and trans. Bart D. Ehrman (LCL; Cambridge, MA: Harvard University Press, 2003), vol. 1.
30. Foster, "The Epistles of Ignatius," 104–106; Carl B. Smith, "Ministry, Martyrdom, and Other Mysteries: Pauline Influence on Ignatius of Antioch," in *Paul and the Second Century*, ed. Michael F. Bird and Joseph R. Dodson (London: T & T Clark, 2011), 40.
31. For more on Ignatius's understanding of the role of the bishop and other ministers, see Foster, "The Epistles of Ignatius," 93–98.
32. For a discussion of other passages that exhibit similarities between Ignatius and Paul, including the weight Ignatius gives to the human suffering of Jesus, see Smith, "Ministry, Martyrdom, and Other Mysteries," 51–55.
33. Todd D. Still, "Shadow and Light: Marcion's (Mis)Construal of the Apostle Paul," in Bird and Dodson, *Paul and the Second Century*, 101.
34. David Salter Williams has questioned how much Marcion did, in fact, alter Luke. "Reconsidering Marcion's Gospel," *JBL* 108 (1989): 477–96.
35. Adolf von Harnack, *Marcion: Das Evangelium vom fremden Gott* (2nd ed.; Leipzig: J. C. Hinrichs, 1924), 89–92, translated in Wayne A. Meeks and John T. Fitzgerald, *The Writings of St. Paul* (2nd ed.; New York: Norton, 2007), 286–88.
36. A conclusion of Harnack's. For questions about that view, see Still, "Shadow and Light," 103.
37. Adolf von Harnack, *History of Dogma*, trans. Neil Buchanan (New York: Dover, 1961), 1:89. On whether or not Marcion was a Gnostic, see Pervo, *The Making of Paul*, 20. For a helpful introduction to the history of scholarship on Marcion, see Still, "Shadow and Light."
38. Chapter 4 above.
39. Neil Elliott and Mark Reasoner, eds., *Documents and Images for the Study of Paul* (Minneapolis: Fortress Press, 2011), 316.

40. Elaine H. Pagels, *The Gnostic Paul: Gnostic Exegesis of the Pauline Letters* (Philadelphia: Fortress Press, 1975), 1.

41. The language comes from Nicholas Perrin, "Paul and Valentinian Interpretation," in Bird and Dodson, *Paul and the Second Century*, 127.

42. For an introduction to Valentinus's life and thought, see Bentley Layton, *The Gnostic Scriptures: A New Translation with Annotations and Introductions* (Garden City, NY: Doubleday, 1987), 217–22.

43. Pagels, *The Gnostic Paul*, 3.

44. Perrin, "Paul and Valentinian Interpretation," 129.

45. From *The Nag Hammadi Library in English*, ed. James M. Robinson (4th rev. ed.; Leiden: Brill, 1996).

46. Jacqueline A. Williams, *Biblical Interpretation in the Gnostic Gospel of Truth from Nag Hammadi* (SBLDS 79; Atlanta: Scholars, 1988), 182, 186–87.

47. Perrin, "Paul and Valentinian Interpretation," 139.

48. Andrew Gregory, "The *Acts of Paul* and the Legacy of Paul," in Bird and Dodson, *Paul and the Second Century*, 171.

49. Pervo's preferred date. *The Making of Paul*, 156.

50. Ibid., 157–58. For further introduction and a translation, see Wilhlem Schneemelcher and Rodolphe Kasser, "The Acts of Paul," in *New Testament Apocrypha*, ed. Edgar Hennecke and Wilhelm Schneemelcher; English trans. ed. R. M. Wilson, 2:213–70 (rev. ed.; Louisville: Westminster John Knox, 1992).

51. Pervo, *The Making of Paul*, 164.

52. See the study by Dennis Ronald MacDonald, *The Legend and the Apostle: The Battle for Paul in Story and Canon* (Louisville: Westminster, 1983); the author of the Pastorals is arguing against the radical Paul of the legends that lie at the basis of the *Acts of Paul and Thecla* as well as those (women) who are spreading them (p. 77).

53. Pervo prefers Clementines rather than Pseudo-Clementines as the name of the literature. *The Making of Paul*, 344 n. 237.

54. Joel Willitts, "Paul and Jewish Christians in the Second Century," in Bird and Dodson, *Paul and the Second Century*, 161.

55. On the complexity of Jewish Christian groups, see Matt Jackson-McCabe, ed., *Jewish Christianity Reconsidered: Rethinking Ancient Groups and Texts* (Minneapolis: Fortress Pres, 2007). On the Pseudo-Clementines, see F. Stanley Jones, "The Pseudo-Clementines," in McCabe, *Jewish Christianity Reconsidered*; Jones, "Jewish Christianity of the Pseudo-Clementines," in *A Companion to Second-Century Christian "Heretics,"* ed. Antti Marjanen and Petri Luomanen, 314–34 (VCSup 76; Leiden: Brill, 2005).

56. From Alexander Roberts and James Donaldson, eds., *The Ante-Nicene Fathers* (repr. ed.; Grand Rapids: Eerdmans, 1950), vol. 1. On the Ebionites, see Sakari Hakkinen, "Ebionites," in Marjanen and Luomanen, *A Companion to Second-Century Christian "Heretics,"* 247–78.

57. Quotations and references to the *Recognitions* and *Homilies* are from Alexander Roberts and James Donaldson, eds., *The Ante-Nicene Fathers* (repr. ed.; Grand Rapids: Eerdmans, 1951), vol. 8.

58. Quoted from Johannes Irmscher and Georg Strecker, "The Pseudo-Clementines," in Hennecke and Schneemelcher, *New Testament Apocrypha*, 2:494.

59. Giorgio Agamben, *The Time That Remains: A Commentary on the Letter to the Romans*, trans. Patricia Dailey (Stanford, CA: Stanford University Press, 2005).

General Index: Authors and Subjects

1 Clement, 106, 195, 198, 230
2 Clement, 22, 106
2 Thessalonians, 21, 23, 25, 28, 31, 111, 289, 290–92, 300, 302
1 Timothy, 21, 23, 28, 31, 289, 297–99
2 Timothy, 21, 23, 28, 31, 289, 297–99
3 Corinthians, 22, 303

Aageson, James W., 112
Abraham, 145, 146, 148–49, 151, 152–53, 203, 217, 239, 245, 300
Achaicus, 103, 119, 167, 171, 185
Achtemeier, Paul, 236–37, 253
Acts, New Testament book of
    as introduction to Paul, 297
    source of Paul's life and thought, 27–34
    view of Paul, 295–97
    "we" sections, 30–31
Acts of John, 49
Acts of Paul, 303
Acts of Paul and Thecla, 31, 63, 289, 303–4
Adam, 114, 184, 241, 268
admonition, 112, 129, 199, 311
adoption
    Christ-believers as God's adopted children, 244
aedile, 165, 311
Aelius Aristides, 41
Agamben, Giorgio, 7, 307
Agrippa, 128
Aland, Kurt, 34
Alexander the Great, 45, 71, 156
already—not yet, 167, 183, 185, 203, 240, 293, 297
amanuensis, 117, 311
ambassadors for Christ, 211–12
American School of Classical Studies at Athens, 188
Amezaga, Louis D., Jr., 309
analogy, 114, 311
Anaximenes, 15
Andronicus, 49, 86
Aphrodite, 76, 163
Apocalypse of Paul, 303
Apollo, 37, 70, 76, 163
Apollos, 103, 162, 168, 185
apologia/apology, 201, 311

apostle, 85, 87–88, 144, 204, 311
Apostolic Council, 27, 29, 32, 33, 38, 40, 120, 147, 154
Apphia, 104, 107, 280, 283, 285
Aquila, 86, 94, 103, 162, 185, 231, 249
Archippus, 107, 278, 280, 283
Aretas IV, 37–38, 40
Aristarchus, 103
Aristophanes, 163–64
Aristotle, 15, 109, 111, 280
Artemis, 47, 76, 163
artisans, 60–62, 162, 163
ascetic/asceticism, 64, 67, 74, 182, 303–4, 311
Asclepius, 70–71, 128, 161, 163
Ascough, Richard S., 97
astrology, 67, 68
atonement, 54, 238–39, 311
atrium, 95, 101, 312
Attridge, Harold W., 309
Augustine, 3, 306
Aune, David E., 19, 109

Badiou, Alain, 7
Bailey, James L., 123
Balch, David L., 72, 89
baptism, 55, 72–73, 87, 96, 99, 100, 101, 112, 115, 131, 150–52, 167, 183, 195, 199, 211, 242–44, 245, 246, 292, 299, 300–301, 305
    baptismal formulas, 116
Barnabas, 32, 38, 103–4, 147
Barnabas, Epistle of, 22, 106
Barnett, Paul, 163, 198, 199, 220
Barrett, C. K., 34, 50, 89, 194
Barrier, Jeremy W., 309
Bartchy, S. Scott, 176
Barth, Karl, 3
Barth, Markus, 288, 308
Baur, F. C., 307
Beal, T. K., 19
Beardslee, William A., 19
Beck, James, 218
Beker, J. Christiaan, 83, 88, 291, 295, 296
Best, Ernest, 308

Betz, Hans Dieter, xiii, 59, 110, 151, 155, 159, 166, 169, 193, 198
Bible
    cultural anthropological study of, 14, 312
    feminist study of, 12, 17, 313
    historical study of, 11–13, 314
    literary study of, 15–17, 315
    narrative critical study of, 16–17, 315
    political study of, 13, 316
    rhetorical study of, 15, 316
    social-scientific study of, 13–14, 316
    sociological study of, 14, 316
    theological study of, 17–18, 317
bishop, 6, 97, 230, 265, 288, 297, 298, 299, 305
Blanke, Helmut, 288, 308
blessing, 79, 108, 116, 121, 130, 149, 151, 304
boasting, 51, 65, 88, 100, 131, 133, 157, 164, 182, 191, 192, 203, 208, 214, 216-17, 220, 226, 237, 239, 261, 271, 290
body
    of Christ, 25, 174, 179–80, 181, 186, 242–43, 294–95, 298
    in Lord's Supper, 72
    human, 67, 74, 148, 157, 167–68, 171, 173–74, 175, 186, 272
    resurrection body, 169, 183, 184–85, 211, 272
    spiritual body, 184
de Boer, Martinus C., 159, 307
Bornkamm, Günther, 197–99
Bowker, J. W., 218
brothers
    translated as *brothers and sisters*, 128
Bruce, F. F., 194, 263
build/building up, 92–93, 137, 176, 178, 182
Bultmann, Rudolf, 3, 198, 307

Caesar, as god, 134
Caesar Augustus (Octavian), 41, 63, 77–80, 119, 128, 178, 224, 256, 312

Caligula, 41
call, 82, 312
Calvin, John, 307
canon, 21, 27, 53, 54, 297, 300, 301, 312
captatio benevolentiae, 214, 312
Carter, Warren, 39, 50, 89
Cassidy, Richard J., 39, 248, 262, 263, 264, 281
catechetical material, 116, 312
catholic/catholicity, 300, 301
Cenchreae, 162, 235, 249
Cephas (Peter), 30, 38, 86, 87, 147, 168, 183
challenge and riposte, 42, 43, 96, 312
charlatan, 61, 130–31, 138
Charlesworth, James H., 34
chiasm, 112, 176, 312
Chloe, 105, 165, 166, 171
Christ, 312
    dying and rising, 72–73, 267–69
    hymn to, 266–69, 272
    as a title, 5
Christ-believer instead of Christian, 5–6
Christian/Christianity
    problem with using during Paul's lifetime, 5–6
    used by Ignatius, 299
church, 312
    as body of Christ, 25, 174, 179–80, 181, 186, 242–43, 294–95, 298
    as bride of Christ, 216, 294
    as cosmic entity, 294
    as fictive family, 95–97, 101, 121, 122, 128–29, 132, 285–86, 288, 313
    house church, 93–95, 166
    as institution, 295–96
    as siblings, 96
    threat to Roman Empire, 97
    tradition, 115–16
    as voluntary association, 97
Cicero, 15, 41, 78, 106, 117, 280
circumcision, 52, 83, 145, 147, 148, 149, 152, 154, 155, 164, 175, 203, 237, 240, 259, 263–64, 271, 305, 312
circum-Mediterranean, 42, 312

city
    Greco-Roman, 44–46
    Greek, 44–45
    Hellenistic, 45
Clabeaux, John J., 309
Clarkson, J. Shannon, 188
Claudius, 36–37, 41, 225, 227, 230–31, 232, 249
Clement (New Testament person), 103
Clement of Alexandria, 72, 74, 86, 302
Clement of Rome, 305
collection, 32, 38, 92, 102, 104, 120–23, 154, 157–58, 185, 193, 195, 197, 198, 200, 201, 202, 213–14, 219, 248
Collins, Raymond F., 188, 308
Colossae, 278, 280, 281
Colossians and Ephesians, 292–95
confessional statement/creed, 115–16, 133, 150, 183, 225, 269, 312
Corinth, 162–64, 235, 249, 256
Corinth Computer Project, 188
Cousar, Charles B., 84, 108, 123, 275
covenant, 52, 115, 145, 146, 148, 149, 180, 206, 208–11, 228, 238, 239, 240, 247, 259, 294, 300, 312
Cranfield, C. E. B., 228
creed/confessional statement, 115–16, 133, 150, 183, 225, 269, 312
Crispus, 162, 165
cross, crucifixion, 55, 74, 103, 157, 169–70, 172, 182, 183, 268, 299
cross, theology of, 172, 210
Crossan, John Dominic, 89, 297
Cynicism, 64–65, 156

Danker, Frederick W., 198, 220
David (King), 5, 18, 224, 225
Davies, W. D., 89
day of the Lord, 128, 135–38, 171, 184, 208, 248, 290–91, 292
deacon, 48, 249, 265, 297, 299
Dead Sea Scrolls, 53, 55, 115, 134, 193, 195, 312
debt, 227, 282, 285–86, 288
Deissmann, Adolf, 106–7

deliberative rhetoric, 109, 111, 128, 155, 169, 193, 201, 213, 260, 267, 280, 283, 312
Demas, 103
Demeter, 71–72, 163
deuteropauline letters, 289–90, 301, 313
diaspora, 56–58, 73, 84, 98, 313
diatribe, 59, 64, 65, 112, 113, 235, 241–42, 244, 313
Dibelius, Martin, 273
Didachē, The (Teaching of the Twelve Apostles), 48
Dio Chrysostom, 64–65
Diogenes (the Cynic), 64, 156
Diogenes Laertius, 67, 151, 156
Dionysus, 72, 85, 163
divination, 68
domestic cult, 68
domus/villa, 46, 95, 97, 101, 166, 179, 313
Donfried, Karl P., 32, 139, 141, 253, 307
doxology, 116, 198, 246, 313
Dozeman, Thomas B., 19
Dunn, James D. G., 145, 146, 228, 240, 253, 281, 288, 308
dyadic personality, 43, 312

Ebionites, 305
Ehrman, Bart D., 27
elder (presbyter), 29, 297, 299
Eleusinian mystery religion, 71–72
elites, 42, 59, 76, 77, 166, 267, 313
Elliott, John H., 18, 42, 43
Elliott, Neil, xiii, 18, 50, 89, 102–3, 120
emperor
    as patron, 45
Engberg-Pedersen, Troels, 66
Epaenetus, 249
Epaphras, 286
Epaphroditus, 103, 105, 119, 256, 258, 260, 269, 271
Ephesians and Colossians, 292–95
Ephesus, 249, 262–63
Epictetus, 65
Epicureanism, 66–67, 129
Epicurus, 66, 67

epideictic rhetoric, 109, 111, 169, 234, 313
Epiphanius, 74
Epistle of Peter to James, 305–6
Erastus, 165, 249
eschatology/eschatological, 87, 92, 115, 151, 229, 273, 291–92, 295, 297, 313
Esler, Philip F., 4–5, 121, 159, 232
Essenes, 51, 313
ethnē
    translated as Gentiles, 5, 225
    translated as nations, 5, 225
    ethnic identity, 152
ethos, 109, 110, 201, 313
Euodia, 103, 104, 257, 259, 272
Eusebius, 39
exegesis/exegetical, 114, 302, 313

faith, 23, 87, 107, 112, 137, 144, 145, 148–51, 156, 182, 204, 227, 229, 238–39, 240, 245–46, 248, 266, 271, 283, 286, 290, 292
    faith in or faith of, 145–47
    obedience of, 108, 225–26, 241
Fee, Gordon D., 263, 275, 307
fictive family, 67, 91–92, 313
    alternative to Roman Empire, 96
    church as, 95–97, 101, 121, 122, 128–29, 132, 285–86, 288
Fiore, Benjamin, 19, 308
first fruits, 183–84
Fitzgerald, John T., 9, 259, 263
Fitzmyer, Joseph A., 188, 236, 253, 288, 308
flesh, 74, 148, 156, 157, 172, 202, 211, 218, 243, 258, 259, 263, 268, 271, 280, 282, 284, 286, 292, 294, 302, 304
food sacrificed to idols, 176–78
form (pattern of discourse), 110, 112–16, 313
Fortunatus, 103, 119, 167, 171, 185
Foster, Paul, 309
freedom, 64, 80, 151, 155, 156–57, 174, 175–76, 177, 242
Furnish, Victor Paul, 13, 141, 191, 194, 195, 199, 220

Gaius, 249
Galen, 70
Gallio, 36–37, 40, 162, 170
Gamaliel, 56, 61
Gaventa, Beverly Roberts, 141
Gehring, Roger W., 102
Georgi, Dieter, 198
Glancy, Jennifer A., 282
glossolalia (speaking in tongues), 93, 102, 167, 181–82, 313
Gnosticism, 31, 73–75, 169, 301–3, 313
God-fearers, 57, 98–99, 162, 166
gods, Greek and Roman, 76
Goodacre, Mark, 123
gospel, 14, 60, 69, 85, 87, 99, 100, 138, 144, 147, 153, 154, 155, 157, 163, 171, 202, 203, 204, 216, 217, 224–29, 231, 234, 235, 244, 246, 257, 260, 265, 266, 272, 291, 292, 295, 296, 300, 302, 313
Gospel of Truth, 302
grace, 82, 107, 108, 121, 144, 169, 171, 208, 213, 219, 238, 240, 241, 246, 250, 292–93, 313
Greco-Roman dinners, 179
Greek language
    Hellenistic, 45
    Koine, 45
Green, Joel B., 18
Gregory, Andrew, 303
group identity, 52, 147, 233
Gruen, Eric, 57
Gunther, John J., 263

Hades, 71–72
Haenchen, Ernst, 34, 308
Hansen , Bruce, 152
Harder, Kenneth J., 309
Harnack, Adolf von, 300, 301, 309
Hata, Gohei, 309
Hausrath, Adolf, 196
Haustafel/n (tables of household duties), 67, 293, 314
Hawthorne, Gerald F., 275
Hayes, Holly, 276

Hayes, John H., 19, 34
Hays, Richard B., 146, 188
Headlam, Arthur C., 24
healing cults, 70–71
heaven, 66, 74, 134, 218–19, 257, 266, 269, 272, 293, 294
Hellenism, 45, 56, 65, 314
Hellenistic Greek, 45
Hellenization, 45, 56, 314
Hellerman, Joseph, 95, 123, 267–69
Hennecke, Edgar, 309
Hermes, 76, 163
Herod, 128
Hesiod, 79
Hestia, 68
Hippocrates, 70
Hippolytus, 74
Hisey, Alan, 218
Hock, Ronald F., 50, 59, 60, 61
Hoffmann, R. Joseph, 309
Hofius, Otfried, 245, 246
Holladay, Carl R., 12, 15–16, 17, 18
holy ones/saints
    Christ-believers as, 55, 171, 226
Holy Spirit, 55, 100, 174, 243–44, 314
    how received, 147–48
Homilies, 305–6
honor and shame, 14, 42–43, 44, 64, 96, 98, 101, 122, 179, 202, 212, 214, 217, 224, 227, 247, 265–66, 267–69, 270, 271, 272, 283, 284, 314
Hoover, R. W., 267
hope, 88, 131, 133, 138, 185, 239, 265, 291
Horsley, Richard A., 18
house church, 92, 93–95, 96–97, 98, 99, 102, 103, 107, 166, 169, 231, 273, 279, 294, 314
Hultgren, Arland J., 92, 123, 226, 240, 253, 308
humanitas, 41
humility/humiliation, 213, 260, 266, 268, 272
hymn, 116
    to Christ, 266–69, 272

Ignatius of Antioch, 6, 31, 106, 198, 288, 289, 295, 298–99
imitate/imitation, 131, 173, 178, 272, 273, 298–99
indicative-imperative, 247, 314
insula, 46, 95, 314
interpolation, 182, 199, 212, 314
Irenaeus, 74, 301, 305, 306
Irmscher, Johannes, 309
Isis, 72, 128
Israel's Bible, 4
  apocalyptic application of, 115
  Marcion's view of, 300
  Paul's view of, 112
  Paul's use of, 112–15

James, brother of Jesus, 27, 32, 38, 87, 147, 296, 305–6
Jeffers, James S., 50, 89
Jefford, Clayton N., 309
Jesus
  appearance, 297
  death for humanity, 83, 137, 209, 238–39
  designated as God, 297
  Lord, 82, 128, 257, 268–69
  poverty, 212
  return of (imminent), 115, 131–34, 138, 140, 171, 184, 259, 273, 291, 292, 297, 314
  Son of God, 82, 225, 297
Jewett, Robert, 85, 110, 117, 224, 231, 235, 253
Johnson, Luke Timothy, 15, 308
Jones, F. Stanley, 309
Josephus, 37, 69
Joshua, 18, 224
Judaizers, 154–55, 156, 158, 203
Judas Iscariot, 27, 179–80
Judean as translation of *Ioudaios*, 4–5, 314
judgment, 55, 67, 133, 135, 173, 180, 227, 237, 248, 291–92
judicial rhetoric, 111, 155, 169, 201, 314
Julius Caesar, 41, 77, 79, 163, 256, 314
Junia, 86, 104

Juno, 45, 46, 76, 77
Jupiter, 45, 46, 76, 77
justify/justification, 23, 54, 82, 92, 144, 145, 146, 147, 149, 167, 227–29, 238, 239, 240, 244, 246, 250, 271, 314
Juvenal, 46

Käsemann, Ernst, 228, 229, 307
Keck, Leander E., 12–13, 34, 229
Keefer, K. A., 19
Kennedy, George A., 19, 193, 201
Kilpatrick, G. D., 259
Klauck, Hans-Josef, 65, 89, 196, 309
Kloppenborg, John, 97
Knox, John, 29
Koester, Helmut, 198, 224
Koine Greek, 45
Kore, 71–72
Krentz, Edgar, 18
Krodel, Gerhard, xiii, 34, 307, 308, 309
Kümmel, Werner, 198

Lactantius, 151
de Lagarde, Paul, 4
Lampe, Peter, 95
Law (of Moses), 5, 30, 52, 53, 54–55, 81, 115, 145, 147, 149–50, 153, 154–56, 167, 209, 238, 239, 240, 300, 305
  as disciplinarian, 150
  Paul's view of, 54, 83, 151, 157, 173, 227, 228, 237, 242, 244–45
Lechaeum, 162
Lendering, Jona, 276
Letter of Tears, 104, 105, 194, 195, 196, 197, 198, 199, 200, 202, 204, 205, 206, 208, 213, 215
letters, 105–20, 314. *See also* Paul, letters
  collection of, 120–23
  delivery of, 119
  determining authorship, 22–25
  friendship, 260
  genre (epistle versus letter), 106–7, 313, 314
  production of, 116–19
  reading of, 119–20

secretary, use of, 117–19
structure, 107–8
Levine, Amy-Jill, 19
Linafelt. T., 19
Lincoln, Andrew T., 308
literary seam, 170, 190–94, 199, 257–59, 314
logos, 110, 201, 315
Lord's Supper (Eucharist), 55, 73–75, 94, 101, 115, 116, 122, 147, 166, 168, 177, 179–80, 301
love, 88, 122, 128, 129, 156–57, 176–77, 181–82, 185, 211, 212, 214, 238, 244, 245, 247, 248, 283, 286, 293, 300
Lucian, 67
Luke (associate of Paul's), 103
Luke (gospel of), 27, 29, 30, 47, 56, 151, 300
Luther, Martin, 3, 228, 229, 307

MacDonald, Dennis R., 309
MacDonald, Margaret Y., 123, 298, 308
Mack, Burton L., 19
magic, 68–70
Majercik, Ruth, 19
Malherbe, Abraham J., 66, 141, 307
Malina, Bruce J., 18, 19, 42, 43, 50
Marc Antony, 41, 256, 311
Marcion, 31, 195, 250, 289, 299–301
Marcus Aurelius, 65
Mark (associate of Paul's), 103, 104
marriage, 11, 55, 86, 129, 174–75, 214
Marshall, I. H., 34, 141, 282, 307
Martin, Michael, 276
Martin, Ralph P., 193, 194, 195, 199, 221, 275
Martyn , J. Louis, 34, 155, 159
Martyrdom of Paul, 303
Mary, 103, 104
Matera, Frank J., 159, 221
Matthews, Shelly, 309
McCant, Jerry, 218
meat sacrificed to idols, 176–78
Mediterranean culture, 42–44
Meeks, Wayne A., 9, 99

Meyer, Marvin W., 71
Messiah (as a title), 5, 315
midrash, 114, 149, 315
Minerva, 45, 46, 76
Mitchell, Margaret, 105, 166, 169
Mithras, 72–73
Moll, Sebastian, 309
Moses, 18, 114, 150, 201, 209, 224, 238, 245
Moule, C. F. D., 267
Moxnes, Halvor, 96
Murphy-O'Connor, Jerome, 188
mystery religions, 71–73, 97

Nag Hammadi documents, 74–75, 315
  Apocalypse of Paul, 303
  Gospel of Truth, 302
  Prayer of the Apostle Paul, 303
  Treatise on Resurrection (*Epistle to Rheginus*), 303
  Tripartite Tractate, 303
Nanos, Mark D., 145
neo-Pythagoreanism, 67
Nero, 39, 41, 248, 263, 264, 269, 315
Neusner, Jacob, 89
New Perspective on Paul, 240
Newsom, Carol A., 19
Neyrey , Jerome H., 19, 199
Nietzsche, Friedrich, 4
Nisbet, Patricia, 218

obligation, 43, 65, 86, 97, 100, 121, 122, 285–86, 288
O'Brien, Julia, 263
O'Brien, Peter T., 275
Octavian (Caesar Augustus), 41, 63, 77–80, 119, 128, 178, 224, 256, 312, 315
Olbricht, T. H., 19
omens, 68
one, God as, 150
Onesimus, 101, 119, 277–88
oracles, 68
Origen, 74
orthodox/orthodoxy, 301

Osiek, Carolyn, 123, 288

Pagels, Elaine, 301, 302, 309
Panaetius, 41
Paola, Justin D., 276
Papakyriakou/Anagnostou, Ellen, 188
paraenesis, 108, 112, 127–29, 155–57, 212, 247–48, 315
parousia, 133–134, 135, 139, 184, 291, 315
Pastoral Epistles (1–2 Timothy, Titus), 23, 297–99, 301, 302, 315
pathos, 110, 201, 295, 315
patron-client relationship, 43–44, 61, 216–17, 256, 273, 315
Paul
   Acts as source for Paul's life and thought, 27–34
   Acts' view of Paul, 295–96
   apocalyptic thought, 7–8, 55–56, 83, 87–88, 134, 138, 183, 229, 248, 311
   apostate, 305–306
   apostle, 3, 27, 85, 87–88, 100, 224, 256, 297
   ascetic/asceticism, 303–4
   Bible Paul used, 58
   biblical interpretation, 54
   birth, 38
   body-flesh distinction, 243
   call/conversion, 81–84, 87
   chronology (dating Paul), 27, 35–39
   citizenship, 59–60
   of Christ-believers, 257, 266, 272
   conversation as missionary activity, 100–102
   conversion/call, 81–84, 87
   coworkers, 103–4, 281, 283, 286
   Cynicism, 64–65
   death, 38–39
   determining authentic and pseudonymous letters of, 22–25
   education, 56, 59
   Epicureanism, 66–67
   family as locus of missionary activity, 100–101
   financial support, 177, 217
   fool's speech, 216–19
   Gnosticism, 75
   Gnostic use of Paul, 301–3
   Greco-Roman, as a, 58–81
   holiness, 55
   Holy Spirit, 55, 243–44
   house as locus of missionary activity, 101–2
   Israel's place in God's salvation plan, 244–46, 250
   as a Judean, 51–58, 271
   Law of Moses, 30, 54. *See also (above)* Law of Moses
   leatherworker (artisan), 60–62, 162, 292
   letters, 105–20
      genre, 106–7
      pseudonymous, 22
      structure, 107–8
         body, 108
         conclusion, 108
         paraenesis, 108
         salutation, 107–8
         thanksgiving, 108
   magic, 69–70
   marital status, 11–12
   martyr, 298
   ministry, understanding of, 44, 64–65, 93, 102, 104, 119, 137, 171–72, 177, 202, 204, 205, 206, 208–9, 210, 211, 214, 219, 220
   ministry of a new covenant, 208–11, 294
   ministry of reconciliation, 206, 209–11
   mission, 87–88
   missionary methods and strategy, 27–29, 92–93
   mystery religions, 72–73
   names, 84–85
   Neo-Pythagoreanism, 67
   non-canonical sources for Paul's life and thought, 31
   nurturing congregations, 102–3

old man, 283
painful visit to Corinth, 103, 105, 195, 196, 197, 202, 208
patron-client relationships, 61, 216, 256, 273, 275
persecutor of the church, 53, 54, 81, 93
personal visits to congregations, 102–3
Pharisee, as a, 11, 53–56, 271
pillar epistles, 22–23, 316
preaching, 98–100
prisoner, 257, 261–62, 264, 265, 279, 281
reason to study Paul, 6–8
rhetoric, 108–111
    confirmatio, 110
    ēthos, 110
    exordium, 109
    logos, 110
    narratio, 110
    pathos, 110
    peroratio, 110
    probatio, 110
    propositio, 110
    refutatio, 110
Roman imperial theology, 80
sinner, 297
slave/slavery, 6, 12–18, 85, 151, 152, 156–57, 175–76, 209, 217, 62, 224, 242, 265, 288
social standing, 59–62
sources for Paul's life and theology, 21–34
status inconsistency, 62
Stoicism, 65–66, 273
suffering, 65, 88, 172, 203, 204, 205, 206, 207, 208, 209, 210, 212, 217, 220, 244, 257, 259, 266, 294–95
synagogues, 98–99
theology, 29–30
    theology of the cross, 172, 210
    thorn in the flesh, 62, 203, 218–19
    travel, 46–50
        land travel, 47–48
        sea travel, 48–50
    undisputed letters, 22–23, 317
    universal apostle, 294
    visits to congregations by associates, 103–5
    weakness, 60, 88, 102–3, 164, 172, 191, 202, 203, 204, 207, 213, 215, 218, 219
    what Paul looked like, 62–63
    women, 104, 151–52, 178, 182, 256, 272, 298
    work/trade, 60–62
    workplace as site of missionary activity, 100
Pax Romana (Peace of Rome), 8, 46, 315
peristaseis, 112, 315
Perrin, Nicholas, 303, 309
Persis, 103
personal religion in Greco-Roman world, 67–75
Pervo, Richard I., 289, 294, 303, 304, 307, 308
pesher, 115, 315
Peter, 27, 28, 30, 32, 33, 39, 85, 120, 230, 298, 305–6
Peterman, G. W., 259
Petersen, Norman R., 19, 277, 285–86, 288
Pharisees, 53–56, 183, 315
    apocalyptic expectation, 55–56
    canon, 53
    holiness, 55
    Law of Moses, understanding of, 54, 242
    ways to interpret the Bible, 53–54
Pharoah Ptolemy II Philadelphus, 58
Philemon (person), 6, 101, 103, 107, 119, 277–88
Philippi, 255–56
Philo, 38, 163
philosophy, 64–67
Phoebe, 48, 104, 117, 119, 249
Pilch, John J., 19, 43
Plato, 22, 73, 151, 163–64

Plummer, Alfred, 196
Plutarch, 150
Polaski, Sandra Hack, 19
political religion, 75–81
Polycarp, 106, 198
Porter, S. E., 19
Poseidon, 76, 163
Powell, Mark Allan, xiii, 19, 30, 34
Praetorium (Praetorian Guard), 261, 262, 263
Prayer of the Apostle Paul, 303
preaching, 98–100
Price, Robert, 218
Priene inscription, 78–79, 224
princeps, 44, 316
Prisca (Priscilla), 86, 94, 103, 104, 162, 185, 231, 249
prophecy, 79, 102, 182, 291, 300, 316
Pseudo-Clementines, 31, 305–6
   Epistle of Peter to James, 305–6
   Homilies, 305–6
   Recognitions, 305–6
Pseudo-Demetrius, 109
Pseudo-Libanius, 109
pseudonymity, 22–26, 28, 316
Puskas, Charles B., Jr., 123, 279
Pythagoras, 22, 67
Pythagoreanism, 22

Quinn, Jerome D., 308
Quintilian, 15, 109, 280
Qumran, 53, 55, 115, 137, 193, 195, 199, 282, 316

Rastoin, Marc, 58
realized eschatology, 291, 293, 297, 316
Reasoner, Mark, 50, 89
reciprocity, 86, 96, 121, 175
Recognitions, 305–6
reconciliation, 167, 191, 192, 196, 197, 204, 205, 206, 209, 239
redemption, 54, 238, 244, 316
Reed, Jonathan L., 89, 297
resurrection, 5, 55, 72, 73, 82–83, 87, 92, 103, 133, 167, 169, 171, 173–74, 183–85, 211, 228, 242, 243, 271, 292, 303, 304, 316
retainer class, 59, 166, 316
Reumann, John, xiii, 273, 275, 276
rhetoric, 15, 59, 106, 108–11, 118–19, 202, 203, 244, 259, 316
Richard, Earl J., 139, 141, 308
Richards, E. Randolph, 117, 118, 119
righteous/righteousness, 23, 53, 54, 83, 145, 147, 149, 150, 227–29, 238, 239, 240, 242, 245–46, 271, 316
   of God, 227–29
Ringe, Sharon H., 19
Robinson, J. A. T., 246
Roetzel, Calvin J., 8, 56, 154
Roma, 163
Roman Empire, 8, 16, 39–42, 64, 92, 97, 224, 225, 226, 257, 282, 296, 304
   citizenship, 41
   Golden Age, 79
   imperial cult, 76–81, 163, 256, 314
   political theology, 76–81, 96
   propaganda, 135
Ryan, Judith, 276, 288

sacrifice, 54, 68, 76, 98, 178, 179, 247–48, 238–39, 299, 316
Sadducees, 53, 55, 316
salutation, 107–8, 316
salvation, 25, 29, 56, 71, 137, 139, 156, 178, 203, 227, 232, 239–40, 246, 250, 264, 269, 293, 297
Sampley, J. Paul, 89
Sanday, William, 24
Sanders, E. P., 228, 240
Sarah, 149, 239
Saul (name of Paul), 84–85
Schnackenburg, Rudolf, 308
Schneemelcher, Wilhelm, 49, 309
Schnelle, Udo, 198, 262
Schoedel, William R., 309
Schüssler Fiorenza, Elisabeth, 19
Schweitzer, Albert, 307
Schweizer, Eduard, 67
secretary, 117–19

Segal, Alan F., 309
Semler, Johann S., 194
Seneca, 22, 39, 65, 106
Septuagint, 58, 93, 128, 226, 265, 269, 316
shame and honor, 14, 42–43, 44, 64, 96,
    98, 101, 122, 179, 216, 217, 224, 227,
    247, 265–266, 267–69, 270, 271, 272,
    283, 284, 316
Shaw, George Bernard, 4
Shepherd of Hermas, 230
siblings, 96, 102, 121, 122, 128, 285–86
Silvanus (Silas), 104, 128, 130
Simon the Magician (Simon Magus), 69,
    306
sin, 3, 83, 183, 211, 228, 239, 241–43, 246,
    268, 316
    universal sinfulness of humanity,
    236–37
slavery, 175–76, 224, 282. *See also* Paul,
    slavery
slaves, Christ-believers as, 157, 242
social history, 13, 316
social network, 91–123
    as counter to Roman Empire, 92
sociological exegesis, 14
Socrates, 99, 151
Sosthenes, 162
speaking in tongues. *See* glossolalia
spiritual gifts, 180–82
Stambaugh, John E., 72, 89
Stephanas, 99, 101, 103, 119, 165, 166,
    167, 171, 185
Stirewalt, M. Luther, 107, 117
Stoicism, 65–66, 112, 156, 173, 273
Stowers, Stanley, 99, 106
Strabo, 163–64
Strecker, Georg, 309
Stuhlmacher, Peter, 232, 253
Suetonius, 63, 230–31
Sumney, Jerry L., 308
Syntyche, 103, 104, 257, 259, 272

tables of household duties (Haustafel/n),
    67, 293, 314
Tacitus, 139

Talbert, Charles, 240
Taylor, Walter F., Jr., 19, 253, 308, 309
temple, 5, 38, 45, 47, 53, 54, 67, 70–71,
    76, 77, 80, 94, 163, 199, 238, 291, 299,
    305
    Christ-believers as God's temple, 172,
    174 212
Tertius, 117, 249
Tertullian, 301, 303
Thales, 151
Theodotus, 74
theology of glory, 172, 210
Thessalonica, 130, 163
Theudas, 302
Thiselton, 169–70, 188
Thrall, Margaret, 194, 195, 199, 221
Thurston, Bonnie B., 276, 288
Tiberius, 37, 41
Timothy, 103, 104, 128, 130, 131, 139,
    185, 200, 249, 256, 260, 265, 269, 271,
    281, 285, 297, 304
Titius Justus, 162
Titus (New Testament letter), 21, 23,
    28, 31, 75, 198, 289, 297–99, 301,
    302
Titus (person), 32, 38, 103, 104, 119, 120,
    147, 192, 193, 195, 196, 197, 198, 200,
    202, 204, 208, 213, 214, 297
topos/topoi, 112, 137, 317
Torah, 5, 52, 61, 240, 317. *See also* Law of
    Moses
treason, as a charge against Christ-
    believers, 135, 263
Treatise on Resurrection (Epistle to Rheginus), 303
triclinium, 95, 317
Tripartite Tractate, 303
Tryphaena, 103, 104
Tryphosa, 103, 104
Tulloch, Janet H., 123
typology, 114–15, 317

unity
    with bishop, 299
    with Christ, 151–52

unity (*continued*)
  in the church, 38, 96, 103, 121, 122–23, 154, 168–70, 185, 193, 233, 257, 259–60, 266, 275, 294, 295, 299
  of humanity, 65, 123
Urbanus, 103

Valentinian Gnosticism, 302–3
Valentinus, 302, 303
Vander Broek, Lyle D., 123
Vielhauer, Philipp, 34, 295
Virgil, 77, 79–80
virginity as a protest against the Empire, 304
virtue and vice lists, 112
voluntary association, 97–98, 267, 317

Wacker, William C., 308
Wagner, Walter H., 80
Wallace, Richard, 89
Wan, Sze-kar, 221
Wanamaker, Charles A., 141, 308
Watson, Duane F., 19, 259
Watson, Francis, 232

weakness, 60, 88, 102–3, 164, 172, 191, 202, 203, 204, 207, 213, 215, 218
Wedderburn, A. J. M., 233
Wesley, John, 3
widow (as a church office), 297–98
Wiefel, Wolfgang, 232
Williams, Wynne, 89
Wilson, Robert M., 288, 308, 309
Winter, Bruce W., 43
wisdom, 54, 76, 78, 109, 167, 171–72, 181, 208, 294
Witherington, Ben, III, 109, 117, 141, 155, 159, 188, 198, 221, 263, 276
women, 104, 151–52, 178, 182, 256, 272, 298
  honor and shame, 43
  in Marcionite churches, 300
word of the Lord, 116, 133
works of the law, 54, 144–45, 147–48, 240
wrath of God, 139, 236
Wright, N. T., 96, 122, 232, 233

Zealots, 51, 317
Zeno, 65
Zeus, 68, 71, 76

www.ingramcontent.com/pod-product-compliance
Lightning Source LLC
Chambersburg PA
CBHW051933290426
44110CB00015B/1959